Teach Yourself
MFC Library Programming
in 21 Days

Teach Yourself
MFC Library Programming
in 21 Days

Robert Shaw
Dan Osier

201 West 103rd Street
Indianapolis, Indiana 46290

To my wife, Kathy, the love of my life, and my daughter, Katie, the life of our love. Their love, beauty, and understanding made this book possible. To my parents, Don and Shirley, who I can never hope to repay for a lifetime of love and nurturing. And to my teachers and friends, for I am a reflection of you all. —Bob Shaw

To my beautiful wife, Diane, and daughter, Nathalia. Without their love and humor, the world would be a boring place. To my parents, Jim and Darlene, who taught me that anything is within my reach, and the impossible just takes a little longer. And finally, to my lifelong friend Scott, who has shown me that striving for excellence and a clarity of vision are in themselves a reward. —Dan Osier

Copyright © 1995 by Sams Publishing
FIRST EDITION

All rights reserved. No part of this book shall be reproduced, stored in a retrieval system, or transmitted by any means, electronic, mechanical, photocopying, recording, or otherwise, without written permission from the publisher. No patent liability is assumed with respect to the use of the information contained herein. Although every precaution has been taken in the preparation of this book, the publisher and author assume no responsibility for errors or omissions. Neither is any liability assumed for damages resulting from the use of the information contained herein. For information, address Sams Publishing, 201 W. 103rd St., Indianapolis, IN 46290.

International Standard Book Number: 0-672-30462-7

Library of Congress Catalog Card Number: 93-86960

98 97 96 95   4 3 2 1

Interpretation of the printing code: the rightmost double-digit number is the year of the book's printing; the rightmost single-digit, the number of the book's printing. For example, a printing code of 95-1 shows that the first printing of the book occurred in 1995.

Composed in AGaramond, Bodoni, and MCPdigital by Macmillan Computer Publishing

Printed in the United States of America

Trademarks

All terms mentioned in this book that are known to be trademarks or service marks have been appropriately capitalized. Sams Publishing cannot attest to the accuracy of this information. Use of a term in this book should not be regarded as affecting the validity of any trademark or service mark.

Microsoft is a registered trademark of Microsoft Corporation.

Windows is a registered trademark of Microsoft Corporation.

Visual C++ is a trademark of Microsoft Corporation.

Publisher
Richard K. Swadley

Acquisitions Manager
Greg Wiegand

Development Manager
Dean Miller

Managing Editor
Cindy Morrow

Marketing Manager
Gregg Bushyeager

Assistant Marketing Manager
Michelle Milner

Acquisitions Editor
Christopher Denny

Development Editors
Dean Miller
Phillip W. Paxton

Production Editor
Gayle L. Johnson

Technical Reviewer
Jeff Perkins

Editorial Coordinator
Bill Whitmer

Formatter
Frank Sinclair

Cover Designer
Tim Amrhein

Book Designer
Alyssa Yesh

Page Layout
Carol Bowers
Charlotte Clapp
Mary Ann Cosby
Terri Deemer
Shawn MacDonald
Steph Mineart
Jill Tompkins
Tina Trettin
Dennis Wesner

Proofreaders
Georgiana Briggs
Michael Dietsch
George Hanlin
Paula Lowell
Donna Martin
SA Springer
Elaine Voci-Reed

Indexer
Jeanne Clark

Overview

		Introduction	xix
Week 1 at a Glance			**1**
Day	1	The Architecture of a Minimal AppWizard Program	3
	2	Documents 101	21
	3	AppStudio and ClassWizard	49
	4	*CView* Painting	71
	5	*CString*s and Other Helpful Miscellany	99
	6	*CObject:* The Mother of All Classes	127
	7	Dialogs	153
Week 2 at a Glance			**193**
Day	8	Genealogy, Databases, and You	195
	9	The ODBC Classes	227
	10	Data Transfer and Stuff	259
	11	ODBC, Part 2	287
	12	MDI and Multiple Views	315
	13	Colors, Palettes, and DDBs	343
	14	DIBs	363
Week 3 at a Glance			**395**
Day	15	An Overview of OLE 2.0 and Objects	397
	16	OLE Servers	411
	17	Printing	451
	18	OLE Containers	473
	19	Drag and Drop	503
	20	Help Me	527
	21	Future Topics	555
Appendixes			
	A	Answers to Quiz Questions	575
	B	Hungarian Notation	585
	C	Use the Source	589
	D	*printf* Format Codes	595
	E	Windows Types and Constants	597
	F	ANSI Chart	601
	G	ASCII (Also Known as OEM) Chart	605
		Index	609

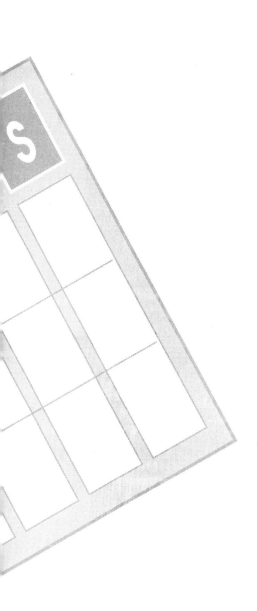

Contents

		Introduction	xix
Week 1 at a Glance			1
Day	1	**The Architecture of a Minimal AppWizard Program**	3
		Building Your First MFC-Based Program	4
		What Did AppWizard Do?	7
		CWinApp	8
		CView and *CDocument*	14
		Summary	18
		Q&A	18
		Workshop	19
		Quiz	19
		Exercises	19
	2	**Documents 101**	21
		Designing Tic-Tac-Toe	23
		Change the Names to Protect the Innocent	24
		The Blank Slate	26
		Storing Our Data	30
		Tic-Tac-Toe Strategy and Win Evaluation	33
		Drawing the Board	38
		Let's Play Tic-Tac-Toe	42
		Summary	45
		Q&A	45
		Workshop	46
		Quiz	46
		Exercises	46
	3	**AppStudio and ClassWizard**	49
		Messages	50
		The MFC and Messages	52
		Sprucing Up Tic-Tac-Toe with AppStudio	55
		Icons	56
		Cursors	58
		Menus	60
		Accelerator Tables	64
		String Tables	66
		Summary	68
		Q&A	69
		Workshop	69
		Quiz	69
		Exercises	69

4	**CView Painting**	**71**
	OnDraw! OnPaint! OnDonner? OnBlitzen?	72
	Oh Say Can You *CDC*?	75
	Pens, Brushes, and Colors	84
	Create and Destroy Your Own CDC Objects	96
	Summary	97
	Q&A	97
	Workshop	98
	Quiz	98
	Exercises	98
5	**CStrings and Other Helpful Miscellany**	**99**
	CString—the Only Way to Go!	100
	Message Boxes	112
	Exceptional Programming	115
	Do You Know What Time It Is?	121
	Summary	125
	Q&A	125
	Workshop	126
	Quiz	126
	Exercises	126
6	**CObject: The Mother of All Classes**	**127**
	What Can *CObject* Do for You?	128
	So You Want to Make Your Own Class	130
	Diagnostics	139
	CRuntimeClass	143
	Dynamic Creation and Serialization	146
	Summary	150
	Q&A	151
	Workshop	152
	Quiz	152
	Exercises	152
7	**Dialogs**	**153**
	Dialog Pieces	155
	Nurturing a Meaningful Dialog	161
	DoModal( ): Our Portal to Conversation	171
	Collecting Data	175
	Getting Information	182
	Software Lister	187

	Summary	190
	Q&A	190
	Workshop	191
	Quiz	191
	Exercises	191

Week 2 at a Glance — 193

8 Genealogy, Databases, and You — 195

This Week's Application—Genealogically Speaking 196
Database Theory 201
ODBC Classes 206
Database Construction 207
'Tis Nothing Lovely as a Tree...Application 219
Summary 225
Q&A 225
Workshop 226
    Quiz 226
    Exercises 226

9 The ODBC Classes — 227

The Genealogical View/Dialog 228
CFormView...CRecordView...CShoreView? 231
That's *CRecordset*, Not *CRecordSet!* 236
I Vant to Connect Your Blood Relations 247
Parameterization 248
Summary 256
Q&A 256
Workshop 257
    Quiz 257
    Exercises 257

10 Data Transfer and Stuff — 259

Dialog Data Exchange (DDX) 260
Dialog Data Validation (DDV) 265
DDX_Field Functions 266
Record Field Exchange (RFX) 267
The Bucket Brigade 271
Remember *CDate?* 272
The DDX Date Transfer Function 277
The *DDX_Field* Date Transfer Function 277
The RFX Date Transfer Function 278
Installing *CDate* Support 279
Summary 283
Q&A 284
Workshop 285
    Quiz 285
    Exercises 285

11	**ODBC, Part 2**	**287**
	Adding New Persons and Other Random Issues	288
	Record Manipulation Procedures	289
	Dialog Controls: The Sequel (No, Not SQL!)	296
	Unions Table Support Installation	298
	Double-Click Support	304
	*CDBException*s	309
	Summary	311
	Q&A	312
	Workshop	313
	Quiz	313
	Exercises	313
12	**MDI and Multiple Views**	**315**
	MDI	316
	Document Templates	317
	Default Multiple Views	317
	A Different Point of View	321
	Collections: Specifically, *CStringArray*	329
	Multiple Documents	330
	AddDocTemplate()	339
	Summary	340
	Q&A	340
	Workshop	341
	Quiz	341
	Exercises	341
13	**Colors, Palettes, and DDBs**	**343**
	A Thousand Points of Light	344
	My Memory Fails Me	347
	Palettes	348
	A *CBitmap* Is Worth a Thousand *WORD*s	351
	CBitmap Member Functions and Attributes	353
	Paint Me a Picture (or, Everything I Learned About Art I Learned in Kindergarten)	358
	A Point of View	361
	Summary	361
	Q&A	362
	Workshop	362
	Quiz	362
	Exercises	362
14	**DIBs**	**363**
	The Problem	364
	DIBs to the Rescue	364
	Two DIB Formats	365
	Thanks for the Memories	368

Teach Yourself MFC Library Programming in 21 Days

Call Me When You Got Some Class	371
Implementing DIB Loading	375
Tying *CDIBitmap*s to the Database	380
CLongBinary and BLOBs	381
Implementing *CDIBitmap* Conversions Associated with *CLongBinary*	382
Implementing DIB Drawing	385
Tying It All Together	388
Summary	392
Q&A	393
Workshop	394
Quiz	394
Exercises	394

Week 3 at a Glance   395

15   An Overview of OLE 2.0 and Objects   397

Olé 2...No Bull!	398
Microsoft's Object Technology Strategy	398
Object-Oriented Programming: It's not Nerdvana	398
Object-Oriented System Software	399
Prehistoric OLE (1.0)	400
The Revolution: OLE 2.0	401
OLE's Component Object Model	401
OLE Automation	402
OLE Controls	403
OLE Drag and Drop	404
OLE Component Management	404
OLE Documents	404
The Price	406
OLE 2.0 Sans MFC	407
OLE 2 Using the MFC	407
Summary	409
Q&A	410
Workshop	410
Quiz	410
Exercises	410

16   OLE Servers   411

A Bare-Bones Server	412
Much Ado About Nothing	416
OLE Foundation Classes	418
OLE Classes à la AppWizard	420
Adding Server Functionality	422
Mapping Modes	426
Back to OLE	431
*HIMETRIC*izing Our Server	432
Hexpad: A Real Application	434

	Loading a File	440
	A Document Is a Thousand Words	442
	Viewing the Document	445
	Scroll View	447
	Summary	449
	Q&A	449
	Workshop	450
	Quiz	450
	Exercises	450

17 Printing 451

	It's Not Just for Displaying Anymore	452
	Implementing Minimal Printing Support	453
	What AppWizard Did for You	453
	CPrintInfo	454
	Advanced Printing	456
	Mapping Modes	456
	Change Fonts (*HexpadView*)	456
	The *Extent* of the Problem	468
	Multiple Pages	470
	Summary	470
	Q&A	470
	Workshop	471
	Quiz	471
	Exercises	471

18 OLE Containers 473

	Containers—by AppWizard	474
	The Whole Is More Than the Sum of Its Parts	480
	CWingrepCntrItem (Also Known as *COleClientItem*)	483
	CWingrepView (Also Known as *CView* with an OLE Attitude)	486
	CWingrepDoc (Also Known as *COleDocument*)	489
	A Better Container	490
	Enhancing *WingrepView*	492
	Hit Testing and Getting Mousy	496
	Summary	501
	Q&A	501
	Workshop	502
	Quiz	502
	Exercises	502

19 Drag and Drop 503

	The Grep Application	504
	Two Views Are Better Than One	508
	File Manager Drag and Drop	512
	OLE Drag and Drop	515
	Bringing Wingrep and Hexpad Together	519

	Summary	525
	Q&A	525
	Workshop	525
	Quiz	525
	Exercises	526
20	**Help Me**	**527**
	Introducing Help	528
	Features of Help	528
	Tools and Source Files	528
	The Process	531
	A User's Perspective	531
	A Developer's Perspective	532
	Planning is Everything	532
	The Creation	537
	Pick Your Poison	537
	Another Language?	539
	Linking Topics	541
	Nonscrolling Regions	542
	Graphical Interpretation	543
	File Formats	543
	Pasting Pictures	544
	Ooh, That's the Spot: Hotspots	545
	Any Size Will Do: MRBs	546
	Macros	547
	Run on Open	547
	Run on Topic	547
	Run from Hotspot	547
	Rules of the Road for Coding	548
	DLLs	548
	Building Help	548
	Project Files	549
	Options	549
	Aliases	551
	Context-Sensitive Mapping	551
	.BMP by Reference	551
	Window Attributes	552
	External Files	552
	Compiling Help Files	552
	Testing and Debugging Help Files	553
	Integrating Help into Your Application	553
	Summary	553
	Q&A	554
	Workshop	554
	Quiz	554
	Exercises	554

21	**Future Topics**	**555**
	Windows 9x	556
	The Wicked Witch Is Dead	556
	The Windows 95 Logo Program	557
	A Virtual World (VxDs)	560
	Plug and Play (PnP)	560
	Flash BIOS	561
	PCMCIA	562
	Win32 and Win32s	563
	Windows NT 3.5	564
	Windows NT 4.0 (Cairo)	566
	WOSA	567
	Common Application Services	567
	Communication Services	568
	Vertical Market Services	569
	MFC 3.x and OLE	569
	OpenGL	570
	WinG	571
	WinToon	571
	Microsoft Network	571
	Intel's P6 and Beyond	572
	Delphi	572
	Conspiracy Theory	573
	Summary	573
	Workshop	573
	Exercises	573
A	**Answers to Quiz Questions**	**575**
	Chapter 1	576
	Chapter 2	576
	Chapter 3	576
	Chapter 4	577
	Chapter 5	577
	Chapter 6	578
	Chapter 7	578
	Chapter 8	578
	Chapter 9	579
	Chapter 10	579
	Chapter 11	580
	Chapter 12	580
	Chapter 13	581
	Chapter 14	581
	Chapter 15	582
	Chapter 16	582
	Chapter 17	582
	Chapter 18	582
	Chapter 19	583
	Chapter 20	583

Teach Yourself MFC Library Programming in 21 Days

B	Hungarian Notation	585
C	Use the Source	589
D	*printf* Format Codes	595
E	Windows Types and Constants	597
F	ANSI Chart	601
G	ASCII (Also Known as OEM) Chart	605
	Index	609

Acknowledgments

We would like to acknowledge the contributions of the following people:

Chris Denny, our acquisitions editor, for not giving up on this effort even after he should have.

Gayle Johnson, our production editor, for having the fortitude to decipher our scribblings and convert them to English.

Dean Miller, our development editor, for making it all come together.

Walt Beck, Dan's supervisor, for giving Dan enough slack to finish this project.

Dan's coworkers at Intel, who tolerated Dan roaming the hallways mumbling "OLE" all day.

And, of course, the families of both Bob and Dan for tolerating their absence (both physical and mental) during this ordeal.

About the Authors

Bob Shaw has been immersed in programming ever since he got his first computer—a TRS-80. He was hooked from the start. In the intervening years he has owned a couple of old Apple machines, but he finally resigned himself to the world of IBM PCs. Shaw has three undergraduate degrees and two master's degrees. He is sometimes hard-pressed to name them all, but suffice it to say that computer-related disciplines are well represented. Shaw has worked in and around the software industry for 15 years, the last three of which have been in his own software business. He also finds time to teach the occasional class at a local community college. Shaw lives in Seattle with his wife, Kathy, and brand-new baby daughter, Katie. He can be reached on CompuServe at 74003,1146.

Dan Osier is a Senior Systems Programmer with Intel Corporation, working on enterprise-wide networked applications. He also has worked as a software engineer for the Air Force, designing real-time aircraft simulations. After receiving his master's degree in software engineering, Osier taught undergraduate and graduate courses in computer science. He has been writing software since the age of 12, and he had his first contract programming job at 15. In his spare time, Osier enjoys immersing himself in new technology, and he suffers from what his colleagues term "techno-lust"—the love of anything new and high-tech. His first love is virtual reality (Silicon Graphics), with Doom II running a distant second. Osier can be reached on CompuServe at 72724,710.

Introduction

This book is all about learning how to use the Microsoft Foundation Class (MFC) Library. You will need the following tools for this endeavor: a Visual C++ compiler (the professional version is recommended) and a computer with enough moxie to run the compiler. The skill you require to get the most out of this book is an understanding of C++. You don't have to be a C++ expert. You don't have to be a world leader in object-oriented technology. If you've made it through a book on C++, you qualify. If you happen to be Mr. or Ms. C++, well, you qualify too, but be warned that this is an introductory book on MFC. Although we will go far into the details of the MFC, don't mistake this book for an advanced treatise on MFC internals.

The MFC Library is a set of C++ classes that encapsulate and ease Windows programming. I've tried to touch on most of the foundation classes in this book, but invariably things get left out. The MFC Library is quite large, so a sacrifice to breadth must be made if comprehension, at an introductory level, is to be gained.

Why MFC?

People have been programming computers (at least what we think of as computers) for only a handful of decades. But, as anyone who has been around computers can tell you, even a couple of years is a long time in technological terms. Times and technology change; people don't. The method of programming has changed very little from those early beginnings. However, rather recently there has been a large shift in the accepted programming doctrine.

Around 1960, when a programmer was given a task, he or she plopped down in front of a CRT and started coding. The tasks were small and the coding was fast. Those were the good old days. It was a time when, if you needed to get something done, you could just sit up all night and get it done. It was a time of thousand-line programs—good programs, too. It was a time when a single person working at home could tap along and come up with a million-dollar program. It was, literally, the golden age of programming. But all good things must come to an end, and there is no better example of this than in the arena of programming.

As computers became more sophisticated, so too did their users. The tasks foisted upon the programmer became larger, and so did the associated coding time. Then a funny thing happened. After a program reached a certain size, the time it took to code it turned out to be much longer than expected (based on smaller programs). If a program was twice as long as another program, it was assumed that it would take twice as long to code. The actual time it took turned out to be more than twice as long! Whether it was the fundamental unfairness of the universe or Murphy's Law, the fact of the matter was that when a program reached a certain size, the human brain couldn't keep track of all the complexity. Complexity was the culprit, all right, and there was nothing we could do about it (at least not directly). It was a hard truism to accept. But case after case, program after program, it was proven to be true.

As you might have noticed, there are quite a few very complex programs running around your local software store. Therefore, we must have beaten complexity, right? Well, yes and no.

Complexity is like the sea: you can't tame it or beat it. You have to ride out complexity, take advantage of calm times, and take shelter in protected harbors when you can. Okay, okay, I've milked that analogy as much as I can. But the essence is true: you can't beat complexity. How many of those whiz-bang, extremely complex programs are error-free? Very, very few! A bug is complexity's way of telling you that you haven't beaten it. And just think, we get bugs even in small programs. Only after quite a bit of work can we say that even the smallest program is truly error-free. What hope can we have of putting together a large program that doesn't fall apart at the seams? Well, the trick to beating complexity is to write small "error-free" programs and put them together, building a large "error-free" program. Of course, this is easier said than done, but this modular approach helps us manage complexity in programming. Note that I put quotes around "error-free." "Error-free" is much the same as "100% pure"—for any nontrivial sample, there is no such thing!

Now, I'm not telling you anything new. Modules have been around quite a while. Any modern, high-level programming language has some type of module structure. You've seen them in C++ as functions and, more important, classes. But modules alone won't solve the complexity problem. What was needed in the 1960s (and some say what's still needed) was a programming discipline—a set of rules that would guide the troubled programmer. Enter software engineering. A software engineer is very different from a programmer. A software engineer talks to the intended user and formally writes down what the user needs from the software. The software engineer then formally writes down what must be done to build this piece of software. Then, and only then, will the software engineer start writing code. Sounds dull? Sounds like a lot of work? Sounds like it will make very clean, robust code? Yes, yes, and sometimes, if the software engineer knows what he's doing. It's a lot more fun to sit down in front of the computer and start hacking out code, but for large systems, it's a lot more fun to have a working product down the road. At any rate, software engineering is the disciplined approach to programming. It even comes with its own doctrine—well, sort of, anyway. This doctrine is called the Software Engineering Principles. When we (the authors) were working on our master's degrees in software engineering, one of our professors, Mr. Shepherd, had us memorize these principles for practically all of our tests. It only seems fair that you at least see them. Shepherd—what better name for a teacher guiding his flock through the perils of programming?

Here are the seven Software Engineering Principles:

Modularity
Localization
Abstraction
Information Hiding
Confirmability
Uniformity
Completeness

These principles are supported in the C++ class structure. Some are a natural consequence of classes, while others must be consciously introduced by the programmer. Modularity and localization come easily from the class structure. Classes are inherently modular. And localization refers to keeping modules logically organized—each module should be a grouping of logically related code. Abstraction and information hiding have very good support in C++ classes. The private and protected keywords allow two levels of support for hiding information from objects outside a particular class. Abstraction is supported through information hiding and through the interface/implementation nature of class files. We allow only the abstracted nature of the class to be public. The implementation details are hidden. Confirmability is attained through a combination of strong type checking and the building of testable modules. Type checking is a way for the compiler to confirm that a given variable is used properly. Testable modules allow the programmer to logically test individual modules for accuracy. Remember, it's a lot easier to build small "error-free" programs than large "error-free" programs. Uniformity and completeness fall totally under the domain of the programmer. Code is easier to read and maintain if it's written and commented in a uniform manner (see Appendix B for a discussion of Hungarian notation). Modules that were complete when originally written don't need to be rewritten or appended when a new need arises—and new needs always arise. Completeness is a lot like "error-free": it's hard to attain. But if you're mindful of the need for completeness, you can maximize the adaptability of your code and minimize changes that are needed later. Changes are an open invitation for errors to creep into your application.

Every one of the Software Engineering Principles is intended to fight complexity. When you build your classes, keep these principles in mind. They will help you and your code. Also keep them in mind when you're looking at the foundation classes. Now and again, you'll find yourself asking why Microsoft did such an odd thing in a particular foundation class. You can usually find the answer in the Software Engineering Principles (sometimes not—Microsoft is human too). The MFC Library is a good example of software engineering. I'll try to keep reminding you of this as we proceed through this book. But the answer to the original question lies with software engineering. Why MFC? Because it's a method of programming in Microsoft Windows that is well-founded in software engineering.

CObject and Friends

The MFC Library is a vast collection of C++ classes that allows us easy access to Windows programming. But vast collections of things are often hard to understand all at once. Fortunately, most of the classes in the MFC Library have a common ancestor: CObject. If you examine the Quick Reference Chart to the MFC Library that came with your compiler, you can see that almost everything in sight has descended from CObject. CObject encapsulates some functionality that practically all the other classes need. This functionality includes runtime class support and serialization.

An object with runtime class support will allow a program to obtain information about its class, such as object size and the class name. This can be very valuable, especially in cases where polymorphism is afoot. Later in this book we will discuss the container classes in depth. For now, we can say that they are C++ encapsulations of data structures that are very useful in computer

science. These container classes use polymorphism to store objects descended from CObject. Polymorphism allows the storage of objects of different classes in the same structure (in this case, different classes descended from CObject). However, runtime class support allows you to determine the class of the object you retrieve from such a polymorphic structure.

CObject serialization is the built-in mechanism by which CObject-derived classes may be saved to disk. With a modicum of effort, you can transform a CObject-derived class into a fully serialized class and reap all the benefits of saving your work. Naturally, you can provide your own mechanism for saving to disk files, but why not use the prewritten code? The whole idea of the MFC Library is to save you coding effort. Here is one place where it saves you a lot of work and frustration. Take advantage of it. Don't worry. There's plenty more code for us to write.

Knowing CObject is a big step toward understanding most of the other classes! In Chapter 5, we will inherit a class from CObject and experiment with these concepts.

CCmdTarget and Friends

The next step in the evolution of the CObject class is the CCmdTarget class. CCmdTarget adds a number of useful features to CObject. The most notable (you can discern it from the name) is that its objects are targets for commands. In other words, objects of CCmdTarget are the recipients of command notifications. In fact, these objects form the backbone of the whole messaging structure. The messaging system, in turn, forms the backbone of Windows. Needless to say, CCmdTarget is a very important foundation class!

CWnd and Friends

The Visual C++ programming vernacular is replete with the word *object*. The C++ side of things has already contributed an object-oriented nature to our programming process. A C++ object refers to a variable instance of a class. One of the reasons C++ is such an ideal programming language for Windows is that Windows deals with objects as well. Every window in the Windows operating system is thought of as an object. To make things more confusing, there are more windows in Windows than you might think. Of course, the big windows that have title bars and that can be moved around are obviously windows. But every button, status bar, scroll bar, and control unit is a window. In fact, practically every displayable and self-contained unit on your Windows screen is a Windows object. So you can see that when we talk about objects in this book, we could be talking about anything. I will make an effort to distinguish Windows objects from C++ class objects, but be aware that there is a difference.

The CWnd class is where the MFC library truly starts supporting Windows programming. We will use classes derived from CWnd to work with the windows you see on-screen. However, the CWnd class objects aren't the same as window objects! There is certainly a connection between them, but they are distinct. One of the attributes of a CWnd object is m_hWnd—a handle (connection) to the associated window object. Most of the CWnd functions are dedicated to providing you access

to the underlying window functionality, but be aware that these functions are really operating on the window that is pointed to by m_hWnd.

Future Directions of Windows

Perhaps the best reason to adopt the MFC architecture is the benefit of seeing into the future of Windows programming. Microsoft is forging ahead along the Windows programming road, and they have a good idea of what direction that is. As time goes by, enhancements to the MFC will reflect the future of Windows programming. Even the short distance that the MFC has come has shown changes indicative of the newest ideas at Microsoft. Object database connectivity (ODBC) and object linking and embedding (OLE) are two examples of these forward-thinking MFC changes. These two concepts are so fundamental to the future of Windows programming that I have dedicated the last two weeks of this book to projects centering around them. I believe that if you will be working in the Windows programming field in the next few years, you *must* know one, if not both, of these programming paradigms.

Where This Book's Code Can Be Found

For your convenience, the code listings in this book are available on the Internet and CompuServe.

Internet: World Wide Web

http://www.mcp.com/sams

Internet: Anonymous FTP

ftp.mcp.com

/pub/sams/books/TYMFC/tymfc.zip

Remember that directory names on the Internet are case-sensitive.

CompuServe

"GO" keyword: SAMS

Library 9, Programming

File: TYMFC.ZIP

Conventions Used in This Book

This book uses the following conventions:

- All code appears in monospace.
- All placeholders in code appear in *italic monospace*.
- All new terms appear in *italic*.

- Menu names and menu options are separated by a vertical bar. For example, File | Open means to access the File menu and choose the Open option.
- Filenames appear in all uppercase.
- In code and figures, a group of three vertical dots represents information that has been omitted for the sake of brevity.

A Note About Windows 95

Note: The programming information in this book is based on information for developing applications for Windows 95 made public by Microsoft as of 9/9/94. Since this information was made public before the final release of the product, there may have been changes to some of the programming interfaces by the time the product is finally released. We encourage you to check the updated development information that should be part of your development system for resolving issues that might arise.

The end-user information in this book is based on information on Windows 95 made public by Microsoft as of 9/9/94. Since this information was made public before the release of the product, we encourage you to visit your local bookstore at that time for updated books on Windows 95.

If you have a modem or access to the Internet, you can always get up-to-the-minute information on Windows 95 direct from Microsoft on WinNews:

On CompuServe: `GO WINNEWS`

On the Internet:
`ftp://ftp.microsoft.com/PerOpSys/Win_News/Chicago`
`http://www.microsoft.com`

On AOL: keyword `WINNEWS`

On Prodigy: jumpword `WINNEWS`

On Genie: `WINNEWS` file area on Windows RTC

You can also subscribe to Microsoft's WinNews electronic newsletter by sending Internet e-mail to `news@microsoft.nwnet.com` and putting the words `SUBSCRIBE WINNEWS` in the text of the e-mail.

WEEK 1 AT A GLANCE

In this first week, you will explore the fundamentals of MFC programming. Here we lay a firm foundation so that you may confidently exploit the advanced features of the MFC in the last two weeks. Chapter 1 is an overview of how to use the AppWizard included with Visual C++ to generate a minimal Windows application. You will explore AppWizard's options and get a feel for your new life as an MFC programmer. In Chapter 2 you will learn what a document is from an MFC perspective. You will be compared to a super spy (a little overdramatization on our part) as parallels are made between your MFC document and the top-secret documents Mr. Spy (that's you) carries around. Chapter 3 will lead you to AppStudio and ClassWizard. These two utilities provide a quick and easy way to create resources (dialog boxes, icons, and so on) and connect them to your application. These are some *very* useful tools. Chapter 4 teaches you to view life a little differently (a little pun) by introducing the CView class. Here you will examine the mechanism that controls how the user interacts with the data. We will string you along in

Week 1 at a Glance

Chapter 5 (another bad pun) by introducing the `CString` class and some other fun tidbits that will come in handy later. In Chapter 6 you will meet `CObject`, the mother of all classes, the big cheese, the head honcho, numero uno, the top dog, the big salami...you get the idea. You will examine existing `CObject`-derived classes as well as derive a class on your own. `CObject` will show you the MFC's true power. Finally, Chapter 7 gives you tips for creating dialogs in all their glory. We hope you find this first week a solid introduction to the MFC. It will prepare you for Week 2.

The Architecture of a Minimal AppWizard Program

WEEK 1

DAY 1
The Architecture of a Minimal AppWizard Program

In this chapter you will become familiar with AppWizard and its options. You will build and run a minimal application using AppWizard. By the end of this chapter, you should know the components of a minimal AppWizard application and how they're related. All the programs and examples in this book start off as minimal AppWizard applications. Understanding the architecture of these minimal applications is an important first step toward understanding MFC programming.

Building Your First MFC-Based Program

In order to expedite your understanding of the MFC, I want to stress the hands-on approach to learning. As you read, perform the actions specified. This will reinforce the concepts presented and give you confidence in their application. But before we jump into program building, let's take care of a little file housekeeping. You need a subdirectory on your hard drive in which to store this book's programs. Open File Manager and create the subdirectory C:\TYMFC. (In case you're wondering, TYMFC is short for Teach Yourself MFC.) As you proceed through this book, you will fill C:\TYMFC with project directories containing the programs you build.

Tip: If you're already in Visual C++, that's okay. You can press Alt-Tab to scroll through open Windows applications. This will allow you to go to Program Manager, launch File Manager, create a new subdirectory, and return without exiting Visual C++ (or any application). Consult your Windows *User's Guide* for more information.

Now let's let Visual C++ construct an application for us by using the MFC library.

Invoke AppWizard by selecting it from the Project menu in Visual C++. The AppWizard dialog appears, asking you for the name of your new project and its path (see Figure 1.1).

Type `hello` in the Project Name edit box. As you type, your keystrokes are reflected in the New Subdirectory edit box. Unless you specify differently, AppWizard will use the project name to create a subdirectory for your application files. Changing the New Subdirectory name won't affect the application files. It will only change their destination. Accept the default name of `hello` as the New Subdirectory name. This generally is the best thing to do, because it reduces the chance of confusion when you have a number of projects.

We also need to specify where this new subdirectory will be created. Find and double-click on the TYMFC subdirectory in the Directory list box. You might have to adjust the Drive selection if you created the TYMFC subdirectory on a drive other than C:.

Figure 1.1.
AppWizard's main dialog.

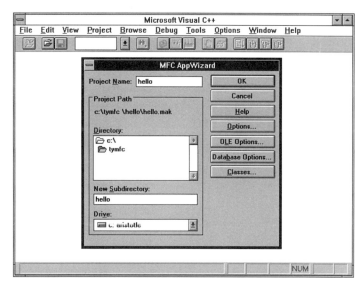

You should see c:\tymfc \hello\hello.mak at the top of the Project Path box. If you don't see this path, double-check the steps you took to get to this point.

There is a row of buttons on the right side of the MFC AppWizard dialog. The OK, Cancel, and Help buttons are probably familiar to you. They're self-explanatory, in any case. The Options..., OLE Options..., Database Options..., and Classes... buttons might not be so obvious.

The Database Options... and OLE Options... buttons are advanced features that we will discuss in detail in the second and third weeks, respectively. For now, we can ignore them. If you're curious, experiment with them and see what happens. You can even take a sneak peek ahead in the book. However, if this is your first exposure to MFC, it's advisable to avoid confusion and take this book one chapter at a time.

Clicking on the Options... button brings up a dialog that allows you to customize the skeletal application that AppWizard constructs. (See Figure 1.2.) For your first MFC program, select only Initial Toolbar, the Medium Memory Model, and Generate Source Comments. As we progress through this book, we will select more and more options, but for this first program, the fewer distractions, the better.

Finally, the Classes... button provides a means to customize the classes and names of the files AppWizard creates. We'll discuss this ability after you've been exposed to AppWizard's default classes and files.

You're now ready to accept the options you've selected for your first MFC program. Click on the OK button.

The Architecture of a Minimal AppWizard Program

Figure 1.2.
AppWizard's Options dialog.

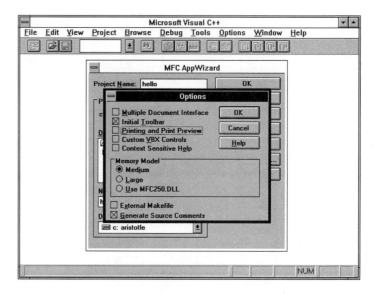

At this point, AppWizard shows you a summary of what will be created and what features will be supported. In this summary, you can see the options that you specified in the Options dialog. The summary also tells you what specific classes and associated files will be created. You now have the option of allowing AppWizard to create your minimal application or aborting the whole process. Go ahead and look over the summary (see Figure 1.3) and then click on Create.

Figure 1.3.
AppWizard's summary screen.

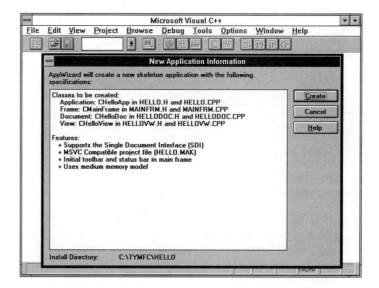

AppWizard has now built the minimal application you've specified. Some books call this minimal application a *skeletal application* since it's up to you to put the flesh on its bony frame in order to bring it to life. In this book, I use *minimal* and *skeletal* interchangeably.

The next step is to compile, link, and run your minimal application. Click on the Run icon (the fourth button from the right on the toolbar). You will be asked if you want the compiler to create HELLO.EXE. Let it proceed. An output window appears that shows you the progress of the compile/link process. Soon it will be done. Click on the Run icon again and your program is launched. Go ahead and take the time to play around with your application. It doesn't do much, does it? Well, neither did you. Considering how much effort you put into the program, it looks pretty good.

What Did AppWizard Do?

There are certain things that every Windows program must have and there are certain things that every Windows program must do. The reason why the MFC library is such a boon to Windows programming is that it consists of code you need that you don't have to write. The MFC insulates you from the confusing details of the Windows Application Programmer's Interface (API). The Windows API is a powerful set of tools that allows you to construct a Windows program, but it does so much that it's hard to know where to start. The MFC encapsulates the API with the required framework to make a Windows program. AppWizard automates the building of a Windows program by putting pieces of the MFC together properly.

For our Hello program, AppWizard created a set of source code files that consists of class definitions and implementations derived from the MFC. Table 1.1 summarizes the specific files that AppWizard created for our Hello program.

Table 1.1. The files AppWizard created for the Hello program.

.H and .CPP	Derived From	Description
Hello	CWinApp	The main class that invokes all the others.
Mainfrm	CFrameWnd	The outermost frame class.
HelloDoc	CDocument	The document class where your data resides.
HelloVW	CView	The view class that manages what you see.

These classes form the skeletal framework around which we can build a usable application. This entire book revolves around manipulations of these four classes. The MFC library consists of many more classes than these four, but none of the others are as crucial to application development. In the context of these four foundation classes, we will discuss much of the MFC library.

The Architecture of a Minimal AppWizard Program

One of the ways these classes are related is through interdependencies. Figure 1.4 shows the inclusion relationship between the classes (that is, which files are included in which other files). From this diagram, you can see that there is a strong interdependence between an application's files. This figure also shows you what effect a modification to one of these files would have on a recompilation. For example, if HELLOVW.CPP was modified, only HELLOVW.CPP would need to be recompiled. However, if HELLO.H were changed, HELLO.H and all the .CPP files would have to be recompiled since HELLO.H is included in all the .CPP files.

Figure 1.4.
Interdependencies between files.

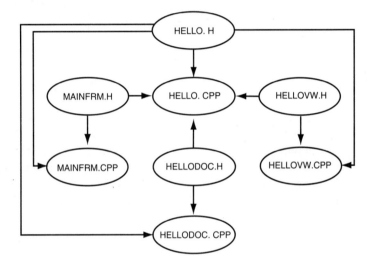

CWinApp

The files HELLO.H and HELLO.CPP, created by AppWizard, define the class CHelloApp. CHelloApp contains the code that is first initiated when you run your program. It does the initialization required before any of the other classes can perform their duties.

Let's take a look at HELLO.H, shown in the following listing. At first glance, it hardly even looks like a C++ program. Half of the lines of code are either preprocessor directives (the lines beginning with #) or seemingly encrypted comment lines. We want to concentrate on the architecture, so we'll ignore the preprocessor directives and the unusual comment lines for now. What's left is the CHelloApp class definition. We see that CHelloApp is derived from the foundation class of CWinApp and that it has a constructor and two functions defined. We will discuss these functions when we discuss their implementation, but for now, note the unusual declaration of the OnAppAbout() function. The preprocessor strips away the afx_msg prefix, which is used as a flag for the message map macros. What remains for the compiler is a normal C++ function definition—void OnAppAbout();. The point is that HELLO.H is not so strange after all.

```
// hello.h: Main header file for the HELLO application
//

#ifndef __AFXWIN_H__
#error include 'stdafx.h' before including this file for PCH
#endif

#include "resource.h"        // Main symbols

/////////////////////////////////////////////////////////////////////////////
// CHelloApp:
// See hello.cpp for the implementation of this class
//

class CHelloApp : public CWinApp
{
public:
CHelloApp();

// Overrides
virtual BOOL InitInstance();

// Implementation

    //{{AFX_MSG(CHelloApp)
afx_msg void OnAppAbout();
// NOTE: ClassWizard will add and remove member functions here.
// DO NOT EDIT what you see in these blocks of generated code!
//}}AFX_MSG
DECLARE_MESSAGE_MAP()
};

/////////////////////////////////////////////////////////////////////////////
```

Examining the HELLO.CPP file (shown next) can yield some important insight into the MFC world. As with HELLO.H, HELLO.CPP has some very arcane lines of code. These strange lines (such as the message map lines) are discussed later in this book. For now, we must concentrate on the fundamental architecture, so try to ignore them.

From the `#include` statements (or Figure 1.4) we can see that HELLO.CPP has access to all the other header files in our application. This important fact lends credence to the statement that the hello files are responsible for initializing the application. CHelloApp needs to see the main frame, the document, and the view in order to set them up.

HELLO.H defines a constructor and two other functions. In HELLO.CPP we can see the implementation of these functions. The constructor is empty, waiting for you to add construction code. AppWizard is so smart that it puts comments in the code blocks, telling you what goes where. Via comments, AppWizard tells you to avoid putting initialization code in the constructor but to put it into the InitInstance() function instead.

There is an important difference between a class constructor and an InitInstance() function. The constructor is called only once, when the application is executed, whereas InitInstance()

The Architecture of a Minimal AppWizard Program

is called every time an instance of that class is created. If you're new to the Windows multitasking environment, this distinction might be hard to discern. Think of it this way: Every time you double-click on an application icon, a new instance of the application is created; hence, `InitInstance()` is called for each double-click. However, no matter how many instances are running around, the class constructor for that application was called only once.

Between the constructor and `InitInstance()` code is a one-line declaration that is easy to miss but extremely important. It is the declaration for the "one and only CHelloApp object." theApp is the handle for your application. It is the means by which Windows accesses your application.

```
// hello.cpp: Defines the class behaviors for the application
//

#include "stdafx.h"
#include "hello.h"

#include "mainfrm.h"
#include "hellodoc.h"
#include "hellovw.h"

#ifdef _DEBUG
#undef THIS_FILE
static char BASED_CODE THIS_FILE[] = __FILE__;
#endif

/////////////////////////////////////////////////////////////////////////////
// CHelloApp

BEGIN_MESSAGE_MAP(CHelloApp, CWinApp)
    //{{AFX_MSG_MAP(CHelloApp)
    ON_COMMAND(ID_APP_ABOUT, OnAppAbout)
    // NOTE: ClassWizard will add and remove mapping macros here.
    // DO NOT EDIT what you see in these blocks of generated code!
    //}}AFX_MSG_MAP
    // Standard file based document commands
    ON_COMMAND(ID_FILE_NEW, CWinApp::OnFileNew)
    ON_COMMAND(ID_FILE_OPEN, CWinApp::OnFileOpen)
END_MESSAGE_MAP()

/////////////////////////////////////////////////////////////////////////////
// CHelloApp construction

CHelloApp::CHelloApp()
{
    // TODO: Add construction code here
    // Place all significant initialization in InitInstance
}

/////////////////////////////////////////////////////////////////////////////
// The one and only CHelloApp object

CHelloApp NEAR theApp;

/////////////////////////////////////////////////////////////////////////////
```

```cpp
// CHelloApp initialization

BOOL CHelloApp::InitInstance()
{
    // Standard initialization
    // If you are not using these features and wish to reduce the size
    // of your final executable, you should remove from the following
    // the specific initialization routines you do not need.

    SetDialogBkColor();        // Set dialog background color to gray
    LoadStdProfileSettings();  // Load standard .INI file options
                               // (including MRU)

    // Register the application's document templates. Document templates
    // serve as the connection between documents, frame windows, and
    // views.

    CSingleDocTemplate* pDocTemplate;
    pDocTemplate = new CSingleDocTemplate(
        IDR_MAINFRAME,
        RUNTIME_CLASS(CHelloDoc),
        RUNTIME_CLASS(CMainFrame),   // Main SDI frame window
        RUNTIME_CLASS(CHelloView));
    AddDocTemplate(pDocTemplate);

    // Create a new (empty) document
    OnFileNew();

    if (m_lpCmdLine[0] != '\0')
    {
        // TODO: Add command line processing here
    }


    return TRUE;
}

/////////////////////////////////////////////////////////////////////////////
// CAboutDlg dialog used for App About

class CAboutDlg : public CDialog
{
public:
    CAboutDlg();

// Dialog data
    //{{AFX_DATA(CAboutDlg)
    enum { IDD = IDD_ABOUTBOX };
    //}}AFX_DATA

// Implementation
protected:
    virtual void DoDataExchange(CDataExchange* pDX);  // DDX/DDV support
    //{{AFX_MSG(CAboutDlg)
        // No message handlers
    //}}AFX_MSG
```

The Architecture of a Minimal AppWizard Program

```
    DECLARE_MESSAGE_MAP()
};

CAboutDlg::CAboutDlg() : CDialog(CAboutDlg::IDD)
{
    //{{AFX_DATA_INIT(CAboutDlg)
    //}}AFX_DATA_INIT
}

void CAboutDlg::DoDataExchange(CDataExchange* pDX)
{
    CDialog::DoDataExchange(pDX);
    //{{AFX_DATA_MAP(CAboutDlg)
    //}}AFX_DATA_MAP
}

BEGIN_MESSAGE_MAP(CAboutDlg, CDialog)
    //{{AFX_MSG_MAP(CAboutDlg)
    // No message handlers
    //}}AFX_MSG_MAP
END_MESSAGE_MAP()

// App command to run the dialog
void CHelloApp::OnAppAbout()
{
    CAboutDlg aboutDlg;
    aboutDlg.DoModal();
}

/////////////////////////////////////////////////////////////////////////////
// CHelloApp commands
```

The InitInstance() function is where we place application-specific initialization code. Looking at the default InitInstance(), you see that the first two commands instruct the application to set the dialog background color to gray and to load the .INI file information. This is precisely the kind of code that belongs here, because each instance of the application must perform these functions. On the other hand, code that confirms specific system settings or initializes a database server might need to be executed only once for all instances. This type of code would be appropriately put in the application's constructor.

The next thing InitInstance() does is to logically connect the CDocTemplate-, CMainFrame-, CView-, and CDocument-derived classes. The CDocTemplate-derived class is the glue that binds the other classes together. For our Hello program, the document template we use is CSingleDocTemplate. This single document template class gives our application the ability to have one, but only one, document open at a time (hence *single* document template). We asked for this restriction in AppWizard when we deselected the Multiple Document Interface (MDI) check box (see Figure 1.2). We will learn about MDI in Chapter 12.

In the InitInstance() function, our application creates an instance of CSingleDocTemplate. The document template creates a main frame window and a document. Finally, the main frame creates a view (see Figure 1.5). Naturally, all this creating doesn't occur all at once or on its own.

Object creation occurs as the result of Windows messages that are the product, ultimately, of user commands. Document template objects are created during the application's `InitInstance()` function. Document templates create documents and frame windows when prompted by the application (usually as the result of an `OnFileNew()` or `OnFileOpen()` command). For example, say you, the user, choose to create a new document in a Single Document Interface (SDI) application. You do this by selecting File | New. The application responds by "telling" the document template to create a main frame window and a document object. The frame window, in turn, creates a view object. While the user only sees a new document appear, the programmer must be aware of the mechanics that occur behind the scenes. You should realize that things are a little different with an MDI application, as we shall see in later chapters.

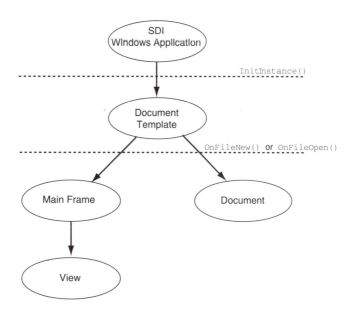

Figure 1.5.
The SDI application creation hierarchy.

Let's get back to `InitInstance`. After registering the document template with Windows, `InitInstance()` calls the `OnFileNew()` command to create a new document. `OnFileNew()` is a member function of `CWinApp` that automates the creation of new documents. It's also the exact same function that is called when the user chooses File | New.

The final commands in `InitInstance()` concern themselves with processing the command line. If your application uses command-line parameters, this is where you would want to extract them and perform any necessary actions.

`InitInstance()` ends with a `return TRUE` statement, which tells the caller that the initialization proceeded successfully.

The Architecture of a Minimal AppWizard Program

The final function defined in HELLO.H is `OnAppAbout()`. This function invokes the About dialog box. The remainder of HELLO.CPP is the definition, implementation, and execution of the About dialog box. Ignore this code for now. We will explore the mysteries of dialog boxes in depth in the chapters to come.

CView and *CDocument*

If there were an MFC popularity contest, `CView` and `CDocument` would tie for first place. You will change and manipulate the code in classes derived from `CView` and `CDocument` more than you will the code in any other class. The reason for this is that documents hold data and views display data. That's programming in a nutshell—holding and displaying data. Everything else in programming exists to support these two functions. Needless to say, a view and a document must have a very close working relationship. The fact of the matter is that every view is tied to one and only one document. A view's sole purpose in life is to display the data held in its document. However, the monogamous relationship that so fills the view's existence can be a one-way street. Any one document can have multiple views! As shocking as this may seem, it can be of enormous benefit to us. In essence, this ability of the document to keep one or more views "on the side" allows us to see and manipulate two portions of the document at once. This can be handy, as we shall see.

We will examine `CDocument` in detail later. Understanding `CView` presents us with enough of a challenge for now. Let's look at the HELLOVW.H file, shown next. As expected, it derives the class `CHelloView` from `CView`. The explanation of many of the lines is postponed until later. Remember, we want to concentrate on the architecture.

The first thing we see in HELLOVW.H is the class constructor. There's nothing strange here, but immediately following it is one of those strange lines we've been ignoring. We will discuss this line (and others like it) in detail when we discuss `CObject` in Chapter 6.

The next function we find is `GetDocument()`. This function will become an old friend. It's the way you get a pointer to the document associated with this view. As I mentioned earlier, `CDocument` and `CView` work together closely, and this is one of the means they employ. Note that at the end of HELLOVW.H is the implementation of `GetDocument()`. It merely returns m_pDocument, which is a pointer to your document object. But note the typecast in the return statement. Actually, m_pDocument (an attribute of `CView`) is a pointer to `CDocument`, not `CHelloDoc`. But the derived classes of `CHelloView` and `CHelloDoc` are the ones that work together. We therefore want to return a pointer to `CHelloDoc`—hence the typecast.

Moving on, we find the `CHelloView` destructor and a function called `OnDraw()`. As you might guess, `OnDraw()` is the function we use to draw things in the view. We will discuss this function shortly.

The next two functions we encounter are debug functions: `AssertValid()` and `Dump()`. You will often see code like this between the `#ifdef _DEBUG` and `#endif` commands. This pair of preprocessor commands indicate that the code they surround is to be used only when the compiler is in debug mode. Likewise, if the first preprocessor command is `#ifndef _DEBUG`, the surrounded code will be ignored when the compiler is in debug mode.

The last thing we see in the class definition is the message map block. This will be put off until Chapter 3.

```
// hellovw.h: Interface of the CHelloView class
//
/////////////////////////////////////////////////////////////////////////////

class CHelloView : public CView
{
protected:   // Create from serialization only
    CHelloView();
    DECLARE_DYNCREATE(CHelloView)

// Attributes
public:
    CHelloDoc* GetDocument();

// Operations
public:

// Implementation
public:
    virtual ~CHelloView();
    virtual void OnDraw(CDC* pDC);  // Overridden to draw this view
#ifdef _DEBUG
    virtual void AssertValid() const;
    virtual void Dump(CDumpContext& dc) const;
#endif

protected:

// Generated message map functions
protected:
    //{{AFX_MSG(CHelloView)
    // NOTE: ClassWizard will add and remove member functions here.
    //    DO NOT EDIT what you see in these blocks of generated code!
    //}}AFX_MSG
    DECLARE_MESSAGE_MAP()
};

#ifndef _DEBUG  // Debug version in hellovw.cpp
inline CHelloDoc* CHelloView::GetDocument()
    { return (CHelloDoc*)m_pDocument; }
#endif

/////////////////////////////////////////////////////////////////////////////
```

Taking a look at this implementation of `CHelloView`, we see the usual strange lines (some of which, hopefully, are becoming less indecipherable). After the message map, we see the constructor and destructor just sitting there empty. Empty means never having to say you're sorry (or explain code, as it turns out), so we move on to the next function.

The Architecture of a Minimal AppWizard Program

OnDraw() is the next function, but let's leave the best for last. The remainder of HELLOVW.CPP consists of the implementations of the debug functions Dump() and AssertValid(), as well as the GetDocument() function. We've already postponed the discussion of Dump() and AssertValid() to a later chapter, so we don't need to talk about them further. But wait a minute, GetDocument()? GetDocument() already has an implementation in the header file! How can we have two implementations of the same function? Recall our discussion of #ifndef _DEBUG a few paragraphs ago. That's right! The GetDocument() function in the header is the nondebug version, and the one in the implementation is the debug version. Note that they are pretty much the same, except that in the debug version, there is some extra debug code. That seems reasonable, doesn't it?

```
// hellovw.cpp: Implementation of the CHelloView class
//

#include "stdafx.h"
#include "hello.h"

#include "hellodoc.h"
#include "hellovw.h"

#ifdef _DEBUG
#undef THIS_FILE
static char BASED_CODE THIS_FILE[] = __FILE__;
#endif

/////////////////////////////////////////////////////////////////////////////
// CHelloView

IMPLEMENT_DYNCREATE(CHelloView, CView)

BEGIN_MESSAGE_MAP(CHelloView, CView)
    //{{AFX_MSG_MAP(CHelloView)
    // NOTE: ClassWizard will add and remove mapping macros here.
    // DO NOT EDIT what you see in these blocks of generated code!
    //}}AFX_MSG_MAP
END_MESSAGE_MAP()

/////////////////////////////////////////////////////////////////////////////
// CHelloView construction/destruction

CHelloView::CHelloView()
{
    // TODO: Add construction code here
}

CHelloView::~CHelloView()
{
}

/////////////////////////////////////////////////////////////////////////////
// CHelloView drawing

void CHelloView::OnDraw(CDC* pDC)
{
```

```
    CHelloDoc* pDoc = GetDocument();
    ASSERT_VALID(pDoc);

    // TODO: Add draw code for native data here
}

/////////////////////////////////////////////////////////////////////////////
// CHelloView diagnostics

#ifdef _DEBUG
void CHelloView::AssertValid() const
{
    CView::AssertValid();
}

void CHelloView::Dump(CDumpContext& dc) const
{
    CView::Dump(dc);
}

CHelloDoc* CHelloView::GetDocument()   // Nondebug version is inline
{
    ASSERT(m_pDocument->IsKindOf(RUNTIME_CLASS(CHelloDoc)));
    return (CHelloDoc*)m_pDocument;
}
#endif   //_DEBUG

/////////////////////////////////////////////////////////////////////////////
// CHelloView message handlers
```

Now let's get on to the fun stuff. `OnDraw()` has some obvious attraction. It's only natural for us to want to view something. `OnDraw()` will help us with that endeavor. We will conclude this chapter by changing `OnDraw()` so that `CHelloView` will display (yes, you guessed it) Hello World.

AppWizard prepares the `OnDraw()` function with a few lines of code that most `OnDraw()` functions will need. The first is the call to `GetDocument()`. Remember, generally our `CDocument` class has the data. Therefore, we must get our data from `CDocument` before we can display it. The second line is a debug function that makes sure that the document we get from `GetDocument()` isn't corrupt or faulty in some way. In our simple Hello program, we don't have any data in `CDocument`, or elsewhere, for that matter. Therefore, neither of these lines is needed. All we want to do is print Hello World in our view. How hard can that be? Well, not too hard if you know what you're doing.

Comment out the `GetDocument()` call and the `ASSERT VALID()` call in `OnDraw()`. Below them, insert the following line:

`pDC->TextOut(0, 0, "Hello World");`

That's it. Compile, link, and run the program, and let's see what we've done. How about that? The program printed Hello World as advertised. But what did we do?

The Architecture of a Minimal AppWizard Program

Look at the parameter for `OnDraw()`. `CDC` is another member of the MFC that is responsible for device contexts (DCs). For our purposes, it will be used to draw text and graphics in our document's view. One of the member functions of CDC is `TextOut (x, y, string)`, where *x* and *y* are the coordinates of the upper-left corner of where the text is to be displayed, and where *string* is the text to be printed. `CDC` and `CView` painting are discussed in detail in Chapter 4. Don't go away. The real fun is about to start!

Summary

In this chapter, we created our first MFC-based program via AppWizard. We examined the architecture of that skeletal application and developed a feel for what AppWizard does. We also examined `CWinApp`- and `CView`-derived classes. We even customized `CHelloView` to make it display `Hello World`.

Beginning to learn about something the size of the MFC library can be a daunting task. You must take the first steps toward understanding it carefully and slowly. If you find yourself confused or unsure of where this is all headed, don't worry. It's still early in the game. There's plenty of time for the pieces to fall into place.

Q&A

Q I've heard that all Windows programs have to have a `WinMain()` function. How come our sample program doesn't have one?

A Yes, all Windows programs need a `WinMain()` function. The `WinMain()` function in our skeletal application is imbedded within the MFC, where it belongs. After all, that's what the MFC is all about: encapsulating and hiding Windows routines that come up time and time again.

Q Do I have to use AppWizard to build MFC Windows applications?

A Absolutely not! However, if you don't use AppWizard, you're in for some work just to get a simple program up and running. For newcomers to the MFC, AppWizard is a necessity that allows them to build their MFC skills. For experienced MFC programmers, AppWizard removes a level of drudgery from Windows programming and allows them to concentrate on application building. Be aware that some programmers forego the use of AppWizard altogether. In this book, however, we will take advantage of any tool we can to ease our programming chores.

Q Is AppWizard's minimal application truly the smallest Windows application?

A No. You can create much smaller Windows applications by avoiding the MFC entirely. The MFC is an additional layer of code between you and Windows. It therefore increases the size of the resultant application. This is not a bad thing. That extra layer not only eases the programming burden, but it also embodies many good software engineering techniques, such as reusability and encapsulation.

Q So, is AppWizard's minimal application the smallest MFC Windows application?

A No again. AppWizard produces a very general skeleton on which you may build a wide and varied selection of applications. It's AppWizard's duty to create the smallest program that can serve as the core to these applications, not the smallest program ever. The smallest MFC program would consist of a single module descended from `CWinApp`—the MFC object that encapsulates the `WinMain()` function.

Workshop

Quiz

1. Name the four classes fundamental to any MFC program built by AppWizard.
2. What class is responsible for displaying data, and where does it get this data?
3. What is the purpose of `CDocTemplate`?
4. Why are there two implementations of `GetDocument()` in the `CHelloView` class? How is it possible to have two implementations of the same function in the same class?
5. Briefly explain how the creation process works in an SDI application.

Exercises

1. Experiment with HELLOVW.CPP by changing the coordinates of the `TextOut()` function.
2. Have AppWizard construct a new skeletal application, but this time try different options. Do any changes occur to the AppWizard files? Try the OLE and Database options.
3. Look at the `InitInstance()` function in HELLO.CPP. By reading the comments, speculate as to which lines are needed and which lines may be removed. Put your money where your mouth is—remove the unnecessary lines and see how your program works without them. Don't worry about corrupting your program. It takes AppWizard only a minute to make a new one!
4. Research the `CDC` class in your Class Library Reference. Choose an interesting function (such as `LineTo`) and try and make it work in the Hello program. Experiment and have fun.

WEEK 1

Documents 101

Documents 101

When you hear the word *document,* a printed work immediately springs to mind. You think of a 40- to 50-page bundle of paper with "Secret" or "Confidential" emblazoned across its front cover. You might think of spies and couriers working tirelessly to get said "document" out of enemy territory. Well, that's not exactly what we're talking about here. Our document is a little more mundane than the life of Spy... James Spy. However, before we give up our secret-agent fantasy, let's discuss what similarities there are.

Mr. Spy's document is a container for potentially secret information. Our document is a container for information, perhaps more so than its paper counterpart. Furthermore, our document may contain secret (in C++ we call it `private`) information to which only the document will have access. "Information Hiding" replaces "National Security" as our watchword, but the spirit is the same. You must often ask yourself whether other objects have a "need to know" concerning certain pieces of data. If they don't, those pieces of data must be kept hidden (or secret).

Mr. Spy's document is sometimes coded and always needs to be dispatched up the chain of command for decoding, analysis, and presentation. Our document has very similar needs. Although our document won't need decoding in the same cryptographic manner as alluded to in the spy scenario, it might require some translation. MFC documents hold information in the most convenient manner for storage. The document, therefore, will contain raw information that most likely will be unintelligible without some interpretation. Hence, as in the spy scenario, our document also needs analysis and presentation to those higher up in the chain of command.

Of course, in MFC land, we don't have a true military chain of command. MFC has a sort of anarchist government. Whatever object happens to be running is in command. (Well, this isn't exactly true, but we'll discuss it later.) Naturally, the end user is acknowledged to be the First Citizen—the place where the buck stops, the end-all-be-all of MFC's existence. As such, the end user is the target for the decoded, translated, analyzed, and otherwise prettied-up information contained in the document. It's the duty of every MFC citizen to do his or her part to facilitate the imparting of this information to the user. But when push comes to shove, the `CView`-derived class does most of the analysis and presentation work. `CView` is the translator. It takes the document's efficiently stored data and translates it into a pleasing display for the user. In this chapter, we will build a Tic-Tac-Toe game that will show the interplay between the `CDocument`- and `CView`-derived classes.

Some people think programming is boring. I believe the preceding discussion disproves that supposition. Programming the MFC is practically the same as being an international superspy (for our side, of course). We can expect excitement and adventure around every corner.

Designing Tic-Tac-Toe

Building a new application requires some thought and preparation. Just plopping down in front of your CRT and cranking out code isn't as accepted in programming circles as it once was. So before we start our Tic-Tac-Toe program, let's think about what the final program will entail. It seems reasonable to expect a Tic-Tac-Toe game to provide an interactive Tic-Tac-Toe adversary. A one-line program descriptive might be: "A program that displays a Tic-Tac-Toe board with moves and interactively plays the game." That might seem a simple-enough demand for a program, but a lot of between-the-lines requirements creep in with that statement. Tearing apart our one-line statement of purpose, we can see what, specifically, we are required to do in order to build a Tic-Tac-Toe game.

Statement of Purpose: A program that displays a Tic-Tac-Toe board with moves and interactively plays the game with us.

Breakdown of requirements:

- ☐ Display the Tic-Tac-Toe grid.
- ☐ Display all moves made (the Xs and Os).
- ☐ Keep track of all moves made.
- ☐ Devise some method of user input (mouse clicks, keyboard, and so on).
- ☐ Construct an algorithm so that the computer will be able to play the game.
- ☐ Construct an algorithm to decide when the game is over.
- ☐ Indicate end-of-game results to the user.

Tic-Tac-Toe never seemed this complicated before! That's not the half of it. Be assured that, even in a program as simple as this, you'll find that unexpected requirements pop up at the least convenient times.

Because we're working within the MFC architecture, our design is partially dictated to us. However, we still must assign responsibility of these requirements to MFC objects. Knowing what you know about the interplay of the MFC classes, look over the requirements and determine which requirements fit best with which classes.

Recalling our discussion from Chapter 1 about the `CView` and `CDocument` classes, you can see that all the display and user-oriented requirements fit best within the `CView`-derived object and that the data-intensive requirements fit best within the `CDocument` derived object. The requirements are divided more or less evenly between `CView` and `CDocument`. Because `CView` is closer to the user and thus further up the chain of command than `CDocument`, it makes more sense to look at `CDocument` first. `CView` will display the data in `CDocument`, so getting `CDocument` prepared and accessible is our first priority.

Documents 101

Change the Names to Protect the Innocent

Use AppWizard to build a minimal Tic-Tac-Toe application with the name "TTT." Use the same options as you did with Chapter 1's Hello program, but this time modify the class names. Click on the Classes... button. You should see the dialog in Figure 2.1.

Figure 2.1.
The Classes dialog—examining the `CTttApp` *class.*

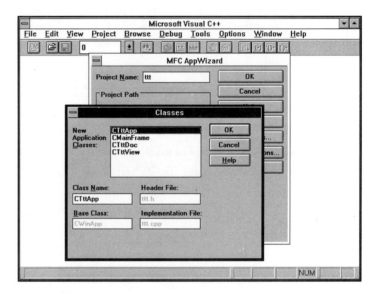

From within the Classes dialog, you may change some of the attributes of the classes constructed by AppWizard. When constructing its default classes, AppWizard capitalizes only the first letter of the project name. In the case of our Tic-Tac-Toe program, TTT is an acronym and therefore should be spelled with all capital letters. This dilemma may be easily solved by changing the class names in this dialog. We are making only a minor name change, but in general, you may rename the classes practically anything you wish. Of course, you should always be practical in these matters; chances are you'll have to live with these class names for the life of the program. Changing the names after AppWizard is finished building your application isn't easy.

The initial Classes dialog screen has the `CTttApp` class highlighted in the New Application Classes list box. Below the list box are four edit boxes: Class Name, Base Class, Header File, and Implementation File. Since this is the application class, only the class name edit box can be edited. The base class must be `CWinApp` (or something derived from `CWinApp`), and the files must be TTT.H and TTT.CPP (because that's our chosen application name). However, there's no reason we can't change the name of the `CWinApp`-derived class. Therefore, let's change the class name from `CTttApp` to `CTTTApp`.

In the New Application Classes list box, move the highlight to CTttDoc. Notice that the CTttApp entry has changed to CTTTApp, as we requested (see Figure 2.2). Also notice that two new edit boxes appear and that all the edit boxes are updated with CTttDoc entries. For the document classes, only the Base Class edit box is disabled. We have a little more freedom with this class. Our class must be derived from CDocument, but our naming conventions are much less restricted. For this program, we won't change the names of the default files that AppWizard built, but note that we can. The new edit boxes that sprang up for our document class are rather interesting. File Extension allows us to specify a default file extension for documents we wish to save and retrieve via the File | Save and File | Open commands. The Doc Type Name edit box allows us to specify a name for our document class that DocTemplate and its derivatives will use. When you have multiple document types running around at the same time, this name can come in handy. For our current program, neither of these new edit boxes will be useful, so we will ignore them. But back to the purpose of this stop: Change the class name from CTttDoc to CTTTDoc.

Figure 2.2.
The Classes dialog—changing CTttDoc to CTTTDoc.

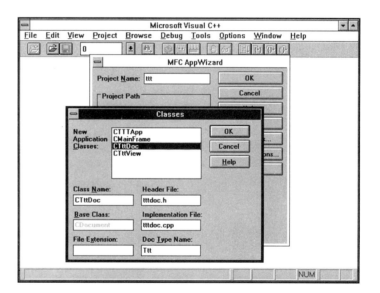

Finally, move the list box highlight to CTttView (see Figure 2.3). The bottom two edit boxes disappear, and we're left with the now-familiar four. You might notice, however, that something is different. The Base Class edit box isn't grayed out. Here in the CView-derived class, you may edit everything if that is your wish. Of course, in our case this is not our wish. We will only change the class name from CTttView to CTTTView (go ahead and do it!) and leave the rest alone. But take a look at the options in the drop-down list box that the Base Class edit box provides. Pretty nifty, huh? The reason that we have a choice of base classes this time is that a number of predefined CView-derived classes are hanging around. CWinApp and CDocument have no predefined descendants that AppWizard recognizes. AppWizard doesn't give you any options for the application

Documents 101

object or the document object because it doesn't know of any. We will exploit some of these `CView` base class options in future programs. For now, let's see what the default classes will do for us.

Figure 2.3.
The Classes dialog—changing `CTttView` *to* `CTTTView`.

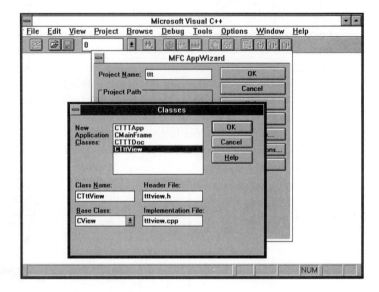

Click on the OK button in the Classes dialog. This brings us back to the AppWizard dialog—familiar territory. Follow through with the application creation process, as we did in Chapter 1. If we try running the application, we should encounter practically the same minimal program as Hello—a blank slate on which we may ply our craft.

The Blank Slate

In order to continue building our Tic-Tac-Toe game, we must alter the document class to meet the document-oriented requirements we listed earlier. But before we stumble into the document class like a tourist in a foreign country, let's first stop, look at the terrain, and do a little reconnoitering. In other words, let's examine the default version of `CTTTDoc` before we alter it. The following listing shows the header file for the `CTTTDoc` class. As in Chapter 1, we encounter quite a bit of strange code that is obviously not normal C++ code. Again, we will close our eyes and hope that we make it through unscathed. Ignorance is bliss, so let's enjoy it while we can.

```
// tttdoc.h: Interface of the CTTTDoc class
//
////////////////////////////////////////////////////////////////////////

class CTTTDoc : public CDocument
{
```

```
protected:  // Create from serialization only
    CTTTDoc();
    DECLARE_DYNCREATE(CTTTDoc)

// Attributes
public:
// Operations
public:

// Implementation
public:
    virtual ~CTTTDoc();
    virtual void Serialize(CArchive& ar);   // Overridden for document I/O
#ifdef _DEBUG
    virtual void AssertValid() const;
    virtual void Dump(CDumpContext& dc) const;
#endif

protected:
    virtual BOOL OnNewDocument();

// Generated message map functions
protected:
    //{{AFX_MSG(CTTTDoc)
        // NOTE: ClassWizard will add and remove member functions here.
        //    DO NOT EDIT what you see in these blocks of generated code!
    //}}AFX_MSG
    DECLARE_MESSAGE_MAP()
};

/////////////////////////////////////////////////////////////////////////////
```

Looking at this listing, we see the normal class declaration structure. Within the structure we can see the familiar constructor and destructor declarations. The next item of interest is the Serialize function. This function, in conjunction with the DECLARE_DYNCREATE macro, provides a slick means for file I/O for the entire application. We will explore serialization in depth when we start deriving our own classes from CObject in Chapter 6. The lines between the #ifdef and #endif statements are strictly debugger links that we will ignore for now. The last function in CTTTDoc is OnNewDocument(). Note that this function is protected.

Note: If you're new to C++, the protected and private keywords can be confusing. The protected keyword indicates that functions and variables (such as OnNewDocument()) can be accessed or called only by objects of the containing class or classes derived from the containing class. private functions or variables can be accessed by objects of the containing class only. Consult a C++ manual for further information.

Day 2: Documents 101

OnNewDocument() is called by the application framework every time a new document is invoked. For most practical purposes, you can say that this function is called when File | New is selected. Place document initialization code in this function; it will be executed for each new document. The remaining clutter near the end of the listing concerns the message map, which we will discuss in the next chapter. It's interesting to note, though, that there are no entries in the message map at present. This will soon change! Stay tuned. At the moment, we have more pressing issues to worry about. For example, how do the functions in the preceding listing work? The answer to this (and other life-affirming questions) lies in CTTTDoc's implementation, found in the next listing.

```cpp
// tttdoc.cpp: Implementation of the CTTTDoc class
//

#include "stdafx.h"
#include "ttt.h"

#include "tttdoc.h"

#ifdef _DEBUG
#undef THIS_FILE
static char BASED_CODE THIS_FILE[] = __FILE__;
#endif

/////////////////////////////////////////////////////////////////////////////
// CTTTDoc

IMPLEMENT_DYNCREATE(CTTTDoc, CDocument)

BEGIN_MESSAGE_MAP(CTTTDoc, CDocument)
    //{{AFX_MSG_MAP(CTTTDoc)
        // NOTE: ClassWizard will add and remove mapping macros here.
        // DO NOT EDIT what you see in these blocks of generated code!
    //}}AFX_MSG_MAP
END_MESSAGE_MAP()

/////////////////////////////////////////////////////////////////////////////
// CTTTDoc construction/destruction

CTTTDoc::CTTTDoc()
{
    // TODO: Add one-time construction code here
}

CTTTDoc::~CTTTDoc()
{
}

BOOL CTTTDoc::OnNewDocument()
{
    if (!CDocument::OnNewDocument())
        return FALSE;

    // TODO: Add reinitialization code here
```

```
        // (SDI documents will reuse this document)

        return TRUE;
}

/////////////////////////////////////////////////////////////////////////
// CTTTDoc serialization

void CTTTDoc::Serialize(CArchive& ar)
{
        if (ar.IsStoring())
        {
                // TODO: Add storing code here
        }
        else
        {
                // TODO: Add loading code here
        }
}

/////////////////////////////////////////////////////////////////////////
// CTTTDoc diagnostics

#ifdef _DEBUG
void CTTTDoc::AssertValid() const
{
        CDocument::AssertValid();
}

void CTTTDoc::Dump(CDumpContext& dc) const
{
        CDocument::Dump(dc);
}
#endif  //_DEBUG

/////////////////////////////////////////////////////////////////////////
// CTTTDoc commands
```

This listing shows the implementation file for the CTTTDoc class. After looking it over, you might come to the conclusion that it's an empty shell. It starts with an empty message map. We then find an empty constructor and destructor. The OnNewDocument() function gives the illusion of substance, but a second glance shows it to be a shell as well, merely containing conditional code waiting to be realized. Even the Serialize() function is devoid of solid code. The last two functions "implemented" are the debug functions. But even without knowing what they're supposed to do, you can tell that they are dummy functions as well. They're just passing the call along to their CDocument counterparts. How disappointing! CTTTDoc is an empty shell that can hardly support its own weight. But consider the blank slate metaphor. AppWizard, our assistant, is too humble to make even the slightest mark on our work. It has prepared this blank slate so that we may fill it with our application. Don't think of the blank slate as a hindrance; think of it as an opportunity.

Day 2
Documents 101

Storing Our Data

Now that we have a feel for what a document class looks like, let's go in and stir our own spices into the soup. The first ingredient we need for our Tic-Tac-Toe program is a place to store all the game moves.

Tip: At the mention of *storing* anything, a little red light should come on in your brain, indicating that this is indeed a document-related function. Always watch for descriptive cues such as *storing* for the document and *displaying* for the view, because they will confirm or deny your choice of placement. If you find yourself trying to force something into a class that doesn't seem to fit, perhaps it's because you've chosen the wrong class!

Storing game moves shouldn't be all that hard, should it? But what exactly *is* a game move? That, my friend, is a design decision we need to make. On the surface, we know that a game move is simply an X or an O placed on the familiar Tic-Tac-Toe game board. There is no need to keep track of the order of the moves, so if we store the character X or O with an associated board coordinate, we'll be home free. Take a look at Figure 2.4. It's a typical Tic-Tac-Toe board with each position marked with a pair of coordinates. It bears a remarkable resemblance to a two-dimensional array! The best data model you can choose is the one that best fits your data. The two-dimensional array fits our data very well. It's unanimous: We'll use a two-dimensional char array to store the game moves (Xs and Os).

In addition to the board, we'll also need an indicator for game status ('X' = X won, 'O' = O won, 'C' = draw, and ' ' = in progress), an indicator for who goes first, and best move coordinates for the computer opponent. Put the following declarations after these lines

```
\\ Attributes
public:
```

in the TTTDOC.H file:

```
char m_acBoard[BOARD_SIZE][BOARD_SIZE];
char m_cGameStatus;
char m_cWhoGoesFirst;
int m_nBestI, m_nBestJ;
```

and put the following statement near the top of TTTDOC.H, after the first comment line:

```
#define BOARD_SIZE 3
```

Figure 2.4.
Tic-Tac-Toe board diagram.

(0,0)	(0,1)	(0,2)
(1,0)	(1,1)	(1,2)
(2,0)	(2,1)	(2,2)

Note: We have used the `#define` directive to specify a constant. This is not really an attempt at generality. It's unlikely that we'll be able to successfully change the board size later in the program. The subtleties of such a change would wreak havoc with some of the Tic-Tac-Toe algorithms. Instead, we are defining the constant in this manner for the purpose of code clarity. Later, you will see BOARD_SIZE and have no trouble identifying it as the array dimension of the Tic-Tac-Toe board. On the other hand, if we had hard-coded a 3 into the program, how could you tell if a particular 3 was board size or an arbitrary number used for some other purpose entirely?

The array will be our Tic-Tac-Toe board. Every mark made will be stored here. The display might look like the true board, but it will only mirror the contents of the m_acBoard array. So our first programming duty, after creating the board, is to initialize it with blank spaces. While we're at it, we'll initialize the other class member variables too. Copy the following code snippet into the implementation of OnNewDocument(), before the return TRUE statement:

```
// Fill the board with blank spaces
for (int i = 0; i < BOARD_SIZE; i++)
    for (int j = 0; j < BOARD_SIZE; j++)
        m_acBoard[i][j] = ' ';
```

Day 2
Documents 101

```
// Initialize the game status indicator
m_cGameStatus = ' ';

// Initialize the computer's best move to the centermost square
m_nBestI = BOARD_SIZE/2;
m_nBestJ = BOARD_SIZE/2;

// If the computer goes first, make the best move
if (m_cWhoGoesFisrt == 'O')
    m_acBoard[m_nBestI][m_nBestJ] = 'O';
```

Note: If the variable prefix notation is unfamiliar to you, consult Appendix B, "Hungarian Notation." I use Hungarian notation throughout the text—at least when it is advantageous to do so. But consider this in the light of the Software Engineering Principle of Uniformity: The more you use Hungarian notation, the more your code becomes uniform, and the more advantageous it becomes.

We didn't initialize m_cWhoGoesFirst in the OnNewDocument() function, but we did use it there. Can you guess why? When we modify this program later, to polish it a bit, we will allow the user to change m_cWhoGoesFirst dynamically. If we initialize m_cWhoGoesFirst here, every time we start a new game, the user's changes will never take effect! This defeats the purpose of the variable. We will place its initialization in the document's constructor, where it will be executed only once during the course of the program. However, we do use this variable in the initialization. If it's the computer's first move, we initialize the array with a move already in place—the computer's move. Place the following code snippet into CTTTDoc's constructor:

```
// Initialize Who Goes First to 'X' -- the human player
m_cWhoGoesFirst = 'X';
```

So far, so good. We have a clean place in our document to store Tic-Tac-Toe moves, and we've initialized the indicators we will need. One requirement down, six to go. What's next on our agenda? Let's stick to document-related requirements for the moment and work on our opponent's brain. This is an interactive program, so we must provide an algorithm that directs the computer's moves based on the board position. The next section covers Tic-Tac-Toe strategy and win evaluation. Read this section for further information about game algorithm construction. There's no harm in bypassing this rather lengthy discussion, but a brief overview of the new code segments would be wise if you wish to understand how they fit into the greater program structure.

Tic-Tac-Toe Strategy and Win Evaluation

The goal of Tic-Tac-Toe is to get three of your marks (Xs or Os) in a row. There are only eight possible unique lines along which you can put your markers and win: three horizontal rows, three vertical columns, and two diagonals. These win lines are central concepts in both the strategy to win as well as win evaluation.

The computer must evaluate the game board between each move to check for game conclusion. This win evaluation algorithm must check the eight win lines for three of the same mark. When three of the same mark are found, the algorithm must flag a win and indicate the winner.

Strangely enough, game strategy and win evaluation are closely related code. Think of the strategy you use when you play Tic-Tac-Toe. First you check to see if there is an imminent win for either you or your opponent. In the case of no imminent situations, you probably favor the center and corners for your mark. But your priority is to act on any imminent situation by making the winning mark or (the next best thing) by blocking your opponent's win. These imminent situations require the checking of the win lines. This is where the game strategy algorithm uses win evaluation techniques and hence similar code. Naturally, we would like to keep code duplication to a minimum, so similar code should become shared code.

Both algorithms center around the win lines and win line sums (see Figure 2.5). A win line sum is the sum of the Xs and Os along a particular win line, where the Xs and Os are considered –1s and +1s, respectively. The absolute value of a win line sum is never larger than 3. A win line sum of +3 or –3 indicates a win. A win line sum of +2 or –2 indicates an imminent win. Win line sums (in absolute terms) of less than 2 are ambiguous. A blank win line and a win line with one X and one O both have sums of zero. Sums of +1 and –1 can also be attributed to multiple situations. However, sums of +2, –2, +3, and –3 can be plenty of help.

While we're summing up win lines, we might as well return a little information we gather along the way. When the win line sum is +2 or –2, it would be nice to know the coordinates of the empty space along that win line. A sum of +2 or –2 can occur only when the line has two of the same mark and one empty space. The empty space is where the winning or blocking move would go.

In order to find the best move or, for that matter, find out if anybody won, we need to iterate through the eight possible win lines. A sum must be performed on each win line and, potentially, the blocking/winning move must be passed back. The eight possible win lines can be divided into three groups: horizontal, vertical, and diagonal. There is no natural iteration that can be performed on all of them. The elegant solution to this problem is a common solution in Windows programming: We must build an iterator.

Documents 101

Figure 2.5.
Win line sums.

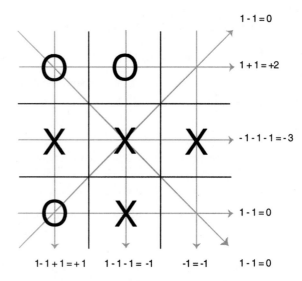

All iterators consist of three parts—an iterator object, an initialization function, and an iteration function. The iterator object acts like a bookmark: It holds your place in the iteration. The initialization function places your bookmark at the beginning of the set over which you're iterating. The iteration function increments your bookmark to the next logical position in the set.

With the preceding discussion in mind, place the following declarations in the CTTTDoc interface:

```
protected:
    int m_nIterator;
    void InitWinSumIterator();
    BOOL NextWinSum (int &nSum, int &nBestI, int &nBestJ);
```

The iterator function NextWinSum() returns a Boolean value to indicate the result of the iteration. The iteration could fail if the iterator object is out of bounds or uninitialized. NextWinSum() also passes back the win line sum and the array coordinates for a winning/blocking move.

The implementations are shown next.

```
void CTTTDoc::InitWinSumIterator()
{
    m_nIterator = 0;
}

BOOL CTTTDoc::NextWinSum(int &nSum, int &nBestI, int &nBestJ)
{
   int i, j;

    if (m_nIterator < 0)
        return FALSE;
        // Iterator was not initialized
```

```
    // Hold the value of the original iterator
    int nPosition = m_nIterator;
    // Increment the iterator for the next pass
    m_nIterator++;

    nSum = 0;

    if (nPosition < BOARD_SIZE)
    {
        // Calculate the appropriate horizontal win sum

        for (j = 0; j < BOARD_SIZE; j++)
            if (m_acBoard[nPosition][j] == 'X')
                nSum--;
            else if (m_acBoard[nPosition][j] == 'O')
                nSum++;
            else   // m_acBoard[i][j] == ' '
            {
                nBestI = nPosition;
                nBestJ = j;
            }

        return TRUE;
    }
```

```
    if (nPosition < 2*BOARD_SIZE )
    {
        // Calculate the appropriate vertical win sum

        // Translate the iterator into array units
        j = nPosition - BOARD_SIZE;

        for (i = 0; i < BOARD_SIZE; i++)
            if (m_acBoard[i][j] == 'X')
                nSum--;
            else if (m_acBoard[i][j] == 'O')
                nSum++;
            else   // m_acBoard[i][j] == ' '
            {
                nBestI = i;
                nBestJ = j;
            }

        return TRUE;
    }

    int nDiagonalWins = 2;   // One for each diagonal
    if (nPosition < 2*BOARD_SIZE + nDiagonalWins)
    {
        // Calculate the appropriate diagonal win sum

        // Translate the iterator into diagonal iteration units
        // n will take on values of 0 and 1
        int n = nPosition - 2*BOARD_SIZE;
```

Documents 101

```
        for (i = 0; i < BOARD_SIZE; i++)
        {
            j = n*(2-2*i) + i;
            if (m_acBoard[i][j] == 'X')
                nSum--;
            else if (m_acBoard[i][j] == 'O')
                nSum++;
            else  // m_acBoard[i][i] == ' '
            {
                nBestI = i;
                nBestJ = j;
            }
        }

        return TRUE;
    }

    return FALSE;
    // m_nIterator went beyond the possible iterations
}
```

Notice how the iterator object, `m_nIterator`, is broken into three pieces. The first, when `m_nIterator` is less than `BOARD_SIZE`, is the horizontal win line sum portion. The second, when `m_nIterator` is between `BOARD_SIZE` and `2*BOARD_SIZE`, is the vertical win line sum portion. The last, when `m_nIterator` is greater than `2*BOARD_SIZE`, is the diagonal win line sum portion. Each of these portions calculates a specific win line sum according to the value of the iterator object. The sum and, if applicable, the array coordinates are passed back to the caller. Note also that the iterator object is also incremented for the next pass of the iterator; this is a key step in any iterator function. Without this incrementing step, the iterator would never stop. It's only when the iterator object exceeds the bounds of the possible iterations that it is not trapped by the `if` statements. Once it gets big enough, it finally makes it to the `return FALSE;` statement that ends the function and, by returning false, ends the iteration.

The iterator will be used in the `AnalyzeBoard()` function, which we will discuss next. `AnalyzeBoard()` is the "brain" behind the game. It determines the best move for the computer opponent and determines the game's completion. The implementation of `AnalyzeBoard()` is shown next, but don't forget to declare it in the interface too.

```
void CTTTDoc::AnalyzeBoard()
{
    int Sum, I, J;

    int BestSum = 0;
    int BestI, BestJ;

    const int ImminentWin = 2;
    const int ImminentLoss = -2;   // For the computer, i.e. for 'O'

    InitWinSumIterator();
    while ( NextWinSum(Sum, I, J) )
    {
```

```
            switch (Sum)
            {
                case 3:
                m_cGameStatus = 'O';
                return;

                case -3:
                m_cGameStatus = 'X';
                return;

                // Keep track of the best sum coordinates for
                // ImminentWin or ImminentLoss
                case ImminentWin:
                BestSum = Sum;
                BestI = I;
                BestJ = J;
                break;

                case ImminentLoss:
                if ( BestSum != ImminentWin )
                {
                    BestSum = Sum;
                    BestI = I;
                    BestJ = J;
                }
                break;

                default:
                break;
            }
    }   // End while

    // Save the imminent win/loss coordinates
    if (abs(BestSum) == 2)
    {
        m_nBestI = BestI;
        m_nBestJ = BestJ;
        return;
    }


    for (int i = 0; i < 3; i++)
        for (int j = 0; j < 3; j++)
            // If there are blanks, the game's still afoot
            if (m_acBoard[i][j] == ' ')
            {
                m_nBestI = i;
                m_nBestJ = j;
                return;
            }

    // If there are no blanks and no wins, it's a draw
    m_cGameStatus = 'C';

}
```

Day 2: Documents 101

The function interacts directly with the document class members m_cGameStatus, m_nBestI, and m_nBestJ. It updates them directly with the information it gleans from the board. This algorithm uses the iterator to cycle through all the possible game win lines. If a win is found, AnalyzeBoard() sets the game status appropriately and immediately returns. It doesn't get any better than a win! If an imminent win or loss for the computer is found (two of the same mark and a blank in a row), AnalyzeBoard() keeps track of the position of the blank space. That blank space is the winning/blocking move. Precedence is given to the imminent win versus the imminent loss because the win is more desirable. After all the win situations have been iterated, AnalyzeBoard() transfers any winning/blocking moves to the document class members m_nBestI and m_nBestJ. Finally, if there are no imminent wins or losses, the algorithm checks to see if the game is still in progress or if it has ended in a draw. It acts on this information accordingly.

That's a lot of code for a little Tic-Tac-Toe program! But that's the way of real programs that actually do something. Real-life programs must work and produce results. One of the intentions of this book is to use nontrivial examples to demonstrate the MFC Library in action. So if you think that these programs are a little long, just remember that real-life programs often are. Of course, this is just the document side of the house. Next we will move on to view what we have stored—to reap what we have sown, if you will.

Drawing the Board

Discussions concerning the document can go only so far before you must talk about the corresponding view. They are two sides of the same coin. The document is the data in storage, and the view is the data on display. It is a marriage. Both can exist separately, but only together can they reach their full potential. That said, let's connect the document's data to the view.

It always comes back to requirements. Out of the seven, we have completed the three document requirements. The most natural view requirement to complete first would be to draw the board with the associated moves. Four straight lines draw the board. This is simplicity itself, especially if you completed Exercise 4 in Chapter 1. As you might recall, in that exercise I asked you to look up the CDC class in your MFC Library reference and play around with some of its functions, namely LineTo(). LineTo() draws a straight line from the current point to the point specified in the parameters. A second CDC function, MoveTo(), allows you to specify the current point. LineTo() working in conjunction with MoveTo() is how we will draw our game board. The CDC class is discussed in much more detail in Chapter 4, but for now, get your feet wet by jumping in—truly the best way to learn.

Place the following declarations in the CTTTView interface:

```
protected:
    const int StartX, StartY;
    const int RegionWidth, RegionHeight;
```

These declarations establish the upper-left starting position of the Tic-Tac-Toe board and the width and height of the board squares. You might be wondering why we're using this particular manner of declaring constants. The answer lies in the Software Engineering Principle of Information Hiding: The constants are protected because only the view's member functions need to see them. However, they aren't private because a class derived from CTTTView would need access. Constants defined using the #define directive would be too public if defined in the interface and too private if defined in the implementation.

These constants need initializing in the view's constructor. Make the following additions to the CTTTView's constructor. Notice (or recall) the interesting method of initializing class constants:

```
CTTTView::CTTTView() :
    RegionWidth(100),
    RegionHeight(100),
    StartX(30),
    StartY(30)
{
    // TODO: Add construction code here
}
```

We may now define some functions that will make our drawing tasks much easier. Place the following function definitions in the public operations section of the CTTTView interface:

```
void DrawBoard (CDC* pDC);
void DrawX (CDC* pDC, int I, int J);
void DrawO (CDC* pDC, int I, int J);
void DisplayStatus (CDC* pDC);
```

The purpose of each of the preceding functions is self-evident. However, look at the parameters. Each function is passed a pointer to a CDC object. The CDC object allows the functions to draw in the client area of the view (this is a preview of Chapter 4). Also note that the DrawX() and DrawO() functions are passed a pair of coordinates (I,J). These coordinates are in Tic-Tac-Toe board array coordinates, not display coordinates. This is done to make the calling routine more abstract, because the Tic-Tac-Toe board coordinates are more abstract than the display coordinates. Take a look at the implementations of these functions:

```
///////////////////////////////////////////////////////////////////////
void CTTTView::DrawBoard (CDC* pDC)
{
    int i;

    // Draw horizontal lines
    for (i = 1; i < BOARD_SIZE; i++)
    {
        pDC->MoveTo (StartX, StartY + i*RegionHeight);
        pDC->LineTo (StartX + nSize*RegionWidth,
                StartY + i*RegionHeight);
    }

    // Draw vertical lines
    for (i = 1; i < BOARD_SIZE; i++)
    {
```

Day 2: Documents 101

```
            pDC->MoveTo (StartX + i*RegionWidth, StartY);
            pDC->LineTo (StartX + i*RegionWidth,
                    StartY + nSize*RegionHeight);
    }
}
```

Examine this code and note the interplay between the functions `MoveTo()` and `LineTo()`. Keep in mind that `LineTo()` draws and `MoveTo()` only moves. Make sure you understand that `LineTo()` does indeed draw the board.

The next two functions draw the game markers:

```
////////////////////////////////////////////////////////////////////////
void CTTTView::DrawX (CDC* pDC, int I, int J)
{
    int AtX = StartX + J*RegionWidth;
    int AtY = StartY + I*RegionHeight;

    pDC->MoveTo (AtX, AtY);
    pDC->LineTo (AtX + RegionWidth, AtY + RegionHeight);

    pDC->MoveTo (AtX, AtY + RegionHeight);
    pDC->LineTo (AtX + RegionWidth, AtY);
}

////////////////////////////////////////////////////////////////////////
void CTTTView::DrawO (CDC* pDC, int I, int J)
{
    int AtX = StartX + J*RegionWidth;
    int AtY = StartY + I*RegionHeight;

    pDC->Ellipse (AtX, AtY, AtX + RegionWidth, AtY + RegionHeight);
}
```

The `DrawX()` function uses the same straight line drawing technique that we used in drawing the board, so there's nothing new here. The `DrawO()` function, however, uses the CDC `Ellipse()` function to make a circle. The `Ellipse()` function inscribes an ellipse within the rectangle specified by passing the upper-left and lower-right coordinates as parameters. `DrawX()` and `DrawO()` allow the view to place Tic-Tac-Toe marks wherever they're needed. In order for `OnDraw()` to use these functions, it must search the board and call the appropriate function when it finds a move.

We still have the game results to post. This is a rather simple process, especially in light of how easy it was to write the `Hello World` message in Chapter 1. The same technique will be applied here, with the addition of some conditional code:

```
////////////////////////////////////////////////////////////////////////
void CTTTView::DisplayStatus (CDC* pDC)
{
    CTTTDoc* pDoc = GetDocument();
    ASSERT_VALID(pDoc);

    int X = StartX;
```

```
            int Y = StartY + BOARD_SIZE*RegionHeight;

        switch (pDoc->m_cGameStatus)
        {
            case 'X':
            pDC->TextOut (X, Y, "You Win!  Congratulations.");
            break;

            case 'O':
            pDC->TextOut (X, Y, "I Win!  Dumb Human.");
            break;

            case 'C':
            pDC->TextOut (X, Y, "Meow! A draw -- Cat's game.");
            break;

            default:
            pDC->TextOut (X, Y, "Game in progress.");
        }
    }
```

Our next step is to incorporate these functions into the OnDraw() function. You might recall this function from Chapter 1's Hello World program. OnDraw() provides us with the CDC object with which we may do our drawing. This is where the rubber meets the road—where we succeed or fail. You can actually feel the excitement in the air! Make the following changes to CTTTView's OnDraw() function:

```
void CTTTView::OnDraw(CDC* pDC)
{
    CTTTDoc* pDoc = GetDocument();
    ASSERT_VALID(pDoc);

    // TODO: Add draw code for native data here

    DrawBoard(pDC);

    // Draw moves
    for (int i = 0; i < BOARD_SIZE; i++)
        for (int j = 0; j < BOARD_SIZE; j++)
            if (pDoc->m_acBoard[i][j] == 'X')
                DrawX (pDC, i, j);
            else if (pDoc->m_acBoard[i][j] == 'O')
                DrawO (pDC, i, j);

    DisplayStatus (pDC);

}
```

Another requirement is satisfied. We are halfway home. If you compile, link, and run the program, you'll be rewarded by an empty Tic Tac Toe board. Of course, this is due to the fact that there aren't any moves on the board and we can't make any moves at present. Yet another requirement rears its ugly head. If you can't wait to see a move on the board, you can change the document's m_cWhoGoesFirst initialization to allow the computer to go first. This should put an O in the center square when the game is started.

Documents 101

Let's Play Tic-Tac-Toe

We have finally come to the interactive portion of our show. There are a number of perfectly valid means of getting moves from the user. We could prompt the user for the coordinates of her move. We could have her use the arrow keys to move a cursor to her chosen square and then press Enter. But in a Windows environment, the obvious choice for our game is mouse input. Using the mouse, the user needs only to point and click to make her move. No fuss, no mess, no keyboard interaction at all. So how do we go about including the mouse in our application? Good question. The answer starts with a trip to our soon-to-be close friend, ClassWizard.

Invoke ClassWizard by selecting Browse | ClassWizard (or press Ctrl-W). The ClassWizard dialog that appears can be a formidable vision at first (see Figure 2.6).

Figure 2.6.
The ClassWizard dialog.

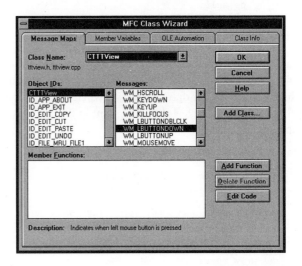

I will leave a detailed explanation of ClassWizard for later. For now, I will say that ClassWizard allows you to add standard functionality to the foundation classes. In this case, we want to add mouse-click recognition support to our view class. Supporting this function means having our view trap the message sent when a mouse click occurs. Sounds confusing and tricky, doesn't it? That's why we use ClassWizard. ClassWizard provides message mapping and the necessary framework so that all we need to do is write the code that gets executed as the result of a mouse click.

At the top of the ClassWizard dialog are file folder tabs: Message Maps, Member Variables, OLE Automation, and Class Info. Clicking on any of these tabs displays a different dialog—it's like having four dialogs in one. Go ahead and click on the tabs and explore. Get the feel of the dialogs. When you're done, however, go back to the Message Maps dialog by clicking on the Message Maps tab.

It is here that we add mouse support. You can see a drop-down list box with a class name selected. Choose CTTTView if it's not already selected. Also select CTTTView in the Object IDs list box. Finally, in the Messages list box, find and select WM_LBUTTONDOWN. You should see the Add Function button become enabled. By clicking on the Add Function button, you add an entry to the Member Functions list box. When you exit from this dialog by clicking on the OK or Edit Code buttons, the respective function(s) will be added to your class(es). In this case, click on the Edit Code button. This will take you to the newly created OnLButtonDown() function in the CTTTView implementation. That's it. We've just put mouse-click support into your application. Of course, it doesn't do anything yet, but that's what we're about to add.

If you're thinking that this ClassWizard procedure is complicated and confusing, you're right. At least, it is at first, but as we work with it more and more, it will become second nature to you. I can remember watching my father drive when I was a kid. I wondered how he could watch the road, shift the gears, tune the radio, and monitor the gauges all at the same time. Now I know that you don't do all those things at the same time. I know what to look for and how to do some of the tasks by feel. It only takes practice and exposure. I can give you the exposure. The practice is up to you.

Modify our newly created function as shown here:

```
void CTTTView::OnLButtonDown(UINT nFlags, CPoint point)
{
    // TODO: Add your message handler code here and/or call default

    CTTTDoc* pDoc = GetDocument();
    ASSERT_VALID(pDoc);

    // Allow moves only if the game is in progress
    if (pDoc->m_cGameStatus != ' ')
        return;

    // Translate logical coordinate into Tic-Tac-Toe array units

    int J = point.x - StartX;
       int I = point.y - StartY;

    // Ignore mouse click if above or to left of board
    if ( (I < 0) || (J < 0) )
        return;

    J = J/RegionWidth;
    I = I/RegionHeight;

    // Ignore mouse click if below or to right of board
    if ( (I >= BOARD_SIZE) || (J >= BOARD_SIZE) )
        return;

    // Accept mouse click only if clicked square was empty
    if (pDoc->m_acBoard[I][J] == ' ')
    {
        pDoc->m_acBoard[I][J] = 'X';
```

Documents 101

```
            pDoc->AnalyzeBoard();

            if (pDoc->m_cGameStatus == ' ')
            {
                pDoc->m_acBoard[pDoc->m_nBestI][pDoc->m_nBestJ] = 'O';
                pDoc->AnalyzeBoard();
            }

            pDoc->UpdateAllViews(NULL);
    }

    CView::OnLButtonDown(nFlags, point);
}
```

This function is an overridden function of the `CWnd` base class. Most of the functions that ClassWizard adds to classes are really just overrides of ancestor functions. `CWnd` has a number of functions for mouse support. These functions are invoked as the result of specific mouse messages generated by the user's mouse interactions. By overriding these functions, we can add our own handling code for certain mouse actions. By calling the base class functions at the end of our handling routine, we can exploit the prewritten code as well. For mouse button clicks, the `CWnd` functions have a form similar to that of the function just shown. Information necessary to a mouse click handler is passed via two parameters.

`nFlags` provides information about the other mouse buttons and the Shift and Ctrl keys on the keyboard. We won't be using the `nFlags` parameter in the Tic-Tac-Toe program. However, this information can be very useful for certain applications. The `nFlags` parameter is constructed from the bitwise ORing of the appropriate combination of the following constants: `MK_CONTROL`, `MK_LBUTTON`, `MK_MBUTTON`, `MK_RBUTTON`, and `MK_SHIFT`. You can retrieve the information stored in `nFlags` by performing a bitwise AND with it and the applicable constant. For example, if you wanted to know if the Shift key was held down at the time of the mouse click, you would use an algorithm comparable to the following:

```
if (nFlags & MK_SHIFT)
    // Shift was held down
    // Other code...
else
    // Shift was not held down
    // Other code...
```

The `point` parameter is a data structure that holds the x- and y-coordinates of the mouse click. From `point` you can determine where in the view the mouse was clicked. This parameter is very useful to our Tic-Tac-Toe program. We want to know if the mouse was clicked on the game board and, if so, in which square. The seven lines after `// Translate` perform the necessary coordinate translation between view coordinates and Tic-Tac-Toe board coordinates.

The remaining code after the line

```
// Accept mouse click only if clicked square was empty
```

actually places the user's move on the board and instructs the computer to make its move. The preceding code snippet contains some view-document subtleties that shouldn't be glossed over. The first thing we do is make sure that the board position on which we clicked was empty—a valid Tic-Tac-Toe move. If the move is valid, we put an X in the appropriate board square. We then have the document analyze the board. If the game is still in progress, we make the computer's move and analyze the board again in light of the change. The last command executed in the valid mouse-click code is a call to the document's `UpdateAllViews()` function. This command informs the document's associated views that the stored data has changed. The views, in turn, update the display with fresh data from the document.

Compile, link, and run the program. You should see a functional Tic-Tac-Toe program that plays a pretty good game. After a bit of observation and play, you should be able to beat it consistently. Enjoy.

Summary

This chapter's main motivation was a Tic-Tac-Toe program. Through the development of this game, we were able to see some of the view-document interactions. An important MFC concept to learn early is the big difference between the task of the view and the task of the document. Distinguishing view requirements from document requirements goes a long way to illustrate this difference in tasks. In this chapter's program, a simple data array was placed in the document, and our view (responding to user commands) was able to retrieve and modify this information. We also took our first steps toward understanding the view's drawing process and its interaction with ClassWizard.

Constructing a nontrivial program like Tic-Tac-Toe from beginning to end can give you an appreciation of the power of the MFC Library and associated Wizards. In one chapter, we have constructed a game that is playable, albeit somewhat plain. In the next chapter, we will use AppStudio and ClassWizard to improve our Tic-Tac-Toe game. In the process, we will learn a great deal about graphical objects and how to connect them into our code.

Q&A

Q All those weird lines of code that AppWizard puts into its files are baffling! They are really breaking my concentration when I try to analyze the classes. Are we ever going to figure out what they're for?

A Yes. As a matter of fact, the next chapter has a whole section on message maps. As you know, message maps constitute a great deal of the weird code.

Documents 101

Q In the Tic-Tac-Toe strategy section, you mentioned that iterators are used in Windows. They seem so weird. Do we really need to know about them?

A Yes. I wasn't lying when I said they're used in Windows. We'll see Windows iterators in action in the chapters to come. By the way, iterators are not weird! They're a lovely programming structure, once you get to know them.

Q Some of the formulas in the Tic-Tac-Toe strategy section looked a little complicated (not to mention weird). I have a medical condition that prevents me from getting close to math. Do we have to do any math in this book?

A No, you don't have to do any math. In this book, all you will have to do is copy the formulas I present. However, the more math you know, the more you'll understand. Math and programming go hand-in-hand—they complement and bolster each other.

Q After analyzing the Tic-Tac-Toe program, I've come to the conclusion that all the real "thinking" is initiated by the `OnLButtonDown()` function. In fact, I believe that all the "thinking" is accomplished between the time I press the mouse button and when the Xs and Os appear on-screen. Can that be right? It looks like the marks are displayed instantly after I press the mouse button.

A Your analysis is correct. To us, the marks appear on-screen instantly, but to the computer, it probably seems like a leisurely stroll. Remember, these newfangled computers can process hundreds of millions of instructions per second.

Workshop

Quiz

1. What is the primary difference between a document's constructor and its `OnNewDocument()` function? Specifically, why would you place code in the `OnNewDocument()` function as opposed to placing it in the constructor?
2. What is an iterator, and what is it used for?
3. Describe the difference between the `MoveTo()` and `LineTo()` functions.
4. Why is the `UpdateAllViews()` function used?

Exercises

1. Change the document class to initialize the `m_cWhoGoesFirst` variable to `'O'`. What do you predict will happen to the application?
2. The Tic-Tac-Toe adversary is a weak player. Work on the strategy algorithm and see if you can make the adversary a better player.

3. Change the constants StartX, StartY, RegionWidth, and RegionHeight. Predict the changes before running the program. Now try changing the BOARD_SIZE constant. What happened that time?

4. The DrawO() and DrawX() functions are somewhat clumsy. See if you can change them so that the marks are drawn without touching the board lines.

5. Put a delay in the OnLButtonDown() function so that it will look like the computer is taking longer to decide its move.

WEEK 1

AppStudio and ClassWizard

AppStudio and ClassWizard

As with most things, we have preconceived ideas about studios. We seem to think of them as places artists go to create works of great entertainment value. Movies come from movie studios. Songs come from recording studios. And starving artists go back and forth between art studios and studio apartments. Studios are the meccas around which art takes form. AppStudio is no different from these other studios. It's the place where much of the visible art that goes into your Windows program is created. Of course, there's plenty of art in the creation of code—the art of programming. But this chapter deals primarily with the visible aspects of our program, how those visible objects are created, and how they are incorporated into our code.

Binding code to the visible objects created with AppStudio is the job of ClassWizard. "Wizard" is a wonderfully appropriate term for this agent. My mental picture of a wizard is a gnarled old man with a conical hat and flowing robes. I see him hunched over a desk, poring over arcane writings all day, searching for magic spells or new potion recipes. This too is the job of ClassWizard! Those cryptic comment statements we found in the classes that AppWizard generates are ClassWizard's arcane writings. Note that it takes wizards to fool around with those odd sections of code—AppWizard to create them and ClassWizard to read and modify them. Don't be intimidated. Someday you too will be a wizard and understand the arcane writings of the Visual C++ wizards!

Messages

One dialect of the arcane writings I just mentioned is the message maps we've been ignoring. Well, the chickens have come home to roost. It's time to start our Wizard training course. The first step to becoming conversant with message maps is to understand Windows messages. Discussing the Windows messaging structure could take up an entire book, but let's see if we can boil it down a bit. Note that in this reducing process I might take a liberty here and there, but it will all be in the name of better understanding.

Just below the surface of Windows, barely hidden from view, is an ongoing exchange of messages. Windows informs window objects of *events* (keyboard activity, mouse manipulation, and so on) by sending the affected window a message. Window objects also can communicate with one another by passing messages. This messaging scheme is like a little e-mail system in your computer, except instead of people sending mail, window objects send each other messages.

Each message is identified by a number—the *message ID*. This number can be anything from 0 to 0xFFFF. Fortunately, we don't have to work with these raw numbers. Windows provides constants for its predefined messages so that we can work with understandable, mnemonic units. It's a good thing Windows does this, because there are well over 200 predefined Windows messages (see the *Windows SDK Programmer's Reference* Volume 3). (This number doesn't include messages defined by standard Windows applications such as File Manager.)

Distinguishing messages by number would be an excruciating exercise—our brains are much better at processing words. Even with the constants, knowing all the messages is no small feat.

To make matters worse, Windows also allows you to define your own messages for use with applications. Now there are even more constants to know! Of course, defining your own messages is a good feature; it allows you to take full advantage of Windows, as we shall see. When you do define a message, it's up to you to provide a properly named constant for the message's ID.

In addition to its ID, a message contains a word parameter (`wParam`) and a long parameter (`lParam`) that are used to pass information pertinent to the specific message. Different messages pass different amounts of information. For example, the BM_GETSTATE message, which is sent to determine the state of a button, passes no information in its parameters. However, the WM_MOUSEMOVE message, which informs a window of a mouse move, has its parameters loaded with information concerning the state of certain keyboard keys and the location of the mouse cursor. There are as many examples as there are Windows messages, and each one is different. However, one message stands apart: WM_COMMAND.

The WM_COMMAND message is special because it carries commands. It could be sent by a Windows control to notify the control's parent window of some change of state. Or it could be sent when a menu option is chosen or an accelerator keystroke is translated. In any of these cases, the primary stimulus is the user issuing menu commands or manipulating controls. WM_COMMAND is really a message within a message. When a window receives a WM_COMMAND message, the message's parameters are examined to determine the command message. See Table 3.1 for a description of the WM_COMMAND parameters.

Table 3.1. A breakdown of the WM_COMMAND parameters.

Parameter	Description
`wParam`	The identifier of the menu item or control.
`lParam` (low word)	The handle to the control, or 0 if not sent by a control.
`lParam` (high word)	The control notification message ID if sent by a control, 0 if sent by a menu selection, or 1 if sent by an accelerator keystroke.

Before you use a menu or work with buttons, edit boxes, or any control, the WM_COMMAND message must be processed. But then, in order to work with Windows at all, you must process messages! The sheer size and complexity of the messaging structure can intimidate you from the start. "How can I possibly keep track of all those messages and protocols?" you might ask. The MFC Library comes to the rescue again.

DAY 3

AppStudio and ClassWizard

The MFC and Messages

Before the existence of the MFC, Windows programmers had no choice but to track and process Windows messages manually. This typically was done using a message-capturing function and a `switch` statement in a message loop. Every Windows program had to have one. It was just part of the overhead needed to program in Windows. This process sounds like a good candidate for encapsulation into the MFC. Well, Microsoft thought so too. Embedded in the `CWinApp` class is a message loop that catches Windows messages and dispatches them to the appropriate class object of the application. The mechanism of distribution is where message maps come into play. Message maps associate messages with message handlers—functions that act on particular messages. Because Windows relies so heavily on message passing, much of the code you write for an application resides in message handlers. In the case of our Tic-Tac-Toe program from Chapter 2, we created (via ClassWizard) and altered the message handler `OnLButtonDown()`. After ClassWizard created this handler, it placed the appropriate entry in the message map:

```
BEGIN_MESSAGE_MAP(CTTTView, CView)
    //{{AFX_MSG_MAP(CTTTView)
    ON_WM_LBUTTONDOWN()
    //}}AFX_MSG_MAP
END_MESSAGE_MAP()
```

The `ON_WM_LBUTTONDOWN()` entry is a message map macro. Pressing the left mouse button is a fairly common occurrence. Catching the left mouse button down message is also common. Therefore, the MFC has defined a set of macros for common Windows messages. These macros have the form `ON_WM_XXXX`, where *XXXX* describes the message. During the compilation process, message map macros are used to associate messages with functions. In the case of the `ON_WM_XXXX` macros, the functions are expected to have the form `OnXxxx()`. This is why it's best to let ClassWizard perform all the housekeeping associated with adding and removing message map entries and message handlers. As we proceed through this chapter, we will see other types of message map macros. But first, let's find out how the message map is used.

When an MFC window object receives a message, it searches through its message map for an associated handler. This searching process is a little more complicated than it sounds, because the search entails not only looking through the message map of the class, but also looking through the message maps of the ancestor classes.

Figure 3.1 is a flowchart of this search process. The ancestor class searched is determined by the `BEGIN_MESSAGE_MAP()` macro. If you take another look at the `CTTTView` message map, you'll see that the `BEGIN_MESSAGE_MAP()` macro takes two class names as parameters. The first parameter is the current class. The second parameter is the current class's immediate ancestor—if that ancestor has a message map. The search leapfrogs up these message maps until no further message map ancestors are referenced. Whenever a handler for the message is found, the search stops and the handler is invoked.

Figure 3.1.
Message map searching.

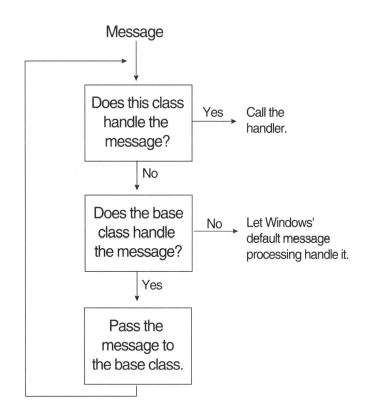

Typically, Windows messages have a specific target. For example, if Windows wants to close a particular window, it sends a `WM_CLOSE` message to that window. Windows messages also are limited. Only objects of classes derived from `CWnd` may be targets of messages. This isn't quite as limiting as it might sound, because `CWnd` is the base class of most of the visible foundation classes. `CView`, `CFrameWnd`, and `CDialog`, just to name a few, are derived from `CWnd`. But `CWinApp`, `CDocument`, and `CDocTemplate` are excluded from the normal message structure.

With the introduction of the MFC library, a new message type came on the scene—the *command*. Commands aren't targeted to a specific window; they're routed over a network of foundation class objects, any one of which may hold a handler. This routing may also extend quite far afield, even to nonwindow objects (that is, objects of classes not derived from `CWnd`). Commands, therefore, have a much wider purview than normal messages. They can be routed to any class with a message map. Message maps are limited to classes derived from `CCmdTarget`.

If Windows messages can't be targeted to non-`CWnd`-derived classes and commands can, it seems obvious that commands can't be Windows messages. Wrong. Although it seems like a contradiction, commands are a form of Windows messages. The explanation for this mind-bending contradiction lies in the `WM_COMMAND` message we explored in the preceding section. The

AppStudio and ClassWizard

menu commands and accelerator keystrokes mentioned earlier are the same commands we're talking about now. Commands are encoded in the `WM_COMMAND` parameters. It's true that the `WM_COMMAND` message can be sent only to `CWnd`-derived class objects. But after the command is extracted, it can be routed by a normal function call, which, of course, isn't limited to `CWnd` classes. The function call in question is the `OnCmdMsg()` function, found in any class derived from `CCmdTarget`. The foundation classes derived from `CCmdTarget` override the `OnCmdMsg()` functions to produce the standard command route shown in Table 3.2. When an object of the type in the column on the left receives a command, it gives itself and other command-target objects a chance to handle the command in the order shown in the column on the right.

Table 3.2. Standard command routing.

Object Type	Order in Which the Command Is Handled
MDI frame window (`CMDIFrameWnd`)	1. Active `CMDIChildWnd` 2. This frame window 3. Application (`CWinApp` object)
Document frame window (`CFrameWnd`, `CMDIChildWnd`)	1. Active view 2. This frame window 3. Application (`CWinApp` object)
View	1. This view 2. Document attached to view
Document	1. This document 2. Document template attached to the document
Dialog box	1. This dialog box 2. Window that owns the dialog box 3. Application (`CWinApp` object)

There is nothing sacred about the standard command route. You can change this routing by overriding the routing function, `OnCmdMsg()`. Be warned that overriding the standard command route is an advanced technique that shouldn't be used without good reason. The standard route works fine for practically every occasion. It won't be changed in this book.

At each point along the route, the message map is searched in the same manner as with normal Windows messages. If no handler is found, the command is passed to the next class on the route. This is what Windows is all about—passing messages and, occasionally, handling messages.

One issue about commands is still unresolved. Where does their routing begin? A typical command is issued by the user through the application's menu. The `WM_COMMAND` message (with the embedded command) is sent to the window that owns the user interface object. In the case of an SDI application being sent a menu command, the CFrameWnd-derived object begins the routing process. The routing continues from object to object, as Table 3.2 indicates. Figure 3.2 diagrams this particular routing, which starts at the frame window.

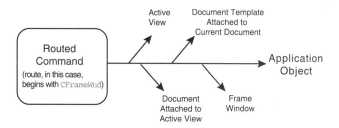

Figure 3.2.
A routed command that starts at CFrameWnd.

What does all this have to do with us? Any discussion of ClassWizard will include at least a little information about messages. Therefore, you need to know the ground rules of messages so that you can appreciate what ClassWizard does for you. Let's look at Tic-Tac-Toe again and see if we can pull some of this information together.

Sprucing Up Tic-Tac-Toe with AppStudio

Our Tic-Tac-Toe game is a neat little program for what it does, but it's also—okay, I'll say it—visually dull. You can play Tic-Tac-Toe for only so long in the first place, but a black-and-white, no-options Tic-Tac-Toe game loses its luster even sooner. By using AppStudio and a bit of imagination, we can breath new life into a program that might already have been pushed aside by the jaded user.

Before we start rewriting Tic-Tac-Toe, use File Manager to copy the whole TTT directory structure, including subdirectories, into a new directory: TTT2. We want to preserve the old Tic-Tac-Toe game so that we can see the difference between the old and new versions.

Note: The name of the project and the name of the directory that contains the project files don't have to be the same! We can copy the TTT directory files to the TTT2 directory verbatim. We don't need to change the names or contents of TTT.H and TTT.CPP to accommodate the new directory. Aside from needing to know where the project is located, the compiler doesn't care how the directory is named. The programmer, on the other hand, had better keep on his toes and make sure he knows which project, old or new, he's working on. This usually isn't a big problem since the environment will automatically open your last working project. However, it's something to keep in mind.

AppStudio and ClassWizard

From the Visual C++ environment, select Project | Open. This allows you to open the Tic-Tac-Toe project in the TTT2 directory. Compile, link, and run the game. Convince yourself that it's the same game (it better be the same—it's the same code!). Finally, reduce the running game's window to an icon by clicking on the little down arrow in the upper-right corner. You should see an icon appear somewhere near the bottom of the desktop. It's not the prettiest thing you've ever seen, but it does the job. Our first task using AppStudio is to try to make that little icon the prettiest thing you've ever seen.

Exit the game and return to the Visual C++ environment. Choose Tools | AppStudio. The AppStudio application should appear on-screen looking something like Figure 3.3. This is the hub of AppStudio: From here you can bring up any of the AppStudio editors.

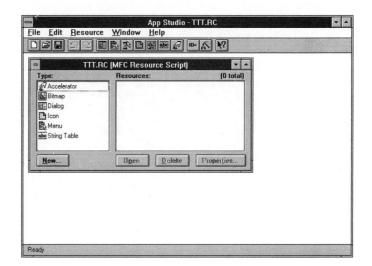

Figure 3.3.
AppStudio.

Icons

At present, we wish to edit the Tic-Tac-Toe icon. By clicking on the icon selection in the TTT.RC (MFC Resource Script) window, we can open the IDR_MAINFRAME resource. This action presents us with the icon editor preloaded with the IDR_MAINFRAME icon—the default AFX icon. Using the icon editor and its floating toolbar, you can transform this dreary little icon into the stunning vision you see in Figure 3.4. (Believe me, it's much better in color.) You don't have to copy my icon. I encourage you to use your imagination and impeccable color sense to create your own tribute to Tic-Tac-Toers everywhere. Once you're finished creating a 32x32 bit masterpiece, exit AppStudio and save your work. That's all there is to it! The default App Wizard code performs all the necessary steps to incorporate the icon into your application. Run it and see!

Figure 3.4.
AppStudio's icon editor.

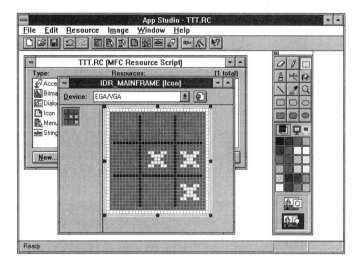

Note that when you edit the default icon, both the desktop icon and the icon incorporated in the About dialog box change automatically. This is so much fun, let's put the icon somewhere else! Of course, putting the icon somewhere else—in the view, for example—requires a snippet of code. But that's why we're here! Add the following lines of code just above the switch statement in the CTTTView::DisplayStatus() function:

```
// Retrieve icon handle and draw icon
HICON hIcon = AfxGetApp()->LoadIcon(IDR_MAINFRAME);
pDC->DrawIcon(X, Y, hIcon);

// Shift text over to accommodate icon
X += 40;
```

Drawing icons is procedurally identical to drawing text. We use a different CDC function, DrawIcon(), and instead of text we pass the icon's handle, but the format and coordinates used are the same. The only tricky part of this procedure is getting the icon's handle. We do this via the CWinApp function LoadIcon(). Before we can make any application calls, we need access to the application object. This navigation problem is a common predicament of beginning MFC programmers: "I'm here but I want to go there." In this case, we're in the view object but we want access to the application object. We accomplish this feat through the global function AfxGetApp(). This function returns a pointer to the application object—a handy function to have.

From the application object we can access the long-awaited LoadIcon() function. This function performs two tasks. It returns a Windows handle to the icon so that we may use it. It also loads the icon into memory if it's not already there. It's a nice safe function to use because it anticipates your next move. It's always funny to hear people say to their computers, "Well, you know what I meant!" Here's an instance where the computer does take the initiative and performs the function you meant it to. The IDR_MAINFRAME icon is preloaded by the application object because

AppStudio and ClassWizard

it's used as the desktop graphic for the application as well as a decoration for the About dialog. So, in this particular case, we're using `LoadIcon()` to merely get the handle to the icon. However, a new icon could be loaded into the application and displayed using this same procedure. Only the `IDR_MAINFRAME` identifier would need to be changed to whatever you named the new icon in AppStudio.

These new lines of code draw the icon to the immediate left of the game status text, but by changing the coordinates you can put the icon anywhere. Anywhere, that is, that happens to be accommodated by the display context—the object pointed to by `pDC`. We'll talk about display contexts in detail in Chapter 4.

Cursors

Our next stop in AppStudio is the cursor editor. Return to the AppStudio hub. Notice that there is no cursor selection in TTT.RC's Type list box. This is because there are no cursors defined in the resource as of yet. Clicking on the New... button in the TTT.RC dialog brings up a list of resource types. Choosing the cursor selection takes you to an edit dialog that is very similar to the icon editor. The first difference you're likely to notice is that the cursor editor is a little wider. This is to make room for a *hotspot* button and coordinates in the top-right section. The cursor hotspot is the pixel on the cursor that determines the cursor's exact coordinates. If you've ever wondered how Windows knew you were pointing to a specific button when only the tip of the arrow cursor was touching the button, now you know. The hotspot on the arrow cursor is on the tip of the arrow. The second difference between the icon editor and the cursor editor is that the cursor editor uses a grayscale palette. With these differences in mind, draw a new cursor for the Tic-Tac-Toe game. The cursor editor and my own cursor creation attempt are displayed in Figure 3.5.

Figure 3.5.
The cursor editor.

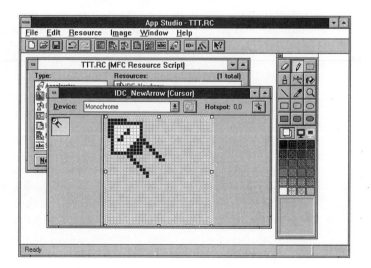

Now that we have a cursor, what do we do with it? A logical approach would be to look up the CWinApp class again. It had a function to load an icon, so maybe it has a function to load a cursor. Cracking open the reference books, we find that, sure enough, CWinApp has a member function called LoadCursor(). However, we're not home yet! The most intuitive thing to do at this point is to put the cursor code into the view class, just as we did with the icon code. Wrong! The reason stems from how Windows implements cursors and our view's position in the MFC architecture.

Every window in Windows has a set of attributes that are specific to that window. One of these attributes is a cursor handle, which the window uses to access the default cursor. In order to change the cursor, we need to change the appropriate attribute of the window. Since I just stated that putting the cursor code in our view doesn't work, you can conclude that the view doesn't own the cursor. We'll discuss the MFC architecture concerning the view classes in the next chapter when we discuss window painting. For the discussion at hand, suffice it to say that the proper place for cursor manipulation is in the view's parent class. In an SDI application such as Tic-Tac-Toe, the view's parent class and the owner of the cursor is the CMainFrame class. It's here that we will load and install the cursor. Place the following code in the CMainFrame::OnCreate() member function:

```
// Set new cursor as default
HCURSOR hC = AfxGetApp()->LoadCursor(IDC_NewArrow);
::SetClassWord(m_hWnd, GCW_HCURSOR, (WORD)hC);
```

You can see that the first line of the new code is very similar to the first line of the icon manipulation code in the preceding section. Basically, it loads the cursor and returns the handle. As in icon loading, if the cursor was already in memory, the loading function is smart enough not to waste time loading it again. In this case, unlike our icon example, the cursor hasn't been loaded. So this is an instance in which actual resource loading does take place. In the icon example, the next step would be to draw the icon. But cursors are a whole different breed of object. We don't draw cursors; Windows has complete control of that task. We change a cursor by providing a different cursor and telling a particular window to use it. You provide the cursor by creating it in AppStudio and loading it via the CWinApp::LoadCursor() function. Instructing a window to use a cursor is done through the ::SetClassWord() function.

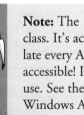

> **Note:** The ::SetClassWord() function is not a member function from a foundation class. It's actually part of the Windows API. Remember, the MFC doesn't encapsulate every API function. But API functions not supported by MFC calls are still accessible! It's just that functions that were included in the MFC are much easier to use. See the *Windows SDK Programmer's Reference* for more information on the Windows API.
>
> The :: scope resolver used this way denotes an API function. It allows you to use API functions that are also covered by the MFC. Otherwise, the compiler will try to use the MFC function.

AppStudio and ClassWizard

In order to set a window's cursor, we must specify the controlling window's handle (m_hWnd) and the new cursor's handle (hC). The middle parameter of ::SetClassWord() indicates which window attribute we intend to change. In this case, GCW_HCURSOR indicates that we are changing the window's cursor. By changing the values of the second and third parameters of ::SetClassWord(), you could also change the style, background color, or default icon of the window specified in the first parameter.

Windows also provides a set of predefined cursors that may be used in your applications. Instead of calling the LoadCursor() function, you can access standard cursors using CWinApp's LoadStandardCursor() function. Table 3.3 describes the standard cursor IDs. LoadStandardCursor() takes the standard cursor ID as its sole parameter.

Table 3.3. Standard cursor IDs.

ID	Description
IDC_ARROW	The standard arrow cursor.
IDC_IBEAM	The usual cursor used in word processing applications.
IDC_WAIT	The hourglass cursor.
IDC_CROSS	The cursor in the shape of a cross hair.
IDC_UPARROW	An arrow cursor pointing straight up.
IDC_SIZE	The cursor used to size windows.
IDC_ICON	The usual cursor used to drag files.
IDC_SIZENWSE	A double-headed arrow cursor that points northwest and southeast.
IDC_SIZENESW	A double-headed arrow cursor that points northeast and southwest.
IDC_SIZEWE	A double-headed arrow cursor that points west and east.
IDC_SIZENS	A double-headed arrow cursor that points north and south.

As soon as they're loaded, the standard cursors may be set in the same way we set our homemade cursors. For example, the following piece of code inserted in the CMainFrame::OnCreate() function would set the application's default cursor to a cross hair. Try it!

```
// Set standard cross-hair cursor as default
HCURSOR hC = AfxGetApp()->LoadStandardCursor(IDC_CROSS);
::SetClassWord(m_hWnd, GCW_HCURSOR, (WORD)hC);
```

Menus

Up to this point, I have carefully chosen examples that don't require menu support. Considering the menu-intensive nature of most Windows programs, this was no small feat. Menus are at the very heart of the Windows command structure. The user interface is centered around them. They are compact and easy to use, yet they are adaptable and powerful. Many things that sound too good to be true often have a dark side—especially in programming. They turn out to consume an inordinate amount of memory or processor cycles. But happily, in this case, there are no real difficulties in using menus.

Let's experience this ease of use firsthand. Bring up AppStudio and select Menu from the Type list box. An interesting thing happens: IDR_MAINFRAME, the same ID that our icon had, appears in the resource list box. Don't be concerned. Windows understands through context what resource type you're using. Opening the IDR_MAINFRAME menu resource brings up the familiar Tic-Tac-Toe menu. (Calling it a Tic-Tac-Toe menu isn't really accurate. Nothing in the menu is particular to our Tic-Tac-Toe game—at least not yet!)

Looking at the menu, even the pull-down parts of the menu, you'll notice that there is always an empty box at the end of the menu. This empty box is the means by which we can add menu selections. The existing menu selections are portable. By clicking and dragging your mouse, you can make menu items switch places. As a demonstration, click and drag the empty box on the main menu to the spot between the Edit and View menu selections. With the empty box still highlighted, type &Options. The ampersand is translated into an underline for the next character, in this case the O. This indicates to Windows that this menu may be selected by pressing Alt-O. As soon as you start typing, a dialog box should appear, as shown in Figure 3.6.

Figure 3.6.
AppStudio's menu editor.

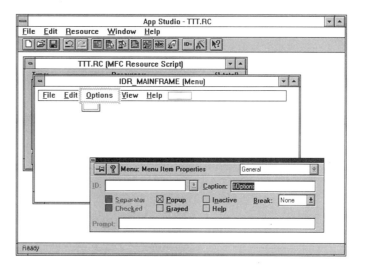

This dialog has a number of interesting features, many of which are not available for main menu selections and hence are grayed out. The Caption edit box, however, is not disabled. It mirrors what is typed as the selection name. There are also a number of check boxes that we will talk about as needed.

AppStudio and ClassWizard

Under the Options menu is a new, empty box. It is an open menu slot that we may fill with a menu item. Click on the empty box and type `&Human Player Starts`. Again the Menu Item Properties dialog appears. This time, however, hardly any of the options are grayed out. For now we will take the conservative approach and just add the bare necessities. Every menu command must have a command ID.

> **Note:** These menu commands are the same ones we discussed at the beginning of this chapter. They are the same commands that get routed from `CCmdTarget` to `CCmdTarget`. The command ID is the same ID that was buried in the `WM_COMMAND` message parameters. So, that earlier discussion is quite applicable here.

The command IDs are of the form `ID_command name`. For menus, it's customary to include both the menu name as well as the option name. In our case, the ID will be `ID_OPTIONS_HUMANSTARTS`. Put this ID name in the ID edit box. The second necessity that I choose to add to this selection is the Prompt at the bottom of the dialog. This is not required, as was the ID, but it's vital for the user's comprehension. The Prompt allows us to communicate the intent of this menu selection directly to the user. The prompt string will appear in the application's status bar when the particular menu selection is highlighted. In this case, type the following string in the Prompt box: `Select this option to change the starting Tic-Tac-Toe player.`

Now that we have this menu selection, what do we do with it? Again, using the Tic-Tac-Toe game as an example, this menu selection will allow the user to change who gets to go first. If you recall from Chapter 2, this was determined by the document variable `m_cWhoGoesFirst`. We tie menu selections to our Tic-Tac-Toe code through ClassWizard. Invoke ClassWizard from AppStudio by choosing Resource | ClassWizard. We now must decide how we will change the `m_cWhoGoesFirst` variable. Actually, making the change isn't so hard. All we have to do is write a little piece of code that changes the `m_cWhoGoesFirst` variable from `'X'` to `'O'` or from `'O'` to `'X'`. Where to place this piece of code takes a bit of thought. Since the `m_cWhoGoesFirst` variable is a document variable and no other classes are involved, the command handler naturally falls into the document class. Not all "where" decisions can be made this easily. Sometimes, if code uses information from many classes, it becomes difficult to determine the best place for the code.

Select `CTTTDoc` from the drop-down Class Name list box. In the Object IDs list box, choose `ID_OPTIONS_HUMANSTARTS`. Two entries appear in the Messages list box: `COMMAND` and `UPDATE_COMMAND_UI`. Select and add both functions to our document class using the Add Function... button. After both functions are added, click on the Edit Code button. This takes you back to the Visual C++ IDE, where the pertinent document code is ready and waiting. Two brand-new functions have been shelled out for us by ClassWizard: `OnOptionsHumanstarts()` and `OnUpdateOptionsHumanstarts()`. Make the following changes to these `CTTTDoc` functions:

```
void CTTTDoc::OnOptionsHumanstarts()
{
    // TODO: Add your command handler code here

    if (m_cWhoGoesFirst == 'X')
        m_cWhoGoesFirst = 'O';
    else
        m_cWhoGoesFirst = 'X';

}
void CTTTDoc::OnUpdateOptionsHumanstarts(CCmdUI* pCmdUI)
{
    // TODO: Add your command update UI handler code here
    pCmdUI->SetCheck (m_cWhoGoesFirst == 'X');

}
```

The command handler `OnOptionsHumanstarts()` is simply a toggling function—`'X'` to `'O'` or `'O'` to `'X'`. The second function, however, requires some explanation.

I'm sure you've seen menu selections grayed out under certain circumstances, indicating that they are disabled. You probably also have seen menu items that have check marks or dots next to them. These marks reflect some kind of status. Have you ever thought about how this part of the menuing system is implemented? I never gave it a second thought until I needed to actually program it. My first instinct was to keep track of all the menu items along with their respective states, continually polling and updating those states as the system's states changed. What a computationally expensive boondoggle that system would have been! I guess we've established how bad my first instincts are. Luckily, the people at Microsoft thought of a better idea.

The trick is to think of the computer as the fast number-crunching machine that it is. To the computer, the time between a mouse click on a menu item and when the user expects to see a pull-down menu is an eternity. Plenty of time to make a few calculations, retrieve a few variables, and even run through a couple of conditional statements. No sweat; computers run hundreds of millions of instructions per second. UPDATE_COMMAND_UI is a command associated with the menu COMMAND, except that its sole purpose is to have a function update the menu. Between the time a main menu item is selected and the associated pull-down menu is displayed, Windows issues the user-interface (UI) update commands for every menu selection on the drop-down menu. Every handler for the UI update command is executed and thus given the chance to change the associated menu selection. Changing the menu selection is made easy through the use of the foundation class CCmdUI.

The OnUpdate*XXXX* functions have a pointer to a CCmdUI object as a parameter. This allows the programmer to concentrate on using the CCmdUI object to alter the menu instead of performing all the housekeeping chores associated with getting the proper CCmdUI object. The CCmdUI class is used for many user-interface items. For the purposes of menus, Table 3.4 contains the CCmdUI functions we need.

AppStudio and ClassWizard

Table 3.4. `CCmdUI` functions in terms of menus.

Function	Description
Enable	Allows you to enable or disable a menu item.
SetCheck	Allows you to check or uncheck a menu item.
SetRadio	Allows you to check or uncheck a menu item in a radio group.
SetText	Allows you to alter the text of a menu item.

In the case of the Tic-Tac-Toe program, the Human Starts menu selection needs to be checked if the human player is currently slated to go first. It needs to be unchecked if the computer player is slated to go first. This is accomplished as just shown in the `OnUpdateOptionsHumanstarts()` function.

Before we go on to accelerator tables, let's take a look at what ClassWizard did to the message map of `CTTTDoc`. Recall from Chapter 2 that the message map for our document was empty. This is what it looks like after we install the menu commands:

```
BEGIN_MESSAGE_MAP(CTTTDoc, CDocument)
    //{{AFX_MSG_MAP(CTTTDoc)
    ON_COMMAND(ID_OPTIONS_HUMANSTARTS, OnOptionsHumanstarts)
    ON_UPDATE_COMMAND_UI(ID_OPTIONS_HUMANSTARTS, OnUpdateOptionsHumanstarts)
    //}}AFX_MSG_MAP
END_MESSAGE_MAP()
```

ClassWizard has placed two new entries in the message map. `ON_COMMAND()` is a macro that is completely dedicated to associating command messages with message handlers. The macro `ON_UPDATE_COMMAND_UI()` is used to associate user-interface update commands with their respective class function handlers. Without these macros in place, commands and messages wouldn't be connected to our code!

Note: It's interesting to note that Microsoft adapted C++ to Windows through a macro structure and avoided altering the C++ language itself. Other compilers make an extension to the language in order to support Windows message handling. Which way is better? Who's to say? But be aware of this fact if you ever take a peek at code intended for other compilers.

Accelerator Tables

Accelerator tables are closely linked to menus. Through accelerator tables you may attach a keyboard hot key or shortcut key to a particular menu item. This allows you to issue a menu command without having to navigate through the menu structure. For example, in the Visual C++ environment, an alternative way of invoking ClassWizard is through the hot key Ctrl-W. In the accelerator table for the Visual C++ application, an association was made between Ctrl-W and the menu selection Browse | ClassWizard. By using the accelerator table, we may add to or even change an application's hot key associations. But accelerator tables are a little more powerful than that. They can associate hot keys with any command, not just menu options! However, this practice should be limited somewhat. Hot keys that aren't reflected in a menu tend to become seldom-used "mystery buttons." You know the saying: "Out of sight, out of mind!"

For the Tic-Tac-Toe example, we will attach a hot key to the Human Starts menu item we installed in the preceding section. To do so, invoke AppStudio and select Accelerator from the Type list box. Open the IDR_MAINFRAME selection that appears in the Resources list box. The accelerator table editor that appears contains all the predefined hot keys that AppWizard established for Tic-Tac-Toe. We want to establish a new hot key, so click on the New button. The dialog that appears is relatively self-explanatory (see Figure 3.7). Choose the menu command ID_OPTIONS_HUMANSTARTS from the ID drop-down list box. Note that any existing command may be chosen from this drop-down list box, not just a command from the menu!

Figure 3.7.
AppStudio's accelerator editor.

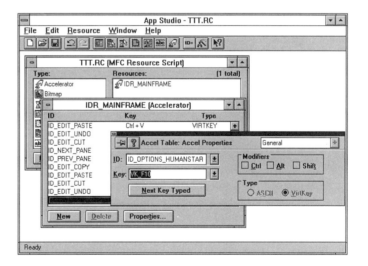

It's now time to choose a hot key for our menu selection. Let's use the F10 key. It's easy to get to, and as of yet it's unused in our application. Click on the Next Key Typed button. This button allows you to enter the key combination, just as you would select it in the application. This is a very handy button, especially when you use complex key combinations such as Shift-Ctrl-Alt-F2. After you press the F10 key, VK_F10 appears in the Key edit box, telling you that the F10 key was accepted. That's all there is to it. Installing accelerator tables isn't very code-intensive,

AppStudio and ClassWizard

at least on our side of Visual C++. Run the program and test the new hot key. Notice that the hot key isn't shown next to the menu selection. This must be done manually. You have to go back to the menu editor, select the menu item in question, and alter the caption. For the current menu item under discussion, you would change &Human Starts to &Human Starts\tF10. The \t inserts a tab in the caption.

String Tables

An application's string table is a central place to store strings. There are two reasons to store strings in this table: internationalization and memory management. When you have a central location for string storage, an application may be translated into a foreign language much more easily. In fact, the programmer doesn't have to be involved with the translation effort at all, as long as this string table storage technique is followed. Internationalizing programs is becoming increasingly important in commercial software development, because more and more foreign markets are becoming available. The modicum of time it takes to put strings in central storage is more than rewarded by the resultant increase in sales.

Even if you're not a commercial software programmer or you don't care about foreign markets, you still can appreciate the second advantage of string tables. String tables allow you to keep your memory consumption down. When the strings are in central storage, they don't clutter up your usable memory. When they are needed, they are loaded from the table, used (usually displayed), and then discarded. This technique is very good for memory conservation, but there is a little overhead in the loading process. The memory advantages are usually well worth this small processing price.

Now, let's take one last look at Tic-Tac-Toe. As you recall, the game status was stored in the document's m_cGameStatus variable. For each situation of game status, a different character string was drawn on-screen. These character strings are ideal candidates for inclusion in the string table.

From the main dialog in AppStudio, click on the New button. Choose String Table from the list of potential new resources. The String Table resource editor appears, containing quite a few strings—some familiar and some not so familiar. Take a moment to scroll through the list of strings. Notice that the prompt string for the menu selection we installed is here. This feature allows the menu to take advantage of the string table the same way we do. It also provides the benefits of internationalization.

Click on the New button in order to create some strings for use with the Tic-Tac-Toe game. Figure 3.8 shows the String Properties dialog that is displayed as a result of clicking on the New button. Place the following strings and associated string IDs into the string table (consecutive uses of the New button are required):

IDS_HUMAN_WIN	You Win! Congratulations.
IDS_COMPUTER_WIN	I Win!! Dumb Human.
IDS_DRAW	Meow! A draw - Cat's game.
IDS_IN_PROGRESS	Game in progress.

Figure 3.8.
String properties.

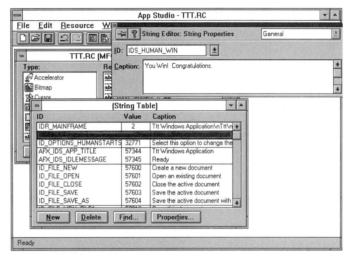

Once the four new strings are placed in the string table, we may use them in the program. Change CTTTView's `DisplayStatus()` function to that shown in the following listing:

```
void CTTTView::DisplayStatus (CDC* pDC)
{
    CTTTDoc* pDoc = GetDocument();
    ASSERT_VALID(pDoc);

    int X = StartX;
    int Y = StartY + BOARD_SIZE*RegionHeight;

    // Icon stuff
    HICON hIcon = AfxGetApp()->LoadIcon(IDR_MAINFRAME);
    pDC->DrawIcon(X, Y, hIcon);

    X += 40;

    CString S;

    switch (pDoc->m_cGameStatus)
    {
        case 'X':
        S.LoadString (IDS_HUMAN_WIN);
        pDC->TextOut (X, Y, S);
        break;

        case 'O':
```

Day 3: AppStudio and ClassWizard

```
            S.LoadString (IDS_COMPUTER_WIN);
            pDC->TextOut (X, Y, S);
            break;

            case 'C':
            S.LoadString (IDS_DRAW);
            pDC->TextOut (X, Y, S);
            break;

            default:
            S.LoadString (IDS_IN_PROGRESS);
            pDC->TextOut (X, Y, S);
        }

    }
```

Converting `DisplayStatus()` to support string table access is accomplished with the addition of a `CString` object. `CString` is a foundation class that is discussed in more detail in Chapter 5. For now, you only need to understand that `CString` objects are variable-length character strings that support the loading of strings from string tables. The loading call is very simple. Pass the string ID we specified in the string table to `CString`'s `LoadString()` function, and the string is loaded. It's that easy! You can use the `CString` object almost everywhere you use character arrays.

Summary

This chapter introduced you to a critical component of the Windows system: the messaging architecture. How Windows uses messages and how the MFC Library interacts with the same messages are important pieces of knowledge. We will use this knowledge a great deal in the chapters to come. You also learned about some of AppStudio's abilities. We created some typical AppStudio objects and incorporated them into our Tic-Tac-Toe program. These examples will come in handy when you decide to put some of these visual objects in your future applications. However, we skipped a couple of very high-visibility AppStudio objects: bitmaps and dialogs. These subjects weren't skipped because they lack importance. Quite the contrary: We skipped them because we couldn't do them justice. Dialogs are so important to Windows programming that I have devoted an entire chapter to them. Bitmap programming can get a bit involved, so I'm postponing the discussion of bitmaps until we can cover device contexts. Don't be concerned. We'll cover both of these interesting topics very soon.

We covered a great deal of information in this chapter. Every bit of it is important to your full understanding of the MFC and Windows. Chapter 4 discusses Windows painting. The drawing we've been doing only scratches the surface of Windows painting. There is a considerable amount of material coming up, so let's move on.

Q&A

Q In the process of changing the cursor for a window, we made a call to `::SetClassWord()`. You said the last parameter in the call was supposed to be the handle to the cursor. But in the third parameter slot, you typecast the handle to a `WORD` type. Why?

A Very observant of you. Yes, the cursor handle is typecast to the 16-bit unsigned integer type `WORD`. The `WORD` type provides a certain anonymity similar to that of the `void` pointer type. `::SetClassWord()` provides support for changing many of the window attributes, but window attributes come in a variety of types. Using a common type like `WORD` as a parameter is a useful way of allowing one function to service many dissimilar attributes.

Q I've heard that icons and cursors are bitmaps. Why didn't we just talk about bitmaps here too? Bitmaps are cool.

A Yes, this is correct. Icons and cursors are special types of bitmaps that have specialized uses. And because they have such specific uses, much of their manipulation is automated by way of predefined functional support. The general bitmap is a much more generalized creature. Many more decisions and preparations go into displaying it. Those extras take a few more sophisticated manipulations, which you will see in the next chapter.

Workshop

Quiz

1. Describe the components of a message.
2. What's so special about the `WM_COMMAND` message?
3. What's the difference between commands and messages?
4. What does the function `AfxGetApp()` accomplish, and why is cursor ownership such an important issue in cursor management?
5. Do accelerator entries have to be tied to menu items?

Exercises

1. Use AppStudio to create a new icon (don't overwrite the old icon as we did in this chapter). Add the new icon to the end of the status text by altering the `DisplayStatus()` function. However, leave the old icon at the beginning of the status text alone. That's right—two different icons in the same view!

AppStudio and ClassWizard

2. In the spirit of Exercise 5 in Chapter 2, put a delay in the `OnLButtonDown()` function. While it's delayed, display the hourglass cursor.

3. Use the `CCmdUI::SetText()` function to toggle the menu selection from Human Starts to Computer Starts. Is this better or worse than the check mark?

4. Try your hand at internationalizing the Tic-Tac-Toe application. For example, you could change "You Win! Congratulations." to the near-French equivalent "Victoire vous. Félicitations." (My apologies to France.)

WEEK 1

CView Painting

DAY 4
CView Painting

Painting in Windows and painting in the real world aren't as dissimilar as you might expect. Of course, our idea of painting is somewhat removed from that of Joe Artist hanging around the Louvre sipping French coffee. Windows painting includes all output to the screen. The `Hello World` that we casually tossed up on the screen in Chapter 1 is included in the all-encompassing Windows term of *painting*. "Even if you frame that sucker, it ain't going in no art gallery!" would be my first reaction if someone told me that `Hello World` was art. Windows isn't that picky. Anything written, drawn, copied, or otherwise transferred to the screen is considered by Windows to be painting. There's no accounting for taste. But what Windows lacks in taste, it more than makes up for in accommodation. Your every painting whim has been anticipated and provided for. (Well, okay, there are some limitations.) Microsoft even went so far as to name the MFC painting objects after the tools used for painting and drawing in the real world. This chapter examines a wide range of foundation classes dedicated to our drawing needs. But before we go too far out into the fancy classes, perhaps we should talk about the mechanisms of painting.

OnDraw! OnPaint! OnDonner? OnBlitzen?

The canvas we paint on can represent any part of the screen, a printer, or even a file. Drawing to these varied and disparate media is very easy. In fact, much of the time the same code will be used for all three device types: screen, printer, and metafile. Drawing on one versus drawing on another is done by way of a *device context* (*DC*). For the most part, the same drawing functions are called for any of the device types. The device context indicates to which device the drawing commands are to be directed. The base device context class is `CDC`. From this class spring all the other device context classes. The `CDC` class contains all the graphical drawing functions you will need. The derived classes inherit this mass of drawing functionality from the `CDC` class; only a modicum of derived class-specific code is added. In your painting routines, the device context objects you will be dealing with will be those derived from the `CDC` class. However, the derived objects will be passed to you as if they were `CDC` objects. The painting functions take advantage of the polymorphic abilities of the C++ classes by passing pointers to `CDC` objects, even though the objects in question are most likely descendants of the `CDC` class. Because the `CDC` class contains the drawing functions, this technique allows one piece of code to be used for multiple output devices. For example, one function can (and will) "draw on" both the printer and the screen. The MFC provides many `CDC`-derived classes intended for specific output jobs. See Table 4.1.

Table 4.1. `CDC`-derived classes.

Class	Description
CWindowDC	Used for accessing the entire screen.
CClientDC	Used for accessing the client area of one window.
CPaintDC	Used only for responding to `WM_PAINT` messages.
CMetaFileDC	Used for recording a sequence of graphical commands.

The CPaintDC class is used exclusively to respond to the WM_PAINT message that is sent by the framework when a window needs redrawing. CPaintDC is customized specifically for this purpose. The CWnd function OnPaint() is the normal and accepted way a window responds to a WM_PAINT message. Consequently, you will seldom see CPaintDC used outside of OnPaint(). Outside of overriding the OnPaint() function, you will rarely use CPaintDC directly in your code. Later in this section we will see that we will indirectly use objects of CPaintDC quite often.

The classes CWindowDC and CClientDC are used when you want to create your own device contexts to access the whole screen or the client area of your window, respectively. In previous examples, output was accomplished through the OnDraw() function of our view class. One of OnDraw()'s parameters was a pointer to a CDC class, so we didn't have to worry about where a DC came from. However, if we need a DC and it's not passed to us via a function parameter, we're responsible for DC construction and destruction—especially destruction, since device contexts are a limited resource. Later in the chapter, the differences between CWindowDC and CClientDC will be illustrated by way of examples and discussion.

Note that no "CPrintDC" class is listed in Table 4.1. This is not an oversight; there is no "CPrintDC" class. Printers are the exception to the derived-class passing rule. An object of the CDC class itself is used for printing, not an object from a derived class. We will discuss printing details in Chapter 17. We will also postpone the discussion of the CMetaFileDC class to Chapters 16 and 18. But to prevent you from bursting from curiosity, I will make a comment or two. Objects of the CMetaFileDC class act like graphical tape recorders. They can hold a recorded copy of your graphical commands for file storage or playback. It's a very interesting and powerful class, as you will see.

If you look up the CDC class in the Class Library Reference, you'll see that it's a big class. CDC encapsulates all the drawing algorithms you're likely to need for quite a while. Through the CDC object, you may draw lines, polygons, ellipses, text, bitmaps, and more. The CDC also allows you to specify colors, fonts, clipping regions, stretching factors, and all manner of styles for drawing. CDC truly allows great flexibility in your drawing options. However, many of the options require you to know something about the drawing objects in order to manipulate their attributes.

The drawing objects in question are CPen, CBrush, CPalette, CFont, CBitmap, and CRgn. These drawing objects are all descendants of CGDIObject (in which *GDI* stands for *Graphics Device Interface*). The GDI objects are your software interface to the graphical hardware devices that are present in your system. GDIs in conjunction with DCs are your means of displaying information on the device of your choice. The remainder of this chapter concentrates on screen output, but bear in mind that these techniques will apply to the printer and metafile device types as well. We will talk about these other devices later in this book.

For convenience, you can think of the canvas as your view class and your drawing implement as a GDI object—a pen, for example. Where does the DC come in? It doesn't seem that we really need a DC to do anything. This is not true! You can't paint on the canvas by yourself. You need a digital familiar—a byte-sized robot, if you will—to perform the actual drawing. (See Figure 4.1.) This drawing robot will take an offered drawing object and respond to your drawing

Day 4

CView Painting

instructions. Just in case no drawing object is offered, the robot comes with a default set of tools so as to always be prepared for drawing commands. As you might have guessed, the drawing robot is the DC. He keeps track of and applies your specified drawing styles as he performs the drawing instructions you provide. He is your drawing assistant. But because good help is always hard to find, Windows has only a limited number of DCs available for use. Therefore, you can keep the robot only for the length of the drawing function for which he was summoned. After that, he must be released back into the general pool of Windows resources, where another function may summon and use him. *Summon* and *release* are the euphemisms I use for the uninspiring words of *create* and *destroy*. We'll talk about these aspects of the DC at the end of this chapter. For now, let's concentrate on DC use.

Figure 4.1.
The DC robot.

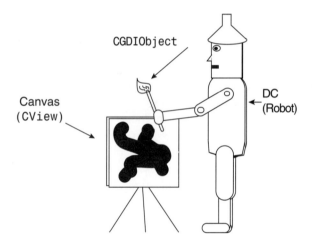

Note: Windows' conservation of resources seems backward. This create-and-destroy paradigm seems very much like the conspicuous consumption that has contributed to our real-world resource problems. Nothing could be further from the truth. By creating and destroying objects like our DC robot, we are actually conserving resources! The reason why this counterintuitive technique works is because of a wonderful recycling program. All objects destroyed are inherently recycled back into the most precious computer resource of all—memory. By not destroying our objects, we are, in effect, shoving them into a landfill where they will never be seen again. Well, not quite. Everything is recycled when Windows restarts, but that can be a long time to wait in computer cycles. I'd hate to have to wait for the sun to go nova before our own environment got cleaned up.

Typically, the canvas on which we spill our paints is the *view*. Of course, there's a lot more to Windows than just our view object. There is the desktop, Program Manager, our application, and potentially lots of other icons and windows cluttering up the display. It's a veritable potpourri of potential painting possibilities (say that three times!). Painting them all would seem to be a formidable proposition. Naturally, the MFC provides ample means to access all portions of the screen.

We want to confine ourselves, at least for the time being, to the predefined painting means available through the CWnd classes. All of the CWnd-derived foundation classes (which, incidentally, doesn't include the CDocument-derived classes), have member functions called OnPaint(). This function, in response to a paint message, performs the painting duties required for that particular window. The OnPaint() function is a natural place to put drawing code. However, our drawing code isn't restricted to OnPaint(). In fact, our view class, the class that will contain most of our drawing code, will have very little new code in its OnPaint() function. The reason for this is that CView has a different function that's called by OnPaint(). You might recall its name from the programs we've already written: OnDraw(). Why on earth would we want another processing layer in such a computation-intensive area as screen painting? What does this layer give us? These are both very good questions.

The answer centers around the issue of device contexts. The OnDraw() function is slightly different from the OnPaint() function in terms of parameter lists. A DC pointer is passed to OnDraw(), whereas OnPaint() has to create (and destroy) its own DC. The implication is that the same OnDraw() function can be used to output information to any DC that it's passed. OnPaint() is specifically intended to output information to the screen, and the application framework treats it as such. When a paint message is encountered, the OnPaint() function is called. The OnPaint() function, in turn, creates an appropriate screen DC, calls OnDraw(), passing the DC, and then destroys the DC. OnPaint() is particular to the screen, but OnDraw() is not. At another time, a print message may invoke an OnPrint() function, which calls OnDraw(), passing a printer DC. Printer output or screen output—it makes no difference to OnDraw(). It goes about its duties, unaware of the final destination of its drawings. Obviously, the DC-independent nature of the OnDraw() function is a very good idea!

The central figure in the whole drawing scenario is the DC. Understanding the role and techniques of the DC is critical to understanding Windows painting.

Oh Say Can You *CDC?*

As I mentioned earlier, the CDC has a mess of functions associated with it. I don't expect you to gain full understanding of them from this chapter. However, I do want you to become familiar with many of them. As a start, let's look at the CDC graphic drawing functions listed in Table 4.2.

CView Painting

Table 4.2. CDC graphic drawing functions.

Function	Description
GetCurrentPosition	Returns the current pen coordinates in a CPoint structure.
MoveTo	Changes the current pen coordinates to those specified.
SetPixel	Sets the pixel at the given coordinates to the specified color.
GetPixel	Returns the color of the pixel at the given coordinates.
LineTo	Draws a line from current coordinates to those specified.
Polyline	Draws line segments connected end-to-end.
Polygon	Draws a polygon.
PolyPolygon	Draws multiple polygons.
Rectangle	Draws a rectangle.
RoundRect	Draws a rectangle with rounded edges.
DrawFocusRect	Draws a rectangle using the current focus attributes.
Ellipse	Draws an ellipse.
Arc	Draws an elliptical arc.
Chord	Draws a chord.
Pie	Draws the specified wedge out of an ellipse.

Each of these functions automates some type of drawing capability. It's interesting to note that the algorithms used in these functions could reside in the actual hardware device. For example, some printers have hardware routines that perform ellipse drawings given the pertinent parameters. Some video cards, on the other hand, don't support the drawing of ellipses as such. Ellipses may still be drawn in a pixel-by-pixel fashion, but the drawing algorithm (the mathematical calculations for the ellipse) exists in the Windows software. Part of the beauty of the Software Engineering Principles of Abstraction and Information Hiding is that it doesn't matter where the algorithm resides. The fact of the matter is, we *shouldn't* know. This knowledge not only brings another bit of information to the surface that adds to the overall complexity, but it also makes the code hardware-dependent. However, a closely related issue is not so easily dismissed. What if the hardware device is truly unsupportive? There are still printers out there that output only text. They are totally graphics-illiterate. Having such a device on your machine constitutes a tidbit of knowledge that you do need to know. Recognize the difference between knowing *if* a capability is supported and knowing *where* a capability is discharged.

These functions, along with the drawing implements themselves, allow you to create some impressive graphics images. To demonstrate the graphics calls, we will need to create a demo program that's simple enough to fit within the confines of this chapter, yet complex enough to demonstrate the CDC functionality. A happy balance can be obtained by using a menu to select drawing options and the mouse to indicate drawing positions. The data in this application will be an array of drawing coordinates (CPoint objects) and the current drawing options. Enough talk. Let's see some action.

Use AppWizard to create another project with the same options we used in the Hello and Tic-Tac-Toe programs—a medium memory model with only toolbar support. Have it generate source comments. Name the project Paint. When AppWizard is through putting the application together, open the document interface (PAINTDOC.H) and add the following define directives at the top of the file:

```
// Shape types supported
#define NO_SHAPE 0
#define ELLIPSE 1
#define ARC 2
#define PIE 3
#define CHORD 4
#define RECTANGLE 5
#define ROUNDRECT 6
#define POLYLINE 7
#define POLYGON 8

// Size of our array: specifies maximum number of points possible
#define MAX_SIZE 8
```

Within the class declaration, add the following data objects:

```
CPoint m_acPoints[MAX_SIZE];
int m_nPointCount;   // Counts how many points are in the array
int m_nNewPoint;     // Indicates the index of the last point entered

int m_nShape;        // Stores the currently selected shape type
BOOL m_bDrawPoints;
```

As the preceding code stands, our point array will hold up to eight CPoint objects. The member variable m_nPointCount will keep a running total of the number of points currently stored (this number can't exceed MAX_SIZE). The member variable m_nNewPoint points to the array position of the most recently added point. This information is valuable because, as we keep adding points via the mouse, we will write over the oldest points. The document will also keep track of the current drawing shape using m_nShape in conjunction with the defined constants. Finally, m_bDrawPoints will indicate to the view whether we want the actual points to be drawn on the display.

> **Note:** CPoint is a very simple foundation class. It consists of two member variables (an x- and a y-coordinate) along with associated member functions. Because many of the CDC functions deal with CPoint and CPoint arrays, it's an ideal choice for our current project.

Day 4

CView Painting

These values must be initialized, so put the following code snippet into the `CPaintDoc::OnNewDocument()` function:

```
m_nPointCount = 0;
m_nNewPoint = -1;

m_bDrawPoints = TRUE;   // Boolean objects may be TRUE or FALSE
m_nShape = NO_SHAPE;
```

We don't have to initialize the array because the point count variable will tell us how many of the values in `m_acPoints` are valid.

Now that we know the players, let's write the script. Use ClassWizard to add the `OnLButtonDown()` function to the `CPaintView` class. Make the following modifications to the newly created mouse button routing:

```
void CPaintView::OnLButtonDown(UINT nFlags, CPoint point)
{
    CPaintDoc* pDoc = GetDocument();
    ASSERT_VALID(pDoc);

    // Increment the new point index
    pDoc->m_nNewPoint++;
    // Remember, if it exceeds MAX_SIZE, cycle back to zero
    pDoc->m_nNewPoint %= MAX_SIZE;

    // Store the point and increment the counter
    pDoc->m_acPoints[pDoc->m_nNewPoint] = point;
    if (pDoc->m_nPointCount < MAX_SIZE)
        pDoc->m_nPointCount++;

    // Instruct the document's views to update their displays with new data
    pDoc->UpdateAllViews(NULL);
}
```

This function stores the mouse point in the array and maintains the housekeeping variables of `m_nPointCount` and `m_nNewPoint`. This is the only function that adds points to the array. If there were more than one input function, it would behoove us to hide the array in the document or encapsulate it in its own class. This would allow us to control access to the array and help prevent misuse. An example of misuse would be if a function added a point but neglected to increment the count. In this case, I chose simplicity (as dangerous as it can be) so that I could concentrate on the lesson at hand. We will cover encapsulation techniques when we discuss the `CObject` class.

We now have an array and the capability to fill that array with points. Our next step is to draw the points on the display. We do this by altering `CPaintView::OnDraw()`. What else is new? Make the following changes to `OnDraw()`:

```
void CPaintView::OnDraw(CDC* pDC)
{
    CPaintDoc* pDoc = GetDocument();
    ASSERT_VALID(pDoc);

    int i;
```

```
        CPoint P1, P2;  // Temporary points

        // Display some text to show text/graphics interaction
        pDC->TextOut(100, 100, "This is the Paint Demo program!!");

        // If there are no points, don't draw anything
        if (pDoc->m_nArraySize <= 0)
            return;

        // Draw points (if selected)
        if (pDoc->m_bDrawPoints)
            for (i = 0; i < pDoc->m_nArraySize; i++)
            {
                P1 = pDoc->m_acPoints[i];
                DrawPoint(pDC, P1.x, P1.y);
            }

        // Draw the appropriate shape
        switch (pDoc->m_nShape)
        {
            // Place the shape-drawing routines here under the appropriate case

            case default:
            break;
        }
}
```

The additions to OnDraw() are easily surmised. We check to make sure we have points. We then draw the points if the m_bDrawPoints flag is set. Finally, we draw the shape selected in the m_nShape member variable. In a few moments, we will add the appropriate cases to this switch statement. The DrawPoint() function isn't included in the MFC, so we must add it (don't forget to include it in the interface too):

```
void CPaintView::DrawPoint (CDC* pDC, int AtX, int AtY)
{
    pDC->Ellipse(AtX-5, AtY-5, AtX+5, AtY+5);
    pDC->MoveTo(AtX-10, AtY);
    pDC->LineTo(AtX+10, AtY);
    pDC->MoveTo(AtX, AtY-10);
    pDC->LineTo(AtX, AtY+10);
}
```

This little routine draws a circle around the point (AtX, AtY) and then puts cross hairs over it. It's very simple, but it makes a distinct point. Run the program and see how things are going. The application should respond to mouse clicks by displaying one of our little points at the position of the mouse click. After you click more than eight times, the oldest point disappears when the newest point appears. If all is going well, let's work on the menu.

Invoke AppStudio. In the menu editor, add a &Shapes menu between Edit and View. Under the Shapes menu, add the menu items listed in Table 4.3.

DAY 4

CView Painting

Table 4.3. The Shapes menu.

ID	Caption	Prompt
ID_SHAPES_ELLIPSE	&Ellipse	Change to ellipses.
ID_SHAPES_ARC	&Arc	Change to arcs.
ID_SHAPES_PIE	&Pie	Change to pies.
ID_SHAPES_CHORD	&Chord	Change to chords.
ID_SHAPES_RECTANGLE	&Rectangle	Change to rectangles.
ID_SHAPES_ROUNDRECT	R&ound Rect	Change to round rectangles.
ID_SHAPES_POLYLINE	Poly&line	Change to a polyline.
ID_SHAPES_POLYGON	Poly&gon	Change to a polygon.

Also add an &Options menu between Shapes and View. Under Options, add a single menu item: UID_OPTIONS_DRAWPOINTS. Its caption will be &Draw points, and its prompt will be "Toggle the drawing of points." Save your work and exit AppStudio.

Use ClassWizard to add all the menu commands and UI update commands to the CPaintDoc class. Yup, you read it right. Add *all* the ON_COMMAND and *all* the ON_UPDATE_COMMAND handlers for the menu items just added. After ClassWizard has added these 18 functions, it's your job to make them work! It's not as bad as you might think. These functions are one, maybe two, lines long at the most. They are also very similar. With the proper employment of cut and paste, you can get this nasty business concluded in no time.

The OnOptionsDrawpoints() and OnUpdateOptionsDrawpoints() functions have a slightly different mission than do the other menu commands we installed. The draw points functions deal with the m_bDrawPoints variable:

```
void CPaintDoc::OnOptionsDrawpoints()
{
    m_bDrawPoints = !m_bDrawPoints;
    UpdateAllViews(NULL);
}
void CPaintDoc::OnUpdateOptionsDrawpoints(CCmdUI* pCmdUI)
{
    pCmdUI->SetCheck(m_bDrawPoints);
}
```

The draw points command toggles the m_bDrawPoints variable and calls the now-familiar UpdateAllViews() function. The associated UI update function sets or resets the check mark on the menu item as per the value of m_bDrawPoints.

The remainder of the menu commands bear an uncanny resemblance to the procedure seen in the draw points functions, except that they concern themselves with the m_nShape variable. Each of the On*XXXX*() command functions ClassWizard added to the document class is responsible for revising the m_nShape member variable to the appropriate value. For example:

```
void CPaintDoc::OnShapesArc()
{
    m_nShape = ARC;
    UpdateAllViews(NULL);
}

void CPaintDoc::OnUpdateShapesArc(CCmdUI* pCmdUI)
{
    pCmdUI->SetRadio(m_nShape == ARC);
}
```

The command function merely sets m_nShape to the ARC constant and refreshes the display. The UI update function places a dot in front of its menu item if ARC is the currently selected shape. Each command/UI update function pair is practically identical to these two functions. As I said, with the proper application of cut and paste, you're in business.

We now have a framework in which we may readily add the actual routines that will illustrate CDC drawing. Since we've seen ellipses before, let's begin with them. In the CDC Ellipse() function, ellipses are defined by a bounding rectangle. This can be done in two ways. In the ellipse calls we have made so far, we have passed the upper-left and lower-right corner coordinates of this bounding rectangle. Alternatively, we could pass the rectangle in toto. This is done through the foundation class CRect, which is just the encapsulation of those same corner coordinates. It's really just six of one versus half a dozen of the other. But you might have an inclination to one parameter over four. This preference might soften a bit, though, since you have to declare another variable, namely one of CRect. It's good to know about CRect, however, because some functions will take only objects of this stripe.

Place the following piece of code into CPaintView::OnDraw()'s switch statement:

```
case ELLIPSE:
for (i = 0; i < pDoc->m_nArraySize/2; i++)
{
    P1 = pDoc->m_acPoints[2*i];
    P2 = pDoc->m_acPoints[2*i+1];
    pDC->Ellipse(P1.x, P1.y, P2.x, P2.y);
}
break;
```

This piece of code demonstrates a common technique that we will be using for points in the array. We require two points for the definition of a bounding rectangle. Therefore, an array of eight points will provide points enough for only four ellipses. The same is true of rectangles and round rectangles:

```
case RECTANGLE:
for (i = 0; i < pDoc->m_nArraySize/2; i++)
{
    P1 = pDoc->m_acPoints[2*i];
    P2 = pDoc->m_acPoints[2*i+1];
```

Day 4: CView Painting

```
        pDC->Rectangle(P1.x, P1.y, P2.x, P2.y);
    }
    break;

case ROUNDRECT:
    for (i = 0; i < pDoc->m_nArraySize/2; i++)
    {
        P1 = pDoc->m_acPoints[2*i];
        P2 = pDoc->m_acPoints[2*i+1];
        pDC->RoundRect(P1.x, P1.y, P2.x, P2.y, 30, 50);
    }
    break;
```

Note the difference in the CDC::RoundRect() call. It has two extra parameters tacked on the end. These last two parameters specify the width and height, respectively, of an ellipse that's used to round the corners. I found that 30 and 50 did nicely, but feel free to experiment.

The Arc(), Chord(), and Pie() functions are very similar in form and substance. They all are closely associated with ellipses. In fact, the first four parameters of each function specify the particular ellipse on which the shape will be based. The final four parameters of each function specify the two points along the ellipse where a break will be made. The nature of the break is determined by the shape. For example, the pie shape will remove a pie-shaped wedge from the ellipse at these break points. The break points don't have to be on the ellipse, but it makes sense to at least place them close. However, wherever the break points are, the computer will do its best to perform the break. A picture is worth a thousand words. Playing around with this program will give you a feel for what these shape algorithms can do. Enter the following into the switch statement:

```
case ARC:
    for (i = 0; i < pDoc->m_nArraySize/4; i++)
    {
        P1 = pDoc->m_acPoints[4*i];
        P2 = pDoc->m_acPoints[4*i+1];
        CPoint P3 = pDoc->m_acPoints[4*i+2];
        CPoint P4 = pDoc->m_acPoints[4*i+3];
        pDC->Arc(P1.x, P1.y, P2.x, P2.y, P3.x, P3.y, P4.x, P4.y);
    }
    break;

case CHORD:
    for (i = 0; i < pDoc->m_nArraySize/4; i++)
    {
        P1 = pDoc->m_acPoints[4*i];
        P2 = pDoc->m_acPoints[4*i+1];
        CPoint P3 = pDoc->m_acPoints[4*i+2];
        CPoint P4 = pDoc->m_acPoints[4*i+3];
        pDC->Chord(P1.x, P1.y, P2.x, P2.y, P3.x, P3.y, P4.x, P4.y);
    }
    break;

case PIE:
```

```
for (i = 0; i < pDoc->m_nArraySize/4; i++)
{
    P1 = pDoc->m_acPoints[4*i];
    P2 = pDoc->m_acPoints[4*i+1];
    CPoint P3 = pDoc->m_acPoints[4*i+2];
    CPoint P4 = pDoc->m_acPoints[4*i+3];
    pDC->Pie(P1.x, P1.y, P2.x, P2.y, P3.x, P3.y, P4.x, P4.y);
}
break;
```

You should be able to discern the difference between arc, chord, and pie by selecting between them on the Shapes menu. See Figures 4.2, 4.3, and 4.4.

Figure 4.2.
Arcs.

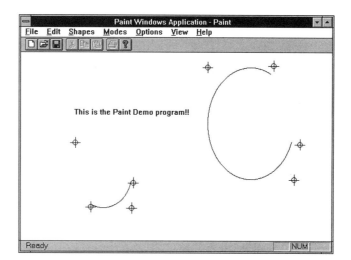

Figure 4.3.
Chords.

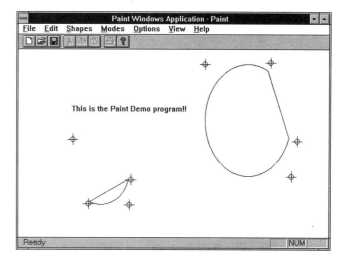

CView Painting

Figure 4.4.
Pies.

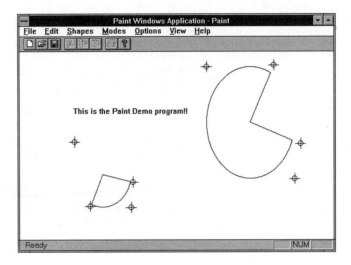

The final two menu selections, Polyline and Polygon, might seem the most difficult to code. In fact, they're probably the easiest by virtue of our choice of point storage. Both `Polyline()` and `Polygon()` take an array of points as a parameter. Enter the following code into the `switch` statement:

```
case POLYLINE:
if (pDoc->m_nArraySize >= 2)
    pDC->Polyline(pDoc->m_acPoints, pDoc->m_nArraySize);
break;

case POLYGON:
if (pDoc->m_nArraySize >= 2)
    pDC->Polygon(pDoc->m_acPoints, pDoc->m_nArraySize);
break;
```

In both cases, we pass an array of points and the number of points contained therein. Happily, both of these objects are easily obtained from the document. The `Polyline()` and `Polygon()` functions are practically identical. They both draw line segments from point to point in the array. They differ in that `Polygon()` connects the last point to the first and fills the interior. You might have noticed that your polygons haven't been filled. *Au contraire.* They *have* been filled—with white! All the closed shapes we've been dealing with fill their interiors using the default white brush. This brings us back to the subject of painting utensils.

Pens, Brushes, and Colors

In my `CDC` robot analogy, I mentioned that the robot came with his own equipment so as to always be ready for painting. Of course, any type of standard equipment is usually conservative and, yes, boring. The `CDC` standard equipment is a thin black pen and a white painting brush—

a boring pair if I ever saw one. Needless to say, this must change if we are to have any fun at all. But before we go changing things around, let's find out a little more about pens, brushes, and colors.

I know what you're thinking: "I know about colors. I learned about them in kindergarten. How different could they be?" Fortunately, computer colors aren't that different from the crayon colors with which we grew up. One of the differences is that we usually have to mix them ourselves. The three primary colors of the computer world are red, green, and blue—*RGB*. By mixing these three colors, we can construct practically any hue you desire. You mix your colors by way of the RGB macro. RGB takes three parameters holding the amount of red, green, and blue, respectively, and it returns a 32-bit COLORREF value with the desired color encoded. Each of the parameters is a BYTE value that ranges from 0 to 255, where 0 is the minimum amount of color. For example, the following code statement would store the color of purest green in the variable MyColor:

```
COLORREF MyColor = RGB(0, 255, 0);
```

Performing a couple of quick calculations will reveal that the RGB macro will provide 16,777,216 different color possibilities. Of course, your particular video hardware might place some limitations on your color choices. In fact, it's not unlikely that you'll have a choice of only 16 pure colors. Wow, that's what I call a letdown—from 16 million to 16. All is not lost. If you happen to ask RGB to construct one of the 16 million colors that your system doesn't support, it will do its best to accommodate you. That's where dithering comes in.

Dithering is the process of creating the illusion of a new color by weaving the pure colors into a pattern. If you alternate dots of red and blue, for example, you will make a dithered purple color. The whole process is pretty well automated, so you really don't have to worry about it unless you're doing something fancy. In fact, there is even a predefined dialog that allows you to bring up a palette of colors currently available. When called upon, this dialog provides your users with a dynamic way to choose colors from the currently selected palette. These palettes also can be customized. One of the fancy things that you can do is define your own palette of colors. This can be accomplished through the use of the foundation class CPalette. Unfortunately, CPalette is a topic that's a bit too advanced for this book—a single introductory book can do only so much. In this book, we will use the colors available on the default color palette (the system palette).

In drawing our shapes, our CDC robot has been using a thin black CPen object. This is about to change. There are two general ways of producing a new pen for your CDC robot. The easiest is to give him one of the stock pen objects that Windows has tucked away for just such an occasion. The beauty of using stock objects is that all the details are managed by Windows; all you have to do is point and shoot. The problem with using stock objects is that there are so few of them, especially pens. The following is a list of stock pens and brushes:

Day 4: CView Painting

Pens	Brushes
BLACK_PEN	BLACK_BRUSH
NULL_PEN	DKGRAY_BRUSH
WHITE_PEN	GRAY_BRUSH
	HOLLOW_BRUSH
	LTGRAY_BRUSH
	NULL_BRUSH
	WHITE_BRUSH

You instruct the device context to use a stock object (not just pens, either) by calling the `CDC::SelectStockObject()` function. For example, the following line of code will give the DC a black pen:

```
pDC->SelectStockObject (BLACK_PEN);
```

Big whoop; it already had a black pen. Now it has another one. Well, stock objects are commonly used objects that Windows packaged and provided for use. Not everyone thinks that a fuchsia pen five pixels wide is the cat's meow. Windows doesn't have the time, memory, or inclination to anticipate every possible pen type. If you want a special pen, you have to create a special pen. You can create your own pen with whatever style, width, and color suits your needs. The following code snippet has the form of a typical pen creation and assignment:

```
CPen NewPen(style, width, color);
CPen* pOldPen = pDC->SelectObject(&NewPen);

// Code that uses the DC (now improved with NewPen)
.
.
.
// Put back the old pen
pDC->SelectObject(pOldPen);
```

The first line creates the new pen with style, width, and color specified. The style can be any of the styles described in Table 4.4. Width corresponds to the width of the pen line in pixels. And color, of course, specifies the COLORREF value.

Table 4.4. CPen styles.

Style	Description
PS_SOLID	Solid line.
PS_DASH	Dashed line.
PS_DOT	Dotted line.
PS_DASHDOT	Line alternating with dashes and dots.
PS_DASHDOTDOT	Line alternating with dashes and two dots.
PS_NULL	No line drawn.
PS_INSIDERFRAME	Line drawn just within the border of a closed shape.

The second line in the code snippet instructs the DC to use our new pen. Note that only the address of the new pen is passed and that the call returns a pointer to the previously selected pen. We keep the previous pen's address so that in the last line we may restore the DC to its original state. Remember, you must always clean up after yourself; no one else will do it.

The `CDC` select object functions also allow you to specify `CBrush` objects for your `CDC` robot. Whereas pens draw lines, brushes paint areas of the screen such as window backgrounds and the interiors of closed shapes. Unlike the stock pens, there are a few stock brushes that you can use. However, like `CPen` objects, "rolling your own" is the best way to produce the exact effects you want. The creation/selection process is very similar to that of `CPen`. Only the names have been changed:

```
CBrush NewBrush(style, color);
CBrush* pOldBrush = pDC->SelectObject(&NewBrush);

// Code that uses the DC (now improved with NewBrush)
.
.
.
// Put back old brush
pDC->SelectObject(pOldBrush);
```

There are only a couple of differences between the this code segment and the associated `CPen` code segment. First, the creation of the new brush required only two parameters. Width is irrelevant with brushes. The second difference is that the style of brush is given by a different set of constants. These constants are described in Table 4.5.

Table 4.5. `CBrush` hatch styles.

Constant	Description
HS_BDIAGONAL	Diagonal lines parallel to a backslash.
HS_CROSS	Horizontal and vertical crossing lines.
HS_DIAGCROSS	Diagonal crossing lines.
HS_FDIAGONAL	Diagonal lines parallel to a forward slash.
HS_HORIZONTAL	Horizontal lines.
HS_VERTICAL	Vertical lines.

You may notice that a seemingly essential brush type is missing from Table 4.5—the solid brush. The solid brush is not a hatch style, so it has a slightly different creation procedure. In order to get a solid brush, you must omit the style parameter. The `CBrush` constructor is overloaded to take one parameter in the case of solid brushes or two parameters in the case of hatched brushes. There is something odd about how similar the `CBrush` code is to that of the `CPen` example. It's the fact that we are using the same `CDC` function to load two very different things: `CPen` and `CBrush`. The `SelectObject()` and `SelectStockObject()` functions are overloaded to provide support to both `CPen` and `CBrush` (as well as the other GDI objects, for that matter).

CView Painting

In addition to the drawing functions, there is a set of functions that allow you to change the drawing attributes of the DC object. Table 4.6 lists the drawing attribute functions.

Table 4.6. `CDC` graphic drawing attribute functions.

Function	Description
`GetBkColor`	Returns the current background color.
`SetBkColor`	Sets the background color.
`GetBkMode`	Returns the current background mode.
`SetBkMode`	Sets the background mode.
`GetPolyFillMode`	Returns the current polygon fill mode.
`SetPolyFillMode`	Sets the current polygon fill mode.
`GetROP2`	Gets the binary raster operation (ROP) mode.
`SetROP2`	Sets the binary raster operation mode.

These functions bear some explanation. All the functions come in get/set pairs. The get function returns the appropriate value, and the set function makes the appropriate assignment with the proffered value. The get/set pair motif is a common occurrence in the MFC.

Background color and background mode definitions are intertwined. Background mode determines whether the background color is to be used. Background color is the color that shows through the hatches when a hatched brush is painting. It's also the color that shows through the cracks when you're drawing with a nonsolid pen. And this same color provides the background for text. If the background mode is `OPAQUE`, the background color is used to fill in the blanks. If the mode is `TRANSPARENT`, whatever was under the drawing shows through the cracks. The issue of background color and mode is moot for the drawing of solid lines or brushes since there are no holes that the color can peek through.

The polygon fill mode attribute is a little tricky to describe. It centers around the issue of what parts of a polygon should be filled with a brush. The default value of this attribute is `ALTERNATE`. In this mode, areas to be filled are determined by following an imaginary line across the screen that passes through the polygon. Windows fills in the areas between the pairs of polygon sides it encounters. Another way of looking at this technique is to think of the polygon as a group of distinct closed areas. Alternate areas in the polygon are filled—no two adjacent areas are filled. The only other value of this attribute is `WINDING`. The concept of winding (or winding number) is a measure of how many times and in which direction the polygon goes around a point. A line is drawn from a given point to an area outside the polygon. A count is made of how many polygon sides the line crosses and in which direction the sides cross. The count is incremented when the side crosses from right to left, and it is decremented when the side crosses from left to right. The area is filled if the count is nonzero. A zero count implies that the point is on the exterior of the polygon. See Figure 4.5 for graphical examples.

Figure 4.5.
ALTERNATE *and* WINDING *polygons.*

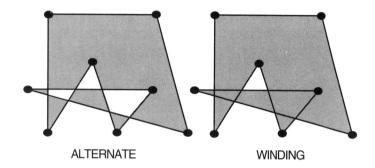

The final get/set function pair concerns the ROP2 modes. ROP2 stands for *binary raster operation;* the 2 refers to the binary nature of these modes. The ROP2 attribute determines how the pixels that make up the drawing interact with the pixels already on the display. In the default mode, R2_COPYPEN, the current pen and brush are used to paint the drawing over the display without interaction. In contrast, drawing with the R2_MERGEPEN mode is done by logically ORing pixels in the drawing with corresponding pixels on the display. Understanding the entire ROP2 mode set is an exercise in computer logic and permutations. For those less mathematically inclined, a cursory understanding can still be obtained by viewing the results of the ROP2 modes. We will add ROP2 functionality to our running example soon. Table 4.7 lists the possible values of the ROP2 attribute.

Table 4.7. ROP2 attribute values.

Value	Description
R2_BLACK	Paints black regardless of the display, pen, or brush.
R2_WHITE	Paints white regardless of the display, pen, or brush.
R2_NOP	No operation is done! No drawing.
R2_NOT	Inverse display pixel.
R2_COPYPEN	Pen pixel.
R2_NOTCOPYPEN	Inverse of pen pixel.
R2_MERGEPENNOT	(Inverse display pixel) OR (pen pixel).
R2_MASKPENNOT	(Inverse display pixel) AND (pen pixel).
R2_MERGENOTPEN	(Inverse pen pixel) OR (display pixel).
R2_MASKNOTPEN	(Inverse pen pixel) AND (display pixel).
R2_MERGEPEN	(Pen pixel) OR (display pixel).
R2_NOTMERGEPEN	Inverse (pen pixel OR display pixel).
R2_MASKPEN	(Pen pixel) AND (display pixel).

continues

CView Painting

Table 4.7. continued

Value	Description
R2_NOTMASKPEN	Inverse (pen pixel AND display pixel).
R2_XORPEN	(Pen pixel) XOR (display pixel).
R2_NOTXORPEN	Inverse (pen pixel XOR display pixel).

Let's reflect some of this theory into our code. Add the following variable declarations to the document class interface:

```
COLORREF m_nBColor, m_nPColor;   // Brush and pen colors
int m_nBStyle, m_nPStyle;        // Brush and pen styles

// Descriptions of current brush and pen styles
CString m_csBStyle, m_csPStyle;

int m_nPolyFill;    // Polygon fill mode
int m_nROP2Mode;    // ROP2 mode
CString m_csROP2;   // Description of ROP2 mode
```

These variables will hold the current drawing colors and modes. The CString variables will hold descriptions of the current modes so that they may be displayed efficiently in the menu text. The following code initializes these variables and should be added to the OnNewDocument() function:

```
m_nPColor = m_nBColor = RGB (0, 0, 0);
m_nPStyle = PS_SOLID;
m_csPStyle = "PS_SOLID";
m_nBStyle = -1;    // Solid brush
m_csBStyle = "SOLID";

m_nPolyFill = ALTERNATE;
m_nROP2Mode = R2_COPYPEN;
m_csROP2 = "R2_COPYPEN";
```

Experimenting with these modes is as easy as changing the initialization of the preceding variables. However, in Windows, we like things a little more interactive than change and recompile. With our current skills, the menu is the natural place to provide attribute alteration support. Add the following items to the Options menu:

ID_OPTIONS_PCOLOR	Change pen color.
ID_OPTIONS_BCOLOR	Change brush color.
ID_OPTIONS_PSTYLE	Change pen style.
ID_OPTIONS_BSTYLE	Change brush style.
ID_OPTIONS_POLYFILL	Change polygon fill mode.
ID_OPTIONS_ROP2	Change ROP2 mode.

Use ClassWizard to add the command functions of the color selections to the view class. Also have ClassWizard add the command and update UI functions for the last four menu items in the preceding list. Make the following alterations to the new functions added to the view class:

```
void CPaintView::OnOptionsBcolors()
{
    CPaintDoc* pDoc = GetDocument();
    ASSERT_VALID(pDoc);

    CColorDialog Dlg;

    if (Dlg.DoModal() == IDOK)
    {
        pDoc->m_nBColor = Dlg.GetColor();
        pDoc->UpdateAllViews(NULL);
    }

}
void CPaintView::OnOptionsPcolors()
{
    CPaintDoc* pDoc = GetDocument();
    ASSERT_VALID(pDoc);

    CColorDialog Dlg;

    if (Dlg.DoModal() == IDOK)
    {
        pDoc->m_nPColor = Dlg.GetColor();
        pDoc->UpdateAllViews(NULL);
    }
}
```

The preceding functions invoke a standard color dialog that allows the user to select a color. It then takes this choice and updates the appropriate color variable. Mysteries of this dialog will be covered in detail in Chapter 7.

Now make the following alterations to the new functions added to the document class:

```
void CPaintDoc::OnOptionsPolyfill()
{
    if (m_nPolyFill == ALTERNATE)
        m_nPolyFill = WINDING;
    else
        m_nPolyFill = ALTERNATE;

    UpdateAllViews(NULL);
}

void CPaintDoc::OnUpdateOptionsPolyfill(CCmdUI* pCmdUI)
{
    if (m_nPolyFill == ALTERNATE)
        pCmdUI->SetText("PolyFill: ALTERNATE");
    else
        pCmdUI->SetText("PolyFill: WINDING");
}

void CPaintDoc::OnOptionsRop2()
```

Day 4: CView Painting

```cpp
{
    switch (m_nROP2Mode)
    {
        case R2_BLACK:
            m_nROP2Mode = R2_WHITE;
            m_csROP2 = "R2_WHITE";
            break;

        case R2_WHITE:
            m_nROP2Mode = R2_NOP;
            m_csROP2 = "R2_NOP";
            break;

        case R2_NOP:
            m_nROP2Mode = R2_NOT;
            m_csROP2 = "R2_NOT";
            break;

        case R2_NOT:
            m_nROP2Mode = R2_COPYPEN;
            m_csROP2 = "R2_COPYPEN";
            break;

        case R2_COPYPEN:
            m_nROP2Mode = R2_NOTCOPYPEN;
            m_csROP2 = "R2_NOTCOPYPEN";
            break;

        case R2_NOTCOPYPEN:
            m_nROP2Mode = R2_MERGEPENNOT;
            m_csROP2 = "R2_MERGEPENNOT";
            break;

        case R2_MERGEPENNOT:
            m_nROP2Mode = R2_MASKPENNOT;
            m_csROP2 = "R2_MASKPENNOT";
            break;

        case R2_MASKPENNOT:
            m_nROP2Mode = R2_MERGENOTPEN;
            m_csROP2 = "R2_MERGENOTPEN";
            break;

        case R2_MERGENOTPEN:
            m_nROP2Mode = R2_MASKNOTPEN;
            m_csROP2 = "R2_MASKNOTPEN";
            break;

        case R2_MASKNOTPEN:
            m_nROP2Mode = R2_MERGEPEN;
            m_csROP2 = "R2_MERGEPEN";
            break;

        case R2_MERGEPEN:
            m_nROP2Mode = R2_NOTMERGEPEN;
```

```
                m_csROP2 = "R2_NOTMERGEPEN";
                break;

            case R2_NOTMERGEPEN:
                m_nROP2Mode = R2_MASKPEN;
                m_csROP2 = "R2_MASKPEN";
                break;

            case R2_MASKPEN:
                m_nROP2Mode = R2_NOTMASKPEN;
                m_csROP2 = "R2_NOTMASKPEN";
                break;

            case R2_NOTMASKPEN:
                m_nROP2Mode = R2_XORPEN;
                m_csROP2 = "R2_XORPEN";
                break;

            case R2_XORPEN:
                m_nROP2Mode = R2_NOTXORPEN;
                m_csROP2 = "R2_NOTXORPEN";
                break;

            default:
                m_nROP2Mode = R2_BLACK;
                m_csROP2 = "R2_BLACK";
                break;
        }

        UpdateAllViews(NULL);

}

void CPaintDoc::OnUpdateOptionsRop2(CCmdUI* pCmdUI)
{
    pCmdUI->SetText("ROP2 Mode: " + m_csROP2);
}

void CPaintDoc::OnOptionsBrushstyle()
{
    switch (m_nBStyle)
    {
        case HS_BDIAGONAL:
            m_nBStyle = HS_CROSS;
            m_csBStyle = "HS_CROSS";
            break;

        case HS_CROSS:
            m_nBStyle = HS_DIAGCROSS;
            m_csBStyle = "HS_DIAGCROSS";
            break;

        case HS_DIAGCROSS:
            m_nBStyle = HS_FDIAGONAL;
            m_csBStyle = "HS_FDIAGONAL";
            break;
```

Day 4: CView Painting

```cpp
            case HS_FDIAGONAL:
            m_nBStyle = HS_HORIZONTAL;
            m_csBStyle = "HS_HORIZONTAL";
            break;

            case HS_HORIZONTAL:
            m_nBStyle = HS_VERTICAL;
            m_csBStyle = "HS_VERTICAL";
            break;

            case HS_VERTICAL:
            m_nBStyle = -1;
            m_csBStyle = "SOLID";
            break;

            default:
            m_nBStyle = HS_BDIAGONAL;
            m_csBStyle = "HS_BDIAGONAL";
            break;
    }

    UpdateAllViews(NULL);
}

void CPaintDoc::OnUpdateOptionsBrushstyle(CCmdUI* pCmdUI)
{
    pCmdUI->SetText("Brush &Hatch: " + m_csBStyle);
}

void CPaintDoc::OnOptionsPenstyle()
{
    switch (m_nPStyle)
    {
        case PS_SOLID:
        m_nPStyle = PS_DASH;
        m_csPStyle = "PS_DASH";
        break;

        case PS_DASH:
        m_nPStyle = PS_DOT;
        m_csPStyle = "PS_DOT";
        break;

        case PS_DOT:
        m_nPStyle = PS_DASHDOT;
        m_csPStyle = "PS_DASHDOT";
        break;

        case PS_DASHDOT:
        m_nPStyle = PS_DASHDOTDOT;
        m_csPStyle = "PS_DASHDOTDOT";
        break;

        case PS_DASHDOTDOT:
        m_nPStyle = PS_NULL;
```

```
            m_csPStyle = "PS_NULL";
            break;

        case PS_NULL:
            m_nPStyle = PS_INSIDEFRAME;
            m_csPStyle = "PS_INSIDEFRAME";
            break;

        default:
            m_nPStyle = PS_SOLID;
            m_csPStyle = "PS_SOLID";
            break;
    }

    UpdateAllViews(NULL);
}
void CPaintDoc::OnUpdateOptionsPenstyle(CCmdUI* pCmdUI)
{
    pCmdUI->SetText("Pen Style: " + m_csPStyle);
}
```

Each of the preceding command functions, when selected, cycles through the list of possible options for the variable it manages. Their associated UI update function reflects the appropriate information in the menu selection itself using the `CCmdUI::SetText()` function. Note that we use a `CString` value to store the current styles to minimize the number of computations made in the update UI functions. Also note the use of a `switch` statement in the command functions. The styles are just numbers, so why don't we just increment them? The first reason is so that we may store the text string describing the style. The second reason is that the actual values of the constants associated with styles or any constants in Windows are subject to change. The constant names will stay the same, but the actual values can differ from one version of Windows to another. So their numerical order or the fact that they are sequential at all might not be immutable. Using the constants without depending on their actual values is important if you want to be able to upgrade your application to the next version of Windows. Of course, nothing guarantees that the values will change, but nothing guarantees that they will remain the same, either!

Our last duty is to tie in the color and mode variables into the paint demo code. This involves adding the following lines to the `CPaintView::OnDraw()` function immediately after the drawing of the points:

```
// Set colors
CPen pen(pDoc->m_nPStyle,0,pDoc->m_nPColor);
CPen* pOldPen = pDC->SelectObject(&pen);

// Declare the brush and then initialize it to solid or hatched
CBrush brush;
if (pDoc->m_nBStyle == -1)   // If solid brush
    brush.CreateSolidBrush(pDoc->m_nBColor);
else
```

Day 4: CView Painting

```
        brush.CreateHatchBrush(pDoc->m_nBStyle, pDoc->m_nBColor);
CBrush* pOldBrush = pDC->SelectObject(&brush);

// Set polyfillmode: ALTERNATE or WINDING
pDC->SetPolyFillMode(pDoc->m_nPolyFill);

// Set ROP2 mode
pDC->SetROP2(pDoc->m_nROP2Mode);
```

The preceding code is readily understandable, with the exception of the `CBrush` initialization. Because there are two separate and distinct ways of constructing the brush (solid and hatched) and we wish to have both available, the code must be split on the `m_nBStyle` condition. In one branch, we initialize the brush to be solid, and in the other, we initialize it to be hatched. Note that these create functions will work only on uninitialized brushes.

To complete the introduction of the modes, place the following code at the end of the `CPaintView::OnDraw()` function:

```
pDC->SelectObject(pOldPen);
pDC->SelectObject(pOldBrush);
```

It's important to note that the pens and brushes selected at the beginning of `OnDraw()` are deselected in favor of the original objects at the end of `OnDraw()`.

Create and Destroy Your Own CDC Objects

Thus far in the book we have been lucky to have a `CDC` object pointer passed to us just when we needed it. What would we do if we wanted to display something from a function that didn't have a `CDC` parameter? "Shiver and crouch in abject fear" is not the proper attitude! The correct answer is, "We would create and manage our own `CDC` object." There are a number of instances where we would like to have direct access to the screen. In a dialog box, we might have cause to make modifications to the window screen. In such a case, we would have to produce our own CDC object. The key decision to be made in any CDC creation choice is whether you want access to the whole screen or just the client area of a window. The `CWindowDC` class is used to make alterations to any part of the screen. Drawing to coordinates (0,0) using a `CWindowDC` object would affect the upper-left pixel of the computer display. The `CClientDC` class is used to make alterations to the client area of a particular window. Drawing to coordinates (0,0) using the `CClientDC` object would affect the leftmost pixel in the current window just under the menu (or just under the toolbar, if one is present). The two DC classes have specific uses, but you will typically utilize the `CClientDC` class. The following code snippet illustrates its use:

```
void MyDraw()
{
    CClientDC MyDC(pW);

    // MyDC drawing code
    MyDC.Ellipse (20, 20, 50, 70);
}
```

This little function declares a device context and draws an ellipse. Because `CClientDC` accesses the client area of a specific window, that particular window must be identified at the time of DC construction. Therefore, the declaration must include a window pointer (the `pW` variable). It's not uncommon to see this window pointer in the form of a `this` pointer (a pointer to the current object). Of course, the `this` pointer will work in this capacity only if your function happens to be a member function of a `CWnd`-derived class. Concerning the memory clean-up issues, `MyDC` is automatically deleted at the end of the function because it was declared locally. Other means of creating a DC can lead to more concern over memory problems, but we will worry about that when the time comes. As far as creating `CWindowDC` objects, a window pointer isn't needed because the whole screen is referenced, not a specific window. Aside from this small difference, the procedure is the same as that just shown.

Summary

This chapter focused on the techniques and operations of the `CDC` class. The analogy of the robotic drawing assistant was used to illustrate the role of the `CDC` in drawing. Pens, brushes, colors, and a large number of the `CDC` drawing functions were demonstrated. We neglected to discuss the text-oriented functions of the `CDC`, such as advanced text output, text color, regions, fonts, and so on. These topics will be examined in chapters to come.

Q&A

Q The brushes are ugly and uninspired. Can I make my own brush designs?

A Yes, you can produce your own brush designs. You can create interesting brushes by using bitmap objects as templates. We will discuss bitmaps and their various uses in Chapters 13 and 14.

Q If I use the same brush or pen throughout my program, is there a way of saving the object so that I don't have to create it at the start of every function that uses it?

A Yes, there are ways of saving the data associated with a `CGDIObject` for future use. Alternatively, there are ways of converting GDI object handles to the stable Windows object handles. Either method would accomplish your goal. For more information, read about `CGDIObject` in the Class Library Reference.

CView Painting

Workshop

Quiz

1. What's the purpose of the `UpdateAllViews(NULL)` call?
2. Describe the difference in the use of the `CClientDC` and the `CWindowDC` classes.
3. The rectangle and ellipse drawing functions require two points to define their dimensions. Why do the pie, arc, and chord functions require four points?
4. Compare and contrast the two polygon filling modes.

Exercises

1. Add a random element into your program so that each graphical object is displayed in a different color.
2. Change the underlying data structure to an array of `CPoint` arrays so that you may display multiple polygons on the same screen.
3. Add right mouse button support that will allow the movement of specific points.
4. Use the experience gained in this chapter to add `CDC::SetPixel()` support to the paint program.

WEEK 1

CStrings and Other Helpful Miscellany

DAY 5

CStrings and Other Helpful Miscellany

Character strings have always been a burden to programmers. I can't think of a programming language I've used where I haven't thrown up my arms in disgust at the manner in which character strings were implemented. Most of the time, my disgust sprang from the frustration inherent in static-length character strings. You often don't know in advance how long a string is going to be. For example, if you query a user, you can only guess as to the length or shortness of her name. Choose a string length too short and you'll lose data; choose one too long and you'll waste memory. There are always good reasons why particular implementations are adopted. Usually, the reasons center around efficiency. It's more efficient to pass the problem on to the programmer so he can find a solution or at least a work-around. The solution to this dilemma used to be to program a dynamic-length string that grows and shrinks, as necessary, to accommodate the programmer's needs. Programming the first two or three variable-length strings is kind of fun, but after that it gets tedious. Enter CString, the MFC solution to dynamic-length character strings.

In this chapter we will talk about CString and a number of other foundation classes that make our programming chores a lot easier and sometimes even fun. Some of the classes we have worked with before, and some are entirely new. There isn't one large program in this chapter. Each section contains code snippets that you can incorporate into your own code. Feel free to test these snippets by creating a special "Misc" program. This will be a fun chapter, so sit back and enjoy.

CString—the Only Way to Go!

We caught a glimpse of CString in earlier chapters, where we used it as a normal string and for loading strings from the string resource table. These two functions alone are enough to make CString worth using, but there is so much more it can do for you. Table 5.1 lists CString's general abilities.

Table 5.1. CString's abilities.

Ability	Description
Attributes	Gets and sets string attributes.
Comparison	Compares one string to another.
Concatenation	String-related appending and prepending.
Extraction	Extracts substrings from the original string.
Conversion	Support for many kinds of conversions.
Searching	Finds substrings/characters in a string.
Buffering	Provides for normal string buffering.
Archiving	Built-in serialization support.
Loading	Loads strings from a string table resource.
OLE	Support for object linking and embedding.

From this list of abilities, you can see that the `CString` class is a formidable exercise in object-oriented programming. Considerable time and effort was invested in this class so that you wouldn't have to do as much. There is a lot to be learned from this class. Not just the `CString` particulars, though that's important too. The real lesson here is the design of the class. Take notes! In the next chapter we will be making our own class, not too dissimilar from this one, that will encapsulate dates (a very handy class, as we shall see).

Our first duty with `CString` is to examine the plethora of construction options. There are many ways of constructing and initializing a `CString` object. The most common method is by using the default constructor and performing an assignment:

```
CString S = "CStrings are fun!!";
```

An equivalent approach would be to use the constant string within the constructor:

```
CString S("CStrings are fun!!");
```

These methods are equivalent, except in the area of error handling, which we will discuss in the section "Exceptional Programming." At the moment, I wish to stress that multiple types of constructors are available for your use. Table 5.2 contains a list of constructor options. Examples in this section will demonstrate most of these constructor techniques.

Table 5.2. `CString` constructor options.

Option	Description
`CString()`	The default constructor. The string will be empty.
`CString(const CString&)`	Initializes the string with a `CString` parameter.
`CString(const char*)`	Initializes with data from a `char` pointer.
`CString(const char*, int)`	Initializes with data from a `char` pointer, but is constrained to `int` length.
`CString(const char FAR*)`	Initializes with data from a `far char` pointer.
`CString(const char FAR*, int)`	Initializes with data from a `far char` pointer, but is constrained to `int` length.
`CString(char, int)`	Fills the string with `int` number of `char`s.

The first set of `CString` functions we will examine are the attribute functions. Table 5.3 describes them.

Day 5
CStrings and Other Helpful Miscellany

Table 5.3. CString attribute functions.

Function	Description
GetLength	Returns the length of the string.
IsEmpty	Returns FALSE if the string's length is greater than zero.
Empty	Reduces the string to zero length.
GetAt	Returns the character at the specified position.
SetAt	Writes a new character to the specified position.
operator[]	Provides arraylike support for the dynamic string.

The attribute functions provide access to fundamental information about the string. GetLength() and IsEmpty() provide string length information to the caller. Empty() actually effects change on the string by setting the length to zero. GetAt() and SetAt() allow you to retrieve or change, respectively, the values in the string by specifying the zero-based index of the character to access. operator[] encapsulates the GetAt() function, allowing you read access to the string as if it were a normal zero-based array. This operator doesn't furnish indexed write access to the string, as does the SetAt() function. This limitation is shown as follows:

```
CString S = "MOUSE";
char C;

C = S[1];     // Equivalently, we could use C = GetAt(1); result C=='O';
S[2] = C;     // ###ERROR: Cannot set elements with operator[]
S.SetAt(2, C); // This is the proper way to change elements of S
// The string becomes "MOOSE"
```

Note: It can be confusing when you must deal with CStrings and standard character arrays in the same program block. Naturally, standard character arrays allow full access through operator[], while CStrings allow only reading through this mechanism. Observe:

```
CString S = "01234";
char p[6] = "abcde";

p[2] = S[2];  // Perfectly legal
S[3] = p[3];  // ERROR! Can't assign CString elements with operator[]
```

Considering this potential for confusion, you may opt to use only the GetAt() and SetAt() functions for your primary mode of CString access, especially if standard strings are nearby.

We will see more illustrations of the attribute functions at work in the examples to come. The next set of CString functions are the comparison functions. No new class is complete without some way of comparing objects of that class. CString is no exception to this rule. In fact, CString has a large number of comparison operators and functions, as shown in Table 5.4.

Table 5.4. CString comparison functions.

Operator or Function	Description
==, !=, <=, >=, <, >	Performs a case-sensitive comparison.
Compare	Returns 0 if the parameter is equal to the calling object's string, –1 if the parameter is greater, or +1 if the parameter is less.
CompareNoCase	Same return as Compare, except that case is not considered.
Collate	Same return as Compare, except that the comparison is based on locale.

These common operators use an alphabetical ordering to compare CString objects. You will often use these functions in sorting algorithms and in the addition functions of sorted data structures. In order to make a thorough test of these functions, the ASSERT macro is employed. The ASSERT macro is used in the debug version of the Visual C++ environment to validate variable values. If the Boolean expression passed to ASSERT is true, program control proceeds as normal. If, on the other hand, a false expression is passed to ASSERT, the program halts and a diagnostic message is displayed. Liberal use of the ASSERT macro can assure a higher level of program robustness. Examples showing the usage of the comparison operators follow:

```
char sz1[6] = "AAAAA";
char sz2[] = "Aardvark";
char sz3[6] = "Zebra"
CString S1('A', 5);   // Fills S1 with five As
CString S2(sz2);      // Fills S2 with the string contained in the z2 array
CString S3 = "Apt #15";

ASSERT (sz1 == S1);       // "AAAAA" equals "AAAAA"
ASSERT (S2 == sz2);       // "Aardvark" equals "Aardvark"
ASSERT (S1 != S2);        // "AAAAA" doesn't equal "Aardvark"
ASSERT (S2 < sz3);        // "Aardvark" comes before "Zebra"
ASSERT (S2 <= sz3);       // "Aardvark" still comes before "Zebra"
ASSERT (S3 > "Apt #112"); // "Apt #15" comes after "Apt #112"
```

Almost all the permutations of CStrings and standard strings have comparison operators defined. The only operators missing from the possible combinations are the ones not involving CString. In order to compare two standard strings, you have to use functions from the runtime library or first convert the standard string to a CString. Why, you ask? Remember, these functions are defined for the CString class. To use them, you must have a CString object present.

Day 5: *CStrings* and Other Helpful Miscellany

Another question might be buzzing around your mind after you looked at the last ASSERT statement in the preceding code. Why does "Apt #15" come after "Apt #112"? In any list I've ever seen, it would be the other way around! However, if you perform the comparison, the computer will sort it as shown. The answer lies in a seldom-stated and, outside of the industry, rarely-known fact: Computers are stupid. Computers don't know that the character string of "15" is treated by the human mind as the number 15. Nor does it know the same fact about the character string of "112." We know that if you see a string of numbers embedded within a string, you can just cluster them together and treat them as a single entity. Computers won't do that unless you tell them to. Ah, that sounds like a future programming exercise! And so it is.

The last three comparison functions are very similar to the operators we've been discussing. These functions accept a string to compare to the current object's string. They return a code that indicates the result of the comparison. If 0 is returned, the strings are equal. If –1 is returned, the string object is less than the passed string. If +1 is returned, the string object is greater than the passed string. The differences between the three functions arise from the underlying runtime function used to implement them. Compare() uses the runtime function strcmp(). This forces a character-by-character comparison of the two strings. CompareNoCase() is based on the stricmp() runtime function. This provides the same functionality as the Compare() function, except that the case of the letters is ignored. Finally, the Collate() function is based on the strcoll() function. Collate() provides a means to compare strings using the current locale setting (the national language selected). Collate() is another vehicle for providing internationalization support for your Windows programs. At the time of this writing, only one locale is available. The Collate() function is no different from Compare(). However, keep in mind that using this function now will save you a great deal of time if you decide to internationalize your program later. Examples of the compare functions follow:

```
CString S1("George");
CString S2("GEORGE");
CString S3("Susan");

ASSERT(S1.Compare(S2) == +1);       // Capital letters are greater than lowercase
ASSERT(S1.Compare(S3) == -1);       // "George" comes before "Susan"
ASSERT(S3.CompareNoCase(S1) == +1); // NoCase works the same,
ASSERT(S1.CompareNoCase(S2) == 0);  // except that it ignores case
```

The next group of CString functions are the assignment/concatenation operators. These operators provide a means of assigning, appending, and prepending string-like objects to one another. By "stringlike," I mean CStrings—standard character strings—as well as single characters. These operators are extremely overloaded, but in a consistent way. Table 5.5 lists the operators in question.

Table 5.5. Assignment/concatenation operators.

Operator	Description
operator =	Assigns a stringlike object to a CString.
operator +	Concatenates a CString with a stringlike object.
operator +=	Appends a stringlike object to the end of a CString.

We will see examples of these functions throughout this chapter as well as throughout the book. These are big-time operators. You will make heavy use of them in almost every application. But to give you a taste of their use, here are a couple of examples:

```
CString S1 ("Puppy");
CString S2 ("Dog");
CString S3;
char sz1[] = " Gone";

S3 = S1 + ' ' + S2;
ASSERT (S3 == "Puppy Dog");

S2 += sz1;
ASSERT (S2 == "Dog Gone");
```

Note that the following will fail on the compile:

```
CString S = "Cat";
char sz2[] = "Fluffy";

S = sz2 + " the " + S;   // Error!!!
// The first two strings are standard and therefore
// don't have the operator + defined for them
```

The next set of CString functions we will look at are the extraction functions, shown in Table 5.6. These functions allow you to copy specific portions of a string to another string.

Table 5.6. CString extraction.

Function	Description
Mid	Extracts a substring from the middle of the parent string.
Left	Extracts a substring from the left side of the parent string.
Right	Extracts a substring from the right side of the parent string.
SpanIncluding	Extracts a substring that includes members of a specific set.
SpanExcluding	Extracts a substring that excludes members of a specific set.

DAY 5
CStrings and Other Helpful Miscellany

If you're a BASIC programmer, the first three functions might look very familiar. Just slap a dollar sign on the end of them and they would turn into their BASIC equivalents. It's been a good many years since I've done any BASIC programming, but I still find myself wanting to put a dollar sign on the end of these functions. Old habits die hard. Fortunately, these functions operate the same way in both languages. They extract a substring from the left, right, or middle of the host string. For example:

```
CString S = "Coffee";

ASSERT(S.Right(3) == "fee");
// Right(3) extracts the three rightmost characters

ASSERT(S.Mid(1, 3) == "off");
// Mid(1,3) extracts the three middle characters,
// starting at position 1 (zero-based index)

ASSERT(S.Left(4) == "Coff");
// Left(4) extracts the four leftmost characters.
// And yes, I know, "Coff" != "Cough." But I had to make "Coffee" stretch!
```

The last two extraction functions involve spanning a set of characters. In both functions, a string holding a set of characters is passed as the sole parameter. Using this set as a guide, each function finds the largest contiguous substring starting at the leftmost position that either includes or excludes all the members of this set. This might seem to be a very specialized and infrequently used type of function, but actually it can be quite useful. The following example shows `SpanIncluding` used for hex manipulation:

```
CString S1 = "7F2A";
CString S2 = "HELLO";
CString S3 = "2B ¦¦ !2B";   // Logical Shakespeare
CString Set = "0123456789ABCDEF";

ASSERT(S1. SpanIncluding(Set) == "7F2A");
// Returns the whole string, indicating a valid hex number

ASSERT(S2.SpanIncluding(Set) == "");
// Returns a null string, indicating no leftmost hex digits

ASSERT(S3.SpanIncluding(Set) == "2B");
// Returns the leftmost valid hex digit string
```

This example shows a `SpanExcluding` stripping function:

```
CString Strip (const char* pszS, const char* pszSet)
{
    CString S = pszS;
    CString Result;

    while (!S.Empty())
    {
        CString temp = S.SpanExcluding(pszSet);
        if (temp == "")
```

```
                // Strip the first character from S
                S = S.Right(S.GetLength() - 1);
            else
                // Otherwise, remove temp from S
                S = S.Right(S.GetLength() - temp.GetLength());
            Result += temp;
        }

    return Result;
}
```

Here's an example of the use of `Strip()`:

```
CString Set = "? *" // Question mark, space, and asterisk
CString InitialString = "** You talking to me? **";

ASSERT(Strip(InitialString, Set) == "Youtalkingtome");
// All members of Set are stripped from the initial string!
```

> **Note:** The `Strip()` function brings up a different point. What is the protocol for passing objects of type `CString` to and from functions?
>
> Passing `CString` objects to functions can be accomplished in two ways: with `const char*` or with `CString&`. Declaring a parameter to be a `const char*` type allows a `CString` object to be passed as a constant value. Once passed, the object may be reassigned to a local `CString` object and manipulated as such. This technique has the added benefit of providing functionality to standard strings as well. However, the parameter is still constant. If you want to be able to effect changes to the original `CString` object, you must use the second option. Declare the parameter to be of type `CString&`. Passing the address of the `CString` object will allow you to change the `CString` object directly from within the called function.
>
> The semantics for returning `CString` objects are much less complicated. You may treat them as you would any primitive data type.

The next set of functions, shown in Table 5.7, loosely involve some sort of `CString` conversion.

Table 5.7. CString conversion.

Function	Description
MakeUpper	Converts all characters in the string to uppercase.
MakeLower	Converts all characters in the string to lowercase.
MakeReverse	Reverses the order of the string.
AnsiToOem	Converts all characters from the ANSI to the OEM character set.
OemToAnsi	Converts all characters from the OEM to the ANSI character set.

Day 5

CStrings and Other Helpful Miscellany

The first two functions concern changing the case of the characters in the string. `MakeUpper()` converts all the characters in the host string to uppercase. `MakeLower()` converts all the characters in the host string to lowercase.

The `MakeReverse()` function doesn't exactly change the characters themselves, but it does affect their order. This function reverses the order of the characters in the string. It comes in handy for the commonly assigned string exercise of making a palindrome-checking function:

```
BOOL IsPalindrome (const char* pszPotentialPalindrome)
{
    CString S1(pszPotentialPalindrome);
    CString S2 (S1);
    S2.MakeReverse();
    return (S1 == S2);  // MakeReverse() reverses the order
}
```

Note: If you're not familiar with palindrome routines, they're usually used to demonstrate string manipulation techniques and sometimes recursion. A palindrome is a word or phrase that is spelled the same backward and forward. Typically, punctuation is ignored. Some palindrome examples are "BOB," "MADAM, I'M ADAM," and "A MAN, A PLAN, A CANAL: PANAMA."

The final two conversion routines, `AnsiToOem()` and `OemToAnsi()`, provide additional support for internationalization. They allow conversion between the normal ANSI character set we use in Windows and the character set installed with MS-DOS, identified by Windows as the *OEM* (original equipment manufacturer) character set. The OEM character set installed on your machine could very well support a foreign language, but the OEM character set installed on most U.S. machines is known as code page 437. This character set includes the characters we're used to with U.S. MS-DOS machines. However, code page 437 is *not* the same as the ANSI character set used in Windows. Therefore, these last two conversion routines not only support internationalization, but they also support proper conversion of strings between Windows and DOS. For example, if you needed to transfer a Windows string to DOS, you would use the `AnsiToOem()` function:

```
CString S1 = "These are foreign letters: éâàå";
CString S2 = S1;

S2.AnsiToOem();
```

If you use the S2 string in Windows, you will see a very strange thing. The OEM string displays black blocks instead of foreign letters. Well, we converted the string to OEM, after all. Displaying in Windows is done with ANSI. There is a certain overlap with standard letters and numbers, but when we start working with some of the funky letters such as é, the overlap ceases.

However, in DOS, the OEM string will look like the ANSI string does in Windows.

The next CString functions concern themselves with searching a string. Table 5.8 lists the three CString find functions.

Table 5.8. CString searching.

Function	Description
Find	Finds the position of the specified substring or character.
ReverseFind	Same as Find, except that the search is begun at the opposite end.
FindOneOf	Finds the position of the first occurrence of a specific set.

After it's given a string to search for, Find() makes a sequential search through the host string, starting with the leftmost position. If the string is found, Find() returns the zero-based position of the string's first occurrence. If the string isn't found in the host string, –1 is returned. ReverseFind() operates in the same way as Find(), except that it starts its search with the rightmost position. Note that these find functions, like most of the CString functions, are overloaded to take strings or characters as parameters.

Here's a simplified AutoCorrect() function that checks for and corrects often misspelled words:

```
void AutoCorrect(CString& S)
{
    CString str1 = "teh";
    CString str2 = "the";
    // Better yet, make this a list of misspelled
    // words and their corrections

    int i;  // Index holding the position of str1 in the S string

    // Find all occurrences of str1 in the S string
    while( (i = S.Find(str1)) >= 0)
    {
        // Replace str1 with str2 in the S string
        S = S.Left(i) + str2 + S.Right(S.GetLength() - str1.GetLength() - i);
    }
}
```

The FindOneOf() function requires a set of characters to be passed. It searches through the host string until it finds any one of the characters in the set. It returns the position of the character found. An immediate application of this function that comes to mind is in a wildcard processing function, like that used in some DOS functions. In such a function, embedded wildcard characters can represent single (?) or multiple (*) character strings that may contain anything. With this wildcard matching algorithm, the strings "A*k" and "Aardvark" and "Aa?dv*" would all be equivalent.

Day 5: CStrings and Other Helpful Miscellany

The following is the implementation of a simple wildcard matching function, IsEquivalent(), in which only a single wildcard is processed per pszWildStr:

```
BOOL IsEquivalent(const char* pszPureStr, const char* pszWildStr)
{
    CString Pure = pszPureStr;
    CString Wild = pszWildStr;

    int i = Wild.FindOneOf("*?");

    if (i < 0)    // Wildcard NOT found
        return Pure == Wild;
    else if (Wild.GetAt(i) == '*')
    {
        int len = Wild.GetLength();
        return ( (Wild.Left(i) == Pure.Left(i)) &&
                 (Wild.Right(len - i - 1) == Pure.Right(len - i - 1)) );
    }
    else  // Wildcard found was '?'
    {
        int len = Pure.GetLength();

        if (len != Wild.GetLength())
            return FALSE;
        // This is invalid if we allow more than one wildcard

        return ( (Wild.Left(i) == Pure.Left(i)) &&
                 (Wild.Right(len - i - 1) == Pure.Right(len - i - 1)) );
    }
}
```

CString buffering is the next order of string business. Table 5.9 lists the functions related to CString buffering. These functions provide a certain amount of access to the actual implementation of the CString.

Table 5.9. CString buffering.

Function	Description
GetBuffer	Returns a temporary pointer to the underlying char buffer.
GetBufferSetLength	The same as GetBuffer, except that you specify the buffer length.
ReleaseBuffer	Indicates that you are finished with a GetBuffer buffer.
operator const char*	Typecasts the string to a temporary const char* string.

The underlying representation of CString is what you might think—a null-terminated consecutive string of memory locations holding the ANSI codes representing the characters held. Gee, that's the same representation for the standard character array. What's the big deal about CString? Well, don't forget about the variable nature of CString as opposed to the static nature of standard strings. This ability of CString is accomplished by the reallocation of memory when a significant change to the `CString` object occurs. However, between changes in the `CString` object, the underlying representation is static. `GetBuffer()` and `GetBufferSetLength()` provide access to a temporary structure that underlies the `CString` object.

Each function takes a buffer size as the sole parameter. `GetBuffer()` requires this parameter to specify the minimum buffer size. If the existing buffer is smaller than this size, `CString` creates a new, larger buffer that meets the requirement. If the buffer is already larger than that specified, a new buffer isn't needed.

On the other hand, `GetBufferSetLength()` takes the proffered size as gospel. If the underlying buffer isn't the specified size, `CString` creates a new buffer that meets this requirement. In both cases, the buffer remains in effect until another `CString` function forces a memory reallocation. Both functions also return a pointer to this buffer so that you may have direct access to `CString`.

The `ReleaseBuffer()` function updates the `CString` object with any changes made via the pointer and then releases the memory allocated for the buffer—the `CString` object goes back to the lean mean memory machine that is its nature. A `CString` object allocates a default amount of memory for the underlying buffer that holds its data. The buffer functions circumvent this predisposition to a certain extent by forcing a minimum buffer length regardless of the size of the actual string buffer. The buffering functions are rather advanced functions for direct manipulation of the `CString`. Casual tinkering with these functions is discouraged. If you work with these functions, be sure of what you're doing! Here are a couple of examples to start you down this precarious road:

```
CString S = "Hello";   // S holds the null-terminated string "Hello"
char* pS = S.GetBuffer(50);   // A 50-character buffer is allocated
S += " Dude?";   // Convert the string to "Hello Dude?"

// Note that pS is still valid because the 50-character
// buffer still holds the string

pS[10] = '!';   // Using the pointer, we may directly change the '?' to a '!'
S.ReleaseBuffer();
// Release the excess buffer memory and update S with any changes
```

When directly accessing the string through the buffer pointer, you must keep in mind a couple of points. First, you must manually null terminate any string you create through the buffer pointer. If, for example, you directly enter more text at the end of the `"Hello Dude!"` string, you would write over the existing ending null. In order to keep the string null-terminated, you would have to append a null to your addition. The second point you must keep in mind is that after you directly modify the buffer, you must call the `ReleaseBuffer()` functions to effect those changes to the `CString` object. As I said, this is advanced stuff. Unless you have a specific need, use the higher-level functions to access the string—that's what they're there for.

Although `operator const char*` isn't really a buffering function, it's closely related to the intent of the buffering functions; hence, it is included here. This operator returns a temporary pointer to the null-terminated string underlying the `CString`. This pointer is a constant value, so you

Day 5: CStrings and Other Helpful Miscellany

may use it for read access only. The pointer is temporary in the sense that changing the `CString` might invalidate any existing constant character pointers you might have obtained before the change. An example follows:

```
CString S ("Nerds rule!");
const char* pS = (const char*)S;

S += "  And slide rules are cool!";
// A change to S might cause a memory reallocation, thereby
// invalidating pS. Any access to pS after such a change to S
// is suspect and very possibly erroneous. Beware!
```

The rest of the `CString` functions will be discussed when the appropriate topic is broached in the remainder of this book.

Message Boxes

Windows isn't the only entity that gets to send messages. Sometimes we want to send a quick little message to the user. The usual method for communicating with the user is through a dialog. But often we don't want to go through the trouble of constructing a dialog resource and the associated dialog class. It takes a bit of work to make a dialog. Of course, when they're needed, they're the best thing since sliced bread. At this point, even though we haven't gotten to dialogs yet, we will discuss the quick, predefined means of sending messages—message boxes.

Actually, message boxes are simple, predefined dialogs that return only the most cursory of information. We may do a modicum of customization to the message box, but this is a drop in the bucket compared to normal dialogs, however. This customization is accomplished through the passing of constant parameters that indicate the presence of standard icons and buttons. The return values indicate which of the standard buttons displayed were pressed. They have a very limited use, but when they can be used, they are lifesavers (well, at least codesavers).

Message boxes come in two flavors: `AfxMessageBox()` and `MessageBox()`. `AfxMessageBox()` is a global function (as are all `Afx` functions) and therefore can be used anywhere in your program. `MessageBox()` is a member function of the class `CWnd` and therefore can be called only from a `CWnd`-derived class. These two varieties use the following parameter formats:

```
AfxMessageBox(MessageText, CustomizationCodes, HelpID);
MessageBox(MessageText, WindowTitle, CustomizationCodes);
```

Aside from the scope differences between the two message box functions, they also differ somewhat in abilities. In both functions you specify the message text, which is the main purpose of the object. Both flavors also use the same constant customization codes described in Table 5.10. But the remaining parameters are where these functions differ. The `AfxMessageBox()` function allows you to specify a help code so that you may tie the message box into the context-sensitive help system that we'll discuss in Chapter 20. You will often see this code omitted. Its default value is –1, which indicates that no help is available. The `MessageBox()` function doesn't have the help code option, but it does allow you to specify the title appearing at the top of the message box. For our immediate purposes, the differences are slight. At the moment, let's concentrate on the similarities between these functions, starting with the customizing code constants.

Table 5.10. Some `MessageBox()` customization codes.

Customization Code	Description
MB_ABORTRETRYIGNORE	Three buttons: Abort, Retry, Ignore
MB_OK	One button: OK
MB_OKCANCEL	Two buttons: OK, Cancel
MB_RETRYCANCEL	Two buttons: Retry, Cancel
MB_YESNO	Two buttons: Yes, No
MB_YESNOCANCEL	Three buttons: Yes, No, Cancel
MB_ICONEXCLAMATION	Uses an "!" icon
MB_ICONINFORMATION	Uses an "i" icon
MB_ICONQUESTION	Uses a "?" icon
MB_ICONSTOP	Uses a stop sign icon

These codes allow you to adapt the look and feel of your message box to your own needs. You may use these codes singly or in a bitwise ORed combination of an icon code and a button code. Proper use of these codes can present a handsome interface to the user that's simplicity itself to incorporate into your code. Be aware that Table 5.10 is not a complete list of customization codes, although it does include the most popular ones. For more information about the other codes, consult your Class Library Reference.

There is one last similarity between the two message box types. Each message box function returns one of the codes in Table 5.11, indicating which button the user pressed. This is the way information, albeit limited, is retrieved from the user via the message box. We use the `MessageText` parameter to transmit information to the user, and the user uses the buttons to respond to our message. Message box button clicks result in the return of one of these codes.

Table 5.11. `MessageBox()` return codes.

Return Code	Description
IDABORT	Indicates that the Abort button was pressed.
IDCANCEL	Indicates that the Cancel button was pressed.
IDIGNORE	Indicates that the Ignore button was pressed.

continues

CStrings and Other Helpful Miscellany

Table 5.11. continued

Return Code	Description
IDNO	Indicates that the No button was pressed.
IDOK	Indicates that the OK button was pressed.
IDRETRY	Indicates that the Retry button was pressed.
IDYES	Indicates that the Yes button was pressed.

Let's take a look at these message boxes in action. Say that from our view class we want to confirm an action by the user. Because CView is derived from CWnd, we could use either of the message box types. I'll choose MessageBox() so that I can demonstrate it, but you will have better reasons in the context of your program. The following code snippet, placed in any CWnd-derived class, will invoke the message box shown in Figure 5.1:

```
if (MessageBox( "Do you really want to ...",  "Confirm ...",
        MB_YESNO | MB_ICONQUESTION) == IDYES)
    // The Yes button was pressed. Go ahead and perform operation.
else
    // The No button was pressed. Do not perform operation.
```

Figure 5.1.
*CWnd::MessageBox()
example.*

Note that we combined the customization codes of MB_YESNO and MB_ICONQUESTION using the bitwise OR. This resulted in both the Yes and No buttons being present, as well as the question mark icon being displayed. Also note that the first string parameter did in fact become the title of the message box.

A second scenario could be that you want to warn the user of some impending data loss, and you want this warning to spring from the holder of the data—the document class. CDocument is not derived from CWnd, so the MessageBox() function is not accessible. Fortunately, there is the AfxMessageBox() function.

The following code snippet may be placed anywhere in your program, and it will result in the message box shown in Figure 5.2:

```
if (AfxMessageBox("Warning: Data loss is possible!",
        MB_ICONSTOP | MB_OKCANCEL) == IDOK)
    // The OK button was pressed. Continue with operation.
else
    // The Cancel button was pressed. Cancel operation.
```

Figure 5.2.
AfxMessageBox example.

It's up to you to determine which message box is best for your particular situation. Experiment with them and have fun. Both are very handy things to have around.

Exceptional Programming

Exceptional programming is always a goal for programmers. The MFC certainly aids us in this endeavor. But in this particular case, we must take exceptions to our code. No, not the computerese version of exception. I'm talking about the "exceptional condition" that can occur during the execution of your code. Catching and handling these exceptional conditions before they reach the user is crucial for robust programs. An out-of-memory error popping up and crashing your program can drastically erode the user's confidence in you. It may even have the

CStrings and Other Helpful Miscellany

added payoff of losing data—that's bad news even if you're the only user. Many people call this process error handling, but I don't like that term. Error implies that someone has done something wrong. There aren't that many people to blame. The user has an ironclad alibi—he isn't here yet. Besides, you've heard the expression "The customer's always right." The user is the customer. If he wants to try to enter letters in a numeric field, it's up to us to kindly correct him. Really, the only error that exists is the unhandled exceptional condition. If we handle the problem, it isn't an error. Of course, you might have *error* inexorably chiseled into your mind. If that's the case, you can think of exceptions as errors with an attitude. But they really aren't just errors; they are something more, as we shall see.

The key idea in exception handling is an alternate flow of control. When an exception is encountered in a program unit, the sequential flow within that unit is halted. A separate flow is started—that of exception processing. If no handlers are found, the exception propagates to the MFC framework, where the exception becomes an error. An error message is displayed, and your program remains halted (or, more appropriately, dead). The whole idea of exception handling is to catch these exceptions before they reach the framework (and hence become errors). In Bjarne Stroustrup's C++ and in the proposed ANSI C++, exception handling is wired into the language. In Visual C++ 1.5, exception handling is accomplished via macros and the exception objects themselves. In Visual C++ 2.0, Microsoft has incorporated exception handling into the language proper. Fortunately, the Visual C++ 1.5 macros closely match the exception handling facilities that are built into the later product, so the eventual migration of code to the new compiler can be done with little effort.

As far as foundation classes are concerned, our primary interest will be in the classes derived from the abstract base class `CException`. Objects of these derived classes will be the exceptions manipulated by the exception handling macros. Each derived class specializes in a particular type of exceptional condition. Table 5.12 describes the predefined `CException`-derived classes.

Table 5.12. Predefined `CException`-derived classes.

Class	Description
`CArchiveException`	Problem with serialization.
`CDBException`	Problem with the database (ODBC exception).
`CFileException`	Problem with file manipulation.
`CMemoryException`	Not enough memory.
`CNotSupportedException`	Requested service is not supported.
`COleException`	Problem with OLE.
`CResourceException`	Problem with resource.
`CUserException`	Application-specific uses.

Of course, the exception objects are only half the story. Catching and responding to the exceptions is the other half. Table 5.13 lists the exception handling macros of Visual C++ 1.5.

Table 5.13. Exception handling macros.

Macro	Description
TRY	Starts a block of code in which you may catch exceptions.
CATCH	Used to catch the first type of exception in a TRY block.
AND_CATCH	Used to catch any additional exception types after a catch.
END_CATCH	Ends the catch portion of an exception handler.
THROW	Allows you to throw a specified exception.
THROW_LAST	Throws the last exception caught to the next outer handler.

The exception handling macros you will use the most are the TRY, CATCH, AND_CATCH, and END_CATCH quartet. Using these four macros, you may tackle practically all your exception handling needs. Just as a picture is worth a thousand words, so is a piece of sample code. The following is the framework for exception handling:

```
TRY
{
    // Code that may cause an exception
}
CATCH(ExceptionClass, ExceptionPointer)
{
    // Code that responds to an exception
}
AND_CATCH(ExceptionClass, ExceptionPointer)
{
    // Code that responds to another exception type
}
END_CATCH
```

Any code from which you anticipate exceptions should be surrounded with TRY blocks. The CATCH statement, which immediately follows the TRY block, requires two parameters: the class of the anticipated exception, and a variable in which to place the pointer to the exception. This pointer variable should not be declared. The declaration is done within the CATCH macro. The associated CATCH block contains the code that will respond to the exception. There is a possibility that a single piece of code might be able to generate many different types of exceptions. In these cases, multiple exception types need to be anticipated, and different types of handling must be provided. The AND_CATCH macro block is added to provide this multiple exception handling support. The AND_CATCH macro has the same functionality as the CATCH macro. However, there can be only one CATCH macro in an exception handler, whereas there can be as many AND_CATCH macros as necessary. This is because the CATCH macro indicates the beginning of all the CATCH blocks, and AND_CATCH indicates an additional CATCH block. Finally, END_CATCH indicates that there are no further CATCH blocks and that the exception handling code is at an end.

Day 5: CStrings and Other Helpful Miscellany

The following is a real exception handler that traps `CMemoryException`:

```
void TestFunction()
{
    CString S;   // Don't initialize here because an exception might result

    TRY
    {
        // If memory is low, the following assignment
        // will throw an exception
        S = "Once upon a time, there were three programmers ...";

        // Any code after the line that throws
        // the exception will not be executed
    }
    CATCH(CMemoryException, e)
    {
        AfxMessageBox("Memory is low!!", MB_ICONSTOP | MB_OK);
    }
    END_CATCH

}
```

If the memory resources of the system are sufficiently strained, even a small assignment can cause the memory to be exhausted. In such a case, a memory exception would be generated and, for this function, caught. You may respond to your exceptions in any number of ways. In this particular case, I decided to send a message indicating the memory status to the user. For memory exceptions, there really is only one possible cause: An attempt was made to allocate more memory than was available. The `CMemoryException` class has no visible members for us to query. All the information we need is in the fact that the exception was thrown. However, many of the other exceptions aren't so black-and-white. File exceptions, for example, could be thrown due to a number of conditions such as the file not being found or file access being denied. These more-complicated exceptions will have data members and functions designed to aid you in responding to the exception. We will get into the specifics of an exception when we deal with the associated class that throws the exception. For now, let's concentrate on general exception handling issues.

One such issue is the alternate flow of control, which I mentioned earlier. Every program equipped with exception handling has two processing paths. There is the standard processing path to which we are accustomed, and there is an alternate path that carries exceptions. Once an exception is thrown, standard processing is halted and control is passed to the alternate path. Alternate path processing continues until an exception handler is encountered. Within the exception handling code, processing control may be returned to the standard processing route. It is important to note that while on the alternate path, commands on the standard path may very well be permanently bypassed! You must take this into consideration when designing your exception handling code. Figure 5.3 diagrams this alternate flow.

Figure 5.3.
The alternate flow of control.

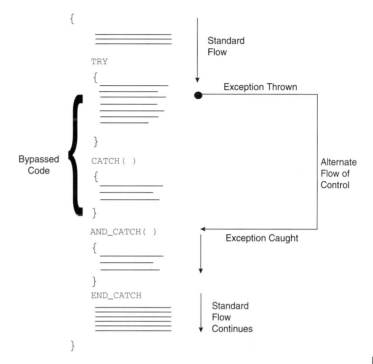

One of the most important considerations regarding the alternate flow of control is memory allocation. It is crucial that all memory issues be resolved, regardless of the control path taken. If the bypassed code includes some memory cleanup commands, then when the alternate route is taken, you will have memory problems. This problem doesn't become as apparent until you let exceptions propagate out of your block of code. Consider the following example:

```
void MyFunction()
{
    CString Name = "Filename.ext";
    char* pLetter = new char;  // Allocated memory for character

    OpenFile(Name);
    // File doesn't exist. A file exception is thrown.
    // No exception handler, so the exception is propagated up and out
    // and the remainder of the code in this code block is bypassed!

    // Perform file stuff, including closing the file

    delete pLetter;  // Free the allocated memory

}   // Name's memory is automatically freed
```

Day 5: CStrings and Other Helpful Miscellany

Meanwhile, somewhere else in your program...

```
TRY
{
    MyFunction();
}
CATCH(CFileException, e)
{
    // Handle the file exception
}
END_CATCH
```

In this example, you intentionally let an exception propagate out of `MyFunction()`, knowing that it's the calling function's responsibility to catch the exception. There's no problem with that approach, but care must be taken with regard to memory allocations. In this particular case, `pLetter` is allocated but never destroyed since the `delete` statement was bypassed when the exception was thrown. The memory allocated to `pLetter` would be unavailable for use for the life of this program. This situation is called a *memory leak*. Just like a leak in a boat, memory leaks can over time cause your program to go under. You might consider avoiding this problem by avoiding the overt memory allocation of calling the new operator whenever an exception is possible. Not only is this measure obscenely extreme, it also won't save you. There is another memory leak in the preceding example. The `CString` object's memory is also never reclaimed. The exception also bypasses the end of the function. The objects declared in the function aren't destroyed. This isn't important for primitive types, but it's important for any object that requires its destructor to be called for memory reclamation. `CString` dynamically allocates memory to accommodate its string data. It therefore requires explicit memory cleanup, which is encapsulated in its destructor. You can't avoid the memory problem—you just have to take care of it.

An example of the proper method of memory cleanup in exception handlers follows:

```
CMyClass* pC = new CMyClass;
TRY
{
    // Code block dealing with pC

    delete pC;
}
CATCH (CException, e)
{
    // Handle the exception

    // Since the delete pC line will not be executed in the
    // case of an exception, we have to delete it here too
    delete pC;
}
END_CATCH
```

This exception handler not only demonstrates proper memory management, but it also uses the `CException` base class as an exception catchall. By using the `CExecption` class instead of one of the derived classes in the `CATCH` macro, you will catch all the exceptions thrown in the `TRY` block.

From within the CATCH block, you may use CObject class functions to determine the actual type of the exception object caught. This technique uses the polymorphic nature of C++ classes to abstract the CATCH macro. You will learn more about these issues in the next chapter, when we discuss CObject, the ancestor of CException.

The foundation classes aren't the only ones that get to have fun throwing exceptions. We too can have that honor. The THROW and THROW_LAST macros provide the means for us to get in on the active side of exceptions. The THROW macro requires a pointer to the exception to be thrown. It then starts the exception on its way. This procedure works for predefined exceptions and any exception that you create. THROW is your entrance to the alternate control path. The THROW_LAST macro is used within a CATCH block to rethrow an exception. This is handy if you're catching only a certain subtype of exception. For example, you might just want to catch invalid filename exceptions in a certain block, but you want to propagate the rest of the file exceptions to the next level of handler. THROW_LAST would be ideal for this situation:

```
TRY
{
    // Code that throws a file exception
}
CATCH(CFileException, e)
{
    if (e->m_cause == CFileException::invalidFile)
    // Handle the problem
    else
        THROW_LAST
}
END_CATCH
```

You will see many more exception handling examples as we progress through this book. If you still feel uneasy about exceptions, don't worry. They seem strange at first. But with a little more exposure, you'll be catching and throwing exceptions like a pro.

Do You Know What Time It Is?

You might not know what time it is, but your computer sure does. At the core of every computer is a clock. This clock is the heartbeat of the computer's logic. It gives the computer the synchronized timing required to perform computations. True, our clock and its clock are different, but the difference is slight. Almost all modern personal computers also have an on-board, battery backed-up, human-type clock. From this internal human clock, the computer can tell time with the best of them. Using the runtime library functions that come with your Visual C++ compiler, you too can access this onboard chronometer. Of course, our preferred method of computing is through the MFC Library. CTime is a foundation class that holds and manipulates date/time information.

CStrings and Other Helpful Miscellany

CTime encapsulates both date and time information. Unfortunately, for efficiency reasons, CTime places some restrictions on the year portion of the date. The CTime components have the following bounds:

Year	1970 to 2038
Month	1 to 12
Day	1 to 31
Hour	0 to 23
Minute	0 to 59
Second	0 to 59

When you access the CTime components directly, these are the ranges of the values you can receive or supply. Read-only access to these components may be obtained through the following CTime functions:

```
GetYear()
GetMonth()
GetDay()
GetHour()
GetMinute()
GetSecond()
```

CTime also provides a number of constructors with which you may construct CTime with a number of different types, as enumerated in Table 5.14.

Table 5.14. CTime constructor parameters.

Parameter	Description
Nothing	The default constructor initializes CTime to an invalid date and time.
const CTime&	Constructs CTime from another CTime object.
time_t	Constructs CTime from a time_t object. Used by many runtime functions.
ints for year, month, day, hour, minute, and second	Specifies the date and time the long way.
WORD for DOS date and WORD for DOS time	Initializes CTime with date and time from DOS functions.

Each of these constructors can be useful to you at one time or another. However, you will often need to specify a date or time the long way, by passing each piece of the date/time structure. This particular route is so popular, I'll provide the following example:

```
CTime NewCentury (2000, 1, 1, 0, 0, 0);   // Midnight of Jan 1, 2000
```

This is one of those instances where the CTime limitation raises its ugly head. An object of CTime can't precede midnight of January 1, 1970, and it can't exceed 11:59 p.m. and 59 seconds of December 31, 2038. For most uses, this limitation is rarely encountered. After all, current times and file timestamps are well within this range. However, database applications can often include dates that fall outside this range. The bottom line is that you must make sure that the values passed in this constructor fall within the valid range of values.

Back to the issue that started this whole date/time discussion: How do you get the current system date and time? CTime provides a function for this very operation. Calling the CTime::GetCurrentTime() function will return a static CTime object containing the current date and time. It's that simple. The equivalent runtime function procedure requires many more lines and is considerably more complicated than this one-line, no-parameter call. Trust the MFC to simplify your life.

Now that we have a date and time, how can we display it? Enter the CTime functions of Format() and FormatGmt(). Both functions are given a format string containing the format codes in Table 5.15, and both functions return a CString object representing the date and time. The only difference between these two functions is that Format() converts the object to local time before formatting it, whereas FormatGmt() formats the object as is. Which one you use is dictated by your particular application.

Table 5.15. Format codes (see `strftime` in the runtime library reference).

Code	Description
%A	Weekday name.
%a	Three-letter weekday abbreviation.
%B	Month name.
%b	Three-letter month abbreviation.
%c	Locale time and date representation.
%d	Day of month (01 to 31).
%H	Hour of day, military (00 to 23).
%I	Hour of day, standard (01 to 12).
%j	Day of year (001 to 366).
%M	Minute (00 to 59).
%m	Month (01 to 12).
%U	Week of year (00 to 51), with Sunday as first day of week.
%W	Week of year (00 to 51), with Monday as first day of week.

continues

Day 5

CStrings and Other Helpful Miscellany

Table 5.15. continued

Code	Description
%W	Decimal value of weekday (0 = Sunday).
%X	Locale time representation.
%x	Locale date representation.
%Y	Year (four digits).
%y	Year (two digits).
%Z	Time zone name. Null if the time zone isn't known.
%%	Percent literal.

The following example demonstrates the `CTime` format technique:

```
CTime T;
T = CTime::GetCurrentTime();

CString strTime = T.Format ("The current date is: %d %B %Y");

AfxMessageBox(strTime, MB_OK);
```

Figure 5.4 shows the output message box.

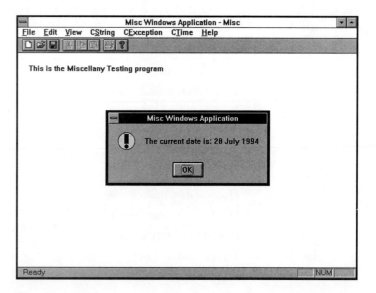

Figure 5.4.
CTime format example.

`CTime` also contains the usual plethora of assignment, comparison, and arithmetic operators. They are relatively self-explanatory, so I will let you explore them on your own—perhaps gently prompted by an exercise or two.

Summary

This has been an eventful and, hopefully, fun chapter. We explored the extremely useful CString class in depth. Almost every aspect of the variable-length CString was detailed—from construction to searching. You will find this class so helpful in your MFC programming efforts that you won't know how you survived without it. After looking at CString, we moved on to an easy means of communicating with the user: the message box. Message box invocation and customization techniques were explored and demonstrated. This is another class that will fast become one of your close programming buddies. The next stop on this whirlwind tour was exception handling. I placed emphasis on catching and handling exceptions, since this will be your primary relationship with exceptions. We briefly covered exception throwing. You will be afforded further exposure to THROW macros in the chapters to come. Finally, we discussed the date/time structure of CTime and its associated functions. We uncovered an interesting limitation of CTime: Dates in CTime can't precede January 1, 1970. This is a serious limitation if you ever intend to set up a database that might include birthdates. But this gives us a good excuse to remedy the situation by creating our own date class in the next chapter. I can't wait!

Q&A

Q Every time you called a message box, you passed an MB_ button constant. What happens if you pass an MB_ icon constant only?

A No problem. You can do that. The default message box comes equipped with an OK button. If you don't specify a button with a customization code, you'll get an OK button. In fact, you can omit the customization code entirely and still get the standard OK message box. In the case of MessageBox(), you may also leave out the WindowTile parameter. Both message box functions can be called with a single parameter— MessageText.

Q I noticed that sometimes you tested the message box return code and sometimes you didn't. Is there any hard and fast rule for when this return code must be tested?

A Usually, you test the return code when a multiple choice is possible. I often don't test the return value of a message box if it has a lone button, simply because it has only one possible return value. If a message box is customized with a Yes and a No button, for example, it's advisable to examine the return value. If it doesn't matter what the return value is, perhaps you should reevaluate the wisdom of having two buttons in the first place.

Q It seems to me that exception handling is more trouble than it's worth! Why do we even bother with two control paths?

A Two control paths might sound like a bother now. But, like the event-driven paradigm of Windows, after you use them awhile, you come to understand and appreciate

Day 5: CStrings and Other Helpful Miscellany

them. The second flow of control allows you to treat exceptional conditions as the aberrant events they are. It allows you to separate the code that normally is executed from the code required to clean up after unusual conditions. This code separation is where the true beauty of exception handling can be seen. However, if elegance is not enough of a reason, consider the fact that the MFC throws exceptions whether or not you are prepared for them. By using the MFC, you have already given up your right to avoid exceptions. I guess I should have put a warning in the Introduction.

Q You said that `CTime` is limited to date/time values between 1970 and 2038. Why is it more efficient to restrict `CTime` to these bounds?

A It's more efficient in terms of memory. By restricting the date to these bounds, `CTime` can cram all the date/time information in a single integer value. This integer value, in its rawest form, represents the number of seconds since midnight on January 1, 1970. This particular representation was inherited from the structure `time_t` that is still used heavily in the Visual C++ runtime functions.

Workshop

Quiz

1. What purpose do the `AnsiToOem()` and `OemToAnsi()` functions serve?
2. Compare and contrast the `AfxMessageBox()` function with the `MessageBox()` function.
3. What is meant by the term *alternate flow of control*?
4. Why should you use the `ASSERT` macro in your code?
5. Is it possible to have a `CATCH` block without a `TRY` block?

Exercises

1. Explore the `AnsiToOem()` and `OemToAnsi()` functions by setting up a loop, passing all the possible characters through the conversion, and observing the results.
2. Modify the `AutoCorrect()` function to accommodate a list of misspelled or corrected words so that it may auto-correct multiple words instead of just "teh."
3. Rewrite the wildcard processing function `IsEquivalent()` so that it will process more than one wildcard. Hint: Try using recursion.
4. Write a program that causes an out-of-memory error to occur. Add a handler to catch the exception and print your own message using a message box.
5. Declare a handful of `CTime` objects and initialize them with dates and times that have some special significance to you. Use the `ASSERT` macro to confirm that the `CTime` comparison operators work the way you expect.

WEEK 1

CObject: The Mother of All Classes

DAY 6

CObject: The Mother of All Classes

With all the power built into the MFC framework, it would be unnecessarily limiting if it didn't allow you to create your own "MFC" classes. Of course, you may create a class over an existing foundation class such as CView or CDocument and inherit much of your code. This technique is extremely useful. In fact, AppWizard does precisely this when it creates a new application. However, you will often find that you need a completely new and different class. The designers of the MFC couldn't possibly have considered every contingency, so they didn't try. Instead, they recognized this natural limitation and decided to provide a universal base class—CObject, the mother of all foundation classes. From this class you may inherit functionality that any MFC-cognizant class should have. Minimal foundation class functionality is the mainstay of this chapter. We will explore what CObject provides and why we want it in our own classes.

Note: It would be more accurate, although less dramatic, to say that CObject is the mother of *most* foundation classes. A few foundation classes aren't derived from CObject. CString and CTime are the most notable examples.

What Can *CObject* Do for You?

Ask not what you can do for CObject; ask what CObject can do for you! (My apologies to JFK.) Before getting into the syntax and semantics of creating CObject classes, let's put the whole operation in the perspective of why we want to do it. This is a valid question. You've seen enough of MFC programming to get an inkling of its power. So it's important to question a regression to building our own classes. After all, MFC provides all manner of classes for us to use. But there's the rub. It doesn't provide *all* manner of classes, just the ones you will most likely need. In Chapter 5, we came across the limitation of MFC's date/time structure. CTime is limited to a date range of 1970 to 2038. This is fine for most applications, but as I pointed out, birthdates can easily slip back to dates preceding modern computers. Back to a simpler time of slide rules and vinyl records—but I date myself and digress. As for my younger audience, 2038 might not seem too far off—graduation, perhaps. In any case, how do we overcome CTime's inherent limitation? You guessed it—we'll make our own class that handles a wider range of dates. This new class (let's call it CDate) will encapsulate all the functionality that we might require from a date class.

That's a good reason to build a new class, but why derive it from CObject? C++ has already supplied the ability for us to create our own classes. What does CObject do for us? CObject provides a number of essential hooks to standard MFC processing. CObject's provisions are listed in Table 6.1 in an increasing progression of support.

Table 6.1. CObject's progression of functionality.

Level	Support
Level 1	Diagnostic support
Level 2	Runtime class information support
Level 3	Dynamic object creation support
Level 4	Serialization support

Each level of support includes the functionality from the preceding level. The level of support you incorporate into your class will depend on the nature of the object in question. We will build CDate with the highest level of CObject functionality. But first, let's find out what each level of functionality will do for your class.

The lowest level of CObject functionality is diagnostic support. As you may know, diagnostics are used in the debugger for tracking down errors and general troubleshooting of your code. The only real impact that diagnostic support has on the final product is one of fewer errors and faster repair of post-release bugs (or undocumented features, as they are called in the industry). These diagnostic abilities are invaluable during the construction and maintenance phases of your application.

The next level of CObject functionality is runtime class information. An object of a class graced with this level of support may be queried for class information such as class name and memory size. This class information has a number of uses, not the least of which is class identification. If you place objects from different CObject-derived classes in the same polymorphic structure, the identity of the objects becomes ambiguous. You know that all of them have CObject ancestry, but beyond that, your information is limited. Runtime class support can give you this information and more.

At the third level, we encounter support for dynamic object creation. A CObject-derived class with this level of functionality allows its objects to be dynamically created and destroyed by the application framework. This is especially valuable in serialization, because while loading previously saved object data, the framework must create the appropriate class objects to serve as receptacles for the data.

The highest level of CObject support is serialization. *Serialization* refers to the conversion of class objects to disk file data. The reason serialization is such a hot topic is because of the power of this conversion. Class objects may have an intricate, nonlinear structure, whereas disk data is a serial procession of bits on a magnetic media. Because of the serial nature of magnetic disks, this conversion of object data to disk data is called serialization. A CObject-derived class with this ability may be saved and retrieved from disk automatically through the MFC framework. Enabling your classes with serialization makes them fit in the framework seamlessly. This melding is so lovely and so painless, you won't believe it.

DAY 6

CObject: The Mother of All Classes

Now that you know what `CObject` can do for you, you can intelligently ask what you can do for `CObject`! JFK would be proud.

So You Want to Make Your Own Class

Before we delve too deeply into the `CObject` vernacular, let's take a moment to examine what we want to encapsulate within our `CObject`-derived class. To be more precise, what requirements and limitations will the `CDate` class embody? `CDate` will be limited to dates. We're not trying to compete with `CTime`; we're trying to complement `CTime`'s functionality. Although `CTime` will serve us well in the arena of date- and time-stamping files and other time-oriented issues, `CDate` will allow us to model a broader range of dates. We must design `CDate` in terms of supporting `CTime` as opposed to supplanting `CTime`. During this design process, as in any software process, we must bear the Software Engineering Principles in mind. Completeness is especially important for the high-visibility, widely-used classes such as `CDate`. Consider completeness while looking at the `CDate` class interface in the following listing.

```
#ifndef __DATE_H__
#define __DATE_H__

typedef short int SWORD;
typedef unsigned short int UWORD;

class CDate : public CObject
{
protected:

    // Attributes
    SWORD m_nYear;
    UWORD m_nMonth;
    UWORD m_nDay;

public:

    // Constructors
    CDate();  // Default constructor
    CDate(CDate& Date);   // Copy constructor
    CDate(CTime& Time);
    CDate(SWORD y, UWORD m, UWORD d);

    // Assignment operator
    CDate& operator= (CDate& Date);

    // Selectors: providers of controlled visibility to the attributes
    SWORD Year()
        {return m_nYear;}
    UWORD Month()
        {return m_nMonth;}
    UWORD Day()
        {return m_nDay;}
```

```cpp
    // Functions that increment the date by one day
    CDate& operator++();      // Prefix notation
    CDate& operator++(int);   // Postfix notation
    void AddDay();

    // Functions that decrement the date by one day
    CDate& operator--();      // Prefix notation
    CDate& operator--(int);   // Postfix notation
    void SubtractDay();

    // Sum and difference operators
    CDate& operator+ (int Days);    // Add Days to date
    CDate& operator- (int Days);    // Subtract Days from date
    int operator- (CDate& Date);    // Return difference between dates in days

    void Add (SWORD Years, SWORD Months = 0, SWORD Days = 0);

    // Comparison operators
    BOOL operator== (CDate& Date);
    BOOL operator!= (CDate& Date);
    BOOL operator> (CDate& Date);
    BOOL operator>= (CDate& Date);
    BOOL operator< (CDate& Date);
    BOOL operator<= (CDate& Date);

    // Miscellaneous functions

    // Returns 0 if Date is invalid
    int IsValid();

    // Changes date to closest valid date
    void MakeValid();

    // Returns TRUE if y is a leap year
    BOOL IsLeapYear(SWORD y);

    // Returns the number of days in the month
    UWORD DaysInMonth();

    // Returns a CString object representation of the date
    // Format is the same as in strftime(). See MS Visual C++
    // runtime library reference.
    CString DateString (CString& Output, const char* Format = "%d %b %Y");

    // Sets the date to the value held in the string.
    // A string-to-date conversion is performed.
    // Returns TRUE if successful.
    BOOL StringToDate (const char* strDate);
};

#endif
```

Wow! That's one long class interface. No good deed goes unpunished. The punishment for making a class nearly complete, and therefore applicable for a wide variety of uses, is the implementation work. In this case, much of the work is an exercise in C++ class construction.

DAY 6
CObject: The Mother of All Classes

Most of the manufacture of this class should be old hat to you—well, at least you should have seen it before. Because this is a book on MFC, much of this implementation is left as an exercise to the reader. We will concentrate on the portions needed to demonstrate the CObject aspects of this class.

The first interesting features you might notice in CDate's interface are the preprocessor directives. The first two lines and the last line contain directives that instruct the compiler to ignore the code if CDate has already been included. This bit of compiler magic is done through the definition of the constant __DATE_H__. If this constant has been defined, the module must have been previously included. Otherwise, the module hasn't been included, so you must define the constant. This technique is commonly employed in widely used classes that may be included in a number of different modules. If the class is actually included in two different places, the compiler will complain of a redefinition of the class. By using these preprocessor directives, we can eliminate the problem before it even arises.

Two type definition statements just before the class definition provide abbreviations for two commonly used types. Actually, the UWORD and SWORD types are a foreshadowing of some ODBC topics. In fact, the class CDate will serve us well in our database activities during this book's second week. SWORD and UWORD are also defined in one of the ODBC interface files (SQL.H). However, for now we will use the CDate definitions. Later we can switch to the SQL definitions.

Unlike CTime, which is both date and time, our CDate class doesn't practice false advertising. CDate's sole responsibility is date storage and manipulation. Hence, its attributes are m_nYear, m_nMonth, and m_nDay. Using the SWORD and UWORD type definitions serves a dual purpose. First, the short integer base allows a more compact and natural modeling of the attributes. Neither day nor month has any reason to be negative, so an unsigned data model works. Second and more importantly, this data layout closely resembles an ODBC structure that we will exploit in a data exchange mechanism. The closeness of the mapping will allow us to use CDate in the ODBC structure's stead and exchange data directly into and out of CDate. Of course, this similarity of structure isn't something we can count on in future releases of the MFC. In preparation for such a change, the attributes are protected. No other module will have access to this underlying representation. This is a good idea anyway. We might decide later that this particular implementation isn't efficient enough. Perhaps we will change the representation to a single integer value that holds the number of days since January 1, 1900. Doesn't this representation sound familiar? In a lot of ways, this representation would be more efficient. But if the attributes were public, such a change would force a recompilation (perhaps a redesign) of any modules that use CDate.

Making the attributes protected is a valid precaution, but it entails some extra work. Ironically, once we've hidden the attributes, we must provide them with some measure of visibility. Selectors allow hidden attributes a controlled means of accessibility. People sometimes argue that selectors are an unnecessary shell that just adds a burden to the already-busy processor. Every level of protection you can add to make your code more robust and clean should be welcomed. A small impact on the processor is more than made up for by solid, debugged code. In the case of selectors, the impact on the processor can be illuminated by making the selector code in-line. Placing the selector implementation in the class interface automatically makes it in-line. Alternatively, preceding the implementation with the keyword `inline` will achieve the same result in the implementation file. You usually won't have to give up efficiency for good programming technique, but if you do, know that you are doing it for a very good cause.

`CDate` has a number of constructors that ease the object initialization process. The first two constructors are the most crucial. The default constructor allows `CDate` objects to be declared without the need of parameters. This ability is especially important when the framework needs to dynamically create `CDate` objects during the loading part of the serialization process. The second constructor is the copy constructor. It provides the ability to copy one `CDate` to another. For normal C++ classes, the compiler will generate a default copy constructor that will construct the new object and copy all member data to that object. However, in the case of `CObject`-derived classes, the compiler won't generate a default copy constructor. Microsoft defined `CObject` in such a way that you must override the copy constructor if you wish to use it in your class. In the same vein, the assignment operator must also be overridden. These overrides are required for `CObject`-derived classes so that you will be aware of and involved in your class definition. These functions are so important to the proper functioning of your class that letting the compiler generate default versions is too dangerous. Implement the constructors and the assignment operator as follows:

```
// Default constructor
CDate::CDate()
{
    m_nYear = 0;
    m_nMonth = 0;
    m_nDay = 0;
    // Null date. Not valid as a date, but handy.
}

// Copy constructor
CDate::CDate(CDate& Date)
{
    m_nYear = Date.m_nYear;
    m_nMonth = Date.m_nMonth;
    m_nDay = Date.m_nDay;
}

CDate::CDate(CTime& Time)
{
    m_nYear = Time.GetYear();
    m_nMonth = Time.GetMonth();
    m_nDay = Time.GetDay();
}

CDate::CDate(SWORD y, UWORD m, UWORD d):
    m_nYear(y),
```

Day 6

CObject: The Mother of All Classes

```
        m_nMonth(m),
        m_nDay(d)
{}

CDate& CDate::operator=(CDate& Date)
{
    m_nYear = Date.m_nYear;
    m_nMonth = Date.m_nMonth;
    m_nDay = Date.m_nDay;

    return *this;
}
```

The increment and decrement functions allow us to add days to and subtract days from a date. Overloading the ++ and -- operators in this way is a very natural extension to the class. These functions are fundamental to the class's utility and should therefore be provided. However, incrementing and decrementing the date is trickier than you might at first think. A major hurdle that must be overcome is the problem with the end and beginning of the month. What happens when you increment past the end of a month or, conversely, decrement past the beginning of a month is an issue that needs resolving. Both of these operations require knowledge of the number of days in the month in question. But the number of days in a month isn't as constant as we might want it to be. Don't forget about leap years! The increment/decrement operations require two additional functions in order to work properly: `IsLeapYear()` and `DaysInMonth()`:

```
BOOL CDate::IsLeapYear(SWORD y)
{
    // Perform standard leap-year calculations
    // Leap years occur in years divisible by 4...
    if (y % 4 != 0)
        return FALSE;
    else
    {
        // ...except for century years...
        if (y % 100 != 0)
            return TRUE;
        // ...that are divisible by 400
        else if (y % 400 != 0)
            return FALSE;
        else
            return TRUE;
    }
}

UWORD CDate::DaysInMonth()
{
    switch (m_nMonth)
    {
        case 2:
        if (IsLeapYear(m_nYear))
            return 29;
        else
            return 28;
```

```
            case 4:
            case 6:
            case 9:
            case 11:
                return 30;

            default:
                return 31;
    } // End switch
}
```

Utilizing these functions, we may implement the increment/decrement functions as follows:

```
void CDate::AddDay()
{
    if (m_nDay < DaysInMonth())
        m_nDay ++;
    else
    {
        m_nDay = 1;
        if (m_nMonth != 12)
            m_nMonth ++;
        else
        {
            m_nMonth = 1;
            m_nYear++;
        }
    }
}

void CDate::SubtractDay()
{
    if (m_nDay > 1)
        m_nDay--;
    else
    {
        m_nDay = DaysInMonth();
        if (m_nMonth <= 1)
        {
            m_nMonth = 12;
            m_nYear--;
        }
        else
            m_nMonth--;
    }
}

    // Prefix operator
CDate& CDate::operator++()
{
    AddDay();
    return *this;
}

// Postfix operator
CDate& CDate::operator++(int)
```

CObject: The Mother of All Classes

```
{
    CDate Old = *this;
    AddDay();
    return Old;
}
```

I will leave the implementation of the decrement operators as an exercise for you. They really aren't that hard if you follow the lead provided by the increment operators. You will also need to implement the sum and difference operators on your own. These might present more of a challenge.

The next function in the interface is the Add() function. This function allows you to increment the date by years, months, and/or days. This functionality is clearly useful, but it also brings up some interesting issues. Add a year and a month to Jan 3, 1990 and you'll end up with Feb 3, 1991. But add a month and a day to Jan 30, 1992, and what do you get? Feb 28, 1992? Mar 1, 1992? In our own parlance, we have no problem saying "a month from now" or "next month" and expecting everyone to understand. But analytically speaking, "one month" is very vague. When you weigh all the options, it becomes clear that if you add a month to any date, the resultant date should stay in the following month. Hence, adding a month to Aug 31 would give you Sep 30. That said, let's look at the implementation of Add():

```
void CDate::Add (SWORD Years, SWORD Months, SWORD Days)
{
    // First, add the years. No problems here.
    m_nYear += Years;

    if (Months < 0)
    {
        // If Months is negative, perform the subtraction,
        // decrementing the year as necessary
        Months = abs(Months);
        while (m_nMonth <= (UWORD)Months)
        {
            Months -= 12;
            m_nYear--;
        }
        m_nMonth -= Months;
    }
    else if (Months > 0)
    {
        // If Months is positive, perform the addition,
        // incrementing the year as necessary
        m_nMonth += Months;
        while (m_nMonth > 12)
        {
            m_nMonth -= 12;
            m_nYear++;
        }
    }

    // Make sure the day is valid
    if (m_nDay > DaysInMonth())
```

```
            m_nDay = DaysInMonth();

    if (Days == 0)
        return;

    if (Days < 0)
        for (int i = 1; i <= abs(Days); i++)
            SubtractDay();
    else
        for (int i = 1; i <= abs(Days); i++)
            AddDay();
}
```

The next group of functions in CDate are the comparison operators. I will implement three and let you implement three. It's good practice.

```
BOOL CDate::operator== (CDate& Date)
{
    return (m_nYear == Date.m_nYear) &&
        (m_nMonth == Date.m_nMonth) &&
        (m_nDay == Date.m_nDay);
}

BOOL CDate::operator!= (CDate& Date)
{
    return !(operator==(Date));
}

BOOL CDate::operator> (CDate& Date)
{
    if (m_nYear == Date.m_nYear)
        if (m_nMonth == Date.m_nMonth)
            return m_nDay > Date.m_nDay;
        else
            return m_nMonth > Date.m_nMonth;
    else
        return m_nYear > Date.m_nYear;
}
```

These operators are straightforward implementations, but you might think that operator> could be made more efficient by using the conditional operator (?:). This might be so. However, the gain in efficiency decreases code understandability. Code clarity translates into fewer bugs and easier maintenance. But understandability is a judgment call. You might find the ?: structure perfectly clear. I do not. I find it cryptic. If you decide to reimplement this function, remember that an efficient but buggy program doesn't hold a candle to a slower yet reliable and maintainable program.

A couple of additional miscellaneous functions are included in the class to aid in supporting the model. Both the IsValid() and MakeValid() functions concern themselves with the validity of the currently stored date. IsValid() reports on this validity, and MakeValid() actually changes the day field to make the date conform to a legitimate value. Both functions will be applicable in future projects. For now, take a look at the implementations:

CObject: The Mother of All Classes

```cpp
BOOL CDate::IsValid()
{
    if (m_nMonth < 1 || m_nMonth > 12)
        return FALSE;
    if (m_nDay > 0 && m_nDay <= DaysInMonth())
        return TRUE;
    else
        return FALSE;

    // Note that a null date is not a valid date
}

void CDate::MakeValid()
{
    if (m_nMonth < 1)
        m_nMonth = 1;
    // Note that m_nMonth can't be less
    // than 0 since UWORD is unsigned

    // Cycle any excess months into years
    while (m_nMonth > 12)
    {
        m_nMonth -= 12;
        m_nYear++;
    }

    // Clip the days to fit in the month
    if (m_nDay < 1)
        m_nDay = 1;
    else if (m_nDay > DaysInMonth())
        m_nDay = DaysInMonth();
}
```

Note: To be painfully accurate, the validation functions must also take into account some of the calendar changes that have occurred throughout history. For example, the calendar introduced by Julius Caesar and used by the world for more than 1,600 years was faulty. It used a year that was over 11 minutes too long. Consequently, over the centuries, this error built up to about 10 days. On October 5, 1582, the Catholic church rectified this problem by fixing the error in the calendar and decreeing the new date to be October 15, 1582. Some predominantly Protestant countries were slow to adopt this Catholic edict. England adopted our modern calendar in 1752, and Russia did so in 1918. The bottom line is this: Dates in this period are highly suspect since they depend on the country of origin. So as not to make our code unwieldy, we will ignore the whole issue.

The last `CDate` function we will discuss is the `DateString()` function. It returns a string containing the date and adhering to the format specified. The format convention is borrowed from the runtime function `strftime()`, which, by the way, happens to be the same format used in CTime. Implementing this function is made quite easy by using the `strftime()` function as follows:

```
CString CDate::DateString (const char* Format)
{
    const BuffLen = 128;
    CString Output;
    char* pszS = Output.GetBuffer(BuffLen);

    int nWeekday = 0;   // Sunday
    // You might wish to make nWeekday just a tad more accurate

    int nDaysSinceJan1 = operator-(CDate(m_nYear,1,1));
    struct tm Date = {0, 0, 0, m_nDay, m_nMonth-1,
                      m_nYear-1900, nWeekday,
                      nDaysSinceJan1, 0};

    strftime(pszS, BuffLen-1, Format, &Date);
    Output.ReleaseBuffer();

    return Output;
}
```

Note that we use the tm structure as a way station for the date data because the `strftime()` function uses it as a parameter. Also note that the tm structure holds both date and time data and that it is fundamentally different from the other date/time structures we have encountered. Here, in the construction of the tm structure object, we have zeroed out all the nonapplicable members. This has the effect of making the time portion of the tm structure indicate midnight without daylight savings time. You may also see an opportunity to improve this function by actually calculating the nWeekday variable (see the exercises at the end of this chapter). For more information about the tm structure, consult your runtime library reference.

Thus far we have discussed the basic functionality of CDate. Nothing we have encountered in this discussion is specific to a CObject-derived class. The implementation of CDate up to this point would be practically the same as a date class designed for DOS use. Of course, we have derived it from CObject, so CDate already has started down the MFC road.

Diagnostics

The mere derivation of CDate from CObject is enough to provide minimal diagnostic services to the class. CObject provides two functions for diagnostic support: Dump() and AssertValid(). The Dump() function dumps diagnostic information about the class to a specified output. These diagnostic dumps can be very useful in your debugging efforts. The AssertValid() function concerns itself with the internal validity of the class data. If it determines that class data is invalid, inconsistent, or corrupt, it outputs a diagnostic message to that effect and halts the program. You might think that halting the program is a rather drastic measure. But 'tis better to halt the

Day 6
CObject: The Mother of All Classes

program during debugging and find the source of the corruption than be ignorant of the problem and go on with invalid data.

By default, these two functions provide a certain amount of diagnostic support that we may use, but the true benefit comes when we go to the trouble of overriding them. Place the following code in CDate's interface:

```
#ifdef _DEBUG
    virtual void Dump(CDumpContext& dc) const;
    virtual void AssertValid() const;
#endif
```

The diagnostic support is for the debugger's "eyes" only, so we must enclose any diagnostic code (even declarations) in these preprocessor directives that check for the debug mode. It's important to keep this in mind when you place calls to these functions in your code. When you switch over to a release version of a program, any diagnostic calls visible will cause compiler errors. Enclosing diagnostic calls in the same type of preprocessor directives just shown automatically makes the calls invisible to the release version of the compiler.

Taking another look at the new declarations, you will see that Dump() has a seemingly familiar parameter—a device context! No, not quite. CDumpContext is not a CDC-derived class; hence, it's not a device context. However, this dump context is similar to a device context in that it serves as our attaché to a display/recording object. CDumpContext provides a means to connect our dumped data to a file or the screen. You will typically use afxDump, the predefined CDumpContext object for standard output. Standard output depends upon your configuration, but for most Windows configurations, the standard output will be in the debug output window. Don't be too concerned about this class. We won't use CDumpContexts in this book other than the afxDump object.

Note: In order for the diagnostic routines and macros to work, you must enable them via the MFC Trace Options application included with Visual C++. This application is found in the Visual C++ program group.

Without the trace options enabled, you won't see any diagnostic output. However, when they are enabled, they can show up in a variety of places, depending on your system's configuration. Typically, the diagnostic output will appear in the debugger's output window—the same window where the compile/link results appear. If you invoke the DBWin application (also found in the Visual C++ program group), diagnostic output will be channeled to the DBWin window.

CObject::Dump() displays data about the class. You override the Dump() function to customize this data. If you don't override it, Dump() will display only the class name and object address. Even this trifle of information is limited. Without the runtime information, the next level of support, the only class name available is CObject. Until you provide a detailed dumping mechanism in an override of Dump(), its output for a CDate object is the information shown in Figure 6.1. The following code snippet demonstrates a typical Dump() call:

```
CDate theDate(1962, 9, 13);

#ifdef _DEBUG
    theDate.Dump(afxDump);
#endif
```

Figure 6.1.
The default CDate Dump() output.

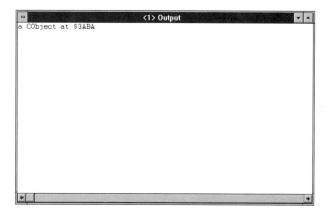

After you override the diagnostic functions as follows, the same call to Dump() will result in the information displayed in Figure 6.2.

```
#ifdef _DEBUG

void CDate::Dump(CDumpContext& dc) const
{
    // First, call the ancestor's Dump()
    CObject::Dump(dc);

    dc << "Year: " << m_nYear << " Month: " << m_nMonth
        << " Day: " << m_nDay << "\n";
}

void CDate::AssertValid() const
{
    CDate* pD = (CDate*)this;

    // First, call the ancestor's AssertValid()
    CObject::AssertValid();

    // If date is null, don't halt the program
    // A null date is valid in this sense
    if ( pD->operator==(CDate()) )
        return;
```

CObject: The Mother of All Classes

```
        ASSERT(pD->IsValid());
}

#endif
```

Figure 6.2.
Overridden CDate diagnostic data.

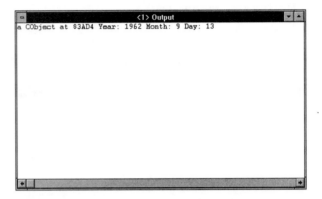

The AssertValid() function has quite a different mission than Dump(). AssertValid() doesn't actively provide any information unless something is very wrong. Class data being very wrong is particular to the class in question. In the case of CDate, it's rather complicated to determine whether the data is valid or not. Most of the confusion centers around the issue of leap years. Is Feb 29, 1900 a valid date? As it turns out, it is not. However, Feb 29, 1904 *is* valid. Checking these types of conditions is a job for AssertValid(). Internal consistency of the CObject object can be done in the implicit AssertValid() function, but you must explicitly check the class-specific data in the override of AssertValid().

When you override AssertValid() for your own classes, you will use the ASSERT macro to confirm invariant conditions associated with the class data. For CDate, we use the ASSERT macro in conjunction with the IsValid() function created earlier. Because of the simple data representation, CDate's AssertValid() function is trivial. However, if you embed other CObject-derived class objects within your class, you may wish to call the appropriate AssertValid() function on the embedded object. This chaining of the AssertValid() functions isn't always recommended because infinite loops are possible. However, this is another instance of the specific nature of the application determining your best course of action. Constructing the best AssertValid() function really isn't hard once you get the hang of it.

Note: Microsoft provides a macro as an alternative to calling the AssertValid() member function directly. The ASSERT_VALID macro takes a pointer to a CObject-derived object, makes sure the pointer isn't NULL, and then calls the object's

AssertValid() member function. ASSERT_VALID encapsulates all the safety checks you normally would have to perform prior to a direct AssertValid() call (including checking for debug mode). Needless to say, using the ASSERT_VALID macro is much more convenient:

```
CDate d(1969, 4, 20);
ASSERT_VALID(&d);
```

Another convenient macro to keep in mind is TRACE. This macro allows you to dump diagnostic information directly to the debug output. TRACE takes the same parameters as Visual C++'s printf function. Note that there are a few subtle differences between the Visual C++ printf function and the ANSI C printf function. To be warned is to be prepared. The TRACE macro is automatically ignored by the release version of the compiler:

```
char szA[] = "hello";
int nB = 5;
float fC = 3.1415;
TRACE("String: %s; Integer: %i; Float %f\n", szA, nB, fC);
```

You can see that CObject's diagnostic support can be as powerful as you wish to make it. The key to utilizing the power of the diagnostic functions is to use them in your code. Putting Dump()s, AssertValid()s, ASSERTs, and other diagnostic calls in your code during the writing process might at first seem to be more trouble than it's worth. But the first time the diagnostic routines catch a problem, you'll understand that they are well worth the effort. Usually these precautionary measures catch small problems before they become big ones.

CRuntimeClass

Enhancing CDate to include runtime information support is a relatively easy procedure. The first step is to add a pair of macros to the class code. The runtime support macros are DECLARE_DYNAMIC and IMPLEMENT_DYNAMIC. Placing these macros in the interface and implementation, respectively, will result in runtime information support. It's just that simple, as shown:

```
// Interface file
class CDate : public CObject
{
.
.
.
    DECLARE_DYNAMIC (CDate)
.
.
.
```

Day 6 CObject: The Mother of All Classes

```
};

// Implementation file
.
.
.
IMPLEMENT_DYNAMIC (CDate, CObject)
.
.
.
```

With the preceding changes, `CDate` will have runtime class support. These macros instruct the compiler to make the appropriate arrangements for runtime class information. Every class derived from `CObject` has an associated `CRuntimeClass` object that holds runtime class information. The parameters passed to the macros indicate the current class and the immediate ancestor class. This information is transferred to the associated `CRuntimeClass` object. But `CRuntimeClass` holds more data than just class names. The `CRuntimeClass` structure has the following attributes:

- `m_lpszClassName`: A null-terminated string holding the current class name.
- `m_nObjectSize`: The size of the object in bytes.
- `m_wSchema`: A class version number used in serialization.
- `m_pfnConstruct`: A void pointer to the class's default constructor.
- `m_pBaseClass`: A pointer to the CRuntimeClass structure of the base class.

As you can see, the information stored in the `CRuntimeClass` object is varied and useful. The first attribute does in fact give us a character string that holds the current class name. From this, we may resolve ambiguities that some objects might have as a result of void pointer passing or polymorphism. The second attribute is the size of the object in bytes. This information can be very useful when determining memory consumption and/or allocation. The third and fourth `CRuntimeClass` attributes are used in serialization. We'll discuss them in the next section. The last attribute is a pointer to the `CRuntimeClass` object associated with the base class. The `CRuntimeClass` objects in a series of `CObject` derivations form a linked list from the newest class back to `CObject`. Traversing this chain allows you to examine the entire `CObject`-derived ancestry of a particular class. Because `CObject` is a common ancestor to most of the MFC library, all these `CRuntimeClass` linked lists are like lines converging on `CObject`. See Figure 6.3 for a small piece of this converging-line picture.

Figure 6.3.
CRuntimeClass linked lists converging on CObject.

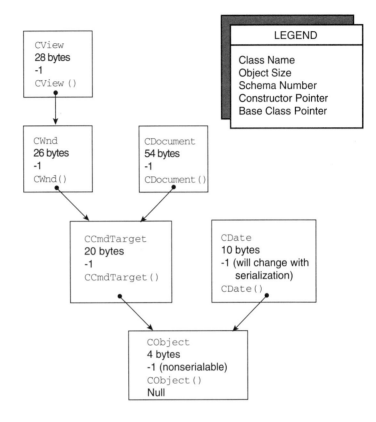

The CObject methods that afford access to this runtime information are KindOf() and GetRuntimeClass(). Both of these functions use the underlying CRuntimeClass structure to accomplish their tasks. The following code snippet demonstrates these functions:

```
CDate d1(1904, 2, 29);

// CDate objects are both CDate and CObject class types
ASSERT( d1.IsKindOf(RUNTIME_CLASS(CObject)) );
ASSERT( d1.IsKindOf(RUNTIME_CLASS(CDate)) );

#ifdef _DEBUG
d1.Dump(afxDump);
#endif

CRuntimeClass* pRTC = d1.GetRuntimeClass();   // For CDate
```

CObject: The Mother of All Classes

```
// Try other runtime CObject-derived classes, such as...
//CRuntimeClass* pRTC = GetRuntimeClass();      // For our view
//CRuntimeClass* pRTC = pDoc->GetRuntimeClass();  // For our document

// Display runtime information for the current class and all
// ancestor classes
while (pRTC)
{
    TRACE("Class Name: %Fs; ObjectSize: %d; Schema #: %d\n",
        pRTC->m_lpszClassName, pRTC->m_nObjectSize, pRTC->m_wSchema );

    pRTC = pRTC->m_pBaseClass;
}
```

Executing this code from within your view class will result in the following output:

```
a CDate at $3B2C Year: 1904 Month: 2 Day: 29
Class Name: CDate; ObjectSize: 10; Schema #: -1
Class Name: CObject; ObjectSize: 4; Schema #: -1
```

Note that the Dump() function displays the true class name now that we have enabled CDate's runtime support. Runtime checking is certainly not limited to our own classes. If we started pRTC at our document's runtime class object in the preceding code segment, we would get the following output:

```
a CDate at $3B2C Year: 1904 Month: 2 Day: 29
Class Name: CDatesDoc; ObjectSize: 54; Schema #: -1
Class Name: CDocument; ObjectSize: 54; Schema #: -1
Class Name: CCmdTarget; ObjectSize: 20; Schema #: -1
Class Name: CObject; ObjectSize: 4; Schema #: -1
```

Use this code snippet in your applications to investigate CObject-derived classes.

Dynamic Creation and Serialization

The next level of CObject functionality is support for dynamic creation. At this level, the framework can create objects dynamically. This ability is especially important during the view/document pair creation that occurs for each File | New command. The practicality of this ability will become obvious to you when we start working with the Multiple Document Interface (MDI), where multiple view/document pairs can be seen concurrently. If you take a look at the view classes in some of our past applications, you will see the dynamic creation macros in the interface and implementation. These macros provide the dynamic creation ability to the framework. Let's upgrade CDate to take advantage of the dynamic creation ability provided by CObject. Replace the DECLARE_DYNAMIC macro in CDate's interface with the DECLARE_DYNCREATE macro. Likewise, replace the IMPLEMENT_DYNAMIC macro in CDate's implementation with the IMPLEMENT_DYNCREATE macro. The macro parameters stay the same. With these macros in place, a new CObject-derived class needs only one more addition to be able to invoke the dynamic creation ability—a default constructor. Through incredible foresight, our CDate class already meets this requirement and therefore can be created dynamically.

The actual mechanism of dynamic creation resides in the CRuntimeClass structure. In addition to its attributes, CRuntimeClass has a single function: CreateObject(). This function is used to create instances of CObject-derived class objects during runtime. It uses the information contained in the CRuntimeClass object to allocate the appropriate structure, and it uses the fourth CRuntimeClass attribute, m_fnConstruct, to perform the default initialization. The following code snippet demonstrates the use of CreateObject():

```
CRuntimeClass* pRTC = RUNTIME_CLASS(CDate);
CObject* pOb = pRTC->CreateObject();

// pOb is a CObject pointer that points to a CDate object
```

The dynamic creation ability is also very important during serialization. When data is being loaded from disk during the serialization process, it must be placed in the appropriate empty objects. If these objects don't exist, the framework must create them by calling the CreateObject() function of the appropriate CRuntimeClass object. After being built by CreateObject(), the objects are filled with the previously saved data. Dynamic creation is a central issue in the serialization process.

When we build new classes, we rarely stop at dynamic creation. Typically, once we have come this far, it is to our benefit to go on and make the class serializable. Of course, this decision is based on the particulars of the class in question.

Serialization is accomplished through the interplay of the CObject::Serialize() function and an object of the class CArchive. In a typical serialization, the framework establishes a CArchive object and passes it to the document's Serialize() function, usually in response to a File | Save command. You must flesh out your document's Serialize() function in order to exploit this means of serialization. Don't be put off. Remember, CDocument is just another CObject-derived class. You implement its Serialize() function using the same techniques we use on our own classes.

Within any Serialize() function, class data is passed between the archive object and the class object. Storage or retrieval of class data is determined by the state of the archive object. The CArchive class has two functions that allow you to determine the state of the archive object: IsStoring() and IsLoading(). These functions are mutually exclusive, so you need to access only one of them to determine the state of the archive object. Either the archive is storing information to a file or it is loading information into the class object. There is no in-between.

In this book, our dealings with CArchive will be limited to that of users of an existing object. As such, the operators of most interest to us are the storage (<<) and retrieval (>>) operators. We shall use these operators in our override of CObject's Serialize() function to store and retrieve class data. Both of these operators are heavily overloaded to accommodate a number of different types. However, a few types are conspicuously missing. See Table 6.2.

CObject: The Mother of All Classes

Table 6.2. << and >> allowable types.

BYTE (also known as unsigned char)
WORD (also known as unsigned short)
LONG (also known as long)
DWORD (also known as unsigned long)
float
double
CString
CSize and SIZE
CPoint and POINT
CRect and RECT
CTime
CTimeSpan
CObject (in certain circumstances)

Many of these types will be unfamiliar to you. Don't be alarmed. A complete list is bound to have unfamiliar types. Other types, such as integer, are missing altogether from the list. integer seems to be a very fundamental type to leave out. Unfortunately, C++ defines the int type in system-dependent terms. Therefore, the size of int might change from system to system. Archiving needs stability in the objects it stores. The types listed in Table 6.2 fit the bill. However, you may still store and retrieve integer values using CArchive. The trick is to convert them to one of the CArchive-friendly types. You must be very careful not to lose data in this typecasting. If you typecast an integer value to a WORD value, you will lose some bits because integers tend to be much longer, bitwise, than WORD values. With care, you can successfully make your types fit into the archive paradigm.

A disclaimer flags the CObject entry in Table 6.2. If you have CObject-descended objects embedded in the class you're serializing, there are two routes you may take. The most obvious, in light of the current chapter, is calling the object's own Serialize() function. This will invoke the code specifically written to store or retrieve that class's data. However, an alternative approach is implied by CObject's presence in Table 6.2. Using the << and >> operators instead of calling the object's Serialize() function is based on the information you have about the object to be stored or retrieved. In most cases, the object is a member variable of your class and you know all there is to know about it. Here you use the Serialize() function. Sometimes, however, you know very little about the object. Your class might be using polymorphism to keep its options open about the exact nature of a member object. The member variable in question may be a CObject pointer. At compile time, you don't know exactly which descendent of CObject will be stored. In these cases, you must utilize the << and >> operators.

Let's make our date class serializable. This procedure is slightly more complex than the upgrade to dynamic creation. Two functions are required in a serializable class: a default constructor and an override of the `Serialize()` function. Dynamic creation already required a default constructor for `CDate`, so that requirement is met. Overriding the `Serialize()` function is where the rubber meets the road. It is in the `Serialize()` function that we will perform the actual saving and restoring of data. Place the following declaration in `CDate`'s interface:

```
virtual void Serialize( CArchive& ar);
```

and place the following code in `CDate`'s implementation:

```
void CDate::Serialize( CArchive& ar)
{
    // Serialize the base class first
    CObject::Serialize( ar );

    // Convert m_nYear to a CArchive-friendly type
    long y = (long)m_nYear;

    if ( ar.IsStoring() )
        ar << y << m_nMonth << m_nDay;
    else
    {
        ar >> y >> m_nMonth >> m_nDay;
        m_nYear = (int)y;
    }
}
```

From the `Serialize()` function, you can see the general form of the serialization process. Note the typecast of `m_nYear`. This must be done to make it `CArchive`-friendly (see the `CArchive` discussion earlier in this section). Once the data is prepared for archival, we use the `IsStoring()` function (or you could use the `IsLoading()` function with opposite logic) to determine the direction of data flow. Depending on data direction, the << or >> operators are used to store and retrieve the class data. It is crucial that the format for storage is exactly the same as that for retrieval. Mixing these up will literally mix up your data. This mix-up will be especially pronounced in classes whose data members come from differing data types. Be warned: Keep your data straight!

The final touch that makes `CDate` serializable is the replacement of the previous macros with the serialize macros, `DECLARE_SERIAL` and `IMPLEMENT_SERIAL`. This time, however, we will have a parameter change for the implementation macro. `IMPLEMENT_SERIAL` has an additional parameter whose value is the schema number:

```
// CDate implementation file
.
.
.
IMPLEMENT_SERIAL(CDate, CObject, 0)
.
.
.
```

CObject: The Mother of All Classes

In this case, the schema number is zero. This number is arbitrary, although –1 is reserved to indicate that no serialization is present. It's customary to start at 0 and increment for each new version of the class. I like to think of the schema number as the version number of your class. It's used during the load process to distinguish between objects of the same class but different versions. Consider the following scenario. You finish CDate, and it's so successful that everyone in your company decides to use it in their program (it's nice when that happens). Then you realize that CDate is just too big. You decide to change the data representation to a single integer value—perhaps the number of days since Jan 1, 1970. No problem. The users of CDate couldn't access the underlying representation anyway, so that won't affect their code. However, the serialization process is greatly affected. The difference between one value and three is distinctly different in the serialization business. Any CDate objects serialized with the old CDate representation couldn't be properly retrieved into the new CDate representation. It's the old round-peg-in-a-square-hole syndrome. If the attempt is made, erroneous data will result. This is where the schema numbers come in. The second representation of CDate will be assigned a new schema number—1, for example. When the framework encounters a different schema number during a load, it throws a CArchiveException. The framework knows better than to load the old data representation into an object with CDate's new representation—at least, it knows better when schema numbers are used properly.

One last thing must be said about the process I chose to make CDate serializable. It's not necessary to incrementally go from the bare diagnostic supporting CObject-derived class to runtime support to dynamic creation support to serialization. You can jump to the precise level of support that your class needs. Just remember that each level provides support for all the previous levels. Therefore, even though you're jumping to the serialization level, you still must provide a default constructor for the dynamic creation level of support. And you are advised, though not required, to override the diagnostic functions so that you may receive optimal debugger information.

Summary

In this chapter, we derived our own CDate class from the universal base class—CObject. This derivation took us through the concepts of diagnostic routines, runtime information support, dynamic creation of objects, and serialization. Each of these concepts has its own quirks and benefits. Only through use will you get a good understanding of what they can do. Before you're through with this book, you will get a number of other opportunities to see CObject derivations up close.

Producing your own classes using CObject is the most fundamental way to extend the capabilities of the MFC library. For this reason, deriving a CObject is a valuable skill to have in your repertoire. But there is another reason to study the CObject class. An understanding of CObject prepares you for a better understanding of the classes derived from CObject. Since most of the MFC library is derived from CObject, knowing CObject translates to a knowledge of the MFC! And, of course, that's why you're here.

Q&A

Q Why are the diagnostic functions declared as constant functions?

A By declaring `Dump()` and `AssertValid()` as constant functions, `CObject` ensures that class data won't be changed in these diagnostic functions. Diagnostics should be totally passive with respect to the data held in the classes. Passive observation of data is essential to maintain a minimal impact on the actual code and thereby preserve the integrity of the observation. The constant nature of the functions also forces the odd conversion of the `this` pointer that is present in both functions. This conversion is necessary to gain access to the class data via the nonconstant functions in order to perform the diagnostic duties.

Q The progression of the `CDate` files from level 1 of `CObject` functionality to level 4 is very interesting. However, why didn't you use the C++ mechanism of inheritance to add each new layer of `CObject` functionality to the base `CDate` class?

A Actually, this was a tricky decision to make. On one hand, I wanted to provide a simple class to demonstrate the ideas of `CObject` functionality. On the other hand, I wanted to construct a class that you could use beyond the scope of this book. I felt that using inheritance to incorporate increasing levels of `CObject` functionality would be an unnecessary complication of the `CDate` class. I used the class file renaming technique so that you could look back at the changes but still have a clean class to use in your own applications. Outside of demonstrating the levels of `CObject` functionality, the first three `CDate` classes we've constructed have limited use. Only the last class, `CDate` enabled with serialization, will be used. When you construct your own classes from `CObject`, you will select the level of support you want and implement it without going through all the levels we did.

Q I noticed that you didn't enclose any of the runtime support or serialization functions in debug-mode–checking preprocessor blocks. Don't all those types of functions need to be so enclosed?

A No. Only the diagnostic calls should be enclosed in debug-mode–checking preprocessor blocks. The diagnostic macros may be placed anywhere. `ASSERT` and `ASSERT_VALID` are automatically ignored in a release build of your application. You only have to worry about explicit references to `Dump()` and `AssertValid()`.

 *CObject:* **The Mother of All Classes**

Workshop

Quiz

1. What should you use the diagnostic functions for?
2. How does the addition of runtime class support change Dump()'s output?
3. Describe the purpose of the CRuntimeClass object.
4. How is the schema number used in serialization?

Exercises

1. Many of the CDate functions were left as an exercise. Here is the exercise in question: Implement the remainder of CDate.
2. Use AppWizard to create an application to test the operation of CDate.
3. Improve the DateString() function by calculating the weekday of the date and passing it to the strftime() function.
4. Serialize some CDate objects by including them in your document's Serialize() function. Change the schema number, recompile, and try to load the old objects. Observe the exception that halts your program. Alter the program to catch the exception and display a message when this condition is encountered.

Dialogs

WEEK 1

Day 7

Dialogs

According to Webster's Ninth New Collegiate Dictionary, a dialogue (or dialog) is "2 a : a conversation between two or more persons... b : an exchange of ideas and opinions." We carry on dialogues all the time. Practically every interaction we make with the world involves some sort of dialogue. We have dialogues with coworkers, with family members, and even with the machines that interrupt our smoothly flowing existence. Our machine dialogues might consist of exchanging information with such basic things as ATMs or microwave ovens. Of course, the machine dialogues that concern us here are the information exchanges that occur between ourselves and computers—specifically, computers that run the Windows operating system. Dialogs in Windows, like real-world dialogues, are communications. We use them to retrieve data, clarify points, update information, and so on. Dialogs have a million and one uses. However, in Windows there is a standard way to conduct dialogues—a specialized dialog window.

There are two types of dialogs: *modal* and *modeless*. Modal dialogs are like demanding children: They prevent you from doing anything else until you respond to their requests. Unlike children, however, they have the power to enforce their wishes. When a modal dialog is activated, you can't do anything else in your application. You can switch applications to get away from normal modal dialogs. But when you come back to the original application, the dialog will still be waiting for you. On the other hand, some modal dialogs are so demanding that escape to another application is impossible. These extra-needy dialogs are called *system modal dialogs*. You must respond to these dialogs before you do anything else in Windows. In either case, the term *modal* refers to this uncompromising demand for attention.

We have seen this modal effect before. Message boxes use the modal technique to force the user's attention on the information at hand. Is there a connection between message boxes and modal dialogs? Yes! Beneath the easy-to-use facade of the message box lurks a modal dialog. Although they have been packaged in a programmer-friendly wrapping and the user doesn't explicitly transfer any information to them, message boxes are still modal dialogs. However, in message boxes the dialogue is rather one-way—from the computer to the user. This attests to the flexibility of the dialog paradigm.

The flip side of this issue deals with modeless dialogs. These dialogs have the same functionality as modal dialogs. In fact, a dialog is designated modal or modeless within the invoking code. The distinction between the two types of dialogs is evident at runtime. Modeless dialogs, as opposed to modal dialogs, don't demand the user's attention. They are available at the user's convenience, but they don't balk if they are ignored. Modeless dialogs are contained within, but are practically independent of, the application. During its life, you have full access to the modeless dialog, but you don't need to close it to continue working with the parent application. From the descriptions of these two types of dialogs, it would seem that the modeless dialog would be the dialog of choice hands-down. Actually, the reverse is true. Modeless dialogs certainly have their place, but more often than not, a program requires certain data in order to proceed. The modal dialog is, therefore, the dialog of choice.

This chapter is limited to discussing modal dialogs. However, the topics discussed in this chapter are applicable to both types of dialogs. For further information about modeless dialogs, consult the Visual C++ User's Guides.

Dialog Pieces

A Windows dialog consists of three parts: the dialog window, the dialog resource, and the dialog code. The dialog window holds the graphical elements of the dialog (the dialog controls) during runtime. The dialog resource is the information held in the resource file that specifies which graphical elements are to be included and where they are to be placed within the dialog. This information is stored in the resource file in response to our creation of a dialog resource via AppStudio. Before resource editors were invented, Windows programmers had to design their dialogs (and other resources) by hand. They would work them out on paper and manually insert the information into the resource file. (Three cheers for these more civilized and enlightened times.) The dialog code—the brains behind the dialog—is where the dialog is given life. In terms of the MFC, the dialog code resides primarily in the CDialog class. Additional dialog code is found within the classes that underlie the dialog's graphical elements. These elements are control items that provide the user with a controlled means of entering and retrieving data. Table 7.1 lists predefined MFC dialog control classes.

Table 7.1. Dialog control classes.

Class	Description
CStatic	Static text, box, icon, or rectangle. No user interaction.
CEdit	An editable box that allows the user to add to or alter the text contents.
CButton	A general pushbutton interface that has multiple button styles.
CListBox	A selection box with multiple text selections.
CComboBox	An editable selection box that is a hybrid of edit and list box controls.
CScrollBar	A scroll bar control like those on the edges of windows.
CVBControl	A Visual Basic control soon to be obsolete due to OLE.

Each of these control classes is derived from the CWnd class. All the dialog controls are therefore windows in and of themselves with the rights and privileges thereto. You heard that right. Each control is yet another window. Isn't that incredible? Even a small application could have nearly a hundred windows doing their thing. That's why they call it Windows! This is an important point, so I will emphasize it. Because each dialog and each dialog control is derived from CWnd, they inherit all the functionality of "normal" windows. As a rule, you treat them as controls, but if that doesn't serve your purpose, you may treat them like windows. Don't forget this fact.

Dialogs

Somewhere down the line, a dialog or control will give you some difficulty. Understanding that they are also windows will give you an extra set of inherited functions to draw on.

A common structure runs throughout dialog controls. Each control is built around an object of type RECT, the rectangle structure. This rectangle provides the spatial dimensions of the control window (actually, the controls inherit this need from CWnd objects, which also require spatial dimensions via RECT). In addition to the window dimensions, every control needs a parent window, typically a dialog, to which will be sent control notification messages. These messages allow the controls to keep the parent window apprised of the current situation. Each control type also has a specific style that determines the look and feel of the interface. The specific style choices might differ from class to class, but the general style remains the same. Control types may be customized by their style attribute. Each control also has its own unique identification number. This number is chosen for us when we select an ID constant name in AppStudio. However, if you decide to create your own controls from scratch, it's up to you to make sure that these ID numbers are unique. Now that we have a glancing idea of what the control classes are like, let's explore some of the details involved with each class.

Static controls are just that—static. They are inaccessible to the user. No matter what you try to do to them, they just sit there. Static objects are window dressing (no pun intended). Their sole purpose is to make the associated dialog (or whatever happens to be the parent window) more understandable and attractive. The most frequently used static controls are the static text controls. These usually serve as labels for other, nearby controls. They appear as text written directly on the dialog. Of course, this isn't the case because the text is actually contained within the control's window. However, typical control windows for static text are invisible, so it appears that the text is resting directly on the underlying window. Perhaps less used, but by no means less useful, is the static icon box. A static control can be associated with an icon resource. In this case, the control becomes the container for the icon. The control automatically adjusts to the size of the icon. In AppStudio, you may select the icon to be associated with the static control. Once the icon is selected in this manner, the icon is loaded and displayed automatically. The static control may also be used as a destination of a bitmap. AppStudio's picture control is actually a static control rectangle. The picture control isn't automated. If you want to display a bitmap in a static control rectangle, you must do so manually.

The next control class on our list is CEdit. Edit controls are the common means to receive information from the user. They appear as boxes on-screen and, when selected, provide a vertical-line cursor to indicate where text may be inserted. The user employs the keyboard (or Clipboard) to fill edit boxes with the most valuable of commodities—information. Once data has been written to the edit control, it's available to the parent window. The parent window is alerted to this data entry by notification messages streaming from the control. A good number

of these messages go to the parent window from the edit control (as is the case with most controls). Table 7.2 lists the edit control notification messages.

Table 7.2. CEdit control notification messages.

Message	Description
EN_CHANGE	User changes have been updated to the display.
EN_ERRSPACE	Text entry has caused the edit control to run out of memory.
EN_HSCROLL	The user has clicked on the horizontal scroll bar.
EN_KILLFOCUS	The control has lost the input focus.
EN_MAXTEXT	Insertion of more text than that allotted has occurred.
EN_SETFOCUS	The control has gained the input focus.
EN_UPDATE	User changes are about to be updated to the display.
EN_VSCROLL	The user has clicked on the vertical scroll bar.

You may have your dialog class tap into these messages by instructing ClassWizard to add the appropriate message handler. We will use this technique later in this book.

The CButton class provides a simple way of adding a point-and-shoot flavor to your windows. The only information that the button sends to its parent window is a button-clicked message or a button-double–clicked message. The internal state of a button consists of a check state (for check and radio buttons only), a highlight state (an intermediate state that occurs while the button is pressed), and a focus state (indicating whether the button has the focus). These states are in addition to the states inherent in CWnd. The state of a button's label is actually a hangover state from CWnd. The button's label is really the window's title.

Buttons are a very simple form of user interface but also a very valuable one. They are an extremely common, even essential, part of every dialog. The standard interface that Windows presents requires that you design your dialogs with buttons so that your users may specify control choices. The default buttons that AppStudio puts in your dialogs are OK and Cancel. These two buttons are very important for the standard Windows dialog interface. It makes sense to give your users the ability to specify whether they wish to proceed with the current operation (OK) or change their mind and abort the current operation (Cancel). After all, it's their program too. They should have the ultimate say over how their data is handled.

The big, fat, friendly pushbuttons are just the tip of the iceberg when it comes to CButton possibilities. Table 7.3 shows the possible styles of CButton objects.

Dialogs

Table 7.3. `CButton` styles.

Style	Description
BS_AUTOCHECKBOX	An automatic version of CHECKBOX.
BS_AUTORADIOBUTTON	An automatic version of RADIOBUTTON.
BS_AUTO3STATE	An automatic version of 3STATE.
BS_CHECKBOX	A check box button with associated text to the right.
BS_DEFPUSHBUTTON	A highlighted pushbutton with a heavy outer line.
BS_GROUPBOX	A hollow button that encloses controls in a group.
BS_LEFTTEXT	Makes the text of a check box or radio button fall on the left side of the control.
BS_OWNERDRAW	Just like it says, you get to draw the button.
BS_PUSHBUTTON	A standard pushbutton that, when pushed, causes a WM_COMMAND message to be sent to the parent.
BS_RADIOBUTTON	As with a car radio, when one button goes in, the rest in the group go out. Associated text appears on the right.
BS_3STATE	A three-state button: checked, unchecked, or dimmed.

These button styles are pretty much automated in AppStudio when you select your button choice. However, it's a good idea to look over the list just to see your options. This is an especially good idea if you ever intend to implement your own buttons without AppStudio's assistance.

The list box control is a way to show the user the list of possible selections. The user may then choose one or more selections. This is ideal for a fixed and known number of possible choices. Asking the user to choose a month from the 12 possible would be a good use for the list box. After the user makes a selection or selections, the information is available to the parent window and thus to your application. As with the edit box control, the list box uses notification messages to keep the parent window up to date with the control's status. These messages may be captured and exploited by using ClassWizard to build the empty shells of the message-handling functions and filling them with application-specific code. Table 7.4 lists the notification messages.

Table 7.4. List box notification messages.

Message	Description
LBN_DBLCLK	The user double-clicked on a list box selection.
LBN_ERRSPACE	Cannot allocate enough memory for the command.
LBN_KILLFOCUS	The list box has lost the input focus.
LBN_SELCANCEL	The list box selection has been canceled.

Message	Description
LBN_SELCHANGE	The list box selection has changed.
LBN_SETFOCUS	The list box has gained the input focus.

Note: Only list boxes with the LBS_NOTIFY style set will send the LBN_DBLCLK, LBN_SELCANCEL, and LBN_SELCHANGE messages.

The list box has a number of styles from which to choose. List boxes may have multiple columns or multiple selections. They may be sorted or sport an owner-draw feature. The number of list box options can make your head spin. Luckily, AppStudio automates the style choices, so we needn't trouble ourselves with them here.

The combo box control is a combination of a list box control and an edit box (or static) control. Like the list box, a combo box may take on quite a few styles. However, you may break down the combo box class into three distinct classes: the simple combo, the drop-down combo, and the drop-down list.

The simple combo and drop-down combo boxes are the result of connecting a list box to an edit box. The connection is both proximal and logical. The edit box is immediately above the list box. A selection made in the list box is immediately reflected in the edit box. The only difference between these two types of combo boxes is the visibility of the list box. The drop-down combo box has its list box concealed until the user activates it. The list box in the simple combo box is always visible. Needless to say, this difference is hardly more than aesthetic.

These two types of combo boxes afford you the opportunity to select an item from the list or enter your own value. These types of controls are used when the selections aren't limited to a fixed number of entries yet there is still a common set of responses. Selecting a budget category in a personal finance program would be a good situation in which to use these types of combo box controls. You should provide many standard categories such as Electricity, Natural Gas, and Groceries. But every household is different, so you must provide the flexibility of allowing unique categories as well, such as Llama Food, Computer Games, or Clock Parts. These combo box types merge the convenience of the list box with the generality of the edit box.

The third type of combo box is the drop-down list box. This type of combo box is a combination of a list box and a static control. It's a dead ringer for the drop-down combo box, except that it doesn't allow the user to add a new selection. In other words, the box on top of the list box can't be edited—it is to display the user's selection only. Aside from the visual gymnastics, the drop-down list box does nothing that the normal list box doesn't do. Actually, the normal list box has more functionality, because drop-down list boxes don't support multiple selections.

Dialogs

Despite the minor differences between the combo box types, each has its own unique place among the dialog controls. Combo boxes also have more than their share of notification messages. They have so many messages, in fact, that I will neglect to list them here. Basically, their messages are an amalgam of edit box notifications and list box notifications, except with conditions based on the combo box style. As usual, AppWizard takes care of style management and ClassWizard takes care of message-handler management.

The scroll bar control is a portable version of the scroll bar found on the edges of scrollable windows. It typically is a long, narrow control that allows you to graphically specify a value in a range. The length of the control represents the range in question. The position along that range is specified by a moveable box called a *thumb*. Scroll bars are so common that it is rare indeed to find a Windows application that doesn't have them. However, stand-alone scroll bars are not so common. Admittedly, they have less applicability than do most of the other controls, but, for sake of completeness, they must be covered.

No doubt due to their limited application, stand-alone scroll bars aren't heavily supported in the wizards. The scroll bar controls aren't automatically wired in by AppStudio, as are most of the other controls. AppStudio allows you to place the control in a dialog, but even the simplest functionality must be programmed manually. Another piece of evidence that shows this lack of support is CScrollBar's notification message scheme. Regardless of how many scroll bar controls are contained within a dialog, only one vertical scroll bar event and one horizontal scroll bar event are sent to the dialog. This limitation is most likely due to the fact that a window usually has only one vertical and one horizontal scroll bar. Within the WM_VScroll or WM_HScroll event notification message is a scroll code. Table 7.5 shows the codes for a WM_VScroll message. Similar codes are used with a WM_HScroll message. Using these codes, you may animate the scroll bar. Such animation will be demonstrated shortly.

Table 7.5. Vertical scroll bar message codes.

Code	Description
SB_BOTTOM	The thumb has hit the bottom of the scroll bar.
SB_ENDSCROLL	A scroll sequence has ended.
SB_LINEDOWN	The down-arrow button was clicked.
SB_LINEUP	The up-arrow button was clicked.
SB_PAGEDOWN	The area below the thumb was clicked.
SB_PAGEUP	The area above the thumb was clicked.
SB_THUMBPOSITION	The thumb has been released from tracking.
SB_THUMBTRACK	The thumb itself is being moved (tracked).
SB_TOP	The thumb has reached the top of the scroll bar.

The final control type on the list is CVBControl. Even though Visual Basic controls were developed, surprisingly enough, for use with Visual Basic, with certain restrictions they can be used in Visual C++. These controls allow you to design and implement your own controls and incorporate them into the dialog editor as if they were standard controls. This is a wonderful concept, but unfortunately this technology is being swept away by the advent of the newer and more powerful technology of object linking and embedding (OLE). Due to their forthcoming obsolescence, we won't delve into the mysteries of Visual Basic controls. However, we will discuss OLE controls in Chapter 15.

Nurturing a Meaningful Dialog

This chapter's example is a Software Lister. The program is a simple one. Information concerning software products is retrieved from the user, held in memory, and, at the user's request, stored to disk. Naturally, we will use a dialog as the data-gathering mechanism. The dialog may also serve as a device for displaying data. This program also employs a CObject-derived class as the data's receptacle. These data objects are held in one of the standard collection objects designed for storage and serialization of CObject-derived classes. Disk storage of this information is accomplished through the framework's typical serialization route. For this particular design, the software information that will be stored is shown in Table 7.6.

Table 7.6. Software Lister data.

Data	Description
Title	The software's title.
Registration #	The software's registration number.
Publisher	The software's publisher.
Support Phone #	The technical support phone number.
Purchase Date	The date the software was purchased.
Purchase Price	The price paid for the software.
Joystick	The enumerated type holding the level of joystick support—Not Used, Supported, or Required.
Media	The media included with the software package—3 1/2-inch high-density disks, CD-ROM, and so on.
Minimum Resolution	The minimal resolution required for the software—CGA, EGA, VGA, and so on.
Rating	Your personal rating of the product.
Software Category	The category that the product falls under—Games, Business, and so on.
Windows Compatible	The Boolean flag indicating Windows compatibility.

Dialogs

Enter AppWizard and construct the Software Lister application with our usual set of options (Toolbar, Medium Memory Model, and Generate Source Comments). Using the software product data set as a guide, produce the dialog resource shown in Figure 7.1 via AppStudio.

Figure 7.1.
Software Lister's Add Software dialog.

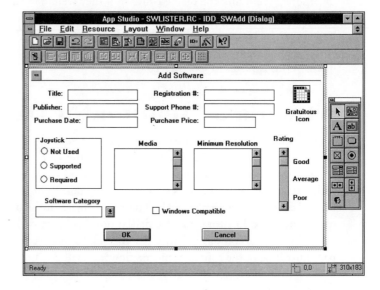

The important thing to remember while constructing the dialog is that every window associated with the dialog has a choice of properties and, sometimes, styles. Double-clicking on any control or on the dialog itself produces the appropriate properties dialog. If the control also has a choice of styles, you may change the aspect of the properties dialog to that of the styles dialog. This change is accomplished through the control on the upper-right of the properties dialog. It is through this little dialog that you may alter the properties and styles of a particular control or of the dialog under construction. See Figures 7.2 and 7.3 for the properties and styles dialogs for the dialog under construction.

Figure 7.2.
The properties dialog for the dialog.

Figure 7.3.
The styles dialog for the dialog.

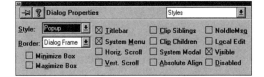

The actual building of the dialog is rather simple. You select a control type from the floating toolbar. You position the cursor over the spot on your dialog where you wish to drop the control. You click the mouse, and voilà, the selected control appears. At this point, you would adjust the size and position of the control to suit your needs. You would also double-click on the control in order to manipulate its properties, the most important of which is the control ID. The control ID is the name you call the control. This is your link to the control from the application code. Control IDs start with the prefix IDC_ and end with a descriptive name. If you don't provide a name, AppStudio will. Of course, the names AppStudio comes up with are not very inspired, nor are they particularly illuminating as to the purpose behind the control. Typical AppStudio-generated names are IDC_EDIT1, IDC_EDIT2, and IDC_RADIO1. You can discern the nature of the control, but the purpose behind the control is lost. Give your controls meaningful names so that later, during development, you won't have to guess which control is which. The properties and styles of each control are relatively self-explanatory given our earlier discussion of control types.

The most common control type in our dialog (and in most dialogs) is the static control, which is used for labeling. Being good programmers, we use labels very liberally. Figure 7.4 shows the properties dialog for a typical static text control. However, as I mentioned, static controls have other uses. As an example, I placed a static icon control in the upper-right of our dialog. Within the properties dialog of this control, shown in Figure 7.5, you can see how the icon resource and the icon control are linked. Note that this link is not truly evident until runtime. Also in the example, the icon identified by IDI_Abstract must be created prior to this linkage.

Figure 7.4.
The static text control properties dialog.

Figure 7.5.
The static icon control properties dialog.

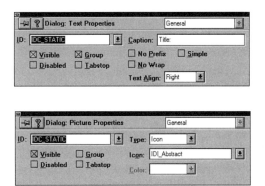

Day 7: Dialogs

The second most commonly used dialog control is the edit control. Half of the controls in our Software Lister dialog are edit box controls and associated static control descriptors. The reason for this is the highly textual nature of our data. You should use the edit box controls for nearly all string and numeric data entry. Edit boxes are ready-made for this type of use. Figures 7.6 and 7.7 show the properties and styles dialogs for a typical edit control.

Figure 7.6.
The edit control properties dialog.

Figure 7.7.
The edit control styles dialog.

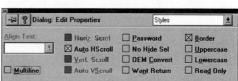

Although edit box controls are very popular, we often have occasion to use the more esoteric controls for special purposes. The Media, Minimum Resolution, and Software Category data are really sets of choices for the user. Hence, the best retrieval mechanism for that data is a list or combo box control. In the case of Media, a software product may include multiple sets of diskettes of various sizes. Although the media selections available are known beforehand, the Media control must allow the user to choose more than one selection. Therefore, a multiple-selection list box is used. Figures 7.8 and 7.9 show the properties and styles dialogs for the Media list box control.

Figure 7.8.
The Media list box control properties dialog.

Figure 7.9.
The Media list box control styles dialog.

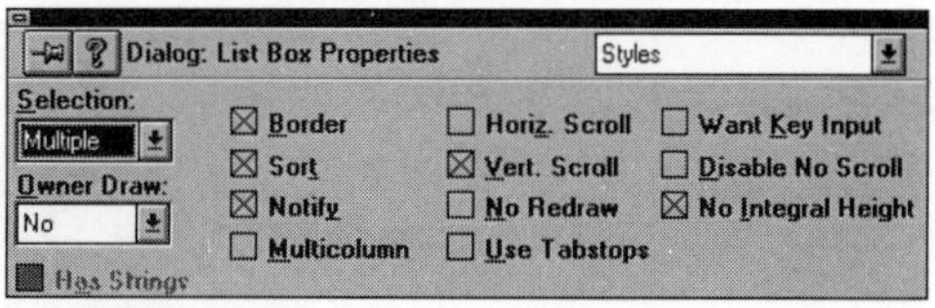

For the Minimum Resolution data, we're concerned with the minimal resolution that the software product supports. Because of the nature of the data, there can be only one minimum. Because we know the possible resolutions ahead of time, a single-selection list box will do the job nicely. The Minimum Resolution list box properties dialog is nearly identical to that for the Media list box. But the styles dialog is distinct and therefore is shown in Figure 7.10.

Figure 7.10.
The resolution list box control styles dialog.

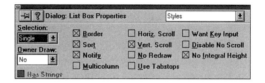

The Software Category data set is a little more flexible than the previous two we discussed. We will choose a set of software categories from which the user may select, but due to the general nature of the data, we can't include every possibility. Therefore, a combo box control is the most appropriate. I'll make it a drop-down combo box so as to meet the increasing space restrictions in our dialog. Drop-down combo boxes are also more fun. Figures 7.11 and 7.12 show the properties and styles dialogs for the Software Category drop-down combo box.

Figure 7.11.
The combo box control properties dialog.

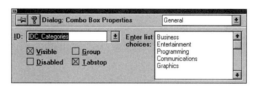

Figure 7.12.
The combo box control styles dialog.

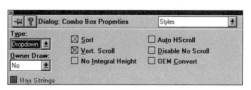

Joystick support is a mutually exclusive choice between three possible values: Required, Supported, and Not Used. There is no reason, other than aesthetics, why joystick support couldn't be chosen from a single-selection list box. For our dialog, we will use three radio buttons. Typically, buttons are chosen over other types of selection mechanisms for their direct nature. When a specific button is pressed, a message is immediately sent to the parent window. The parent window knows immediately which button was pressed. Of course, the other controls send messages too, but for those messages, more processing is required to discern the specific cause. Button messages are direct—*ButtonX* was pressed. Three radio buttons are used to represent the possible joystick choices. They are surrounded by a group box that ensures that

Dialogs

they are treated as a group—both visually and logically. See Figure 7.13 for an example of a properties dialog for a radio button control.

Figure 7.13.
The radio button control properties dialog.

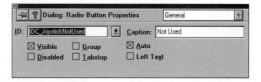

The Rating control allows you to graphically rate the software from poor to good. This graphical rating mechanism is nicely provided by a vertical, stand-alone scroll bar. Note that all the scroll bar labels are external static controls; none are intrinsic to the scroll bar. As a matter of fact, as we discussed earlier, not much is intrinsic to a scroll bar, either visually or functionally. Figure 7.14 shows the properties dialog of the scroll bar control.

Figure 7.14.
The scroll bar control properties dialog.

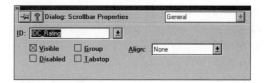

Finally, we come to the last data item on the list. The Windows Compatible data item is a Boolean flag that indicates whether the software product is compatible with Windows. Why anyone would buy a piece of software not compatible with Windows is beyond me, but then, I am a bit biased. Check box controls are ideal for representing Boolean values, so that's what we'll use. Figure 7.15 shows the properties dialog for a check box control.

Figure 7.15.
The check box control properties dialog.

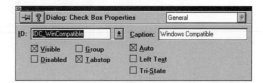

For easy reference, Table 7.7 lists the controls and their associated IDs.

Table 7.7. Software Lister's dialog control IDs.

Data	Control Type	Control ID
Title	Edit control	IDC_Title
Registration #	Edit control	IDC_Registration

Data	Control Type	Control ID
Publisher	Edit control	`IDC_Publisher`
Support Phone #	Edit control	`IDC_Phone`
Purchase Date	Edit control	`IDC_PurchaseDate`
Purchase Price	Edit control	`IDC_PurchasePrice`
Joystick Not Used	Radio button	`IDC_JoystickNotUsed`
Joystick Supported	Radio button	`IDC_JoystickSupported`
Joystick Required	Radio button	`IDC_JoystickRequired`
Media	Multiple-selection list box	`IDC_Media`
Minimum Resolution	Single-selection list box	`IDC_Resolution`
Rating	Scroll bar	`IDC_Rating`
Software Category	Drop-down combo box	`IDC_Categories`
Gratuitous Icon	Static	`IDI_Abstract`
Windows Compatible	Check box	`IDC_WinCompatible`

Note: In your first attempt at dialog building, you might find that your controls are askew and not uniform. This is nothing to worry about. They will still work fine. Getting a knack for control placement and sizing can be a lifelong pursuit. It still takes me much longer than I think it should to get just the right look for a dialog. However, the dialog editor does provide tools to help you clean up your act. At the top of the dialog edit window is a toolbar chock full of control alignment aids, including my personal favorite—the grid control. Using these aids will allow you to rapidly polish your dialog's look. Consult your user manuals for the particulars.

As soon as all the dialog components are in their proper places, it's a good idea to make sure that the tab order is correct. The tab order is the sequential order in which the dialog controls gain the input focus. Select Layout | Set Tab Order in AppStudio or press Ctrl-D. This command displays the tab order on the dialog (see Figure 7.16) and allows you to resequence it through a series of mouse clicks.

Day 7 Dialogs

Figure 7.16.
Dialog tab order.

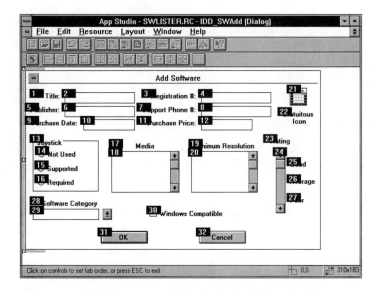

The dialog resource is now ready to be tied to code. To accomplish this, you must invoke ClassWizard to create the `CDialog`-derived class associated with this new resource. ClassWizard automatically prompts you to supply the appropriate dialog class names so that it can create the class. I chose the dialog class name of `CSWAddDlg`. See Figure 7.17.

Figure 7.17.
ClassWizard's Add Class dialog.

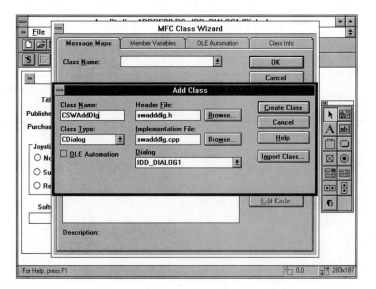

After the new dialog class is created, you may manipulate the class in ClassWizard as you would any other class. In this case, we will make dialog class member variables to help us manage the dialog controls. ClassWizard provides two general types of member variables: value variables and control variables. Value variables are very handy for controls that are fully automated, such as edit and check box controls. ClassWizard connects the value variable with the dialog control via a data exchange and validation scheme. All the little details of data transfer and control execution are provided for. The value variable route is the best route when you don't need direct control of the control. However, sometimes the controls we use aren't as automated as we might like. Scroll bars, being an extreme, can't even adjust the position of their thumb without help. Control variables provide access to the control itself. They allow us to directly affect the control. This ability is crucial for controls that require hands-on manipulation, such as list boxes.

Having ClassWizard install these member variables is a relatively smooth operation. After clicking on the Member Variables file tab at the top of the ClassWizard dialog, you merely highlight the desired control ID and click on the Add Variable button. This causes the Add Member Variable dialog to appear. In this dialog you may specify the variable name, the variable property (value or control), and the variable type. For our purposes, select the Value property for the check box control and each edit box control. The rest of the controls will need direct manipulation, so we will use control variables for them. The value controls have a choice of types, ranging from CString to integer to floating-point types. Use CString for all the value variables except Purchase Price and Windows Compatible; use float and BOOL for those variables, respectively. The control variables don't have the range of types that value variables do. They are set to the type of the underlying control, such as CEdit.

Figures 7.18 and 7.19 show examples of the Add Member Variable dialog in action with both value variables and control variables. Figure 7.20 shows the resulting ClassWizard Member Variable Dialog screen after all the variables have been entered.

Note that radio button control IDs aren't listed in ClassWizard. This is because radio button controls are treated differently than the other controls. Because they act as members of a group, they must be controlled in a group manner. CWnd-derived classes have special functions for dealing with child radio button groups. We'll see some of these functions in the dialog class implementation later in this chapter. At that time we will also see some methods of tying the more esoteric classes to our code.

That's all there is to building a dialog—at least a simple one. Of course, there is still the issue of dialog control manipulation, but for now our first priority is to learn how to call up a dialog from our code. This will allow us to see some return on this lengthy dialog-building investment.

Dialogs

Figure 7.18.
ClassWizard's Add Member Value Variable dialog.

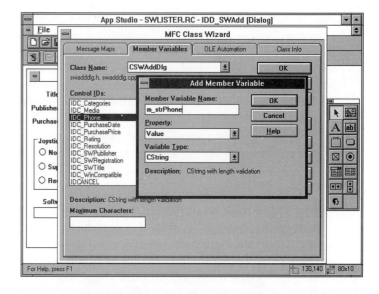

Figure 7.19.
ClassWizard's Add Member Control Variable dialog.

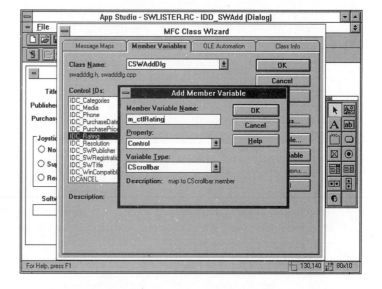

Figure 7.20.
Software Lister's dialog member variables.

DoModal(): Our Portal to Conversation

After producing a fine dialog like the one in the preceding section, it's important to know how to use it. The typical procedure we will use to bring up a dialog is through a variation of the following code snippet:

```
CSWAddDlg Dlg;

if (Dlg.DoModal() == IDOK)
{
    // Data has been transferred to the dialog class members
    // so that you may access the new data at this time!
    AfxMessageBox("Dialog OK button pressed! Title = "
                + Dlg.m_strTitle);
}
else
{
    AfxMessageBox("Dialog was cancelled. No data transferred.");
    // Place code that deals with dialog cancelation here
}
```

Day 7: Dialogs

Go ahead and place this snippet of code somewhere in your application. A good spot for it would be in a new menu item handler built for this purpose. If you do this, make sure that you #include the SWADDDLG.H file in the proper place so that the dialog class will be visible. I will demonstrate this dialog formally after it's complete at the end of this chapter.

Examining the preceding code snippet, we find that the first line constructs a dialog object using the default CSWAddDlg constructor. Within the if statement, the dialog is invoked. All user interaction with the dialog occurs during the execution of this first line of the if statement. Only after the user closes the dialog may normal processing proceed. This is the crux of the dialog's modal nature. The user must respond to the dialog before the proper conditional branch may be determined. Because of their nature, modeless dialogs have a completely different construction and calling process.

The CDialog class has three constructors. Being constructors of the same class, they differ only in their parameter lists:

```
CDialog();
CDialog(LPCSTR lpszTemplateName, CWnd* pParentWnd = NULL);
CDialog(UINT nIDTemplate, CWnd* pParentWnd = NULL);
```

The last two constructors create and initialize modal dialogs with the specified resource. The dialog resource is identified either by an ID number or by a character string name. In either case, a modal dialog is created and initialized from the resource template found in the application's executable file. This technique is called *resource-based dialog box construction*. It is the popular, direct approach to constructing dialogs. We will use resource-based construction exclusively in this book.

The first constructor in the list is CDialog's default (parameterless) constructor. This constructor is used in making modeless dialogs or in making indirect (nonresource-based) modal dialogs. Modeless dialogs will have to wait until a later chapter. However, I will mention a few things about nonresource-based modal dialogs. Indirect modal dialogs are created with CDialog's default constructor. They are then explicitly initialized from a memory-based dialog template. Finally, they are executed normally, through the DoModal() function. Indirect dialogs present a number of complications, not the least of which is the construction of the memory-based dialog template. These complications push indirect modal dialogs outside the scope of our introductory text. Hence, you will not see them in this book.

Wait a minute! In the preceding code snippet, we used the default constructor to make a modal dialog box. Isn't that a use of the indirect modal dialog?

It's true that we used a default constructor in the declaration of the dialog object in the code snippet. However, we didn't use CDialog's default constructor. ClassWizard-created dialog classes such as CSWAddDlg override CDialog's default constructor and its DoDataExchange()

function. These overridden functions provide a smooth connection to the dialog resource constructed in AppStudio. CSWAddDlg's default constructor doesn't call CDialog's default constructor; it calls one of the resource-based constructors with the underlying dialog resource ID. This establishes a connection between the resource and the code. DoDataExchange() also makes connections to the resource. When you instruct ClassWizard to create member variables for your dialog class, it also takes the liberty of connecting them to this data transfer mechanism. At the same time, ClassWizard puts initialization code for the member variables in the default constructor. These extra efforts on the part of ClassWizard make the modal dialog class/resource interface practically seamless. Manipulating a modal dialog has never been so easy. But it gets even easier with a little help from some friendly dialog functions. Table 7.8 lists the modal-specific dialog functions.

Table 7.8. CDialog's modal-specific functions.

Function	Description
DoModal	Executes a modal dialog and returns a result ID.
EndDialog	Terminates a modal dialog.
InitModalIndirect	Initializes a dialog object from a memory template.

Modal dialogs are terminated by a call to the EndDialog() function. However, this termination is not destruction. EndDialog() merely terminates the current modal session and makes the dialog invisible. The dialog and its member variables are still viable. Any data stored in the dialog can still be retrieved after EndDialog() is called. When you call EndDialog(), an integer result must be passed as the sole parameter. The value of the result parameter will be the value returned by the DoModal() function. The OK and Cancel buttons cause EndDialog() to be called with the value of IDOK or IDCANCEL, respectively. You may call EndDialog() in your own dialog functions if the need arises. But remember that what you pass to EndDialog() is passed back to the dialog's caller via DoModal().

The InitModalIndirect() function provides you with an alternative to the popular means of resource-based modal dialog initialization. Use InitModalIndirect() after you have constructed a dialog object with the default CDialog constructor. This function requires a handle to the memory-based dialog template that you have constructed especially for this purpose. Once initialized, the dialog may be executed normally with the DoModal() function.

Many of CDialog's functions work equally well with modal or modeless dialogs. Table 7.9 lists some of the functions available for use with both types of dialogs.

Dialogs

Table 7.9. Some of `CDialog`'s mode-independent functions.

Function	Description
NextDlgCtrl	Moves the input focus to the next control in the tab order.
PrevDlgCtrl	Moves the focus to the previous control in the tab order.
GotoDlgCtrl	Moves the input focus to a specified dialog control.
SetDefID	Sets the default pushbutton to that specified.
GetDefID	Returns the default pushbutton's control ID.
SetHelpID	Establishes the context-sensitive help ID to that specified.

The first three functions allow you to maneuver the input focus to the control of your choice. The last three functions help you to customize the dialog to your tastes. These functions will be explored in future chapters.

For a full understanding of dialog etiquette, we must discuss three very important `CDialog` functions. They are used with both modal and modeless dialogs. Table 7.10 lists the three overridable public member functions of `CDialog`.

Table 7.10. `CDialog`'s important overridable member functions.

Function	Description
OnOK	Called when the user clicks on the OK button.
OnCancel	Called when the user clicks on the Cancel button.
OnInitDialog	Called just before the dialog is displayed.

The `OnOK()` function is called when the user clicks on the dialog's OK button. `CDialog`'s default `OnOK()` function performs two services for you. It calls the `CWnd` function `UpdateData()`, and it terminates the dialog with a call to the `EndDialog()` function passing the `IDOK` value. The `UpdateData()` function transfers data between the dialog controls and the dialog class member functions. `UpdateData()` accomplishes this through a call to the `CWnd::DoDataExchange()` function. `DoDataExchange()` is a virtual function, overridden in your dialog class, that performs data exchange and validation on dialog member variables. Dialog data exchange (DDX) and dialog data validation (DDV) are extremely useful features in your dialogs, especially as they are automated via the `OnOK()` and `InitDialog()` functions. We will discuss DDX and DDV in greater detail in Chapter 10.

Note: Don't confuse dynamic data exchange (DDE), used for interprocess communication, with dialog data exchange (DDX), used for data transfer between a dialog and its controls. They are completely different!

The `OnCancel()` function is called when the user clicks on the dialog's Cancel button. `CDialog`'s default `OnCancel()` function performs only one duty. It terminates the dialog with a call to the `EndDialog()` function passing the `IDCANCEL` value. No exchange of data takes place—you canceled the operation, after all.

Finally, the `OnInitDialog()` function is called every time the `DoModal()` function is called but just before the dialog is displayed. `CDialog`'s default implementation of `InitDialog()` calls `CWnd`'s `UpdateData()` function to transfer data from the member variables to the dialog's controls—the opposite of what it does in `OnOK()`. Just as `OnOK()` updates the member variables with potentially changed dialog data, `OnInitDialog` uses the same mechanism to initialize the dialog controls with data initially present in the member variables. In this sense, `OnOK()` and `OnInitDialog()` are complementary functions.

The `CWnd::UpdateData()` function is not called by just framework functions. You may use this function in your own code whenever you feel it's necessary. `UpdateData()` takes a single Boolean parameter that indicates the direction of data transfer. If the parameter is `TRUE` (which is the default), data will be transferred from the controls to the member variables. If the parameter is `FALSE`, the dialog will be initialized—data will be transferred from the member variables to the dialog controls. We will see this function used quite often in the chapters to come.

Collecting Data

Before we can proceed with our application and implement dialog information transfer, we must have a place to put the data retrieved. It's true that the dialog itself has member variables that hold on to the data. But this is temporary storage. It only serves as a waystation for the data—a waiting room for data shuttling between the dialog controls and our application. We must provide a permanent storage facility for multiple entries of the data coming in via the dialog. Fortunately for us, the MFC comes prepared to help us in this endeavor.

The MFC provides us with a set of collection classes that allow us to store certain objects in a painless way. These collection classes not only store objects in memory, but, for some types of objects, they also provide serialization support. They also vary in size to accommodate as many objects as memory constraints will allow. The collection classes may be divided into three major

Dialogs

groups: the list classes, the array classes, and the map classes. Because each group represents the same structure applied to different types, the member functions of the classes within each group are nearly identical. Once you learn how to use one collection class, you will understand the other classes in the same group. Serious students of computer science might note that these classes correspond to some of the most fundamental and classic data structures around. From these classes, you may build almost any data structure that suits your fancy.

The list collection classes support the storage of CObject pointers, CStrings, and void pointers. Serialization is supported for CObject-derived classes and CStrings. These lists are doubly-linked and manipulated using a head/tail paradigm. Each list has a head (the first element) and a tail (the remaining elements). The head is an element of the list, whereas the tail is a linked list in its own right. Using this idea and the proper functions, you may navigate through and manipulate the list at will. The list classes also provide an iterator mechanism through which you may navigate the list. Table 7.11 describes the list classes in the MFC library.

Table 7.11. MFC list collection classes.

Class	Description
CObList	The list that holds CObject-derived class object pointers.
CStringList	The list that holds CString objects.
CPtrList	The list that holds void pointers. No serialization support.

Anyone familiar with C-style arrays can understand the array collection class immediately. The array collection behaves like a standard array. You may access elements via the standard [ ] operator. It does everything a normal array does, with the added benefit of dynamic length. What CString is to the normal character string, the array collection class is to the normal array. No more fussing with exact lengths of arrays. The array collection does it all internally. It even provides serialization support for most of the array collection types. Table 7.12 lists the array collection classes.

Table 7.12. MFC array collection classes.

Class	Description
CObArray	The array that holds CObject-derived class object pointers.
CStringArray	The array that holds CString objects.
CPtrArray	The array that holds void pointers. No serialization support.
CByteArray	The array that holds BYTE values.
CWordArray	The array that holds WORD values.
CDWordArray	The array that holds DWORD (double word) values.

This last collection class group is no doubt the least familiar of the three. Data maps aren't the same as those flat, folded things that get stuffed in the back of a car's glove compartment. No, the maps I'm talking about are good bit trickier. Maps store logical connections between two objects of potentially different types. The first object in the connection is a simple type that serves as a key (or search field) for the map. Each key is unique because the map doesn't allow duplicate key entries. The second object in the connection is the value object. Value objects hold the actual data. This combination of the small, unique key object and the value object allows for very fast storage and retrieval of data. This speed is partly due to the fact that the map isn't an ordered structure. Very little time is wasted storing the key/value pair in the map. Retrieval is also very efficient because map searching is performed by a hashing algorithm using the key. The down side to this speedy storage/retrieval system is that the map isn't ordered. The questions that should leap to your lips are "How can we go through the map if there is no order?" and "If we don't know a particular key, does that mean the associated value is inaccessible?" The answer lies in a technique we implemented in Chapter 2—the iterator. Maps, like lists, have iterators that allow you to move through the structure item-by-item. At each item, during the iteration, you may perform whatever tasks you need to on the item. The iterator is a very helpful tool, even for structures with order. Table 7.13 shows the various map collection classes available.

Table 7.13. MFC map collection classes.

Class	Description
CMapPtrToPtr	The map that stores void pointer keys to void pointer values.
CMapPtrToWord	The map that stores void pointer keys to WORD values.
CMapStringToOb	The map that stores CString keys to CObject-derived values.
CMapStringToPtr	The map that stores CString keys to void pointer values.
CMapStringToString	The map that stores CString keys to CString values.
CMapWordToOb	The map that stores WORD keys to CObject-derived values.
CMapWordToPtr	The map that stores WORD keys to void pointer values.

Note: CMapPtrToPtr, CMapPtrToWord, CMapStringToPtr, and CMapWordToPtr don't support serialization.

Dialogs

We'll use a CObList collection object to store the information we gather from the user via our dialog. The natural place for this object is in the document class. Place the following declaration in the public attribute section of the CSWListerDoc class interface:

```
CObList m_TheList;
```

Of course, there's more to incorporating the list object into the document class than a simple declaration. There are destruction and serialization issues to worry about (fortunately, initialization is done automatically). Taking care of serializing this new object seems reasonable enough, but destruction? Wouldn't destruction be as automated as the list's construction process? No. As we shall see, when we place new objects in the list, we first create them with the new operator. It's therefore clear that an explicit delete is required within the destructor. The CSWListerDoc destructor and the Serialize() function follow:

```
CSWListerDoc::~CSWListerDoc()
{
    CObject* pOb;

    POSITION Pos = m_TheList.GetHeadPosition();

    while (Pos != NULL)
    {
        pOb = m_TheList.GetNext(Pos);
        delete pOb;
    }

    m_TheList.RemoveAll();
}

void CSWListerDoc::Serialize(CArchive& ar)
{
    m_TheList.Serialize(ar);
}
```

Note the use of the iterator in the destructor. Iterators prove very useful in the collection classes. Also note the unusually brief form the serialization function takes on. Because the only data item serialized is a CObject-derived class itself, the conditional if (IsStoring(ar)) statement isn't needed and therefore was removed from the default Serialize() function.

In order to use this collection object, we must create a CObject-derived class to hold the data. Before you get too anxious about this proposition, let me tell you that it won't be as involved as the CDate class. We're only going to construct a vessel for our data, not a full-blown class that must be complete because of potential widespread use. This new object will need only implementations for the default constructor, the destructor, and the Dump() and Serialize() functions. It will be quick and easy.

Looking at the Software Lister data, we find that nearly all the data in its rawest form takes on simple types, usually CString. However, one data item does present a problem: Media. The Media data item may take on an undetermined number of multiple string values. (There's always one in the crowd who tries to spoil your fun.) The term "undetermined number" should strike a chord with you, especially after our discussion of the collection classes whose individual sizes vary. Yup, you guessed it. We will use another list collection, a CStringList, within our CObject-derived class to hold the Media data. See the next two listings for the class interface and implementation, respectively. Don't forget to add this new class to your make file via the Project | Edit menu command. If the project doesn't know about this neat new class, it won't be able to compile it.

```
// Filename: SWProdct.h
//
// Class definition for CSWProduct

#ifndef __SWPRODUCT_H__
#define __SWPRODUCT_H__

// Enumerated type for Joystick support
typedef enum{JNot_Used, JSupported, JRequired} JS_Support;

// m_wRating constants
#define RATING_MIN 0    // Good rating
#define RATING_MAX 10   // Poor rating

class CSWProduct : public CObject
{
public:
    DECLARE_SERIAL(CSWProduct)

    // Default constructor
    CSWProduct();

    // Destructor
    ~CSWProduct();

    // Attributes
    CString m_strTitle;
    CString m_strPublisher;
    CString m_strRegistration;
    CString m_strPhone;
    CString m_strPurchaseDate;
    float m_fPurchasePrice;
    CString m_strResolution;
    CString m_strCategory;
    WORD m_wRating;
    JS_Support m_nJoystick;
    BOOL m_bWinCompatible;
    CStringList m_lstMedia;

    // Serialization
    virtual void Serialize( CArchive& ar );

#ifdef _DEBUG
    // Diagnostics
    virtual void Dump(CDumpContext& dc) const;
#endif
```

Day 7: Dialogs

```cpp
};

#endif

// Filename: SWProdct.cpp
//
// Class implementation of CSWProduct

#include "stdafx.h"
#include "SWProdct.h"

IMPLEMENT_SERIAL(CSWProduct, CObject, 0)

// Default constructor
CSWProduct::CSWProduct()
{
    CObject::CObject();

    m_fPurchasePrice = 0.0;
    m_wRating = 5;
    m_nJoystick = JNot_Used;
    m_bWinCompatible = TRUE;
}

// Destructor
CSWProduct::~CSWProduct()
{
    // Empty strings
    m_strTitle.Empty();
    m_strPublisher.Empty();
    m_strRegistration.Empty();
    m_strPhone.Empty();
    m_strPurchaseDate.Empty();
    m_strResolution.Empty();
    m_strCategory.Empty();

    // Empty string list
    m_lstMedia.RemoveAll();
}

// Serialization
void CSWProduct::Serialize( CArchive& ar )
{
    CObject::Serialize(ar);
    m_lstMedia.Serialize(ar);

    WORD wCompatible = m_bWinCompatible;
    WORD wJS = m_nJoystick;

    if (ar.IsStoring())
    {
```

```cpp
            ar << m_strTitle << m_strPublisher
                << m_strRegistration << m_strPhone
                << m_strPurchaseDate << m_fPurchasePrice
                << m_strResolution << m_strCategory
                << m_wRating << wJS << wCompatible;
        }
        else
        {
            ar >> m_strTitle >> m_strPublisher
                >> m_strRegistration >> m_strPhone
                >> m_strPurchaseDate >> m_fPurchasePrice
                >> m_strResolution >> m_strCategory
                >> m_wRating >> wJS >> wCompatible;
            m_bWinCompatible = wCompatible;
            m_nJoystick = (JS_Support)wJS;
        }

}

#ifdef _DEBUG
// Diagnostics

void CSWProduct::Dump(CDumpContext& dc) const
{
    dc.SetDepth(1);
    // Allows collections to dump the individual collection elements

    dc << "Title: " << m_strTitle
        << " Publisher: " << m_strPublisher
        << "\nReg #: " << m_strRegistration
        << " Phone: " << m_strPhone
        << "\nPurchase Date: " << m_strPurchaseDate
        << " Purchase Price: " << m_fPurchasePrice
        << " Resolution: " << m_strResolution
        << "\nCategory: " << m_strCategory
        << " Rating: " << m_wRating
        << "\nJoystick Support: ";

    switch (m_nJoystick)
    {
        case JRequired:
        dc << "*Required*";
        break;

        case JSupported:
        dc << "*Supported*";
        break;

        case JNot_Used:
        dc << "*Not Used*";
        break;
    }
```

Day 7

Dialogs

```
        dc << " Win Compatible: ";

        if (m_bWinCompatible)
            dc << "*TRUE*";
        else
            dc << "*FALSE*";

        dc << "Media selections:\n";
        m_lstMedia.Dump(dc);

        dc << "\n\n";
}

#endif
```

From our work in Chapter 6, these listings shouldn't be too hard to understand. However, a point concerning the `m_lstMedia` variable should be made. In the `Serialize()` and `Dump()` functions, the `<<` and `>>` operators are not, and should not be, used with the list object. Direct calls to the `CStringList::Serialize()` and `CStringList::Dump()` functions are made to perform the appropriate operation. The `m_lstMedia` object is finally emptied in the class destructor to ensure memory reclamation.

Getting Information

Now that we have destinations for the dialog data, we may work on the transferal process. For small dialogs with a few simple data controls, we could get away with transferring the data from the dialog within the `DoModal()` conditional statement:

```
CSWAddDlg Dlg;
CString S;

if (Dlg.DoModal() == IDOK)
{
    // Transfer small amounts of simple data, such as...
    S = Dlg.m_strTitle;
}
```

However, with most dialogs this transfer process becomes very complicated. Even if a dialog has only simple controls, the sheer mass of data transfers alone is enough to complicate matters. Dialogs with complex controls, such as multiple-selection list boxes, would be incredibly inconvenient to use if data transfer were the responsibility of the calling code. The transfer mechanism must therefore reside within the dialog class code. For our application, we want the dialog to transfer its information to a `CSWProduct` object. To do this, the dialog class code must have access to a `CSWProduct` object. Add the following line to the `CSWAddDlg` class interface immediately below the `AFX_DATA` list:

```
CSWProduct* m_pSW;
```

This gives the dialog class a destination for its data. There is a danger here, however. This pointer object must point to something. Therefore, the code that invokes the dialog must first initialize the pointer object to an existing CSWProduct object. If that is done, the dialog class code can perform all the transfer duties. These transfer duties are broken into two parts: data initialization and retrieval. Data initialization is done in the OnInitDialog() function, and data retrieval is done in the OnOK() function. Use ClassWizard to set up these functions in the CSWAddDlg class. The next listing shows the implementations of OnInitDialog() and OnOK().

```
BOOL CSWAddDlg::OnInitDialog()
{
    if (m_pSW == NULL)
    {
        TRACE0("Dialog's CSWProduct pointer is NULL!\n");
        EndDialog(IDCANCEL);
        return TRUE;
    }

    // Initialize strings
    m_strTitle = m_pSW->m_strTitle;
    m_strPublisher = m_pSW->m_strPublisher;
    m_strRegistration = m_pSW->m_strRegistration;
    m_strPurchaseDate = m_pSW->m_strPurchaseDate;
    m_strPhone = m_pSW->m_strPhone;

    // Initialize numbers
    m_fPurchasePrice = m_pSW->m_fPurchasePrice;
    m_bWinCompatible = m_pSW->m_bWinCompatible;

    CDialog::OnInitDialog();

    // Multiple-selection list box initialization
    m_ctlMedia.AddString("3.5 inch HD disks");
    m_ctlMedia.AddString("3.5 inch DD disks");
    m_ctlMedia.AddString("5.25 inch HD disks");
    m_ctlMedia.AddString("5.25 inch DD disks");
    m_ctlMedia.AddString("CD ROM");

    POSITION Pos = m_pSW->m_lstMedia.GetHeadPosition();
    int nSelection;
    CString S;
    while (Pos != NULL)
    {
        S = m_pSW->m_lstMedia.GetNext(Pos);
        nSelection = m_ctlMedia.FindString(-1, S);
        if (nSelection != LB_ERR)
            m_ctlMedia.SetSel(nSelection);
    }

    // Single-selection list box initialization
    m_ctlResolution.AddString("CGA");
    m_ctlResolution.AddString("EGA");
    m_ctlResolution.AddString("VGA");
    m_ctlResolution.AddString("Super VGA");
    m_ctlResolution.SelectString(-1, m_pSW->m_strResolution);
```

Day 7

Dialogs

```cpp
    // Combo box selection initialization
    if (m_ctlCategories.SelectString(-1, m_pSW->m_strCategory) == CB_ERR)
    {
        int index = m_ctlCategories.AddString(m_pSW->m_strCategory);
        m_ctlCategories.SetCurSel (index);
    }

    // Initialize scroll bar
    m_ctlRating.SetScrollRange(RATING_MIN, RATING_MAX);
    m_ctlRating.SetScrollPos(m_pSW->m_wRating);

    // Initialize radio buttons
    int nRadioSel;
    switch (m_pSW->m_nJoystick)
    {
        case JRequired:
        nRadioSel = IDC_JoystickRequired;
        break;

        case JSupported:
        nRadioSel = IDC_JoystickSupported;
        break;

        default:
        nRadioSel = IDC_JoystickNotUsed;
        break;
    }

    CheckRadioButton(IDC_JoystickRequired, IDC_JoystickNotUsed, nRadioSel);

    return TRUE;  // Return TRUE unless you set the focus to a control
}

void CSWAddDlg::OnOK()
{
    CString Temp;

    // Retrieve scroll bar data
    m_pSW->m_wRating = m_ctlRating.GetScrollPos();

    // Retrieve combo/list box data
    if (m_ctlResolution.GetCurSel() != LB_ERR)
        m_ctlResolution.GetText(m_ctlResolution.GetCurSel(),
                        m_pSW->m_strResolution);
    if (m_ctlCategories.GetCurSel() != CB_ERR)
        m_ctlCategories.GetLBText(m_ctlCategories.GetCurSel(),
                        m_pSW->m_strCategory);

    m_pSW->m_lstMedia.RemoveAll();
    for (int i = 0; i < m_ctlMedia.GetCount(); i++)
    {
        if (m_ctlMedia.GetSel(i) > 0)
        {
            m_ctlMedia.GetText(i, Temp);
            m_pSW->m_lstMedia.AddHead(Temp);
```

```
            }

        }

        CDialog::OnOK();

        // Retrieve strings
        m_pSW->m_strTitle = m_strTitle;
        m_pSW->m_strPublisher = m_strPublisher;
        m_pSW->m_strRegistration = m_strRegistration;
        m_pSW->m_strPurchaseDate = m_strPurchaseDate;
        m_pSW->m_strPhone = m_strPhone;

        // Retrieve numbers
        m_pSW->m_fPurchasePrice = m_fPurchasePrice;
        m_pSW->m_bWinCompatible = m_bWinCompatible;

        // Retrieve and translate radio selection
        int nJS = GetCheckedRadioButton(IDC_JoystickRequired,
                            IDC_JoystickNotUsed);
        switch(nJS)
        {
            case IDC_JoystickRequired:
            m_pSW->m_nJoystick = JRequired;
            break;

            case IDC_JoystickSupported:
            m_pSW->m_nJoystick = JSupported;
            break;

            default:
            case IDC_JoystickNotUsed:
            m_pSW->m_nJoystick = JNot_Used;
            break;
        }

}
```

These two functions demonstrate a nice selection of initialization and retrieval functions for the featured controls. Each control has its own quirks and idiosyncrasies. Take particular note of the handling of the Media data set control. The Media issue is an especially gnarly one since this control is a list box, the selected items in the control can be a list, and the application storage device is also a list (a `CStringList`, to be precise). Careful study of these functions can shed light on the murky world of data transfer. We will come back to this topic in Chapter 10.

With all the data and controls buzzing around the dialog, sometimes it's necessary to perform a little explicit clean-up of our member variables. It's true that the member variables declared in the dialog class are automatically destroyed when the dialog is destroyed. However, it's better to be safe than sorry. When I compiled and ran this project the first time, I got runtime errors due to improper clean-up of the dialog. If you want something done right...

```
CSWAddDlg::~CSWAddDlg()
{
```

Day 7

Dialogs

```
    // Empty CStrings
    m_strPhone.Empty();
    m_strPublisher.Empty();
    m_strRegistration.Empty();
    m_strTitle.Empty();
    m_strPurchaseDate.Empty();

    // Empty list boxes
    while (m_ctlResolution.GetCount())
        m_ctlResolution.DeleteString(0);
    while (m_ctlMedia.GetCount())
        m_ctlMedia.DeleteString(0);
    while (m_ctlCategories.GetCount())
        m_ctlCategories.DeleteString(0);

    // Call base-class destructor
    CDialog::~CDialog();
}
```

Memory clean-up is crucial to the health of your application. In the preceding destructor, I empty the `CString` objects as well as the list box control objects. This may seem like overkill. But it is recommended that for every object in a class, an explicit effort should be made to ensure its memory reclamation. Never assume that the automated destruction sequence will do this for you. Naturally, objects you create via the `new` operator absolutely require that you destroy them via the `delete` operator. But objects created using either type of memory allocation bear close inspection as to their destruction. The bottom line is that you must keep a careful eye on memory issues when building a class—even when ClassWizard helps you.

There is one last piece of dialog code left to implement—the scroll bar activation code. The next listing demonstrates a way to breathe life into your scroll bar control.

```
void CSWAddDlg::OnVScroll(UINT nSBCode, UINT nPos, CScrollBar* pScrollBar)
{
    // TODO: Add your message handler code here and/or call default

    // If pScrollBar is NULL, it's the window's scroll bar,
    // not a control per se.
    if (!pScrollBar)
        return;

    int nMin, nMax, nCurPos;
    pScrollBar->GetScrollRange(&nMin, &nMax);
    nCurPos = pScrollBar->GetScrollPos();

    switch (nSBCode)
    {
        case SB_LINEDOWN:
        case SB_PAGEDOWN:
            if (nCurPos < nMax)
                pScrollBar->SetScrollPos(nCurPos + 1);
            break;

        case SB_LINEUP:
```

```
    case SB_PAGEUP:
    if (nCurPos > nMin)
        pScrollBar->SetScrollPos(nCurPos - 1);
    break;

    case SB_THUMBPOSITION:
    pScrollBar->SetScrollPos(nPos);
    break;

    default:
    return;
}

CDialog::OnVScroll(nSBCode, nPos, pScrollBar);
}
```

Remember, the scroll bars can't do anything by themselves. From within the parent window, you must capture the appropriate scroll message (either WM_VSCROLL or WM_HSCROLL) and perform some message decoding. For our dialog, the WM_VScroll message is the appropriate one. The OnVScroll() function is passed three parameters: nSBCode, nPos, and pScrollBar. The nSBCode parameter indicates the type of activity being attempted with the scroll bar. These codes were listed in Table 7.5. The second parameter, nPos, is used only if nSBCode holds the value of SB_THUMBPOSITION or SB_THUMBTRACK. When used, nPos holds the current position of the thumb. The final parameter is a pointer to the scroll bar itself. Use this pointer to access the scroll bar from within this function. Most of the work is done by the SetScrollPos() function, which moves the scroll bar's thumb to the specified position.

Software Lister

At this point, all the dialog code is written. All the data object (CSWProduct) code is written, and the collection object is incorporated into our application. The only thing left to do is to call the dialog from our application. Well, that's almost the last thing we have to do. Calling the dialog should be under our control. Placing the call in a menu handler specially built for the purpose will do the trick. Use AppStudio to add the following two menus to Software Lister's menu bar:

```
Iterator Menu:
    Initialize ID_ITERATOR_INITIALIZE
        "Initialize the software list iterator."
    Next       ID_ITERATOR_NEXT
        "Increment the software list iterator."

List Menu:
    Add        ID_LIST_ADD
        "Add a software item to the list."
    Modify     ID_LIST_MODIFY
        "Modify the current software item in the list."
    Dump       ID_LIST_DUMP
        "Display contents of list in the diagnostic window."
```

Day 7: Dialogs

The iterator menu just shown is a quick means of allowing selection in the Software Category list without having to implement a full-blown display. To be true to the document/view architecture, the display portions of the application would be added to the view class. Unfortunately, creating a fully functional display can fill a whole chapter by itself (as we shall see), so we must make do with the iterator trick. In order for the menu-based iterator to work, an iterating element is needed. Add the following `m_nIteratorIndex` declaration to the private attribute section of the document's interface:

```
private:
    int m_nIteratorIndex;
```

This value must also be initialized. Add the following line of code to the `OnNewDocument()` function:

```
m_nIteratorIndex = 0;
```

The second menu will allow us to directly affect the list. You will understand both menus better after you look at the code that serves them.

Use ClassWizard to add the Software Lister menu command handler functions to your document class, and implement them as shown in the following listing.

```cpp
void CSWListerDoc::OnIteratorInitialize()
{
    m_nIteratorIndex = 0;
}

void CSWListerDoc::OnIteratorNext()
{
    m_nIteratorIndex++;
}

void CSWListerDoc::OnUpdateIteratorNext(CCmdUI* pCmdUI)
{
    pCmdUI->Enable(m_TheList.GetCount() > m_nIteratorIndex);
}

void CSWListerDoc::OnListAdd()
{
    CSWAddDlg Dlg;

    CSWProduct* pSW = new CSWProduct();
    Dlg.m_pSW = pSW;

    if (Dlg.DoModal() == IDOK)
        m_TheList.AddTail(pSW);
    else
        delete pSW;
}

void CSWListerDoc::OnListModify()
{
    POSITION Pos = m_TheList.FindIndex(m_nIteratorIndex);
```

```
        CSWProduct* pSW = (CSWProduct*)m_TheList.GetAt(Pos);
        CSWAddDlg Dlg;

        Dlg.m_pSW = pSW;
        Dlg.DoModal();
}

void CSWListerDoc::OnUpdateListModify(CCmdUI* pCmdUI)
{
        POSITION Pos = m_TheList.FindIndex(m_nIteratorIndex);

        if (Pos == NULL)
        {
            pCmdUI->SetText("&Modify");
            pCmdUI->Enable(FALSE);
            return;
        }

        CSWProduct* pSW = (CSWProduct*)m_TheList.GetAt(Pos);
        pCmdUI->SetText("&Modify: " + pSW->m_strTitle);
        pCmdUI->Enable(TRUE);
}

void CSWListerDoc::OnListDump()
{
        TRACE1 ("The SW Product List contains %i items (as shown):\n",
                m_TheList.GetCount());
#ifdef _DEBUG
        POSITION Pos = m_TheList.GetHeadPosition();
        CSWProduct* pSW;
        while (Pos != NULL)
        {
            pSW = (CSWProduct*)m_TheList.GetNext(Pos);
            pSW->Dump(afxDump);

        }
#endif
}

void CSWListerDoc::OnUpdateListDump(CCmdUI* pCmdUI)
{
#ifdef _DEBUG
      pCmdUI->Enable(TRUE);
#else
      pCmdUI->Enable(FALSE);
#endif
}
```

Note the use of the OnUpdateXXXX() functions for the control of invalid states. For example, there is a danger in trying to modify a nonexistent list element. The OnUpdateListModify() function checks the viability of the iterator's position before the OnListModify() function can even be enabled, let alone selected. Also note the interplay of the iterator functions with the list functions. The iterator is used to select an element, and the list functions are used to manipulate it. The OnListDump() function is also a function of note. It serves as the only output, albeit

Dialogs

diagnostic, for our application. Naturally, this type of output isn't acceptable for a finished application, but to convince yourself of the proper functioning of the application, it performs equitably.

That's it for the Software Lister application. It should store and display (after a fashion) software information that you provide through the dialog mechanism. You even have the ability to use disk I/O via the File | Open, File | Save, and File | Save As menu commands at no extra charge. The effort we put into serialization is now paying off. Try entering a few software items, paying close attention to the operation of the dialog controls, and then save your work to disk. Bring up the application later to see that you can indeed restore your work. Not too bad for a little program. It's the power of the MFC at work. As a wise old bird used to say, "It's the only way to fly."

Summary

This chapter was a long haul through the smoky, dimly lit corridors of dialogs. We examined the wide variety of dialog controls and what they can accomplish. To that end, an application was developed that illustrated many of the controls presented. The Software Lister application was an ideal staging ground to show dialog construction, destruction, and all the little bits in between. Dialog invocation and termination techniques were covered in this application. We also took a brief tour of data transfer methods. As an added bonus, the second installment of `CObject`-derived class building was included. This was done to accommodate the newest addition to our storage repertoire—the collection classes. These friendly classes make holding and serializing large quantities of data a breeze.

Q&A

Q Why don't you give the static controls unique IDs in the dialog resource?

A Typically, you won't need access to the static controls from your application. When access isn't needed, unique IDs aren't needed. Unique IDs allow you to access individual controls during runtime. However, there will be times when you might want to modify the static controls on-the-fly. In order to do this, the static controls that you wish to alter will have to have unique IDs. We will use this technique in future chapters.

Q We used `CString` for date entry and storage. Why didn't we use `CDate`?

A It does seem ironic that we put such effort in building the `CDate` class in the previous chapter, yet we neglect to use it when an opportunity arises. Incorporating `CDate` into our application presents some complications that I didn't want to get into in this chapter. This chapter had enough complexity as it was. Be assured, however, that we will use `CDate` to hold and validate dates in applications to come.

Q You mentioned that both the list and map collection classes have iterators. Doesn't the array collection class have an iterator?

A Yes and no. The array collection doesn't have a formal iterator like the other two collection types. But it does have an index structure that performs the same service that an iterator provides. So, no, it doesn't have an iterator, but it also doesn't need one as do the other collection groups.

Workshop

Quiz

1. Name and briefly describe the three pieces of a dialog.
2. Explain the difference between the list box control and the combo box control.
3. What's the difference between modal and modeless dialogs?
4. In `CSWAddDlg::OnOK()`, why are the string data transfers done after the call to `CDialog::OnOK()`? (The string data transfers I'm referring to are the ones of the form `m_pSW->m_fPurchasePrice = m_fPurchasePrice;`.)

Exercises

1. Add a delete option to the list menu and implement it, paying close attention to memory reclamation.
2. Research the control classes presented in this chapter. Pay particular attention to the member functions that allow data transfer and state manipulation. Test your new knowledge by adding a little something of your choice to the application.
3. The application in this chapter only output data to the diagnostics window. Try your hand at implementing a real output display for our Software Lister application.

WEEK 2

AT A GLANCE

In Week 2 you will explore some fascinating concepts. Chapter 8 is a discussion of genealogy. We will talk about database theory and about how ODBC works and fits into the picture of Windows and databases. You will finish the chapter by creating the database for our Week 2 project. In Chapter 9 you will delve into the technical details of how the ODBC is organized, the classes the MFC has for dealing with databases, and how to incorporate ODBC into your applications. Chapter 10 will show you the nuts and bolts of data transfer. I know you've been wondering how data makes it from that dialog box you just filled in to the application itself. You will explore Dialog Data Validation (DDV) (bounds checking) and a number of other data exchange methods. Chapter 11 discusses the ODBC again, giving you a thorough understanding of how to use the ODBC for real-world applications. This is a chapter of variety, so enjoy. Chapter 12 deals with an essential topic, MDI. The Multiple Document Interface, essential to a large number of applications, is explored in depth. Multiple views are also presented. Chapters 13 and 14 deal with one of our favorite subjects—graphics! We will teach you about colors, palettes, and two varieties of bitmaps—DDBs and DIBs. These are fun and useful chapters.

Genealogy, Databases, and You

WEEK 2

DAY 8: Genealogy, Databases, and You

Now that we've gone to all the trouble of learning about serializing objects and enhancing your application to take advantage of serialization, it's time to look at an alternative route to data storage. For certain projects, serialization won't do the job. Usually, you will abandon serialization due to a lack of memory space. Remember, serialization is the process of transferring data between a data structure in memory and a flat file on a magnetic disk. If the data you're storing grows larger than your memory capacity (or more important, the memory capacity of your customers' machines), you're out of luck when it comes to the serialization technique. Other subtle problems inherent with serialization don't appear until large or complicated systems are forced into the simple packaging of serializing. In most cases, these problems won't arise, but in database applications, watch out!

Sometimes you're presented with a database problem that, for one reason or another, doesn't fit within the confines of an existing database product. It seems as though you would be forced to write your own DBMS (database management system). In the old days, that's precisely what you would have had to do. You would either write one from scratch or see if you could scavenge the code you used the last time and exploit some reuse. Every time you see or hear the word *reuse*, I want you to think of MFC. Yes, MFC comes to our rescue again with a set of database classes. Actually, these classes are just a wrapper around the more fundamental database API that implements a DBMS.

Microsoft thought long and hard about this problem of database management and about how programmers need to be able link into a standard database interface in order to communicate with existing databases. As usual, their thinking paid off. They came up with the ODBC (object database connectivity) interface. The ODBC is a standard database interface that can lie on top of most of the popular database systems such as Paradox, Access, FoxPro, dBASE, and so on. Because each of these popular database interfaces is different, a developer would have to target code to a specific database. A program so constructed would be coupled to the respective database. Changing the underlying database of such a system would result in a significant code change and perhaps even a redesign of the system. The ODBC allows for much more generic code.

This Week's Application— Genealogically Speaking

Over the next seven chapters, we will develop a genealogical database. The beauty of genealogy as an application topic is that everyone has a blushing familiarity with the subject. Much of its terminology is recognized and understood. Fathers, grandmothers, cousins, nieces, and the like are all in common usage. Another nice bonus is that most people have a spark of interest in their heritage, so building this application should have some general appeal. Let's first look at the genealogical subject in a little more depth before we plunge into program design. After all, in order to automate a process, you must first know how it's done manually.

Genealogy is the study of family trees. Genealogists research family lines and try to trace ancestries back as far as possible. It's the ultimate in detective work, and it's all about you—more or less. The detective works to put the pieces of a centuries-old puzzle together. The problem is that the further back you go into a history, the colder the trail becomes. Evidence gets harder to find, and witnesses become scarce. Genealogy presents a challenge for even the most skilled of detectives. Of course, when skill is needed for a challenging proposition, complicated terminology isn't far behind. Look at the computer terminology we've become so used to, for instance.

Yes, genealogy has its share of technical terms. Much of the genealogical vernacular centers around familial relationships. As I mentioned earlier, terms concerning immediate family relationships are quite well known: mother, father, cousin, nephew, and so on. But proceeding a bit further, we find that terminology regarding distant relationships is fuzzy to say the least. Who is your third cousin twice removed? Do you even know where in your family tree such a person might be located? Chances are you don't. I didn't before I started this project. Figure 8.1 shows a family relation chart that illustrates, by way of example, the relationship terminology of genealogy.

Figure 8.1.
The relationship terminology chart.

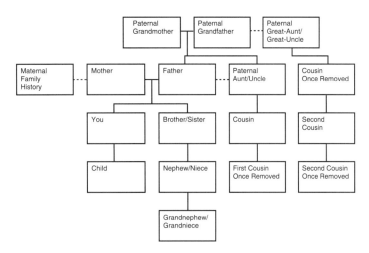

Other terms you might see in genealogic literature appear in Table 8.1. Don't worry. We won't use all these terms during the course of the project. However, it's good to get the lay of the land before you jump into the subject matter.

Table 8.1. More genealogical terminology.

Term	Definition
Affinal	Related by marriage—an in-law.
Agnate	Related by a common male ancestor on the father's side.

continues

Genealogy, Databases, and You

Table 8.1. continued

Term	Definition
Ahnentafel	A numbered, sequential list of a person's family tree.
Cognate	Related by a common ancestor.
Collateral	Related by common descent but through different lines.
Consanguine	Related by blood.
Distaff	The female branch of a family.
Floruit	The period of time during which a person was alive.
Lineal	In a direct line of descent.
Maternal	Concerning the mother.
Paternal	Concerning the father.
Patronymic	A surname derived from that of an ancestor.
Progenitor	An ancestor in a direct line of descent.
Surname	A last name or Christian name.

One term in the list that we will use in a later chapter is *ahnentafel*. One of the types of output that we will produce for our family tree program is the ahnentafel listing, a numbered, sequential list of the family history of a particular person. It restricts its entries to direct ancestors of the subject, and it has a very specific numbering scheme. The *subject,* the first person on the list, is labeled with a 1. The next two people on the list (numbers 2 and 3) are the subject's father and mother. The next four people on the list are the subject's grandparents, starting with the paternal grandfather and grandmother. There is a relationship between the people and the numbers. For any person on the list, their father's number is twice their own number. Likewise, their mother's number is twice their own number plus one. Each person's entry contains a multitude of information that can vary from list to list. Some ahnentafel lists contain only names, and others contain everything from names to marriage dates to occupations. What you put in your ahnentafel is up to you, although a minimum of ancestral names is clearly needed. The following is an ahnentafel list for one famous American:

Ahnentafel Listing for George Washington

1 George WASHINGTON (President): born 22 Feb 1731 Bridge's Creek, Westmoreland, Virginia; died 14 Dec 1799 Mount Vernon, Virginia.

2nd Generation
2 Augustine WASHINGTON (Captain): born 1694 Bridge's Creek, Westmoreland, Virginia; died 12 Apr 1743 Pope's Creek, Westmoreland, Virginia.

3 Mary BALL: born 1708, Lancaster County, Virginia; died 25 Aug 1789 Fredericksburg, Virginia.

3rd Generation

4 Lawrence WASHINGTON (Captain): born Sep 1659, Mattox, Westmoreland, Virginia; died 30 Mar 1697.
5 Mildred WARNER: born 1659, Warner Hall, Gloucester, Virginia; died Feb 1697.
6 Joseph BALL (Colonel): born Epping Forest, Lancaster, Virginia.
7 Mary MONTAGUE: died 1715.

4th Generation

8 John WASHINGTON (Colonel): born Feb 1632, Purleigh, Essex, England; died Sep 1677, Westmoreland, Virginia.
9 Ann POPE: born 1638, St. Mary's, Maryland; died 1668, Westmoreland, Virginia.
10 Augustine WARNER (Colonel): born 3 Jul 1642, Warner Hall, Gloucester, Virginia; died 19 Jun 1681, Warner Hall, Gloucester, Virginia.
11 Mildred READE: born 2 Oct 1643 Williamsburg, Virginia; died 20 Oct 1686 Warner Hall, Gloucester, Virginia.
12 William BALL (Colonel): born about 1615; died about 1680.
13 Hannah ATHEROLD.
14 Richard MONTAGUE: born 1614.
15 Abigail DOWNING.

.
.
.

You can see immediately that in only four generations the amount of data gathered is substantial. As you go back each generation, the amount of data to be stored grows exponentially. Clearly, for any serious genealogist, information storage and retrieval is a major concern. And that's not the half of it. The data included in the ahnentafel listing for George Washington is only a small part of the total data set. Much more information is needed for each ancestor to make a genealogist happy.

Each person in the family tree has a certain standard set of information that must be collected in order to be truly included in the family history. It's the genealogist's job to track down, uncover, and gather this standard set of information, which is shown in Table 8.2.

Genealogy, Databases, and You

Table 8.2. The standard set of genealogical data about a person.

Information	Description
Name	The person's name, including first, last, middle, and maiden.
Sex	The person's sex, male or female. (The name might not indicate this information.)
Birthdate	The date the person was born.
Birthplace	The place the person was born, including city, state, and zip code.
Death date	The date the person died.
Death place	The place the person died, including city, state, and zip code.
Where buried	The place the person was buried, including cemetery, city, state, and zip code.
Mother	A unique identifier for the person's mother, usually full name and birth date.
Father	A unique identifier for the person's father.
Spouse 1	A unique identifier for the person's first spouse.
Date of marriage 1	The date of marriage to spouse 1.
Spouse 2	A unique identifier for the person's second spouse.
Date of marriage 2	The date of marriage to spouse 2.
.	.
.	.
.	.
Child 1	A unique identifier for the person's first child.
Child 2	A unique identifier for the person's second child.
.	.
.	.
.	.
Occupation	The person's primary occupation.
Notes	Miscellaneous information about the person.
Portrait	A picture of the person.

This is a lot of information to collect from every member of your family, past and present. It's no small task to gather this information from your living relatives, let alone gather information about those who have been dead for centuries. Because of the amount of difficulty involved and sentimental concerns, genealogical data has a great deal of value. But not only is it valuable in its own right. It also has value because it contains clues to help you obtain more data. Each genealogical tidbit is but a stepping-stone to other nuggets of your past. It's very much like a ladder in which each rung is harder and harder to find. Consequently, once you go through hell and high water to get this information, it's only right that you should take care of it. Well, taking care of data is what computing is all about. You knew I was going to get back to computers eventually! The subdiscipline of computer science that deals with data storage and retrieval is called *database theory*.

Database Theory

A database is simply an organized storage of data in a computer system. Practically every program you write will, in one way or another, utilize a database. Think of your favorite commercial programs that don't fit under the label "database." Word processors, spreadsheets, aircraft simulators, adventure games, and even operating systems all have database elements hidden beneath their surface. In fact, only the smallest and most trivial of programs avoid using databases—in the most general sense of the term. I'm not saying that most programs use a formal database system as their data repository. I'm saying that most programs store data and that the storage of data is implicitly a database, albeit a rudimentary one.

What separates the men from the boys, in database circles, is the use of a formal database management system (DBMS). This is a commercial product whose sole purpose is to help you efficiently store, retrieve, and organize your data. It's the old story of avoiding reinventing the wheel by going to your local tire retailer. Why write your own database system when there are a dozen prebuilt products out there? Like a popular chicken restaurant, they have the advantage of doing it right, because that's all they do. You, on the other hand, have your application to worry about. Why not take advantage of prebuilt, pretested software to speed your development process? Indeed, isn't that what this book is all about? The whole idea behind the MFC is to provide you with prebuilt software components that facilitate Windows programming. Taking advantage of prebuilt database software is a natural extension.

Nearly all the commercial DBMSs on the market today are of the relational variety. Relational database systems differ from other database systems by the manner of data storage. Simply stated, a relational database system organizes its data as a collection of tables and only tables. The term *relational* comes from *relation*—the other name used for tables. Tables are also known as relations because they form relationships between data elements.

Physically, a database table is usually a file where database information is stored. Logically, however, a database table is a matrix of cells, much like that found in a spreadsheet application.

Genealogy, Databases, and You

Each row of cells in a table is called a *record*, and each column of cells is called a *field*. A table is defined by specifying its field names and types. All the elements of a field have the same name and type, whereas the elements in a record are a composite of field types. See Table 8.3 for a simple example of a table definition and Table 8.4 for the respective, partially filled table.

Table 8.3. An inventory table definition.

Field Name	Type	Size (if Necessary)
Stock No.	Integer	
Name	String	20 characters
Price	Float	
Quantity	Integer	
Date Received	Date	
Perishable	Boolean	

Table 8.4. A partially filled inventory table.

Stock No.	Name	Price	Quantity	Date Received	Perishable
1234	Ballpoint Pens	1.99	100	5/6/94	No
1399	Chewing Gum	0.65	130	8/22/93	No
3312	Milk (2%)	3.50	40	9/1/94	Yes
.					
.					
.					

Note that the preceding database table is sorted on the Stock No. field. This is not by accident. The database system must be told which field is to be the sorting field. This field (or combination of fields) is known as the table's *primary key*. It is used to uniquely identify the record for both searching and retrieval. Using the primary key, the database also ensures that no duplicate records are introduced. It is therefore crucial that these field values are unique to each entry in the table. Each database table must have a primary key defined. Using this primary key, a primary index is created to impose a default order on the table. Because there can be only one default order, there can be only one primary key and only one primary index. In other words, the table can have only one physical ordering at a time. Alternative orderings are permitted through the use of secondary indices. These indices are used in much the same way as book indices. They give you an additional, usually alternative, way of referencing the information in question. They greatly facilitate the searching process. Unlike book indices, you may define multiple secondary indices for different search and sort orderings.

Secondary indices are based on a field (or a combination of fields) that is different from the primary key. A secondary index represents an alternative ordering for the table, but it doesn't affect the physical order. For example, think of a dictionary as a database table. The primary key for a dictionary is the "word" field. A standard dictionary is sorted alphabetically by word. A secondary index could be defined to aid crossword-puzzle solvers. Consider a secondary key of word length. This index, otherwise known as a crossword dictionary, would sort the dictionary in terms of word length. Of course, there are many words with the same length, so this key isn't unique. Unlike the primary key, a secondary key doesn't need to be unique. The database doesn't use secondary keys to avoid duplicate entries, so they aren't required to be unique. This field wouldn't suffice as the primary key. At times, this nonuniqueness creeps into a field that we wish to make primary. Uniqueness is regained by specifying multiple fields for the primary key. Keys that use multiple fields are called *composite fields*. A sort order is determined from a composite key by comparing elements from the first field, then the second, and so on through the composite.

Another issue that needs to be covered is table construction. That is, how do you determine what information to put into which table? In fact, how do you know whether multiple tables are necessary at all? These questions are answered under the topic of table normalization, probably the single most important activity performed on a database. *Normalization* is a fancy term for breaking your database into logical chunks in order to guarantee that each data item resides in one and only one location. Why is this so important? In the words of Grady Booch, the guru of all software engineers, "This eliminates redundancy, simplifies the process of updating the database, facilitates the maintenance of database integrity (that is, self-consistency and correctness), and reduces storage requirements."

Okay, so we have to do it—the guru is always right. But at first glance, normalization seems to be a trivial task. How hard could it be to make sure each data item is stored in a single place? For trivial databases, normalization *is* trivial. However, as you encounter databases of increasing complexity, normalization becomes more and more challenging. Let's take a gander at the genealogical data that we are to collect and store. It might be unclear at first whether the data in Table 8.2 is as of yet normalized. Many of these data items are perfectly suited, as is, for entry into a table. However, many are not. Consider one of the references to other people in the data list—mother. In the field notes, I mention that the mother of the subject is usually uniquely identified by full name and birthdate. Indeed, something to that effect is done with a genealogist's handwritten notes. However, this is a direct violation of normalization! In the genealogical database, the person's mother will form another entry. In that record we will again be forced to enter the full name and birthdate. Redundancy! We can't have multiple instances of the same data running around. Something must be done with each reference to another person. There is a simple solution to this problem. By assigning a unique ID number to each person in the database, we can make references to other family members without duplicating data. (The ID number isn't considered raw data because it is only used internally to the database.)

Genealogy, Databases, and You

What are we to do with the multiple spouse and multiple child entries? This presents a real problem. How can we accommodate an unknown number of potential entries in a database table? Do we lean toward overkill and allow space for 20 children and 10 spouses? This would take up an obscene amount of space in the database. Besides, both parents would have this information about their children, so the overkill would be multiplied by two! Even if we decide to err on the side of caution and allow only five children and two spouses, the redundancy still exists. What's the constructor of a database to do? Actually, there are a number of solutions to this dilemma. One of the better solutions involves the use of multiple tables. The principal table, "Person," will hold the information particular to each individual person. A second table called "Union" is created to hold information associated with marriages. See Tables 8.5 and 8.6 for definitions of these database tables.

Table 8.5. The Person database table.

Field Name	Data Type	Length
ID	Number	
Last	Text	30
First	Text	30
Middle	Text	30
Maiden	Text	30
Is Male	Boolean	
Birthdate	Date	
Where Born	Text	60
Death Date	Date	
Where Died	Text	60
Interred	Text	60
Mother	Number	
Father	Number	
Occupation	Text	30
Notes	Long text	
Portrait	Long binary object (BLOB)	

Table 8.6. The Unions database table.

Field Name	Data Type	Length	Comments
Husband	Number		ID for the husband.
Wife	Number		ID for the wife.
Start	Date		Date the marriage began.
End	Date		Date the marriage ended.
Reason	Text	15	Death, divorce, and so on.

Notice that a person's children aren't explicitly indicated in either table. This isn't necessary. Any children in the database will have the appropriate links to their mother and father. Finding a person's children is done through a query to the database. A man's children are found by matching his ID with father IDs in the database. In a similar manner, female entries may be associated with their children. It might be tempting to place a "Children" flag in the database to alert us that children of this person exist. Resist the urge. Even this sort of Boolean flag would be a duplication of data, which would lead to complications. Namely, the flag and the addition and subtraction of children must be maintained simultaneously. It's an accident waiting to happen. Once the redundant data falls out of sync, the database is corrupt. Rely on queries, not the duplication of data, to retrieve database information. Discussing database queries brings us to the last issue of database theory we will discuss: the language of the query.

I don't doubt that there have been as many database query languages as there have been programming languages—in other words, lots! In the old days, every new DBMS that hit the market had its own query language. Some were good, and others were poor, but the one thing you could depend on was that they were all different. After we played the "endless learning curve" game for a while, someone decided that there were better things to learn (like the MFC). Most database query languages have settled around a standardized version of IBM's Structured Query Language or SQL (pronounced "sequel"). This is one of those languages that has been around seemingly forever. Few outside the database management set have bothered to learn it for fear that the powers that be will choose a different favorite language (it happens). However, SQL, instead of fading away, is gaining popularity and applicability. In some small way, this is due to the fact that the ODBC standard has adopted the SQL standard as the language of choice in communicating with the underlying database drivers. In fact, the ODBC interface even allows you the option of passing your own raw SQL statements to the driver.

Teaching SQL is a bit far afield from this book's topic, and a thorough coverage would constitute a book in itself. However, we can take a quick look at some common SQL keywords used with the ODBC, along with some sample queries. Table 8.7 shows some typical SQL keywords you'll encounter in your ODBC journeys.

Genealogy, Databases, and You

Table 8.7. SQL keywords commonly used with the ODBC.

Keyword	Description
SELECT	Selects a subset of a table specified by parameters.
WHERE	Modifies a SELECT statement with a condition.
ORDER BY	Specifies a sort order for the selected records.
INSERT	Adds records.
DELETE	Removes records.
UPDATE	Updates changes to records.

The SELECT statement is probably the most used and the most useful for our purposes. A few examples of SELECT's usage follow:

```
SELECT {field(s)} FROM {table(s)} WHERE {condition} AND {condition}...

SELECT WIFE FROM UNION

SELECT LAST_NAME, FIRST_NAME FROM PERSON
    WHERE LAST_NAME = "Smith" ORDER BY LAST_NAME
```

The SELECT statement selects a subset of elements from the table specified. The database maintains this selection so that you may view it, modify it, or even perform further selections on it. It is a very powerful statement. We'll see more of its use in future chapters.

Now that you have an understanding of databases, let's look at how the MFC library helps us take advantage of this technology.

ODBC Classes

The ODBC classes are Microsoft's answer to easy database connectivity. They provide the power of commercial database access with the MFC's ease of use. With these classes in your corner, you can concentrate on making your application work and not have to worry about the data—well, not much, anyway! The first item of business is to examine the ODBC architecture. Then we will look at the classes themselves.

Figure 8.2 shows how the ODBC interface fits within the architecture of your program. The actual details of database interaction are hidden from view within the database subset of the MFC. These database classes are summarized in Table 8.8.

Figure 8.2.
The ODBC architecture.

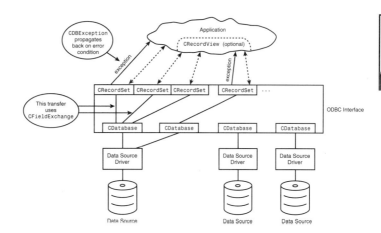

Table 8.8. A summary of the ODBC classes.

Class	Description
CDatabase	The encapsulation of the underlying data source.
CRecordset	The abstraction of a selected set of records from a database.
CFieldExchange	The structure used in data transfer between the CRecordset object and the database.
CLongBinary	The structure used in the storage of bitmaps and other large binary objects (also known as BLOBs).
CRecordView	A CView-derived class specially designed for database use.
CDBException	The derived CException class for the ODBC.

Each of these classes has a role to play in the ongoing drama that is a database application. However, some classes have bigger parts than others. CDatabase, CRecordset, and CFieldExchange are almost always used in an MFC database application. They are the lead actors in MFC database interaction. On the other hand, the CLongBinary class is used only when a specific need arises—typically the storage and retrieval of a bitmap.

We will discuss these classes in detail when the need arises. For now, let's move on to the more pedestrian issues of setting up a database object for use with our application.

Database Construction

It's hard to believe that even with all the automated processes included in the Visual C++ package, you still have to perform some manual chores. Believe it. The manual chore that currently looms before us is data source construction. Before we can perform the usual database

Day 8: Genealogy, Databases, and You

tasks of data storage and retrieval, we must have a data source with which to interact. Data sources represent different things to different database drivers. Basically, they hold information about the data and how to obtain it. Usually, this consists of a location where the database files can be found. Building a working data source for your application is a three-step process. First, you must create a directory to hold the database files. Second, you must use the ODBC Administrator to create the data source associated with the directory created in step one. Finally, you must use the ODBC Query application to create the tables for that data source.

The ODBC Administrator manages the creation and registration of data sources and the installation of database drivers. The ODBC Administrator is the centralized location where applications get information about currently registered data sources. AppWizard and ClassWizard retrieve information from the ODBC Administrator when constructing application-specific, derived MFC database classes. Unless you preregister your data sources with the Administrator, the wizards won't be able to automatically incorporate them into their code. You can manually incorporate data sources in your code, but what's the use in having wizards if you don't use them? Actually, many professional MFC programmers avoid the use of wizards entirely. They feel that they can make more efficient use of the MFC classes if they do the work themselves. For now, however, we will stick to doing it the easy way.

First, we must create the subdirectory where the database files will reside. Use File Manager to create the DB_DATA subdirectory under our TYMFC directory (or anywhere you want). The next step is to use the ODBC Administrator to create a data source. The ODBC Administrator is found in Control Panel in your Main program group if you're using Windows 3.x. It's found in the Microsoft ODBC group if you're using Windows NT. Find and open the Administrator on your system. Your screen should look something like Figure 8.3.

Figure 8.3.
The ODBC Administrator.

The ODBC Administrator window displays all the currently registered data sources for your system. You might be surprised to see that quite a few data sources are already available. Every database driver installed on your system has a default data source defined. These default data sources use your application's directory as the location for the database files, but aside from that small limitation, they're perfectly usable. We will create our own data source, because we want our database files to reside in the DB_DATA directory we created for this specific purpose. This technique is especially useful if multiple applications will be using the same database files. If we used a default data source, the database files would have to reside in each application's directory and therefore couldn't be shared. With a custom-created data source, we specify a single location for the database files regardless of how many applications access them. Some of these multiple applications could even reside on different machines and access the database files over a network. The particular set of data source options available depends on the database driver selected.

Visual C++ comes with a number of database drivers for some of the more popular commercial databases. The following is a list of the drivers available with Visual C++ 1.5:

>   Access
>   Btrieve
>   dBASE
>   Excel
>   FoxPro
>   ORACLE
>   Paradox
>   SQL Server
>   Text files

Note: The Access, dBASE, FoxPro, and Paradox drivers are installed into the ODBC Administrator automatically. The ORACLE and SQL Server drivers are for remote database servers.

The type of information that may be placed in a database table strongly depends on the underlying database driver. This is because each database supports varying data types. Selecting an appropriate database driver is an important decision. Many issues must be weighed. Here are some questions you should ponder: Does the database driver support the types of data your application requires? Is the database driver fast enough for your application? Will the driver support shared network access to the data files? Will your application need access to specific preexisting database files? If so, is there a database driver to accommodate you?

Luckily, for our family tree application, we need only concern ourselves with issues about type support. Our application will hold and store values from a variety of types, so naturally we want the database to be able to accommodate us. Each database driver supports a set of types chosen from a standard master list of possible ODBC types. This master list of types (just shown) was derived from the types used in the SQL language. This list is subdivided into three categories of driver compliance. The first level indicates minimal support—only fixed character strings are supported. The second level is core support. It contains the standard, mainline types that you will commonly use. The third level is extended support. It contains types for more specific uses, such as storing dates and long streams of text. The ODBC SQL types are shown in Table 8.9. They are categorized by driver compliance level.

DAY 8
Genealogy, Databases, and You

Table 8.9. The ODBC type standard—the SQL types.

ODBC SQL Type	Description
The Minimal SQL Data Type for the ODBC	
SQL_CHAR	A fixed-length character string whose length is less than 255.
Core SQL Data Types for the ODBC	
SQL_NUMERIC	A fixed-point value with up to 15 significant digits.
SQL_DECIMAL	A fixed-point value with up to 15 significant digits.
SQL_INTEGER	A standard integer value—32 bits.
SQL_SMALLINT	A small integer value—16 bits.
SQL_FLOAT	A floating-point value with a mantissa precision of 15.
SQL_REAL	A floating-point value with a mantissa precision of 7.
SQL_DOUBLE	A floating-point value with a mantissa precision of 15.
SQL_VARCHAR	A variable-length character string whose length is less than 255.
Extended SQL Data Types for the ODBC	
SQL_BIT	A Boolean type—one or zero.
SQL_DATE	A date structure—year, month, and day.
SQL_TIME	A time structure—hour, minute, and second.
SQL_TIMESTAMP	A combination of date and time.
SQL_LONGVARCHAR	Variable-length character data (for example, a memo). The maximum length is driver-dependent but usually very large.
SQL_LONGVARBINARY	A variable-length binary object (for example, a bitmap). The maximum length is driver-dependent but usually very large.
SQL_BINARY	A fixed-length binary object whose length is less than 256.
SQL_VARBINARY	A variable-length binary object whose length is less than 256.
SQL_BIGINT	A large integer value—64 bits.
SQL_TINYINT	A tiny integer value—8 bits.

Note that the entries in Table 8.9 aren't really types but are identifiers for types. These identifiers are used internally to manage the corresponding type values embedded within the database. Also note that the specific type definitions given in the table aren't necessarily followed religiously within any particular database driver. You must look up the information about the driver you choose to see where liberties have been taken. Variety may be the spice of life, but variation from a standard is the bane of programming. That said, let's look at how the database drivers support the ODBC type standard. The following lists show which standard types are "supported" by which popular database driver. The column on the left is the driver type, and the column on the right is the corresponding ODBC type.

Microsoft Access Driver

BIT	SQL_BIT
CURRENCY	SQL_NUMERIC
DATETIME	SQL_TIMESTAMP
DOUBLEFLOAT	SQL_DOUBLE
LONG	SQL_INTEGER
LONGBINARY	SQL_LONGVARBINARY
MEMO	SQL_LONGVARCHAR
SHORT	SQL_SMALLINT
SINGLEFLOAT	SQL_REAL
TEXT	SQL_CHAR
UNSIGNEDBYTE	SQL_TINYINT

Paradox Driver

ALPHANUMERIC	SQL_CHAR
DATE	SQL_DATE
NUMBER	SQL_DOUBLE
SHORT	SQL_SMALLINT

dBASE Driver

CHAR	SQL_CHAR
DATE	SQL_DATE
LOGICAL	SQL_BIT
MEMO	SQL_LONGVARCHAR
NUMERIC	SQL_DOUBLE

FoxPro Driver

CHAR	SQL_CHAR
DATE	SQL_DATE
GENERAL	SQL_LONGVARBINARY
LOGICAL	SQL_BIT
MEMO	SQL_LONGVARCHAR
NUMERIC	SQL_DOUBLE

Day 8

Genealogy, Databases, and You

Btrieve Driver

DATE	SQL_DATE
FLOAT4	SQL_REAL
FLOAT8	SQL_DOUBLE
INTEGER1	SQL_TINYINT
INTEGER2	SQL_SMALLINT
INTEGER4	SQL_INTEGER
LOGICAL1	SQL_BIT
MONEY	SQL_NUMERIC
NOTE	SQL_LONGVARCHAR
STRING	SQL_CHAR

For the purposes of creating the family tree program, only two of the database drivers will give us the type flexibility we need: Access and FoxPro. Because the MFC database tutorial that comes with Visual C++ utilizes the Access driver, I'll choose the FoxPro driver for some contrast. Click on the Administrator's Add... button in order to add a new data source. This invokes the Add Data Source dialog, shown in Figure 8.4, in which you may choose the driver for your new data source. Select the FoxPro driver and click on the OK button. This brings up the ODBC FoxPro Setup dialog, shown in Figure 8.5, in which you configure the data source.

Note: If the FoxPro driver isn't loaded, insert your MSVC CD-ROM and run Setup. Choose Custom Installation and uncheck all options except ODBC. Click on the Drivers button and choose the FoxPro driver. Continue with the installation, and the driver will be installed.

Figure 8.4.
The Add Data Source dialog.

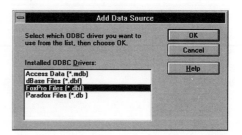

You must do two things in the setup dialog. You must give the data source a unique name—unique in the sense that no other data source registered in this particular ODBC Administrator has the same name. "Family Tree Data Source" should be sufficiently unique, so use that as the Data Source Name. The second thing you must do is establish a location for the data files—you won't be able to okay the dialog without one. You do this by clicking on the Select Directory...

button, which displays the Select Directory dialog. Navigate the directory structure from within this dialog and select the DB_DATA directory that we created earlier. An OK button later, we find ourselves back at the main ODBC Administrator dialog (the Data Sources dialog). You should see our new Family Tree data source sitting among the other choices in the list box. The procedure for establishing a data source from one of the other drivers isn't much different. The other driver setup dialogs are practically the same as the FoxPro dialog. Any differences are mainly due to the inherent variations in the database drivers themselves.

Figure 8.5.
The ODBC FoxPro Setup dialog.

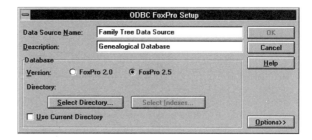

After the data source is created and configured with the ODBC Administrator, the database tables need to be created with ODBC Query. The Query application is found in the Microsoft ODBC group on the desktop. Starting the Query application, you should see something resembling Figure 8.6.

Figure 8.6.
Microsoft Query.

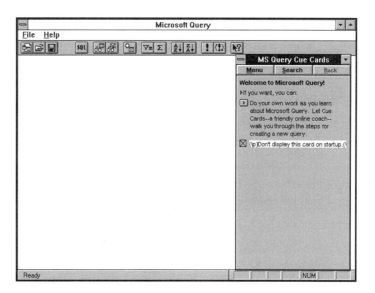

Genealogy, Databases, and You

The Query application has its own tutorial system, the MS Query Cue Cards window. I highly recommend that you use this to gain familiarity with the product. The Cue Cards window has the annoying, yet sometimes helpful, habit of always being the window on top. If this trait annoys you, you can close the window, because it's not necessary for the operation of Query. Query has many uses beyond the mere creation of database tables, and this tutorial system will help you get the most out of Query. However, for now, let's just concentrate on the matter at hand—tables!

Our family tree database consists of two tables: a Person table and a Unions (marriages) table. Let's have Query add these two tables to the Family Tree data source. In Query, choose File | Table Definition.... The Select Data Source dialog appears. Family Tree Data Source isn't among the selections, even though we just put it in! Don't panic! We just have to tell Query to update its list from the Administrator. Click on the Other... button and choose our data source from that list, as shown in Figure 8.7.

Figure 8.7.
Selecting the data source.

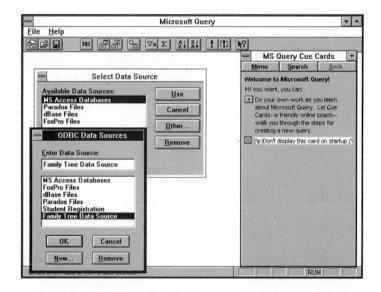

Now we may use the Family Tree data source. Query asks you to select a table from the Select Table dialog, shown in Figure 8.8. No tables yet exist in the Family Tree data source (that is, the DB_DATA subdirectory), so you will have no tables to choose from. However, the New button gives you the opportunity to create tables. It brings up the New Table Definition dialog, shown in Figure 8.9.

Figure 8.8.
The Select Table dialog.

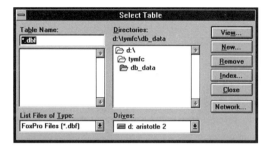

Figure 8.9.
The New Table Definition dialog.

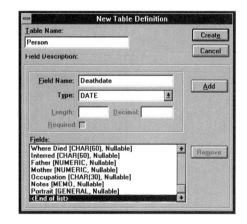

From within this dialog, you may define your table by entering the name and properties of each field and clicking on the Add button. In the case of our Person table, enter Person into the Table Name edit box, then "Add" each Person field (found in Table 8.5) to the table. When you're satisfied that the table is properly constructed, click on the Create button. But take heed. Once you create a table, you *cannot* use Query to edit it. To make changes, you have to delete the table and start fresh. So take the time to go over the table fields a couple dozen times to make sure that they're perfect; otherwise, it's back to square one!

> **Note:** You might be wondering what the New... button in the ODBC Data Sources dialog does. Well, it's actually another route to creating data sources. We took the ODBC Administrator approach because that's where the work is actually done. Even if you create a data source via the New... button, you're really using the Administrator. I figure we might as well call a rose a rose...or rather, an Administrator an Administrator. After all, things are confusing enough. However, I also want to let you know of the shortcuts that are offered. So there you have my compromising position on the subject.

Genealogy, Databases, and You

Use this same procedure to create a database table named Unions. Add the marriage fields from Table 8.6 to this table. Again, look the table over a couple hundred times (once you get burned, you'll be overly cautious too) and make sure it's what you want. If it is, have Query create it.

Now that we have a couple of tables, it's time to establish indices for them. This too is done through Query. Again, select File | Table Definition..., which takes you to the Select Table dialog. Instead of creating a new table at this point, choose the existing Person table and click on the Index... button. This brings up the Create Index dialog, shown in Figure 8.10.

Figure 8.10.
The Create Index dialog.

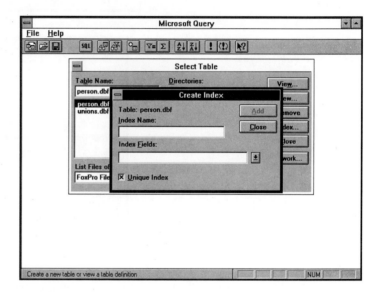

Here you may create an index or multiple indices for a database table. By using the table name as the index name, you tell Query to make a primary index. Any other name will make the index secondary. In the Index Fields edit box, you may put the field or fields that constitute the key for the index. For the Person table, create a primary index from the ID field. The ID field is the best choice for a primary key because it was designed for this explicit purpose! However, no single field in the Union table is unique. Here we must use two fields as a primary key. HUSBAND and START_DATE would constitute a unique combination. Unfortunately, here we encounter a peculiarity in the database driver. The FoxPro driver will allow any field type except the GENERAL and MEMO types to be used as a single-field index. However, when multiple fields are used in an index, the FoxPro driver becomes fussy. Only text fields may be included in a multiple-field index in the FoxPro driver. Such is life. We will just have to forego the use of an index with the Union table.

 Note: The FoxPro driver converted the field names to uppercase. This is just a quirk of the driver; don't be concerned. Other drivers, such as Paradox, don't do this. This is just another example of variations between database drivers.

At this point, we have two empty database tables associated with the Family Tree data source. We could jump right into programming our application at this point, but it's usually best to take these things slowly. Instead of pushing ahead into coding, let's utilize the Query application to put some data into our tables. This will give our fledgling ODBC programming effort something to sink its teeth into. Naturally, adding and manipulating table elements is usually done by the program itself. But with empty tables, we will have to learn how to add and view table data at the same time. If the tables already have information in them, we can concentrate on the program's viewing aspects.

In Query, choose File | New Query.... Query asks you for the data source and then the particular table from that data source. Let's put some information in the Person table. In the Add Tables dialog, shown in Figure 8.11, add the Person table only once and then close the dialog.

Figure 8.11.
Query with the Person table selected.

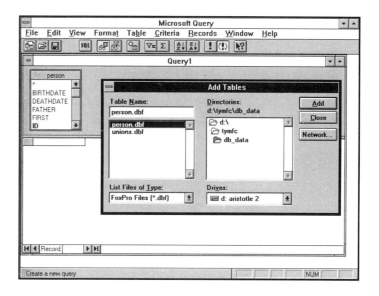

The Person table is visible as a little window within the Query window. From this table you may select the fields you wish to manipulate. Note that ID is highlighted because we identified it as our primary index. For our present purposes, we want to manipulate only certain fields, so

Day 8: Genealogy, Databases, and You

double-click on each of the following fields in the Person table window: ID, FIRST, LAST, MIDDLE, MAIDEN, IS_MALE, FATHER, and MOTHER. This action causes all of Person's fields to be placed in the workspace. Choose Records | Allow Editing in order to place data in the table. Go crazy! Put all the members of your family into the table, taking care to make the IDs unique and to link parents to children. Remember, the parent/child links are established through the ID fields. Eventually, our program will choose unique IDs for us and make these linkages automatically. But here in Query, everything is manual. This exercise will give you some appreciation of what our program will do. When you're finished filling the Person table with your family history, you should see something similar to Figure 8.12. Your exact data will be different from mine (unless I have a long-lost twin that Mom and Dad have been hiding), but its general nature should be the same.

Figure 8.12.
Query with the Person table and some data.

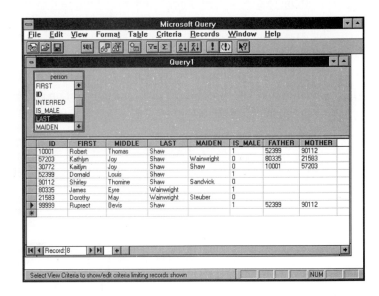

Now we have a data-filled table in the Family Tree data source with which our programs may interact. Of course, first things first—there is the little matter of our application to consider. Nothing's going to interact with anything unless we have an agent of action. Let's go ahead and build a program while there is life left in this chapter.

Note: When you exit Query after adding data to a table, you will be asked whether you want to "save the query." You may safely say no. As you enter the data, it is incrementally added to the table—the actual table, not a memory-based data structure. Consequently, the data is being "saved" or stored in the database as we enter it. What is Query talking about when it asks about saving the query? It's talking about saving the current question (or query) you've posed to the database. This is Query's primary purpose, by the way—retrieving information by posing queries to a database. Anyway, until you understand Query and use it for its intended purpose, you can safely ignore saving queries. I'm afraid any further understanding of Query you gain will be outside the domain of this book, because this is the last I have to say on the matter. I have to draw the line somewhere!

'Tis Nothing Lovely as a Tree...Application

Crank up AppWizard and create the Tree project. For this application, we will choose a different set of options. A new week and a new application deserve some variety. Aside from incorporating database support, we will use AppWizard's default set of options. This includes the Multiple Document Interface (MDI) and Printing and Print Preview selections under the Options... button. Both of these topics and more will be discussed at length in this week's chapters. But our first item on the agenda is the database. Clicking on the Database Options... button will reveal the dialog in Figure 8.13.

Figure 8.13.
The Database Options dialog.

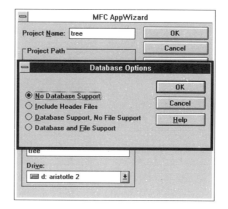

Each option in this dialog gives us an increasing amount of database support. The first radio button, No Database Support, is the default option. It indicates that no database support will be included in your application. This doesn't mean that you can't later add database support manually, but it's always easier if these things are automated. The next level of database support is provided through the Include Header Files radio button. At this level, only the bare minimum of database support is provided. The database header file (AFXDB.H) is incorporated in the STDAFX.H file, which is always included in your applications. Once this visibility is furnished, your application can freely use any of the database classes and constants.

Genealogy, Databases, and You

The next two levels of support truly give our programs database connectivity. As such, they need a bit more information about the data source. To this end, when either of the last two buttons is selected, a pushbutton appears that allows you to specify the data source. When selected, the Database Support, No File Support radio button instructs AppWizard to imbue our application with a number of special features: a special view class (CRecordView), a predefined CRecordset class to hold database record information, menu and toolbar additions for database navigation, and the connections of all these objects to the database. However, this level doesn't include document serialization. It makes sense that if you have full database support, you won't necessarily need the simple file I/O of serialization. Hence, at this level, you won't have the serialization menu commands of File | New, File | Open, File | Save, and File | Save As. On the other hand, sometimes the use of a database and serialization can be valuable. The final radio button, Database and File Support, allows you to exploit both serialization and database manipulations in a single application.

Select Database and File Support from the Database Options dialog, because our program will employ both types of data-saving techniques. This will automatically connect our application to the database while allowing us the normal serialization options. After you click on the Database and File Support radio button, a new button appears in the dialog. This Data Source... button allows you to connect the application to the data source we have been clucking over for practically the entire chapter. Perhaps "allows" is too tame a word. If you choose the Database and File Support option, you *must* connect your application not just to a data source but to a data source table. (Is it any wonder it took almost a whole chapter to get to the point where we could start the application?) Fortunately, all the data source busywork is out of the way, so we may connect our protoapplication to the Person table. That being done, we are all set to create this week's base application. Figure 8.14 shows the new application information screen.

Figure 8.14.
New application information.

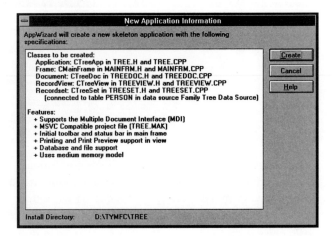

Go ahead and run the application, and let's see just how much of the database connection is automated. Hmmm. Not much! All you'll see if you run the program is the completely inert display shown in Figure 8.15.

Figure 8.15.
The Family Tree application.

Aside from a new look to the toolbar and the MDI interface (which we will discuss in Chapter 12), it doesn't look like it does much! What a disappointment...or is it? Before you give up and leave the computer in a huff or do something drastic with regards to this book, let's fiddle with the application just a little to see if anything can be salvaged.

The answer to animating our application lies in AppStudio. It is here that we may poke holes in the opaque shell of the default implementation and view some of the data hidden in our database. Launch AppStudio and click on the dialog type. Isn't that interesting? There are two dialogs to choose from—this is new! Open the IDD_TREE_FORM dialog to examine this development further. Curiouser and curiouser! Before you is a dialog empty but for a single static control holding the text "TODO: Place form controls on this dialog." That happens to be the same text displayed by our default application. Is there a connection? Of course; it's the same text. When you think about it, it does seem strange that the view automatically displayed anything. It hasn't done this before, but then we did change a lot of stuff when we created this application. Pinning down all the changes that this application introduced will absorb the next six chapters, but this particular addition is due to a database class. Specifically, when we chose the database option, a new view class was used as our default view. This new view class is CRecordView, which traces its ancestry back to CFormView and, of course, CView.

> **Note:** Something else is different about the IDD_TREE_FORM dialog! It has no default dialog buttons. Where are our friends OK and Cancel? This is another change in operating procedures that CRecordView (actually, CFormView) has foisted upon us. The view uses the dialog resource to construct the view, but the view doesn't become a dialog. Certainly, it has aspects of a dialog, but it's a far cry from being a dialog. You can paint spots on your cat, but it's still not a leopard.

Day 8
Genealogy, Databases, and You

> Dialogs, especially modal dialogs, need buttons so that the user can indicate completion. Views don't have such a limited life. They are on display for practically their entire existence. Form views don't necessarily have buttons because they don't really have an immediate completion. They represent a semipermanent view into the document's data, whereas modal dialogs typically represent a fleeting glimpse into the application's data.
>
> Don't get me wrong about form views. They often have buttons to initiate actions. They just don't usually have buttons that cause them to terminate as dialogs do. You will understand the differences between dialogs and form views better as this application progresses.

CFormView makes a few changes to the CView class, the most notable of which is that it merges some dialog functionality with CView. CFormViews have the capability to hold and operate dialog controls just like a dialog. In fact, the visual basis of CFormView is a dialog resource object. In our case, the dialog resource in question is IDD_TREE_FORM. CRecordView builds on the work of CFormView by adding automated database connectivity. The bottom line is that if you use CRecordView as the base class for your view, much of your work is done for you. To demonstrate this ease of use, let's bring our focus back to the dialog hanging on our screen, waiting to be edited.

Delete the static text control from the dialog—we don't need that skulking around. Add three new static control boxes and a surrounding group box, as shown in Figure 8.16. We're going to do something different with the static text controls this time. Assign the following IDs to the static text controls: IDC_FirstName, IDC_MiddleName, and IDC_LastName. That's right, we aren't going to use the default ID of IDC_STATIC! IDC_STATIC is an anonymous identifier used to indicate that we don't intend to use the control in our program. By assigning our own ID, we provide ourselves a handle so that we may alter the caption of even "static" text. In other words, static text controls don't really hold static text (since we can, in fact, change it).

Also clear the caption for the group box since we intend it to be just a box that visually groups the names of our subject. Give the group box an ID of IDC_NameBox. We do this not so that we may later change its caption, although identifying the group box in this way would allow it. It is identified this way so that we may later retrieve its extent in order to aid in mouse hit-testing. Eventually, the application will support a double-click invocation of a Person edit dialog. Knowing the extent of the name boxes is an important first step toward deducing whether they were double-clicked.

Figure 8.16.
The preliminary Family Tree dialog/view.

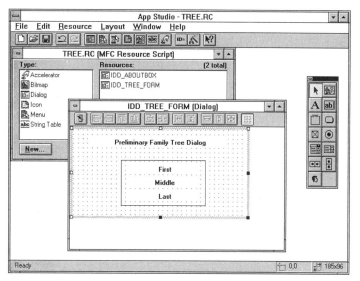

Fire up ClassWizard, and let's see if anything has changed in the class manipulation business. Make sure ClassWizard is looking at the CTreeView class, and you'll see that the Message Maps tab in ClassWizard looks as expected. The OLE Automation tab is no different. Of course, it shouldn't be, because we didn't use any OLE options. However, the remaining two tabs in ClassWizard have some surprises for us. Clicking on the Member Variables tab might not reveal anything new at first glance, but with a little probing, we'll soon see some differences. Add a member variable corresponding to the IDC_FirstName control. While in the Add Member Variable dialog, take a look at the drop-down combo box associated with the variable name (see Figure 8.17).

Figure 8.17.
Adding database member variables.

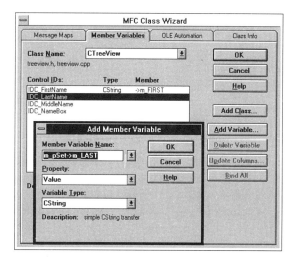

Day 8

Genealogy, Databases, and You

The variable names look familiar! They are the names (preceded by a pointer reference) of the fields in our database. Yes, the connection we made to the database did some good after all. Choose the "First Name" database entry in the combo box and click on OK. Perform the same operation with the IDC_LastName and IDC_Middle_Name controls. You now have at least some of your database linked with the application. It's that simple. Tying the rest of the database entries into dialog controls is accomplished through a similar process, as we shall see.

Looking at the Class Info tab, we also see an addition. There are names in the Foreign Class and Foreign Variable edit boxes, as shown in Figure 8.18.

Figure 8.18.
ClassWizard's Class Info tab.

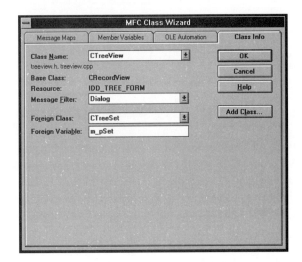

The foreign variable is the same as the pointer reference that preceded the database field names in the Member Variable Name combo box. It is this variable that allows us to connect the dialog/view with the database. Actually, we don't connect directly to the database. We go through an intermediary class of CTreeSet—the foreign class. This class is derived from the database class CRecordset, which is the logical encapsulation of the records in a table. The foreign variable is a pointer to an instantiation of this CRecordset-derived class that allows record manipulation. Fortunately, all the details of this linkage reside within the AppWizard- and ClassWizard-created code. So, for the moment, we can hope for the best and press on. Naturally, we will come back to these details so that we can understand the process. However, for the time being, we've done enough talking. Let's experiment with the application as it stands.

Run the application with the new enhancements. Try out the new toolbar objects that deal with the database—the ones that look kind of like cassette tape controls. Oops—I mean compact disc player controls; what century am I living in? Anyway, back to the toolbar. The plain arrow controls step you forward or backward through the database one record at a time. The arrows

with a vertical line send you to the first or last record of the database table. Corresponding menu commands are found on the Record menu. Step through your database and confirm that this application does indeed perform as advertised. As usual, once we get through the background material, a very small effort is needed to produce a usable product—a product that will grow and become more useful in the chapters to come.

Summary

Databases are repositories for data. Relational databases use the table structure, and only the table structure, as the location for data storage. These tables (also known as relations) are a matrix of cells that hold the actual data. The columns of a table are known as fields, and the rows are known as records. Each record represents a data item—a composite of data from each field. Every table is required to have a primary key, which is a field (or fields) that uniquely identifies the record in the table. The uniqueness of the primary key ensures that there will be no duplicate records in the table. Every record in a table must be distinct. Indices may be defined on table keys. Indices allow for easy searching and sorting of items in a table. There can be only one primary index, but there may be multiple secondary indices. The primary index is used for the physical sorting of the table. Secondary indices are used for additional logical sorting and searching.

The ODBC interface is a standard database connectivity tool that allows applications to access popular databases. The ODBC is a shell of standard database functions that link to predetermined database drivers. This standard interface allows particular database dependencies to be removed from an application. The loose coupling that results from ODBC use causes database driver changes to have minimal impact on the application code.

The MFC database classes encapsulate much of the ODBC's operational functionality. But despite the automation built into Visual C++ and the MFC, some database management tasks still need to be done manually. In this chapter, we saw how to perform this manual linking and how this linking is used in our own genealogical application. The modicum of code written in this chapter is only the tip of the iceberg. We shall continue expanding the family tree application in the chapters ahead.

Q&A

Q Are the ODBC Administrator and ODBC Query applications the only means of configuring a data source?

A No. The ODBC API has function calls you can use to create and register a data source and create tables for your ODBC application. However, these calls are rather complicated and outside the realm of this book.

Genealogy, Databases, and You

Q I've heard that normalization is a complicated business.

A Yep, you are correct! In the normalization business, there are such things as First Normal Form (1NF), Second Normal Form (2NF), Third...well, you get the idea. In professional database manager circles, these are the talk of the town. Database administrators throw around 1NFs and 4NFs while enjoying cucumber sandwiches (crusts removed, of course) and afternoon tea. However, for us mere mortals, the normalization concepts we have discussed are more than sufficient.

Workshop

Quiz

1. Describe the relationships between the concepts of table, field, and record.
2. Compare and contrast key with index.
3. Why do you want a normalized database?
4. What are the duties of the ODBC Administrator?
5. Does the static text control always contain the same text throughout the life of an application?

Exercises

1. Familiarize yourself with Microsoft Query via the Cue Cards.
2. Using Help, investigate another database driver and compare it to the FoxPro driver.
3. Add more dialog items to the application and tie them into the database. See how many you can implement with the information presented so far.

WEEK 2

The ODBC Classes

The ODBC Classes

Everything discussed in the last chapter was background material for the Family Tree application and the ODBC tools required to build the application. We didn't explore the technical details underlying the ODBC, nor did we discuss any coding strategies particular to the ODBC. Technical details are the mainstay of this chapter. Here we will delve deeply into the foundation classes that support ODBC programming. We will also explore various strategies of incorporating the ODBC classes into your applications.

The central topic of this chapter is the CRecordset class. This class is at the heart of MFC's ODBC paradigm. It is through record set objects that we gain access to table data. Because manipulating data is the ultimate goal of almost every program, the CRecordset class has a pivotal role in any MFC database application. We therefore will take the time to do justice to the record set class. In this chapter, you will gain familiarity with most of CRecordset's functionality. You might feel that an inordinate amount of time is spent on CRecordset, and that CRecordView and CDatabase are only touched on at best. When in Rome, it's best if you know how to speak Italian, not Latin. CRecordset functionality is the language of the day in MFC's ODBC land.

The Genealogical View/Dialog

We'll start this chapter by continuing where we left off in Chapter 8. We left our hero in the midst of a burgeoning application without a hint as to what to do next. We had just installed a few static dialog controls into our dialog/view in order to demonstrate the ease of database connectivity. As it turned out, static controls weren't as static as we were led to believe! We can change what's displayed in any control at runtime. We're the programmers, for cryin' out loud. We should be able to change things at will.

Let's continue setting up our main view/dialog in order to display more information. The main view of our application will center around genealogical relationships between the people in the Person table. In this view, we will concentrate on familial ties and avoid the individual person's attributes. These familial ties are found both in the Person table and in the Unions table. The Person table holds blood relationships in the form of mother/father IDs. All other blood relations can be discerned via the mother/father ties. The Unions table gives us the spousal relationships. Both tables must be used to get the information for the main view. Of course, multitable access is a bit complicated, so for the moment we will concentrate on only one table. Don't worry. Everything will fall into place before the week is out.

Place the controls into the dialog as shown in Figure 9.1, and then we'll talk about the connectivity issues that arise. Let me assure you, issues *will* arise!

The IDs corresponding to these controls are listed in Table 9.1.

Figure 9.1.
The completed main view dialog.

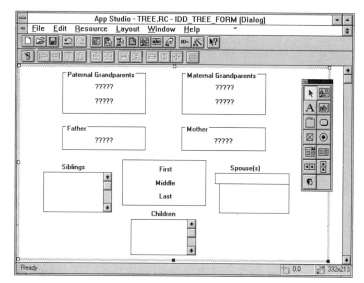

Table 9.1. Main view/dialog control IDs.

ID	Description
IDC_FirstName	The static control that holds the subject's first name.
IDC_MiddleName	The static control that holds the subject's middle name.
IDC_LastName	The static control that holds the subject's last name.
IDC_NameBox	The static group box that surrounds the subject's names.
IDC_Father	The static control that holds the name of the subject's father.
IDC_FatherBox	The static group box that surrounds the name of the subject's father.
IDC_Mother	The static control that holds the name of the subject's mother.
IDC_MotherBox	The static group box that surrounds the name of the subject's mother.
IDC_PGFather	The static control that holds the name of the subject's paternal grandfather.
IDC_PGMother	The static control that holds the name of the subject's paternal grandmother.
IDC_MGFather	The static control that holds the name of the subject's maternal grandfather.
IDC_MGMother	The static control that holds the name of the subject's maternal grandmother.

continues

The ODBC Classes

Table 9.1. continued

ID	Description
IDC_Siblings	The list box control that holds the subject's siblings.
IDC_Children	The list box control that holds the subject's children.
IDC_Spouses	A simple combo box control that holds the subject's spouses. The current spouse is in the top box.

Use ClassWizard to build member variables in CTreeView corresponding to the controls just listed. Take special care to use the Value property for the CString variables and the Control property for the control variables. As ClassWizard establishes these variables, it also connects them to the dialog controls. These variables and connections are summarized in Table 9.2. Note that the group box items are omitted. We will work with the group box controls manually though their control IDs in Chapter 11.

Table 9.2. View controls and associated member variables.

Control ID	Member Variable	Description
IDC_FirstName	m_pSet->m_FIRST	Foreign variable linkage.
IDC_MiddleName	m_pSet->m_MIDDLE	Foreign variable linkage.
IDC_LastName	m_pSet->m_LAST	Foreign variable linkage.
IDC_Father	m_strFather	A CString variable.
IDC_Mother	m_strMother	A CString variable.
IDC_PGFather	m_strPGFather	A CString variable.
IDC_PGMother	m_strPGMother	A CString variable.
IDC_MGFather	m_strMGFather	A CString variable.
IDC_MGMother	m_strMGMother	A CString variable.
IDC_Siblings	m_ctlSiblings	A list box control variable.
IDC_Children	m_ctlChildren	A list box control variable.
IDC_Spouses	m_ctlSpouses	A simple combo box control variable.

So how do these controls get connected to their respective data members? The superficial answer to this question would be a discussion involving ClassWizard to attach the view/dialog's member variable to an associated member variable of a foreign object of CRecordSet descent. That's how we make the connection, but the real issue here is how the connection is made behind the scenes. How is the actual connection made between the database and the view/dialog? Another valid

question at this point is, do we really care? If ClassWizard handles all the messy details, why be concerned? To answer this question, let's look at Table 9.1 again. The first four items in this table are easy enough to hook up to the database. They are straight connections between view variables and record set variables. But the rest of the list consists of items that aren't held in the same record as the subject; some kind of record set manipulation must be done in order to retrieve this information. Okay, so now we *do* care about what goes on behind the scenes, and the connection question remains. In order to find the answer to that question, we must travel down a couple of twisty roads that raise even more questions. Such is the path of learning.

CFormView...CRecordView...CShoreView?

Before you can understand how to connect objects within your application, you must first gain familiarity with the individual objects. Many of these objects will already be familiar. The first seven chapters of this book were dedicated to making you familiar with many of the foundation classes. But the current application has a couple of new and different classes that you haven't seen before. In fact, the central visual object of our application is no longer an immediate descendent of a CView class. Our new view object descends from CRecordView, which descends from CFormView, which, finally, descends from CView.

The first stop on our magical ODBC mystery tour must be the CFormView class. CFormView is a hybrid of the CView and CDialog classes. When I say hybrid, visions of multiple inheritance and migraines no doubt come to mind. Let me put your mind at ease. CFormView is merely a CView class with aspects of a dialog. This isn't too much of a stretch, because both CView and CDialog are immediate descendants of CWnd. The dialog functionality is embedded in overridden CView methods. Consequently, aside from an updated constructor, CFormView has the same interface as CView. The only twist the new constructor presents us with is a dialog resource parameter. CFormView objects are based on dialog resources, so each constructor requires a dialog resource identifier. CFormView-derived classes created via AppWizard or ClassWizard have constructors that automatically tie the particular resource to the class object. The added benefit that these auto-built classes give you is support for tying the dialog controls to code via ClassWizard. The actual functionally involved with data transfer will be discussed at length in the next chapter.

There is a down side to having controls tied to the application's view. Dialog controls don't have any printer support; they can't draw themselves with a printer context. Consequently, CFormView-derived classes don't have default print or print preview support. Printing support must be wired in by hand. The general concepts of printing are discussed in Chapter 17.

Note: A dialog resource used in a CFormView class must be of a certain style. Just any dialog resource won't do. In the dialog editor in AppStudio, select the following styles in the Dialog Properties dialog:

DAY 9: The ODBC Classes

> - Select the Child option from the Style drop-down list box. If the resource were destined for a CDialog object, the option of choice would be Popup, because dialogs are pop-up windows. However, in our case, the resource is destined for a CFormView object, and form views are child windows.
> - None must be selected in the Border drop-down list box. Dialog objects need borders, but view objects are bordered by a frame object. Hence, resources destined for CFormViews must not have borders.
> - Clear the check boxes associated with the Visible and Titlebar attributes. View objects have their visibility managed by the framework, so the resource visibility must start off in a known state—off. Because the resource doesn't have a border, it can't have a title bar.
>
> These styles are automatically set properly when AppWizard prepares your resource-based dialog/view class. You will have to do this yourself if you manually prepare a CFormView-derived class and an associated dialog resource.

Learning about CFormView is all well and good, but our current application involves CRecordView. Going from CView to CFormView seemed easy enough, so it would be reasonable to expect that the transition from CFormView to CRecordView would be just as simple. You might even think that we're halfway home—that this will be a short chapter and that you can spend the rest of the day loafing on the couch. Nope. I'm afraid not. The CFormView explanation went so quickly because we already knew something about both CView and CDialog. CRecordView is the incorporation of CRecordset functionality into the CFormView class. Since we haven't even discussed CRecordset yet, you can see that CRecordView will take some time and pages for a full understanding.

Unlike the transition from CView to CFormView, the CRecordView transformation involves the addition of new functions. CRecordView has some new capabilities that stem from its connection to the data source. Most of this new functionality maps directly to the functionality of the associated CRecordset object. Table 9.3 lists the functions added to CRecordView.

Table 9.3. CRecordView's added functionality.

Function	Description
OnGetRecordset	Returns a pointer to the associated CRecordset object.
IsFirstRecord	Tests to see whether the associated record set is at the first record.
IsLastRecord	Tests to see whether the associated record set is at the last record.
OnMove	Changes the position in the associated record set.

The first function, OnGetRecordset(), returns a pointer to the associated record set object. The other three functions use OnGetRecordset() to obtain access to the database. IsFirstRecord()

checks the record set to see if it's currently positioned at the first record. Likewise, IsLastRecord() checks to see if the record set is positioned at the last record. However, due to the nature of CRecordset, IsLastRecord() will return TRUE only after you have established the end of the record set by moving past the last record. See the section titled "That's CRecordset, Not CRecordSet!" for more information on this quirk. The last new function added to CRecordView is the OnMove() function, which actually affects the underlying record set. You indicate the nature of the move by passing one of four movement command IDs to OnMove(). Table 9.4 lists the four OnMove() command IDs. OnMove() responds to each of these values by calling the appropriate CRecordset function. Normally, when dealing directly with the record set, you must be careful not to move past the last record or before the first, or exceptions will be thrown. OnMove() checks this for you, so you don't need to worry about exceptions.

Table 9.4. OnMove() constants and associated CRecordset commands.

Command ID	Handler	Description
ID_RECORD_FIRST	MoveFirst()	Moves to the first record.
ID_RECORD_LAST	MoveLast()	Moves to the last record.
ID_RECORD_NEXT	MoveNext()	Moves to the next record.
ID_RECORD_PREV	MovePrev()	Moves to the previous record.

Note: From the look of the constants in Table 9.4, you might conclude that they're menu commands. You would be correct; they *are* menu commands (and toolbar commands). The command messages are trapped in the CRecordView implementation and routed to the OnMove() function. This is done through a message map and specialized macros as shown:

```
BEGIN_MESSAGE_MAP(CRecordView, CFormView)
    //{{AFX_MSG_MAP(CRecordView)
    // NOTE - the ClassWizard will add and remove
    // mapping macros here.
    //}}AFX_MSG_MAP
    ON_COMMAND_EX(ID_RECORD_FIRST, OnMove)
    ON_UPDATE_COMMAND_UI(ID_RECORD_FIRST,
        OnUpdateRecordFirst)
    ON_COMMAND_EX(ID_RECORD_PREV, OnMove)
    ON_UPDATE_COMMAND_UI(ID_RECORD_PREV,
        OnUpdateRecordPrev)
    ON_COMMAND_EX(ID_RECORD_NEXT, OnMove)
    ON_UPDATE_COMMAND_UI(ID_RECORD_NEXT,
        OnUpdateRecordNext)
```

The ODBC Classes

```
    ON_COMMAND_EX(ID_RECORD_LAST, OnMove)
    ON_UPDATE_COMMAND_UI(ID_RECORD_LAST,
        OnUpdateRecordLast)
END_MESSAGE_MAP()
```

It's instructive to examine this code. At first glance, everything looks normal, but then you see that the `ON_COMMAND` macros are a little different. The `ON_COMMAND_EX` macro differs from the familiar `ON_COMMAND` macro in that it passes the command ID as a parameter to the associated function in addition to passing control. In this case, the `OnMove()` function is the recipient of both the command ID and the control path, which is exactly why `OnMove()` was designed the way it was. If you're curious as to the context of this message map, look up the DBVIEW.CPP file in your Visual C++ directory. It should be found in the MSVC\MFC\SRC directory.

Notice that the last three `CRecordView` functions rely heavily on the first function. `OnGetRecordset()` is a pure virtual function, so it must be overridden in the derived class. This mechanism ensures that `OnGetRecordset()` delivers only the most current information to its client functions. This is a wonderful illustration of the power of virtual functions. The implementation of the `OnGetRecordset()` function is written long after the implementations of functions that require it! In a sense, it's like passing information back in time—from the current object to an old implementation.

We now have a general idea of the `CRecordView`'s functionality. It's a view with a little bit of dialog and record set sprinkled in. Now that we've had a look at `CRecordView`'s upholstery and bucket seats, it's time to look under the hood. The central function that makes `CRecordView` useful to us is `OnMove()`. It is this function that implements movement commands that emanate from the menu or toolbar. Any measure of control we wish to assert over this movement will begin with an override of `OnMove()`. Recall our original problem: We were in a quandary as to how we were going to get parent and grandparent information from the record set. This information must be obtained and displayed each time we make a move in the record set. Hence, we must put this code in the override of `OnMove()`. But what does `OnMove()` really do? One sure way of finding out what a particular function does is to look up the implementation. Even the MFC library code is available for your perusal (see the preceding note). Of course, it's there only for instructive purposes. No guarantees are made as to its accuracy! However, it does give you a feel for how the function was written, and it can open your eyes to new coding techniques. It's also good to see library code as just plain code. It reminds you that there is nothing all that special about the libraries.

If you take a look behind the scenes at the implementation of the `OnMove()` function, you will see that basically it performs the following tasks:

- ☐ It commits any changes made to the current record.
- ☐ It performs the appropriate move (determined by the parameter).

- If either end condition is violated, it brings the record set back in line to a legitimate state (if possible).
- Finally, it calls `UpdateData(FALSE)` to update the dialog controls in the view with the new record set data.

That seems reasonable for what a move command should do. So reasonable, in fact, that we will call it in our override. ClassWizard doesn't support this function so we must (gasp!) put it in manually. While we're at it, let's also manually install a few other functions that will help `OnMove()`. Add the following two lines to the public operations section of `CTreeView`'s interface:

```
virtual BOOL OnMove (UINT nIDMoveCommand);
void UpdateRelatives();
```

and add the following line to the protected portion of `CTreeView`'s interface immediately after `OnInitialUpdate()`:

```
virtual void OnUpdate(CView* pSender, LPARAM lHint, CObject* pHint);
```

Add the following code to `CTreeView`'s implementation:

```
BOOL CTreeView::OnMove (UINT nIDMoveCommand)
{
    if ( CRecordView::OnMove(nIDMoveCommand) )
    {
        GetDocument()->UpdateAllViews(NULL);
        return TRUE;
    }
    else
        return FALSE;
}

void CTreeView::OnUpdate(CView* pSender, LPARAM lHint, CObject* pHint)
{
    CRecordView::OnUpdate(pSender, lHint, pHint);

    UpdateData(FALSE);
    UpdateRelatives();
}

void CTreeView::UpdateRelatives()
{
    // Add update code here!
}
```

The interaction between these three functions is quite interesting. `OnMove()` is called by the framework in response to a user event. If the base class `OnMove()` call is successful, the function updates all the views (via `UpdateAllViews(NULL)`) associated with our document. Of course, there is only one view at the moment, but we must plan ahead. During the processing of the `UpdateAllViews()` call, the `OnUpdate()` function of each view attached to the document is called. We override the `OnUpdate()` function to do any special preparation work for our view. In this particular case, `OnUpdate()` calls the `UpdateData()` and `UpdateRelatives()` functions. `UpdateData()`

The ODBC Classes

initiates the data transfer between the member variables and the dialog. `UpdateRelatives()` performs some application-specific manipulation of the data. We will discuss these functions in more detail as we progress through this chapter.

For your own edification, you might want to place a `TRACE` macro or a `MessageBox()` call in our override of the `OnMove()` function. This will assure you that `OnMove()` is indeed called when the record set is moved via menu or toolbar commands. It's important that you believe this in your heart—we don't want Tinkerbell's light to go out, do we? Later in this chapter, we'll implement the `UpdateRelatives()` function so that our main view is properly updated. First, however, we must learn about `CRecordset`.

The `CRecordset` connection is what makes `CRecordView` distinct from its predecessor views. Therefore, a true understanding of `CRecordView` can be achieved only through knowledge of `CRecordset`.

That's *CRecordset*, Not *CRecordSet!*

In Table 8.8 in Chapter 8, we described `CRecordset` as the "abstraction of a selected set of records from a database." It is that and more. It's your gateway to a table in a database. Through the record set object, you may select a subset of the table, search the selection, sort the selection, retrieve and edit individual records, and so on. It's a very powerful tool as long as you use it correctly. By the way, using it correctly entails writing it correctly. The class name is written `CRecordset`, not `CRecordSet`, much to my irritation (see the following note).

Note: One thing I must warn you about is the natural tendency to type `CRecordset` as `CRecordSet`. I make this typo every other time I work with the class (I'm improving; I used to do it every time). Why the MFC folks decided not to capitalize `set` is quite beyond me. Every other compound class name is written with mixed case. But not `CRecordset`, nooooo.... Oh well, that's my pet peeve for the day. Needless to say, the compiler doesn't share my peeve. It doesn't like the mixed-case version at all. Beware by being aware!

In AppWizard-generated applications with database support, a record set object is automatically installed into the document class. If you think about it, you'll understand that this is precisely the proper place for the record set. The document holds the application's data, but in the case of an ODBC application, the data is really held in the database itself. The record set does hold a copy of a record of a database table, which may be viewed and altered. This is the closest thing to a data object that your application will be able to access. Therefore, the record set object belongs in the document. However, the view class will need access to the record set object on a very frequent basis. To accommodate the view, AppWizard installs a pointer to a `CRecordset`-derived object in the `CRecordView`-derived class. You will note that the `CTreeView` class has an `m_pSet` attribute that is initialized (in `OnInitialUpdate()`) to point to the document's record set! But this is just a convenience. A reference of `m_pSet` is easier to write and, more important, easier to read than a reference of `GetDocument()->m_treeSet`. Where the record set is and how to gain access to it are two issues of concern to the beginning database class programmer. But what to do once you've gained access is of even greater concern. We will now discuss `CRecordset`'s functionality in detail.

One of the most fundamental issues regarding the `CRecordset` class (or any class, for that matter) is the means of setting up and taking down a particular instance. Each record set instance represents a selection of records from the associated database table. The `CRecordset` class provides the functions listed in Table 9.5 for the construction, initialization, and shutdown of record sets.

Table 9.5. `CRecordset` administrative functions.

Function	Description
`CRecordset`	A constructor that sets up a record set and connects it to a database.
`Open`	Associates the record set with a database, constructs and performs the defined query, and prepares it for interaction.
`Close`	Closes the record set and database connection.
`Requery`	Updates the record set with current database information by resubmitting the record set's query.

`CRecordset`'s constructor serves a dual purpose—it prepares the record set for initialization, and it also connects the record set to a database object. The constructor has a single parameter that is a pointer to an existing `CDatabase` object. If a `NULL` pointer is passed, the constructor creates a new `CDatabase` object associated with the appropriate data source. In most cases, you will let the record set create and connect to a default `CDatabase` object. However, sometimes an instance of the appropriate `CDatabase` object is available. It's much more space-efficient to use an existing `CDatabase` than to create a new one. In these cases, you will want to pass the `CDatabase` object pointer to the `CRecordset` constructor.

Once the record set object is constructed, it must be opened in order to perform any manipulations. These manipulations include moving about within the selection, adding records to the selection, editing records in the selection, testing the status of the record set, testing the status of the current record, testing the status of a specific field in the current record, requerying the record set, and closing the record set. The most important thing to keep in mind is that you may only perform these manipulations on an open record set! Another important tidbit of knowledge is that you must close a record set when you're through with it. What happens to the record set between `Open()` and `Close()` is the primary subject of the remainder of this chapter. But before we get ahead of ourselves, let's take a closer look at `Open()`.

The record set's behavior is determined by the parameters you pass it via the `Open()` function. `Open()` has three parameters, all of which have default values. Therefore, you can open the record set with a simple parameterless call to `Open()`. In fact, you'll find that this is the most common way to open a record set. The default choices are the ones typically desired. Table 9.6 lists `Open()`'s parameters and parameter choices.

Table 9.6. CRecordset::Open() parameter choices.

Parameter	Choices
`UINT nOpenType = snapshot`	Snapshot, dynaset, or `forwardOnly`.
`LPCSTR lpszSql = NULL`	NULL, table name, SQL statement, or the `CALL` statement.
`DWORD dwOptions = defaultOptions`	`defaultOptions`, `appendOnly`, or `readOnly`.

There are two types of `CRecordset` objects: snapshot and dynaset. The distinction between the two lies in how the object reflects the status of the database. A snapshot record set is a static copy of the table subset. Even if other users are manipulating the database, the snapshot remains stable. This is important if you're performing some table-wide computation or if you're constructing a report from disparate elements of the table. The snapshot can be updated with new information quite easily by the `Requery()` function call. The dynaset, on the other hand, reflects the current state of the database. If other users are manipulating the database, you will see the changes in a dynaset simultaneously (or nearly so). Both snapshots and normal dynasets support database reading and writing. However, a variation on the dynaset theme, the `forwardOnly` dynaset, doesn't support changes to the database. This is a read-only dynaset that is restricted to forward scrolling. The `forwardOnly` dynaset is typically used for massive data transfers where only forward scrolling is needed and up-to-date data is a must. Choosing one type over another depends on the needs of your application. For most needs, the snapshot record set is more than adequate. It's the default choice in the `Open()` function, and it's what we will use.

Note: Not only can `CRecordset`-derived classes represent selections from a table, but they also can represent other database entities. You can derive a `CRecordset` class to represent a join of multiple tables from the same data source. This type of object may hold and process data from more than one table. Another type of CRecordset object you can construct is a predefined database query. A database query is a question you pose to the database concerning its data. Most queries return a set of records as a response. Clearly, these queries need a destination where the set of records may be stored—a record set. Other queries don't return anything. You may still represent them as a CRecordset class, but since nothing is returned, it's common to eliminate the unnecessary record set and submit such queries directly to the database via the ExecuteSQL() function.

The second parameter in the Open() function is the string lpszSql. When this parameter is NULL, the record set automatically uses the whole database table associated with the record set. This is usually what we want anyway, so again we choose the default. However, at times you might want to get a little fancy and be more explicit as to the SQL call that underlies the record set. One alternative to the NULL parameter is to specify the table name yourself through the lpszSql parameter. This will connect the record set to whatever table you specify (as long as it's in the previously associated data source). Of course, a true connection can't be made this way unless the DoFieldExchange() function also reflects the specified table's fields. We'll talk more about DoFieldExchange() in the next chapter. Another option for the lpszSql parameter is to directly specify the SQL statement in its entirety. This truly cuts out the middleman. In this scenario, you spell out the query in no uncertain terms. For example, you could pass the following SQL statement string to the record set:

```
"SELECT ID,LAST,FIRST,BIRTHDATE FROM PERSON"
```

Don't get too full of your power. Open() may still append WHERE and ORDER BY clauses to the SQL statement, depending on certain conditions. These other conditions will be explored in a moment.

The last parameter in the Open() function is dwOptions. This parameter specifies the read/write nature of the record set object. The default option (defaultOptions—pretty original, huh!) is the most useful. It allows full access to the records. Using this option, you may edit, delete, and append records. The remaining two options are increasingly more restrictive and self-explanatory. The appendOnly option allows only appending records, not deleting or editing. The readOnly option allows (yes, you guessed it) only the reading of the records. No changes whatsoever can be affected on the database.

Note: You might be wondering where the record set is opened in AppWizard's default application. If you look through the wizard-generated code, you will be hard-pressed to find any Open() statements at all. Your first instinct is to look at the

Day 9 — The ODBC Classes

> document class. This is where the record set object is stored, so this must be where it is initialized, right? Wrong! You can look high and low, but you won't find a call to the record set's `Open()` function. You might eventually conclude that it must be magic. However, when you get stuck, always remember the trick of looking at the predefined class implementations. It's here that you can find the answer. In the `CRecordView::OnInitialUpdate()` implementation, the view class opens the record set by using the same virtual function trick found in `CRecordView`'s movement functions. There's no magic, unless you still find mystery in the way virtual functions work.

Each `CRecordset` object contains six public attributes, which are listed in Table 9.7. These attributes help define the query that will build the record set selection. Proper use of the attributes can mean the difference between an efficient, useful program and a slow, troublesome program.

Table 9.7. CRecordset's public attributes.

Attribute	Description
`m_hstmt`	The handle to the ODBC statement data structure for the record set.
`m_pDatabase`	The pointer to the underlying `CDatabase` object.
`m_nFields`	The number holding the number of fields in the record set.
`m_nParams`	The number holding the number of parameters in the query.
`m_strFilter`	The string specifying the filter that includes records. Used in the SQL WHERE clause.
`m_strSort`	The string specifying the sort order of the query results. Used in the SQL ORDER BY clause.

The first attribute is `m_hstmt`. This is a handle to the ODBC statement data structure for the record set. Fortunately for us, the use of this attribute is practically fully automated within the database classes. Only in certain circumstances is it necessary to manipulate it directly. It is an advanced topic that we will not pursue.

The second attribute, `m_pDatabase`, is a pointer to the underlying `CDatabase` object. It is in this attribute that the constructor places the database connection. The `Open()` function also uses this attribute to enable the `CDatabase` object if necessary. You will use this attribute when you want two record sets to share the same `CDatabase` object. As I mentioned earlier, the sharing of a `CDatabase` object is encouraged for space efficiency reasons.

The next two attributes, m_nFields and m_nParams, hold a count of the record set fields and record set parameters, respectively. The m_nFields parameter holds the number of fields in the record set. This isn't necessarily the number of fields in the associated table. The number of record set fields might differ from the number of table fields, depending on how many field member variables we (or rather, ClassWizard) have installed. The framework uses this information for managing information transfer between the record set and the underlying data source. This attribute is preinitialized through the AppWizard/ClassWizard-generated code. Of course, if you manually add fields, you must manually increment m_nFields.

The other count attribute, m_nParams, concerns itself with the number of parameters. This attribute initially is zero since AppWizard's default application doesn't include parameters. You will manually wire parameters into your application to facilitate changing a particular record set's query (and hence selection) at runtime. In essence, parameters are variables we insert in the SQL statement that constitutes the query. These variables may be changed at runtime to alter such things as sort order and the filtering mechanism. When we add parameters to the record set, we must commensurately increment the m_nParams attribute so that the framework will know of our parameters. Parameters are discussed in the section "Parameterization," which is devoted to parameterizing our record set.

The last two public attributes of a CRecordset object are strings associated with filtering and sorting the selection set. The selection set is assembled through the action of the record set's query. This query is built around a SQL SELECT statement and its modifiers and database table information. The two attributes under discussion are used by two of the SELECT statement's modifiers: WHERE and ORDER BY. The CRecordset object uses the strings contained in m_strFilter and m_strSort to construct, respectively, the WHERE and ORDER BY clauses that are appended to the SELECT statement. You don't have to use these attributes together (or at all, for that matter). You may use one, none, or both. By default, neither of the string attributes is used—they are empty initially. To make use of their abilities, you simply set them to an appropriate value before a query is constructed. Although queries are invoked during both an Open() and a Requery() function call, a query is constructed only in a call to Open(). Hence, in order for any changes to the sort or filter attributes to have an effect, they must be made prior to an Open() call. This restriction on Requery() isn't as bad as it seems as long as you're aware of it! The limitation can be sidestepped altogether through the use of parameters, as we shall see. But first, let's take a look at the following examples, which demonstrate the utility of the sort and filter parameters:

```
// Select all records with last name Shaw and sort on first name
m_pSet->m_strFilter = "LAST = 'Shaw'";
m_pSet->m_strSort = "FIRST";
m_pSet->Open();

// Select all male members of the database with last name Shaw
m_pSet->m_strFilter = "IS_MALE = 1 AND LAST = 'Shaw'";
m_pSet->Open();
```

Day 9: The ODBC Classes

```
// Sort the selection by birthdate
m_pSet->m_strSort = "BIRTHDATE";
m_pSet->Open();
```

Naturally, the preceding code could not exist sequentially as stated because exceptions will be thrown if you attempt to open a record set that's already open. This code is only for demonstration purposes. But surrounding any of the open commands with either an exception handling block or altering it like the following would make it safe:

```
// If the record set is open, close it and reopen it with the
// modified query
if ( m_pSet->IsOpen() )
    m_pSet->Close();
m_pSet->Open();
// The selection now reflects any attribute changes
```

The database classes are especially prone to throw exceptions when erroneous conditions occur. Therefore, you must be extra cautious when performing any database class function calls.

Thus far in our discussion of CRecordset, we have explored functions that affect the record set as a whole. As a rule, our record set manipulations will be on a smaller scale. Since the whole purpose behind the database and record set classes is the storage and retrieval of data, we typically interact with a record set at the level of records and fields. Let's regress for a moment and see where the record set fields originated.

In order for the wizards to be able to create a CRecordset-derived class, the associated database table must be specified. The wizard can then create member variables corresponding to each of the fields in the associated table. By default, all the field members are connected to these member variables. You can, of course, instruct ClassWizard to remove any or all of these variables. But it is through these member variables that you have access to the data held in the database. The collection of member variables constitutes one record in the record set. The CRecordset object provides functions that allow you to move among the records in the database. Table 9.8 lists the CRecordset movement functions. By the way, these are the functions that underlie CRecordView's OnMove() function.

Table 9.8. CRecordset movement functions.

Function	Description
Move	Moves the position of the record set a given number of records forward or back.
MoveFirst	Moves the record set to the first record in the selection.
MoveLast	Moves the record set to the last record in the selection.
MoveNext	Moves the record set ahead one record.
MovePrev	Moves the record set back one record.

 Warning: Trying to move to an illegal position will result in a CDBException!

Indiscriminate movement isn't supported. If you try to move past the last record or before the first record, you'll have problems. Actually, you will have an exception thrown to you. We could construct a TRY-CATCH block around every move statement and handle the problem that way, but the best way to handle a problem is to avoid it in the first place! To that end, the functions in Table 9.9 are provided.

Table 9.9. CRecordset status functions.

Function	Description
CanAppend	Tests whether the record set currently supports appending. It returns TRUE if you can add new records.
CanRestart	Tests whether the record set can be restarted. It returns TRUE if you are allowed to call the Requery() function.
CanScroll	Tests whether the record set can be scrolled. It returns TRUE if the record set supports the movement functions.
CanTransact	Tests whether the record set supports transactions. See the note following this table.
CanUpdate	Tests whether the record set can be updated. It returns TRUE if the record set can be edited.
GetRecordCount	Returns the current record count (not necessarily the total).
GetSQL	Returns the SQL string constructed and used by Open().
GetStatus	Returns a structure containing the current index and a flag that indicates whether all the records have been visited.
GetTableName	Returns the name of the record set's database table.
IsBOF	Tests whether the current record position is before the first record.
IsEOF	Tests whether the current record position is after the last record.
IsOpen	Tests whether the record set is open.
IsDeleted	Tests whether the current record has been deleted. See the discussion of the CRecordset::Delete() function in Chapter 11.

The ODBC Classes

> **Note:** A database transaction is a collection of database interactions that may be made permanent or aborted. A transaction may represent a particular session you've had with the database. Every command, addition, or update you make is held in a transaction. A session stored in this way may be rolled back—the database expression for undone or aborted. Rolling back the database turns back the hands of time; the database will be as if the transaction never took place. On the other hand, if the session went well and you want to keep the changes, you can commit the transaction. This makes the changes permanent and a roll-back impossible. Some databases support the concept of transaction, and others don't. The CanTransact() function distinguishes between the two. If transactions are supported by the database driver, you can realize them through the following CDatabase functions: BeginTrans(), CommitTrans(), and Rollback().

These functions are invaluable for discerning the exact status of your record set. Using these functions, you can determine whether a particular command will work *before* you call the function. Let's see an example of how to use these functions to get information about our CRecordset object.

Use AppStudio to add a new popup menu named Info and a menu item named Recordset. Use ClassWizard to add the command handler for this new menu item to our document class. Its implementation follows:

```
void CTreeDoc::OnInfoRecordset()
{
    TRACE1("Recordset's associated table: %s\n",
           m_treeSet.GetTableName());
    TRACE1("Recordset's SQL statement: \n%s\n",
           m_treeSet.GetSQL());

    TRACE0("\nRecordset Attributes:\n");

    if (m_treeSet.IsOpen())
        TRACE0("Recordset is open.\n");
    else
        TRACE0("Recordset is NOT open.\n");

    if (m_treeSet.CanAppend())
        TRACE0("Can Append\n");
    else
        TRACE0("Can NOT Append\n");

    if (m_treeSet.CanRestart())
        TRACE0("Can Restart\n");
    else
        TRACE0("Can NOT Restart\n");

    if (m_treeSet.CanScroll())
```

```
            TRACE0("Can Scroll\n");
        else
            TRACE0("Can NOT Scroll\n");

        if (m_treeSet.CanTransact())
            TRACE0("Can Transact\n");
        else
            TRACE0("Can NOT Transact\n");

        if (m_treeSet.CanUpdate())
            TRACE0("Can Update\n");
        else
            TRACE0("Can NOT Update\n");

        CRecordsetStatus rssObj;
        m_treeSet.GetStatus(rssObj);
        TRACE1("The index of the current record is: %li\n",
               rssObj.m_lCurrentRecord);

        CString S = "%li is the record count and that's ";
        if (rssObj.m_bRecordCountFinal)
            S = S + "final\n";
        else
            S = S + "NOT final\n";

        TRACE1 (S, m_treeSet.GetRecordCount());

        if (m_treeSet.IsBOF())
            TRACE0("Current position is BOF\n");
        if (m_treeSet.IsEOF())
            TRACE0("Current position is EOF\n");
}
```

Executing this code (by choosing Info | Recordset) results in the following diagnostic output (note that I reformatted the SELECT statement for ease of viewing):

```
Recordset's associated table: PERSON
Recordset's SQL statement:
SELECT ID,LAST,FIRST,MIDDLE,MAIDEN,IS_MALE,
    WHERE_BORN,WHERE_DIED,FATHER,MOTHER,
    OCCUPATION,NOTES,PORTRAIT,INTERRED FROM
    PERSON FOR UPDATE OF

Recordset Attributes:
Recordset is open.
Can Append
Can Restart
Can Scroll
Can NOT Transact
Can Update
The index of the current record is: 0
1 is the record count and that's NOT final
```

This glob of information might not hold a great deal of interest for you right now, but it is all pertinent database information. Trust me, it will peak your interest when you try to code your own ODBC application. Most of the results of the OnInfoRecordset() function should be no

The ODBC Classes

mystery to you, but a couple of functions could use some clarification. The `GetRecordCount()` function returns a count of the records visited by the record set object during the application's immediate execution. Unless you've scrolled the record set through all the records since you've started the application, `GetRecordCount()` won't return the total number of records. If you're thinking that `MoveLast()` will make quick work of this problem, think again. The only way that `GetRecordCount()` will return a correct count is to scroll, one record at a time, through the database from front to back. To determine whether `GetRecordCount()` will return a correct value, you may consult the `GetStatus()` function. `GetStatus()` returns a `CRecordsetStatus` object whose structure is the following:

```
struct CRecordsetStatus
{
    long m_lCurrentRecord;
    BOOL m_bCountFinal;
}
```

The first element of this structure holds the index of the current record. The second element holds a flag that indicates whether the entire record set selection has been traversed. If the selection has been traversed (from front to back), `GetRecordCount()` returns the total number of records in the current record set selection. Experiment with the application, moving the record set position and checking the record set information. Confirm that the `MoveLast()` function doesn't update the record count. In fact, it corrupts the index of the current record! Only moving back to the first item of the record set will restore the integrity of this index.

Also notice that the `IsBOF()` and `IsEOF()` functions always seem to return `FALSE`. This doesn't mean that you can't reach these limits. So far, we've been using the toolbar buttons to navigate through the database table. These buttons have safeguards built into them that prevent us from going past the upper and lower limits of the record set. But the only way for `CRecordView` to know it has reached the upper or lower limit is in the utilization of `IsBOF()` and `IsEOF()`. This is why the toolbar buttons and menu commands aren't grayed out until we try to move past the first or last record. This little quirk of `CRecordView` can be blamed on `CRecordset`'s `IsBOF()` and `IsEOF()` functions. Soon we will be working without a net, so we will need these functions to retain our balance as we walk the fine line of ODBC programming (oooo, what imagery!). See Figure 9.2.

`IsBOF()` and `IsEOF()` have an alternative purpose. Using these functions in tandem, you can determine whether the record set has any records in it. If both functions return `TRUE`, your record set is empty. As clumsy as it looks, this is the easiest way to make that determination. You will often see conditional statements like the following in code that uses the `CRecordset` class:

```
if ( m_pSet->IsBOF() && m_pSet->IsEOF() )
{
    // Record set is empty
    // Do NOT perform any record manipulations
}
else
```

```
{
    // Record set has records available
    // Record manipulations may proceed
}
```

Practical examples of this technique can be found in almost all functions that deal directly with a record set object. As a matter of fact, if you look closely at the implementation of `CRecordView::OnMove()`, you'll find `IsBOF()` and `IsEOF()` featured prominently.

Figure 9.2.
Walking the fine line of ODBC programming.

I Vant to Connect Your Blood Relations

At this point, we can go back to the original problem that launched us into our current exploration of the database classes: What can we do to reflect our familial relations in the record view? The main subject of the view can be connected directly to the document's record set object. This is because the name of the subject is completely contained within the current record of the record set. Blood ancestors, on the other hand, are specified only by reference. In order to obtain their names, we must perform a separate search through the database, looking for their IDs. Once found, their names may be placed in static controls and displayed. A separate search must be made for each blood ancestor! Siblings, children, and spouses present their own problems that we must confront when the time comes. Let's first connect the direct blood ancestors to the record view.

No doubt your first instinct is to use the prepared record set object located in the document—the same record set object we've been using via the `CRecordView` controls. This is not a bad instinct. It's always a good idea, for efficiency reasons, to use existing objects when you can, as long as such use doesn't violate data integrity or code comprehension. You could argue that using an existing record set to obtain information about the table it is already set up to manipulate is a legitimate use. I believe that the document's record set object should always be positioned at the currently displayed subject. Any movement from the current subject would constitute a violation of data integrity. If, for example, something went wrong in the search, the record set

The ODBC Classes

could be left in a different position than that displayed by the view. I also believe that such a double use of the record set would lead to confusing code and a degradation of comprehension. Each engineer has varying degrees of compulsiveness: What one engineer believes to be true, another can, rightfully, shun. Fortunately, I have other reasons to use a second record set object in our secondary searches.

First, it will demonstrate how to set up your own record sets. This is an important ability to cultivate. Second, we will use a parameter to let the database do our searching for us. By parameterizing the record set class and passing an appropriate filter parameter, we can pick out a particular person by specifying his or her ID. To accomplish this feat, the Open() function must be called. Closing and reopening the document's record set is surely over the line in terms of document stability and thus also justifies the use of a second record set. Finally, by using an alternative record set, we may perform our search and not have to worry about positioning the original record set at the previous position so as to resynchronize the record set with the view.

In order to accomplish these separate searches, we need our own autonomous record set. Because our need for the record set object is on a temporary basis, we can declare it local to the particular function that's doing the search and retrieval. The display updates must occur within the context of the view, so it's natural to put the search and retrieval functions in the view class. These decisions set the stage of what happens where, but the breakdown of functionality is still in the air. Let's consider what must be done and how we can efficiently capture it in database class functionality.

One of the most fundamental tasks that must be accomplished in these search-and-retrieval operations is finding a particular ID. Given a person's ID, we would like to be able to dredge up all the pertinent information about that person. The best way to implement a search is to pass the work to someone else—in this case, the database. With proper preparation, we can make the database do our searching for us. We accomplish this through record set parameterization. In the discussion of CRecordset's m_strParam attribute, an allusion was made to parameterization, but no firm information was given. We will remedy that situation presently.

Parameterization

Parameterization of a record set is accomplished through the insertion of variables (parameters) into the SQL statement that defines the record set. These variables may be altered while the record set is open, and a Requery() command will update the record set commensurate with these altered variables. The parameter variables are utilized within the SQL statement through the use of question marks. Each question mark serves as a placeholder for a parameter value. You may place the question marks in any appropriate spot within the SQL statement. Typically, though, you place a question mark in the filter or sort attribute members of the record set. The Open() statement then incorporates the filter/sort strings into the SQL statement—question marks included! Immediately before the query (caused by either Open() or Requery()), the question marks are filled in with the submitted parameter values. For example, if we parameterized our Family Tree record set with a string parameter, we could force the record set's selection to include only records with the last name equaling Smith. We could then change the parameter to select records with the last name Jones. Assuming such a parameterization, this could be accomplished as shown:

```
pSet->m_strFilter = "LAST = ?";
m_strLastNameParam = "Smith";
pSet->Open();
// Record set contains only "Smith" records

m_strLastNameParam = "Jones";
pSet->Requery();
// Record set contains only "Jones" records
```

Parameterization might not seem like such a big deal. All it saves you is having to close and then reopen the record set with an altered SQL command. However, remember that the `Open()` function does more than just rebuild the SQL statement; its implementation is quite involved. `Open()` has to check the validity of the database object. It has to confirm that the underlying driver supports all the options specified in `Open()`'s parameters. And so on... The list is nauseatingly long. Look up the implementation of `Open()` only if you have a strong constitution. I'm glad I didn't have to write it. `Requery()`, on the other hand, is a lean, mean function that doesn't need the overhead that's required in the `Open()` implementation. The bottom line is: `Requery()` is faster than `Open()`. But that shouldn't surprise anyone; the record set must be open before you can use `Requery()` in the first place! Naturally, it would be faster. The beauty of parameterization is that you can take advantage of this speed.

Once you parameterize a record set, searches and sorts can be accomplished easily. But don't think that you've given anything up in your parameterization efforts. If you don't put any question marks in the SQL statement, no parameterization effects will be seen—good or bad. You won't receive error messages for not utilizing your parameters. Just because you parameterized the record set doesn't mean that you have to employ its use for every query! In fact, for our application we will parameterize `CTreeSet`, but we won't use this parameterization on the document's instance of the record set. We will use the parameterization on temporary record sets devoted to searching.

Building parameterization into a record set isn't as complicated as it might at first look. The following steps show the parameterization process in action with `CTreeSet`:

1. Add the following parameter member variable to `CTreeSet`'s interface in the Field/Param Data section but outside ClassWizard's `AFX_FIELD` code block:

   ```
   double m_fIDParam;
   ```

   The naming convention for parameter member variables is to append the word `Param` to each parameter. This convention, along with the usual foundation class naming notation, results in the parameter name you see.

Day 9: The ODBC Classes

2. Add the following two lines to the implementation of `CTreeSet`'s constructor. Again, place them below ClassWizard's code block:

   ```
   m_nParams = 1;
   m_fIDParam = 0;
   ```

   Recall `m_nParams` from our discussion of `CRecordset` attributes. We set it at 1 to indicate to the record set that it now has one parameter. The second line merely initializes the parameter to 0.

3. Finally, you must add the following two lines to `CTreeSet`'s `DoFieldExchange()` function to formalize the passing of parameters to and from the database driver:

   ```
   pFX->SetFieldType (CFieldExchange::param);
   RFX_Double(pFX, "IDParam", m_fIDParam);
   ```

   The first line tells the `CFieldExchange` object to expect parameters. The second line (and potentially subsequent lines) performs the actual transfer of parameter data.

We will discuss the data transfer mechanism in the next chapter. For now, concentrate on the idea of parameters. The particular transfer function used in the final step is dedicated to `double` values, so we used it for our `m_fIDParam` parameter. If you want to install other types of parameters, you must choose the appropriate `RFX_type()` function. Another important issue regarding parameters is that they are ordered. In other words, when you have multiple parameters, the order of their transfer functions is the order in which they will be used in the SQL statement. For example, say we incorporated two parameters in a record set—`m_nOneParam` and `m_strTwoParam`. After constructing an instance of the record set, we set its filter to `FIELD1 = ? AND FIELD2 = ?`. When we open or later requery this record set, the order of placement of the two parameters' values in the SQL statement is determined solely by the order of the RFX transfer functions in `DoFieldExchange()`.

Note: Multiple-word field names present the programmer with a couple of quirks that you must be aware of lest you go insane. When referencing such a field, you must gather the parts of the name within square brackets so that the database driver can recognize the name as a single entity. If you were sorting or filtering on a multiple-name field, you would have to employ brackets like this:

```
pSet->m_strSort = "[Last Name]";
pSet->m_strFilter = "[First Name] = ?";
```

If you leave out the square brackets, you will get a runtime error that is somewhat difficult to track down. This can be maddening, in fact, especially when you don't know about this quirk. When in doubt as to the particulars of this convention, just look up how a wizard does it by examining the `DoFieldExchange()` function in your

> record set. Its transfer functions must deal with the record set fields in the same manner and therefore can serve as examples.
>
> The FoxPro driver we've been working with doesn't allow much flexibility in field names. It is restrictive as to the name's length, case, and number of words. When you create a FoxPro table, the driver will automatically convert the name to uppercase and replace any spaces with underscores. This defeats the problem before it occurs—although it does so at the expense of slightly less readable field names.

CTreeSet is now parameterized, albeit with a single parameter. Its parameterization revolves around the IDs that uniquely identify records in the Person table. One last thing remains to be done to CTreeSet in order to make it even more usable to our application. Our main view consists almost entirely of full names of various relatives. Because the names in the record set are split into three or four respective parts, it's a good idea to make a standard function that will return a formatted full name. This function belongs in CTreeSet. Add the following two lines to a public portion of CTreeSet:

```
enum NameFormat {Casual_Name, Formal_Name};
CString FullName(NameFormat nFormat = Casual_Name);
```

and add the following code to CTreeSet's implementation:

```
CString CTreeSet::FullName(NameFormat nFormat)
{
    CString S;

    switch (nFormat)
    {
        case Casual_Name:
        S = m_FIRST + " " + m_MIDDLE + " " + m_LAST;
        break;

        case Formal_Name:
        S = m_LAST + ", " + m_FIRST + " " + m_MIDDLE;
        break;

        default:
        TRACE0("Undefined case encountered"
            " in CTreeSet::FullName().");
        ASSERT(FALSE);
    }

    return S;
}
```

We may now put together some CTreeView functions that will aid the UpdateRelatives() function in building our view. Add the following lines to CTreeView's interface:

The ODBC Classes

```cpp
private:
    // Reset view's member string names to a constant ("?????")
    void ResetStrings();

    // Given an open CTreeSet object with a filter parameterized as
    // "ID = ?" and a subject ID, GetMomDad will find and pass back
    // the full names of the subject's mom and dad
    void GetMomDad(CTreeSet* pSet, double fSubjectID,
                CString& strMom, CString& strDad);

    // The following three functions will fill their respective controls
    // with the appropriate information
    void FillSpouses();
    void FillChildren();
    void FillSiblings();
```

These functions are defined to be private because their use should be controlled. Their use is intended to be exclusive to the `UpdateRelatives()` function. In particular, the `GetMomDad()` function is merely a functional localization of `UpdateRelatives()` code and therefore assumes certain conditions. If C++ allowed nested functions, I would have included `GetMomDad()` within `UpdateRelatives()`. As it stands, we must be careful of the use of `GetMomDad()`; hence, it is made private. The other functions have similar, though less critical, reasons.

Now we may add the following to `CTreeView`'s implementation:

```cpp
void CTreeView::ResetStrings()
{
    CString Unknown = "?????";

    m_strMother = Unknown;
    m_strFather = Unknown;
    m_strPGFather = Unknown;
    m_strPGMother = Unknown;
    m_strMGFather = Unknown;
    m_strMGMother = Unknown;

}

void CTreeView::GetMomDad(CTreeSet* pSet, double fSubjectID,
            CString& strMom, CString& strDad)
{
    BOOL bMomExists = FALSE;
    double fMom = 0;

    if ( !(pSet->IsOpen()) )
    {
        TRACE0("GetMomDad: Record set is not open!\n");
        return;
    }

    pSet->m_fIDParam = fSubjectID;
    pSet->Requery();
    if ( pSet->IsBOF() && pSet->IsEOF() )
    {
        TRACE0("GetMomDad: fSubjectID is invalid!\n");
        return;
```

```
        }
        // If the mother field is not NULL, save mother data
        if ( !pSet->IsFieldNull(&pSet->m_MOTHER) )
        {
            bMomExists = TRUE;
            fMom = pSet->m_MOTHER;
        }

        // If the father field is not NULL, retrieve the father's name
        if ( !pSet->IsFieldNull(&pSet->m_FATHER) )
        {
            pSet->m_fIDParam = pSet->m_FATHER;
            pSet->Requery();
            if ( pSet->IsBOF() && pSet->IsEOF() )
                TRACE0("Father ID invalid!\n");
            else
                strDad = pSet->FullName();
        }

        // Now go back and retrieve the mother's name if possible
        if (bMomExists)
        {
            pSet->m_fIDParam = fMom;
            pSet->Requery();
            if ( pSet->IsBOF() && pSet->IsEOF() )
                TRACE0("GetMomDad: Mother ID is invalid!\n");
            else
                strMom = pSet->FullName();
        }
}

void CTreeView::FillSpouses()
{
    // Stubbed
}

void CTreeView::FillChildren()
{
    // Stubbed
}

void CTreeView::FillSiblings()
{
    // Stubbed
}
```

The first function, ResetStrings(), simply resets all the strings that hold names of relatives. This ensures that there will be no holdover of names from the previous subject when the user moves the position in the record set. Changing the strings to question marks indicates that no information is available—an important condition for our genealogist users.

As I stated earlier, the GetMomDad() function is very particular as to the state of the record set pointer that is passed as a parameter. This passed record set must be open and parameterized.

The ODBC Classes

Further, its filter attribute must contain the value ID = ?. This allows GetMomDad() to easily search for the appropriate blood relations. The subject ID is also passed to indicate whose mom and dad we wish to obtain information about. The two strings parameters are holders for the names should we find any names. To determine whether a particular mother or father is even linked to the subject, the IsFieldNull() function is employed. Through this function we can determine if the m_MOTHER or m_FATHER field variables are valid. Remember, database NULL and C++ NULL are two different things! You can't determine whether a field variable is NULL by comparing it to the C++ NULL constant! Only passing the address of the record set's field member variable to the IsFieldNull() function will determine if the database field is NULL.

The GetMomDad() function implementation is also a good place to observe the use of Requery(), parameterization, and the IsEOF()/IsBOF() function pair. A close examination of this function can give you some insights into record set manipulation.

The last three functions are stubbed out; we will implement them in Chapter 11. I've included them here so that we may compile the application and get a feel for how our work is proceeding.

With these five helper functions defined, we may proceed to the UpdateRelatives() function:

```
void CTreeView::UpdateRelatives()
{
    // Make sure m_pSet is open
    if (!m_pSet->IsOpen())
    {
        TRACE0("Record set is not open in UpdateRelatives().\n");
        return;
    }

    ResetStrings();

    // Declare a new Person record set object
    // but use the same database object
    CTreeSet TS(m_pSet->m_pDatabase);

    BeginWaitCursor();
    TS.m_strFilter = "ID = ?";
    if ( TS.Open() )
    {
        // Get parent names
        GetMomDad(&TS, m_pSet->m_ID, m_strMother, m_strFather);

        // Get maternal grandparent names
        if ( !m_pSet->IsFieldNull(&m_pSet->m_MOTHER) )
            GetMomDad(&TS, m_pSet->m_MOTHER, m_strMGMother, m_strMGFather);

        // Get paternal grandparent names
        if ( !m_pSet->IsFieldNull(&m_pSet->m_FATHER) )
            GetMomDad(&TS, m_pSet->m_FATHER, m_strPGMother, m_strPGFather);

        TS.Close();
    }

    // Get spouses' names
```

```
    FillSpouses();

    // Get siblings' names
    FillSiblings();

    // Get children's names
    FillChildren();

    EndWaitCursor();

    UpdateData(FALSE);
}
```

A few items of interest should be pointed out in the UpdateRelatives() function implementation. First, note that in the construction of the local record set object, we use the existing CDatabase object constructed for the document's record set. Remember that sharing a CDatabase object is the efficient thing to do—when convenient.

The next item of interest we come to in UpdateRelatives() is the use of the BeginWaitCursor() function. This function is a member of CWnd that automatically loads the hourglass cursor. This cursor is the international Windows symbol for "Hold your horses, I'm working on it!" You use the hourglass cursor whenever you're performing a task that might take a little longer than the user expects. Database accesses can sometimes be slow, so this is an ideal use for the hourglass cursor. By calling EndWaitCursor(), we turn off the wait cursor when we're done with the extended task. You therefore can find the EndWaitCursor() call at the end of the UpdateRelatives() function.

Let's see if this pile of code is worth the electrons and phosphorus is takes to display it. Compile, link, and run the program. You should see something like Figure 9.3. Play around with the application and see if it does what you thought it would.

Figure 9.3.
Running the Family Tree application.

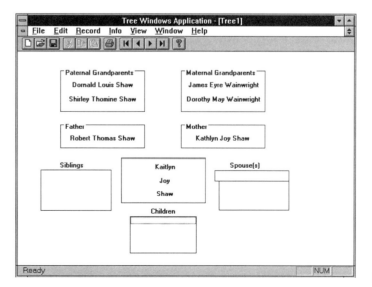

Day 9

The ODBC Classes

Summary

The ODBC database classes are Microsoft's answer to automated database programming. Through the use of CRecordView, CRecordset, CDatabase, CDBException, and CLongBinary, you can manipulate an underlying database in almost every way possible.

The MFC provides CRecordView to automate the abstract process of record scrolling and display. CRecordView is a combination of CView (its ancestor), a dialog, and a record set. It is an amalgam of functionality from all three of these classes. Sometimes it behaves like a dialog, using dialog controls to display and retrieve information about database fields. Other times it behaves like a record set, moving from one record to another in response to user commands (both menu and toolbar). Of course, it is most like its ancestor class, CView; it is a view window that allows us to display our data.

Of the five classes, CRecordset is by far the most important to the programmer. It is through this class that we may take control of the database. In fact, this class is an encapsulation of a selection of records from the database. The selection is determined by a SQL statement that is built by and, in turn, defines the record set. The CRecordset object has attributes that give us the ability to affect how the SQL statement is constructed. In this chapter, we used parameterization of the SQL statement to facilitate searches. Parameterization is a very flexible tool for record set management. It is typically used to make on-the-fly changes to the query, which speeds up changes to the filtering and sorting process.

Record set manipulation is an exacting process that requires the use of many different functions. This chapter explored the bulk of the record set functions, many of which concern the status of the record set. Despite our breadth of CRecordset knowledge, we still haven't gotten to the point of being able to change field data! This subject, as well as further information on the other database classes, will be addressed in the next chapter.

Q&A

Q Why don't the CRecordset functions MoveFirst() and MoveLast() work with the GetRecordCount() function?

A The simple answer to this is: efficiency reasons. Moving the record set position to the last element in the selection should be a quick operation. It would be far from quick if it entailed traversing the entire list of records in order to update the record count that might not even be used.

Q Whoa there, dude! In a previous chapter, you talked about isolating the application's data in the document class and using the view class only for user interface tasks. But in this chapter, you've stored data in the view class. What's the deal?

A You are absolutely correct. Application data should reside in the document class. However, just as in the dialog class, we sometimes need member variables in a form view class to serve as data waystations. We're not permanently storing data in the view; we're using the member variables as temporary storage to facilitate data display. Temporary data storage is certainly acceptable! If you don't believe me, think of the implementations of the dialog controls. They also store data in a temporary capacity for purposes of both display and retrieval.

Q When we perform searches of the database, the secondary record sets are used in a reading capacity only. Wouldn't it be better to open these search record sets as read-only?

A Yes, indeedy! I would like to say that I intentionally neglected to do that to see if anyone would notice. However, I just overlooked it. Good eye! Give yourself an "A" for the day.

Workshop

Quiz

1. Describe the functionality of CRecordView in terms of other foundation classes.
2. In an AppWizard-generated database application, where does the default record set object reside? Why should it reside there? Where is this default record set opened?
3. What are the main differences between CRecordset's Open() and Requery() functions?
4. How are the CRecordset attributes m_strSort and m_strFilter used in a database application?
5. Why would you use the IsFieldNull() function?

Exercises

1. Experiment with the various parameter combinations that Open() allows. See if forwardOnly can be used. If so, see if it is really enforced as forward-only. Try your hand at writing your own SQL statement. See just how much trouble you can get into!
2. Initialize the document's record set object to sort its selection by last name. Run the program to make sure that you've accomplished your task. Then change the sort attribute to order the selection by first name. Again make sure that you've accomplished the task. Now for the challenge. Make the record set sort its selection by both last name and first name.

The ODBC Classes

3. Add a second parameter of type `double` to the `CTreeSet` class. Use both parameters to search for subjects in the Person table with the same mother and father of a particular person. This exercise could form the core for a routine that fills the Children list box in our view.

Data Transfer and Stuff

WEEK 2

Data Transfer and Stuff

This chapter really isn't about any one topic. The last two chapters were based primarily on the ODBC classes, and we will still be exploring this topic here, but not without distraction. This chapter's theme concerns the hows and whys of data transfer. Computers and data transfer go hand in hand, so it's surprising that it has taken us this long to get to this point. But the topics surrounding computers are so intertwined that it's tough to decide which topic should come first. As it stands, we are in a position to tackle some of the most important data transfer issues in Windows.

Data transfer is a deceptively broad subject. It touches a number of different areas. Some we have seen, but others we haven't. In this chapter we will concentrate on the data transfers that occur between internal application objects. Even with this limited view of data transfer, we must still investigate a large number of topics. You know what this means—we're going on another whirlwind tour! We'll make a return visit to the shores of dialogs. The ODBC classes are, of course, a must this time of year. We will take another look at dialog controls. Finally, we will make a surprise visit to our very own CDate class. Oops! I guess it won't be a surprise anymore. Oh well. On our tour we will cover many important things that make our Family Tree application work the way we want it to. So put on your fedora and ready your whip, because we're goin' explorin'.

Dialog Data Exchange (DDX)

There is a special relationship between a dialog window and a dialog class. The dialog window is the "physical" object on your screen, and the dialog class is the abstraction in your code. Okay, okay, the dialog window isn't a physical object in any sense of the word. But in the Windows environment, a dialog window is a real object. The mere fact that the Windows environment itself is an image on your monitor without physical form or substance makes no difference. It's all a matter of perspective. To Windows, the dialog window is the real object. To us, the dialog window is an image, and the dialog class is real. However you look at it, the bottom line is that both objects are separate and distinct. This separation brings up the issue of what spans the gap. In other words, how is data transferred between the dialog window and the corresponding class? Data transfer? Hey, I knew we would get to that eventually!

Data transfer between the dialog window object and an object of CDialog class descent is accomplished through CDialog's (actually CWnd's) virtual function DoDataExchange(). You, however, don't call this function! DoDataExchange() is called as a result of a call to the UpdateData() function, which CDialog also inherits from CWnd. When UpdateData() is called, it is passed a Boolean parameter that indicates the direction of the data transfer. UpdateData(TRUE) initiates a transfer of data from the dialog controls to the associated dialog class member variables. This is done to retrieve information from the dialog window. Conversely, a parameter of FALSE would transfer data from the member variables to the dialog controls. This updates the dialog controls with class data, usually done during initialization. UpdateData() performs this transfer by passing the work on to the DoDataExchange() function.

The `DoDataExchange()` function is the centralized location for data transfer in your dialog classes. Within this function, data transfer is performed for each of the dialog controls individually. In order to support the bidirectional nature of data transfer promised by the `UpdateData()` function, `DoDataExchange()` also supports a bidirectional transfer mechanism. As in `UpdateDate()`, `DoDataExchange()` is alerted to the data direction through a single parameter. However, unlike `UpdateData()`, `DoDataExchange()`'s parameter is much more complicated than a simple Boolean value. `DoDataExchange()` requires more information, so its parameter is a pointer to a whole new class of object: `CDataExchange`.

`CDataExchange` is a class that contains information concerning a specific data transfer. It holds a flag that indicates the data transfer direction. It holds a pointer to the parent window of the controls. And it encapsulates functionality that facilitates the data transfer process. Tables 10.1 and 10.2 list `CDataExchange`'s attributes and operations, respectively.

Table 10.1. `CDataExchange`'s public attributes.

Attribute	Description
m_bSaveAndValidate	A Boolean flag indicating data transfer direction. TRUE implies that data will travel from the controls.
m_pDlgWnd	A pointer to the window holding the dialog controls.

Table 10.2. `CDataExchange`'s public operations.

Operation	Description
PrepareCtrl	Prepares a non-CEdit control for data transfer.
PrepareEditCtrl	Prepares a CEdit control for data transfer.
PrepareVBCtrl	Prepares a Visual Basic control for data transfer.
Fail	Called when a transfer function fails. It sets the input focus to the "failing" control. Warning: `Fail()` throws an exception!

The `m_bSaveAndValidate` attribute is akin to `UpdateData()`'s Boolean parameter; it indicates the direction of data transfer. It is this attribute that alerts the transfer function whether to save or to load data. The `m_pDlgWnd` attribute is a pointer to the parent window that holds the dialog controls. Typically this window is a dialog, but certain applications (like our current application) might use dialog-like containers for controls (`CFormView`, for example).

All but one of the public operations defined for `CDataExchange` concern themselves with dialog control preparation. This preparation is just the localization of a bunch of "housekeeping" busywork that each control must be subjected to in order for it to behave properly within the

Day 10: Data Transfer and Stuff

system. Three different preparations are available: non-`CEdit` control preparation, `CEdit` control preparation, and Visual Basic (VB) control preparation. As I mentioned earlier, Visual Basic controls are becoming obsolete due to OLE technology. We will therefore ignore the issues they bring up. The other two preparatory functions divide themselves between `CEdit` controls and non-`CEdit` controls. Actually, the preparation for `CEdit` controls is just a bit more specialized than the preparation for non-`CEdit` controls. All controls need a certain minimum preparation—`PrepareCtrl()`. This preparation begins with a number of `ASSERT` statements that ensure that the control is valid. `PrepareCtrl()` then saves a handle to the control just in case immediate future access to the control is needed. `PrepareEditCtrl()` calls `PrepareCtrl()` and also sets a flag indicating that the control was of the `CEdit` variety. Knowing that the control was a `CEdit` control allows other functions to make proper assumptions about the nature of the control. For example, if the flag indicates the presence of a `CEdit` control, the `Fail()` function will send a message that tells the edit control to highlight its text. It can do this only because the control is known to be an edit control.

Speaking of the `Fail()` function, what does it do? A transfer function calls the `Fail()` function whenever the transfer fails. The `Fail()` function, in turn, aborts the transfer and positions the input focus at the offending dialog control. If the offending control is an edit control, the associated text is highlighted (as I just mentioned). The transfer is blocked until the user enters the data in the appropriate format (or at least in the format acceptable to the transfer function). Using the `Fail()` function in your transfer functions is a big responsibility. Poor usage of `Fail()` can cause the user to be trapped in a dialog. On the other hand, you don't want to shy away from using the `Fail()` function either. It is a very handy little routine that can truly enhance your application. Another dangerous aspect of using the `Fail()` function is the fact that it generates an exception. That's right. As soon you call the `Fail()` function, an alternate flow of control is produced and you temporarily lose control. This is not a bad thing—as long as you expect it. Later in this chapter, we will see an example of this technique.

`CDataExchange` is a base class—it's not even derived from `CObject`. It is fundamental in this way both because it needs to be lean (what class doesn't?) and because it doesn't require the trappings that come with `CObject`. The `CDataExchange` objects are typically used internally by prebuilt data transfer functions, so the enhancements provided through the `CObject` class aren't necessary.

`CDataExchange` objects aren't used outside functions relating to data transfer, so you will seldom need to use them. Even within the `DoDataExchange()` function, the `CDataExchange` object is passed only to the functions that perform the actual data transfers—the DDX functions. Recall from Chapter 7 that DDX stands for dialog data exchange. Be careful not to confuse it with dynamic data exchange (DDE), which facilitates interprocess communications. Although the `DoDataExchange()` function is the centralized data transfer function, the DDX functions are built with specific data types in mind. Let's take a look at the `DoDataExchange()` function from the dialog class we created in Chapter 7 for the Software Lister application:

```
void CSWAddDlg::DoDataExchange(CDataExchange* pDX)
{
    CDialog::DoDataExchange(pDX);
    //{{AFX_DATA_MAP(CSWAddDlg)
    DDX_Control(pDX, IDC_Resolution, m_ctlResolution);
    DDX_Control(pDX, IDC_Rating, m_ctlRating);
    DDX_Control(pDX, IDC_Media, m_ctlMedia);
    DDX_Control(pDX, IDC_Categories, m_ctlCategories);
    DDX_Text(pDX, IDC_Phone, m_strPhone);
    DDX_Text(pDX, IDC_PurchasePrice, m_fPurchasePrice);
    DDX_Text(pDX, IDC_SWPublisher, m_strPublisher);
    DDX_Text(pDX, IDC_SWRegistration, m_strRegistration);
    DDX_Text(pDX, IDC_SWTitle, m_strTitle);
    DDX_Check(pDX, IDC_WinCompatible, m_bWinCompatible);
    DDX_Text(pDX, IDC_PurchaseDate, m_strPurchaseDate);
    //}}AFX_DATA_MAP
}
```

As you might recall, the Software Lister application was built to track information about your home software library. Its dialog served as the means to gather and alter existing data concerning the software products. For most of the controls, we wired data members directly to the data contained within the dialog controls. For example, the data held by the Purchase Price edit control is connected directly to the floating-point variable m_fPurchasePrice. During a control update, the value of the m_fPurchasePrice variable is used to fill the edit control. During a data retrieval, the m_fPurchasePrice variable is assigned the value contained in the edit control. This data transfer occurs automatically! The member variable serves as a way station for dialog data.

Sometimes you require a more hands-on approach. You might want access to the control itself. You can do this by having the actual control be a member object of the dialog class, where you may manipulate it directly. In the Software Lister application, m_ctlMedia is such a control variable. Access to the Media list box is made directly through the control variable. The variable is the control object!

We made both types of control linkages in Software Lister via ClassWizard. But all ClassWizard did was put the appropriate DDX functions in the DoDataExchange() function of the derived CDialog class. From the preceding code you can see that the DDX routines are used for both data transfer (DDX_Text(), DDX_Check(), and so on) and the establishment of member dialog controls (DDX_Control()). The DDX_Control() function prepares the respective dialog control for use. This preparation entails, among other things, the rerouting of command messages so that the parent class (the dialog class in this case) has the first shot at responding to the messages; any unhandled messages are sent to the control. This altered message processing has the effect of allowing the dialog class to contain dialog control message handlers. The dialog class can then intercept messages destined for a control and respond appropriately. Both approaches to dialog control management have their advantages and disadvantages. The choice of one over the other is determined by your particular needs. However, you will typically choose the automated approach because of its ease of use. The DDX functions are listed in Table 10.3.

Day 10: Data Transfer and Stuff

Table 10.3. DDX functions.

Function	Description
DDX_Control	Used for getting a pointer to the actual control.
DDX_Text	CEdit transfer function. Used for many types, including CString, int, long, float, double, and so on.
DDX_Check	Check box transfer function.
DDX_Radio	Radio button transfer function.
DDX_LBString	List box's selected string transfer function.
DDX_CBString	Combo box's selected string transfer function.
DDX_LBIndex	List box's index transfer function.
DDX_CBIndex	Combo box's index transfer function.
DDX_LBStringExact	List box's exact selected string transfer function.
DDX_CBStringExact	Combo box's exact selected string transfer function.

The entries in this table are relatively self-explanatory. However, the DDX_Text() entry actually represents a plethora of functions that allow transfer of various types of values to and from a CEdit control. Through the magic of overloading, all these functions bear the name DDX_Text(); they are distinguished by their parameter lists. This function is so helpful that you will seldom need to use any of the other functions. Of course, should the need arise, you might want to know what the deal is with the "exact" transfer functions. Why are there two sets of functions that seemingly perform the same transfer task? Specifically, what's the difference between DDX_LBString() and DDX_LBStringExact()? It depends on the direction of data transfer. If the data is coming from the controls, the "exact" functions are identical to the "normal" string transfers. When we are transferring information to the controls, things are different. The difference stems from the nature of list box and combo box controls. Each of these controls has two means of finding a particular string in its list. One method is searching for a prefix of a string. This finds the first string that has this prefix. The other method (which is available only on Windows 3.1 and later) is an exact-match method. Using this method, only exact matches of the string are found. As you have probably guessed, the "exact" string transfer functions select strings in the combo or list boxes only when an exact match is made. The "normal" string transfer functions select the first element in the list that has the appropriate prefix. The following example illustrates the difference.

Elements in a list or combo box (note zero-based index):

0	Yellow Snow
1	Snowman
2	Snowball
3	Snowblower
4	Snow
5	Snowflake

```
CString Snow = "Snow";
CString Snowb = "Snowb";
// Assume pDC->m_bSaveAndValidate = FALSE
DDX_LBString (pDX, IDC_LBItems, Snow);
// Item 1 will be selected in the list box. Selection matches prefix.
DDX_LBStringExact (pDX, IDC_LBItems, Snow);
// Item 4 will be selected in the list box. An exact match.
DDX_LBString (pDX, IDC_LBItems, Snowb);
// Item 2 will be selected in the list box. Selection matches prefix.
DDX_LBStringExact (pDX, IDC_LBItems, Snowb);
// No item is an exact match, so no list box selection is made!
```

Of course, the same results occur when the respective combo box transfer functions are used.

Dialog Data Validation (DDV)

The term *dialog data validation* is somewhat misleading. Data validation, at least in my mind, brings up thoughts of type validation—that is, making sure that an integer is an integer, a float is a float, and a string is a string. Okay, everything is a string, so that's a bad example—or is it? There is a DDV function that validates strings. Obviously my preconceived ideas of data validation don't jibe with DDV! In fact, type validation is done in the DDX functions. Try it with one of our previous applications—the ever-popular Software Lister. If you try putting a nonnumeric string in the Purchase Price edit box and click on the dialog's OK button, the dialog won't close. This action will result in a message box telling you of your error. After you close the message box, the invalid data in the dialog control in question is highlighted. If you look in the Software Lister's code, you will find only DDX functions. DDV functions don't check type; that's DDX's job.

So what kind of validation is performed in the DDV functions? Basically, the DDV functions carry out range or boundary checking. Table 10.4 lists the predefined DDV functions.

Day 10 Data Transfer and Stuff

Table 10.4. DDV functions.

Function	Description
DDV_MinMaxByte	Confirms that the BYTE value is between Min and Max.
DDV_MinMaxInt	Confirms that the int value is between Min and Max.
DDV_MinMaxLong	Confirms that the long value is between Min and Max.
DDV_MinMaxUInt	Confirms that the UINT value is between Min and Max.
DDV_MinMaxDWord	Confirms that the DWORD value is between Min and Max.
DDV_MinMaxFloat	Confirms that the float value is between Min and Max.
DDV_MinMaxDouble	Confirms that the double value is between Min and Max.
DDV_MaxChars	Confirms that the length of CString is less than or equal to the Max value.

You can see that most of the DDV functions concern themselves with numeric range checking. That is, most of the DDV functions check to see if a given number is within a specified range of values. This range checking nature of most of the DDV functions is indicated by the naming convention DDX_MinMax*XXXX*(), where *XXXX* is the particular type name. One DDV function in the preceding table stands out. The last entry, DDV_MaxChars(), is used to check strings for specified length requirements. This function is particularly useful in database applications, since the underlying database fields have a specified maximum length.

Like DDX functions, DDV functions may be installed manually or via ClassWizard. In ClassWizard's main dialog under the Member Variables tab, select a dialog class in the Class Name combo box. This brings up a list of dialog control IDs and corresponding variables (if any are installed). Just below the variable description toward the bottom of the dialog is enough space to hold edit boxes that will accept range restrictions. If you click on a numeric or string member variable in ClassWizard's dialog box, these range edit boxes will appear. By specifying a range for a variable, you are telling ClassWizard to install a DDV function. ClassWizard installs a DDV function in the DataExchange() function immediately after the DDX function corresponding to the same variable.

DDX_Field Functions

The DDX functions we have been discussing are intended for your average, run-of-the-mill application. They transfer data between the dialog window and your dialog class member variables. ODBC applications are far from run-of-the-mill, however. In terms of data transfer, ODBC applications often bypass dialog class member variables altogether. You might recall that in our current application we used "foreign variables" in the dialog class instead of member variables. The foreign variable in question was a pointer to a record set object. Through this pointer, the dialog class's `DoDataExchange()` function was able to connect the dialog directly to record set field members. Let's take a look at `CPersonDlg::DoDataExchange()`:

```
void CPersonDlg::DoDataExchange(CDataExchange* pDX)
{
    CDialog::DoDataExchange(pDX);
    //{{AFX_DATA_MAP(CPersonDlg)
    DDX_FieldText(pDX, IDC_BirthPlace, m_pSet->m_WHERE_BORN, m_pSet);
    DDX_FieldText(pDX, IDC_FatherID, m_pSet->m_FATHER, m_pSet);
    DDX_FieldText(pDX, IDC_FirstName, m_pSet->m_FIRST, m_pSet);
    DDX_FieldText(pDX, IDC_ID, m_pSet->m_ID, m_pSet);
    DDX_FieldText(pDX, IDC_Interred, m_pSet->m_INTERRED, m_pSet);
    DDX_FieldText(pDX, IDC_DeathPlace, m_pSet->m_WHERE_DIED, m_pSet);
    DDX_FieldText(pDX, IDC_LastName, m_pSet->m_LAST, m_pSet);
    DDX_FieldText(pDX, IDC_MaidenName, m_pSet->m_MAIDEN, m_pSet);
    DDX_FieldText(pDX, IDC_MiddleName, m_pSet->m_MIDDLE, m_pSet);
    DDX_FieldText(pDX, IDC_MotherID, m_pSet->m_MOTHER, m_pSet);
    DDX_FieldText(pDX, IDC_Notes, m_pSet->m_NOTES, m_pSet);
    DDX_FieldText(pDX, IDC_Occupation, m_pSet->m_OCCUPATION, m_pSet);
    //}}AFX_DATA_MAP
    DDX_FieldRadio(pDX, IDC_Female, m_pSet->m_IS_MALE, m_pSet);
    DDX_FieldText(pDX, IDC_Birthdate, m_pSet->m_BIRTHDATE, m_pSet);
}
```

From this code we may discern a slight difference between `DDX_` and `DDX_Field` functions (aside from the name). The `DDX_Field` functions have one more parameter than the `DDX_` functions. Take a look at the following two declarations for integer data transfer:

```
void AFXAPI DDX_Text(CDataExchange* pDX, int nIDC, int& value);
void AFXAPI DDX_FieldText(CDataExchange* pDX, int nIDC, int& value,
CRecordset* pRecordset);
```

The first three parameters of both functions are the same: a pointer to the `CDataExchange` object, the ID number of the dialog control, and the data to be transferred. The `DDX_Text()` function gets by fine with only three parameters, but the `DDX_FieldText()` function needs more. Since the `DDX_FieldText()` functions deal directly with record set data, they need a pointer to the record set in question in order to perform the appropriate validity checks. Is the record set pointer valid? Can the particular field we're working with be `NULL`? Can the field be written to? These questions, and others, can be answered only by direct interaction with the record set in question. The `DDX_Field` function performs these extra duties so you don't have to.

Record Field Exchange (RFX)

Once data reaches the record set object, how does it get transported to the database? Conversely, how is data fed into the record set object from the database? The answers to both these questions revolve around the issues of Record Field eXchange (RFX) functions. Actually, most of the record set functions that deal with specific database fields are accomplished through that particular field's RFX function.

Data Transfer and Stuff

There is a close analogy between the DDX and RFX functions, both in form and in function. The following list compares the two types of functions:

- DDX spans the gap between the dialog window and the dialog class. RFX spans the gap between the database and the record set class. Both types of functions span the gap between the real object (dialog window and database) and the abstraction (dialog class and record set class).
- Both DDX and RFX functions are specialized for particular types. In other words, there is a separate function for each distinct type to be transferred.
- The respective prototypes for integer transfer are

    ```
    void AFXAPI DDX_Text(CDataExchange* pDX, int nIDC, int& value);
    ```

    and

    ```
    void AFXAPI RFX_Int(CFieldExchange* pFX, const char *szName, int& value);
    ```

    The first parameter of both functions holds all the particulars for a transfer. The second parameter indicates the object holding the data (nIDC is the dialog control ID and szName is the name of the field). The last parameter is the actual value being transferred. As you can see, the form of the two types of functions is practically identical.

- Even the helper classes of CDataExchange and CFieldExchange are similar in form. Both hold information pertinent to the transfer at hand, and both are critical to the success of the transfer.

The first parameter in each RFX function is a CFieldExchange object. As I just alluded, CFieldExchange does for RFX what CDataExchange does for DDX—in general, that is. The specifics of CFieldExchange are considerably different from CDataExchange due to the huge difference between a database and a dialog. In order to better understand the role of the RFX functions, we must first get an idea of what the CFieldExchange object is all about.

Objects of the CFieldExchange class are used to indicate the specifics of a particular data transfer between the database and a record set class object. Tables 10.5 and 10.6 list the attributes and operations available for the CFieldExchange class, respectively.

Table 10.5. CFieldExchange's public attributes.

Attribute	Description
m_nOperation	The operation to be performed (type enum Operation).
m_prs	The pointer to the record set object.

Table 10.6. CFieldExchange's public operations.

Operation	Description
IsFieldType	Returns TRUE if the operation can be performed.
SetFieldType	Sets the type of record set data—column or parameter.

The m_nOperation attribute holds a value that indicates the operation being requested. This attribute holds one of the enumerated RFX_Operation values we'll discuss in a moment. It's a far cry from the simple Boolean flag used in CDataExchange to indicate the direction of data transfer. The second attribute is a pointer to the host CRecordset object. The record set must be specified in the CFieldExchange object for a complete description of the operation. For example, a StoreField operation is ambiguous in a multiple-record set environment. Besides which, there is still information stored in the record set object that is pertinent to data transfer. The bottom line is this: Access to the record set object is needed during data transfer, so the CFieldExchange object must be able to provide that access when necessary.

The two public member functions provided by CFieldExchange are for the sole purpose of managing the two types of record set data: columns and parameters. "Column" is the RFX word for normal field data—the data you store in your database. "Parameter" has the same meaning as the parameter we worked with earlier that facilitates sorting and searching. It might not seem clear right now why column and parameter types need managing. Actually, this is a very important issue. You might recall from our CTreeSet::DoFieldExchange() function (shown in the following code) that before any RFX transfer call is made, you must call the appropriate CFieldExchange's SetFieldType() specifying that you want to transfer column data.

```
void CTreeSet::DoFieldExchange(CFieldExchange* pFX)
{
    //{{AFX_FIELD_MAP(CTreeSet)
    pFX->SetFieldType(CFieldExchange::outputColumn);
    RFX_Double(pFX, "ID", m_ID);
    RFX_Text(pFX, "LAST", m_LAST);
    RFX_Text(pFX, "FIRST", m_FIRST);
    RFX_Text(pFX, "MIDDLE", m_MIDDLE);
    RFX_Text(pFX, "MAIDEN", m_MAIDEN);
    RFX_Bool(pFX, "IS_MALE", m_IS_MALE);
    RFX_Text(pFX, "WHERE_BORN", m_WHERE_BORN);
    RFX_Text(pFX, "WHERE_DIED", m_WHERE_DIED);
    RFX_Double(pFX, "FATHER", m_FATHER);
    RFX_Double(pFX, "MOTHER", m_MOTHER);
    RFX_Text(pFX, "OCCUPATION", m_OCCUPATION);
    RFX_Text(pFX, "NOTES", m_NOTES);
    RFX_LongBinary(pFX, "PORTRAIT", m_PORTRAIT);
    RFX_Text(pFX, "INTERRED", m_INTERRED);
    //}}AFX_FIELD_MAP
    pFX->SetFieldType (CFieldExchange::param);
    RFX_Double(pFX, "IDParam", m_fIDParam);
}
```

Day 10

Data Transfer and Stuff

After all the "real" data transfers have been completed, another call to SetFieldType() specifies that you now want to transfer parameter data. Once a call to SetFieldType() is made, the CFieldExchange object remains in that state until another SetFieldType() call changes it. The IsFieldType() function is used to determine if the current operation is compatible with the field (parameter or column) in question. Typically, this information is used in the RFX transfer functions to assess whether the current operation is viable for the field under scrutiny.

> **Note:** A CFieldExchange object may have three different values of field type. They are enumerated in this FieldType type:
>
> ```
> enum FieldType
> {
>     noFieldType,
>     outputColumn,
>     param
> };
> ```
>
> The last two values of this enumerated type match what we discussed in the text (outputColumn is the column field type and param is the parameter field type). The first value might seem strange at first, but after a moment's thought, you will see that it must be used as the default uninitialized value; no assumptions are made as to CFieldExchange's initial field type. You must explicitly set the CFieldExchange object to column or parameter—neither will be assumed!

The various operations available to m_nOperation are listed in the enumerated type RFX_Operation. Each enumerated value indicates the operation to be performed during the RFX transfer. Consequently, the RFX transfer functions must respond differently for every value of m_nOperation. Therefore, the main control structure in RFX transfer functions is typically a switch statement. Here is the enumerated type RFX_Operation:

```
enum RFX_Operation
{
    BindParam,    // Register users' fields with ODBC SQLBindCol
    BindFieldToColumn,    // Register users' fields with ODBC SQLBindCol
    Fixup,    // Set string lengths, clear status bits
    MarkForAddNew,
    MarkForUpdate,    // Prepare fields and flags for update operation
    Name,    // Append dirty field name
    NameValue,    // Append dirty name=value
    Value,    // Append dirty value or parameter marker
    SetFieldDirty,    // Set status bit for changed status
    SetFieldNull,    // Set status bit for null value
    IsFieldDirty,    // Return TRUE if field is dirty
    IsFieldNull,    // Return TRUE if field is marked NULL
```

```
    IsFieldNullable,   // Return TRUE if field can hold NULL values
    StoreField,        // Archive values of current record
    LoadField,         // Reload archived values into current record
    GetFieldInfoValue, // General info on a field via pv for field
    GetFieldInfoOrdinal,  // General info on a field via field ordinal
};
```

Microsoft put comments in this declaration to clarify the purpose behind each value. Obviously the RFX transfer functions do a lot more than just transfer data. It is through these functions that the record set manipulates the database. If you look at the implementation of `CRecordset` (see \MSVC\MFC\SRC\DBCORE.CPP), you'll see that some of the operations just shown are implemented via the `DoDataExchange()` function. For example, the function `CRecordset::IsFieldNull()` is implemented by first constructing a `CFieldExchange` object with the `m_nOperation` attribute set to the value `IsFieldNull`. The function then makes the appropriate connections between the `CFieldExchange` object and the field in question. Finally, the function calls the `DoDataExchange()` function, which in turn calls the RFX transfer functions. Although we usually associate the RFX functions with the transfer of "real" data, they are actually used for most communications with the database. Naturally, there are times when a direct SQL call to the database is necessary in both the predefined code as well as your own. However, the functions provided by the record set class are usually more than adequate for your needs.

The Bucket Brigade

All this data transfer can get confusing when you look at it in little piecemeal bites, but if you look at the big picture, everything will become clear. The larger view can be thought of as a data bucket brigade in which each data transfer type is one link. These functions pass data one to the next, trying to quench the user's burning desire for information. Figure 10.1 illustrates the various routes of data transfer.

Note: The data transfers shown in Figure 10.1 are typical data transfers—not the only means of transfer.

Note that the two transfer routes are distinct and separate from one another. The top diagram shows the interaction of a dialog transferring data to its corresponding class. This is the data route you typically see in non-ODBC applications. The bottom diagram illustrates the usual data transfer that occurs between a dialog and record set class and then between the record set class and its respective database. This is the transfer route you will typically see in an ODBC application. But do not misunderstand! You might see both types of transfer occurring in a single ODBC application. You also might not see either type of transfer in a given application.

Day 10: Data Transfer and Stuff

Remember that in the MFC world, there are many ways to skin a cat. (Of course, we will always endeavor to choose the best, most efficient way that's also approved by the ASPCA.)

Figure 10.1.
Data transfer routes.

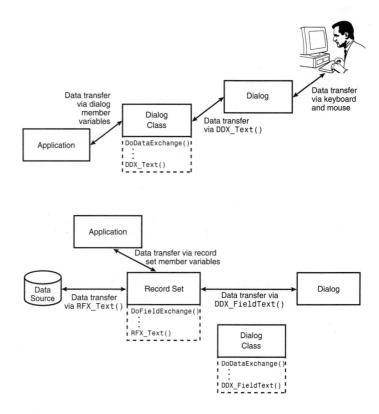

Remember *CDate*?

Now that we have paid lip service to the concepts surrounding Windows' data transfer mechanisms, let's actually get our hands dirty by building a data transfer utility file for CDate. This file will hold all our functional data transfer needs. Specifically, it will contain a DDX_, a DDX_Field_, and an RFX_ function. The interface follows:

```
// This file contains utilities relating to CDate
// Filename : DateUtil.h

#include "date.h"

void AFXAPI DDX_Text(CDataExchange* pDX, int nIDC, CDate& value);

// If the ODBC classes are available, allow the field exchange
// mechanisms to be compiled
```

```
#ifdef __AFXDB_H__
void AFXAPI DDX_FieldText(CDataExchange* pDX, int nIDC, CDate& value,
CRecordset* pRecordset);
void AFXAPI RFX_Date(CFieldExchange* pFX, const char *szName,
CDate& value);
#endif
```

This header file looks much messier than you might have anticipated. What's with the `#ifdef`/`#endif` stuff? Consider the use of this file. We will want to include it whenever we are transferring date data to or from a dialog or record set. Dialogs are used everywhere. You might want to use `DataUtil` in a non-ODBC application. After all, dates and dialogs are in no way exclusive to database applications. However, `CRecordset` *is* exclusive to ODBC applications. If AFXDB.H isn't included in your application, `CReocrdset` won't be available either, and therefore the compiler won't recognize it. The key to minimizing errors is to prevent them whenever possible. By enclosing the references to `CReocrdset` within precompiler directives that check for `__AFXDB_H__`, you can use `DateUtil` in applications regardless of their ODBC predilections.

The documentation that comes with your Visual C++ compiler makes little mention of how these functions are constructed. Only in the technical notes will you find information useful for our current problem. However, even in the technical notes, the final word is to learn from the existing transfer functions. As flippant as this might seem, it's actually sage advice. We learn by doing. Each of the functions in our utility file is based on one of Microsoft's predefined transfer functions. The implementation of DATEUTIL.CPP follows:

```
// This file contains the implementations for utilities
// relating to CDate.
// Filename: DateUtil.cpp

#include "stdafx.h"
#include "DateUtil.h"

#define RFX_DATE_TYPE 15

void AFXAPI DDX_Text(CDataExchange* pDX, int nIDC, CDate& value)
{
    HWND hWndCtrl = pDX->PrepareEditCtrl(nIDC);
    CString tempS;

    if (pDX->m_bSaveAndValidate)
    {
        int nLen = ::GetWindowTextLength(hWndCtrl);
        ::GetWindowText(hWndCtrl, tempS.GetBufferSetLength(nLen), nLen+1);

        if (nLen == 0)
            value = CDate();   // Null date
        else if (!value.StringToDate(tempS))   // Convert string to date
        {
            AfxMessageBox("Invalid Date!");
            tempS.Empty();
            // Fail will throw an exception whose alternate
            // flow of control will bypass the normal end-scope
```

Day 10: Data Transfer and Stuff

```cpp
            // clean-up. Therefore, we must manually destroy
            // dynamic objects such as CString.
            pDX->Fail();
        }
    }
    else
    {
        ::SetWindowText(hWndCtrl, value.DateString());
    }
}

// If the ODBC classes are available, allow the field exchange
// mechanisms to be compiled.
#ifdef __AFXDB_H__
void AFXAPI DDX_FieldText(CDataExchange* pDX, int nIDC, CDate& value,
    CRecordset* pRecordset)
{
    ASSERT_VALID(pRecordset);
    HWND hWndCtrl = pDX->PrepareEditCtrl(nIDC);
    CString tempS;

    if (pDX->m_bSaveAndValidate)
    {
        int nLen = ::GetWindowTextLength(hWndCtrl);
        ::GetWindowText(hWndCtrl, tempS.GetBufferSetLength(nLen), nLen+1);

        if (nLen == 0)
        {
            if (pRecordset->IsFieldNullable(&value))
                pRecordset->SetFieldNull(&value, TRUE);
                // Null DB field
        }
        else if (!value.StringToDate(tempS))   // Convert string to date
        {
            AfxMessageBox("Invalid Date!");
            tempS.Empty();
            // Fail will throw an exception whose alternate
            // flow of control will bypass the normal end-scope
            // clean-up. Therefore, we must manually destroy
            // dynamic objects such as CString.
            pDX->Fail();
        }
    }
    else
        ::SetWindowText(hWndCtrl, value.DateString("%m/%d/%Y"));
}

////////////////////////////////////////////////////////////////////////
// Implementation of the RFX_Date function

// DATE_STRUCT is a portable SQL type for C
// It's defined in sqlext.h

void AFXAPI RFX_Date(CFieldExchange* pFX, const char *szName,
    CDate& value)
{
```

```cpp
    ASSERT(AfxIsValidAddress(pFX, sizeof(CFieldExchange)));
    ASSERT(AfxIsValidString(szName));

    CDate NULL_DATE_OBJ;
    DATE_STRUCT* pds_value = (DATE_STRUCT*)( ((int)&value) + 4 );

    UINT nField;
    if (!pFX->IsFieldType(&nField))
        return;

    LONG* plLength = pFX->m_prs->GetFieldLength(pFX);
    switch (pFX->m_nOperation)
    {
        case CFieldExchange::BindFieldToColumn:
        if (pFX->GetColumnType(nField) != SQL_C_DATE)
            pFX->m_prs->ThrowDBException(
            AFX_SQL_ERROR_FIELD_SCHEMA_MISMATCH);
            // Fall-through

        default:
LDefault:
        pFX->Default(szName, pds_value, plLength, SQL_C_DATE,
            sizeof(*pds_value), 6);
        return;

        case CFieldExchange::Fixup:
        if (*plLength == SQL_NULL_DATA)
        {
            pFX->m_prs->SetFieldFlags(nField,
                AFX_SQL_FIELD_FLAG_NULL,
                pFX->m_nFieldType);
            value = NULL_DATE_OBJ;
        }
        return;

        case CFieldExchange::SetFieldNull:
        if ((pFX->m_pvField == NULL &&
            pFX->m_nFieldType == CFieldExchange::outputColumn) ||
            pFX->m_pvField == pds_value)
        {
            if (pFX->m_bField)
            {
                // Mark fields null
                pFX->m_prs->SetFieldFlags(nField,
                    AFX_SQL_FIELD_FLAG_NULL,
                    pFX->m_nFieldType);
                value = NULL_DATE_OBJ;
                *plLength = SQL_NULL_DATA;
            }
            else
            {
                pFX->m_prs->ClearFieldFlags(nField,
                    AFX_SQL_FIELD_FLAG_NULL,
                    pFX->m_nFieldType);
                *plLength = sizeof(*pds_value);
            }
```

Day 10

Data Transfer and Stuff

```cpp
#ifdef _DEBUG
            pFX->m_bFieldFound = TRUE;
#endif // _DEBUG
        }
        return;

    case CFieldExchange::MarkForAddNew:
        // Can force writing of psuedo-null value (as a non-null) by
        // setting field dirty.
        if (!pFX->m_prs->IsFieldFlagDirty(nField, pFX->m_nFieldType))
        {
            if ( value == NULL_DATE_OBJ )
            {
                pFX->m_prs->SetFieldFlags(nField,
                    AFX_SQL_FIELD_FLAG_DIRTY,
                    pFX->m_nFieldType);
                pFX->m_prs->ClearFieldFlags(nField,
                    AFX_SQL_FIELD_FLAG_NULL,
                    pFX->m_nFieldType);
            }
        }
        return;

    case CFieldExchange::MarkForUpdate:
    case CFieldExchange::StoreField:
        if ( value == NULL_DATE_OBJ )
            pFX->m_prs->SetFieldFlags(nField,
                AFX_SQL_FIELD_FLAG_NULL,
                pFX->m_nFieldType);
        else
            pFX->m_prs->ClearFieldFlags(nField,
                AFX_SQL_FIELD_FLAG_NULL,
                pFX->m_nFieldType);
        goto LDefault;

    case CFieldExchange::GetFieldInfoValue:
        if (pFX->m_pfi->pv == pds_value)
        {
            pFX->m_pfi->nField = nField-1;
            goto LFieldFound;
        }
        return;

    case CFieldExchange::GetFieldInfoOrdinal:
        if (nField-1 == pFX->m_pfi->nField)
        {
LFieldFound:
            pFX->m_pfi->nDataType = RFX_DATE_TYPE;
            pFX->m_pfi->strName = szName;
            pFX->m_pfi->pv = pds_value;
            pFX->m_pfi->dwSize = sizeof(*pds_value);
            // Make sure field found only once
            ASSERT(pFX->m_bFieldFound == FALSE);
            pFX->m_bFieldFound = TRUE;
        }
        return;
```

        }
    }
#endif

A complete description of the preceding implementations could consume a book in their own right. Therefore, I will restrict my discussions to the interesting bits and allow you to flounder around (that is, learn) in the remainder.

The DDX Date Transfer Function

The major control structure in DDX date transfer function is the `if` statement that acts on the `m_bSaveAndValidate` attribute of `CDataExchange`. When the attribute is `TRUE`, the transfer function should retrieve, validate, and save the data held in the edit control. When the attribute is `FALSE`, it should load the edit control with value. Each condition dictates the appropriate `CDate` function to be used: `CDate::StringToValue()` when `m_bSaveAndValidate` is `TRUE` and `CDate::DateString()` when it is `FALSE`.

The most important lesson to learn from this transfer function is the use of the `Fail()` function. As I mentioned earlier, `Fail()` throws an exception. Not "`Fail()` might throw an exception." `Fail()` will throw an exception every time it is called. The alternate flow of control that's evoked will bypass the end-of-transfer function. This might not seem like that big of a deal until you realize that `tempS CString` will never be destroyed. Since `CString` is a dynamic object, you have memory leaks if the `CString`s (or any other dynamically allocated objects) aren't cleaned up. Therefore, just before the call to `Fail()`, `CString`'s `Empty()` function is called, releasing `tempS`'s memory and thereby preventing the memory leak.

The *DDX_Field* Date Transfer Function

Although it's usually described as a wrapper around the ordinary DDX function, the `DDX_Field` function can often be an independent function that partially duplicates the functionality of the respective DDX function. This is the case with our `CDate` field transfer function. Yes, there is a certain amount of duplication between the two transfer functions, but forcing a field function to be a wrapper function at the expense of understandability is not an equitable trade.

The field transfer function bears a striking resemblance to the DDX function immediately preceding it. However, some of the names are changed to protect the database. One of the biggest changes between the two transfer functions is the idea that the database `NULL` is different from the `NULL CDate` we use in the application. If the text in the edit control is of zero length, we duly note that the date is `NULL`. In the normal DDX function, we set the value to `CDate`'s `NULL` (which is just (0,0,0), as you might recall). However, in the field transfer function, we want the database to reflect a `NULL` date. This is accomplished through the record set function `SetFieldNull()`.

Day 10: Data Transfer and Stuff

The RFX Date Transfer Function

As I mentioned earlier, RFX functions have a `switch` statement as their central control block. This central `switch` statement divides the function into bite-sized pieces, each dealing with a unique operation that might crop up in the `CFieldExchange` object. Of course, before we get to the `switch` statement, the requisite plethora of diagnostic tests must be performed in order to validate the various parameters being passed to the function. I don't mean to minimize the importance of these diagnostic statements; they can save your hide when an error rears its ugly head. It's just that they tend to take your attention away from the issues at hand. I breeze by the diagnostics, but you shouldn't. Also, a few statements that set up local variables aid in simplifying the code. The following statement, in particular, deserves some detailed explanation:

```
DATE_STRUCT* pds_value = (DATE_STRUCT*)( ((int)&value) + 4 );
```

What the heck is going on with this statement? Strangely enough, this statement is at the heart of how our RFX function operates with the database. In order for `CDate`s to be able to be stored in the database at all, a compatible data type indigenous to the database is required. Fortunately, we actively selected a database driver that supports dates, so we know that somewhere beneath the surface of the database lurks a date type. If only we could gain access to it! Well, that's what the RFX transfer function is all about.

All database (SQL) types have corresponding C++ types that are defined in SQLEXT.H or SQL.H (both are found in the MSVC\INCLUDE subdirectory). If you peruse SQLEXT.H, you find a defined variable named `SQL_C_DATE`, also known as `SQL_DATE`. Bingo! This is the identifier for a type that we can translate to `CDate`. The actual type that `SQL_DATE` refers to is `DATE_STRUCT`. Its definition follows:

```
/* SQL portable types for C */
/* Transfer types for DATE, TIME, TIMESTAMP */
typedef struct tagDATE_STRUCT
   {
      SWORD year;
      UWORD month;
      UWORD day;
   } DATE_STRUCT;
```

Look familiar? It should. It's identical to the attribute definition of `CDate`. Now you know why we defined `CDate` in this way. We may now reap the benefits of planning ahead. Since the structures of `CDate` and `DATE_STRUCT` are identical, they should be interchangeable with the proper typecast, right? Bzzzzzt. Wrong! The structure of `CDate` and `DATE_STRUCT` are *not* identical! Take a moment and try to figure out why they're different. I'll just sit here and hum the *Jeopardy* song. Okay, time's up. Have you figured it out? `CDate` is built upon `CObject`, which is 4 bytes long (see Chapter 6). `CDate`'s three attributes (which, by the way, are identical to `DATE_STRUCT`) are preceded by the 4 bytes of `CObject`. Therefore, we can't make a direct (typecast) assignment. One way to make the proper conversion is to take the address of a `CDate` object, shift it by 4 bytes, and typecast it to a `DATE_STRUCT` pointer. In other words, perform the following operation:

```
DATE_STRUCT* pds_value = (DATE_STRUCT*)( ((int)&value) + 4 );
```

Once this is done, you have a pointer to the `DATE_STRUCT` object that can be found within the `CDate` object. Having a pointer is important, because we might want to update the `DATE_STRUCT` values within the `CDate` object. A pointer can retrieve and set this information directly.

Now back to the `switch` statement. Every possible operation that the RFX transfer function supports is enumerated in the `switch` statement. Each case block is its own little function that's responding to a particular operation. This RFX transfer function was modeled after the integer RFX transfer function since most of the transfers were the same and those that differed required only minor modifications. This is the easy way to produce RFX functions for your own types: Model them after existing RFX transfer functions.

Installing *CDate* Support

At this point, you might be asking, "Why bother?" It's true that we have expended a great deal of time and effort just to make dates work. Why? To make yourself even crazier, take a look at our application as it stands. Specifically, look at the header file for our `CTreeSet` class. There, in the list of field/param data, are (say it ain't so) the variables `m_BIRTHDATE` and `m_DEATHDATE`! Have we gone to all this work for nothing? Did the Wizards come through for us after all? No, of course not. If for no other reason than the dates are defined as `CTime`s, and `CTime` has that little problem of not supporting dates prior to 1970 (see Chapter 5). Okay, but if we didn't care about this limitation of `CTime`, the Wizards came through for us, right? Well, yes and no. A Wizard did put an appropriate predefined RFX function in `CTreeSet`'s `DoFieldExchange()` function, and it does transfer date information between the record set and the database. But it doesn't work entirely correctly. If you run our application as it stands, you will find no overt problems until you look at the diagnostic output window. If your application is compiled with Visual C++ 1.5, the diagnostic window will be full of memory leak warnings. These memory leaks come from the `CTime` RFX transfer function that came with the compiler. Yes, even Microsoft code is buggy at times. Naturally, this particular bug will be fixed in the next release of the software (I hope), which is probably even now humming happily within your computer. But this problem illustrates a number of important issues:

- Even predefined functions can sometimes be the cause of your problems.
- It's valuable to know about these seemingly arcane subjects (like data transfer) so that you can fix problems when necessary.
- The diagnostic display can be a wonderful tool. Use it often.

Regardless of your version of Visual C++, it is certain that the `CTime` limitation is too restrictive for our application. The `CTime` references must go. Use ClassWizard to remove the `CTime` variables from `CTreeSet`. We must now manually install the `CDate` variables in `CTreeSet`'s

Day 10: Data Transfer and Stuff

interface. This is a three-step process. First, add DATE.CPP to the project's make file. Second, provide date visibility to `CTreeSet` by adding the following line to the beginning of TREESET.H:

```
#include "date.h"
```

Third, put the following two lines immediately after ClassWizard's `AFX_FIELD` block:

```
CDate m_BIRTHDATE;
CDate m_DEATHDATE;
```

Of course, these variables won't do you much good unless they're connected to the database. This is done via our newly created RFX function.

Connecting our new variables to the database is a four-step process. First, the record set must be made aware of the new fields. You do this by incrementing the `m_nFields` attribute by 2—one for each new field. Place the following line in `CTreeSet`'s constructor immediately after ClassWizard's `AFX_FIELD_INIT` block:

```
m_nFields += 2;   // For m_BIRTHDATE & m_DEATHDATE
```

Second, you must add DATEUTIL.CPP to the project's make file. Third, you must include the `DateUtil` file in `CTreeSet`'s implementation file. Add the following line to the beginning of TREESET.CPP:

```
#include "dateutil.h"
```

Fourth, you must add the RFX transfer functions to `CTreeSet`'s implementation. Add the following lines to `CTreeSet`'s `DoFieldExchange()` function after ClassWizard's `AFX_FIELD_MAP` block but before the call to `CFieldExchange`'s `SetFieldType()`:

```
RFX_Date(pFX, "BIRTHDATE", m_BIRTHDATE);
RFX_Date(pFX, "DEATHDATE", m_DEATHDATE);
```

Now we have our `CDate` variables all installed in the record set. It's a good feeling, isn't it? Well, after all this work, it had better feel good at some point. But alas, for all our efforts, we still don't have any tangible proof that we have done anything. That's right. Even though the `CDate` variables are installed in the record set, we haven't done anything with them, so our application has no visible changes. Let's change that right now.

Our current application needs a dialog that allows access to each individual's genealogical data (including dates) that's stored in the record set. Use AppStudio to build the dialog shown in Figure 10.2.

Figure 10.2.
The person data dialog.

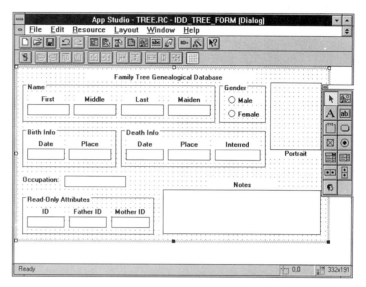

Table 10.6 lists the person data dialog's control IDs and associated controls. Assign these control IDs to the appropriate dialog controls. Use ClassWizard to build the CPersonDlg class associated with the dialog. Then have ClassWizard install m_pSet, a CTreeSet object, as a foreign variable in the CPersonDlg class. You will also have to include the file TREESET.H in the CPersonDlg interface to make CTreeSet available to CPersonDlg. Finally, use ClassWizard to connect as many dialog controls as possible to their record set variable counterparts via the foreign variable. Note that CDate is not automated through ClassWizard. CDates, radio buttons, and the portrait bitmap will all have to be handled manually. For now, let's concentrate on CDate.

Table 10.6. Control IDs for the person data dialog.

Control ID	Control Type	Description
IDC_FirstName	Edit box	Normal text transfer
IDC_MiddleName	Edit box	Normal text transfer
IDC_LastName	Edit box	Normal text transfer
IDC_MaidenName	Edit box	Normal text transfer
IDC_Birthdate	Edit box	Manually installed transfer/conversion

continues

Day 10 — Data Transfer and Stuff

Table 10.6. continued

Control ID	Control Type	Description
IDC_BirthPlace	Edit box	Normal text transfer
IDC_Deathdate	Edit box	Manually installed transfer/conversion
IDC_DeathPlace	Edit box	Normal text transfer
IDC_Interred	Edit box	Normal text transfer
IDC_Occupation	Edit box	Normal text transfer
IDC_Notes	Edit box	Multiline edit box with auto VScroll
IDC_Male	Radio button	
IDC_Female	Radio button	
IDC_Portrait	Static frame	Destination for bitmap picture
IDC_ID	Edit box	Normal double transfer (for diagnostics)
IDC_FatherID	Edit box	Normal double transfer (for diagnostics)
IDC_MotherID	Edit box	Normal double transfer (for diagnostics)

The final connection between the record set CDate variables and the CEdit controls in the dialog is made through the DDX_Field function that we constructed earlier in this chapter. Making this connection is child's play compared to the building of the DDX_Field function. First, we must make CPersonDlg's implementation visible to the DateUtil file. Add the following line to PERSONDL.CPP immediately after the other #include statements:

```
#include "dateutil.h"
```

Second, you must add the following DDX_FieldText() functions to the dialog class's DoDataExchange() function immediately after ClassWizard's AFX_DATA_MAP block:

```
DDX_FieldText(pDX, IDC_Birthdate, m_pSet->m_BIRTHDATE, m_pSet);
DDX_FieldText(pDX, IDC_Deathdate, m_pSet->m_DEATHDATE, m_pSet);
```

Finally, in order to see the dialog in action, you must add a menu item that calls up the dialog for the currently selected person. Using AppStudio, add the following menu item under Record:

    ID   ID_RECORD_EDIT

    Caption   &Edit

    Prompt   View/Edit data concerning the current person.

Next, use ClassWizard to add a command and command UI handler for this new menu item to your document class. Flesh out these functions as follows:

```
void CTreeDoc::OnRecordEdit()
{
```

```
        EditCurrentPerson();
}
void CTreeDoc::OnUpdateRecordEdit(CCmdUI* pCmdUI)
{
    // Enable the command if the record set is
    // open and also has available records
    BOOL bActivate = m_treeSet.IsOpen() &&
        !(m_treeSet.IsBOF() && m_treeSet.IsEOF());

    pCmdUI->Enable( bActivate );
}
```

The function `EditCurrentPerson()` is declared in the document's interface and implemented as follows:

```
void CTreeDoc::EditCurrentPerson()
{
    CPersonDlg Dlg;
    Dlg.m_pSet = &m_treeSet;
    Dlg.DoModal();
}
```

Needless to say, the PERSONDL.H file must be included in the document's implementation file in order for the new dialog class to be visible. Now we can finally see the fruits of our labor. Running the application and choosing the Info | Person menu option will cause the Person Data dialog to be displayed. This dialog should contain all the pertinent data about the current person. Unfortunately, not all of our work is done. The dialog as it stands is a look-but-don't-touch entity. The dialog itself will allow you to edit its controls, but the record set has not been properly prepared. Any changes you make to the fields won't be reflected in the database. Well, we had to leave something for the next chapter.

Summary

This chapter centered around the issues of automated data transfer in the Windows environment. Data transfers are necessary whenever a gap is found to separate distinct elements of your system. Special emphasis was given to the gaps that separate dialog windows from dialog classes and the gaps that separate record set classes from the database information they represent. These gaps are crossed by Dialog Data eXchange (DDX) and Record Field eXchange (RFX) functions, respectively.

When we dealt with ODBC classes, specifically `CRecordset`, it became clear that a hybrid of DDX was needed. A transfer function with knowledge of record sets and dialogs would be ideal for the transfer of data directly between dialogs and record sets. Thus, the `DDX_Field` functions were born. ODBC applications typically have `DDX_Field` functions working in tandem with RFX functions in order to quickly and efficiently transfer information between the various parts of the application.

Day 10: Data Transfer and Stuff

The dry subject matter of data transfer mechanisms was brought to life somewhat at the end of the chapter when you implemented the three types of transfer functions on our old friend `CDate`. However, even with all the work put forth for the implementation of these transfer functions, you still have a long way to go before you have a fully functional ODBC application. So let's keep moving—we have work to do!

Q&A

Q Since the `DoDataExchange()` function is a `CWnd` function, why do we always assume we're using it in the context of a dialog? Is this function ever used in normal windows?

A Since the most common Windows object out there that holds dialog controls is the dialog, the most common application of the `DoDataExchange()` function is with dialog data transfer. It is easiest to focus on a single class of windows, such as dialogs, when explaining the transfer process. However, any `CWnd`-derived window object can use `DoDataExchange()`. Of course, only windows that contain dialog controls will make good use of this function. Our `CRecordView`-derived class is an example of a non-dialog class that utilizes `DoDataExchange()`.

Q In the RFX transfer function, why is there an integer cast during the `CDate*`, `DATE_STRUCT*` conversion?

A The integer cast is very important. It changes `&value` from a `CDate` pointer to an integer. This must be done before we add the 4 bytes representing the `CObject` offset. Recall that when we add integers to object pointers, the addresses are incremented in units of the type pointed to. `CDate` is 10 bytes in size. So `(&value + 4)` would add 40 (4 × 10) bytes to the address of value, whereas `(((int)&value) + 4)` would add only 4 bytes to the address.

Q At the very top of the `DateUtil` implementation, file `RFX_DATE_TYPE` is defined as 15. What is the significance of this definition?

A Each data type used in conjunction with the database must have a unique integer identifier. This identifier is used in the `GetFieldInfo` operations to retrieve the appropriate information. The value of 15 is significant only in the sense that it is unused by the predefined database types.

Workshop

Quiz

1. Under what conditions is `CDataExchange::Fail()` used? Why must you be extra careful when you use `Fail()`?
2. What's the difference between the `DDX_CBString()` and `DDX_CBStringExact()` functions?
3. Name two reasons why we didn't use the default `CTime` implementation for `CTreeSet`'s `m_BIRTHDATE` and `m_DEATHDATE` variables.
4. Can both data transfer routes shown in Figure 10.1 be operating in the same application? Why or why not?

Exercises

1. Rewrite `CDate`'s `DDX_Field` transfer function to actually be a wrapper for the respective DDX transfer function. Justify to yourself that it's more trouble than it's worth. In other words, see for yourself that two separate functions are more understandable than nested functions (in this case).
2. Test `CDate`'s `DDX_Text()` function by installing it in the dialog class you built for the Software Lister application.
3. Try building a DDV function for `CDate` that will check to see if a date is between two other specified dates. If the date doesn't fall within the bounding dates, our new DDV function will abort the transfer and flag the violating control.

WEEK 2

11

ODBC, Part 2

DAY 11

ODBC, Part 2

The previous three chapters were a good introduction to database terminology, ODBC classes, and the associated functionality that makes database applications tick. However, they didn't discuss some of the details that real-world applications require. This chapter extends your ODBC knowledge by looking at some of the advanced topics that lurk just below the ODBC surface. *Advanced* might not be the best word. These topics aren't extremely difficult; they just build upon, and assume that you're knowledgeable about, topics we have already covered.

This chapter finalizes the details of connections displayed in the main view. This entails more manipulation of record set objects—including creating and installing a new record set. But record sets aren't the only ODBC class we will discuss. We will also explore CDBExceptions. Other topics of note in this chapter are random numbers, double-click capturing, and dialog control functions. It's a regular spectacle of Visual C++ delights all loosely centered around ODBC. This will be the last potpourri chapter for a while, so enjoy it while it lasts.

Adding New Persons and Other Random Issues

When last we left our application, we had just enabled the CDate transfer mechanism and constructed a new dialog on which to test our work. The Person dialog seemed to work fine when displaying the data, but we encountered problems when we tried to alter the data. Sometimes when little problems crop up, it's best to ignore them and hope they will go away (this tried-and-true method is used by much of the computing community). However, not having the ability to alter data in a database application is not a little problem. Unfortunately, this is one of those times when you have to face the problem head-on and discover a solution. So you must ask yourself, "Why doesn't the dialog update the record set data with the information the user provides?" The usual answer to such a question is "Because you didn't tell it to!" This answer is nowhere more appropriate than in this case.

In Chapter 10, we neglected to tell the dialog to update the database because we didn't know how. Chapter 9 covered much of CRecordset's functionality, but adding and editing were postponed. Guess what—the wait is over. Table 11.1 lists CRecordset's adding and editing functions.

Table 11.1. CRecordset's record manipulation functions.

Function	Description
AddNew	Adds a new record to the record set.
Delete	Removes the current record from a record set.
Edit	Prepares the current record to be changed.
Update	Accepts an "edit-in-progress."
SetLockingMode	Sets the locking mode for a record set.

Each of these functions has an important role to play in the manipulation of records. These functions act on a record as a whole; they don't distinguish individual field elements. They perform their tasks at the abstraction level of the record.

You can immediately discern the purpose behind the record manipulation functions from their names. However, the interaction between various functions and the choreography necessary to accomplish your tasks is not so obvious. Adding a new record to the database will naturally involve the AddNew() function, but it will also require (less obviously) the use of the Update() function. Similar combinations of functions in the correct order must be called in order to edit or delete a record. The following are step-by-step instructions for each procedure.

Record Manipulation Procedures

Follow these steps to add a new record to the database:

1. Make sure that the record set supports the addition of new records. You do this by using the CanAppend() function. If the record set isn't open or doesn't support appending when AddNew() is called, an exception will be thrown.

2. Knowing that the record set supports appending, you may call AddNew(). This call creates a new, empty record and positions it at the end of the record set (in other words, it *appends* it to the record set).

3. Make whatever changes you wish to the now currently selected and empty record in the record set via direct assignment or dialog interaction.

4. Now comes the moment of truth: Do you accept the changes made in the record set? To accept the record set changes, make a call to Update(). This writes the record set data to the database. Not calling Update() is tantamount to aborting the changes. If you perform a record set move before you call Update(), the added record will be lost. Moving to another record takes the record set out of the AddNew mode. To explicitly exit the AddNew mode, you may call Move with the parameter AFX_MOVE_REFRESH. Any of these methods will legitimately end the AddNew session.

5. In either case (accept or abort), the record set is returned to the record it was previously positioned at. Hence, after you update or cancel your AddNew() command, you are no longer positioned at that record. Further modification or examination of that record can be done only after you move to the record using conventional means (Move(), MoveNext(), and so on).

6. Our application uses a snapshot record set. As you might recall, snapshots are static views of the database—they don't dynamically reflect changes in the database. Well, adding a new record is a significant dynamic change and therefore isn't reflected in a snapshot! In order to see additions to the record set, you must bring the snapshot up to date by calling Requery(). Note that dynasets don't have this problem because they dynamically reflect changes in the database.

DAY 11

ODBC, Part 2

Follow these steps to edit an existing record in the database:

1. Position the record set on the record to be edited. This is in contrast to the AddNew() procedure, which automatically positions the record set to a newly created and appended record.
2. Determine if the record set can be edited by calling the CanUpdate() function. This function will return FALSE if the Update() function is supported. Update() is not supported for read-only record sets.
3. Call the Edit() function. Edit() alerts the record set that the current record may be changed.
4. Make the changes in the record. You may do this directly by assigning values to record set member variables or indirectly through a dialog and its associated transfer functions.
5. Again comes the moment of truth: Do you accept the changes (Update()) or abort the edit (Move(AFX_MOVE_REFRESH) or simply do nothing)?
6. Unlike with AddNew(), after an Edit() interaction, the record set remains positioned on the newly edited record. After all, you manually positioned the record set on the record before calling Edit(), so it's only natural that the record set stays positioned where you last put it.
7. Unlike adding new records, *your* edits are reflected in *your* snapshots. Note the emphasis on the word *your*. Edits made by other users are still not reflected in your snapshots, and your edits are not reflected in other users' snapshots. But since you're doing the editing and you have exclusive access to your snapshots, these changes are visible. Naturally, all edits will be reflected in dynasets. The bottom line is that Requery() does *not* need to be called after an Edit().

Follow these steps to delete a record in the database:

1. Position the record set on the record to be deleted.
2. Call CanUpdate() to ensure that the record set can be updated and thus allows deletions.
3. Remove the current record from the database by calling Delete().

Caution: Unlike AddNew() and Edit(), Delete() takes effect immediately; you don't have a chance to confirm or deny your changes. You can't go back after a deletion.

Caution: While we're on the topic of Delete(), there's a discrepancy you should be aware of. Despite what's printed in the Microsoft documentation, Delete() does *not* return a Boolean value indicating the success of the operation—it is a void function!

4. Move to a new record, because the current record has been deleted and therefore is invalid. A simple MoveNext() or MovePrev() call will suffice to make the current record a valid one. If you remain on a deleted record while making other record set calls, you run the risk of throwing exceptions.

Each of these procedures will be of value in our current application, but our immediate concern is editing the data in the Person dialog. How do we go about translating the edit procedure into code that will accomplish our goal? First, recall that we invoked the Person dialog through the function CTreeDoc::EditCurrentPerson(). It is here that we must place the C++ translation of the edit procedure just described. The revised EditCurrentPerson() function is as follows:

```
void CTreeDoc::EditCurrentPerson()
{
    // The user positions the record set at the
    // desired record before calling this function

    // Make sure the record set is open and updateable
    if ( !(m_treeSet.IsOpen() && m_treeSet.CanUpdate()) )
    {
        TRACE0("m_treeSet not ready in EditCurrentPerson().\n");
        return;
    }

    // Alert the record set that changes may occur
    m_treeSet.Edit();

    CPersonDlg Dlg;

    Dlg.m_pSet = &m_treeSet;

    // Make changes via dialog transfers
    // Accept changes if OK or abort changes if CANCEL
    if (Dlg.DoModal() == IDOK)
        m_treeSet.Update();
    else
        m_treeSet.Move(AFX_MOVE_REFRESH);
        // Note: This call is optional. Not calling
        // Update() is usually sufficient.
}
```

The new EditCurrentPerson() function embodies the edit record procedure mentioned earlier. There is a one-to-one correspondence between the code and the previous description, so I will

Day 11

ODBC, Part 2

forego the detailed explanation. With this function reimplemented, our application will now update changes to person data in the database. Try it out. Make sure our application does everything advertised.

Note: A common error that programmers make with respect to the add and edit record set commands is using `CRecordset::Cancel()` to abort an add/edit in progress. As I stated earlier, you abort add/edit commands with the `Move(AFX_MOVE_REFRESH)` command. The misconception about `Cancel()` is no doubt due to the fact that you often see the `Cancel()` function listed in the same tables as `AddNew()`, `Edit()`, `Delete()`, and `Update()`. `Cancel()` is *not* used with these commands; it is used to cancel asynchronous database tasks (typically long-duration SQL commands sent directly to the database). I don't want to delve into the morass of direct database manipulation, so I won't discuss `Cancel()`. However, I did want to warn you about this point of potential confusion that could be hazardous to your data. Unintended `Cancel()`ing could interrupt some underlying asynchronous operations that might be critical to your database.

The next step is to install a deleting feature that allows us to remove person records from the database. Use ClassWizard to add a command handler to the document class for the Record | Delete menu selection you created in the last chapter. Its implementation follows:

```
void CTreeDoc::OnRecordDelete()
{
    if (!m_treeSet.CanUpdate())
    {
        TRACE0("m_treeSet is not usable in "
               "OnRecordDelete().\n");
        return;
    }

    CString S = "Do you really want to delete: " + m_treeSet.m_FIRST
        + " " + m_treeSet.m_LAST + "?";
    if (AfxMessageBox(S, MB_YESNO) == IDYES)
    {
        m_treeSet.Delete();

        m_treeSet.MoveNext();
        if (m_treeSet.IsEOF())
        {
            m_treeSet.Requery();
            // Requery is usually unnecessary, but with the
            // selected driver, deleting the last record
            // can result in a corrupted state.
            m_treeSet.MoveLast();
        }
        UpdateAllViews(NULL);
    }
}
```

The `OnRecordDelete()` function also follows the procedure outlined earlier for deleting a record. It confirms that a delete can be performed, and then it warns the user about data loss. If confirmation is given, the deletion is performed, followed by a move to get the record set off the deleted record. The record set is moved forward, so the function must check for the end boundary condition. It is here that the function deviates from the spirit of the step-by-step procedure shown earlier. It calls `Requery()`, something that shouldn't have to be done. Well, sometimes theory and practice don't always agree—especially in programming. In this case, the database driver we're using gets confused when the last record is deleted. To unconfuse the driver, you need a call to `Requery()`. The function then calls `MoveLast()` for proper positioning since `Requery()` repositions you at the beginning of the record set. Finally, a call to `UpdateAllViews(NULL)` is made to bring the views up to speed with the document (that is, to refresh the views with the document's current data). Let me re-emphasize: `Requery()` is *not usually needed after a deletion*. In fact, by the time you read this, `Requery()` might not be needed even in this particular instance.

At long last we get to the interesting bits of database adding and editing: adding records to the database. At first glance, adding records to our database doesn't seem too hard; simply convert the addition procedure given earlier into C++ code and compile. Well, you will see that adding new records can get a little stickier than that. Let's take a look at the final function. Use ClassWizard to install a command handler for the Record | Add menu selection in the document class. Complete the implementation as follows:

```
void CTreeDoc::OnRecordAdd()
{
    // Make sure the record set is updateable
    if ( !m_treeSet.CanUpdate() )
    {
        TRACE0("m_treeSet not updateable.\n");
        return;
    }

    // Alert the record set that you are trying to add a record
    m_treeSet.AddNew();
    CPersonDlg Dlg;

    Dlg.m_pSet = &m_treeSet;

    // Fill in record via dialog transfers
    // Accept record if OK or abort the add if CANCEL
    if (Dlg.DoModal() == IDOK)
    {
        m_treeSet.m_ID = GetUniqueRandomID();
        m_treeSet.Update();
        m_treeSet.Requery();
    }
    else
        m_treeSet.Move(AFX_MOVE_REFRESH);
}
```

Day 11: ODBC, Part 2

This function is also the embodiment of the procedure shown earlier for using the AddNew() function. First it makes sure that the record set can be updated, and then it sets the record set in AddNew mode. A dialog is declared and invoked that represents the person data in the record set. If the dialog is canceled, AddNew is aborted. If the dialog is okayed, AddNew is accepted. That's about all there is to it. I guess that wasn't as sticky as I thought—or was it? Let's look again at what happens when the dialog is okayed. The first thing that occurs is that an ID is assigned to the record's ID field. That ID comes from a new function that we have yet to implement: GetUniqueRandomID(). The function then Update()s and Requery()s the record set to confirm the addition and refresh the record set, respectively. Everything the function does is mirrored in the procedure, except this business with GetUniqueRandomID(). What's the deal?

Consider the person ID. We have defined the ID to be the unique attribute of the person record. Unique IDs don't grow on trees; they have to be built. There are a number of different ways we could go about creating an ID that fulfills our requirements. We could keep track of the last ID and add one to it until it was unique in the database. We could form some type of hashing algorithm that transforms a person's name into a number. But, for our purposes, the best bet is to use a random-number generator to produce potential IDs and confirm their uniqueness before assignment. At any rate, to complete our add procedure, we must have a GetUniqueRandomID() function waiting in the wings. To wit:

```
double CTreeDoc::GetUniqueRandomID()
{
    // Assume srand() has already been called to
    // seed the random-number generator
    //CTime time = CTime::GetCurrentTime();
    //srand(time.GetTime());

    // First, set up the record set with ID param
    CTreeSet TS(m_treeSet.m_pDatabase);
    TS.m_strFilter = "ID = ?";

    // Next, place an appropriately sized random
    // number in the parameter
    TS.m_fIDParam = (double)rand() * 3 + 10000;

    if ( TS.Open() )
    {
        // If any records are selected,
        // the ID is NOT unique; hence,
        // increment the ID until it is unique
        while ( !(TS.IsEOF() && TS.IsBOF()) )
        {
            TS.m_fIDParam++;
            TS.Requery();
        }

        TS.Close();
    }
```

```
        // Return the unique ID
        return TS.m_fIDParam;
}
```

This function obtains a random number, scales it appropriately, and uses it as a base from which a unique random ID may be created. The means by which a random number is converted to an ID is simple. The potential ID is searched for (via the parameterization paradigm) in the record set. If it isn't found, it is the unique ID we seek. Otherwise, it is incremented by one and this new value is searched for in the database. This incrementing process is repeated until a suitable ID is found. The questions that should pop into your mind are "What if all the numbers are taken? Wouldn't this create an infinite loop?" Well, strictly speaking, this is true. However, double values can become very large, and our database sample is very small, so we may ignore the risks. In an arbitrarily large database, we couldn't afford to be so cavalier. Let's relish this moment while we can.

The central function we use in GetUniqueRandomID() is the rand() function. This runtime library function returns a random number between zero and RAND_MAX (which, for my system, is 32767). As with most random-number generators, rand() requires a seed value to start the randomizing process. One of the best sources for random seed values is the system time. We seed rand() through the runtime library function srand(). The declarations for rand() and srand() follow. Note that srand() requires an unsigned integer as a parameter and that rand() returns an integer for the random value:

```
void srand( unsigned int seed );
int rand( void );
```

We need to seed the random-number generator only once, so the seeding code may be placed in the application's initialization code. Add the following lines to CTreeApp's InitInstance() function:

```
        // Initialize the random-number generator
        // by using the current time as a seed value
        CTime time = CTime::GetCurrentTime();
        srand((int)time.GetTime());
```

This completes the insertion of the add facility to our application. However, there is still much to be accomplished. Just because we add a new person to the database doesn't mean that the person's data is completely assimilated into the logical structure of the database. Two types of connections are lacking in any newly created person record: parental ties and spousal ties. Needless to say, both types of connections are critical to any genealogist or genealogical program. See the Exercises section for guidance on how to go about implementing these connections.

But before we make these familial connections, we must first activate the view's dialog controls that hold the connection information. Before we can activate the dialog controls, we really should take another look at what the dialog controls are and what they can do.

DAY 11

ODBC, Part 2

Dialog Controls: The Sequel (No, Not SQL!)

It's been a while since we've talked about dialog controls, so let's review what we know:

- ☐ Dialog controls are windows just like everything else (it seems). A number of different control classes are derived from the CWnd class.
- ☐ Dialog controls must have a parent window with which to communicate.
- ☐ This communication is accomplished through a near-steady stream of window notification messages. I say "steady stream" to emphasize that every action the user takes with regard to a control sends a message to the control's parent.
- ☐ Data is passed between dialog controls and their parent window class via a Dialog Data eXchange (DDX) mechanism that's called by the CWnd::UpdateData() function.
- ☐ Dialog boxes are usually (but not always) the parents to these controls.

Probably the most overlooked but important point from this list is the first item: Dialog controls are windows! They are descendants of CWnd, and as such they have CWnd's full complement of windowing functions. You may also conclude from this fact that dialog controls have all the attributes of CWnd objects. They have a specified extent, they have a string title, they have a handle, and so on.

How does all this fit into our current dilemma of making connections? The dialog controls are at the heart of the data connections. These controls display the information that we logically assimilate into our genealogical map. At a more pedestrian level, we need to know about dialog controls in order to fill them with information from our database.

Nearly all the dialog controls are working properly in the person data dialog except for the Gender radio buttons and the Portrait box. I'm saving the implementation of the portrait bitmap code until Chapter 14, where we will discuss bitmaps in detail. However, the radio buttons can be installed immediately. Add the following line to the CTreeView::DoDataExchange() function after the ClassWizard's AFX_DATA_MAP code block:

```
DDX_FieldRadio(pDX, IDC_Female, m_pSet->m_IS_MALE, m_pSet);
```

This line, and the proper assignment of group attributes and tab order within the dialog resource, will enable both radio buttons in the person data dialog. But you might think that this logic is a little out of whack. This line of code seemingly sends the m_IS_MALE attribute of the record set to the IDC_Female dialog control. However, m_IS_MALE is a Boolean value that is implemented zero for FALSE and nonzero (typically one) for TRUE. The DDX_FieldRadio() function works in nearly the opposite way. It takes a zero-based index as a parameter to set a radio button in a group. Therefore, passing zero (when m_IS_MALE is FALSE) to the DDX function will result in the first button in the group (IDC_Female) being set. Likewise, when m_IS_MALE is TRUE (or one), the DDX function will set the second button in the group (IDC_Male). This logic might look reversed, but it actually is correct assuming that the tab order places the female button immediately before the male button.

As with most procedures in Windows programming, this method is by no means the only way to transfer data between the dialog class and its radio buttons. It does have the advantage of being a clean, one-line approach that is more than sufficient for our purposes. However, at one time or another, you might need to retrieve radio button information with a little more hands-on control. Never fear. CWnd functions come to the rescue again. CWnd::CheckRadioButton() and CWnd::GetCheckedRadioButton() allow you to set and retrieve information concerning a group of radio buttons. CWnd has a number of these dialog control-related functions that can help you considerably in dialog manipulations. These CWnd functions are listed in Table 11.2.

Table 11.2. Dialog control-related CWnd functions.

Function	Description
CheckDlgButton	Checks a dialog button.
IsDlgButtonChecked	Determines the state of a dialog button.
CheckRadioButton	Checks a radio button in a specified group.
GetCheckedRadioButton	Determines the state of a group of radio buttons.
SetDlgItemText	Sets the caption of a control to the specified text.
GetDlgItemText	Retrieves the caption of the specified control.
SetDlgItemInt	Sets the caption of a control to the specified integer.
GetDlgItemInt	Translates the caption of a control to an integer.
GetNextDlgGroupItem	Retrieves the next control in a group.
GetNextDlgTabItem	Retrieves the next control in the tab order.
DlgDirList	Fills a list box with a directory listing.
DlgDirSelect	Retrieves the selection of a list box filled by the DlgDirList() function.
DlgDirListComboBox	Fills a combo box with a directory listing.
DlgDirSelectComboBox	Retrieves the selection of a combo box filled by the DlgDirListComboBox() function.
SendDlgItemMessage	Sends a message to a control.
SubClassDlgItem	Attaches a control to a parent window and routes the control's messages through the parent window.

You call these functions through the parent window of the control. You also usually need the control's ID in order to make the call. These are very interesting and powerful routines. Experiment with them and try to figure out what they can do for you.

Day 11 ODBC, Part 2

Unions Table Support Installation

The first order of business in installing support for the Unions table is creating the record set class that encapsulates the Unions table. This is probably something you wouldn't expect. AppWizard built the Person record set automatically when it created the skeletal application. During that process, as I'm sure you'll recall, you were prompted to select the data source as well as the particular table name. That information guided the creation of CTreeSet so that it would interact with the Person table. In a very similar fashion, we will guide ClassWizard when it creates the new record set that will be tied to the Unions table. Enough talk. Let's see some action.

Launch ClassWizard and click on the Add Class... button. In the Add Class dialog, type CUnionSet for the class name and select CRecordset as the Class Type. As you type CUnionSet, the Wizard automatically selects the filenames UNIONSET.H and UNIONSET.CPP for the interface and implementation, respectively (of course, you can change the filenames if necessary). Once you like the choices you've made, click on the Create Class button, which sends ClassWizard on its way to create the Unions record set. Figure 11.1 shows the completed Add Class dialog.

Figure 11.1.
ClassWizard's Add Class dialog.

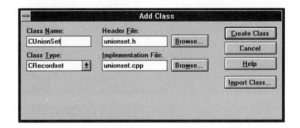

As I stated earlier, ClassWizard still needs our guidance in order to tie CUnionSet to the Unions database table. Select Family Tree Data Source from the SQL Data Sources dialog, and select the UNIONS table from the Tables dialog. With this information, ClassWizard may build the CUnionSet class. But the story doesn't end there! We must do a little cleaning and sprucing up in order to make the class useable.

While we are still in ClassWizard with our new class selected, let's look at the Member Variables tab. What do we have here? As usual, all the fields in the table are represented as member variables—including the dates. Just as with CTreeSet, remove the CTime member variables. We remove them for precisely the same reasons as in CTreeSet: the date limitation and the bug in CTime's RFX function. Once these variables are deleted, you can exit ClassWizard; the remaining sprucing up will be done manually.

The work left to be done to the CUnionSet class is practically identical to the changes we made to enhance CTreeSet. First, let's look at CUnionSet's interface. It will be spruced up in the following ways:

1. New `CDate` variables will be installed to hold the two date fields in the Unions data table.
2. A parameterization variable will be added. As with `CTreeSet`, this variable will facilitate database searches.
3. Precompiler directives will be added to prevent multiple includes of the `CUnionSet` class.

These changes can be seen in the completed `CUnionSet` interface:

```
#ifndef __UNIONSET_H__
#define __UNIONSET_H__

#include "date.h"

class CUnionSet : public CRecordset
{
public:
    CUnionSet(CDatabase* pDatabase = NULL);

// Field/Param Data
    //{{AFX_FIELD(CUnionSet, CRecordset)
    double      m_HUSBAND;
    double      m_WIFE;
    CString m_REASON;
    //}}AFX_FIELD
    CDate    m_START;
    CDate    m_END;
    double    m_fIDParam;

// Implementation
protected:
    virtual CString GetDefaultConnect();    // Default connection string
    virtual CString GetDefaultSQL();        // Default SQL for record set
    // RFX support
    virtual void DoFieldExchange(CFieldExchange* pFX);
    DECLARE_DYNAMIC(CUnionSet)
};

#endif
```

With the interface properly prepared, we may now make the commensurate changes to the interface. These changes to the implementation are limited to the constructor and the `DoFieldExchange()` function, and they revolve around the installation of date support and parameterization. The modified `CUnionSet` functions are as follows:

```
CUnionSet::CUnionSet(CDatabase* pdb)
    : CRecordset(pdb)
{
    //{{AFX_FIELD_INIT(CUnionSet)
    m_HUSBAND = 0;
    m_WIFE = 0;
    m_REASON = "";
    m_nFields = 3;
```

DAY 11
ODBC, Part 2

```
    //}}AFX_FIELD_INIT
    m_nFields += 2;    // One for each of the new CDate variables
    m_nParams = 1;
    m_fIDParam = 0;
}

void CUnionSet::DoFieldExchange(CFieldExchange* pFX)
{
    //{{AFX_FIELD_MAP(CUnionSet)
    pFX->SetFieldType(CFieldExchange::outputColumn);
    RFX_Double(pFX, "HUSBAND", m_HUSBAND);
    RFX_Double(pFX, "WIFE", m_WIFE);
    RFX_Text(pFX, "REASON", m_REASON);
    //}}AFX_FIELD_MAP
    RFX_Date(pFX, "START", m_START);
    RFX_Date(pFX, "END", m_END);
    pFX->SetFieldType (CFieldExchange::param);
    RFX_Double(pFX, "IDParam", m_fIDParam);
}
```

There shouldn't be anything new about these functions that you haven't seen in our work with CTreeSet. Just as in CTreeSet, you must include DATEUTIL.H at the beginning of the implementation file in order to gain visibility for the RFX_Date() functions. Now we are in a position to discuss the manipulation of Union record set objects. Actually, as we shall see, CUnionSet object manipulation isn't really any different from the manipulation of localized CTreeSet objects.

Before you implement the actual marriage process between consenting person records (as suggested in the Exercises section), perhaps we had better wire in the Spouses list box. It's always a good idea to write code that implements visibility to data before you write code that changes the data. In other words, it's nice to see what you're doing before you do something damaging. We do this, if for no other reason, to be better able to assess the damage we inflict. This is a cynical view of programming, but an apt one.

While we're at it, let's finish off the rest of our CTreeView class's dialog controls as well. Implement the Fill functions as follows. Note that you must include the file UNIONSET.H in the implementation of CTreeView in order for these functions to compile:

```
void CTreeView::FillSpouses()
{
    double fTempID;
    int nTemp;
    CString S;

    if ( !m_pSet->IsOpen() )
    {
        TRACE0("Record set is not open in FillSpouses()!");
        return;
    }

    // Declare record set objects but
    // use the existing database object
```

```cpp
        CTreeSet TS(m_pSet->m_pDatabase);
        CUnionSet US(m_pSet->m_pDatabase);

        // Clear the Spouses combo box
        m_ctlSpouses.ResetContent();

        // Prepare TS for ID searching
        TS.m_strFilter = "ID = ?";
        if ( !TS.Open() )
        {
            TRACE0("Tree set failed to open in FillSpouses()!");
            return;
        }

        if (m_pSet->m_IS_MALE)
            US.m_strFilter = "HUSBAND = ?";
        else
            US.m_strFilter = "WIFE = ?";

        US.m_fIDParam = m_pSet->m_ID;
        if ( US.Open() )
        {
            if ( !(US.IsBOF() && US.IsEOF()) )
            {
                US.MoveFirst();
                while ( !US.IsEOF() )
                {
                    if (m_pSet->m_IS_MALE)
                        fTempID = US.m_WIFE;
                    else
                        fTempID = US.m_HUSBAND;

                    TS.m_fIDParam = fTempID;
                    TS.Requery();
                    if ( !(TS.IsBOF() && US.IsEOF()) )
                    {
                        S = TS.FullName();
                        nTemp = m_ctlSpouses.AddString(S);
                        m_ctlSpouses.SetItemData(nTemp, (DWORD)fTempID);
                    }
                    else
                        TRACE1("DB Corruption: ID [%f] not"
                            " in PERSON Table", fTempID);

                    US.MoveNext();
                }
                // select the first string in the box
                m_ctlSpouses.SetCurSel(0);
            }
            US.Close();
        }

        TS.Close();
}

void CTreeView::FillChildren()
```

ODBC, Part 2

```cpp
{
    int nTemp;
    CString S;

    if ( !m_pSet->IsOpen() )
    {
        TRACE0("Record set is not open in FillChildren()!\n");
        return;
    }

    // Declare a new Person record set object
    // but use the same database object
    CTreeSet TS(m_pSet->m_pDatabase);

    // Clear the Children list box
    m_ctlChildren.ResetContent();

    if (m_pSet->m_IS_MALE)
        TS.m_strFilter = "FATHER = ?";
    else
        TS.m_strFilter = "MOTHER = ?";

    TS.m_fIDParam = m_pSet->m_ID;
    if ( TS.Open() )
    {
        if ( !(TS.IsBOF() && TS.IsEOF()) )
        {
            // Fill child list box with elements of record set
            TS.MoveFirst();
            while ( !TS.IsEOF() )
            {
                S = TS.FullName();
                nTemp = m_ctlChildren.AddString(S);
                m_ctlChildren.SetItemData(nTemp, (DWORD)TS.m_ID);
                TS.MoveNext();
            }
        }

        TS.Close();
    }
    else
        TRACE0("Tree set failed to open in FillChildren()!\n");
}

void CTreeView::FillSiblings()
{
    int nTemp;

    if ( !m_pSet->IsOpen() )
    {
        TRACE0("Record set is not open in FillSiblings()!\n");
        return;
    }

    // Declare a new Person record set object
    // but use the same database object
```

```
            CTreeSet TS(m_pSet->m_pDatabase);

            // Clear the Siblings list box
            m_ctlSiblings.ResetContent();

            TS.m_strFilter = "FATHER = ?";
            TS.m_fIDParam = m_pSet->m_FATHER;

            if ( TS.Open() )
            {
                if ( !(TS.IsEOF() && TS.IsBOF()) )
                {
                    // Fill sibling list with elements of record set
                    TS.MoveFirst();
                    while ( !TS.IsEOF() )
                    {
                        if (TS.m_ID != m_pSet->m_ID)
                        {
                            nTemp = m_ctlSiblings.AddString( TS.FullName() );
                            m_ctlSiblings.SetItemData(nTemp, (DWORD)TS.m_ID);
                        }
                        TS.MoveNext();
                    }
                }

                TS.Close();
            }
            else
                TRACE0("Tree set failed to open in FillSiblings()!\n");

            // Note that the above code will load up only siblings
            // on your father's side. Half-siblings on your mother's
            // side will not be included! I smell an exercise!

}
```

Each of these functions makes use of, potentially, multiple local record sets that share the same database object as the document's record set. Using these alternative record sets, complex searches are made to retrieve data pertinent to the still-current record positioned in the document's record set. The data gathered is stored in the appropriate dialog control object, where it is visible to the user. The particulars of each function are different, but you should be able to see the common thread amidst the changing tapestries.

An important aspect of these functions is the manner in which data is stored in the list/combo boxes. Not only can these controls store the text strings we see them display, but they can also store an associated data value. This is particularly useful in this instance since each name in the list boxes has an ID that we use for search and retrieval operations. The SetItemData() function is used to attach an associated number to a list box item. Later in this chapter we will see this data being retrieved through the use of the GetItemData() function. Look for it at the end of the next section, "Double-Click Support."

DAY 11

ODBC, Part 2

Note: You will note that I support only heterosexual relationships in the `FillSpouses()` function. I am not passing judgment on anyone by way of C++ code. For legitimate genealogical reasons, it only makes sense to track natural mothers and fathers. It still takes both a man and a woman to make a baby, so, genealogically speaking, heterosexual relationships are the only ones of interest. When you get right down to it, keeping track of babies is what genealogy is all about.

My presumption that mommies and daddies must be married (that is, *espoused*) is my own view of the world. Disregard it if you wish, or, better yet, enhance the program to include your own views. Just remember that I made this presumption so that the design would be cleaner.

Double-Click Support

Navigating through the records in a record set has been a serial task up to now. We have been using the arrow toolbar buttons to move from one record to the next. True, we do have the `MoveFirst()` and `MoveLast()` buttons, but for the most part we have been moving through the records in sequence. The bottom line is that if you have a large number of records, serial movement is not enough! A more natural approach to maneuvering within the record set springs from the genealogical aspects of our program. Wouldn't it be nice if we could just double-click on the mother, father, sibling, children, or spouse control and immediately make that person the current selection? Wouldn't it also be nice if we could bring up the edit box for the current person simply by double-clicking on the central name box? Implementing these wishes is the purpose of this section.

Double-clicking is a tried-and-true method of initiating change in Windows. Sadly, double-clicking will soon be something of the past due to the advent of the next generation of Windowing (that is, Windows 95). But you know me: I like to live in the past. Actually, altering the code in this section to instead support single-clicking wouldn't be that difficult; I just prefer the feel of double-clicking.

We will be applying two distinct approaches to installing double-click support in our application. The first method captures any double-clicks made on the view window itself. These double-clicks are evaluated as to position, and, depending on where the double-click took place, different actions can be performed. The second method is to capture the double-click notification messages that were destined for a dialog control. Naturally, the second method is limited to handling double-clicks concerning dialog controls, whereas the first method can be used anywhere in the view. Which method you choose depends on your needs. Because of the layout of our view, we will use the first method to invoke the edit dialog for the current person and to navigate to the mother or father. The second method will be used for the spouses, children, and siblings dialog controls.

In most of the double-click handlers, we move the position of the document's record set to another record. For example, if we double-click on the father box, the current selection will change to the person record corresponding to the father of the previously selected person. This movement procedure is an ideal candidate for a localized function. The best home for this function is the document class, since here any other housekeeping chores may also be done (such as keeping the views current). Install the following function in the CTreeDoc class:

```
BOOL CTreeDoc::MoveTo (double ID)
{
    CTreeSet TS(m_treeSet.m_pDatabase);
    TS.m_strFilter = "ID = ?";
    TS.m_fIDParam = ID;
    if (TS.Open())
    {
        if (TS.IsBOF() && TS.IsEOF())
            return FALSE;   // ID not valid
        TS.Close();
    }
    else
    {
        TRACE0("MoveTo failed upon tree set open.\n");
        return FALSE;
    }

    // At this point, we know that the ID exists
    // in the record set

    // Make sure that m_treeSet has records in it.
    // It could have a different filter.
    if ( m_treeSet.IsBOF() && m_treeSet.IsEOF() )
        return FALSE;

    m_treeSet.MoveFirst();
    while ( !m_treeSet.IsEOF() )
    {
        if (m_treeSet.m_ID == ID)
        {
            UpdateAllViews(NULL);
            return TRUE;
        }
        else
            m_treeSet.MoveNext();
    }

    // If the ID isn't found, there must be an inconsistency
    // between m_treeSet and TS. So...
    TRACE0("Record Set Inconsistency Error!\n");
    ASSERT(FALSE);   // Abort the program when in the debugger

    // If the application is in a release stage (i.e. no debugger),
    // alert the user of the problem and return false
```

Day 11

ODBC, Part 2

```
        AfxMessageBox("Record Set Inconsistency Error in "
                "CTreeDoc::MoveTo().");
        return FALSE;
}
```

This function first checks to make sure the ID is valid. It then starts at the first record and scrolls the record set until the ID is found. This might seem like a very inefficient way of moving to the proper record, but without any order imposed on the record set, any other method would be unduly complicated. However, since you brought it up, take a look at the Exercises section for motivation to make this routine faster.

> **Note:** This is a good opportunity to mention a couple of points regarding debugging macros such as TRACE and ASSERT. At the end of the MoveTo() function are a couple of debugging macro statements followed by some seemingly redundant debugging code. What's more confusing is that the ASSERT(FALSE) statement will abort the program, so the following lines in the function will never get executed. Curiouser and curiouser! However, a close look at the comments will illuminate the purpose of this code. Only while in debugging mode will the TRACE and ASSERT macros actually do anything. In a release product, these debugging statements will be no-ops ("no-operations," or null lines). Therefore, control will fall through to the latter statements.
>
> This brings up another point regarding ASSERT. In the release version of your application, ASSERT won't do anything—including evaluating the expression you give it. If you require the expression to be evaluated for the proper functioning of your application, either evaluate the expression outside of the ASSERT macro and pass the result to ASSERT, or call the VERIFY macro. VERIFY will always evaluate its expression and then act on the result in the same way ASSERT does. In other words,
>
> VERIFY (*expression*);
>
> is equivalent to
>
> BOOL bTemp = expression;
> ASSERT (bTemp);

Now that we have the MoveTo() function, we can go about installing the double-click support. Use ClassWizard to add a handler in CTreeView that will capture double-clicks in the view window. In ClassWizard, select CTreeView in the Class Name list box. Then select CTreeView in the Object IDs list box. Finally, select WM_LBUTTONDBLCLK in the Messages list box. Once ClassWizard installs the stubbed OnLButtonDblClk() in CTreeView, you may fill it in as shown next:

```
void CTreeView::OnLButtonDblClk(UINT nFlags, CPoint point)
```

```
{
    CTreeDoc* pDoc = GetDocument();

    CWnd* pCtl = GetDlgItem(IDC_FatherBox);
    CRect CtlRect;

    pCtl->GetWindowRect(&CtlRect);
    ScreenToClient(&CtlRect);

    // Check to see if the point is in the Father box
    if ( CtlRect.PtInRect(point) )
    {
        // If there is no father ID, there is nothing to do
        if (pDoc->m_treeSet.IsFieldNull(&pDoc->m_treeSet.m_FATHER))
            return;

        if ( !pDoc->MoveTo(pDoc->m_treeSet.m_FATHER) )
            TRACE("DB Corruption: Father ID : %i NOT "
                "FOUND\n", pDoc->m_treeSet.m_FATHER);

        return;
    }

    pCtl = GetDlgItem(IDC_MotherBox);
    pCtl->GetWindowRect(&CtlRect);
    ScreenToClient(&CtlRect);

    // Check to see if the point is in the Mother box
    if ( CtlRect.PtInRect(point) )
    {
        // If there is no mother ID, there is nothing to do
        if ( pDoc->m_treeSet.IsFieldNull(&pDoc->m_treeSet.m_MOTHER) )
            return;

        if ( !pDoc->MoveTo(pDoc->m_treeSet.m_MOTHER) )
            TRACE("DB Corruption: Mother ID : %i NOT "
                "FOUND\n", pDoc->m_treeSet.m_MOTHER);

        return;
    }

    CRecordView::OnLButtonDblClk(nFlags, point);

    pCtl = GetDlgItem(IDC_NameBox);
    pCtl->GetWindowRect(&CtlRect);
    ScreenToClient(&CtlRect);

    // Check to see if the point is in the Name box
    if ( CtlRect.PtInRect(point) )
        pDoc->EditCurrentPerson();

    // Alternatively, we could send a WM_COMMAND message
    // to the main frame with the associated notification
    // message ID_RECORD_EDIT. Recall the messaging
    // discussions earlier in this book. This command will
    // be routed through to the document. If you're wondering,
```

Day 11

ODBC, Part 2

```
    // "Why not cut out the middleman and send a message
    // directly to the document?", remember that the document
    // is not a window class. It is derived from CCmdTarget.
}
```

The `OnLButtonDblClk()` function is effectively divided into three sections—one for each static box we're checking for a double-click hit. Each of these sections is broken into the following procedure:

1. Get a pointer to the control in question.
2. Retrieve the extent of the control window via the control pointer. The window extent is held in a `CRect` object.
3. Convert the `CRect` coordinates from screen coordinates to client window coordinates.
4. Determine if the double-click point falls within the extent of the particular control. This is accomplished through the `PtInRect()` function.
5. Perform whatever tasks are appropriate for the clicked control.

More-detailed discussions of `CRect` and `CRect`-related functions will have to wait for a later chapter. We will also postpone the discussion of coordinate transformations until we discuss printing in Chapter 17. Both of these topics are important to the Windows programmer, so stay tuned.

The next item on the agenda is installing double-click support for the remaining controls in the view window. Each of these controls will have its own double-click handler function. Use ClassWizard to install these handlers in the view class. Under ClassWizard's Message Maps tab, select `CTreeView` in the Class Name list box. Select `IDC_Children` from the Object IDs list box, and select `LBN_DBLCLK` from the Messages list box. Click on the Add Function button to add the double-click handler for the Children list box. Through similar procedures, add double-click handlers for `IDC_Siblings` and `IDC_Spouses`. Implement these functions with the following code:

```
void CTreeView::OnDblclkChildren()
{
    CTreeDoc* pDoc = GetDocument();

    double fID = (double)m_ctlChildren.GetItemData(m_ctlChildren.GetCurSel());
    pDoc->MoveTo(fID);
}

void CTreeView::OnDblclkSiblings()
{
    CTreeDoc* pDoc = GetDocument();

    double fID = (double)m_ctlSiblings.GetItemData(m_ctlSiblings.GetCurSel());
    pDoc->MoveTo(fID);
}

void CTreeView::OnDblclkSpouses()
```

```
    {
        CTreeDoc* pDoc = GetDocument();

        double fID = (double)m_ctlSpouses.GetItemData(m_ctlSpouses.GetCurSel());
        pDoc->MoveTo(fID);
    }
```

Note the use of the GetItemData() function for retrieving the person ID associated with the name that was visible in the list box. Recall that the IDs were placed in their respective list boxes by one of these functions: FillChildren(), FillSiblings(), or FillSpouses().

*CDBException*s

The CDBException class is a CException-derived class specifically designed to work with the database classes. A large number of database class functions utilize the CDBException class to warn the user of unusual conditions that could lead to errors. This new exception class is treated like any of the other exception classes we have dealt with. The TRY-CATCH paradigm is still the means of catching and processing these exceptions. However, the CDBException class does have some additions. Three new public attributes included in the CDBException class will aid you in determining the whats and whys of a particular exception. Table 11.3 lists these new attributes.

Table 11.3. CDBException's public attributes.

Attribute	Description
m_nRetCode	ODBC-related error codes.
m_strError	A string containing a human-readable explanation of the exception.
m_strStateNativeOrigin	A string that contains ODBC codes explaining the nature of the condition.

The first attribute, m_nRetCode, is the actual error code returned by the ODBC API. This code can take on any of the values listed in Table 11.4 under the appropriate conditions. This value is a very precise way of determining what went wrong.

Table 11.4. CDBException return codes.

AFX_SQL_ERROR_API_CONFORMANCE

AFX_SQL_ERROR_CONNECT_FAIL

AFX_SQL_ERROR_DYNASET_NOT_SUPPORTED

AFX_SQL_ERROR_EMPTY_COLUMN_LIST

AFX_SQL_ERROR_FIELD_SCHEMA_MISMATCH

continues

ODBC, Part 2

Table 11.4. continued

AFX_SQL_ERROR_ILLEGAL_MODE
AFX_SQL_ERROR_MULTIPLE_ROWS_AFFECTED
AFX_SQL_ERROR_NO_CURRENT_RECORD
AFX_SQL_ERROR_NO_ROWS_AFFECTED
AFX_SQL_ERROR_ODBC_LOAD_FAILED
AFX_SQL_ERROR_RECORDSET_FORWARD_ONLY
AFX_SQL_ERROR_SNAPSHOT_NOT_SUPPORTED
AFX_SQL_ERROR_SQL_CONFORMANCE
AFX_SQL_ERROR_SQL_NO_TOTAL
AFX_SQL_ERROR_RECORDSET_READONLY
SQL_ERROR
SQL_INVALID_HANDLE

Note that the SQL_-prefixed codes are error conditions propagated directly from the ODBC, whereas the AFX_-prefixed codes are local to the database foundation classes. For more information about all the codes listed in Table 11.4, consult the database class reference manual (*Database Classes for the MFC Library,* Microsoft Press, page 202).

The second attribute of CDBException is m_strError. This string contains an English description of what went wrong. This string is ideal for screen output. It can be used to alert the operator of an erroneous condition if all recovery efforts fail. This attribute is also a valuable addition for your testing efforts. Errors in English are usually hard to come by, so shunting m_strError to the diagnostic screen in place of a raw error code can be an illuminating experience.

The final public attribute found in CDBException is m_strStateNativeOrigin. This string attribute encapsulates the information provided by the SQLError() function found in the ODBC API. The string has the form State:%s, Native:%ld, Origin:%s, where each of the % format codes is replaced by data that comes from the SQLError() function. In our dealings with CDBException objects, we will use the first two attributes. The particulars of the m_strStateNativeOrigin attribute may best be discerned by examining the SQLError() function. SQLError() may be found in *The ODBC SDK Programmer's Reference* (Microsoft Press, 1994).

Let's take a look at database exceptions from the perspective of their use. The following example illustrates how exceptions may be captured and examined during a record set's Open() command:

```
TRY
{
    m_pSet->Open();
}
CATCH( CDBException, e )
{
    // Display the human-readable description of the error
    AfxMessageBox (e->m_strError);
    // Display the encoded, yet more specific, description of the error
    AfxMessageBox(e->m_strStateNativeOrigin);
}
END_CATCH
```

Note that the variable e is a pointer to a CDBException object that is loaded with the information pertinent to the exception at hand. Use of this exception data can mean the difference between having a stubborn error break you into an empty shell of a programmer, and finding the error, bending it to your will, and eventually crushing it out of existence. Trust me on this one: It's better to break the error. Capture exceptions frequently. You won't be sorry.

Summary

This chapter continued a discussion of the ODBC classes and associated topics. It primarily used the Family Tree application as a sounding board for a discussion of advanced ODBC techniques. This discussion focused on a number of issues.

The first item of interest was the record set routines for adding and editing database records. This topic is crucial to any working database application, yet providing this support presented us with some unexpected subtleties. One complication arose in the form of the need for a unique ID for new person records. This in turn opened the door for a discussion of random-number generators and determining ID uniqueness.

Another look at dialog controls allowed us an excuse to put a few more touches on the near-complete person data dialog. This time we added support for the Gender radio buttons through the DDX_FieldRadio() function. But this function is far from the only means by which radio button controls can be affected. The CWnd functions CheckRadioButton() and GetCheckedRadioButton() may be used for more immediate access. This fact further revealed the existence of a suite of CWnd functions dedicated to manipulating dialog controls.

At our next stop, we looked at creating and installing a new record set class that encapsulated the Unions database table created in Chapter 8. This table holds the spousal connections between people in the Person database table. Although this was very similar to the work we did on CTreeSet, installing functionality for the new record set illustrated the techniques involved with a multiple record set environment.

We then added double-click support to the main view of the application. This provided a nonserial means of database navigation that was more in tune with the problem domain (in other words, it was more in sync with the genealogical nature of the application). Two methods of

ODBC, Part 2

capturing double-click messages were explored: capturing all the double-clicks in the view window versus capturing double-click notifications for dialog controls. Both methods have their uses.

Finally, database exceptions were examined. `CDBException` is an advanced form of its ancestor class `CException`. It holds numeric and string data that further specifies the exception under scrutiny. This extra data can help immeasurably in the debugging process.

That's it. We have a working database application with practically all the functionality we could ever want. Actually, that's a bold-faced lie. Of course, we have more to do. There are three more chapters in this week; we have to fill them with something. The next chapter concerns the ideas behind the MDI paradigm and what it can do for you. Tune in next time—same bat time, same bat channel!

Q&A

Q In the installation of the double-click support, why did we separate the handlers for the dialog controls the way we did? For example, why did we use `OnLButtonDblClk()` for the `IDC_MotherBox` control and use `OnLButtonDblClk()` for the Children list box?

A This is an interesting point. You will note that all the controls that have separate double-click handlers are working controls. The controls that we grouped under the `OnLButtonDblClk()` function were static in nature. Static controls come under the purview of the button controls. Through ClassWizard you can install individual click and double-click handlers for these static controls, but they assume that the controls are real buttons. Real buttons generate notification messages when they are clicked or double-clicked, but static controls don't. Static controls are more or less inert. Therefore, we have to use the all-encompassing `OnLButtonDblClk()` handler to support `IDC_NameBox`, `IDC_MotherBox`, and `IDC_FatherBox`.

Q What would happen if we didn't seed the `rand()` function?

A The `rand()` function isn't really a random-number generator at all. Its actual designation is pseudo-random-number generator. Given a random seed, it will continue to produce random-like numbers—random-like since the same initial seed will always produce the same series of "random" numbers. Not seeding the `rand()` function removes the random element—do you know why? Write a short program to find the answer to this question experimentally. (Yeah, I know this isn't the Exercises section. But who's the author here, anyway?)

Workshop

Quiz

1. How do you abort an `AddNew()` or `Edit()` in progress? How do you abort a `Delete()`?
2. What's the difference between the List box functions `AddString()` and `SetItemData()`?
3. What's the difference between the `VERIFY` macro and the `ASSERT` macro?

Exercises

1. Select one of the `CWnd` functions from Table 11.2. Research it and use it, meaningfully, in one of your programs.
2. Enhance (in other words, fix) the `FillSiblings()` function so that it reflects siblings on both the mother's and the father's side. Caution: Make sure you don't place double entries in the Siblings list box.
3. Add Update UI command handlers for the menu items implemented in this chapter.
4. Impose an order on the document's record set (through the `m_strSort` attribute) and rewrite the `CTreeDoc::MoveTo()` function so that it takes advantage of this new ordering.
5. Implement the parental and spousal connections by adding menu item selections and constructing dialogs for this purpose. Parental connections are straightforward once you have the dialogs and menu items ready. The spousal connections can be a little trickier simply because of the extra data needed to specify the union. Follow the same procedures we did in the person dialog in order to enable the START and END dates associated with the Unions table. Care and a little creative programming will see you through.

WEEK 2

MDI and Multiple Views

Day 12

MDI and Multiple Views

The Multiple Document Interface, or MDI, is one of the most common user interfaces you'll see in Windows applications. The reason for its popularity is the same reason for Windows' popularity: People like to be able to interact among and between multiple objects on their "desktop." This is especially true of objects within the context of an application. In a word processor, for example, users like to be able to move (cut and paste) groups of words from one document to another. Clipboard certainly is the main player in this procedure, but if the application allows both documents to be visible while the move is occurring, this is an extra added plus. If the user can see the source and destination side by side, he can better determine exactly what to extract and exactly where it will go. This is just one example in one potential application. The benefits of MDI, when taken in total, are mind-boggling.

This chapter explores our application's existing MDI capabilities as well as how to add new MDI functionality. But be warned: The treatment you will find here is only the tip of the iceberg. MDI programming is a very rich and complex subset of MFC programming. I will give you at least enough knowledge to get yourself in trouble.

MDI

Before we travel any farther down this application's road, we really must talk about the new Multiple Document Interface. Nothing is as fundamentally new and different about our application as its multiple document ability. Before Chapter 8, we were dealing only with Single Document Interfaces (SDIs). Those were the salad days—a simpler time. Under SDI, your application had one and only one currently active document or view. An SDI application's view was displayed in that application's one and only mainframe window. It was simple, clean, and efficient. Now, enter MDI! Multiple documents also mean multiple views and associated view windows. Our main application window now hosts a potential multitude of child windows, each of which represents a view to a document. Finding a particular view or document now takes a conscious effort.

> **Note:** It's not entirely true that under SDI your application has one and only one currently active document or view. Under SDI, you are constrained to a single document by definition, but multiple view classes may still be provided. Visibility to these alternative views can be on a one-by-one basis or multiply through the use of a splitter window.

Not only does MDI introduce window quantity to your application, but it also introduces window variety. The windows in this potential plethora of child windows don't all have to contain the same document/view class pair. Under MDI you may have multiple types of documents floating around, and attached to each document you may have multiple types of views. This ability adds some dramatic flexibility and potential to your application, but it comes at the price of complexity. MDI applications are typically more complicated to program than their SDI counterparts. Naturally, the MFC does its best to buffer you from as many of the confusing details as possible, but in order to build applications that exploit the full power of Windows, access to some of the details is necessary. One such detail essential to conscientious MDI programming is the document template.

Document Templates

Document templates are the choreographers of the MDI dance. They determine which types of documents and views get paired up. Behind the scenes they provide the appropriate registration to the Windows environment that gives the respective documents seeming autonomy while preserving the integral nature of their connection to Windows.

Document templates provide the following document/view combinations:

- Primary document and view: The default AppWizard combination.
- Primary document and second view: The default AppWizard application automatically supports this ability via the Window | New Window menu option.
- Primary document and second different view: This must be installed manually. This combination allows multiple different views of the same document (and hence data).
- Secondary document and view: In this case, a new and different document (and hence data) is introduced into the application. The new document necessitates a new view. Multiple different views may be incorporated into the secondary document paradigm just as they were in the primary document.

Each unique pairing of document class to view class requires a `CDocTemplate`-derived object, typically declared and initialized in the application class (in our case, a `CMultiDocTemplate` is declared and initialized in `CTreeApp`). Throughout this chapter you will see the utilization of document templates make all aspects of MDI come to life.

Default Multiple Views

Multiple views are very easy to implement. In fact, our application already provides multiple view support! That's right. The default AppWizard MDI application automatically includes the ability to produce multiple views on a document through the Window | New Window menu option. Go ahead and try it out on our current application. Isn't it interesting? Of course, in this particular case, the multiple-view capability doesn't really give us anything new. Two copies of a picture of the current person's immediate family doesn't help us much. However, in some circumstances, two identical views on the same document can be a benefit. For example, if the two views can be scrolled, they could represent different portions of the same document. We will see this demonstrated when we implement the ahnentafel document/view later in this chapter.

Day 12
MDI and Multiple Views

As you play around with these new views, you might encounter a problem. If you highlight one view window, move to a different person record, highlight the other view window, and move the record set from within the context of the second window, you will see a problem—and it's not a small problem, either. It's a data-corrupting, hair-pulling, throw-your-computer-out-the-window type of problem. The most serious adjective in the preceding sentence is "data-corrupting." Yes, the one thing that's totally unacceptable in a database application is corruption of data. Yet simply using one of the predefined capabilities in the default application that AppWizard built causes this sin of sins. Your first instinct is to conclude that multiple views are crap and to avoid them at all costs. I assure you that this is an overreaction. Although it's true that our application's use of multiple views can cause data corruption, it's not the fault of the default application code. The fault lies in our additions to the code. First, let's look at what's going wrong. Then we will fix the problem. This process will be instructive both in the sense of repairing the problem and in terms of gaining more insight into the MFC architecture.

So, what exactly causes this data corruption? You will note that any data corruption is limited to a change in first, middle, and last names. In fact, the changes that occur are simply the copying of one person's names to another person's record. (If you don't believe me, fiddle around with multiple views in the manner just described until there is obviously a corruption. Then invoke Microsoft Query and view the Person table's data. The copying of names becomes clear from this view.) Couple the nature of the corruption with its cause (alternatively moving the record set in different views), and you should be able to pinpoint where in the code the problem is. Any guesses? Actually, the mere fact that the corruption is caused by record set movement should direct you to the view's OnMove() function. The copying of names from one record to the next might be a bit more perplexing. But note that the three fields affected are precisely the same three fields whose data was transferred via the DDX_FieldText() functions in CTreeView::DoDataExchange(). Coincidence? No. Where do OnMove() and DoDataExchange() intersect? OnMove() calls UpdateData(), which in turn calls DoDataExchange(). Bingo! Obviously, something is screwy in the UpdateData() call, but what? Let's take a look at CTreeView's OnMove() function, which we wrote in an earlier chapter:

```
BOOL CTreeView::OnMove(UINT nIDMoveCommand)
{
    if( CRecordView::OnMove(nIDMoveCommand) )
    {
        UpdateRelatives();
        return TRUE;
    }
    else
        return FALSE;
}
```

Nothing seems amiss in this code—at least with regard to UpdateDate(). However, the call to CRecordView::OnMove() might hold our problem. CRecordView::OnMove() is part of the MFC library code, so we can't change it directly, but there's no reason we can't look at it. The code is found in the file \MSVC\MFC\SRC\DBVIEW.CPP and is shown here:

```cpp
BOOL CRecordView::OnMove(UINT nIDMoveCommand)
{
    if (CDatabase::InWaitForDataSource())
    {
#ifdef _DEBUG
        if (afxTraceFlags & 0x20)
            TRACE0("Warning: ignored move request\n");
#endif // _DEBUG
        return FALSE;
    }

    CRecordset* pSet = OnGetRecordset();
    if (pSet->CanUpdate())
    {
        pSet->Edit();
        if (!UpdateData())
            return FALSE;

        pSet->Update();
    }

    switch (nIDMoveCommand)
    {
        case ID_RECORD_PREV:
            pSet->MovePrev();
            if (!pSet->IsBOF())
                break;

        case ID_RECORD_FIRST:
            pSet->MoveFirst();
            break;

        case ID_RECORD_NEXT:
            pSet->MoveNext();
            if (!pSet->IsEOF())
                break;
            if (!pSet->CanScroll())
            {
                // Clear screen since we're sitting on EOF
                pSet->SetFieldNull(NULL);
                break;
            }

        case ID_RECORD_LAST:
            pSet->MoveLast();
            break;

        default:
            // Unexpected case value
            ASSERT(FALSE);
    }

    // Show results of move operation
    UpdateData(FALSE);
    return TRUE;
}
```

Day 12: MDI and Multiple Views

This `OnMove()` function is considerably more complicated than our implementation. Is it any wonder that we opted to call the ancestor function within our own? However, this ancestor call doesn't come without a price, especially if we didn't know all the details of the original function. Look at the `if` block immediately preceding the `switch` statement. This `if` statement checks to see if the record set can be updated. If it can be updated, the record set is prepared for editing, and `UpdateData()` is called without a parameter. Ah ha! We finally get to the point where `UpdateData()` comes into the picture. The default parameter for `UpdateData()` is a `TRUE` value. `UpdateData(TRUE)` means to transfer data from the dialog (or in this case, the record view) to the class (in this case, the record set). This is the crux of the problem. A mismatch of data occurred when multiple views holding different sets of dialog data were connected to a single document holding a single record set. When a switch of views was made and an implicit call to `OnMove()` was made, the `UpdateData()` function transferred old view data into a different record in the record set. Ouch! Data corruption!

Two solutions are immediately apparent. Completely rewrite `CTreeView::OnMove()` so that `CRecordView::OnMove()` is not called but the functionality remains intact, or massage the existing `CTreeView::OnMove()` so that the problem disappears. Both solutions have pros and cons. Massaging `OnMove()` is a bit on the hackish side of programming and results in two useless calls to `UpdateData()`. Completely rewriting `OnMove()` is a longer process that duplicates existing code and that can consequently introduce new errors. Which of the two methods is worse depends on your software engineering predilections. However, in terms of the ease of the fix and the resulting readability, the massage technique wins out. It also continues to rely on library code that is stable and tested. On the other hand, the complete rewrite would streamline `OnMove()` by removing two `UpdateData()` calls. The resulting application would be that much more efficient and customized toward our application. However, the additional programming time and effort required for the complete rewrite might seem unnecessary. Also, you could argue that abandoning pretested library code for a marginal gain in efficiency is folly. You're experienced enough in programming to be able to judge for yourself. I opted for the massaging route since it added only a single line of code to `OnMove()`. However, feel free to do the complete rewrite if you think that's the best route. I firmly believe that the less you monkey around with working code, the happier you will be. The massaged `CRecordView::OnMove()` function is as follows:

```
BOOL CTreeView::OnMove(UINT nIDMoveCommand)
{
    UpdateData(FALSE);
    if( CRecordView::OnMove(nIDMoveCommand) )
    {
        UpdateRelatives();
        return TRUE;
    }
    else
        return FALSE;
}
```

The preemptive call to UpdateData(FALSE) forces the view back in line with the record set before CRecordView::OnMove() gets a chance to call UpdateData(TRUE), pushing the data in the opposite direction and potentially causing database corruption. As I said, this is much less efficient than the complete rewrite, but you've got to admit that the solution is extremely compact.

A Different Point of View

As we saw in the preceding section, the default implementation of multiple views can be a little trickier than you might think. Far from being the mindless exercise that the word "default" connotes, an understanding of the architecture and the implementation details is necessary to properly use the default implementation of multiple views in your application. Ironically, you don't need much more knowledge to install a completely new and different view into your application. This new view is different because it will be instantiated from a new view class that we will build. By creating a new view class, we may customize and tune a second view to our exact specifications. For our immediate purposes, the second view class will simply present all the data of the current record of the record set. Nothing special is required to accomplish this goal, so we may derive our class directly from CView.

Invoke ClassWizard and click on the Add Class... button. This brings up the Add Class dialog. Select CView from the Class Type combo box and type CPersonView in the Class Name edit box. Now you may click the Create Class button. ClassWizard constructs the new view class for you, but you must make any connections to your application. So it is written; so shall it be done:

```
// personvi.h: header file
//

/////////////////////////////////////////////////////////////////////////////
// CPersonView view

class CPersonView : public CView
{
    DECLARE_DYNCREATE(CPersonView)
protected:
    CPersonView();   // Protected constructor used by dynamic creation

// Attributes
public:

// Operations
public:

// Implementation
protected:
    virtual ~CPersonView();
    virtual    void OnDraw(CDC* pDC);
    // Overridden to draw this view
```

DAY 12
MDI and Multiple Views

```
    // Generated message map functions
protected:
    //{{AFX_MSG(CPersonView)
    // NOTE: ClassWizard will add and remove member
    // functions here.
    //}}AFX_MSG
    DECLARE_MESSAGE_MAP()
};
```

The implementation of CPersonView is as follows:

```
/////////////////////////////////////////////////////////////////////////////
// personvi.cpp: implementation file
//

#include "stdafx.h"
#include "tree.h"
#include "personvi.h"
#include "treeset.h"
#include "treedoc.h"

#ifdef _DEBUG
#undef THIS_FILE
static char BASED_CODE THIS_FILE[] = __FILE__;
#endif

/////////////////////////////////////////////////////////////////////////////
// CPersonView

IMPLEMENT_DYNCREATE(CPersonView, CView)

CPersonView::CPersonView()
{
}

CPersonView::~CPersonView()
{
}


BEGIN_MESSAGE_MAP(CPersonView, CView)
    //{{AFX_MSG_MAP(CPersonView)
    // NOTE: ClassWizard will add and remove mapping macros here.
    //}}AFX_MSG_MAP
END_MESSAGE_MAP()


/////////////////////////////////////////////////////////////////////////////
// CPersonView drawing

void CPersonView::OnDraw(CDC* pDC)
{
    CDocument* pDoc = GetDocument();
    CTreeSet* pSet = &((CTreeDoc*)pDoc)->m_treeSet;
    CString S;
    int X = 10, Y = 10;
```

```
    int offset = 20;

    pDC->TextOut(X, Y, "Full Name: " + pSet->FullName());
    pDC->TextOut(X, Y += offset, "Maiden: " + pSet->m_MAIDEN);
    if (pSet->m_IS_MALE)
        S = "Person is Male.";
    else
        S = "Person is Female.";
    pDC->TextOut(X, Y += offset, S);
    pDC->TextOut(X, Y += offset, "Birth Place: " + pSet->m_WHERE_BORN);
    pDC->TextOut(X, Y += offset, "Birthdate: " +
        pSet->m_BIRTHDATE.DateString());
    pDC->TextOut(X, Y += offset, "Death Place: " + pSet->m_WHERE_DIED);
    pDC->TextOut(X, Y += offset, "Deathdate: " +
        pSet->m_DEATHDATE.DateString());
    pDC->TextOut(X, Y += offset, "Interred: " + pSet->m_INTERRED);
    pDC->TextOut(X, Y += offset, "Occupation: " + pSet->m_OCCUPATION);

    pDC->TextOut(X, Y += offset, "Notes: ");
    S = pSet->m_NOTES;
    // Divide the notes string into bite-sized (60-character) chunks
    // so that it may be read on one screen.
    while (S.GetLength() > 60)
    {
        pDC->TextOut(X+10, Y += offset, S.Left(60));
        S = S.Right(S.GetLength() - 60);
    }
    pDC->TextOut(X+10, Y += offset, S);
}

//////////////////////////////////////////////////////////////////////
// CPersonView message handlers
```

As you can see, the CPersonView class is little more than a minimal descendent of CView. Only the OnDraw() function is customized for our application, and it has the simple function of dumping the current record's data to the screen. The one tricky part of the code in OnDraw() is splitting the Notes field into 60-character lines so that it will be more readable. The rest of the function is straightforward.

Now that we have a new view class, how can we incorporate it into our current application? The tried-and-true method of answering these "How can we..." questions is to look at how someone else did it. The someone else in this case is Microsoft: How does the default application deal with the Window | New menu option? Our search through the MFC source code eventually takes us to the implementation of CMDIFrameWnd found in your \MSVC\MFC\SRC directory. Toward the beginning of the WINMDI.CPP file, you will find the message map shown here:

```
BEGIN_MESSAGE_MAP(CMDIFrameWnd, CFrameWnd)
    //{{AFX_MSG_MAP(CMDIFrameWnd)
    ON_WM_DESTROY()
    ON_MESSAGE(WM_COMMANDHELP, OnCommandHelp)
    ON_MESSAGE(WM_IDLEUPDATECMDUI, OnIdleUpdateCmdUI)
    ON_WM_SIZE()
```

DAY 12

MDI and Multiple Views

```
    // MDI Window messages
    ON_UPDATE_COMMAND_UI(ID_WINDOW_ARRANGE, OnUpdateMDIWindowCmd)
    ON_UPDATE_COMMAND_UI(ID_WINDOW_CASCADE, OnUpdateMDIWindowCmd)
    ON_UPDATE_COMMAND_UI(ID_WINDOW_TILE_HORZ, OnUpdateMDIWindowCmd)
    ON_UPDATE_COMMAND_UI(ID_WINDOW_TILE_VERT, OnUpdateMDIWindowCmd)
    ON_COMMAND_EX(ID_WINDOW_ARRANGE, OnMDIWindowCmd)
    ON_COMMAND_EX(ID_WINDOW_CASCADE, OnMDIWindowCmd)
    ON_COMMAND_EX(ID_WINDOW_TILE_HORZ, OnMDIWindowCmd)
    ON_COMMAND_EX(ID_WINDOW_TILE_VERT, OnMDIWindowCmd)
    // WindowNew = NewWindow
    ON_UPDATE_COMMAND_UI(ID_WINDOW_NEW, OnUpdateMDIWindowCmd)
    ON_COMMAND(ID_WINDOW_NEW, OnWindowNew)
    //}}AFX_MSG_MAP
END_MESSAGE_MAP()
```

The last line of this message map is pertinent to our discussion. This line maps the OnWindowNew() function to the ID_WINDOW_NEW command message, which is sent in response to the Window | New Window menu option. An examination of the OnWindowNew() function will demonstrate the technique of creating multiple views:

```
void CMDIFrameWnd::OnWindowNew()
{
    CMDIChildWnd* pActiveChild = MDIGetActive();
    CDocument* pDocument;
    if (pActiveChild == NULL ||
      (pDocument = pActiveChild->GetActiveDocument()) == NULL)
    {
        TRACE0("Warning: No active document for WindowNew command\n");
        AfxMessageBox(AFX_IDP_COMMAND_FAILURE);
        return;  // Command failed
    }

    // Otherwise, we have a new frame!
    CDocTemplate* pTemplate = pDocument->GetDocTemplate();
    ASSERT_VALID(pTemplate);
    CFrameWnd* pFrame =
        pTemplate->CreateNewFrame(pDocument, pActiveChild);
    if (pFrame == NULL)
    {
        TRACE0("Warning: failed to create new frame\n");
        return;  // Command failed
    }

    pTemplate->InitialUpdateFrame(pFrame, pDocument);
}
```

What on earth is going on here? All we want to do is tack another view to the current document. The process can't be this involved, can it? Well, as a matter of fact, it can. Remember, this code is supposed to conform to whatever MDI situation might arise. This could include multiple types of documents and views. This piece of code will handle any combination of document/view marriages (of course, it is limited to document/view combinations that are already in existence). We will have to modify the code to actually create new combinations. But before we do that, let's look at an overview of what OnWindowNew() does in the first place:

1. It gets the active MDI child window.
2. It gets the document associated with the active MDI child window.
3. It gets the document template associated with the document.
4. It uses the template to create a new frame window associated with the current document and current MDI child window. (See Figure 12.2 later in this chapter.)
5. It uses the template to initialize the frame window.

Using OnWindowNew() as a guide, we can construct a couple of functions that will conjure up the document/view combination of our choice.

> **Note:** Actually, we're not free at this point to choose *any* combination. This particular technique will allow us to construct any new document/view pair as long as a document object currently exists in the application. Instantiating new document objects will be explained shortly.

As the first step toward this goal, place the following two menu items on the Window menu immediately after New Window:

ID	ID_WINDOW_NEWRELATIVEWINDOW
Caption	New Relative Window
Prompt	Opens another relative window for the current document.

ID	ID_WINDOW_NEWDATAWINDOW
Caption	New Data Window
Prompt	Opens another data window for the current document.

Use ClassWizard to add command handlers to the CMainFrame class for these new menu items. Fill out these handler functions in the manner shown here:

```
void CMainFrame::OnWindowNewrelativewindow()
{
    CMDIChildWnd* pActiveChild = MDIGetActive();
    CDocument* pDocument;
    if (pActiveChild == NULL ||
      (pDocument = pActiveChild->GetActiveDocument()) == NULL)
    {
        TRACE0("Warning: No active document for WindowNew command\n");
        AfxMessageBox(AFX_IDP_COMMAND_FAILURE);
        return;   // Command failed
    }
```

Day 12

MDI and Multiple Views

```cpp
    // Otherwise, we have a new frame!

    // The only thing that needs to be changed from the original
    // OnWindowNew() function is the source of the document
    // template!
    // CDocTemplate* pTemplate = pDocument->GetDocTemplate();
    CDocTemplate* pTemplate = ((CTreeApp*)AfxGetApp())->m_pRelativeTemplate;

    ASSERT_VALID(pTemplate);
    CFrameWnd* pFrame = pTemplate->CreateNewFrame(pDocument, pActiveChild);

    if (pFrame == NULL)
    {
        TRACE0("Warning: failed to create new frame\n");
        return;  // Command failed
    }

    pTemplate->InitialUpdateFrame(pFrame, pDocument);
}

void CMainFrame::OnWindowNewdatawindow()
{
    CMDIChildWnd* pActiveChild = MDIGetActive();
    CDocument* pDocument;
    if (pActiveChild == NULL ||
      (pDocument = pActiveChild->GetActiveDocument()) == NULL)
    {
        TRACE0("Warning: No active document for WindowNew command\n");
        AfxMessageBox(AFX_IDP_COMMAND_FAILURE);
        return;  // Command failed
    }

    // Otherwise, we have a new frame!

    // The only thing that needs to be changed from the original
    // OnWindowNew() function is the source of the document
    // template!
    // CDocTemplate* pTemplate = pDocument->GetDocTemplate();
    CDocTemplate* pTemplate = ((CTreeApp*)AfxGetApp())->m_pPersonTemplate;

    ASSERT_VALID(pTemplate);
    CFrameWnd* pFrame = pTemplate->CreateNewFrame(pDocument, pActiveChild);

    if (pFrame == NULL)
    {
        TRACE0("Warning: failed to create new frame\n");
        return;  // Command failed
    }

    pTemplate->InitialUpdateFrame(pFrame, pDocument);
}
```

Even a cursory examination of these command handlers will tell you that they're a rip-off of the OnNewWindow() code from the CMDIFrameWnd implementation shown earlier. Only a small change in the middle of these functions makes each uniquely capable of providing the new view support that we require.

Of course, we must provide definitions for the template objects we reference in these functions. Add the following template variables to `CTreeApp`'s interface:

```
// Attributes
public:
    CMultiDocTemplate* m_pRelativeTemplate;
    CMultiDocTemplate* m_pPersonTemplate;
```

Also, alter `CTreeApp`'s `InitInstance()` and `ExitInstance()` functions as follows:

```
BOOL CTreeApp::InitInstance()
{
    // Standard initialization
    // If you are not using these features and wish to reduce the size
    // of your final executable, you should remove from the following
    // the specific initialization routines you do not need.

    SetDialogBkColor();    // Set dialog background color to gray
    LoadStdProfileSettings();
    // Load standard INI file options (including MRU)

    // Register the application's document templates. Document
    // templates serve as the connection between documents, frame
    // windows, and views.

        m_pRelativeTemplate = new CMultiDocTemplate(
            IDR_TREETYPE,
            RUNTIME_CLASS(CTreeDoc),
            RUNTIME_CLASS(CMDIChildWnd),
            RUNTIME_CLASS(CTreeView));
    AddDocTemplate(m_pRelativeTemplate);

        m_pPersonTemplate = new CMultiDocTemplate(
            IDR_TREETYPE,
            RUNTIME_CLASS(CTreeDoc),
            RUNTIME_CLASS(CMDIChildWnd),
            RUNTIME_CLASS(CPersonView));

    // Create main MDI frame window
    CMainFrame* pMainFrame = new CMainFrame;
    if (!pMainFrame->LoadFrame(IDR_MAINFRAME))
        return FALSE;
    m_pMainWnd = pMainFrame;

    // Initialize the random-number generator
    // by using the current time as a seed value
    CTime time = CTime::GetCurrentTime();
    srand((int)time.GetTime());

    // Create a new (empty) document
    OnFileNew();

    if (m_lpCmdLine[0] != '\0')
    {
        // TODO: Add command-line processing here
    }
```

Day 12: MDI and Multiple Views

```
    // The main window has been initialized, so show and update it
    pMainFrame->ShowWindow(m_nCmdShow);
    pMainFrame->UpdateWindow();

    return TRUE;
}

int CTreeApp::ExitInstance()
{
    // Delete m_pRelativeTemplate;
    // Since m_pRelativeTemplate is registered, Windows
    // takes care of its destruction.
    delete m_pPersonTemplate;

    return CWinApp::ExitInstance();
}
```

We place the document template pointers in the interface of our application so that they will be visible and available for use from anywhere in the application (in our case, from `CMainFrame`). In the application's `InitInstance()` function, we initialize the pointers by allocating new `CMultiDocTemplate` objects (`CMultiDocTemplate` is the flavor of document template custom-designed for MDI use). Within the allocation call, we pass a number of parameters to the `CMultiDocTemplate` constructor. These parameters specify the logical connections to be made between the document template object, the view class, the frame window class, the document class, and the particular resource to be used. Here's the new call we added to the preceding code:

```
m_pPersonTemplate = new CMultiDocTemplate(
    IDR_TREETYPE,
    RUNTIME_CLASS(CTreeDoc),
    RUNTIME_CLASS(CMDIChildWnd),
    RUNTIME_CLASS(CPersonView));
```

Notice that the `CMultiDocTemplate` object, `m_pPersonTemplate`, associates the default resource ID, the `CTreeDoc` document class, the `CMDIChildWnd` frame window class, and the `CPersonView` class. Thus, a call to `m_pPersonTemplate`'s `CreateNewFrame()` function from within one of the `OnWindowNewXXXX()` functions discussed earlier will cause a new `CPersonView` object to be attached to an existing `CTreeDoc` object and be displayed in a new `CMDIChildWnd` object. The actual creation process is shown in Figure 12.1. This diagram is analogous to the SDI window creation hierarchy we saw in Figure 1.5 in Chapter 1.

With these changes to our application in place, a second, different type of view may be attached to the current document! This can be very useful when different types of views into a document are needed. For example, if you designed stock-tracking software in which a great deal of numeric data is stored for analysis, you might want both a view to the raw data (daily stock prices) and a graph of a stock's price over time. Both views represent the same data (hence the same document), but they present it in vastly different ways.

Figure 12.1.
The MDI creation hierarchy.

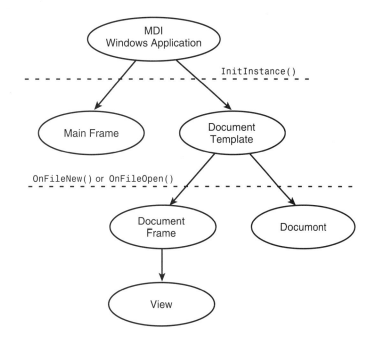

Note: In this particular application, the person view might seem to be a useless view of the data since our edit dialog duplicates this functionality. However, if you wanted to install printer support for our application, this would be an ideal starting point. View classes were designed for printing, but dialogs were not. So this new view is both instructive in terms of a second view attached to a document as well as handy for any future addition of printer support.

Now that we have talked about multiple different views attached to a given document class, it's time to look at installing true multiple document support—that is, support for different multiple document classes in a single application.

Collections: Specifically, *CStringArray*

`CTreeDoc`, the document class currently in use in the Family Tree application, is really just a shell around an object of the `CTreeSet` class. One could say that `CTreeDoc` is a sorry excuse for a document class, since it doesn't really hold any data other than a reference to a record set object. Our actual data is buried deep within a database file, access to which is gained through ODBC calls. This lack of a "real"—dare I say "manly"—document class should be reason enough to whip together a second document class and install it into our application. However, if you require more than a silly reason for creating yet another class and throwing it into our already overstuffed application, there is a legitimate reason for a second document class. Recall our original discussion of genealogy in Chapter 8. One of the constructions useful in genealogical work was the ahnentafel listing (a listing of a person's direct blood ancestry). Think about how such a list must be retrieved from our existing database. Yuck! Not a pleasant thought. Trying to maintain a view of such a list given the single record tool of CRecordSet isn't trivial. Therefore, for practical reasons, the ahnentafel list should be compiled from the database into a separate document class—the CAhnenDoc class.

The CAhnenDoc object must be able to hold the complete blood ancestry of any person in the database. This requirement will have different resource needs depending on circumstances. Some people will have a long ahnentafel list, and others will have a short list. Obviously, some sort of dynamic allocation of memory must be managed so as to efficiently accommodate our needs while also providing for a worst-case scenario. We need a class that provides a data structure suited to our use while providing this dynamic allocation behind the scenes. How many of you out there have been anxiously awaiting the chance to code a dynamically allocated linked list or array class? What's that? You've coded enough data structures to last a lifetime? This particular task does seem an ideal choice for some bright-eyed Microsoft programmer right out of Computer Science school who wants to code the MFC libraries. Indeed, this is exactly what the MFC library is all about: providing reusable code so that we don't have to! Happily, MFC didn't let us down. It provides three major superclasses of collections—arrays, lists, and maps—which will be discussed in detail later in this book. The particular class that we will use as the destination for our ahnentafel list is a string array class (CStringArray) that we will embed in CAhnenDoc.

The CStringArray class encapsulates an array structure dedicated to the storage of CString objects. All of your memory allocation and management needs are anticipated and provided for. Most of this is done behind the scenes, nearly transparent to the programmer. Again, we will talk about the collection classes in detail later in this book, so don't expect a detailed discussion of CStringArray in this chapter. For now, let's just see how CStringArray will fit within the purview of CAhnenDoc.

Multiple Documents

This section will put the "MD" in our MDI application. When we talked about multiple views earlier in this chapter, we found that AppWizard's default application gave us a limited implementation of multiple views. Should we expect anything less from AppWizard when we speak of multiple documents? Of course not! Yes, multiple documents are available from the default application using the File | New menu option. Surprise, surprise: File | New does this in commercial applications too! Consistency is such a nice bonus. Go ahead and try File | New on our current application. Hmmmm, not too different from the Window | New command that creates new views. Well, it doesn't look different, but there is all the difference in the world under the hood. File | New actually creates a new document object and attaches a new view object (and associated frame window). Every time you use the File | New command in the current state of our application, a new instance of CTreeDoc is created, and with it, a new record set object. In other words, the problems we encountered with mismatched data in our multiple-view discussion won't be evident in our discussion of multiple documents. Remember, multiple views share a single instance of a document, whereas multiple documents have separate and distinct data sets. Of course, since our CTreeDoc data is just a record set object, the data referenced by any instance of CTreeDoc will be out of the same database. But each CTreeDoc object will at least have its own record set with which to reference the data (a crucial difference illustrated by the problems we faced while analyzing the data corruption caused by our multiple views). The bottom line: AppWizard's default implementation of multiple documents works just fine.

Although the default implementation of multiple document support works, that's not really where we were headed. Multiple documents mean something a little more sophisticated to us. Not only do we want multiple documents, but we also want the documents to be fundamentally different. As described in the preceding section, we would like our second document to be the ahnentafel list document (CAhnenDoc). Before we talk about how to incorporate CAhnenDoc into our application, perhaps we should build it.

Use ClassWizard to create CAhnenDoc, an immediate descendent of CDocument. Alter the default CAhnenDoc interface and implementation as follows:

```
// ahnendoc.h: header file
//

/////////////////////////////////////////////////////////////////////////////
// CAhnenDoc document

#ifndef __AHNENDOC_H__
#define __AHNENDOC_H__

#include "treeset.h"

class CAhnenDoc : public CDocument
{
    DECLARE_SERIAL(CAhnenDoc)
protected:
    CAhnenDoc();   // Protected constructor used by dynamic creation

// Attributes
public:
    CStringArray m_arrAhnentafel;
    CTreeSet m_treeSet;

// Operations
public:
    void LoadAncestry (double ID, int Ahnen_Number = 1);
```

Day 12: MDI and Multiple Views

```cpp
// Implementation
protected:
    virtual ~CAhnenDoc();
    virtual void Serialize(CArchive& ar);   // Overridden for document I/O
    virtual    BOOL OnNewDocument();

    // Generated message map functions
protected:
    //{{AFX_MSG(CAhnenDoc)
    // NOTE: ClassWizard will add and remove member
    // functions here.
    //}}AFX_MSG
    DECLARE_MESSAGE_MAP()
};

#endif

// ahnendoc.cpp: implementation file
//

#include "stdafx.h"
#include "tree.h"
#include "ahnendoc.h"
#include "treedoc.h"

#ifdef _DEBUG
#undef THIS_FILE
static char BASED_CODE THIS_FILE[] = __FILE__;
#endif

/////////////////////////////////////////////////////////////////////////////
// CAhnenDoc

IMPLEMENT_SERIAL(CAhnenDoc, CDocument, 0 /* schema number*/ )

CAhnenDoc::CAhnenDoc()
{
}

CAhnenDoc::~CAhnenDoc()
{
    // Make sure the CStrings in the array are emptied
    for (int i = 0; i < m_arrAhnentafel.GetSize(); i++)
        m_arrAhnentafel[i].Empty();
    // Empty the array
    m_arrAhnentafel.RemoveAll();
}

BOOL CAhnenDoc::OnNewDocument()
{
    if (!CDocument::OnNewDocument())
        return FALSE;

    double Seed_ID;  // Initial ID on which to base ahnentafel list
    CString S;   // Temporary string storage
```

```cpp
    // Navigate the MFC architecture to get to the current document
    CTreeApp* pApp = (CTreeApp*)AfxGetApp();
    CFrameWnd* pChild = ( (CMDIFrameWnd*)(
        pApp->m_pMainWnd) )->GetActiveFrame();
    CDocument* pDoc = pChild->GetActiveDocument();

    // Find ID of the current person selected in the
    // previous document if there is one. Otherwise,
    // abort operation.
    if ( (pDoc != NULL) )
    {
        S = pDoc->GetRuntimeClass()->m_lpszClassName;
        if (S == "CTreeDoc")
        {
            TRACE0 ("Current document is CTreeDoc.\n");
            TRACE1 ("Current person is %f.\n",
                    ((CTreeDoc*)pDoc)->m_treeSet.m_ID);
            Seed_ID = ((CTreeDoc*)pDoc)->m_treeSet.m_ID;
        }
        else
        {
            TRACE0 ("Current document is not CTreeDoc.\n");
            return FALSE;
        }
    }
    else
    {
        TRACE0 ("No current document is available.\n");
        return FALSE;
    }

    m_treeSet.m_strFilter = "ID = ?";
    m_treeSet.m_fIDParam = Seed_ID;
    m_treeSet.Open();

    if ( !(m_treeSet.IsBOF() && m_treeSet.IsEOF()) )
        LoadAncestry(Seed_ID);
    else
    {
        TRACE1("ID %f is invalid!\n", Seed_ID);
        m_treeSet.Close();
        return FALSE;
    }

    m_treeSet.Close();

    return TRUE;
}
BEGIN_MESSAGE_MAP(CAhnenDoc, CDocument)
    //{{AFX_MSG_MAP(CAhnenDoc)
    // NOTE: ClassWizard will add and remove
    // mapping macros here.
    //}}AFX_MSG_MAP
END_MESSAGE_MAP()
```

DAY 12: MDI and Multiple Views

```cpp
////////////////////////////////////////////////////////////////////////
// CAhnenDoc support functions
CString Ahnentafel_String(double ID, CTreeSet* pSet)
{
    CString S = pSet->FullName();

    if (!pSet->IsFieldNull(&pSet->m_OCCUPATION))
        S += '(' + pSet->m_OCCUPATION + ')';

    S += ": born ";
    if (!pSet->IsFieldNull(&pSet->m_BIRTHDATE))
        S += pSet->m_BIRTHDATE.DateString();
    else
        S += "????";
    if (!pSet->IsFieldNull(&pSet->m_WHERE_BORN))
        S += ", " + pSet->m_WHERE_BORN;

    S += "; died ";
    if (!pSet->IsFieldNull(&pSet->m_DEATHDATE))
        S += pSet->m_DEATHDATE.DateString();
    else
        S += "????";
    if (!pSet->IsFieldNull(&pSet->m_WHERE_DIED))
        S += ", " + pSet->m_WHERE_DIED;

    return S;
}

void CAhnenDoc::LoadAncestry (double ID, int Ahnen_Number)
{
    // Filter the record set for the given ID
    m_treeSet.m_fIDParam = ID;
    m_treeSet.Requery();

    if ( m_treeSet.IsBOF() && m_treeSet.IsEOF() )
    {
        TRACE1("Database corrupt: Invalid ID reference -- %f!\n", ID);
        return;
    }

    // Construct the ahnentafel string and insert it into
    // the appropriate place in the array (checking for
    // memory exceptions, of course)
    CString S = Ahnentafel_String(ID, &m_treeSet);
    TRY
    {
        m_arrAhnentafel.SetAtGrow(Ahnen_Number-1, S);
    }
    CATCH(CMemoryException, e)
    {
        TRACE1("LoadAncestry: memory exception on %s!\n", m_treeSet.m_FIRST);
        return;
    }
    END_CATCH

    // Recursively call LoadAncestry for Father and Mother
    // if they are available (i.e. not NULL). Note that
```

```
    // the Ahnen_Number is appropriately changed for each parent.

    if (!m_treeSet.IsFieldNull(&m_treeSet.m_FATHER))
        LoadAncestry(m_treeSet.m_FATHER, Ahnen_Number*2);

    m_treeSet.m_fIDParam = ID;
    m_treeSet.Requery();
    // Why must we do this again?  See the Q&A section.

    if (!m_treeSet.IsFieldNull(&m_treeSet.m_MOTHER))
        LoadAncestry(m_treeSet.m_MOTHER,
                Ahnen_Number*2+1);
}
/////////////////////////////////////////////////////////////////////////////
// CAhnenDoc serialization

void CAhnenDoc::Serialize(CArchive& ar)
{
    if (ar.IsStoring())
    {
        // TODO: Add storing code here
    }
    else
    {
        // TODO: Add loading code here
    }
}


/////////////////////////////////////////////////////////////////////////////
// CAhnenDoc commands
```

Much of the previous code is self-explanatory, but a few points of interest should be touched upon. First, note that a `CStringArray` object and `CTreeSet` object are declared in the interface of `CAhnenDoc`. The `CStringArray` object, of course, is the repository for our data. The `CTreeSet` object, on the other hand, is used merely as a data source to initialize our string array.

In the `CAhnenDoc` implementation, the major function of interest is our override of `OnNewDocument()`. This function, as you might recall, will be invoked once for every new document created. It is here, therefore, that we include code for the one-time initialization of the document's data. The first confusing block of code that you encounter in the `OnNewDocument()` function concerns itself with navigating to the previously current document and retrieving its current person ID:

```
// Navigate the MFC architecture to get to the current document
CTreeApp* pApp = (CTreeApp*)AfxGetApp();
CFrameWnd* pChild = ( (CMDIFrameWnd*)(
    pApp->m_pMainWnd) )->GetActiveFrame();
CDocument* pDoc = pChild->GetActiveDocument();
```

This navigation code starts with a call to `AfxGetApp()`, which returns a pointer to the application object. From `CTreeApp` you can get the main window object (`m_pMainWnd`), which is a `CMDIFrameWnd` object pointer. A call to `CMDIFrameWnd::GetActiveFrame()` will return a pointer to the active child window, which is associated with a document class that is obtained through a call to `GetActiveDocument()`. Phew! MFC navigation should be a book unto itself. Figure 12.2 shows the new architecture that underlies an MDI application.

Day 12 — MDI and Multiple Views

Figure 12.2.
MDI application architecture.

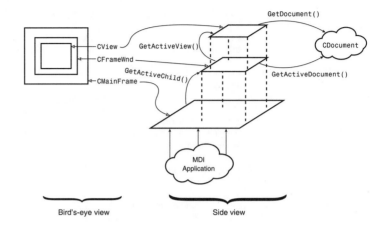

Anyway, now that we have a pointer (pDoc) to the current active document object, you'd think that retrieving the current person's ID would be a cake walk. Of course, if you've learned anything from this book, you should know that sometimes the easiest-sounding tasks can be the most difficult. So why can't we just bop into the CTreeDoc class and grab the m_treeSet.m_ID? One reason is that in our current age of multiple documents, we have no assurance that the document in question is a CTreeDoc at all! Fortunately, in an earlier chapter we made a thorough analysis of the CObject and CRuntimeClass classes, and we found that the actual class names of polymorphic objects can be retrieved via the GetRuntimeClass() call. This is the technique we employ to verify the identity of a potential CTreeDoc object. If the document is not a CTreeDoc object, or if there is no active document at all, the new document procedure is aborted. But if we do have a CTreeDoc object, we can retrieve the current person's ID and use that as a seed to build the ahnentafel list.

The ahnentafel list is constructed by the recursive function LoadAncestry(). This function takes the seed ID, puts together an ahnentafel string (via the Ahnentafel_String() function), stores it in the CStringArray object, and then calls itself with the person's father and mother IDs. Aren't recursive functions both fun and compact? If you're shaky on recursion, spend some extra time analyzing this function. Pay close attention to the Q&A question referred to in the code.

A document class does us little good without a view class to display its data. Use ClassWizard to create a CView-derived class called CAhnenView. I don't discuss the default implementation of CAhnenView in this chapter, except for our slight modification of the OnDraw() function, shown here:

```
/////////////////////////////////////////////////////////////////
// CAhnenView drawing

void CAhnenView::OnDraw(CDC* pDC)
```

```
{
    CAhnenDoc* pDoc = GetDocument();
    CString temp;
    int offset = 30;

    for (int i = 0; i < pDoc->m_arrAhnentafel.GetSize(); i++)
    {
        _itoa(i+1, temp.GetBuffer(20), 10);
        temp.ReleaseBuffer();
        pDC->TextOut(5, offset*i, temp);
        pDC->TextOut(50,offset*i, pDoc->m_arrAhnentafel[i]);
    }
}
```

Nothing should be too surprising in this function. In fact, it should be sufficiently boring to prompt us to move on to integration.

Integrating the new document/view pair into our application is very similar to the approach we used to add a new, second view to CTreeDoc. Any new pairing requires the assistance of a document template object. Therefore, to provide visibility, we add a new CMultiDocTemplate pointer to the CTreeApp interface immediately below the other public pointers:

```
CMultiDocTemplate* m_pAhnenTemplate;
```

The next step is to initialize the m_pAhnenTemplate pointer in the CTreeApp::InitInstance() function immediately below the other new pointer calls:

```
m_pAhnenTemplate = new CMultiDocTemplate(
    IDR_AHNENTYPE,
    RUNTIME_CLASS(CAhnenDoc),
    RUNTIME_CLASS(CMDIChildWnd),
    RUNTIME_CLASS(CAhnenView));
AddDocTemplate(m_pRelativeTemplate);
```

We looked at this code snippet briefly for m_pPersonTemplate when we were installing the new view support, but now let's take a closer look at what's happening. This snippet breaks down into two calls: the CMultiDocTemplate constructor call and the call to AddDocTemplate(). We will discuss what's going on with AddDocTemplate() in the next section. The CMultiDocTemplate class constructor (invoked upon the new call) takes parameters that associate (within the context of the template) the CAhnenDoc class, the CMDIChildWnd class, the CAhnenView class, and the Windows resource identifier IDR_AHNENTYPE. CAhnenView and CAhnenDoc are the classes we have just constructed for this explicit purpose—an understandable inclusion in the constructor. The CMDIChildWnd class is a generic MDI child frame window class whose default implementation is perfect for our purposes of containing the view display   again, nothing too earth shattering. However, where did this IDR_AHNENTYPE identifier come from, and what is it for?

This is interesting: Why does the CMultiDocTemplate constructor need a resource ID? Think about it. Each unique document/view class pairing will have specific resource needs. Typically, these needs are most readily seen in the menu resource (although any resource type can be

Day 12: MDI and Multiple Views

customized to fit a requirement). Often you will find that a particular document/view pair will need specific menu items to support its unique functionality. Consider the earlier case of the second view class, `CPersonView`, that we attached to `CTreeDoc`. There is little fundamental difference between `CTreeView` and `CPersonView`—at least from a resource perspective—so we let them both use the same resource ID. But think about the differences between `CTreeDoc` and `CAhnenDoc`. They are worlds apart. `CTreeDoc` holds a reference to a changing database. The user has full access to move through and change the records in the database. This functionality is mirrored in the menu resource. What is the charter for `CAhnenDoc`? It is a static structure that holds the ancestry construction built from the database. No record scrolling or changing is allowed—what you see is what you get! Therefore, many of the menu items from the default resource are out of context when used with a `CAhnenDoc` document. A new menu, and potentially many other resource items, are obviously needed.

Let's work on the menu resource first. Start AppStudio and click on the menu type to see the menu resources currently defined. You should see two menu resource items: `IDR_MAINFRAME` and `IDR_TREETYPE`. `IDR_MAINFRAME` identifies a bare-bones menu that presents the options available when no documents are available. `IDR_TREETYPE` identifies the menu resource for our default document/view pair (`CTreeDoc`/`CTreeView`). This menu resource has options specifically designed for interactions with `CTreeDoc` and `CTreeView` (record set scrolling, for example). We want a menu somewhere in between these two extremes for our `CAhnenDoc`/`CAhnenView` pair. While still in AppStudio with the menu type selected, choose the `IDR_TREETYPE` resource identifier in the Resources area. Use the Clipboard to copy `IDR_TREETYPE` by selecting Edit | Copy and then Edit | Paste. A new menu resource should appear with the name `IDR_TREETYPE2`. Using the Properties... button, rename the resource `IDR_AHNENTYPE`. Now, open the resource and remove the following menu items: the entire Record and Info pull-down menus, the Window | New Relative Window menu option, and the Window | New Data Window menu option. Now we have an `IDR_AHNENTYPE` menu resource that reflects the capabilities of our `CAhnenDoc`/`CAhnenView` pair.

But menus aren't the only resource in need of duplicating and updating. You should perform the same operation on the icon resource. In other words, use AppStudio and the Clipboard to copy, paste, and rename the `IDR_TREETYPE` icon resource to `IDR_AHNENTYPE`. The icon resource can remain an exact duplicate of the default icon, or you may want to customize it to the particular needs of your new document/view pair. In our case, we will leave it alone.

Only one resource addition remains. In order for our application to be able to retrieve and use pertinent information about our document/view pair, such information must be available on-file. This information is filed away as a string resource under a specific ID. When AppWizard constructs our default document template, it also supplies a default document template string resource containing a set of default information. When we construct our own document template objects, the assembly of the document template string resource is up to us.

Add the following string to the string resource via AppStudio:

ID	IDR_AHNENTYPE
Value	4
Caption	\nAhnen\nAhnentafel Document\n\n
(Up to 255 chars)	\nAhnentafel Document\nAhnentafel Document

Note: There are no newlines (returns) in the actual caption string. They are included here only for ease of display.

Each substring in the caption (delimited by a \n character) corresponds to a particular string used by the framework. For example, the substring Ahnen is used as a base string for the view window titles in our application. Every other substring has a similar use.

AddDocTemplate()

Of course, we still have to register the new document/view pair with the framework so that the new document may be invoked and used seamlessly in the Windows paradigm. This registration was accomplished in the last line of the most recent piece of code we installed. It was accomplished through a call to AddDocTemplate().

By registering your document template objects, you are telling the framework that this particular document template is available for automated document/view creation. The framework, when prompted, will use a registered document template as a means of creating a document/view pair and displaying it in the MDI mainframe window. The framework is prompted to do this whenever you select the File | New menu option.

What do you suppose will happen if the framework has more than one document template registered? It will ask you, on-the-fly, which one you want invoked. It does this through the dialog shown in Figure 12.3. (For a slightly different approach to multiple document templates, see the checkbook program provided in the MSVC sample code.)

Figure 12.3.
The multiple document template (New) dialog.

DAY 12 MDI and Multiple Views

From this dialog you may choose any of the document template objects that the framework has available. The framework then has enough direction to build a document/view/frame trio.

Summary

The whole idea of the multiple document interface is intended to give the most flexibility to applications and application builders. MDI applications are very useful, so it's only right that MFC gives us the tools needed to exploit this powerful technology.

The central idea behind the MDI architecture is the document template. This object associates the key elements of MDI child windows: a frame, a document, a view, and a resource. When registered, a document template is used by the framework in response to a File | New menu option, which creates a new document object with the associated view and frame. The framework, in such a case, also takes the responsibility for managing all aspects of the document/view pair's existence—even to the point of managing the memory associated with the registered document template.

Despite the help provided by the framework and document templates, MDI applications are still a complicated morass of seemingly unrelated classes interacting in a way that's difficult to understand. We need a road map just to get from one class object to another. Here you will see how to travel from one class to another with a minimum of effort.

Q&A

Q Why is the second `Requery()` necessary in the `LoadAncestry()` function?

A Since `LoadAncestry()` is a recursive function utilizing the static member attribute `m_pSet`, there are no guarantees about the state of `m_pSet` after a recursive call. Therefore, we must reset the record set object after each recursive call.

Q During the Window | New command handler, a document template is retrieved from the document. What if more than one document template is associated with a document? How will `OnWindowNew()` know which document template to use?

A This is true. Many document template objects may relate to a single document class. In the Family Tree application, `CTreeDoc` is related to `CTreeView` by the `m_pRelativeTemplate` object, and it is also related to `CPersonView` by the `m_pPersonTemplate`. Which template is retrieved in the `GetDocTemplate()` call? Actually, `GetDocTemplate()` will return templates that are registered with Windows by the `AddDocTemplate()` command used in `CTreeApp::InitInstance()`.

Q I noticed that only one of the document template objects allocated (newed) in `CWinApp::InitInstance()` is deallocated (deleted) in `CWinApp`'s destructor. Won't we get memory leaks if we don't deallocate all the memory we allocate?

A Yes, you are correct that it is extremely important to deallocate all the memory we allocate. However, you will note that the document template objects that we don't deallocate happen to be the same document template objects that we register with the framework. We don't delete the template objects added via `AddDocTemplate()` because they are managed through the framework. Once we register a document template by calling `AddDocTemplate()`, we relinquish responsibility for it.

Workshop

Quiz

1. Are multiple views and multiple documents automatically installed in the default application?
2. What's the difference between installing multiple-view support and installing multiple-document support?
3. Name the four entities that an MDI document template object associates.
4. Why were the template pointers placed in the application's specification and not in the mainframe, document, or view classes?
5. What's the difference between `CTreeDoc` and `CAhnenDoc`?

Exercises

1. In `CPersonView::OnDraw`, change the `int offset=20` line to `int offset=0`. What effect does this have and why?
2. Change some of the substrings in the document template string resource and experimentally discover what each one does. Confirm your guesses by doing a little research using the manuals that came with your compiler.
3. Create and attach a second view class to the `CAhnenDoc` class that displays the ahnentafel list in a graphical tree structure. Use the `CDC` drawing capabilities discussed in Chapter 4.

Colors, Palettes, and DDBs

WEEK 2

DAY 13
Colors, Palettes, and DDBs

In the use of the personal computer, nothing rates higher on the "fun" scale than good graphics and animation. For many PC users, the day begins with word processing and ends with e-mail, but almost everyone manages to squeeze in a game of Solitaire or to frag a couple of imps in Doom II (my personal favorite). It's only natural that the visual side of computing be attractive to us. We're visual creatures. We like color and motion. We like a graphical user interface much more than a text-based, command-line interface. That's the point of Windows, isn't it? Pointing at and clicking pictures (bitmaps) is much easier than typing commands (especially since you have to remember the command first). Chances are, the entire reason you're currently reading about MFC programming is because you want to exploit the power of Windows and its graphical interface. In that sense, an understanding of bitmaps is very central to our goal of understanding Windows and MFC programming.

Bitmaps are the pictures that make up Windows and its Graphical User Interface (GUI). All the icons, cursors, pictures, and views are (at least at some level) bitmaps. If you program in the Windows environment, there is no getting away from this topic. Because of this dependence, the Windows 3.1 operating environment offers a rich collection of tools and techniques to promote the creation, display, and storage of pictorial images. This chapter is intended to demystify the world of bitmaps by clearing the smoke (and maybe even some of the mirrors)!

A Thousand Points of Light

Before we go crazy with bitmaps, a few terms should be defined. Let's start with the basics. The unit of measure for video display is the *pixel*. The pixel is one dot in one of many rows of dots on your screen that make up the video image. If you put your nose right up to the monitor, you might be able to distinguish a single dot. If you did, you would be looking at a pixel, the smallest definable unit on a video display. The actual size of a pixel varies according to the video screen technology being employed. That is why monitor manufacturers advertise .28 dot pitch or .30 dot pitch monitors. The smaller the number, the smaller the pixel. The smaller the pixel, the more of them you can fit on-screen, and the better the picture quality. Figure 13.1 shows that the letter T on your screen would seem clearer if made up of more pixels.

Figure 13.1.
Low and high DPI.

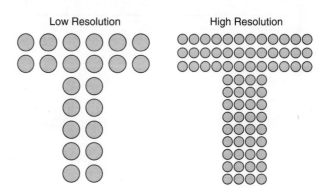

This concept is similar to printed output. A picture printed on a 300 dpi (dots per inch) printer will look grainy. The same picture printed at 600 dpi looks significantly better.

Now let's talk about the next piece of the puzzle. Now that we have a pixel on-screen, we need to power it up. On a monochrome monitor, this is pretty easy. The pixel is either on or off. On a color monitor, things get a little more complicated. If we turn a color pixel on, what color will it be? The color the pixel appears to be on-screen is determined by mixing three basic colors: red, green, and blue. You can think of these colors as the knobs on a stereo. The volume, bass, and treble controls all affect the sound coming out of the speakers. Change any or all of the knobs, and the music sounds different. The same applies to a pixel's color. By mixing different levels or strengths of each of the three colors, you get a different result. These RGB (red, green, blue) combinations form the foundation of color management. The individual strengths of these colors can be any value between 0 and 255. If you're binary-literate, you will immediately recognize that this range can be exactly contained within an 8-bit value (one character). Therefore, three 8-bit values are enough to specify a unique RGB combination for each pixel. However, not all video cards are created equal!

When using Windows with a standard VGA card, you get the default palette of 16 standard colors. These 16 colors are certain mixtures of RGB combinations. Table 13.1 lists the RGB combinations and the resulting colors for the standard palette.

Table 13.1. Core colors for a 16-color video driver.

Red	Green	Blue	Resulting Color
0	0	0	Black
0	0	255	Bright blue
0	255	0	Bright green
0	255	255	Cyan
255	0	0	Bright red
255	0	255	Magenta
255	255	0	Bright yellow
255	255	255	White
0	0	128	Dark blue
0	128	0	Dark green
0	128	128	Blue-green
128	0	0	Brown
128	0	128	Dark purple
128	128	0	Olive
128	128	128	Dark gray
192	192	192	Light gray

Day 13
Colors, Palettes, and DDBs

This is a far cry from the total number of possible color combinations. Three values each having 256 possible values produces 16,777,216 (256 × 256 × 256) possible values. (Sixteen colors seems kind of cheesy in comparison.) What happened to the remaining 16,777,200 colors? Well, that's a long story that will be told in the next few pages. But take heart. Just because our video card will support only 16 colors doesn't mean we can't fool ourselves into thinking that we have more colors. We can generate more colors from the original 16 by mixing them. If we fill an area with an alternative pattern of two different colors, from a distance the area looks like a smooth combination of the two colors. This technique is called *dithering*. We can weave a considerable variety of colors from our meager original 16 by dithering. If you look closely at the colors in your favorite painting program, you should be able to distinguish the dithered colors from the pure (nondithered) colors.

Another way to obtain more colors is to get a better video card. A 256-color VGA video card will give you access to four more pure (nondithered) colors. Wait a minute! Only four more colors? What happened to 256? Is this a case of false advertising? Don't panic. Your new card does have the capability to display 256 different colors, but the standard palette has room for only four extra colors. These colors are listed in Table 13.2.

Table 13.2. Additional "pure" colors available from a 256-color driver.

Red	Green	Blue	Resulting Color
192	220	192	Pale (money) green
166	202	240	Light (sky) blue
255	251	240	Off-white (cream)
160	160	164	Medium gray

Windows wouldn't leave you out in the cold with no way of displaying your new colors. You're just required to expend a little more effort if you want to exploit your new technology. This extra effort centers around a palette that will contain your colors. Dealing with palettes can be a little tricky, but we won't have to face it alone; the MFC will be with us. The MFC class CPalette will help us work with Windows palettes and the associated API calls.

Even our new VGA card with its 256 colors is still a long way from the ultimate capacity of over 16.7 million. What about all the colors in between? Dithering to the rescue! If 256 colors isn't enough, we can always dither our way to hot pink, rusty chartreuse, or any other wacky color you can think of.

If you really wanted the ultimate video experience, you could buy a 24-bit video card. It gives you the luxury of specifying absolute colors, and you don't have to worry about using palettes at all. A 24-bit graphics card has direct access to all 16.7 million colors! Sounds too good to be true? The catch is that although your graphics card can now accommodate 24-bit graphics, you still need a Windows graphics driver (software) that supports the video hardware. This really isn't that big of a limitation. After all, you don't have even close to 16.7 million pixels on-screen anyway. Also, those 256 colors can now come from any of the 16.7 million—well, almost. Windows itself requires 20 basic colors to draw screen backgrounds, borders, and so on, which leaves 236 colors (using a 256-color display driver) for you to manipulate with your own palette. This enables you to write your applications knowing that you will have access to the 20 basic colors regardless of what another application might do to the other 236 colors with its palette manipulations.

My Memory Fails Me

Now that we have defined the pixel and talked about how to determine the color of that pixel, let's look at what's involved with combining pixels into images. Like all artists, the first thing we need is a palette of colors to work with. As with an artist's palette, there is room for only so many colors. In our case, the "room" restriction is a matter of memory (RAM), not physical space. When memory was incredibly expensive, most people weren't willing to put 512K of RAM on a video card when their PC had only 256K of main memory! As memory prices dropped, the amount of memory that people could reasonably attach to a video card went up. Table 13.3 shows how much RAM is really needed for an image of a specific size and desired number of colors.

Table 13.3. Video memory needed versus image size and colors desired.

Width (Pixels)	Height (Pixels)	Bits per Pixel	Colors Desired	Memory (Bytes)
320	200	1	2	8,000
320	400	1	2	16,000
320	400	4	16	64,000
640	480	1	2	38,400
640	480	4	16	153,600
640	480	8	256	307,200
640	480	24	16,777,216	921,600
800	600	1	2	60,000
800	600	4	16	240,000
800	600	8	256	480,000
800	600	24	16,777,216	1,440,000

continues

Day 13: Colors, Palettes, and DDBs

Table 13.3. continued

Width (Pixels)	Height (Pixels)	Bits per Pixel	Colors Desired	Memory (Bytes)
1024	768	1	2	98,304
1024	768	4	16	393,216
1024	768	8	256	768,432
1024	768	24	16,777,216	2,359,296
1280	1024	1	2	163,840
1280	1024	4	16	655,360
1280	1024	8	256	1,310,720
1280	1024	24	16,777,216	3,932,160

You can see that about 3.9M of video memory is required to display a 1280x1024, 16.7-million-color bitmap. Although video memory is getting cheaper, it still adds a considerable amount to the cost of a video card.

Now that we have talked about colors, let's look at transforming colors into palettes.

Palettes

Palettes are a colorful subject. They play an important role in the bitmap world and in Windows as a whole. But so far I have used the word "palette" without really defining what one is! A *palette* is a structure in Windows that holds color information. There can be only one active palette at any given time. When you start Windows, it loads a default palette of colors (let's say 256, assuming that you have a 256-color card). Except for the 20 standard colors discussed earlier, all the colors in that palette are negotiable.

You might ask, "Who does the negotiation?" The answer is the palette manager. Oh no—you know what happens when management gets involved! Well, the result here is similar. The palette manager compares your palette needs to the needs of other programs. All these color needs are then mapped to Windows' current palette, and you are given the colors closest to the ones you requested. Constant compromise is the art of middle management!

There is some saving grace to all this. When your Windows application is in the foreground (when it is the active application), the palette manager tries to rearrange the physical (active) palette to better accommodate your application's color needs (your logical palette). This means that the applications in the background get a revised palette that probably doesn't suit their needs. You might have seen the effect of this on your own PC. When you bring an application into the foreground, the background applications look a little weird. When another application is brought into the foreground (and, consequently, the current application becomes a background application), the palette manager goes through the same renegotiation of the palette, and your application will be given a revised palette that might not look so great. This is the solution Microsoft came up with to deal with colors on a system that could be running many different applications simultaneously. The bottom line is that you can't always get what you want.

There is another way to deal with the palette problem. From within your application, you can create a new palette and tell Windows that you want this new palette to replace the old one. This is a complete physical palette replacement. If your application creates a palette of 236 (remember, 20 colors are reserved) shades of purple, other applications (provided they aren't as mean) will have to deal with a nearly unworkable palette.

The palette manager will still try its best to help the other applications get the colors they need, but with only 236 shades of purple to choose from, the palette manager might end up mapping the other applications' color requirements to the 20 reserved colors. This might be the closest it can get.

How can we tie this back to the MFC? The MFC's answer to palettes and palette management is the CPalette class. This class encapsulates a Windows palette object (of type LOGPALETTE) and the associated palette-related API functions. CPalette provides a number of member functions to manipulate palettes. These are listed in Table 13.4.

Table 13.4. CPalette member functions.

Function	Description
CPalette	Constructs a CPalette object with no attached Windows palette. You must initialize the CPalette object with one of the other member functions (such as CreatePalette) before it can be used.
CreatePalette	Initializes a CPalette object by creating a Windows color palette and attaching this palette to your CPalette object.
FromHandle	Returns a pointer to a CPalette object when given a handle to a Windows palette object. If a CPalette object isn't already attached to the Windows palette, a temporary CPalette object is created and attached.
GetPaletteEntries	Retrieves a range of palette entries in a logical palette.
SetPaletteEntries	Sets RGB color values and flags in a range of entries in a logical palette.
AnimatePalette	Replaces entries in the logical palette identified by the CPalette object. The application doesn't have to update its client area because Windows maps the new entries into the system palette immediately.

continues

Day 13: Colors, Palettes, and DDBs

Table 13.4. continued

Function	Description
GetNearestPaletteIndex	Returns the index of the entry in the logical palette that most closely matches a color value.
ResizePalette	Changes the size of the logical palette specified by the CPalette object to the specified number of entries.

There's some good stuff here. First, we would instantiate a CPalette object. This gives us an empty object. We then would need to use CreatePalette() to create a palette and attach it to the CPalette object. The culmination of this process is the call to CDC::RealizePalette(), which takes the CPalette object and makes it the current Windows palette. The CPalette class provides a clean interface to the world of palettes.

The palette information that CreatePalette() needs is held in a structure called LOGPALETTE. Its structure is

```
typedef struct tagLOGPALETTE {    /* lgpl */
    WORD         palVersion;
    WORD         palNumEntries;
    PALETTEENTRY palPalEntry[1];
} LOGPALETTE;
```

The LOGPALETTE structure defines a logical color palette in Windows. This structure has three components. The palVersion entry specifies the Windows version number for the structure. This value should be 0x300 for Windows 3.0 and later. The entry palNumEntries specifies the number of palette color entries. (You don't always have to have a palette of 256 colors. A palette need only include the colors you are actually using.) palPalEntry specifies an array of PALETTEENTRY structures that define the color and usage of each entry in the logical palette. The colors in the palette entry table should appear in order of importance, because entries earlier in the logical palette are most likely to be placed in the system palette. Earlier entries will be given a higher priority during negotiations with the palette manager.

The PALETTEENTRY structure is defined as

```
typedef struct tagPALETTEENTRY {      /* pe */
    BYTE   peRed;
    BYTE   peGreen;
    BYTE   peBlue;
    BYTE   peFlags;
} PALETTEENTRY;
```

The PALETTEENTRY structure specifies the color and usage of an entry in a logical color palette. peRed specifies the intensity of red for the palette entry color. peGreen specifies the intensity of green for the palette entry color. peBlue specifies the intensity of blue for the palette entry color. peFlags specifies how the palette entry is to be used. The peFlags member can be set to zero (which informs Windows that the palette entry contains an RGB value and that it should be mapped normally) or set to one of the values in Table 13.5.

Table 13.5. peFlag options.

Value	Description
PC_EXPLICIT	Specifies that the low-order word of the logical palette entry designates a hardware palette index. This flag allows the application to show the contents of the palette for the display device.
PC_NOCOLLAPSE	Specifies that the color will be placed in an unused entry in the system palette instead of being matched to an existing color in the system palette. Once this color is in the system palette, colors in other logical palettes can be matched to this color. If there are no unused entries in the system palette, the color is matched normally.
PC_RESERVED	Specifies that the logical palette entry will be used for palette animation. Because the color will change frequently, using this flag prevents other windows from matching colors to this palette entry. If an unused system-palette entry is available, this color is placed in that entry. Otherwise, the color will not be available for animation.

Hopefully, the connection is clear. peRed, peGreen, and peBlue correspond to the RGB color values I mentioned earlier. peFlags allows us to mark a color entry as something we want treated specially. So ends our overview of palettes. Let's move on to the bigger picture (no pun intended) and look at bitmaps.

A *CBitmap* Is Worth a Thousand *WORD*s

The actual pictures that we see in Windows are conglomerations of the colorful pixel objects we have been talking about in this chapter. We arrange pixels with particular colors in a particular order to form shapes. This imposed order is preserved and stored in Windows through the use of a BITMAP structure, defined as follows:

```
typedef struct tagBITMAP {
    int        bmType;
    int        bmWidth;
    int        bmHeight;
    int        bmWidthBytes;
    BYTE       bmPlanes;
    BYTE       bmBitsPixel;
    void FAR*  bmBits;
} BITMAP;
```

DAY 13: Colors, Palettes, and DDBs

Each of `BITMAP`'s fields contains a crucial bit of information regarding the image. Naturally, the most important field is the last field—`bmBits`. This field contains the actual data that makes up the image. It points to an array of values, which contains color codes for our pixels. The conversion of a linear array of color values into the two-dimensional matrix of the image is an interesting process. The conversion is heavily dependent on the width and height of the bitmap (in pixels)—`bmWidth` and `bmHeight`, respectively. The `bmBitsPixel` field also plays a significant role in this conversion. It holds the number of bits allotted to each pixel for its color definition (1 bit for two colors, 2 bits for four colors, and so on up to 24 bits for 16.7 million colors). But how the array is actually mapped to the image depends on the physical hardware and hence on the display driver. It is clear that the data contained in the `BITMAP` structure is very dependent on the video hardware. They are therefore called *device-dependent bitmaps,* or *DDBs.*

> **Note:** The remaining fields in the `BITMAP` structure play less of a role in our work, but let's say a few words about them anyway. The `bmType` field is an indicator for the bitmap type. This field will typically be zero (indicating a logical bitmap). The `bmPlanes` field indicates the number of color planes used in the bitmap. In our work, we will use only a single color plane; color will be determined exclusively by RGB values. This value is therefore set to one.
>
> The `bmWidthBytes` field concerns itself with the underlying structure of the bitmap data. It answers the question of how wide, in bytes, the bitmap is. A naive first guess might be the `bmWidth` value. The `bmWidth` field holds the width of the bitmap in terms of pixels; a pixel might or might not be determined by one byte. The bitmap width (in bytes) must also take into account the number of color bits required for each pixel. Each consecutive grouping of `bmBitsPixel` (the number of color bits per pixel) bits in `bmBits` defines a pixel. Therefore, the width in bytes of the bitmap can be computed by multiplying `bmWidth` by `bmBitsPixel` and dividing this number by the number of bits in a byte (typically 8). However, that's not the end of the story. There's no rule that the product of pixel width and the number of bits per pixel will be divisible by 8! But there *is* a rule that the byte width of bitmaps must be rounded up to the next `DWORD` boundary. Taking all this into account results in the following formula:
>
> ```
> bmWidthBytes = (((bmWidth*bmBitsPixel) + 31) & ~31) >> 3;
> ```
>
> `bmWidth*bmBitsPixel` gives us the bitmap width in bits. `+ 31) & ~31)` rounds up to the next `DWORD` boundary. `>> 3` divides by 8 to convert bits to bytes. We won't be using this formula, but if you hang around bitmaps enough, you *will* encounter it. Be warned.

The MFC class that encapsulates the BITMAP structure is CBitmap. It is a descendent of the CGDIObject class, which encapsulates a Windows graphics device interface (GDI) object. A GDI object can be anything from a font to a cursor to a bitmap. Naturally, the GDI bitmap object is what we're interested in. A GDI bitmap is "tuned" for a specific device context. It's a bitmap that's device-dependent.

> **Note:** CBitmap and CPalette are siblings derived from the master class CGDIObject. Both classes encapsulate a Windows structure with associated API calls. CBitmap centers around the BITMAP structure, which is the storage device for bitmap data. CPalette centers around the LOGPALETTE structure, which is the storage device for palette data. The similarity between the two classes is not coincidental! Other CGDIObject-derived classes also have a similar look and feel: CFont, CBrush, CPen, and CRgn. Study the CGDIObject class for a better insight into these classes and concepts.

CBitmap Member Functions and Attributes

Now for an overview of how CBitmap can be used. CBitmap provides member functions to manipulate a bitmap. These member functions allow us to construct the CBitmap object, install a bitmap in it with one of the initialization member functions, and then manipulate the bitmap. A number of public initialization functions and operations can be accessed. Table 13.6 highlights these.

Table 13.6. CBitmap functions.

Function	Description
LoadBitmap	Initializes the object by loading a named bitmap resource from the application's executable file and attaching the bitmap to the object.
LoadOEMBitmap	Initializes the object by loading a predefined Windows bitmap and attaching the bitmap to the object.
CreateBitmap	Initializes the object with a device-dependent memory bitmap that has a specified width, height, and bit pattern.
CreateBitmapIndirect	Initializes the object with a bitmap that has the width, height, and bit pattern (if one is specified) given in the BITMAP structure.

continues

Day 13: Colors, Palettes, and DDBs

Table 13.6. continued

Function	Description
`CreateCompatibleBitmap`	Initializes the object with a bitmap so that it is compatible with a specified device.
`CreateDiscardableBitmap`	Initializes the object with a discardable bitmap that is compatible with a specified device.
`FromHandle`	Returns a pointer to a `CBitmap` object when given a handle to a `BITMAP` object.
`SetBitmapBits`	Sets the bits of a bitmap to the specified bit values.
`GetBitmapBits`	Copies the bits of the specified bitmap into the specified buffer.
`SetBitmapDimension`	Assigns a width and height to a bitmap in 0.1-millimeter units.
`GetBitmapDimension`	Retrieves the width and height of the bitmap. Warning: Don't use this unless width and height were previously set using `SetBitmapDimension()`.

We're old hands at looking at lists of class functions. Running down the preceding list of functions, you should be able to nod your head, make a serious-sounding grunt now and then, and finally come to the end of the list thinking that it seems a reasonable attempt at functionality. It provides for the construction, initialization, and loading of bitmap data. It provides access to the underlying `BITMAP` structure as well as the bits themselves. It allows access to some of the pertinent bitmap statistics. It even has a couple of arcane functions that must have some crucial use for someone. But isn't there something odd about this list? We're talking about bitmaps here! There isn't a member function that displays our bitmap on the screen. The one thing that every good American bitmap has to do is be displayed. Not to worry: We will fix this particular oversight. No doubt there was some compelling reason that a `DrawBitmap()` function wasn't included as a member of `CBitmap` (but the rationale escapes me).

Are there any other enhancements to `CBitmap` that are immediately apparent? Hmmmm, what about the `SaveToFile()` and `LoadFromFile()` functions? The `LoadBitmap()` and `LoadOEMBitmap()` functions only initialize the `CBitmap` object by loading a bitmap from the application's resource or by loading a Windows standard bitmap. This is a very handy capability, but it won't help us load from files. It seems that loading and saving are candidates for a `CBitmap` enhancement. However, the loading and saving of bitmap files is a very complicated business and, as it turns out, doesn't logically fall within the purview of `CBitmap`. Therefore, the loading and saving functionality will be encapsulated in another class. This topic is postponed until the next chapter. Nothing else springs to mind, so we can derive a new class from `CBitmap` that exports drawing functionality for bitmaps.

Let's create a wrapper class for `CBitmap`. Before you rush off and invoke ClassWizard to create this new class, you should know that ClassWizard won't help you. ClassWizard will let you derive only from certain "preferred" classes. Needless to say, `CBitmap` is not one of the elite. You might recall a similar dilemma when we were constructing the `CDate` class. `CDate` was derived from `CObject`, another MFC class not supported by ClassWizard. We have to manually write a class definition and implementation for classes derived from unsupported MFC classes such as `CBitmap` and `CObject`. Manually? In this age of automated programming support and Visual C++, the word "manually" should send a chill through your veins. Oh well, it can't be helped—at least with the current release of the compiler. The following is the interface and implementation for `CDDBitmap` (our device-dependent bitmap class):

```
// Filename: DDBITMAP.H

#ifndef __DDBITMAP_H__
#define __DDBITMAP_H__

class CDDBitmap : public CBitmap
{

// Constructors and destructors
public:
    CDDBitmap();
    ~CDDBitmap();

// Operations
public:
    BOOL DrawOnDC (CDC* pDC, int x, int y);
    BOOL StretchOnDC (CDC* pDC, int x, int y, int newWidth, int newHeight);

};

#endif

// Filename: DDBitmap.cpp

#include "stdafx.h"
#include "DDBitmap.h"

// Constructors and destructors
CDDBitmap::CDDBitmap()
{
    // Place any one-time construction code here
}

CDDBitmap::~CDDBitmap()
{
    // Place any destruction code here (i.e. clean-up)
}

// Operations
BOOL CDDBitmap::DrawOnDC (CDC* pDC, int x, int y)
```

Day 13: Colors, Palettes, and DDBs

```cpp
{
    // Note: This function should really call
    // the StretchOnDC() function so as to minimize
    // code duplication. However, implementing this
    // second method demonstrates the BitBlt()
    // function of the CDC class.

    // Make sure the CDC pointer is usable
    ASSERT_VALID(pDC);

    // Get bitmap info
    BITMAP bm;
    GetObject(sizeof(bm), &bm);

    // Create bitmap memory context
    CDC dcBM;
    dcBM.CreateCompatibleDC(pDC);

    // Select the bitmap into the DC
    CBitmap* pOldBM = dcBM.SelectObject(this);

    // Block transfer the bitmap onto the screen
    BOOL Result = pDC->BitBlt(x, y, bm.bmWidth,
            bm.bmHeight, &dcBM, 0, 0, SRCCOPY);

    // Return the DC to its original state
    dcBM.SelectObject(pOldBM);

    return Result;
}

BOOL CDDBitmap::StretchOnDC (CDC* pDC,
    int x, int y, int newWidth, int newHeight)
{
    // Make sure the CDC pointer is usable
    ASSERT_VALID(pDC);

    // Get bitmap info
    BITMAP bm;
    GetObject(sizeof(bm), &bm);

    // Create bitmap memory context
    CDC dcBM;
    dcBM.CreateCompatibleDC(pDC);

    // Select the bitmap into the DC
    CBitmap* pOldBM = dcBM.SelectObject(this);

    // Stretch the bitmap onto the screen
    BOOL Result = pDC->StretchBlt(x, y,
            newWidth, newHeight, &dcBM, 0, 0,
            bm.bmWidth, bm.bmHeight, SRCCOPY);

    // Return the DC to its original state
    dcBM.SelectObject(pOldBM);

    return Result;
}
```

Aside from the housekeeping code, we have implemented two functions that facilitate the drawing of bitmaps on-screen: DrawOnDC() and StretchOnDC(). Both of these functions perform the same basic function: They copy the bitmap data to the device context so that it may be beheld in all its glory. These functions differ in that DrawOnDC() copies the bitmap to the display while maintaining the bitmap's dimensions. StretchOnDC(), on the other hand, may stretch the bitmap image (in a specified way) during the transfer. The DrawOnDC() function is a specialized version of the StretchOnDC() function, so by all rights, DrawOnDC() should call StretchOnDC(). We didn't implement it in that way for the sole purpose of demonstrating an alternative means of bitmap transfer. In fact, one of the exercises asks you to rewrite DrawOnDC() so that it does call StretchOnDC().

Looking at the code for these two functions, you will notice that the listings are identical except for the actual bit transfer call. Therefore, I need to explain only one of the functions. The StretchOnDC() function is slightly more complicated, so I will take you through it step-by-step. The first line of code validates the pDC object so as to ensure that we're working with a usable device context. The second function call retrieves the underlying BITMAP object through the use of CGDIObject::GetObject(). This function will retrieve whatever underlying object is appropriate for the particular CGDIObject-derived class. For example, a call to GetObject() from a CFont object would retrieve a LOGFONT object. Once we have the BITMAP structure, we may probe its depths by using what we know of BITMAP. The data we need, in this case, is the height and width. The next piece of code instantiates a bitmap memory context (simply a CDC object) and makes it compatible to the pDC object passed in as a parameter. Compatibility is a big issue at the heart of DDBs. Device dependence means that our bitmap format is peculiar to a given device and hence to a device context. Making our bitmap compatible to the current output device (pDC) is an important step. The next line of code, the SelectObject() call, actually transfers our bitmap to the bitmap memory context we just created. During this process, we also save the old bitmap so that we can restore the context to its original state in the second-to-last line of code. Remember, we must leave everything as we found it, or things might get lost. In terms of computers, lost "things" result in memory leaks.

Finally, we get to the actual transfer of bits to the screen: the StretchBlt() function. StretchBlt() is a block transfer function that copies bitmaps from one device context to another (in our case, it copies the bitmap from dcBM to pDC). Its parameter list is given in Table 13.7.

Table 13.7. StretchBlt() parameters.

Parameter(s)	Description
int x, int y	The destination coordinates for the bitmap.
int nWidth, int nHeight	The new height and width values for the destination (stretched) bitmap.

continues

Colors, Palettes, and DDBs

Table 13.7. continued

Parameter(s)	Description
`CDC* pSrcDC`	A pointer to the device context containing the bitmap to be transferred.
`int xSrc, int ySrc`	The top-left coordinates from which to start reading the bitmap from the source context (`pSrcDC`).
`int nSrcWidth, int nSrcHeight`	The width and height of the rectangle to copy from the source context (`pSrcDC`).
`DWORD dwRop`	A raster operation (ROP) code that determines the interaction of the bitmap with the destination background. See Chapter 4 for more information on ROP codes.

Note that the `BitBlt()` function takes the same parameters except for the new width and height (`nWidth` and `nHeight`), because they aren't needed for a nonstretched transfer. Also note that these two transfer functions will operate correctly only if the two device contexts involved stem from the same device. In other words, don't try to use these functions to transfer bitmaps from a screen device context to a printer device context. At best, your program will experience unpredictable behavior!

Paint Me a Picture (or, Everything I Learned About Art I Learned in Kindergarten)

I have a fun exercise to help you understand one of the first bitmap concepts. We are going to create two bitmap resources that we can use as default photos when a real photo isn't available from our Family Tree database. Start by going into AppStudio and creating two 32x32-bit bitmaps. Look at Figures 13.2 and 13.3 for inspiration. (I never said I was an artist!) The female default photo resource should be named `IDB_DEF_FEMALE`, and the male should be named `IDB_DEF_MALE`.

Now that we have a set of default pictures as resources, let's hook them in so they are displayed. We will base our choice of photos on the gender field in the record set. Let's concentrate on getting the bitmap to show on our data window. Displaying bitmaps where predefined device contexts aren't available will have to wait.

Figure 13.2.
Default female photo.

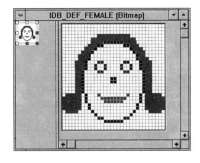

Figure 13.3.
Default male photo.

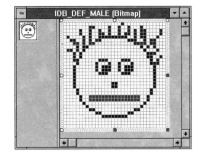

Okay, back to getting `CDDBitmap` support installed into our Family Tree application. Make the following changes to `CPersonView`'s `OnDraw()` function:

```
void CPersonView::OnDraw(CDC* pDC)
{
    CTreeDoc* pDoc = (CTreeDoc*)GetDocument();
    CTreeSet* pSet = &pDoc->m_treeSet;
    CString S;
    int PortraitID;

    int X = 10, Y = 10;
    int offset = 2*(pDC->GetTextExtent("Wpqit", 5)).cy;

    if (pDC->IsPrinting())
    {
        Y += 2*offset;
    }

    pDC->TextOut(X, Y, "Full Name: " + pSet->FullName());
    pDC->TextOut(X, Y += offset, "Maiden: " + pSet->m_MAIDEN);

    if (pSet->m_IS_MALE)
    {
        S = "Person is Male.";
        PortraitID = IDB_DEF_MALE;
    }
    else
```

Day 13: Colors, Palettes, and DDBs

```
    {
        S = "Person is Female.";
        PortraitID = IDB_DEF_FEMALE;
    }

    // Draw bitmap on pDC object
    if (!pDC->IsPrinting())
    {
        if (pSet->m_PORTRAIT.m_dwDataLength != 0)
        {
            // Place database bitmap display code here
        }
        else
        {
            CDDBitmap DDB;
            DDB.LoadBitmap(PortraitID);
            DDB.DrawOnDC(pDC, 300, 10);
            DDB.DeleteObject();
        }
    }

    pDC->TextOut(X, Y += offset, S);
    pDC->TextOut(X, Y += offset, "Birth Place: " + pSet->m_WHERE_BORN);
    .
    .
    .
}
```

Everything here should be relatively self-explanatory. A couple of items of interest do stand out: the call to DeleteObject() and the reference to m_dwDataLength. DeleteObject() is a GDIObject function that cleans up the memory sullied by GDI objects. This call is necessary to the health of your application because it cleans up after the LoadBitmap() call. This is another one of those instances where we must be careful to prevent memory leaks. It's not a big deal unless you forget to do it! The second item that might have you scratching your head is the reference to m_dwDataLength. This variable is a member of the CLongBinary class, which is the MFC database storage receptacle for bitmaps (among other things). We check the length of the CLongBinary object to determine if a bitmap portrait is available for our current subject. If not, we display the generic, handmade portrait found in the application's resource.

Some words of warning concerning any new class that you create: Be sure to #include the interface file (DIBITMAP.H in this case) in the appropriate application file (PERSONVI.CPP in this case). Also make sure you have added the new class's implementation file (DIBITMAP.CPP) to your project files. Either of these oversights will prevent an executable from being built. So go to it! Compile, link, and run. How do you like that! A girl picture for the girls and a boy picture for the boys. It actually worked the first time. Break out the champagne!

A Point of View

Okay, let's get our feet back on earth. Yes, we did have a success and yes, we should always celebrate successes when we can, but the CDDBitmap class is not the end-all, be-all of bitmap manipulation. It all goes back to the name "device-dependent bitmap." The word "dependent" in the real world has very few good connotations; in computer-speak, it has even fewer. The word "independent" connotes strength and vitality, whereas "dependent" connotes weakness and inferiority. Our CDDBitmap class is looking less and less attractive by the minute. Don't bemoan our work on this class. Indeed, we knew of some of its limitations from the start. But CDDBitmap still has uses. The code we just installed in our application will remain as it is because the CDDBitmap implementation does what is needed.

In the world of bitmaps, especially prior to Windows 3.1, bitmaps were created as device-dependent bitmaps, or DDBs. These DDBs contained information (tuned to a specific device) about the bits that make up the image.

The problem with DDBs is that they don't contain a copy of the color palette that existed when the DDB was created. Yes, you heard me right! After all we learned about palettes, DDBs don't even use them (don't worry; we will use palettes soon). This is like trying to touch up the paint on your wall after throwing out the paint can. You buy some new paint, but the color doesn't quite match. That's the way it is here too. The palette that was present during the creation of the DDB had all the current colors being used. When the DDB is saved as a file, the color palette isn't saved with it. As a result, when the DDB is read back into memory, the palette manager in Windows has to map the colors in the DDB as closely as possible to the colors in the current palette. This doesn't always look so great.

So lies the problem with DDBs. They are all constructed from the point of view of a particular machine with a particular palette of colors.

Summary

The device-dependent bitmap was a good start in getting the graphics world going. It provided a way to store graphical data. Since that time we have become much smarter about how we do business. The realization that bitmap data will transcend the 4 bpp (bits per pixel) world into something grander brought the realization that we had to prepare. In the next chapter we will explore device-independent bitmaps (DIBs). This format provides a way to store data in a format we all can love.

Colors, Palettes, and DDBs

Q&A

Q You just said that DDBs are very limiting due to the lack of an included color palette and that DIBs are better. Why are we learning about DDBs?

A DDBs are much faster. This is because the DDB is already "tuned" to the device context. Also, the MFC still supports DDBs, so I felt that a broad knowledge of bitmaps could only help. What doesn't kill us (or bore us to death) will make us stronger.

Workshop

Quiz

1. If we created a new screen resolution of 420x551, how many bytes of video memory would you need to display a 16-color bitmap of that size?
2. When using `CreatePalette()`, do we always have to fill all available entries (for example, 256 colors in a 256-color palette)? Why or why not?
3. Is there a surefire way of making sure that your application gets all the colors it needs in order to display properly when it's in the foreground?
4. Why is the `CBitmap` attribute `bmBitsPixel` so crucial in the data conversion process of `bmBits`?

Exercises

1. Rewrite `DDBitmap`'s `DrawOnDC()` function so that it calls the `StretchOnDC()` function.
2. Write an application that shows all the colors in the current (active) palette.

WEEK 2

DIBs

DIBs

We found in the last chapter that the CBitmap class left much to be desired in terms of ease of display. The solution to this dilemma was the CDDBitmap class, which derived itself from CBitmap. This new class retained all the good features of CBitmap while adding a draw function.

In this same vein, we must now overcome CBitmap's file loading/saving limitation by creating a new class. This new class will provide all the housekeeping chores necessary for loading and saving bitmaps. On the surface, this doesn't seem to be a huge chore, but as we shall see, this simple statement of functionality will take up practically this entire chapter.

The Problem

What's the big deal about transferring bitmaps to and from a file? Can't we just read the bitmap data directly into the memory defining the CBitmap object? No. Think about what a CBitmap object is: a device-dependent bitmap. Do we want bitmap files to be dependent on the device on which they were created? No again. We want to be able to load any bitmap we happen to come across. Of course, that particular wish is a little grandiose. It seems that every program that deals with bitmaps has its own format for storage and compression. However, the thousand-and-one different bitmap formats (BMP, GIF, PCX, and TIFF, just to name a few) would be a drop in the bucket compared to the number of formats needed to further accommodate device dependence.

So what do we do about this device dependence problem? Luckily, Microsoft had its thinking cap on. It created a device-independent bitmap standard: DIB. This standard allows Windows bitmaps to be stored in a file the same way no matter which device creates them.

DIBs to the Rescue

Device dependence isn't confined to the physical ordering of the pixel bits. There is also the matter of color. Bitmap device dependence has its roots in the ordering of the bits, but actual color codes for each bit are also dependent on the specific palette used during bitmap creation. The palette, of course, is highly dependent on the hardware device.

The DIB format contains the actual data bits that make up the bitmap and also contains the color palette used to create the DIB. What a breakthrough! Now when your application reads in the DIB file, it will also read in the color palette and know what colors were used to create the original.

The end result of this new format is a bitmap that looks as good now as the day it was created. Well, most of the time. We still have to deal with the issue of sharing "the" palette with other applications and swapping our palette in and out (as we discussed in Chapter 13).

Two DIB Formats

Just when you thought it was safe to DIB, there are actually two DIB file formats. Yes, two. The difference in these two formats is based on the intended target. One file format is based on the 32-bit Windows world, and the other is based on the 24-bit PM (OS/2 Presentation Manager) world. Let's first examine the PM file format, shown in Figure 14.1.

Figure 14.1.
The PM DIB file structure.

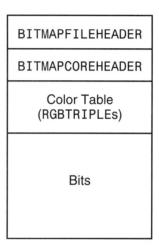

The PM file format includes a `BITMAPFILEHEADER` structure, a `BITMAPCOREHEADER`, and a series of two or more `RGBTRIPLE` structures (the 24-bit part) that describe the colors in the color palette. All of this is followed by the actual bit data. I will show you the guts of all these structures in a minute.

The Windows DIB file format, shown in Figure 14.2, is a little different. It starts out with the same `BITMAPFILEHEADER`. It's followed by a `BITMAPINFOHEADER`, and then a series of two or more `RGBQUAD` structures (the 32-bit part) that describe the colors in the color palette. All of this is followed by the actual bit data.

Let's examine the pieces. First, the `BITMAPFILEHEADER`. This structure has five fields, listed in Table 14.1.

Table 14.1. The `BITMAPFILEHEADER` structure.

Field	Size	Description
bfType	UINT	The bytes BM for a bitmap that is 4D42 hex.
bfSize	DWORD	The total size of the file.
bfReserved1	UINT	Set to 0 (do not change).
bfReserved2	UINT	Set to 0 (do not change).
bfOffBits	DWORD	Offset to the actual data bits from the beginning of the file.

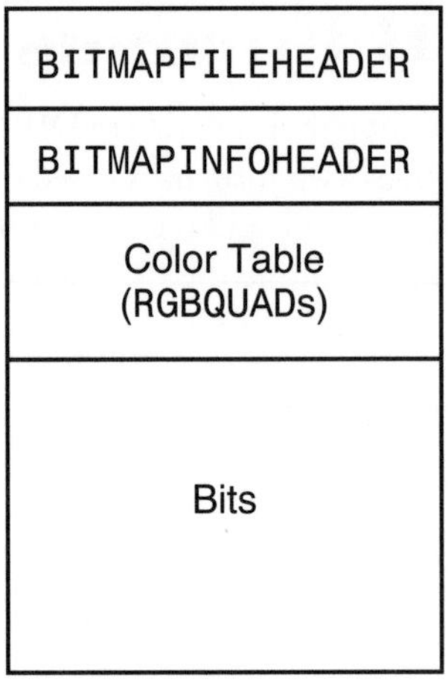

DIBs

Figure 14.2.
The Windows DIB file structure.

```
┌─────────────────────┐
│  BITMAPFILEHEADER   │
├─────────────────────┤
│  BITMAPINFOHEADER   │
├─────────────────────┤
│     Color Table     │
│     (RGBQUADs)      │
├─────────────────────┤
│                     │
│                     │
│        Bits         │
│                     │
│                     │
└─────────────────────┘
```

When reading in the bitmap file, you should ensure that the bfType is BM. This tells you that the file is DIB as opposed to PCX, IMG, or some other format. bfSize is useful in telling us the total size of the file. bfOffBits lets us know where in the file the actual bit data starts. These pieces of information are critical for breaking the file into its constituent parts.

The next block of information in the DIB file is the bitmap header. The BITMAPINFOHEADER and BITMAPCOREHEADER structures differ a little. The BITMAPCOREHEADER (for the PM DIB) consists of the data shown in Table 14.2.

Table 14.2. The BITMAPCOREHEADER structure.

Field	Type	Description
bcSize	DWORD	The size of the BITMAPCOREHEADER structure in bytes.
bcWidth	short	The width of the bitmap in pixels.
bcHeight	short	The height of the bitmap in pixels.
bcPlanes	WORD	The number of color planes defined for the bitmap. For our uses, set to 1.
bcBitCount	WORD	The number of bits per pixel (1, 4, 8, or 24).

bcSize gives the size of the BITMAPCOREHEADER structure. This can help us determine the offset toward reading the bit data (if, for some reason, the file header is unavailable). It also allows us to confirm that the structure we read in is, in fact, a BITMAPCOREHEADER as opposed to a BITMAPINFOHEADER (we couldn't tell otherwise). bcBitCount gives us the number of bits per pixel. This could help us determine the number of RGBTRIPLE structures in the color table. The remaining fields correspond exactly to fields in the BITMAP structure described in Chapter 13.

The `BITMAPINFOHEADER` structure contains much more information about the bitmap. See Table 14.3.

Table 14.3. The `BITMAPINFOHEADER` structure.

Field	Size	Description
`biSize`	DWORD	The size of this structure in bytes.
`biWidth`	LONG	The width of the bitmap in pixels.
`biHeight`	LONG	The height of the bitmap in pixels.
`biPlanes`	WORD	The number of color planes defined for the bitmap. For our uses, set to 1.
`biBitCount`	WORD	The color bits per pixel (1, 4, 8, or 24).
`biCompression`	DWORD	The compression scheme (0 for none).
`biSizeImage`	DWORD	The size of the bitmap in bytes (required only if `biCompression` is less than or greater than 0).
`biXPelsPerMeter`	LONG	The horizontal resolution in pixels per meter.
`biYPelsPerMeter`	LONG	The vertical resolution in pixels per meter.
`biClrUsed`	DWORD	The number of colors used in the image.
`biClrImportant`	DWORD	The number of important colors used in the image.

This header provides a wealth of information about the bitmap. Again, `biSize` provides the size of the `BITMAPINFOHEADER` in bytes. The height and width of the bitmap are contained in `biHeight` and `biWidth`, information that could be useful in sizing a window prior to applying the bitmap to it. The `biBitCount` field tells how many bits per pixel (bpp) were used in creating the file. If `biBitCount` is 1 bpp, two RGBQUAD structures are needed. Sixteen RGBQUADs are required for a 4 bpp bitmap, and 256 RGBQUADs are needed for an 8 bpp bitmap. The 24 bpp bitmap is special case. Since 24 bits hold enough information for three 8-bit values, no mapping is necessary. The 24 bits give the three 8-bit RGB values directly. No palette is necessary. `biCompression` and `biSizeImage` are used only if the image is compressed. We won't deal with compressed images in this book. Therefore, `biCompression` will be set to `BI_RGB` (indicating straight RGB values and hence no compression), and `biSizeImage` will be set to 0 (indicating that the image size is the same as that calculated from the file header data: `bfSize – bfOffBits`).

To reduce the size of the bitmap file, `biClrUsed` may be used. If it's nonzero, `biClrUsed` indicates how many colors are used in the bitmap and how many RGBQUAD structures are present in the color map. This saves space over assuming that an 8 bpp bitmap actually uses the entire palette. If we

DIBs

put only enough RGBQUAD structures as necessary for the number of colors we used instead of how many we have to choose from at the time, this will cut down on the file size.

If a color table is used, the next item in the DIB file is an array of color values. Each item in the array is an RGBQUAD or RGBTRIPLE structure, depending on the DIB format (Windows or PM). These structures are nearly identical. They both describe the RGB values for each color in the color table. See Tables 14.4 and 14.5.

Table 14.4. The RGBTRIPLE structure.

Field	Size	Description
rgbtBlue	BYTE	The blue intensity.
rgbtGreen	BYTE	The green intensity.
rgbtRed	BYTE	The red intensity.

Table 14.5. The RGBQUAD structure.

Field	Size	Description
rgbBlue	BYTE	The blue intensity.
rgbGreen	BYTE	The green intensity.
rgbRed	BYTE	The red intensity.
rbgReserved	BYTE	Set to 0.

As you can see, there are differences between the two formats. You might wonder why you should care. Well, I'll tell you. We are going to have to load these DIB files (we are going to stick with the Windows DIB format instead of PM) from the disk into memory and use them to display scanned family photos in our Family Tree application. Later we will do even more (oh, the suspense!).

The last item in the DIB file is the data bits themselves. Like the data bits found in the BITMAP structure, the DIB's data bits are the representation of the image in terms of color codes.

Thanks for the Memories

Gee, you've never heard that expression before, have you? Well, what I lack in originality, I'll try to make up for in clarity. Memory management is one of those topics that seems to creep into every book that talks about Windows programming. This book is no exception. But why here? Why now? Unfortunately, we can't put the topic off any longer. In order to pull the DIBs from their cozy little nest on our hard drive and splash them across the screen, we must make room

for them (at least temporarily) in our main memory. I know what you're thinking: "Big deal! Just use the new operator to allocate your memory and move on." However, things are a bit more complicated than that.

In order to use the new operator, we need a type or class that will serve as the receptacle for our DIB data. Which type or class did you have in mind for that role? Certainly no types will work, because the data stored in a DIB will vary depending on the size of the bitmap. So we need a dynamic class that will accommodate any bitmap size we wish to throw at it. One of our collection classes should be the first thing that comes to mind. Good thought, but it won't work—at least not efficiently. We're talking bitmaps here—big, huge, honking masses of data just waiting to bog down our resources. If there were ever a time to worry about efficiency, it's when dealing with bitmaps. So we can use types and our dynamic classes aren't efficient enough. (Actually, there's another reason we can't use the collection classes, but we'll talk about that in a moment.) What can we do? We can allocate our own memory.

A wave of nausea passes through you. Yes, I said allocate our own memory. I know, one of the reasons we moved to C++ was to get away from low-level coding (or "coding on the bare metal"). Memory is a thing best managed though multiple layers of operating system and hidden compiler code. Normally, I couldn't agree more. However, there are times when you need a little more control over your environment. Sometimes you must get down and dirty with your machine and actually code in (gasp) C.

We've had it easy with all the dainty frills that come with C++. We haven't had to think about the many old demons that used to lurk for us around every C corner. The old days are back. We need contiguous blocks of memory whose size is determined at runtime. Hence, we need to use the precursors to the new and delete operators: the `malloc()` and `free()` functions. If you're still bemoaning the loss of the days of pure C, don't underestimate what we are giving up by going back to `malloc()` and `free()`. The most crucial loss is that of automated memory leak detection. If you use `malloc()` and don't use `free()`, you will be perpetrating a memory leak. But unlike the implementation of the new/delete paradigm, you won't be alerted to the fact! Ouch!

If you decided to learn C++ cold and skipped over C, I have the highest respect for you. However, you will notice that a few things now and again will jump up and bite you in the butt. To alleviate that problem somewhat, I provide a brief table (no pun intended) describing the direct memory manipulation functions. See Table 14.6.

Table 14.6. Direct memory manipulation functions.

Function	Description	What It Returns
`malloc(size)`	Allocates a block of memory. `size` is the memory size to be allocated.	A pointer to the new block of memory, or NULL if unsuccessful.

continues

DIBs

Table 14.6. continued

Function	Description	What It Returns
free(pMem)	Frees a given block of memory previously allocated by malloc. pMem is a pointer to the memory to be freed.	Nothing.
realloc(pMem, size)	Reallocates a block of memory. pMem is a pointer to the memory block to be resized. size is the new size requested.	A pointer to the new memory block if successful; otherwise, NULL.
memcpy(dest, src, count)	Copies a block of memory from a source to a destination. dest is a pointer to the destination buffer. src is a pointer to the source buffer. count is the size of the transfer in characters.	dest.
memset(dest, char, count)	Sets a block of memory to the given character value. dest is a pointer to the destination buffer. char is the character value in question. count is the size of the memory block affected.	dest.
memcmp(blk1, blk2, count)	Compares two blocks of memory. blk1 is a pointer to the first block of memory. blk2 is a pointer to the second block of memory. count is the size of the memory to be compared.	A negative number when blk1 is less than blk2, a positive number when blk1 is greater than blk2, and 0 when the two are equal.

Call Me When You Got Some Class

We are going to venture off and create our own class. This new class, CDIBitmap, will encompass all of our DIB manipulation needs—specifically, housekeeping, loading, saving, and drawing. We want to create a one-stop shopping solution for DIB "I/O" and display. We will also include the functionality of initializing a specified CPalette object. Palette support is a mighty handy functional addition in light of the role colors play in bitmap display.

What we are trying to achieve is encapsulating functionality specific to DIBs in a single entity. This class can be used to load, save, and display any bitmap. Our software engineering side is showing itself again. Truly reusable code is always a high priority. Why reinvent the wheel each time? Our new CDIBitmap class interface is as follows:

```
// Filename: DIBitmap.h

#ifndef __DIBITMAP_H__
#define __DIBITMAP_H__

class CDIBitmap : public CObject
{
    DECLARE_DYNAMIC( CDIBitmap )

// Attributes
protected:
    BITMAPINFO* m_pBitmapInfo;
    BYTE* m_pBits;
    WORD m_wNumColors;
    WORD m_wBMISize;
    DWORD m_dwBitsSize;

// Operations
public:
    // Constructors and destructors
    CDIBitmap();
    ~CDIBitmap();
    void DestroyDIB();

    // Determines if a DIB is currently loaded and available
    BOOL DIBIsLoaded();

    // Initializes a CPalette object with the DIB's colors
    BOOL GetPalette(CPalette* pPal);

    // Returns the number of colors currently used in the DIB
    WORD NumberOfColors();

    // Selectors for DIB data
    DWORD DIBDataSize();      // In bytes
    WORD BitmapInfoSize();    // In bytes
    DWORD BitsSize();         // In bytes

    // File loading and saving support
    BOOL LoadFromDIB(const char* lpszFileName);
    BOOL SaveToDIB(const char* lpszFileName);
```

Day 14: DIBs

```
    // Memory loading and saving support
    BOOL LoadFromHandle(HGLOBAL &hgDIB, DWORD dwSize);
    BOOL SaveToHandle(HGLOBAL &hgDIB);

    // Display your DIB
    BOOL DrawOnDC (CDC* pDC, int x, int y);
    BOOL StretchOnDC (CDC* pDC, int x, int y, int newWidth, int newHeight);

#ifdef _DEBUG
    virtual void AssertValid() const;
    virtual void Dump( CDumpContext& dc ) const;
#endif

};

#endif
```

Just as advertised, our `CDIBitmap` class provides the functionality needed to work with device-independent bitmaps. Well, at least we have the interface for the functionality needed to work with device-independent bitmaps—a subtle difference not lost on the compiler. Nothing in the specification should be surprising, except perhaps the save/load handle functions. These two functions provide support for the `CLongBinary` class that we use to work with ODBC bitmap objects. More on the `CLongBinary` class later.

Let's implement our `CDIBitmap` class, at least with respect to the housekeeping chores (constructors, destructors, diagnostic routines, and so on). The code that follows is the partial implementation that "stubs out" any difficult functions. (No, you won't get away that easily. Full implementations will be constructed later—maybe by you!)

```
// Filename: DIBitmap.cpp

#include "stdafx.h"
#include "DIBitmap.h"

IMPLEMENT_DYNAMIC( CDIBitmap, CObject )

///////////////////////////////////////////////////////////////////////
// Constructors and destructors

CDIBitmap::CDIBitmap()
{
    m_pBitmapInfo = NULL;
    m_pBits = NULL;
    m_wNumColors = 0;
    m_wBMISize = 0;
    m_dwBitsSize = 0;
}

CDIBitmap::~CDIBitmap()
{
    DestroyDIB();
}
```

```cpp
void CDIBitmap::DestroyDIB()
{
    free(m_pBits);
    free(m_pBitmapInfo);
    m_pBits = NULL;
    m_pBitmapInfo = NULL;
    m_wNumColors = 0;
    m_wBMISize = 0;
    m_dwBitsSize = 0;
}
///////////////////////////////////////////////////////////////////////
// Selectors

BOOL CDIBitmap::DIBIsLoaded() const
{
    return ((m_pBits != NULL) &&
            (m_pBitmapInfo != NULL) &&
            (m_dwBitsSize > 0) &&
            (m_wBMISize > 0));
}

WORD CDIBitmap::NumberOfColors() const
{
    ASSERT( DIBIsLoaded() );

    return m_wNumColors;
}

DWORD CDIBitmap::DIBDataSize() const
{
    // ASSERTs will be made in calling routines

    return BitmapInfoSize() + BitsSize();
}

WORD CDIBitmap::BitmapInfoSize() const
{
    ASSERT( DIBIsLoaded() );

    return m_wBMISize;
}

DWORD CDIBitmap::BitsSize() const
{
    ASSERT( DIBIsLoaded() );

    return m_dwBitsSize;
}
///////////////////////////////////////////////////////////////////////
// Operations

BOOL CDIBitmap::GetPalette(CPalette* pPal)
```

DAY 14: DIBs

```cpp
{
    // This function is stubbed!
    return FALSE;
}

WORD BMIColorCount(BITMAPINFOHEADER* pInfoHeader)
{
    // This function is stubbed!
    return 0;
}

BOOL CDIBitmap::LoadFromDIB(const char* lpszFileName)
{
    // This function is stubbed!
    return FALSE;
}

BOOL CDIBitmap::SaveToDIB(const char* lpszFileName)
{
    // This function is stubbed!
    return FALSE;
}

BOOL CDIBitmap::LoadFromHandle(HGLOBAL &hgDIB, DWORD dwSize)
{
    // This function is stubbed!
    return FALSE;
}

BOOL CDIBitmap::SaveToHandle(HGLOBAL &hgDIB)
{
    // This function is stubbed!
    return FALSE;
}

BOOL CDIBitmap::DrawOnDC (CDC* pDC, int x, int y)
{
    // This function is stubbed!
    return FALSE;
}

BOOL CDIBitmap::StretchOnDC (CDC* pDC, int x, int y,
                    int newWidth, int newHeight)
{
    // This function is stubbed!
    return FALSE;
}

#ifdef _DEBUG

void CDIBitmap::AssertValid() const
{
    CObject::AssertValid();

    ASSERT( DIBIsLoaded() );
}
```

```cpp
void CDIBitmap::Dump( CDumpContext& dc ) const
{
    CObject::Dump(dc);

    if (m_pBitmapInfo == NULL)
    {
        dc << "m_pBitmapInfo == NULL\n\n";
    }
    else
    {
        dc << "\nBITMAPINFOHEADER DATA:\n"
            << "Size: " << m_pBitmapInfo->bmiHeader.biSize
            << "\nWidth: " << m_pBitmapInfo->bmiHeader.biWidth
            << "\nHeight: " << m_pBitmapInfo->bmiHeader.biHeight
            << "\nPlanes: " << m_pBitmapInfo->bmiHeader.biPlanes
            << "\nBit Count: "
            << m_pBitmapInfo->bmiHeader.biBitCount;
        dc << "\nCompression: "
            << m_pBitmapInfo->bmiHeader.biCompression
            << "\nImage Size: "
            << m_pBitmapInfo->bmiHeader.biSizeImage
            << "\nXPels/Meter: "
            << m_pBitmapInfo->bmiHeader.biXPelsPerMeter
            << "\nYPels/Meter: "
            << m_pBitmapInfo->bmiHeader.biYPelsPerMeter
            << "\nColors Used: "
            << m_pBitmapInfo->bmiHeader.biClrUsed
            << "\nImport. Clrs: "
            << m_pBitmapInfo->bmiHeader.biClrImportant << "\n\n";
    }
}

#endif
```

The stubbed-out version isn't so bad. Most of the functions that are actually implemented are housekeeping functions—functions that take care of memory allocation/deallocation and diagnostic output, and simple selector functions that return attributes. These functions are very necessary for the healthy execution of our application, but they aren't central to the topic of CDIBitmaps. These functions have very simple implementations, so we won't discuss them further.

Implementing DIB Loading

The impetus that lead us to DIBs was the problem of bitmap file retrieval and storage. Therefore, these two topics should be high on our implementation agenda. The code that follows is the implementation of CDIBitmap's LoadFromDIB():

DIBs

```cpp
BOOL CDIBitmap::LoadFromDIB(const char* lpszFileName)
{
    CFile fileDIB;   // File handle
    CFileException e;
    DWORD dwBOF;     // Beginning Of File position holder

    // Intermediate variables for bitmap information
    BITMAPFILEHEADER fileHeader;
    BITMAPINFOHEADER infoHeader;
    WORD wNumColors;
    BITMAPINFO* pbmInfo = NULL;
    WORD wBMISize;
    BYTE* pbmBits = NULL;
    DWORD dwBitsSize;

    // Open the file
    if ( !fileDIB.Open(lpszFileName, CFile::modeRead, &e) )
    {
        TRACE0 ("File could not be opened!\n");
        return FALSE;
    }

    // Store Beginning Of File (BOF) position
    dwBOF = fileDIB.GetPosition();

    // Read in the file header
    fileDIB.Read(&fileHeader, sizeof(BITMAPFILEHEADER));

    TRY
    {
        // Make sure it's a bitmap file
        if (fileHeader.bfType != 0x4D42) // 0x4D42 == "BM"
        {
            TRACE0 ("File is not a bitmap!\n");
            AfxThrowNotSupportedException();
        }

        // Read in the info header
        fileDIB.Read(&infoHeader, sizeof(BITMAPINFOHEADER));

        // Make sure it's in Windows format
        if ( infoHeader.biSize != sizeof(BITMAPINFOHEADER) )
        {
            // Most likely, the file is a Presentation Manager bitmap
            // file. This file is structured using the BITCOREHEADER
            // type. Consult your manuals for more information.
            TRACE0 ("File is not a Windows Bitmap File!\n");
            TRACE0 ("PM bitmaps not currently supported.\n");

            AfxThrowNotSupportedException();
        }

        // Analyze and retrieve the color table
        wNumColors = BMIColorCount(&infoHeader);
        wBMISize = sizeof(BITMAPINFO) + wNumColors*sizeof(RGBQUAD);
        pbmInfo = (BITMAPINFO*)malloc( wBMISize );
        if (wNumColors != 0)
```

```cpp
        {
            fileDIB.Read(pbmInfo->bmiColors, wNumColors * sizeof(RGBQUAD));
        }

        // Finish initializing pbmInfo structure
        memcpy(pbmInfo, &infoHeader, sizeof(BITMAPINFOHEADER));

        // Calculate memory needed for the image bits
        dwBitsSize = (DWORD)(fileHeader.bfSize - fileHeader.bfOffBits);

        if (dwBitsSize > 64000)
        {
            TRACE0("Memory allocation too big for malloc!\n");
            AfxThrowMemoryException();
        }

        // Allocate enough memory for the bits
        pbmBits = (BYTE*)malloc((int)dwBitsSize);

        if (pbmBits == NULL)
        {
            TRACE0("Not enough memory for bits!\n");
            AfxThrowMemoryException();
        }

        // Now we can read in the actual bitmap bits!
        fileDIB.Seek( dwBOF + fileHeader.bfOffBits, CFile::begin );
        fileDIB.Read( pbmBits, (int)dwBitsSize );

        fileDIB.Close();

        // Destroy (and free) old DIB info
        DestroyDIB();

        // Commit the changes
        m_pBitmapInfo = pbmInfo;
        m_pBits = pbmBits;
        m_wNumColors = wNumColors;
        m_wBMISize = wBMISize;
        m_dwBitsSize = dwBitsSize;

        return TRUE;
    }
    CATCH(CException, e)
    {
        // If a fatal error occurs, clean things up.
        fileDIB.Close();

        if (pbmBits != NULL)
            free(pbmBits);

        if (pbmInfo != NULL)
            free(pbmInfo);
    }
    END_CATCH

    return FALSE;
}
```

Day 14 DIBs

Not a trivial function, is it? No one ever said that bitmaps were easy. But everyone knows bitmaps are cool, so you have to take the good with the bad. The LoadFromDIB() function isn't so complicated if you take it one step at a time and realize that each step involves either fetching something from a file or analyzing data already fetched. Let's go through the steps.

The first step LoadFromDIB() takes is preparing the file object. The file (specified through the parameter string) is opened, and the BOF position is saved. Of course, error conditions are checked here as they are throughout the function. LoadFromDIB() then reads in the first piece of data from the file. From our earlier discussion of DIB formats, you should understand that the first part of every DIB file is the BITMAPFILEHEADER. This structure holds a great deal of information we need to process the file. Using this data, we check to see if the file is indeed a bitmap (we check for the "magic" number 0x4d42). If it's a bitmap, we continue on our merry way. If not, we must abort the whole process. Aborting the process might seem simple (like just returning FALSE), but things are a little more complicated than that. We use the exception handling facilities provided by Visual C++ to accomplish abnormal termination of this function. The exceptions we throw will take us to a predefined error block that closes our file, cleans up memory, and returns FALSE to indicate failure. Needless to say, we will use this block for general cleanup when we encounter a fatal error. See the following note for details about the exceptions thrown.

> **Note:** Aborting a function like LoadFromDIB() is always troublesome. There are so many little loose ends to tie up—closing the file, freeing memory, and so on. The best place to do these housekeeping chores is in a single location toward the end of the function. There are two ways to accomplish this technique: gotos and exceptions. Probably your first inclination is to use a goto. As distasteful as gotos are, this would be one of the few legitimate places to use one. However, the designers of C++ anticipated this problem and came up with an even better solution: exceptions.
>
> So far we have looked at only the receiving end of exception handling. In this function we must be able to throw exceptions as well. This is not nearly as complicated as you might think. In fact, we will use some of Visual C++'s predefined exception throwers. Each of these functions (listed next) creates and throws an exception object of the appropriate type. No muss, no fuss. One-stop shopping!
>
> ```
> AfxThrowArchiveException()
> AfxThrowFileException()
> AfxThrowMemoryException()
> AfxThrowNotSupportedException()
> AfxThrowResourceException()
> AfxThrowUserException()
> ```
>
> Consult Chapter 5 for a more thorough discussion of exceptions and exception handling.

At this point in the code, we know we have a legitimate bitmap file, and we also have a bunch of data concerning the file. The next thing that LoadFromDIB() must do is read in the next block of DIB data. Thinking back to the DIB file definition, you might recall that a DIB file could have as the next data structure a BITMAPINFOHEADER structure or a BITMAPCOREHEADER structure. Which one depends on the type of DIB! The way to solve this problem is to read in one of the two structures and compare its size field to the actual size of the structure. I chose BITMAPINFOHEADER because we aren't supporting the Presentation Manager (PM) bitmap format. So if the file is of the PM format, we abort the procedure.

Once we know that we have a Windows DIB file, we can begin loading in the color table. From the BITMAPINFOHEADER object, we can obtain enough information about the color table to allocate the appropriate amount of memory and read in the color table. Deciphering the BITMAPINFOHEADER object is not a trivial task and is not unique to LoadFromDIB(). Either of these reasons would be enough to warrant it a function of its own. We will get to the implementation of BMIColorCount() in a moment, but suffice it to say that it analyzes the "info header" data and figures out how many colors are stored in the file. With this information, LoadFromDIB() can intelligently prepare for the colors.

After the colors are loaded, the only thing left is the actual image bits! From the file header data, we can compute the size of the remainder of the file (that's how much we must read in to get the image bits). LoadFromDIB() then reads in the bits. The only thing left to do is commit the transaction. This involves deleting the old data and copying the new data to the attribute variables. A final return TRUE and the function is done (except for the error handling block already discussed).

Well, one mystery is left in the loading process: the function BMIColorCount(). Ask and ye shall receive:

```
WORD BMIColorCount(BITMAPINFOHEADER* pInfoHeader)
{
    WORD numRGBQUADS;

    // If 24 bits per pixel and no colors are used,
    // there is no color table information
    if ( (pInfoHeader->biBitCount == 24) && (pInfoHeader->biClrUsed == 0) )
    {
        numRGBQUADS = 0;
    }
    else
    {
        // Compute number of colors held in the DIB file
        if (pInfoHeader->biClrUsed == 0)
        {
            // Find 2 to the power of biBitCount
            numRGBQUADS = 2 << (pInfoHeader->biBitCount-1);
        }
        else
```

DIBs

```
        {
                numRGBQUADS = (WORD)pInfoHeader->biClrUsed;
        }

    } // End if. Load RGB quads from DIB.

    return numRGBQUADS;
}
```

`BMIColorCount()` uses the pointer to a `BITMAPINFOHEADER` object to analyze the color data contained therein. From this information, it discerns the number of colors associated with the bitmap. When you first glance at this description, you might think that this is a trivial task. Indeed, if there were a "number of colors" field in the info header object, this function would be trivial. But the "number of colors" information is a bit more encrypted within the structure than we might want. It depends on the number of colors used as well as the number of bits per pixel. The "number of bits per pixel" field, `biBitCount`, can provide us with the ultimate number of possible colors (2 to the `biBitCount`-1 power). But this value is valid for the bitmap under only two circumstances: when `biClrUsed` is 0 and when `biBitCount` is not 24. If `biBitCount` equals 24, we know (from an earlier discussion) that no color table is necessary since the 24 bits will describe three 8-bit RGB values—no translation is necessary. However, if the `biClrUsed` field is nonzero, this tells us that only `biClrUsed` colors are needed for the bitmap (regardless of the value of `biBitCount`). Remember, just because a palette has a 256-color capacity doesn't mean that we have to fill it up. We must share the palette with other applications when we can, because we expect other applications to share with us.

Still confused about this function? Well, don't worry. It usually takes a couple walk-throughs of the code and a couple readings of the description to finally figure it out. Be patient. This function's complicated nature is a big reason why it's a separate function. The other reason is that another function must make use of it, as we shall see shortly.

The next logical function to implement would be the `SaveToDIB()` function. But that would rob you of the fun (and learning) that comes with writing and debugging a piece of bitmap code. Again, I will leave that task as an exercise for you. Luckily, the lack of that particular function won't stand in the way of the completed application. So if you postpone implementing the `SaveToDIB()` function until the end of the chapter (or indefinitely, for that matter), you will still have a working Family Tree application.

Tying *CDIBitmap*s to the Database

We can load DIBs from a file. Now what do we do with them? Recall the reason behind our attack on bitmaps. We wanted to figure out how to use bitmaps in the context of our Family Tree application. In essence, we wanted to load bitmaps from a file, display them on-screen, and save them to a database. It's a bit premature to talk of DIB display, so let's put our DIBs in the database for safekeeping until we figure out how to paint them on-screen.

CLongBinary and BLOBs

From our ODBC discussions you might be able to recall a reference to the class `CLongBinary`. This class will be the waystation for bitmap data traveling between the database and our application. Of course, `CLongBinary` isn't dedicated to bitmap data! It can serve as a bucket for any piece or grouping of data that we care to dump in it. In that sense it is the most general and flexible class we have—it can hold anything. However, `CLongBinary` was designed to be a database intermediary for BLOBs (binary large objects). BLOBs are usually large and unwieldy. They don't necessarily come in a given size. And typically, they aren't defined in terms of a recognizable type. This doesn't mean that integers, for example, are prohibited from being stored in a `CLongBinary` object. But the effort needed to convert a standard data type to a `CLongBinary` type and back again is prohibitive (especially since the predefined types have automated database storage mechanisms available, as we have seen). Bitmaps happen to be a favorite example of a large, unwieldy object of unpredictable size (a perfect match for `CLongBinary`). Another good candidate for storage using `CLongBinary` is an executable file. It too is large, unwieldy, and of unpredictable size.

Understanding `CLongBinary` is the next step on the road to bitmap database storage. Let's take a look at `CLongBinary`'s attributes and methods in Table 14.7.

Table 14.7. `CLongBinary`'s attributes and member functions.

Attribute or Member Function	Description
m_hData	Contains a Windows HGLOBAL handle to the data object.
m_dwDataLength	Contains the actual size in bytes of the data object whose handle is stored in m_hData.
CLongBinary	Constructor.
~CLongBinary	Destructor.

Amazing! For once we have an almost trivial class that we can view at a glance! Don't get too confident. `CLongBinary` still has some subtleties. Its first attribute, `m_hData`, is a handle to a global memory block that contains the data. Its second attribute, `m_dwDataLength`, is just what it says—the size (in bytes) of the memory block containing the data. The only two member functions we have to worry about are the constructor and destructor. So, except for the complication of global memory blocks, this class is pretty simple. Indeed, the only difficulty in dealing with `CLongBinary` objects is the potential unfamiliarity of global memory manipulation.

Upon seeing `CLongBinary`'s `m_hData` attribute, you can see where the `CDIBitmap` functions `LoadFromHandle()` and `SaveToHandle()` come in: They save and load DIBs to and from `CLongBinary` objects.

DIBs

Implementing *CDIBitmap* Conversions Associated with *CLongBinary*

Now that we know how the functions LoadFromHandle() and SaveToHandle() fit into the greater scheme of things, let's see how they are implemented.

```
BOOL CDIBitmap::LoadFromHandle(HGLOBAL &hgDIB, DWORD dwSize)
{
    // Far pointer to the global memory object
    BYTE FAR* lpDIB = NULL;

    // Intermediate variables for bitmap information
    WORD wNumColors;
    BITMAPINFO bmiData;
    BITMAPINFO* pbmInfo = NULL;
    WORD wBMISize;
    BYTE* pbmBits = NULL;
    DWORD dwBitsSize;

    // Make sure handle is valid
    if ( (hgDIB == NULL) || (dwSize == 0) )
    {
        TRACE0("NULL handle was passed to LoadFromHandle().\n");
        return FALSE;
    }

    // Lock memory and retrieve the pointer
    lpDIB = (BYTE FAR*)::GlobalLock(hgDIB);

    if (lpDIB == NULL)
    {
        TRACE0("LoadFromHandle: GlobalLock failed.\n");
        return FALSE;
    }

    // Get BITMAPINFO structure from block of global memory
    _fmemcpy( &bmiData.bmiHeader, lpDIB, sizeof(BITMAPINFOHEADER) );

    TRY
    {
        // Make sure it's in Windows format
        if (bmiData.bmiHeader.biSize != sizeof(BITMAPINFOHEADER))
        {
            // Most likely, the mem block is a Presentation Manager
            // bitmap. This is structured using the BITCOREHEADER
            // type. Consult your manuals for more information.
            TRACE0 ("Memory block is not a Windows Bitmap!\n");
            TRACE0 ("PM bitmaps are not supported.\n");

            AfxThrowNotSupportedException();
        }

        wNumColors = BMIColorCount(&bmiData.bmiHeader);
        wBMISize = sizeof(BITMAPINFO) + wNumColors*sizeof(RGBQUAD);
```

```
            pbmInfo = (BITMAPINFO*)malloc( wBMISize );
            if (wNumColors != 0)
            {
                _fmemcpy( pbmInfo->bmiColors, lpDIB + sizeof(BITMAPINFOHEADER),
                    wNumColors * sizeof(RGBQUAD) );
            }

             // Finish initializing pbmInfo structure
             memcpy(pbmInfo, &bmiData.bmiHeader, sizeof(BITMAPINFOHEADER));

            // Now we can read in the actual bitmap bits!
            dwBitsSize = (DWORD)(dwSize - wBMISize);

            if (dwBitsSize > 64000)
            {
                TRACE0("Memory allocation too big for malloc!\n");
                AfxThrowMemoryException();
            }

            pbmBits = (BYTE*)malloc((int)dwBitsSize);

            if (pbmBits == NULL)
            {
                TRACE0("Not enough memory for bits!\n");
                AfxThrowMemoryException();
            }

            _fmemcpy( pbmBits, lpDIB + wBMISize, (int)dwBitsSize );

            ::GlobalUnlock(hgDIB);

            // Destroy (and free) old DIB info
            DestroyDIB();

            // Commit the changes
            m_pBitmapInfo = pbmInfo;
            m_pBits = pbmBits;
            m_wNumColors = wNumColors;
            m_wBMISize = wBMISize;
            m_dwBitsSize = dwBitsSize;

            return TRUE;

    }
    CATCH(CException, e)
    {

    // If a fatal error occurs, clean things up

            ::GlobalUnlock(hgDIB);

            if (pbmBits != NULL)
                free(pbmBits);

            if (pbmInfo != NULL)
                free(pbmInfo);

    }
```

```
    END_CATCH

    return FALSE;
}
```

Does this code look familiar? It should. It's practically identical to the `LoadFromDIB()` code we wrote a few pages ago! The only difference between the functions is that the file references in `LoadFromDIB()` become global memory references in `LoadFromHandle()`. We've already talked about memory functions, so let's move on to `SaveToHandle()`:

```
BOOL CDIBitmap::SaveToHandle(HGLOBAL &hgDIB)
{
    ASSERT( DIBIsLoaded() );

    // Free the memory (if any) currently
    // associated with hgDIB
    if (hgDIB != NULL)
        ::GlobalFree(hgDIB);

    // Allocate enough global memory to accomodate
    // the size of our DIB
    hgDIB = ::GlobalAlloc( GHND, DIBDataSize() );
    if (hgDIB == NULL)
    {
        TRACE0("SaveToHandle: GlobalAlloc failed!\n");
        return FALSE;
    }

    // Retrieve a pointer to the global block of memory
    BYTE FAR* lpDIB = (BYTE FAR*)::GlobalLock(hgDIB);

    if (lpDIB == NULL)
    {
        TRACE0("SaveToHandle: GlobalLock failed.\n");
        return FALSE;
    }

    // Copy the DIB data into the global block of memory
    _fmemcpy( lpDIB, m_pBitmapInfo, BitmapInfoSize() );
    _fmemcpy( lpDIB+BitmapInfoSize(), m_pBits, (int)BitsSize() );

    // Release the memory. lpDIB is no longer valid.
    ::GlobalUnlock(hgDIB);

    // Global memory is freed elsewhere.
    // In our case, during the ODBC cleanup.

    return TRUE;
}
```

This function is very straightforward. We make the usual validation call assuring that a DIB is loaded. We then make sure that any global memory currently allocated to `hgDIB` is freed. An allocation of enough global memory is then made to accommodate the DIB data. We lock the global memory so that we can get a pointer to the memory block. Then we dump the DIB data into the memory object. The only thing left to do is to unlock the global memory. Note that freeing the memory is the job of whoever owns the global handle that was passed to us. In our application, that job falls to the ODBC. It can have as many jobs as it likes!

Implementing DIB Drawing

Once we have a DIB loaded into the database, what do we do with it? Again, the whole purpose behind bitmaps is putting them on-screen so that they may be seen, admired, and otherwise used. In our CDDBitmap class, we accomplished this through the DrawOnDC() and StretchOnDC() functions. Surprisingly enough, since we want the same functionality in our CDIBitmap class, we implement the same functions.

Unlike the CDDBitmap::DrawOnDC() function, in CDIBitmap we'll be a bit more frugal with our code by calling StretchOnDC() from DrawOnDC():

```
BOOL CDIBitmap::DrawOnDC (CDC* pDC, int x, int y)
{
    // Make sure bitmap data exists
    ASSERT( DIBIsLoaded() );

    // Call StretchOnDC() with the current width and height
    return StretchOnDC(pDC, x, y,
        (int)m_pBitmapInfo->bmiHeader.biWidth,
        (int)m_pBitmapInfo->bmiHeader.biHeight);
}
```

Obviously, this function is highly dependent on the implementation of StretchOnDC(). But that was the intent—changes to the drawing implementation need to be made in only one place! However, the question remains: How is StretchOnDC() implemented? The answer follows:

```
BOOL CDIBitmap::StretchOnDC (CDC* pDC, int x, int y,
                             int newWidth, int newHeight)
{
    BOOL Result;

    // Make sure the CDC pointer is usable
    ASSERT_VALID(pDC);

    // Make sure bitmap data exists
    ASSERT( DIBIsLoaded() );

    // Select and realize the palette
    CPalette CurPalette;
    CPalette* pOldPalette = NULL;
    if (GetPalette(&CurPalette))
    {
        if (pOldPalette = pDC->SelectPalette(&CurPalette, FALSE))
            pDC->RealizePalette();
        else
        TRACE0("DrawOnDC: Error in Selecting Palette.\n");
    }
```

Day 14

DIBs

```
    else
    {
        // No palette available
        TRACE0("DrawOnDC: GetPalette returns FALSE.\n");
    }

    // Block transfer the bitmap to the screen
    int Width  = (int)m_pBitmapInfo->bmiHeader.biWidth;
    int Height = (int)m_pBitmapInfo->bmiHeader.biHeight;
    Result = ::StretchDIBits(pDC->GetSafeHdc(),
                x, y, newWidth, newHeight, 0, 0,
                Width, Height, m_pBits, m_pBitmapInfo,
                DIB_RGB_COLORS, SRCCOPY);

    // Return dc to original state
    if (pOldPalette)
        pDC->SelectPalette(pOldPalette, FALSE);

    return Result;
}
```

This function starts out with the usual verification ASSERT statements, but then it launches right into palette manipulation. A CPalette object is declared that will hold the palette information associated with our DIB. We use the CDIBitmap function GetPalette() to construct a palette from the information contained in the BITMAPINFO structure. (GetPalette() will be discussed in a moment.) Once we have the palette, we use the CDC functions SelectPalette() and RealizePalette() to copy the palette into the device context and to start palette negotiations with the Palette Manager. After the palette is selected and realized, we are ready to copy the bitmap to the screen. This is accomplished through the StretchDIBits() function. It's important to realize that a simple CDC::BitBlt() call won't suffice to display the bitmap. BitBlt() will copy the bits to the screen, but they won't necessarily have the proper ordering. This is due to device dependence. However, StretchDIBits() understands both the DIB standard as well as the peculiarities of the current video driver, so it acts as our translator. Finally, we must reset the device context to its original state before returning the result of our attempts. It shouldn't surprise you that this function bears remarkable resemblance to the corresponding CDDBitmap function. After all, they perform practically the same task!

One last thing is left regarding the drawing code: GetPalette(). Will this calling nest ever end? What does GetPalette() call? Don't worry. This is the last function we need to look at before finishing this section.

```
BOOL CDIBitmap::GetPalette(CPalette* pPal)
{
    ASSERT_VALID (pPal);
    ASSERT( DIBIsLoaded() );

    WORD numRGBQUADS = NumberOfColors();

    // If there are no colors, there is no palette!
    if (numRGBQUADS == 0)
```

```
    {
        return FALSE;
    }

    // Construct a CPalette-compatible temporary destination
    // for the color info
    LOGPALETTE* pLP = (LOGPALETTE*)malloc(sizeof(LOGPALETTE) +
                        numRGBQUADS*sizeof(PALETTEENTRY));
    if (pLP == NULL)
    {
        // malloc failed to allocate memory for pLP
        TRACE0("GetPalette: Out of memory!\n");
        return FALSE;
    }

    // Fill the LOGPALETTE structure with the color data
    pLP->palVersion = 0x300;    // Windows version 3.0 (or better)
    pLP->palNumEntries = numRGBQUADS;
    for (DWORD i = 0; i < numRGBQUADS; i++)
    {
        pLP->palPalEntry[i].peRed   = m_pBitmapInfo->bmiColors[i].rgbRed;
        pLP->palPalEntry[i].peGreen = m_pBitmapInfo->bmiColors[i].rgbGreen;
        pLP->palPalEntry[i].peBlue  = m_pBitmapInfo->bmiColors[i].rgbBlue;
        pLP->palPalEntry[i].peFlags = 0;
    }

    // Detach and reallocate any LOGPALETTE structure that might
    // already be associated with the CPalette object.
    // Note: CreatePalette() will fail with an assertion if the
    // CPalette object already has a palette.
    pPal->DeleteObject();

    // Create the new palette based on the LOGPALETTE structure built above
    if (!pPal->CreatePalette(pLP))
    {
        TRACE0("GetPalette: Palette creation failed!\n");
        free(pLP);
        return FALSE;
    }

    // Reallocate LOGPALETTE structure memory since
    // all its info has been copied to the palette
    free(pLP);

    return TRUE;
}
```

This function has one purpose: to convert the RGBQUAD data (held in the BITMAPINFO structure) into the PALETTEENTRY data (found in the LOGPALETTE structure). This is accomplished, simply enough, by allocating enough memory for the LOGPALETTE object and copying the RGBQUAD data into it. The only wrinkle in all this is that RGBQUAD and PALETTEENTRY have a very similar structure but are not an exact match. Therefore, field-by-field copying must be done. Surround that core functionality with some diagnostic calls and some memory housekeeping, and we have a GetPalette() function!

DIBs

Hey, guess what? We're in a position to load a DIB, store it in the database, and display it on-screen! What are we waiting for?

Tying It All Together

Happy days are here at last. The hard part is over. All we need to do now is exploit the CDIBitmap functionality in the Family Tree application. Compared to the writing of CDIBitmap, this integration is easy.

Using AppStudio, add a new pull-down menu called Portrait. Add the following items to this new menu resource (they will provide a user interface for our new bitmap functionality):

ID	D_PORTRAIT_LOADFROMFILE
Caption	&Load From File
Prompt	Load bitmap portrait into the database from a .BMP file.
ID	ID_PORTRAIT_SAVETOFILE
Caption	&Save To File
Prompt	Copy the current bitmap portrait to a specified file.
ID	ID_PORTRAIT_DELETE
Caption	&Delete
Prompt	Remove the bitmap portrait from the current record.

Have ClassWizard construct the following CTreeDoc functions that handle the new commands we just put in our menu. Also make the indicated additions to ClassWizard's default handlers:

```
void CTreeDoc::OnPortraitLoadfromfile()
{
    CFileDialog dlg(TRUE, NULL, "C:\\WINDOWS\\*.bmp");
    CDIBitmap DIB;

    if (dlg.DoModal() == IDOK)
    {
        BeginWaitCursor();

        // Get the filename selected in the file dialog
        if ( DIB.LoadFromDIB(dlg.GetPathName()) )
        {
            // Failed to load DIB from file
            AfxMessageBox("Couldn't load DIB!");
            EndWaitCursor();
            return;
        }

        // Prepare the record set for editing
        m_treeSet.Edit();

        // Transfer the DIB data to the CLongBinary object
        if ( DIB.SaveToHandle(m_treeSet.m_PORTRAIT.m_hData) )
        {
            // Failed to save DIB to global handle
```

```cpp
                EndWaitCursor();
                return;
            }
            m_treeSet.m_PORTRAIT.m_dwDataLength = DIB.DIBDataSize();

            // Tell the database that we changed the field.
            // Note: The CLongBinary field is so long that automatic
            // updating is turned off. You must explicitly tell the
            // record set to update this field.
            m_treeSet.SetFieldDirty(&m_treeSet.m_PORTRAIT);
            m_treeSet.SetFieldNull(&m_treeSet.m_PORTRAIT, FALSE);

            // Commit the changes (write them to the database)
            m_treeSet.Update();

            EndWaitCursor();
        }

        // Tell all the attached views that the data changed
        UpdateAllViews(NULL);
}

void CTreeDoc::OnUpdatePortraitLoadfromfile(CCmdUI* pCmdUI)
{
        // Disable the load portrait command when
        // -- the record set is not open
        // -- no current record exists
        // -- a portrait already exists for the current record

        BOOL bDisable = !m_treeSet.IsOpen() ||
                m_treeSet.IsEOF() || m_treeSet.IsBOF() ||
                (m_treeSet.m_PORTRAIT.m_dwDataLength != 0);

        // Note: Yes, I did use a logical OR instead of AND above.
        // I'm testing to see if any record is selected as
        // opposed to testing for an empty database.

        pCmdUI->Enable(!bDisable);
}

void CTreeDoc::OnPortraitSavetofile()
{
        CFileDialog dlg(FALSE, "bmp", "Face.bmp");
        CDIBitmap DIB;

        if (dlg.DoModal() == IDOK)
        {
            BeginWaitCursor();

            // Get the filename selected in the file dialog
            // and save the DIB to that file
            if (!DIB.SaveToDIB(dlg.GetPathName()))
                TRACE0("Portrait NOT saved!!\n");

            EndWaitCursor();
        }
```

```cpp
}

void CTreeDoc::OnUpdatePortraitSavetofile(CCmdUI* pCmdUI)
{
    // Disable the load portrait command when
    // -- the record set is not open
    // -- no current record exists
    // -- a portrait doesn't exist for the current record

    BOOL bDisable = !m_treeSet.IsOpen() ||
        m_treeSet.IsEOF() || m_treeSet.IsBOF() ||
        (m_treeSet.m_PORTRAIT.m_dwDataLength == 0);

    // Note: Yes, I did use a logical OR instead of AND above.
    // I'm testing to see if any record is selected as
    // opposed to testing for an empty database.

    pCmdUI->Enable(!bDisable);
}

void CTreeDoc::OnPortraitDelete()
{
    BeginWaitCursor();

    // Prepare the record set for editing
    m_treeSet.Edit();

    // Free the memory associated with the bitmap
    ::GlobalFree(m_treeSet.m_PORTRAIT.m_hData);
    m_treeSet.m_PORTRAIT.m_hData = NULL;
    m_treeSet.m_PORTRAIT.m_dwDataLength = 0;

    // Tell the database the bitmap is deleted
    m_treeSet.SetFieldNull(&m_treeSet.m_PORTRAIT, TRUE);
    m_treeSet.SetFieldDirty(&m_treeSet.m_PORTRAIT, TRUE);

    // Commit the changes (write them to the database)
    m_treeSet.Update();

    EndWaitCursor();
}

void CTreeDoc::OnUpdatePortraitDelete(CCmdUI* pCmdUI)
{
    // Disable the load portrait command when
    // -- the record set is not open
    // -- no current record exists
    // -- a portrait doesn't exist for the current record

    BOOL bDisable = !m_treeSet.IsOpen() ||
        m_treeSet.IsEOF() || m_treeSet.IsBOF() ||
        (m_treeSet.m_PORTRAIT.m_dwDataLength == 0);

    // Note: Yes, I did use a logical OR instead of AND above.
    // I'm testing to see if any record is selected as
    // opposed to testing for an empty database.
```

```
         pCmdUI->Enable(!bDisable);
}
```

Nothing is too surprising in this code. It all comes directly out of our discussions of the CDIBitmap member functions. One last alteration remains—modifying CPersonView::OnDraw() to display the bitmap.

```
void CPersonView::OnDraw(CDC* pDC)
{
    CTreeDoc* pDoc = (CTreeDoc*)GetDocument();
    CTreeSet* pSet = &pDoc->m_treeSet;
    CString S;
    int PortraitID;

    int X = 10, Y = 10;
    int offset = 2*(pDC->GetTextExtent("Wpqit", 5)).cy;

    if (pDC->IsPrinting())
    {
        Y += 2*offset;
    }

    pDC->TextOut(X, Y, "Full Name: " + pSet->FullName());
    pDC->TextOut(X, Y += offset, "Maiden: " + pSet->m_MAIDEN);

    if (pSet->m_IS_MALE)
    {
        S = "Person is Male.";
        PortraitID = IDB_DEF_MALE;
    }
    else
    {
        S = "Person is Female.";
        PortraitID = IDB_DEF_FEMALE;
    }

    // Draw bitmap on pDC object
    if (!pDC->IsPrinting())
    {
        if (pSet->m_PORTRAIT.m_dwDataLength != 0)
        {
            CDIBitmap DIB;
            DIB.LoadFromHandle(
                pDoc->m_treeSet.m_PORTRAIT.m_hData,
                pDoc->m_treeSet.m_PORTRAIT.m_dwDataLength);
            if (!DIB.DrawOnDC(pDC, 300, 10))
                TRACE0("CDIBitmap::DrawOnDC() failed.\n");
        }
        else
        {
            CDDBitmap DDB;
            DDB.LoadBitmap(PortraitID);
            BITMAP bm;
            DDB.GetObject(sizeof(bm), &bm);
            DDB.StretchOnDC(pDC, 300, 10, bm.bmWidth*2, bm.bmHeight*2);
```

```
            DDB.DeleteObject();
        }
    }

    pDC->TextOut(X, Y += offset, S);
    pDC->TextOut(X, Y += offset, "Birth Place: " + pSet->m_WHERE_BORN);
.
.
.
}
```

This change should be self-explanatory and obvious.

Well, that concludes the bitmap additions to the Family Tree application (and thus concludes the Family Tree application itself). Play with your new toy. Isn't it wonderful that we can reach out and grab one of those .BMP files and display it at will? Continue to play for a while to get used to your new-found power. But always remember that wielding the power of bitmaps is an awesome responsibility. Wield it in the service of good! Beware of the dark side.

Summary

The topic of this chapter was device-independent bitmaps, or DIBs. The DIB format is a standard for the storage of bitmap data. Actually, there are two DIB standards: one for OS/2 Presentation Manager bitmaps and one for Windows bitmaps. We emphasized the Windows DIB format by constructing a class dedicated to this type of DIB. CDIBitmap encapsulated the underlying Windows DIB format as well as providing a number of useful functions for DIB manipulation.

In addition to implementing a DIB file loader, we also provided the functionality for displaying previously loaded DIBs on-screen. We found that drawing DIBs wasn't all that different from drawing DDBs. There was only a slight difference in terms of the actual calling function.

Finally, we discussed how to convert DIBs to CLongBinary objects and back again. This was accomplished through the CDIBitmap functions LoadFromHandle() and SaveToHandle(). You developed an understanding of memory functions to aid in this endeavor. The CLongBinary objects were the key to bitmap database storage and retrieval.

This chapter was a long row to hoe, but I hope that you have gained a good understanding of device-independent bitmaps.

Q&A

Q Do I really need to know about DIBs? Can't I just use DDBs exclusively and avoid the whole DIB mess?

A As a matter of fact, you *can* use DDBs exclusively in your applications. That's why the MFC provides you with `CBitmap` and not `CDIBitmap`. Almost all your graphics needs can be met with DDBs—unless, of course, you want to use a picture generated by a product other than AppStudio. Or perhaps you want to scan in an image; you'd need a DIB to transfer the image into your application. Or...well, you get the picture (pun intended). DIB functionality is just a handy thing to have around.

Q I don't get the concept of color planes. Is this something I should know more about?

A My opinion is that everyone should know more about everything. This theory has been proven time and time again in the computer world, since every aspect of the computer is seemingly tied to every other aspect. However, since there is so much computer-related information out there, we have to set priorities. Color planes shouldn't be too high on your priority list. But since you asked...

The whole idea behind color planes boils down to another means of assigning colors to the bits in a bitmap. Think of your bitmap as a sheet of paper. You can visualize the bitmap being colored by covering the paper with sheets of transparent plastic on which specific bits have a certain color. Each transparency is dedicated to a single color—either red, green, or blue. When bits overlap from transparency to transparency, the colors are merged just as they are in the standard coloring scheme (for example, red + blue = purple, depending on intensity). Instead of having all the colors of each bit next to one another, they are separated into color planes.

Q Why didn't we define `CDIBitmap`'s functions `SaveToHandle()` and `LoadFromHandle()` to work directly with `CLongBinary` objects?

A First of all, converting DIBs to global memory handles and back again is much more general and therefore should be able to be applied in more situations. But there is another reason. `CLongBinary` is an MFC database class, which means that it isn't available to us unless we include the AFXDB.H file. Converting a DIB back and forth between our DIB class and global memory is not unique to a database application. Therefore, there is no reason to force a user of `CDIBitmap` to fool around with `CLongBinary`.

 **DIBs**

Workshop

Quiz

1. What are the two types of DIBs, and how do they differ?
2. What is the purpose behind the `SaveToHandle()` and `LoadFromHandle()` functions?
3. What is the purpose of the `CLongBinary` class?
4. What is the structure of a Windows DIB file?

Exercises

1. Implement `CDIBitmap::SaveToDIB()`. Hint: Use `LoadFromDIB()` as a guide.
2. Research the memory allocation routines (if you're fuzzy on their workings) and upgrade `CDIBitmap` to handle large (bigger than 64K) bitmaps. Hint: Use `huge` pointers and their corresponding memory functions.
3. The `CDIBitmap` class doesn't provide for any direct manipulation of its data. It was originally designed to serve as a transfer class used only to move bitmaps from a file, to the display, to a memory block, or back to a file. With what you now know about bitmaps and display contexts, you should be able to make `CDIBitmap` flexible enough to allow for direct manipulation.

WEEK 3

AT A GLANCE

15
16
17
18
19
20
21

Week 3 is some real programming "meat." You will go where many fear to tread—OLE. Chapter 15 gives you a good overview of what OLE 2.0 is and how it works. This chapter is meant to whet your appetite for more. It shows you OLE's features and capabilities and how they improve your life. Chapter 16 gets down and dirty into actually creating an OLE server. This server will be a part of your completed application for Week 3. Chapter 17 tackles the toughest task in Windows—printing. We show you how the Windows printing cycle works and how to survive it. Chapter 18 gets you back to creating an OLE container that holds the server from Chapter 16. Chapter 19 teaches you how that magical drag and drop works. It seems so easy to drag a file from File Manager to Notepad. Now you will see the engine behind the scenes. Chapter 20 shows you how to integrate help into your Week 3 application. The ins and outs of the help compiler, as well as some development ideas, are presented. Chapter 21 finishes Week 3 by talking about the future. There is no crystal ball included with this book, so we thought a little discussion of the future was in order. We hope this week will propel you forward in your overall understanding of the MFC.

WEEK 3

An Overview of OLE 2.0 and Objects

An Overview of OLE 2.0 and Objects

Olé 2...No Bull!

One of the first things any beginning OLE 2 programmer should learn is how to properly pronounce "OLE 2." When you're talking with colleagues, never refer to OLE 2.0 as "O-L-E 2." The accepted pronunciation is "Olé 2." It's what a matador would say to the second bull. (Microsoft gurus use such terms as passwords to their inner sanctums.)

Microsoft's Object Technology Strategy

To understand the importance of OLE, it might help you to have an idea of how Microsoft views objects. This view will dictate how Microsoft treats object-oriented technology and how it is integrated into end-user products, as well as programming and support tools. In talking about objects, we will discuss two areas of interest: OOP (object-oriented programming) and OOSS (object-oriented system software). It's important to differentiate between them even though they share a common ancestry. Because you're reading this book, I assume you have some experience in C++ and understand at least a little about objects. We will build upon this knowledge.

Object-Oriented Programming: It's not Nerdvana

Before we talk about OOP, let's define an object. This word has been seriously overused. According to Grady Booch, god of all that is object-oriented and author of *Software Engineering with Ada*, Second Edition (1986), an object is "an entity that has a state; that is, it has some value...the behavior of an object is defined by the actions it suffers and vice versa...every object is actually an instance of some class of objects." There is the first answer to the first question of your first quiz in your first graduate software engineering class. Since you're writing C++ code, I assume you have some idea of what an object is. Let's examine how OOP has affected life as we know it.

Object-oriented programming has been around for a number of years and has reared its head (I bet you thought I was going to say "ugly head") in such programming languages as Ada, Smalltalk, and, of course, C++. The magical term "object" has conjured up such a name for itself that the mere mention of it, especially in the same sentence as the words "software engineer," makes IS managers drool with anticipation.

The reality is just that—reality. I have seen object-oriented code that is far worse than any standard C code could ever be. I have also seen beautiful object-oriented code. OOP is a means to an end, a tool to be used for good or evil. The problem with OOP is that it defines a source code (programming language) standard. This means that the objects are dependent on both the

language and the specific compiler. You might ask "Why should I care?" Because an incredible dependency is implied here. The "gotcha" is that the applications that interact with your newly upgraded application will need to be recompiled and redistributed simultaneously with your new application. This might be realistic with three or four applications running on a single machine at a single site, but it's nearly impossible to accomplish if your software is on tens, hundreds, or thousands of systems in a distributed environment (networked). To make matters worse, consider that your new application might interact with applications from several other vendors, and you might not even have access to their code for recompilation.

Okay, maybe OOP won't solve the world's problems, but it can make a contribution toward the common good. The object mentality is a good one, filled with promise of a more organized and orderly world. Let's see how Microsoft has jumped on the object bandwagon by providing a foundation for you to grab your OOT (object-oriented trumpet) and do the same.

Object-Oriented System Software

There must be a way to achieve compatibility with other objects (preferably all of them) without having to worry about whether your object was written in C++ or Ada or on Windows NT or Windows 3.1. Well, you're in luck. Object-Oriented System Software (OOSS) defines a binary standard that specifies how objects interact with each other. This accomplishes a great deal. Because the standard is a binary one, it assures that all objects created to the standard will be able to interoperate freely, regardless of the operating system they run under, the language they were written in, or the company that created them. This standard allows for the creation of what is termed "component" software, which addresses several critical needs:

- ☐ The need for a single, well-defined object model that promotes objects that can communicate between applications, even if the applications are on different machines (distributed computing)
- ☐ The need to integrate components written by diverse companies, in many languages, in a smooth and seamless fashion
- ☐ The need to be able to upgrade a single object component without disturbing the operation of the distributed system

It's a Floor Wax and a Dessert Topping

You might ask, "How is Microsoft going to help me achieve this state of object 'nerdvana'?" Here is the strategy Microsoft uses for delivering innovations in object technology:

- ☐ Deliver value today. OLE (a subject we will deal with shortly) provides the foundation for component-based software. Microsoft is using, and will continue to use, OLE as its strategic object technology throughout its operating systems, development tools, and its end-user applications.

DAY 15

An Overview of OLE 2.0 and Objects

- Provide the most open solution. Microsoft will ensure that all future enhancements to OLE are published through the Open Process. The Open Process is a method whereby Microsoft distributes and discusses preliminary technology specifications with software architects, OEMs, hardware and software vendors, and corporate developers. This happens at least one year prior to the release of a new technology. These Open Process members can then provide feedback or alternative approaches to the problem and help shape the end product into something that is as useful as possible. This also gives the participants early access to technologies so that their products can take full advantage of these new technologies.
- Provide the most comprehensive cross-platform support. Microsoft has vowed to ensure that OLE works across multiple platforms and incorporates many market-driven standards.
- Protect existing customer investments. Many users and developers alike are afraid that their investment will be obsolete in just a few years (or less). Future versions of Windows will provide extensive OLE services. Also, today's OLE applications will inherit tomorrow's capabilities.
- Eliminate world hunger and the national debt.

All this sounds great, but will Microsoft hold up its end of the deal (everything except the world hunger thing)? The proof can be seen when looking at Microsoft's product line.

- Microsoft Office products. Word 6.0, Excel 5.0, PowerPoint 4.0, and Access 2.0 are all OLE-enabled. They support drag and drop, visual editing, and automation.
- Programming languages and development environments. Visual C++ can be used to build complete OLE-enabled applications (as you will do in later chapters). The MFC reduces the number of lines of code necessary to write an OLE-enabled application. Visual Basic provides an OLE container capability and allows you to quickly write applications that exploit OLE methods.

As you can see, Microsoft is committed to providing a robust object-enabled base of tools and environments. I know this sounds like an advertisement for Microsoft, but they really are trying to provide the tools we need to make this work. And no, I don't own any Microsoft stock (well, not much). I hope this little introduction has given you a better feel for how Microsoft treats the world of objects and where they are going with it. Now let's explore OLE in particular.

Prehistoric OLE (1.0)

OLE 1.0, commonly known as *oleis minimus* (to me, anyway), was a new and wonderful technology. It was introduced as part of Windows 3.1 and provided for both object linking and embedding. This meant that the user could now create complex compound documents capable of containing objects from a variety of sources. You could edit embedded objects just by double-clicking on them. For instance, if you double-clicked on an Excel spreadsheet embedded in a Word document, the spreadsheet would come up in a separate window, and you could edit it. When you were done editing, Excel would let you save the changes to the embedded Excel object in the Word document.

Another feature was object linking. This allowed a spreadsheet to be linked into a Word document (basically, this was nothing more than a pointer to the spreadsheet in the Word document). If you updated the data in the original spreadsheet, the next time the Word document was loaded, the link would update the document and reflect the changes. Think of the benefits for the manager who had a Word document with embedded Excel spreadsheets from his employees. He could tell his workers to update their data by 10:00 a.m. on Monday, bring up his document at 10:05 (all the data would be self-updating), print the statistics for the week, give them to his boss, and look like a pro. It always comes back to image. It's much better to look good than to feel good, but with OLE you can have both!

OLE 1.0 provided much-needed relief for the weary end user who desperately needed a way to decrease the "manual" in manual labor.

The Revolution: OLE 2.0

OLE 2.0 has come a long way in helping us solve some of the key problems in component-based software. Let's look at some of the features of OLE 2 and the functionality they provide.

OLE's Component Object Model

Every structure needs a foundation. OLE 2.0's foundation is the Component Object Model (COM), a system software object model that allows complete interoperability between components that are written by different companies and in different languages. The modularity of these components is the key to their success. These components can be purchased, upgraded, or replaced individually or in groups without affecting the performance of the whole (sort of like the Borg, if you're a fan of *Star Trek: The Next Generation*). All are part of the collective contributing to the good of the whole (resistance is futile). COM is the backbone or nerve center of OLE. COM's primary responsibility is to ensure that components behave in a well-known and predictable manner. This should be done at the smallest cost to the programmer, maximizing the options in component implementation. The COM accomplishes this by defining a binary interface (which I spoke of earlier) that is completely independent of the programming language used in implementing the component. A component written to comply with the binary COM interface specifications can communicate with another component without really knowing any specific information about the other component's implementation.

Day 15: An Overview of OLE 2.0 and Objects

OLE relies on COM to provide all the basic communication between components. Again, this is an example of the object mentality. OLE uses the functionality of COM instead of reinventing the wheel. Remember, reuse is a programmer's best friend! This communication by COM is what allows you to embed a Visio drawing in a Word document. Word knows nothing of Visio's implementation (the products are even from different companies), yet COM allows the two to talk enough to get the job done.

OLE Automation

Automation is a wonderful new feature integrated into OLE 2.0 that allows you to access and manipulate another application's objects from outside that application. These objects "exposed" for external use are called OLE automation objects. The types of objects that can be "exposed" are as varied as the Windows applications themselves. A word processor could expose a document, paragraph, or sentence as an automation object. A spreadsheet could just as easily expose a spreadsheet, chart, cell, or range of cells.

The major difference between the normal OLE objects and automation objects is that automation objects can only be accessed programmatically. This could be accomplished using a programming language such as Visual Basic or a macro-based language such as Access 2.0. These objects aren't exposed to the end user and are used primarily to automate tasks that might be repetitive in nature. Normally there would be no user intervention in the task performed between your application and the exposed object. Figure 15.1 illustrates this concept.

Figure 15.1.
Automation at work.

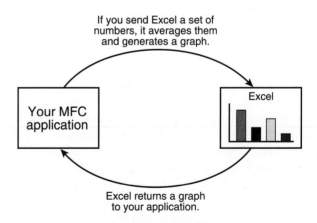

The result of this programmatic interface is that automation objects can't really be linked or embedded into your application; they can be accessed only by preprogrammed remote control. Why? Because they are created and used by preprogrammed code, and are therefore "temporary" in nature. They might exist for only a small portion of your program's execution time.

OLE Controls

OLE custom controls are software components (again, the modular mentality) that can be purchased off-the-shelf or written by you. These controls are used to give your application additional functionality. A number of custom controls are available, ranging from button and list box controls to complex network management and interface controls.

Many of these custom controls are currently implemented as VBXs. The VBX is just a special form of DLL. The OLE custom control (which has an extension of .OCX) is a major improvement over the VBX. The VBX is a 16-bit implementation, whereas the OLE control supports both 16- and 32-bit and is platform-independent. The OLE custom control specification is equally applicable to Windows, Windows NT and successors, and the Apple Macintosh. It even encompasses the potentially difficult issue of internationalization. For example, how do you spell the name of the color property—color, colour, coulcur, colore? This gives the OLE control a distinct advantage in the new 32-bit market.

Every OLE custom control possesses three sets of attributes:

- Properties: Named attributes such as color, font, and caption.
- Events: Actions that occur based on an external action directed to the control from outside the control itself. This could be the user clicking on the OLE control or pressing a key while the control is in focus.
- Methods: Functions in the control itself that allow external code to change the control's behavior or appearance. This could be as simple as modifying the current text entry in a text control.

The result of these three sets of attributes is the extreme flexibility of OLE controls to "become" whatever you need them to be. This is the beauty of OLE custom controls. This flexibility allows the software developer to create applications whose existence is based almost solely on other OLE controls. It makes the job more of an integration effort than a creation effort, as shown in Figure 15.2.

Figure 15.2.
OLE + OLE = application.

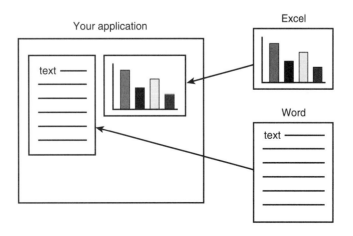

An Overview of OLE 2.0 and Objects

OLE Drag and Drop

You use OLE's drag and drop features almost without noticing them. Taking a file from File Manager and dropping it into Notepad (a lame excuse for a text editor, with a nearly 0.0 byte file size limit) is a prime example. This gives the user a great deal of flexibility and control. If you don't want to use Notepad, you can drag FOO.TXT from File Manager to Write and use it instead. Drag and drop gives us choices.

OLE Component Management

Because of the autonomous nature of OLE (having individual components), we may upgrade or replace an OLE component without having to recompile all the applications that rely on that component. Remember that everyone deals with OLE components through a defined set of interfaces. The internal structure is invisible to the developer. This means that as long as the interface remains consistent, the internals of the component could be rewritten completely, and the user would never know the difference.

OLE Documents

An OLE Document is a form of compound document that can incorporate data created in any OLE-enabled application. For instance, an OLE-enabled word processor (such as Microsoft Word) can accept tables and charts from an OLE-enabled spreadsheet (such as Microsoft Excel). OLE Documents allow users to convey their ideas more effectively by incorporating many different types of information into any business document. In addition to incorporating static information such as charts and tables, OLE Documents can also incorporate live data such as sound, video, and animation. OLE Documents also make users more productive by simplifying the process of creating compound documents. The following sections discuss features specific to OLE Documents.

OLE Object Linking and Embedding

This feature was supported in OLE 1.0, as I mentioned earlier, and it is still supported in OLE 2.0. This is more proof that Microsoft is committed to providing consistency throughout its product development (the object strategy).

OLE Visual Editing

Visual editing is probably the greatest feature of OLE 2. Visual editing allows users to create robust, compound documents easily, incorporating text, graphics, sound, video, and many other diverse objects. Instead of constantly switching between applications to create different parts of a compound document, users can work within a single application that holds the context of their document. As the user begins to edit an object that originated in another application, such as a spreadsheet or graphic, the container application's menus and tools automatically change to the menus and tools of that object's native application. The user can then edit the object in the context of the document without worrying about activating and switching to another application. See Figure 15.3.

Figure 15.3.
Visual editing.

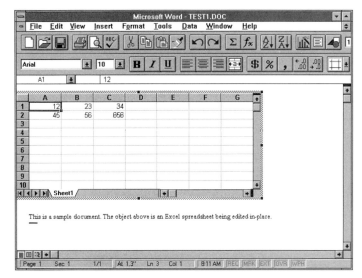

This particular feature provides a smooth path for users to follow when creating a compound document. Visual editing is also referred to as *in-place activation*. This term makes sense, because the menus and toolbars change as the OLE server is activated for the particular object being edited. This provides a similar look and feel for the user—always a plus.

Object Conversion

Objects can be converted to different types so that different applications can be used with the same object. For example, an object created with one brand of spreadsheet can be converted so that it can be interpreted by a different spreadsheet application for editing.

Nested Object Support

In a truly object-based system, you should be able to nest objects in multiple layers within other objects. Also, users should be able to access and manipulate objects that are nested inside other objects and establish links to them. It just so happens that OLE 2.0 provides all these features! This too adds to the flexibility of object-based software.

An Overview of OLE 2.0 and Objects

Optimized (Persistent) Object Storage

With OLE 1, the entire object had to be loaded from disk into memory, even if you only wanted to draw the object's border on the screen. This was a huge waste of our two most precious resources: memory and CPU cycles. This problem has been overcome in OLE 2. In OLE 2, objects remain on disk until needed, and they aren't loaded into memory each time the container application is opened. The great part is that now an OLE 2 object need only load the portion of itself that is required at that point in time.

A relevant example of this would be a Word document with an embedded Excel spreadsheet that would load the spreadsheet only if you were editing the page on which that spreadsheet resided. This also would help speed your application's responsiveness, because you would be carrying only a portion of the document around with you, not the entire thing. Also, OLE has complete transacted object storage, which supports commits and rollbacks (no, I'm not talking about SQL Server) of objects to disk. This ensures that data integrity is maintained as objects are stored in the file system.

Storage-Independent Links

This feature allows objects to update each other's information. Not a big deal, right? Well, it is when those objects are embedded in other documents. Simply put, my Excel spreadsheet embedded in a Word document can exchange data with another Excel spreadsheet embedded in yet another document. All this occurs even though neither embedded object exists as a straight disk file. Pretty cool.

Wow! The flexibility, the power! Okay, enough is enough. OLE 2.0 opens new doors for programmers who want to complete complex software applications in a short period of time. It allows the mere mortal programmer to include the power of Excel in his or her application without having to write it! This is why component-based software development tools such as Visual Basic 3.0 have sold so well, and why the next generation of OCX-enabled (again, .OCX is the extension given to an OLE custom control) Visual Basic will sell even better. There is a large ROI (return on investment) here. A little integration work with a huge payoff.

The Price

Of course, there is a little up-front investment on your part. You must study and understand OLE. After hundreds of hours of mind-numbing work, you might begin to glean a faint understanding of where OLE is headed. The details of OLE are at least as complicated as the details of Windows programming. Why couldn't someone write a set of C++ classes that hides most of the OLE details? It would show us only the essential details we need to make OLE work. Why couldn't someone write this set of classes so that it would do for OLE programming what the MFC library did for Windows programming? Someone did, and they had the good taste to hide it among the other classes of the MFC. Yes, we've had it all along, and unlike Dorothy, we didn't need a tornado and a yappy little dog to show us the light. So how does the MFC support OLE 2.0? Read on!

OLE 2.0 Sans MFC

You may choose to use only the raw OLE API when constructing your application. These types of tasks are given to the brainiacks at Microsoft (you know—the guys they keep in locked offices with six workstations, feeding them Twinkies and Mountain Dew). What you are up against if you try the "I write everything myself" mentality is that the raw OLE API makes little to no assumptions about your application. This is more a curse than a blessing (an MFC-based opinion). It allows you more flexibility, but it also does little of the work for you. It gives you only the core structure and defines many of the standard interfaces. The rest of the job is up to you. This definitely puts the "manual" in manual labor.

The benefit of using the raw OLE API is that you have many choices. You need to decide which of the standard interfaces you will need, and how they will talk to the rest of your program. You even have a choice of programming language. I recommend C++, of course, but an OLE 2 application could be written in C, Ada, BASIC, or Assembly. Programming the OLE 2.0 API gives you the ultimate in flexibility. It's sort of like playing SimCity: You create the culture from the ground up.

In my humble opinion, it's always better to let someone else do the work for you. You can then concentrate on making your "killer" application.

OLE 2 Using the MFC

The MFC has a number of significant achievements, not the least of which is OLE 2.0 support. The MFC again shields you from what you don't need to know. This assumption is based on Microsoft's assumptions about what you're going to do.

I can assume that if you're using the MFC, you're building a Windows application using C++. You're also taking advantage of classes (such as CObject, which we used earlier). So far we have used the MFC to add everything from ODBC database support to printing support, so why not add OLE 2?

When you select Project | AppWizard, you will see an OLE Options... button. See Figure 15.4.

This option allows you to pick the OLE-specific options you would like implemented in your application. When you click on this button, you see the dialog shown in Figure 15.5.

An Overview of OLE 2.0 and Objects

Figure 15.4.
The AppWizard dialog.

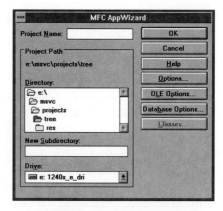

Figure 15.5.
The OLE Options dialog.

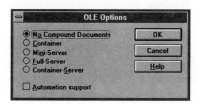

Wow! After hearing about all of OLE's features, isn't it amazing to see that things like OLE automation are just a check box away? As you can see, the options are there for the picking. A recent Microsoft article estimated that more than 19,000 lines of code in the MFC are dedicated to the implementation of OLE. This code helps mesh OLE into the document and view structure we have already been using. So much for writing it yourself.

If that isn't reason enough to use the MFC, how about this: The OLE API differs between 16- and 32-bit versions. This should be expected. 16-bit OLE uses 8-bit ANSI characters, whereas 32-bit OLE uses 16-bit Unicode characters. If you aren't using the MFC and are writing OLE applications, you have to worry about handling both types of strings. With MFC 3.0 (the next version), you can use your old MFC application and simply recompile for 16- or 32-bit execution. The MFC takes care of string conversions for you.

The MFC supports visual editing (in-place activation) as well as drag and drop and structured storage (compound files). The MFC provides two sets of C++ classes that support visual editing. The first class supports the creation of an OLE server. I mentioned this briefly earlier. The server exports it services to others. An example of a server would be a linked spreadsheet linked in a Word document.

The second set of classes supports the creation of an OLE container—the container designed to "hold" an OLE server. The container application knows how to harness the power of the OLE server. This explanation is a little simplistic, of course, but this is an overview chapter. In later chapters we will implement an OLE server and an OLE container. We will also learn how to create and use them.

The other OLE feature supported by the MFC is OLE automation. I have already explained what automation is, but here is what the MFC can do about it. It helps you export your automation interfaces and expose your member variables and functions as properties and methods. Notice the terms *properties* and *methods*. These come directly from the custom control discussion (what a small world). ClassWizard (in the OLE Automation tab) also lets you import libraries from other applications, which allows you to control other automation servers from your C++ application. See Figure 15.6.

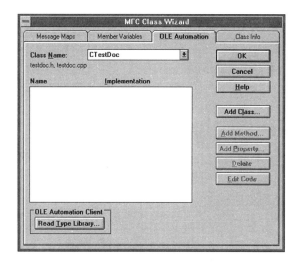

Figure 15.6.
ClassWizard OLE automation.

As with any other technology, the more you know, the better. You can use the MFC to generate your OLE application, but a thorough understanding of OLE 2 can never hurt. It's akin to our earlier experiences with Windows MFC programming. Simply knowing how to use the MFC is only one side of the coin; understanding the underlying technology (Windows or OLE) is the other side. Only through comprehending both sides can you really exploit the power.

Summary

We could only scratch the surface of OLE in this chapter (or in this book, for that matter). OLE is a complex and rich subject worthy of in-depth study. I highly recommend looking at the OLE tutorials that come with Visual C++. I also recommend Brockschmidt's *Inside OLE 2* (Microsoft Press, 1994), over 900 pages of light reading. It seems that OLE is the wave *to* the future, and your knowledge is the surfboard.

An Overview of OLE 2.0 and Objects

Q&A

Q I thought linking was a continuous updating mechanism, but you said it updates only during application loading. Is there any way to update while remaining in the application?

A Yes! You can update a link while in an application if the link is supported by the application, usually by selecting Link | Update.

Q I haven't seen much about OCX controls. How can I get more information?

A The Microsoft Developer's Network CD (a quarterly subscription service from Microsoft) is the single largest source of information I have ever seen in one place. It gives you access to thousands of articles, white papers, and specifications dealing with many issues, including OCX technology.

Workshop

Quiz

1. Describe the difference between linking and embedding.
2. What are the inherent limitations of VBX technology?

Exercises

1. Demonstrate to yourself the concepts of linking and embedding using your favorite application (Word, Excel, and so on).
2. To demonstrate to yourself drag and drop (if you haven't used it before), open File Manager and drag a .TXT file to the Notepad icon.

WEEK
3

OLE Servers

Day 16

OLE Servers

Now that we have a bird's-eye view of what OLE 2.0 does for us, let's get our hands dirty and make some OLE magic. In this chapter we will start constructing an OLE server application that will serve as a simple ASCII/hex file viewer. In Chapter 17 we will expand on this application by adding printing support. But before we do anything else, we must instruct AppWizard to build a default server.

A Bare-Bones Server

In the AppWizard dialog box, type the name of our new server application: Hexpad. Then invoke the OLE Options... dialog and select the Full-Server option, as shown in Figure 16.1.

Figure 16.1.
The OLE Options dialog.

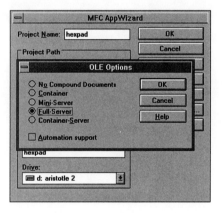

Invoke the Options dialog and deselect the MDI check box because we want an SDI application. Invoke the Classes dialog and make a minor change in the view class: Have AppWizard derive our view from `CScrollView`. The rest of the AppWizard options may remain as their default values, so click on the appropriate number of OK and Create buttons and let the wizard do its work. Now go ahead and compile. When the dust settles and your hard drive is through grinding, you will be left with a bare-bones server application. Just like all the other AppWizard-generated applications, it won't look like much. However, it is a full-blown server application that can be run stand-alone or embedded in a container application.

Let's test it. Run the application in the Visual C++ environment to make sure that it runs as a stand-alone application. Sure enough, it does. Now start your favorite container application. You can choose from one of the big professional containers such as Word or Excel, or you might want to set your sights a little lower and try Write or Contain. We will stick to the last two choices because I know you have them. Write comes with Windows (look in the Accessories group) and Contain (version 1.0) comes with your compiler (look under the MFC Samples group).

Note: Actually, I'm being somewhat sneaky here. Implementing the "full-blown" server might seem like I'm doing you a big favor. But the fact that full servers can stand alone makes some things very easy. You see, the easy way to register an OLE server is to run it. Running a server automatically registers it with Windows. Once registered, a server can be "seen" by a container. If a server isn't registered (that is, it hasn't been run in the current instance of Windows), Windows and container applications can't know of the server's existence. That's why I had you run the stand-alone version of our server before having you embed it. If you move your server to another machine, you have to reregister it with that instance of Windows! What if you build a mini-server (a server that can only be embedded)? Well, you can't register it just by running it because it can't run stand-alone. It can only be run embedded, but you can't embed it until you register it. A catch-22! Enter the setup program. When you install your application, you can register it directly during setup.

Start the Write application. It will contain Hexpad. To that end, embed a Hexpad document in the Write document by selecting Edit | Insert Object. You will be prompted with the OLE Insert Object dialog box, shown in Figure 16.2.

Figure 16.2.
The Insert OLE Object dialog.

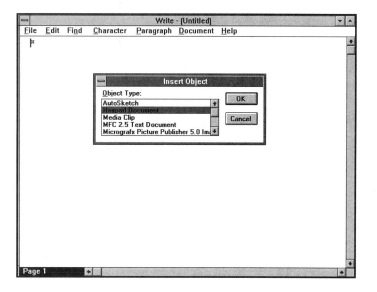

DAY 16

OLE Servers

Hexpad is one of the choices in this dialog. Yes, this is our brand-new Hexpad application that does nothing. Choose it and click on OK. You should see the Hexpad application come up, just as it did in the Visual C++ environment (see Figure 16.3).

Figure 16.3.
Editing Hexpad within Write.

If you close Hexpad, you will return to Write. However, there is now an embedded version of a Hexpad document within the Write document, as shown in Figure 16.4.

Figure 16.4.
An inactive Hexpad document within Write.

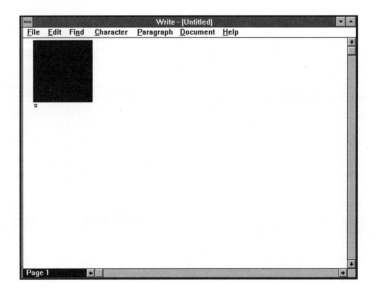

Double-clicking on the embedded Hexpad document will again bring up the Hexpad application. The Hexpad object is embedded in the Write document.

Using a similar process, we can embed a Hexpad document within the Contain application. Start Contain and select Edit | Insert New Object. You see a slightly different OLE Insert Object dialog. However, you still have the same selection of potential server applications to choose from (see Figure 16.5).

Figure 16.5.
Contain's Insert OLE Object dialog.

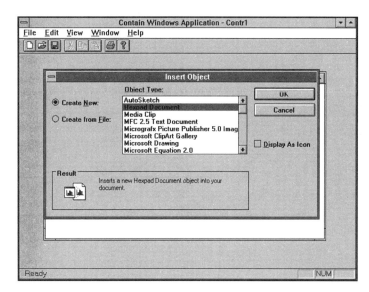

Choose the Hexpad application and click on OK. Isn't that interesting? The Hexpad application is not invoked! We just get a new little box in the current Contain child window, as shown in Figure 16.6.

This little box is the Hexpad document. The difference between Contain and Write is in how they allow editing of their embedded server documents. Contain supports in-place editing—that is, the document may be edited as it sits in the Contain document. Write doesn't support in-place editing, so when you want to edit the Hexpad document, Write just starts the stand-alone application and hands it the document, which you edit in its native environment. Both methods are legitimate OLE, but in-place editing is much more satisfying from a user's perspective.

OLE Servers

Figure 16.6.
Hexpad in-place editing.

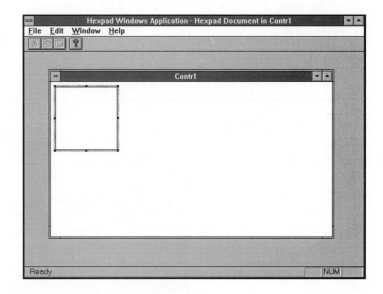

Much Ado About Nothing

So we have let AppWizard do our work by building a bare-bones server that does absolutely zip! Its only redeeming value is that it does in fact act like an OLE server. We can embed it at will, and everywhere we do, it still does nothing. At least it's consistent! So how is this default OLE "nothing" accomplished? The answer to this question could be your life's work, but you should be able to glean a superficial understanding of the default "nothing" from this chapter.

The default AppWizard server application is still based on the idea of the document/view architecture. AppWizard servers have documents that hold data. They have views that display data. They have `CMainFrame` and `CWinApp`-derived classes. In fact, a cursory examination would reveal that a full server is simply a non-OLE application with some extra OLE classes tacked on. This isn't quite correct, but from an architecture point of view, it's pretty close. Figures 16.7 and 16.8 show the MFC MDI server and the SDI server architectures, respectively.

You can see from these diagrams that as long as a server document is not embedded, its architecture is identical to the corresponding non-OLE application document. It acts and responds the same because it uses practically the same classes. However, once a document is embedded in a container, different classes are used. Just like Jekyll and Hyde, the embedded document might have a significantly different personality. Naturally, we strive to minimize this difference, but the fact remains that embedded documents use different classes than documents in their native environment.

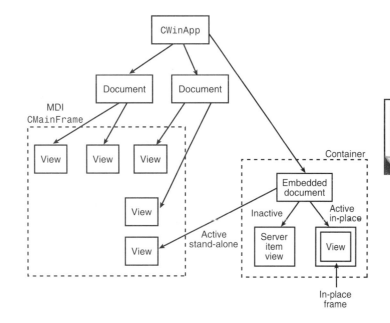

Figure 16.7.
The MFC MDI server architecture.

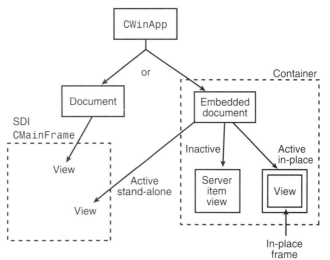

Figure 16.8.
The MFC SDI server architecture.

OLE Servers

A plethora of new classes that have been added to the MFC provide connections to OLE 2.0. These classes are described briefly in the following section.

OLE Foundation Classes

The advent of MFC support for OLE 2.0 brought forth a number of new classes. These classes can be split into several groups:

- Container support
- Server support
- Both container and server support
- Data transfer support
- Dialog box support
- Miscellaneous

Tables 16.1 through 16.6 enumerate each of these groupings.

Table 16.1. MFC container support classes.

Class	Description
COleLinkingDoc	The base class for your container document if you want linking support.
COleClientItem	The container-side hook to a server item.
CRectTracker	Used by the container object as an aid in manipulating in-place server objects.

Table 16.2. MFC server support classes.

Class	Description
CIPFrameWnd	The window frame for an in-place server.
COleObjectFactory	The base class encapsulating the OLE class factory functionality. It allows one object to create another.
COleResizeBar	The resize bar for the in-place server window.
COleServerItem	The base class for server-side objects that provide for embedding and linking.
COleServerDoc	The base class for your server document.
COleTemplateServer	The document template class for your server application.

Table 16.3. MFC OLE general (container and server) support classes.

Class	Description
COleDocument	The base class for both server and container documents.
COleDocItem	The abstract base class for both container and server items (COleClientItem and COleServerItem).

Table 16.4. MFC data transfer support classes.

Class	Description
COleDataObject	The destination actor in OLE data transfer associated with the Clipboard or drag and drop.
COleDataSource	The source actor in OLE data transfer associated with the Clipboard or drag and drop.
COleDropTarget	Represents the destination window of a drag-and-drop operation. It determines whether a drop is acceptable.
COleDropSource	Represents the object of a drag-and-drop operation. It controls the visual feedback associated with potential drops.

Table 16.5. MFC OLE dialog box support classes.

Class	Description
COleDialog	The abstract base class for all the OLE dialog classes.
COleBusyDialog	Notifies the user of a busy or nonresponsive server application.
COleChangeIconDialog	Allows the user to select a new icon for a given, currently embedded, or linked server application.
COleConvertDialog	Allows the user to convert an OLE object from one type to another.
COleInsertDialog	Prompts the user to choose from a list of registered servers after the user tries to insert an OLE object.
COleLinksDialog	Allows the user to manipulate OLE links.
COlePasteSpecialDialog	Allows the user to control the Edit	Paste Special menu option.
COleUpdateDialog	Notifies the user of the status of the requested link update.

OLE Servers

Table 16.6. MFC miscellaneous OLE support classes.

Class	Description
COleException	The OLE customized CException class.
COleDispatchException	An exception class designed for use with OLE automation.
COleMessageFilter	A class used to manage message flow in the concurrent environment of multiple servers and containers.
COleStreamFile	A class supporting OLE 2.0 structure storage.

We have a veritable smorgasbord of new classes from which to choose. And, as with a buffet, we must take care to budget what we pile on our plates. Some of these classes aren't very palatable at first; you might have to develop a taste for them. But when you do, "Mmmmmm... OLE-licious," as Homer Simpson would say. Let's start out easy and look at the classes that even AppWizard can handle. I will introduce and explain any additional classes as the need arises.

OLE Classes à la AppWizard

Table 16.7 shows the classes created for our default server and from where they were derived.

Table 16.7. Default Hexpad classes (built by AppWizard).

Class	Files	Description
CHexpadView	HEXPAVW.H, HEXPAVW.CPP	The good old CView-derived class that implements the native display.
CHexpadDoc	HEXPADOC.H, HEXPADOC.CPP	The document class derived from COleServerDoc that supports server functionality.
CMainFrame	MAINFRM.H, MAINFRM.CPP	The good old CMDIFrameWnd-derived class that supports multiple documents and views.
CHexpadApp	HEXPAD.H, HEXPAD.CPP	The good old application class derived from CWinApp.
CHexpadSrvrItem	SRVRITEM.H, SRVRITEM.CPP	A brand-new class derived from COleServerItem that implements the embedded, inactive display.

Class	Files	Description
CInPlaceFrame	IPFRAME.H, IPFRAME.CPP	A brand-new class derived from COleIPFrameWnd that implements the in-place frame window.

The first four classes are somewhat familiar. No, CHexpadDoc isn't the same class we have come to love. It's derived from COleServerDoc, but for our immediate concern, you can ignore its additions to CDocument. Really, it's just CDocument with an OLE attitude. The last two classes, however, are completely new! The CHexpadSrvrItem class will be our server's representative in the container application. It will be the server item's responsibility to draw a picture of the embedded document when that document is inactive. Only when the embedded document is active (editable) will the server's view take over; otherwise, the view is cut out of the loop. The last class implements the frame window for in-place editing. Although it's important to our application, CInPlaceFrame need not be customized. The default version is usually more than adequate for most applications. The default COleServerItem-derived class, on the other hand, is far from adequate!

To see where CHexpadSrvrItem is lacking, let's examine what it does by looking at its interface:

```
// srvritem.h: Interface of the CHexpadSrvrItem class
//

class CHexpadSrvrItem : public COleServerItem
{
    DECLARE_DYNAMIC(CHexpadSrvrItem)

// Constructors
public:
    CHexpadSrvrItem(CHexpadDoc* pContainerDoc);

// Attributes
    CHexpadDoc* GetDocument() const
        { return (CHexpadDoc*)COleServerItem::GetDocument(); }

// Implementation
public:
    ~CHexpadSrvrItem();
#ifdef _DEBUG
    virtual void AssertValid() const;
    virtual void Dump(CDumpContext& dc) const;
#endif
    virtual BOOL OnDraw(CDC* pDC, CSize& rSize);
    virtual BOOL OnGetExtent(DVASPECT dwDrawAspect, CSize& rSize);

protected:
    // Overridden for document I/O
```

OLE Servers

```
    virtual void Serialize(CArchive& ar);
};
```

//

It bears a remarkable resemblance to our view classes, but it also has aspects you would normally attribute to a document class. This duality is due to the fact that the server item is responsible for drawing our embedded object as well as serializing it in the container document. Both `OnDraw()` and `Serialize()` are implemented in the same way as their counterparts in the view and document classes. Another interesting function that is visible in the interface is `OnGetExtent()`. This function provided the container with a means of determining the size of the embedded document. The container needs this information if it is to make room for the embedded object. All three of these functions will need to be customized.

Let's back up a minute. The view class has an `OnDraw()` function and the server item class has an `OnDraw()` function. Both functions draw the same thing in (hopefully) the same manner—we want the two displays to be consistent. Doesn't that sound like a maintenance nightmare waiting to happen—two separate drawing implementations of the same thing? After all, we want the inactive, embedded document to look like the document in its native environment. There is a way to minimize code duplication while ensuring consistency between the native view and the server item view. The trick is to put the drawing code in a location accessible to both views and the server item. This location is the document class. Yes, I know. We should avoid putting drawing code in the document—we should separate the document and the view. But considering the alternative that breaks even more rules, we make the sacrifice.

Adding Server Functionality

Add the following function to CHexpad's document class:

```
void CHexpadDoc::DrawStuff(CDC* pDC, CRect rect)
{
    // Draw stuff on pDC
    CBrush brush = (RGB(0, 0, 255));  // Blue brush
    CBrush* pOldBrush = pDC->SelectObject(&brush);
    pDC->Rectangle(&rect);
    pDC->Ellipse(&rect);
    pDC->TextOut(20, 20, "Hello Big, Blue World.");
    pDC->TextOut(20, 50, "I do like the color blue!");
    pDC->SelectObject(pOldBrush);
}
```

This is a brand-new function (so don't forget to add it to the interface) that performs the drawing for both the server item and the view class. You will note that our old friend, the `CDC` pointer, is passed as an argument. But we are also passing an object of `CRect`. The `CRect` class is little more than a structure holding the x-y coordinates of the top-right and bottom-left corners of a rectangle. This object is passed to indicate the size of the drawing space. In the current implementation of DrawStuff(), it is used to paint the view blue using the Rectangle() function. The blue color is accomplished by creating a blue brush and selecting it into the device context (are you getting bitmap flashbacks, too?). All CDC filling will subsequently be done in blue. Just to get a feel for server drawing and its responsibilities, we call the Ellipse() function and draw two lines of text. The final line, where you reselect the old brush, should be somewhat familiar from our bitmap experiences. Always leave things as you found them.

Now that we have the drawing code, what do we do with it? Well, we must painlessly insert it into the OnDraw() functions found in the view and server item classes. Putting the DrawStuff() call into the view class is very simple:

```
void CHexpadView::OnDraw(CDC* pDC)
{
    CHexpadDoc* pDoc = GetDocument();
    ASSERT_VALID(pDoc);

    // Draw "stuff" in the client area
    CRect rc;
    GetClientRect(&rc);
    pDoc->DrawStuff(pDC, rc);
}
```

We declare a CRect object and set it equal to the current client area (via the GetClientRect() function). Then we simply call the document's DrawStuff() function. However, slipping our new call into the server item's OnDraw() might seem more difficult due to the complicated nature of the default function:

```
// Add the indicated lines to the server item's OnDraw function
BOOL CHexpadSrvrItem::OnDraw(CDC* pDC, CSize& rSize)
{
    CHexpadDoc* pDoc = GetDocument();
    ASSERT_VALID(pDoc);

    // TODO: Set mapping mode and extent
    // (The extent is usually the same as
    // the size returned from OnGetExtent)
    pDC->SetMapMode(MM_ANISOTROPIC);
    pDC->SetWindowOrg(0,0);
    pDC->SetWindowExt(3000, 3000);

    // TODO: Add drawing code here. Optionally, fill in the
    // HIMETRIC extent.
    // All drawing takes place in the metafile device context (pDC).

    CRect rc(0, 0, 3000, 3000);
    pDoc->DrawStuff(pDC, rc);

    return TRUE;
}
```

OLE Servers

The first three default `CDC` function calls might seem straight out of the blue (no application-related pun intended). These calls concern mapping modes—specifically, the `MM_ANISOTROPIC` mapping mode. If you were hoping to escape from learning about mapping modes, I'm sorry to disappoint you. They are rather central to OLE server implementation. The code we have added to the server's `OnDraw()` function is relatively simple. We simply construct a rectangle (of hard-coded size) and pass it and the `CDC` pointer to `DrawStuff()`.

Ignoring the new mapping mode code for a moment, let's see what's going on with the application at this point. Compile, link, and run Hexpad. Cool, huh?

Figure 16.9 shows our MDI application with a blue child window that contains part of an ellipse as well as some text. That's nice, but so what? This isn't anything new. We could do this before OLE. Ah, true, but could you now turn around and embed this application in a container? Let's do that. Figure 16.10 shows Hexpad immediately after you have inserted it into the Contain application. Note that the embedded document is active and that it looks just like one of the child window documents in the stand-alone version.

By clicking inside the Contain application but outside of the embedded item's box, you force the Hexpad object into its inactive state, as shown in Figure 16.11.

Figure 16.9.
Stand-alone Hexpad version 0.0.

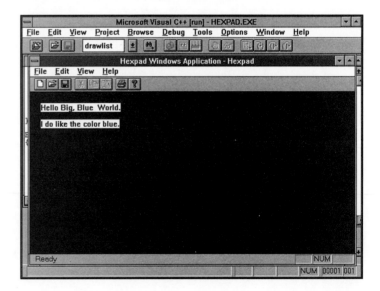

Figure 16.10.
Embedded and active Hexpad version 0.0.

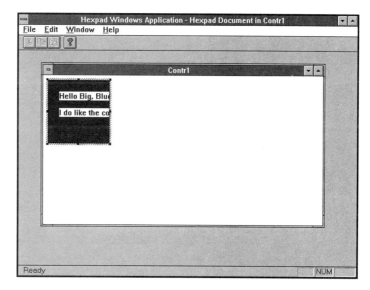

Figure 16.11.
Embedded and inactive Hexpad version 0.0.

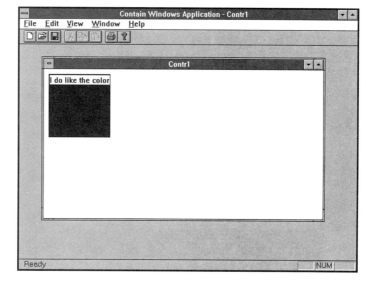

OLE Servers

When embedded and inactive, the server item code is used to draw the document. And look at the difference! The whole area isn't painted blue; the ellipse is scrunched up in the corner, a shadow of its former self; and the first line of text is missing. What happened? The two drawing functions use precisely the same code. The difference is in that illusive topic of mapping modes that we have so gladly ignored in the past.

Mapping Modes

At the risk of boggling your mind with a seemingly non sequitur topic, we will now delve into the hidden depths of mapping modes. "Why," you might ask, "are you about to prattle on about mapping modes when we have a real problem with our OLE application?" The brush-off answer to this question would be "Patience is a virtue, Grasshopper. In time, all will become clear!" However, I hate being brushed off myself, and since we're not learning a martial art, I can reveal the answer early. To wit: Due to the nature of OLE—that is, objects within objects—it's very important to establish a common ground with respect to display coordinates and scaling. This common ground may be partially achieved through the use of a standard mapping mode. Windows has many mapping modes to choose from (see Table 16.8), but OLE uses only one: MM_HIMETRIC.

Table 16.8. Windows mapping modes.

Mode	Description
MM_ANISOTROPIC	Customizable mapping mode. No holds barred.
MM_ISOTROPIC	Customizable mapping mode. x and y directions must have the same units.
MM_HIMETRIC	Fixed, high-granularity, metric-unit mapping mode.
MM_LOMETRIC	Fixed, low-granularity, metric-unit mapping mode.
MM_HIENGLISH	Fixed, high-granularity, English-unit mapping mode.
MM_LOENGLISH	Fixed, low-granularity, English-unit mapping mode.
MM_TEXT	Default mapping mode. Unique axis directions and device-dependent units.
MM_TWIPS	Used in printing. Units based on font points.

Thus far in our windowing experiences, we have been content to ignore mapping modes. Whatever the default mapping mode was (the default mapping mode for GDI functions is MM_TEXT), that is what it remained. For our limited use of the display, the "ignore" technique served us well. Now, however, we want to play with the big boys and make OLE work. Learning mapping modes is one of the prices we have to pay. Another place where mapping modes come in handy is printing. We will discuss printer-related mapping mode techniques in the next chapter.

The default mapping mode that we have been working with so far is MM_TEXT. Whenever we wrote text to the screen via the CDC::TextOut() function or displayed a geometric object via one of the CDC shape functions, we were using MM_TEXT. You know, therefore, that the MM_TEXT mapping mode is defined as shown in Figure 16.12.

Figure 16.12.
The MM_TEXT mapping mode.

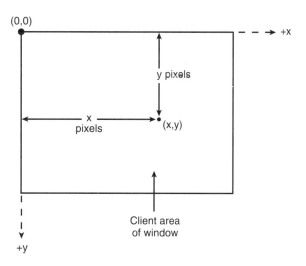

MM_TEXT has a default origin of (0, 0), corresponding to the upper-left corner of the window in question. Some point, (x, y), is located *x* units to the right of the origin and *y* units down from the origin. The unit of measurement in MM_TEXT is the pixel, which just happens to be the unit of measurement of the video device (as we saw in our dealings with bitmaps). In Windows literature, you will see units divided into two categories: device units and logical units. Device units are the screen pixels, whereas logical units are dependent on the particular mapping mode. Equating the logical units to the device units in MM_TEXT made it easy for us to draw the predefined CDC shapes and deal directly with coordinates on the screen. The pixel is a very intuitive unit—at least from a programming perspective. But tying your mapping mode units to device units (pixels) can have some undesirable consequences—namely, going from one video device to the next will change the size of your drawing! In general, different video hardware will have different pixel dimensions. You don't want your application to look different from machine to machine! Consistency is expected in quality applications. To help you provide a consistent application, the other mapping modes were made to be device-independent. In fact, their mapping units are based on real-world distances, as shown in Table 16.9.

Day 16: OLE Servers

Table 16.9. Mapping mode units and axis directions.

Mode	Units	Axis Directions
MM_ANISOTROPIC	Roll your own	Roll your own
MM_ISOTROPIC	Roll your own	Roll your own
MM_HIMETRIC	0.01 millimeter	x-axis right, y-axis up
MM_LOMETRIC	0.1 millimeter	x-axis right, y-axis up
MM_HIENGLISH	0.001 inch	x-axis right, y-axis up
MM_LOENGLISH	0.01 inch	x-axis right, y-axis up
MM_TEXT	Pixel	x-axis right, y-axis down
MM_TWIPS	1/1440 of an inch	x-axis right, y-axis up

From this table you can see that the y-axis direction for the other mapping modes is opposite that of the familiar MM_TEXT. The other mapping modes have the positive y-axis going up (a familiar sight if you're mathematically inclined). This is illustrated in Figure 16.13.

Figure 16.13.
The MM_HIMETRIC mapping mode.

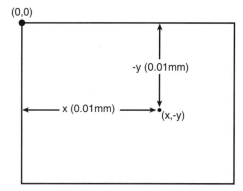

Wait a second! If you want to specify a coordinate in the middle of a window using one of the mapping modes other than MM_TEXT, you'll have to use a negative value for the y-coordinate? Well, yes and no. Without making any other calls except the switch to the new mapping mode, the answer is yes. However, you can specify a new origin: a new (0,0) point in the window. Since all the (x, y) coordinate pairs are relative to the origin, you can again use positive values to specify actual window points in a non-MM_TEXT mode. See Figure 16.14 for an example of a changed viewport origin.

Figure 16.14.
A changed viewport origin.

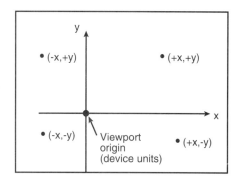

Changing the viewport origin is just one of the many different manipulations you can perform on the device context's mapping mode. Table 16.10 describes the CDC functions that relate to mapping modes.

Table 16.10. CDC mapping mode functions.

Function	Description
GetMapMode	Returns the current mapping mode.
SetMapMode	Sets the mapping mode.
GetViewportOrg	Returns the current viewport origin in device coordinates.
SetViewportOrg	Sets the viewport origin to the specified device coordinates.
OffsetViewportOrg	Moves the current viewport origin by the x and y offsets specified in device units.
GetViewportExt	Returns the x and y dimensions (extents) of the viewport in device units.
SetViewportExt*	Sets the x and y dimensions of the viewport in device units.
OffsetViewportExt*	Resizes the viewport dimensions by the x and y offset specified in device units.
GetWindowOrg	Returns the current window origin in logical coordinates.
SetWindowOrg	Sets the window origin to the specified logical coordinates.
OffSetWindowOrg	Moves the current window origin by the x and y offsets specified in logical units.
GetWindowExt	Returns the x and y dimensions of the window in logical units.

continues

OLE Servers

Table 16.10. continued

Function	Description
SetWindowExt*	Sets the x and y dimensions of the window in logical units.
ScaleWindowExt*	Resizes the window dimensions by the x and y offsets specified in logical units.

*These functions apply only to the MM_ANISOTROPIC and MM_ISOTROPIC mapping modes; they have no effect when applied in the other modes. These four functions are the means by which you "roll your own" mapping mode.

You will note in this table that there are really two sets of functions that seem to do the same thing; the only difference is the word Window versus the word Viewport. Whenever you see Viewport, think of device coordinates. Whenever you see Window (at least with regard to mapping modes), think of logical coordinates.

Two of the most important functions listed here are SetMappingMode() and GetMappingMode(). SetMappingMode() allows you to change your current mapping mode to one of the other seven possibilities. GetMappingMode() allows you to determine which mapping mode is currently in effect. It's important to be familiar with both.

An example of these mapping modes can be demonstrated through the following code snippet and corresponding screen, shown in Figure 16.15.

```
pDC->SetMappingMode(MM_HIMETRIC);
pDC->Ellipse(0, 0, 200, -1000);   // Note the negative y value
// Draws an ellipse 2mm by 10mm in the upper-left corner of the window

pDC->SetMappingMode(MM_LOENGLISH);
pDC->Ellipse(0, 0, 20, -100);   // Note the negative y value
// Draws an ellipse 0.2 inch by 1.0 inch
// in the upper-left corner of the window

pDC->SetMappingMode(MM_TEXT);
pDC->Ellipse(0, 0, +200, +1000);   // The +'s are just for emphasis
// Draws an ellipse 200 pixels by 1000 pixels
// in the upper-left corner of the window
```

I have ignored the two "roll your own" mapping modes up to this point because I wanted you to get a feel for the other modes first. MM_ANISOTROPIC and MM_ISOTROPIC are called *variable-scale* mapping modes because you can define their scale. The other modes have a fixed scale based on their definition and are therefore called *fixed-scale* modes (that is, MM_LOENGLISH is fixed to 1 logical unit = 0.01 inches). The difference between the two variable-scale mapping modes is that

MM_ISOTROPIC must have its x units equal to its y units. In other words, a square in logical units will look like a square on-screen. MM_ANISOTROPIC is not restricted in any way. You will often see variable-scale mapping modes used when a drawing must be scaled to fit within a window.

Figure 16.15.
The MM_HIMETRIC *mapping mode.*

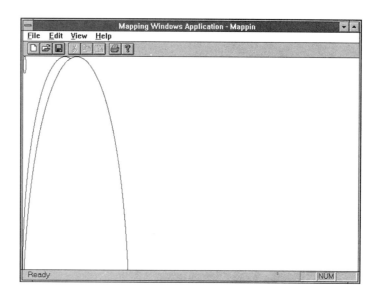

After spending the majority of this book tacitly assuming MM_TEXT, it might be a little difficult for you to switch gears to these other mapping modes. Don't worry. The more you use them, the more they too will seem like second nature.

Back to OLE

Okay, now that you're an expert on mapping modes, we can take another look at our server item drawing problem and try to find out what was going wrong. I mentioned that the problem centered around mapping mode issues. By examining the symptoms of the ailment (the shrinkage of the rectangle and ellipse and the disappearance of the first line of text), one might conclude that the cause of this problem is a mismatch of scale between the native environment of the document and the embedded environment. In the preceding section I mentioned that OLE assumes a default mapping mode of MM_HIMETRIC. In our native environment, the default mapping mode is MM_TEXT. No wonder the inactive, embedded object looked so funny! The way to fix this problem is to make appropriate conversions to and from the MM_HIMETRIC mapping mode. Luckily, these conversions can be done very easily by utilizing a set of CDC functions custom-designed for this purpose (see Table 16.11).

OLE Servers

Table 16.11. CDC unit conversion functions.

Function	Description
DPtoHIMETRIC	Converts device units to MM_HIMETRIC units.
DPtoLP	Converts device units to the current logical units.
HIMETRICtoDP	Converts MM_HIMETRIC units to device units.
HIMETRICtoLP	Converts MM_HIMETRIC units to the current logical units.
LPtoDP	Converts the current logical units to device units.
LPtoHIMETRIC	Converts the current logical units to MM_HIMETRIC units.

Alternatively, you could just use the MM_HIMETRIC mapping mode in your server application and not worry about conversions. Both approaches have their advantages and disadvantages. We'll try this second, alternative approach first and see how we do. Don't worry. Somewhere along the line you'll use some of the unit conversions just shown.

*HIMETRIC*izing Our Server

Make the following modifications to CHexpadSrvrItem::OnDraw():

```
BOOL CHexpadSrvrItem::OnDraw(CDC* pDC, CSize& rSize)
{
    CHexpadDoc* pDoc = GetDocument();
    ASSERT_VALID(pDoc);

    pDC->SetMapMode(MM_HIMETRIC);
    TEXTMETRIC tm;
    if (pDC->GetTextMetrics(&tm) == FALSE)
        TRACE0("GetTextMetrics() failed!\n");

    short cxChar, cyChar;
    cxChar = tm.tmAveCharWidth;
    cyChar = tm.tmHeight + tm.tmExternalLeading;
    TRACE1("tmHeight in the inactive embedded server is %d.\n",
            tm.tmHeight);

    // TODO: Add drawing code here. Optionally,
    // fill in the HIMETRIC extent.
    // All drawing takes place in the metafile device context (pDC).

    CRect rc(0, 0, 3000, -3000);
    pDoc->DrawStuff(pDC, rc);

    return TRUE;
}
```

If you run the code as it stands, we still have a problem! The inactive, embedded server doesn't display the text correctly! Well, if you look back at the DrawStuff() function, you will see that we hard-coded the y-coordinates into the TextOut() functions (you'd think we would know better). Of course, the coordinates of the text will depend on two things: the height of the text in the particular device context and the direction of the coordinate axes for the particular mapping mode. Both of these considerations must be taken into account when displaying text. For our problem, the size of text changes dramatically and the y-axis values decrease going down in MM_HIMETRIC as opposed to increasing going down in MM_TEXT. So let's smarten-up DrawStuff():

```
void CHexpadDoc::DrawStuff(CDC* pDC, CRect rect)
{
    int nCharHeight, nAveCharWidth;
    int x, y;

    // Draw stuff on pDC
    CBrush brush = (RGB(0, 0, 255));   // Blue brush
    CBrush* pOldBrush = pDC->SelectObject(&brush);
    pDC->Rectangle(&rect);
    pDC->Ellipse(&rect);

    // Determine character height and width for current device context
    TEXTMETRIC tm;
    if (pDC->GetTextMetrics(&tm) == FALSE)
        TRACE0("GetTextMetrics() failed!\n");
    nCharHeight = tm.tmHeight + tm.tmExternalLeading;
    nAveCharWidth = tm.tmAveCharWidth;
    TRACE1("nCharHeight = %d.\n", nCharHeight);
    TRACE1("nAveCharWidth = %d.\n", nAveCharWidth);

    // Take into account coordinate axis direction
    if (rect.Height() < 0)
        nCharHeight = -nCharHeight;
    if (rect.Width() < 0)
        nAveCharWidth = -nAveCharWidth;

    x = LEFT_MARGIN*nAveCharWidth;
    y = TOP_MARGIN*nCharHeight;
    pDC->TextOut(x, y, "Hello Big, Blue World.");
    y += nCharHeight;
    pDC->TextOut(x, y, "I do like the color blue!");

    pDC->SelectObject(pOldBrush);
}
```

You'll note that a couple of new items have cropped up. We now have a TOP_MARGIN and a LEFT_MARGIN, which shift the display by that many character units from the top-left corner. These constants are defined in the document's interface:

```
#define LEFT_MARGIN 0
#define TOP_MARGIN 1
```

You can see that now DrawStuff() is actually smart enough to determine and use both character extent and coordinate axis direction. If you run the application, you will see that both the stand-alone server as well as the inactive, embedded server display the same information. All is right with the world.

DAY 16

OLE Servers

Hexpad: A Real Application

Now that we have a little OLE experience under our belts, it's time to tackle a real server problem. Suppose we want a server that will load a file and display its contents in a window in either ASCII or hex. Furthermore, we want this application to be able to be embedded in other applications so that we may reuse this capability at will. Sounds like a reasonable application to have on hand. How do we do it?

As you might have guessed by the name of our current application, we're about to modify it so that it will, in fact, perform this exact function. First, let's concentrate on getting the file loaded into the application. To accomplish this feat, we must prepare a destination for the file data. For this task, we will use one of the MFC's predefined collection classes in conjunction with a new class we will create.

The loading procedure will consist of reading bytes from the file one line at a time, storing each line in some type of structure (for example, CTextLine), and then storing each line in our collection class. The interface of CTextLine follows:

```
// Filename: TextLine.h

#ifndef __TEXTLINE_H__
#define __TEXTLINE_H__

class CTextLine : public CObject
{

DECLARE_SERIAL(CTextLine)

protected:
    BYTE* m_pText;
    WORD m_wByteCount;
    BOOL m_bTerminated;

public:
    // Constructors
    CTextLine();   // Default
    CTextLine(CTextLine& TL);   // Copy
    CTextLine(const char* lpszText, WORD count);
    CTextLine(BYTE* pBytes, WORD count);

    // Destructor
    ~CTextLine();

    // Assignment
    CTextLine& operator=(CTextLine& TL);
    BOOL SetTo(BYTE* pBytes, WORD count);
    BOOL SetTo(const char* lpszText, WORD count);
    BOOL SetAt(WORD position, BYTE value);
    void SetTerminated(BOOL flag = TRUE);
```

```
    // Selectors
    WORD ByteCount();
    BOOL GetAt(WORD position, BYTE& value);
    CString GetString();
    BOOL IsTerminated();
    // Keeps track of artificial termination from ReadFromArchive

#ifdef _DEBUG
    virtual void Dump(CDumpContext& dc) const;
    virtual void AssertValid() const;
#endif

    virtual void Serialize( CArchive& ar);
    void WriteToArchive (CArchive& ar);
    void ReadFromArchive (CArchive& ar,
        WORD wMaxCount, BYTE byTerminator = 10);
    // ReadFromArchive() reads a text line directly
    // from the archive. nMaxCount indicates
    // the maximum number of bytes to be loaded and
    // bTerminator specifies an "end-of-line"
    // byte (default is 10 -- linefeed).

};

#endif
```

This is the typical form of a CObject-derived class with application-specific particulars. The mission of this class is to hold, and provide access to, text lines retrieved from a file. The tricky part of the code is the file storage and retrieval mechanism. Using the ReadFromArchive() and WriteToArchive() functions, CTextLine can store or load a line of text to or from the given archive object. In the ReadFromArchive() call, we specify both the maximum count to be read as well as an end-of-line (terminator) byte. These two parameters will prove useful when we integrate this class into our application. The implementation of CTextLine follows:

```
// Filename: TextLine.cpp

#include "stdafx.h"
#include "TextLine.h"
#include "ctype.h"

IMPLEMENT_SERIAL(CTextLine, CObject, 0)

////////////////////////////////////////////////////////////////////////
// Constructors
CTextLine::CTextLine()
{
    m_pText = NULL;
    m_wByteCount = 0;
    SetTerminated(FALSE);
}
```

DAY 16
OLE Servers

```cpp
CTextLine::CTextLine(CTextLine& TL)
{
    SetTo(TL.m_pText, TL.m_wByteCount);
    SetTerminated(TL.m_bTerminated);
}

CTextLine::CTextLine(const char* lpszText, WORD count)
{
    SetTo((BYTE*)lpszText, count);
}

CTextLine::CTextLine(BYTE* pBytes, WORD count)
{
    SetTo(pBytes, count);
}


////////////////////////////////////////////////////////////////////////
// Destructor
CTextLine::~CTextLine()
{
    free(m_pText);
}


////////////////////////////////////////////////////////////////////////
// Assignment
CTextLine& CTextLine::operator=(CTextLine& TL)
{
    SetTo(TL.m_pText, TL.m_wByteCount);
    SetTerminated(TL.m_bTerminated);

    return *this;
}

BOOL CTextLine::SetTo(BYTE* pBytes, WORD count)
{
    ASSERT ( (count == 0) || (pBytes != NULL) );

    SetTerminated(FALSE);

    if ( (count > 0) && (pBytes != NULL) )
    {
        free(m_pText);
        m_pText = (BYTE*)malloc(count);
        if (m_pText == NULL)
        {
            m_wByteCount = 0;
            return FALSE;
        }
        memcpy(m_pText, pBytes, count);
        m_wByteCount = count;
    }
    else
    {
```

```
            m_pText = NULL;
            m_wByteCount = 0;
        }

        return TRUE;
}

BOOL CTextLine::SetTo(const char* lpszText, WORD count)
{
        return SetTo((BYTE*)lpszText, count);
}

BOOL CTextLine::SetAt(WORD position, BYTE value)
{
        if (position >= m_wByteCount)
            return FALSE;
        else
        {
            m_pText[position] = value;
            return TRUE;
        }
}

void CTextLine::SetTerminated(BOOL flag)
{
        m_bTerminated = flag;
}

////////////////////////////////////////////////////////////////////////
// Selectors
WORD CTextLine::ByteCount()
{
        return m_wByteCount;
}

BOOL CTextLine::GetAt(WORD position, BYTE& value)
{
        if (position >= m_wByteCount)
            return FALSE;
        else
        {
            value = m_pText[position];
            return TRUE;
        }
}

CString CTextLine::GetString()
{
        CString S;

        for (WORD i = 0; i < m_wByteCount; i++)
        {
            if ( isprint(m_pText[i]) )
                S += (char)m_pText[i];
        }

        return S;
```

OLE Servers

```
}

BOOL CTextLine::IsTerminated()
{
    return m_bTerminated;
}

////////////////////////////////////////////////////////////////////////
// Diagnostic routines
#ifdef _DEBUG
void CTextLine::Dump(CDumpContext& dc) const
{
    dc << m_wByteCount << (WORD)m_bTerminated;
    for (WORD i = 0; i < m_wByteCount; i++)
        dc << m_pText[i];
}

void CTextLine::AssertValid() const
{
    ASSERT ( (m_wByteCount == 0) ||
             (m_pText != NULL) );
}

#endif

////////////////////////////////////////////////////////////////////////
// Serialization functions
void CTextLine::Serialize(CArchive& ar)
{
    if (ar.IsStoring())
    {
        ar << m_wByteCount << (WORD)m_bTerminated;
        for (WORD i = 0; i < m_wByteCount; i++)
            ar << m_pText[i];
    }
    else
    {
        free(m_pText);
        WORD tempTerm;

        ar >> m_wByteCount >> tempTerm;
        SetTerminated((BOOL)tempTerm);

        m_pText = (BYTE*) malloc(m_wByteCount);
        if (m_pText == NULL)
        {
            TRACE0("CTextLine::Serialize -- Out of Memory.\n");
            m_wByteCount = 0;
            SetTerminated(FALSE);
            return;
        }
        for (WORD i = 0; i < m_wByteCount; i++)
            ar >> m_pText[i];
    }
}
```

```
void CTextLine::WriteToArchive (CArchive& ar)
{
    ar.Write(m_pText, m_wByteCount);
}

void CTextLine::ReadFromArchive (CArchive& ar,
        WORD wMaxCount, BYTE byTerminator)
{
    free(m_pText);
    m_wByteCount = 0;
    m_pText = (BYTE*) malloc(wMaxCount);
    if (m_pText == NULL)
    {
        TRACE0("CTextLine::ReadFromArchive");
        TRACE0(" -- Out of Memory.\n");
        return;
    }

    WORD i = 0;
    SetTerminated(FALSE);
    while (ar.Read(&m_pText[i], 1) == 1)
    {
        i++;

        // If we reached the maximum line size, stop reading
        if (i == wMaxCount)
            break;

        // If we have reached the specified terminator, stop reading
        if ( m_pText[i-1] == byTerminator )
        {
            SetTerminated();
            break;
        }
    }

    m_wByteCount = i;

    realloc(m_pText, m_wByteCount);
    // This realloc is safe from out-of-memory errors since
    // m_wByteCount will always be less than or equal to
    // wMaxCount -- the original size of m_pText.
}
```

As you can see, most of the code is straightforward. Almost all of the standard CObject fare is very close to our previous work with CObject (for example, CDate). However, the two unfamiliar functions in the serialize ranks, ReadFromArchive() and WriteToArchive(), need some additional discussion. These two functions are doing new and interesting things with the archive object that we haven't seen before. Instead of using the predefined << or >> operators to store data to or retrieve data from the archive, here we are using the CArchive::Read() and CArchive::Write() functions. These two functions give us direct access to the underlying file. Using these functions, we gain direct control over the reading and writing of bytes. Of course,

OLE Servers

this direct control comes at the price of having to know what you're doing. Study `ReadFromArchive()` and `WriteToArchive()` to understand this new facet of `CArchive` interaction.

Now that we have the `CTextLine` class implemented, we can move to the next step in our application. Where do these text lines go? How will they be incorporated into our application? How will we load them with data? The answers to all these questions will come in time, but first let's see what the default application does when loading a file. This knowledge will be valuable for us because it will show us what we must do to seamlessly incorporate our application into the standard Windows user interface.

Loading a File

Before we whip together a brand-new loading routine, let's take a look at how the default loading is accomplished. When the user selects File | Open, the framework responds by calling `CWinApp`'s `OnFileOpen()` function:

```
void CWinApp::OnFileOpen()
{
    // Prompt the user (with all document templates)
    CString newName;
    if (!DoPromptFileName(newName, AFX_IDS_OPENFILE,
        OFN_HIDEREADONLY | OFN_FILEMUSTEXIST, TRUE, NULL))
        return; // Open cancelled

    OpenDocumentFile(newName);
        // If it returns NULL, the user has already been alerted
}
```

As you can see, this function is understandable; it calls only a couple of other functions. The first function, `DoPromptFileName()`, prompts the user for the name of the file to open, and then it passes the filename back to the caller through its parameters (as shown next). If `DoPromptFileName()` concludes with the user clicking on the OK button, `OnFileOpen()` will pass the filename on to `OpenDocumentFile()`, which opens the file in question:

```
// Prompt for filename. Used for Open and Save As.
BOOL CWinApp::DoPromptFileName(CString& fileName,
    UINT nIDSTitle, DWORD lFlags,
    BOOL bOpenFileDialog, CDocTemplate* pTemplate)
    // If pTemplate==NULL => all document templates
{
    CFileDialog dlgFile(bOpenFileDialog);

    CString title;
    VERIFY(title.LoadString(nIDSTitle));

    dlgFile.m_ofn.Flags |= lFlags;

    CString strFilter;
    CString strDefault;
    if (pTemplate != NULL)
```

```
        {
            ASSERT_VALID(pTemplate);
            AppendFilterSuffix(strFilter, dlgFile.m_ofn,
                    pTemplate, &strDefault);
        }
        else
        {
            // Do for all doc templates
            POSITION pos = m_templateList.GetHeadPosition();
            while (pos != NULL)
            {
                AppendFilterSuffix(strFilter, dlgFile.m_ofn,
                        (CDocTemplate*)m_templateList.
                            GetNext(pos), NULL);
            }
        }

        // Append the *.* all files filter
        CString allFilter;
        VERIFY(allFilter.LoadString(AFX_IDS_ALLFILTER));
        strFilter += allFilter;
        strFilter += (char)'\0';   // Next string, please
        strFilter += "*.*";
        strFilter += (char)'\0';   // Last string
        dlgFile.m_ofn.nMaxCustFilter++;

        dlgFile.m_ofn.lpstrFilter = strFilter;
        dlgFile.m_ofn.hwndOwner = AfxGetMainWnd()->GetSafeHwnd();
        dlgFile.m_ofn.lpstrTitle = title;
        dlgFile.m_ofn.lpstrFile = fileName.GetBuffer(_MAX_PATH);

        BOOL bRet = dlgFile.DoModal() == IDOK ? TRUE : FALSE;
        fileName.ReleaseBuffer();
        return bRet;
}
```

Much of `DoPromptFileName()`'s work is in preparation for the underlying file dialog's `DoModal()` call. Careful study of this code can illuminate many interesting techniques for `CFileDialog` manipulation. Now let's take a look at the `OnOpenDocument()` code:

```
BOOL CDocument::OnOpenDocument(const char* pszPathName)
{
    if (IsModified())
    TRACE0("Warning: OnOpenDocument replaces an unsaved document\n");

    CFile file;
    CFileException fe;
    if (!file.Open(pszPathName,
        CFile::modeRead | CFile::shareDenyWrite, &fe))
    {
        ReportSaveLoadException(pszPathName, &fe,
            FALSE, AFX_IDP_FAILED_TO_OPEN_DOC);
        return FALSE;
    }
```

OLE Servers

```
    DeleteContents();
    SetModifiedFlag(TRUE);   // Dirty during deserialization

    CArchive loadArchive(&file,
        CArchive::load | CArchive::bNoFlushOnDelete);
    loadArchive.m_pDocument = this;
    loadArchive.m_bForceFlat = FALSE;
    TRY
    {
        BeginWaitCursor();
        Serialize(loadArchive);   // Load me
        loadArchive.Close();
        file.Close();
    }
    CATCH_ALL(e)
    {
        file.Abort();   // Will not throw an exception
        DeleteContents();   // Remove failed contents
        EndWaitCursor();

        TRY
            ReportSaveLoadException(pszPathName, e, FALSE,
                AFX_IDP_FAILED_TO_OPEN_DOC);
        END_TRY
        return FALSE;
    }
    END_CATCH_ALL

    EndWaitCursor();
    SetModifiedFlag(FALSE);   // Start off with unmodified
    return TRUE;
}
```

Careful study of this code can reveal the mysteries behind the standard method of file opening. The first thing OnOpenDocument() does is open the file associated with the filename we chose in DoPromptFileName(). This is necessary, because in order to create an archive object, you need an existing, open CFile object. The virtual document function, DeleteContents(), is then called. It cleans up the document and prepares it for new data. Now the CArchive object can be created, which will serve as the data conduit connecting our application data to the file. Finally, the function calls the serialization function, which actually does the data transfer. From this code we can see that in order to utilize the standard and default File | Open code, we merely have to implement the document's serialization function and utilize the archive as if it were a file. Indeed, we will use the same method illustrated in the CTextLine class—that's why we did it that way there in the first place.

A Document Is a Thousand Words

Before we can serialize the document, we need something in the document to serialize. Add the following code line to the public attributes section of the CHexpadDoc interface:

```
CObList m_lstText;
```

This will be our container object that will hold the CTextLine objects that hold the lines of text collected from the file. Each of these text line objects will be constrained to a specified size. This constraint will be a defined constant found at the very beginning of CHexpadDoc's interface:

```
#define DOC_WIDTH 32
```

Reading and storing the data in m_lstText will be accomplished through two new serialization functions. Add the following lines of code to the public implementation section of CHexpadDoc's interface:

```
void ReadFromArchive(CArchive& ar);
void WriteToArchive(CArchive& ar);
```

These two routines will provide the functionality to store and retrieve information held in the CObList object to and from the archive (and hence the file). The implementation of these functions follows:

```
void CHexpadDoc::ReadFromArchive(CArchive& ar)
{
    // Use CArchive's Read() function to
    // read the actual bytes from the file

    DeleteContents();

    while(TRUE)
    {
        CTextLine* pTL;

        TRY
        {
            pTL = new CTextLine;
            pTL->ReadFromArchive(ar, DOC_WIDTH);
            if (pTL->ByteCount() == 0)
            {
                // EOF was reached
                delete pTL;
                break;
            }
            m_lstText.AddTail(pTL);
        }
        CATCH (CMemoryException, e)
        {
            // File too large. Reallocate
            // memory and notify user!
            delete pTL;
            DeleteContents();
            AfxMessageBox(
                "File too large to fit in free memory!");
            break;
        }
        END_CATCH
    }
}

void CHexpadDoc::WriteToArchive(CArchive& ar)
```

OLE Servers

```
{
    POSITION pos = m_lstText.GetHeadPosition();
    CTextLine* pTL;

    while (pos != NULL)
    {
        pTL = (CTextLine*)m_lstText.GetNext(pos);
        pTL->WriteToArchive(ar);
    }
}
```

Certainly we make great use of the read and write to archive functions we created in the `CTextLine` class. This should remind you to include the TEXTLINE.H file at the top of the document's implementation file. We have also made use of the virtual `DeleteContents()` function that is a part of every document class. However, in order for `DeleteContents()` to be truly useful, we must override it. Place the following line in the public implementation section of `CHexpadDoc`'s interface:

```
virtual void DeleteContents();
```

and place the following code in `CHexpadDoc`'s implementation file:

```
void CHexpadDoc::DeleteContents()
{
    while (!m_lstText.IsEmpty())
    {
        CTextLine* pTL = (CTextLine*)m_lstText.RemoveHead();
        delete pTL;
    }
}
```

Again, the override is a very simple function that I won't take time to describe in detail. However, note that it's a very handy class to have when you want to destroy all the information in the document. Hmmmm. Doesn't that mean we should put it in the destructor? No! The framework automatically calls this class just before the destructor, so you needn't explicitly make the call. This also means that if you put all your destructor code in `DeleteContents()`, you don't have to put any in the destructor.

The last thing we need to do to get our File | Open menu command working is to connect our archive reading and writing functions to the `Serialize()` function as shown:

```
void CHexpadDoc::Serialize(CArchive& ar)
{
    if (ar.IsStoring())
    {
        WriteToArchive(ar);
    }
    else
    {
        ReadFromArchive(ar);
    }
}
```

Now if you run the application, you can load files into the document. Of course, we haven't reflected any of this into the view class, so nothing we have done is visible. Our next step is clear.

Viewing the Document

Because we're talking about an OLE server, we need to make a general drawing routine that will display the `m_lstText` item in both the `CHexpadView` and `CHexpadSrvrItem` classes. First, change the calls in `CHexpadSrvrItem::OnDraw()` and `CHexpadView::OnDraw()` from `DrawStuff()` to `DrawList()`. Then install this general drawing function, `DrawList()`, as follows:

```
void CHexpadDoc::DrawList(CDC* pDC, CRect rect)
{
    POSITION pos = m_lstText.GetHeadPosition();
    // pos == NULL if the list is empty

    CString S;
    TEXTMETRIC tm;
    int nCharHeight;
    int nCharWidth;
    WORD wLineNumber = 1;
    WORD wLineCount = 1;
    const WORD wRightJust = 5;

    pDC->GetTextMetrics(&tm);
    nCharHeight = tm.tmHeight + tm.tmExternalLeading;
    nCharWidth = tm.tmAveCharWidth;

    if (rect.Height() < 0)
        nCharHeight = -nCharHeight;
    if (rect.Width() < 0)
        nCharWidth = -nCharWidth;

    while (pos != NULL)
    {
        CTextLine* pTL = (CTextLine*)m_lstText.GetNext(pos);
        char buffer[20];
        _itoa(wLineNumber, buffer, 10);
        S = buffer;
        unsigned int len = S.GetLength();
        S = "     " + S + ": ";
        S = S.Right(wRightJust + 2);

        if (m_bHexView)
        for (WORD i = 0; i < pTL->ByteCount(); i++)
        {
            BYTE b;
            if(!pTL->GetAt(i, b))
            {
            TRACE0(
            "CHexpadDoc::DrawList -- Error in text line.\n");
                return;
                break;
            }
```

Day 16: OLE Servers

```
            CString Buff;
            _itoa(b, buffer, 16);
            Buff += buffer;
            if (Buff.GetLength() == 1)
                S += '0' + Buff + ' ';
            else
                S += Buff + ' ';
        } // End for i = 0 to ByteCount()-1
        else
            S += pTL->GetString();

        pDC->TextOut(LEFT_MARGIN*nCharWidth,
            nCharHeight*(TOP_MARGIN+wLineCount-1), S);

        if (pTL->IsTerminated())
            wLineNumber++;
        wLineCount++;
    } // End while pos != NULL

    pDC->SelectObject(pOldFont);
}
```

There are many similarities between this function and the drawing routine `DrawStuff()`. We still compute the text metrics and position the text based on the height and width measurements. We still check the direction of the mapping mode axes so we know which way is up.

But there is something new. A Boolean flag has been added to the document's interface, indicating whether the document is in ASCII or hex mode. This Boolean flag is used in `DrawList()` to determine if the application will show ASCII values or hexadecimal numbers for the file display. Place the following line in `CHexpadDoc`'s interface:

```
BOOL m_bHexView;
```

This value must be initialized in `CHexpadDoc`'s constructor. We initialized it to `FALSE`, but the choice is arbitrary. While we're talking about the `m_bHexView` variable, we might as well implement it. In AppStudio, add a new pull-down menu named Hexpad to the `IDR_MAINFRAME` menu resource. Add a new menu item to the Hexpad menu:

ID	ID_HEXPAD_TOGGLE
Caption	&Hex View
Prompt	Toggle between ASCII and Hex views.

Using ClassWizard, add the command and command UI handlers for this menu item to the document class. Modify these functions as shown:

```
void CHexpadDoc::OnHexpadToggle()
{
    m_bHexView = !m_bHexView;
    UpdateAllViews(NULL);
}
```

```
void CHexpadDoc::OnUpdateHexpadToggle(CCmdUI* pCmdUI)
{
    if (m_bHexView)
        pCmdUI->SetText("&ASCII View");
    else
        pCmdUI->SetText("&Hex View");
}
```

These functions will toggle the m_bHexView variable and display the current state of the m_bHexView variable in the menu, respectively.

This brings us to another position where we may compile, link, and run. How are we doing? Well, pretty good unless you load a file that is longer than the current display. What would be ideal is a scrollable display so that we may move the display to the location of our choice. What a transition.

Scroll View

As you might recall, we did in fact have AppWizard derive our current view from the CScrollView class. However, nothing is for free in this world. We must do a few things in order for the scrolling to work. One thing the scroll window needs to know is the size of the document. Add the following code to CHexpadDoc:

```
CSize CHexpadDoc::GetDocSize()
{
    CSize csDocExtent;
    if (m_bHexView)
        csDocExtent.cx = DOC_WIDTH*3 + 7;
    else
        csDocExtent.cx = DOC_WIDTH + 7;

    csDocExtent.cy = m_lstText.GetCount();

    return csDocExtent;
}
```

Well, that wasn't too bad. The document's width is constant and its length is tracked by the list object. Returning the CSize object with these values is relatively simple. Now we need to create a function on the view side of the house to take advantage of this newfound information about the document's size. Add the following function to CHexpadView:

```
void CHexpadView::ResizeScrollBars()
{
    CClientDC dc(this);
    CHexpadDoc* pDoc = GetDocument();
    TEXTMETRIC tm;
    CSize csTotal;
    CSize csPage;
    CSize csLine;
    WORD wRowHeight, wRowWidth;
```

OLE Servers

```
    dc.GetTextMetrics(&tm);

    csDoc = pDoc->GetDocSize();

    wRowHeight = tm.tmHeight + tm.tmExternalLeading;
    wRowWidth = tm.tmAveCharWidth * csDoc.cx;

    csLine.cx = tm.tmAveCharWidth * 5;
    csLine.cy = wRowHeight;

    csPage.cx = csLine.cx * 4;
    csPage.cy = csLine.cy * 20;

    csTotal.cx = wRowWidth;
    csTotal.cy = wRowHeight * csDoc.cy;

    SetScrollSizes(MM_TEXT, csTotal, csPage, csLine);
}
```

`ResizeScrollBars()` computes the text height and width in pixels and then uses the document size, retrieved from `GetDocSize()`, to set the scroll sizes. This function must be called whenever there is a change in the document. The document notifies its views of any changes through the `UpdateAllViews()` function, which calls the view's `OnUpdate()` function. We must override our view's `OnUpdate()` function so that `ResizeScrollBars()` is called.

```
void CHexpadView::OnUpdate(CView* pSender, LPARAM lHint, CObject* pHint)
{
    ResizeScrollBars();

    Invalidate(TRUE);  // Invalidate the entire window
}
```

This function simply calls `ResizeScrollBars()` to compute the potentially new scroll sizes and then invalidates the window.

We're almost done. Only one final bit of clean-up remains. It turns out that the default implementation of `OnInitialUpdate()` uses hard-coded sizes to initialize the scroll bars. The fix is very simple: We delete the offending code (I just commented it out so that you could see the initial offending code):

```
void CHexpadView::OnInitialUpdate()
{
   CScrollView::OnInitialUpdate();

   // ResizeScrollBars() has already been called via OnUpdate()

   //CSize sizeTotal;
   // TODO: Calculate the total size of this view
   //sizeTotal.cx = sizeTotal.cy = 100;
   //SetScrollSizes(MM_TEXT, sizeTotal);
}
```

We didn't have to replace the hard-coded values with anything because that little bit of housekeeping is already done in the `OnUpdate()` function we talked about earlier.

The Hexpad application now works as an embeddable, scrolling, ASCII/hex file viewer. That's quite a bit for a single chapter, so we'll stop here. But stay tuned for further enhancements in the chapters to come.

Summary

In this chapter we looked at the behavior and architecture of the default AppWizard-generated server application. We then attempted to customize this default application to be the server of our dreams. The addition of code to accomplish this customization was less than intuitive. However, with the proper understanding of the technology, you can build your own dream server application.

The whole idea of OLE technology is epitomized in the server. A server application is the object that gets embedded or linked. Therefore, most of the work associated with building OLE applications rests on the shoulders of the server developer. In the next chapter we will add printing support to Hexpad. Here we will detour slightly from the pure OLE topics and discuss issues concerning the incorporation of printing to any application. In Chapter 18, we will come back as strong as ever in OLE issues and concern ourselves with the other side of the OLE coin: containers.

Q&A

Q Is there any preference in building MDI server applications over SDI server applications?

A MDI servers are preferred to SDI servers if it's likely that multiple documents from the application will be embedded in various containers simultaneously. With an MDI server, each embedded document will be supported by the single mother server application. If the server were using SDI, every embedded document would need its own instance of the server to be invoked. Obviously, more overhead is needed for multiple SDI application instances as opposed to a single MDI application instance and multiple documents.

Q I'm having trouble loading files into Hexpad when it's embedded. Did I do something wrong?

A No. This isn't an error; it's an exercise. For more information about this problem, consult Exercise 2 and reread the "Loading a File" section of this chapter.

OLE Servers

Q Why did you derive Hexpad's view from `CScrollView` instead of `CEditView`? Isn't `CEditView` designed to be the base view class for word-processing applications?

A `CEditView` is a good class to use for certain applications, but it is by no means a generic base for even editor-like applications. It has too many limitations. Of course, our editor has many of these same limitations, but in our application the limitations are explicitly visible, which means we can overcome them. With `CEditView` the limitations are built-in and therefore are much harder to overcome. From a learning perspective, it is also beneficial to use `CScrollView` rather than `CEditView` because you get an opportunity to see some programming techniques that are used behind the scenes in `CEditView`.

Workshop

Quiz

1. Name the new OLE classes involved with the default AppWizard-generated server application.
2. Why does the server need two separate and distinct `OnDraw()` functions?

Exercises

1. Experiment with `CHexpadDoc`'s defined constants. Change these constants, predict the results of these changes, and verify your predictions.
2. Using the `ReadFromArchive()` function, implement a `LoadFromFile()` function for Hexpad. Don't use `ReadFromArchive()` as a template; call it from your function and pass it a `CArchive` object you create, associated with a particular file. Introduce a new menu selection to support `LoadFromFile()`. Test your creation in both stand-alone and embedded circumstances.

WEEK 3

Printing

Printing

Printing is a very slippery topic. In the early days of Windows programming, printing information was sparse and only talked about in whispers. I remember poring over many books and magazine articles, trying to decipher this arcane craft. At the time, I was programming in Pascal using "the other compiler" (let's call it Buckland's Turbo).

Windows has helped us come a long way toward simplifying printing. In DOS-based programs, we had to write our applications to provide for many different types of printers. Hence, only the strong survived. Because the Epson printers prevailed, I could never get a software package that would support the Star printer. And I wondered why companies like Star made sure their printers had an Epson mode! No more. Now print drivers provide an interface between the printer and Windows, and we just print, not worrying about whether we're printing to an HP Laserjet IV or a Star dot-matrix printer.

It's Not Just for Displaying Anymore

So far in our travels, we have found great uses for CScrollView concerning the display of data held in the CHexpad classes. However, we have neglected a major area of CScrollView functionality—printing. CScrollView has a number of member functions dedicated to the support of printed output. Table 17.1 lists these methods.

Table 17.1. CScrollView **printing support functions.**

Function	When It's Called	When It's Overridden
OnPreparePrinting	Before a document is printed or previewed.	To initialize the Print dialog box.
OnBeginPrinting	When a print job begins.	To allocate GDI resources.
OnEndPrinting	When a print job ends.	To deallocate the GDI resources allocated in OnBeginPrinting.
OnEndPrintPreview	When preview mode is exited.	
OnPrepareDC	Before the OnDraw member function is called for screen display or before the OnPrint member function is called for printing or for print preview.	
DoPreparePrinting	When you override OnPreparePrinting, this displays a Print dialog box and creates the printer device context.	
OnPrint	To print or preview a specific page of the document.	

Each of these functions plays a pivotal part in a great printing loop that converts your document's data into output. This great printing loop (much like the Great Pumpkin) is something of an imaginary entity. It's really just a sequence of events resulting from the interaction of a number of individual objects.

Implementing Minimal Printing Support

Recall from the last chapter that when we had AppWizard create the default application, we told it to add printer and print preview support. Well, it's time for us to cash in our printing chip and find out if AppWizard is worth its weight. Crank up the application and try to print something. Uh oh—tiny little print. Your eyes could really get tired reading that all day. Has AppWizard has let us down again? Let's see what went wrong.

> **Note:** Actually, we're lucky to have anything print at all. If we had tried to add printing to our Family Tree application, we would have been hurting. As we discussed in Chapter 9, the `CRecordView` class is a descendent of `CFormView`, a `CView` class with dialog support added. Unfortunately, printing isn't supported for dialogs. After all, dialogs are meant to pop up on-screen and give or ask for information, and thus they don't constitute printable material. This means that because we added dialog enhancements to our `CView` class, which gave us `CRecordView` as an end product, we have been robbed of our print and print preview capabilities!

What AppWizard Did for You

When you created the project using AppWizard, you checked the printer support option. This option placed the two entries necessary for printing in the message map of `CHexpadView`:

```
BEGIN_MESSAGE_MAP(CHexpadView, CScrollView)
        //{{AFX_MSG_MAP(CHexpadView)
        ON_WM_CREATE()
        ON_WM_DROPFILES()
        //}}AFX_MSG_MAP
        // Standard printing commands
        ON_COMMAND(ID_FILE_PRINT, CScrollView::OnFilePrint)
        ON_COMMAND(ID_FILE_PRINT_PREVIEW, CScrollView::OnFilePrintPreview)
END_MESSAGE_MAP()
```

The two `ON_COMMAND` macro calls tie the File | Print and File | Print Preview menu options to `CHexpadView`'s default `OnFilePrint()` and `OnFilePrintPreview()` functions, which we will discuss shortly. First, let's get our application printing.

Printing

Note the following code in the protected section of CHexpadView's interface:

```
// Printing support
virtual BOOL OnPreparePrinting(CPrintInfo* pInfo);
```

Note the following code in CHexpadView's implementation:

```
/////////////////////////////////////////////////////////////////////////////
// Printing support

BOOL CHexpadView::OnPreparePrinting(CPrintInfo* pInfo)
{
    // Default preparation
    return DoPreparePrinting(pInfo);
}
```

This function (put in by AppWizard) adds the printing. The OnPreparePrinting() function is the bare minimum necessary to install printing support in an MFC application. It must be overridden so that a call to DoPreparePrinting() is made (the default CHexpadView implementation of DoPreparePrinting() is empty). DoPreparePrinting() must be called before either printing or print previewing because it invokes the Print dialog box and also creates the printer device context that is used to print the document.

The behavior of DoPreparePrinting() depends on whether you're printing or doing a print preview. DoPreparePrinting() determines this by examining the m_bPreview member of the pInfo parameter passed to it. If the file destination is the printer, DoPreparePrinting() invokes the Print dialog box using the parameters from the CPrintInfo structure to populate the dialog box defaults. (We will talk about the CPrintInfo structure itself in a moment.) After the user changes the defaults in the Print dialog box, the new settings are passed back in the pInfo parameter and are used for printing the document. If the destination is the print preview window, DoPreparePrinting() simply creates a printer device context used to simulate the printer during the print preview operation. This minimal printer support lets us print.

CPrintInfo

In order for you to better understand how printing works, I need to give you some background information on CPrintInfo. CPrintInfo stores information about a print or print preview job. The framework creates an object of CPrintInfo each time the Print or Print Preview command is chosen and destroys it when the command is completed.

CPrintInfo contains information about the print job, such as which pages are to be printed, and the current status of the print job, such as which page is currently being printed. Some information is stored in an associated CPrintDialog object, which retains the print preferences the user entered in the Print dialog box.

A CPrintInfo object is passed between the framework and your view class during the printing process and is used to exchange information between the two. An example would be when the framework informs the view class of whether the document is being printed or previewed by assigning a value to the m_bPreview member of CPrintInfo. The view class retrieves the value and performs the actual previewing of the specified page.

CPrintInfo has several data members. They are listed in Table 17.2.

Table 17.2. CPrintInfo's public data members.

Member	Description
m_pPD	Contains a pointer to the CPrintDialog object used for the Print dialog box.
m_bPreview	Contains a flag indicating whether the document is being previewed.
m_bContinuePrinting	Contains a flag indicating whether the framework should continue the print loop.
m_nCurPage	Identifies the number of the page currently being printed.
m_nNumPreviewPages	Identifies the number of pages displayed in the preview window—either 1 or 2.
m_lpUserData	Contains a pointer to a user-created structure.
m_rectDraw	Specifies a rectangle defining the current usable page area.
m_strPageDesc	Contains a format string for page-number display.

There are also several attributes you can use to set or retrieve page information. They are listed in Table 17.3.

Table 17.3. Attributes—public members.

Attribute	Description
SetMinPage	Sets the number of the first page of the document.
SetMaxPage	Sets the number of the last page of the document.
GetMinPage	Returns the number of the first page of the document.
GetMaxPage	Returns the number of the last page of the document.
GetFromPage	Returns the number of the first page being printed.
GetToPage	Returns the number of the last page being printed.

We will use the CPrintInfo data members later to gather information before printing.

Printing

Advanced Printing

I'm sure you'd like to improve the quality of our output. Well, there are a few things we can do to spice it up. We need to delve into the depths of mapping modes in order to make sure that what you see is what you get (WYSIWYG).

Mapping Modes

The only additional comment I can make to Chapter 16's treatment of mapping modes is that they apply to all device contexts, including printer DCs. We will use the default mapping mode MM_TEXT. This mode is simple in that it maps coordinates to pixels directly. It doesn't support scaling, and the origin can be moved only with SetWindowOrg and SetVieportOrg calls. This mode is simple and serves our purpose.

Change Fonts (*HexpadView*)

Allowing the user to change the font before printing or print preview is fun. Although Microsoft did help us by providing a flexible set of font tools, the hours I spent researching the font interaction material discussed next were comparable to having my wisdom teeth pulled out one at a time by a tow truck.

CFont

This is the place to start. The CFont class encapsulates a Windows graphics device interface (GDI) font and includes member functions for changing or manipulating that font. In order to use a CFont object, we need to construct a CFont object and attach a Windows font to it with CreateFont or CreateFontIndirect, and then use the object's member functions to manipulate the font. You might wonder why we need to do all this. Well, the answer is flexibility. Windows allows you to use many different fonts in a document at the same time, multiple fonts for printing, and so on. The price we pay for that flexibility is a little more work to set them up. The first thing we need to do is instantiate a pointer to CFont so that we can use it later. Add the code necessary to HEXPADVI.H so that the attributes area looks like this:

```
// Attributes
public:
        CFont* pFont;
```

We also need to override the OnPrepareDC(), OnBeginPrinting(), and OnEndPrinting() calls because we're going to add some cool stuff to these too!

Ensure that your HEXPADVI.H looks like this (additions appear in bold):

```
// hexpavw.h: Interface of the CHexpadView class
//
////////////////////////////////////////////////////////////////////////

class CHexpadView : public CScrollView
{
protected: // Create from serialization only
        CHexpadView();
        DECLARE_DYNCREATE(CHexpadView)

// Attributes
public:
        COleDropTarget m_dropTarget;
        CHexpadDoc* GetDocument();

        // Added to support user's font selection
        CFont* pFont;

public:

// Implementation
public:
        virtual ~CHexpadView();
        virtual void OnUpdate(CView* pSender, LPARAM lHint, CObject* pHint);
        virtual void OnDraw(CDC* pDC);   // Overridden to draw this view
        void ResizeScrollBars();

public:
        // Drag-and-drop functions
        BOOL OnDrop(COleDataObject* pDataObject,
                DROPEFFECT dropEffect, CPoint point);
        DROPEFFECT OnDragEnter(COleDataObject* pDataObject,
                DWORD grfKeyState, CPoint point);
        DROPEFFECT OnDragOver(COleDataObject* pDataObject,
                DWORD grfKeyState, CPoint point);
        void OnDragLeave();

#ifdef _DEBUG
        virtual void AssertValid() const;
        virtual void Dump(CDumpContext& dc) const;
#endif

protected:
        virtual void OnInitialUpdate();   // Called first time after construct

        // Printing support
        virtual BOOL OnPreparePrinting(CPrintInfo* pInfo);
        virtual void OnBeginPrinting(CDC* pDC, CPrintInfo* pInfo);

        // Added to support user printing
        virtual void OnPrepareDC(CDC* pDC, CPrintInfo* pInfo = NULL);
        virtual void OnPrint(CDC* pDC, CPrintInfo *pInfo);
        // End addition

        virtual void OnEndPrinting(CDC* pDC, CPrintInfo* pInfo);
```

Day 17: Printing

```
// Generated message map functions
protected:
        //{{AFX_MSG(CHexpadView)
        afx_msg int OnCreate(LPCREATESTRUCT lpCreateStruct);
        afx_msg void OnDropFiles(HDROP hDropInfo);
        //}}AFX_MSG
        DECLARE_MESSAGE_MAP()
};

#ifndef _DEBUG  // Debug version in hexpavw.cpp
inline CHexpadDoc* CHexpadView::GetDocument()
   { return (CHexpadDoc*)m_pDocument; }
#endif
```

///

Now we're ready to include our font enhancements in the `CHexpadView()` code. Let's let the user choose the font at print time by displaying the Font dialog box and letting him choose. Let's look at the `CFontDialog` class to get a better understanding of how to bring up a dialog box and what our options are.

CFontDialog

The `CFontDialog` class allows us to incorporate a font selection dialog box into our application (see Figure 17.1). This dialog box provides a list of the fonts currently installed in the system. The user can select the font and size, as well as italic and bold features for that font. The user's selections are passed back to the application.

Figure 17.1.
The Font dialog box.

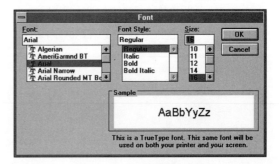

The `CFontDialog` class is outlined as follows. It can also be found in the class library reference manual.

```
CFontDialog( LPLOGFONT lplfInitial = NULL,
DWORD dwFlags = CF_EFFECTS | CF_SCREENFONTS,
CDC* pdcPrinter = NULL,
CWnd* pParentWnd = NULL );
```

The lplfInitial parameter is a pointer to a LOGFONT data structure that allows you to set some of the font's characteristics. The LOGFONT structure defines the attributes of a font. Think of it as the keeper of all relevant font style information. The structure follows:

```
typedef struct LOGFONT {   /* lf */
    int     lfHeight;
    int     lfWidth;
    int     lfEscapement;
    int     lfOrientation;
    int     lfWeight;
    BYTE    lfItalic;
    BYTE    lfUnderline;
    BYTE    lfStrikeOut;
    BYTE    lfCharSet;
    BYTE    lfOutPrecision;
    BYTE    lfClipPrecision;
    BYTE    lfQuality;
    BYTE    lfPitchAndFamily;
    BYTE    lfFaceName[LF_FACESIZE];
} LOGFONT;
```

dwFlags specifies one or more choose-font flags. What this means is that you can choose one or more options from a predefined set of options to affect the user's ability to choose items in the dialog box. You can combine these flags using the ¦ or bitwise OR operator. For instance, combining the CT_TTONLY and the CF_NOSIZESEL flags would allow the user to choose only TrueType fonts and prohibit him from varying from the current size. Table 17.4 describes the flags and their uses. These can also be found in the Windows 3.1 SDK reference manuals.

Table 17.4. dwFlags and their meanings.

Value	Meaning
CF_APPLY	Specifies that the ChooseFont function should enable the Apply button.
CF_ANSIONLY	Specifies that the ChooseFont function should limit font selection to fonts that use the Windows character set. If this flag is set, the user can't select a font that contains only symbols.
CF_BOTH	Causes the dialog box to list the available printer and screen fonts. The hDC member identifies either the device context or the information context associated with the printer.
CF_TTONLY	Specifies that the ChooseFont function should enumerate and allow the selection of only TrueType fonts.

continues

Day 17: Printing

Table 17.4. continued

Value	Meaning
CF_EFFECTS	Specifies that the Choosefont function should enable strikeout, underline, and color effects. If this flag is set, the lfStrikeOut and lfUnderline members of the LOGFONT structure and the rgbColors member of the CHOOSEFONT structure can be set before calling Choosefont. If this flag isn't set, the Choosefont function can set these members after the user clicks on the OK button to close the dialog box.
CF_ENABLEHOOK	Enables the hook function specified in the lpfnHook member of this structure.
CF_ENABLETEMPLATE	Indicates that the hInstance member identifies a data block containing the dialog box template pointed to by lpTemplateName.
CF_ENABLETEMPLATEHANDLE	Indicates that the hInstance member identifies a data block that contains a preloaded dialog box template. If this flag is specified, the system ignores the lpTemplateName member.
CF_FIXEDPITCHONLY	Specifies that the Choosefont function should select only monospace fonts.
CF_FORCEFONTEXIST	Specifies that the Choosefont function should indicate an error condition if the user attempts to select a font or font style that doesn't exist.
CF_INITTOLOGFONTSTRUCT	Specifies that the Choosefont function should use the LOGFONT structure pointed to by lpLogFont to initialize the dialog box controls.
CF_LIMITSIZE	Specifies that the Choosefont function should select only font sizes within the range specified by the nSizeMin and nSizeMax members.
CF_NOFACESEL	Specifies that there is no selection in the Font (face name) combo box. Applications use this flag to support multiple font selections. This flag is set on input and output.
CF_NOOEMFONTS	Specifies that the Choosefont function should not allow vector-font selections. This flag has the same value as CF_NOVECTORFONTS.

Value	Meaning
CF_NOSIMULATIONS	Specifies that the Choosefont function should not allow graphics device interface (GDI) font simulations.
CF_NOSIZESEL	Specifies that there is no selection in the Size combo box. Applications use this flag to support multiple size selections. This flag is set on input and output.
CF_NOSTYLESEL	Specifies that there is no selection in the combo box. Applications use this flag to support multiple style selections. This flag is set on input and output.
CF_NOVECTORFONTS	Specifies that the Choosefont function should not allow vector-font selections. This flag has the same value as CF_NOOEMFONTS.
CF_PRINTERFONTS	Causes the dialog box to list only the fonts supported by the printer associated with the device context or information context that is identified by the hDC member.
CF_SCALABLEONLY	Specifies that the Choosefont function should allow the selection of only scalable fonts. Scalable fonts include vector fonts, some printer fonts, TrueType fonts, and fonts that are scaled by other algorithms or technologies.
CF_SCREENFONTS	Causes the dialog box to list only the screen fonts supported by the system.
CF_SHOWHELP	Causes the dialog box to show the Help button. If this option is specified, hwndOwner must not be NULL.
CF_USESTYLE	Specifies that the lpszStyle member points to a buffer that contains a style-description string that the Choosefont function should use to initialize the Font Style box. When the user clicks on the OK button to close the dialog box, the Choosefont function copies the style description for the user's selection to this buffer.
CF_WYSIWYG	Specifies that the Choosefont function should allow the selection of only fonts that are available on both the printer and the screen. If this flag is set, the CF_BOTH and CF_SCALABLEONLY flags should also be set.

Wow! What a variety! The only thing it seems you can't control is the way the user holds the mouse. These flags may be set when the structure is initialized (unless the description specifies otherwise). You can see the level of control and flexibility we have been given. This is just another way in which Microsoft has created a more usable system.

Printing

Back to the `CFontDialog` class calls. The `pdcPrinter` parameter is a pointer to a printer-device context. If supplied, this parameter points to a printer device context for the printer on which the fonts are to be selected. This implies that if we pick the `CF_PRINTERFONTS` flag, we should get only fonts that are compatible with the `pdcPrinter` device context we have passed in. Lastly, the `pParentWnd` parameter is a pointer to the font dialog box's parent or owner window.

Now it's time to implement the changes to `CHexpadView` to accommodate the selection of fonts by the user. We need to override several of `CScrollView`'s support functions (recall Table 17.1). The first is `OnBeginPrinting()`. This is overridden if you need to allocate GDI resources for printing. The font we're going to use is a GDI resource. We will allocate it here, and it will be destroyed after we use it. Look at the following code:

```
void CHexpadView::OnBeginPrinting(CDC* pDC, CPrintInfo* pInfo)
{
        pFont = new CFont;

        LOGFONT lf;
        LPLOGFONT plf = NULL;

        CFontDialog dlg(plf, CF_PRINTERFONTS, pDC);

        if (dlg.DoModal() == IDOK)
        {
                lf = dlg.m_lf;
                TRACE1("font selected %s\n", lf.lfFaceName);
                pFont->DeleteObject();
                pFont->CreateFontIndirect(&lf);
        }

}
```

A lot is going on here. First, we instantiate a new pointer to a `CFont` object, `pFont`. This is so that we will have a structure to place the user's selections in after the Print dialog box has done its thing. We then create `lf`, which is a `LOGFONT` structure (from our earlier `CFontDialog` discussion). `plf`, a long pointer to a `LOGFONT` structure, also is created.

Finally the rubber meets the road! We create an object `dlg`, which is of the `CFontDialog` class. When we create this object, we pass three things: `plf`, a pointer to a `LOGFONT` structure that could hold default values you wish to populate the dialog box with; `CF_PRINTERFONTS`, which tells the Print dialog box to display only fonts; and `pDC`, the printer device context. At this point, the dialog box is displayed and the user selects a preferred font, size, and so on. The `if` statement simply says that if the user clicked on the OK button to close the dialog box, submit the font change request.

From the dialog object we extract `m_lf`, which is a `LOGFONT` structure, and put it into `lf` (our `LOGFONT` structure). By the way, `m_lf` isn't documented in the online help, but it's used in sample MFC programs. The specification for `CFontDialog()` reveals this little jewel:

```cpp
///////////////////////////////////////////////////////////////////
// CFontDialog.  Used to select a font.

class CFontDialog : public CDialog
{
        DECLARE_DYNAMIC(CFontDialog)

public:
// Attributes
        // Font choosing parameter block
        CHOOSEFONT m_cf;

// Constructors
        CFontDialog(LPLOGFONT lplfInitial = NULL,
                DWORD dwFlags = CF_EFFECTS | CF_SCREENFONTS,
                CDC* pdcPrinter = NULL,
                CWnd* pParentWnd = NULL);

// Operations
        virtual int DoModal();

        // Retrieve the currently selected font while dialog is displayed
        void GetCurrentFont(LPLOGFONT lplf);

        // Helpers for parsing information after successful return
        CString GetFaceName() const;    // Return the face name of the font
        CString GetStyleName() const;   // Return the style name of the font
        int GetSize() const;            // Return the point size of the font
        COLORREF GetColor() const;      // Return the color of the font
        int GetWeight() const;          // Return the chosen font weight
        BOOL IsStrikeOut() const;       // Return TRUE if strikeout
        BOOL IsUnderline() const;       // Return TRUE if underline
        BOOL IsBold() const;            // Return TRUE if bold font
        BOOL IsItalic() const;          // Return TRUE if italic font

// Implementation
        LOGFONT m_lf;   // Default LOGFONT to store the info

#ifdef _DEBUG
public:
        virtual void Dump(CDumpContext& dc) const;
#endif

protected:
        virtual void OnOK();
        virtual void OnCancel();

        char m_szStyleName[64];    // Contains style name after return
};
```

Note that a call to GetCurrentFont is available. It returns a LOGFONT structure, but that is only while the dialog box is present on-screen. After the dialog box leaves the screen, the only way to retrieve information is by getting the data in pieces using the other operators, such as GetSize, GetColor, and so on. This method of data retrieval could result in success if we retrieved each

Printing

font attribute individually, constructed a font using CreateFont(), and fed all those parameters in. What a pain! This method is easier and cleaner. So we use the undocumented m_lf to return a LOGFONT structure and move on!

If pFont were a persistent object (not just created and soon to be destroyed), we would need to do a pFont->DeleteObject() call to clear any old font information before placing new information in pFont. The pFont-> CreateFontIndirect (&lf) call creates a font based on a pointer to a LOGFONT structure (&lf), and that is fed into pFont. Hooray! We have just taken the user's input and created a font based on the printer device context. Now let's use pFont.

OnPrepareDC()

OnPrepareDC() is the call we override if we wish to change the viewport origin or device context in any way. In our case, we wish to apply the new font we have constructed in pFont to the printer device context. Before we put this line of code in, we need to check for something. That is, we need to see if we're printing. OnPrepareDC() is called for screen display too. So imagine if we took a pFont tuned to a specific printer device context and forced it into a display device context. Try leaving out the checking line, and see what happens (but save your work first). We will apply the code as follows:

```
void CHexpadView::OnPrepareDC(CDC* pDC, CPrintInfo* pInfo)
{
        CView::OnPrepareDC(pDC, pInfo);

        if (pDC->IsPrinting() && pFont)
        {
                pDC->SelectObject(pFont);
        }
}
```

The if (pDC->IsPrinting() && pFont) line says that if the device context is a printing one, and pFont isn't null, load the font. We load the font by doing a SelectObject() and feeding it pFont, and then loading that into the printer device context. Now we're ready to print with our newly loaded font.

The printing operation takes place using the printing cycle shown in Figure 17.2.

Note that after we feed the font into OnPrepareDC(), the StartPage()-OnPrint()-EndPage() loop gets the job done. OnPrepareDC() is in the loop to see if the end of the document has been reached.

When the job is done, EndDoc() is called, and then OnEndPrinting() is called. This is where we should deallocate any GDI resources we have created for our print job. pFont was just such an animal, so we override OnEndPrinting() to the following:

```
void CHexpadView::OnEndPrinting(CDC* pDC, CPrintInfo* pInfo)
{
        delete pFont;
}
```

This call deletes the pFont object and frees up the resources for later use. Again note that if we had defined pFont as a persistent object, we wouldn't destroy it, but would continue to reuse it.

Figure 17.2.
The printing loop.

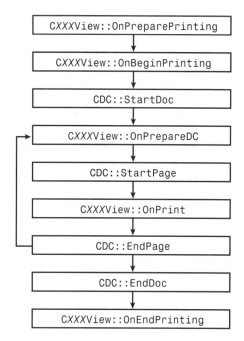

If you try to print or print preview the document, everything will work, but you will find that the font on the print preview screen (or the printed page) will be significantly smaller than the font on the display. Fourteen-point Arial text ends up looking like 8-point in the output. What happened? The answer is scaling. We need to ensure that the scale (the number of logical pixels) is the same for both the screen and the printed output. Look at our additions to OnBeginPrinting():

```
void CHexpadView::OnBeginPrinting(CDC* pDC, CPrintInfo* pInfo)
{
        pFont = new CFont;

        LOGFONT lf;
        LPLOGFONT plf = NULL;

        CFontDialog dlg(plf, CF_PRINTERFONTS, pDC);
```

Day 17: Printing

```
        if (dlg.DoModal() == IDOK)
        {
                lf = dlg.m_lf;
                TRACE1("font selected %s\n", lf.lfFaceName);
                        // Map the log font to the screen metrics
                CDC dcScreen;
                dcScreen.Attach(::GetDC(NULL));
                lf.lfHeight = MulDiv(lf.lfHeight,
                   pDC->GetDeviceCaps(LOGPIXELSY),
                   dcScreen.GetDeviceCaps
(LOGPIXELSY));
                lf.lfWidth = MulDiv(lf.lfWidth,
                   pDC->GetDeviceCaps(LOGPIXELSX),
                   dcScreen.GetDeviceCaps
(LOGPIXELSX));
                        // Create the font
                pFont->CreateFontIndirect(&lf);
        }

}
```

We perform a few tricks here. We first create a screen device context and attach it to the current display context using `Attach` and `GetDC()`. `MulDiv(p1,p2,p3)` is simply a way to take (p1*p2/p3) and wrap it into an easy function call (see the Windows 3.1 SDK documentation for details). This call sets the LOGFONT font height equal to its height times the printer's device context logical pixel height and divides the result by the screen's logical pixel height. Remember, the LOGFONT structure we are scaling is the user's choice from the Font dialog box. This means that we are scaling the user's selection by the screen font and ensuring that the printer font is the same scale. The end result is WYSIWYG! Try it now and see what happens.

Well, we were close. The reason the text is still small is that our user's font selection is being overridden by calls we put into the code in Chapter 16. We need to remove the bold text from `ResizeScrollBars()` in HexpadView():

```
void CHexpadView::ResizeScrollBars()
{
        CClientDC dc(this);
        CHexpadDoc* pDoc = GetDocument();
        TEXTMETRIC tm;
        CSize csTotal;
        CSize csPage;
        CSize csLine;

        // Commented this out so as not to overwrite
        // CFontDialog's font selection
        // CFont* pOldFont = (CFont*)dc
        //          SelectStockObject((int)pDoc->m_lStockFont);
```

We also need to remove the following bold code from HEXPADDOC.CPP:

```
void CHexpadDoc::DrawList(CDC* pDC, CRect rect)
{
TRACE0("CHexpadDoc::DrawList -- First line\n");
```

```
// Comment this out so we can pick the font with CFontDialog
// and not have that font get overwritten
// CFont* pOldFont = (CFont*)pDC->
//              SelectStockObject((int)m_lStockFont);
```

and

```
// Comment this out so we can pick font with CFontDialog
// pDC->SelectObject(pOldFont);
```

This will take care of our size problem. Try running the application now.

Overriding *OnPrint()*

Adding a header and footer to this document isn't difficult (famous last words). In order to print a simple header and footer, we need to override the OnPrint() call. Examine the following code, and then we will discuss what's happening:

```
void CHexpadView::OnPrint(CDC *pDC, CPrintInfo* pInfo)
{
        CString strHeader = "Teach Yourself the MFC in 21 Days";
        CString strFooter = "Hexpad Data Printout";
        int MyChar = 2*(pDC->GetTextExtent("Wpqit", 5)).cy;
            CRect ThePage = pInfo->m_rectDraw;

        // Draw and exclude space for header
        if (!strHeader.IsEmpty())
        {
                pDC->TextOut(ThePage.left, ThePage.top, strHeader);
                ThePage.top += MyChar + MyChar / 4;
                pDC->MoveTo(ThePage.left, ThePage.top);
                pDC->LineTo(ThePage.right, ThePage.top);
                ThePage.top += MyChar / 4;
        }

        // Allow space for footer
        pInfo->m_rectDraw = ThePage;
        if (!strFooter.IsEmpty())
                pInfo->m_rectDraw.bottom -= MyChar + MyChar/4 + MyChar/4;

        // Draw body text
        CHexpadView::OnDraw(pDC);

        // Draw footer
        if (!strFooter.IsEmpty())
        {
                ThePage.bottom -= MyChar;
                pDC->TextOut(ThePage.left, ThePage.bottom, strFooter);
                ThePage.bottom -= MyChar / 4;
                pDC->MoveTo(ThePage.left, ThePage.bottom);
                pDC->LineTo(ThePage.right, ThePage.bottom);
                ThePage.bottom -= MyChar / 4;
        }
}
```

Printing

What do you think? It looks worse than it really is. Here are the steps that were used:

1. Create two strings to hold our header and footer text.
2. Use the `GetTextExtent()` call to get the height of our text using the current printer device context.
3. Get the drawing area of the page from the `pInfo` structure being passed to `OnPrint()`, which we call ThePage. Note that `pInfo` is a `CPrintInfo`, which we discussed at the beginning of this chapter. Bet you never thought you would see that again! This structure contains a data member called `m_RectDraw`. This member contains information we will use about the size of the drawing area on the page (for instance, top, bottom, left, and right).
4. Providing that the header string isn't empty, we put the header string at the top-left corner of the page. We move the top of the page to a new top of the page, which is 1.25 character heights below where it originally started. This means that now when something gets the top-of-page measurement, it won't write over the header.
5. Draw a line from the left to the right edge of the drawing area, and then adjust the new top of the page to .25 character heights below the line.
6. Leave room for the footer on the page by "bringing up" the bottom of the page by about 1.5 times the character height. This leaves room for the footer and the line above it.
7. Call on the parent class's `OnPrint()`, which will print the body of the text (the data).
8. Draw the footer by coming up from the bottom of the page a character's height, and then put the footer out to the page at the bottom-left corner of the drawing area. Adjust the bottom of the drawing area to be .25 character heights from the old bottom (so that the line doesn't overwrite the footer) and draw the line. Readjust the bottom of the page to be .25 above the line.

This should give you a pretty good idea of how to add your own header/footer combination to your document.

The *Extent* of the Problem

You might wonder why the `GetTextExtent` call in step 2 was used. The answer is spacing. You might find that magic offset that makes the header look just great when using 10-point Courier, but what if we change fonts? If you were trying to make the header/footer look like a double-spaced typewriter document, when you changed to a bigger font, the spacing would decrease. With a smaller font, the spacing would increase. I have a solution for this dilemma (that's why I get the big bucks).

The solution to this problem is the `GetTextExtent` function. Its specification follows:

`CSize GetTextExtent( LPCSTR lpszString, int nCount ) const;`

- lpszString   Points to a string of characters. You can also pass a `CString` object for this parameter.
- nCount   Specifies the number of characters in the string.

This computes the height and width of a line of text (which we provide in the `lpzString` parameter) using the currently selected font and returns it to us as a `CSize` structure. We also need to give it the `nCount` parameter, which is the number of characters in our `lpzString`. This means that if we call it with "WjyB" (and any other tall or low-hanging characters), it should return some good information on the dimensions of our text. Now that we have the `CSize` info back, what do we do with it? Let's look at the `CSize` specification:

```
CSize( );
CSize( int initCX, int initCY );
CSize( SIZE initSize );
CSize( POINT initPt );
CSize( DWORD dwSize );
```

- initCX   Sets the cx member for `CSize`.
- initCY   Sets the cy member for `CSize`.
- initSize   The `SIZE` structure or `CSize` object used to initialize `CSize`.
- initPt   The `POINT` structure or `CPoint` object used to initialize `CSize`.
- dwSize   The `DWORD` used to initialize `CSize`. The low-order word is the cx member, and the high-order word is the cy member.

The `CSize` class (besides having facilities to change data members) has two public members: cx and cy. These members represent, in this case, the height (cy) and the width (cx) of the `lpzString` we fed `GetTextExtent`. cy is what we're interested in. If we put the cy member in our `MyChar` variable, it would change automagically (a new word that really applies to computers) to accommodate scaling for any font. Notice that our document header/footer looks like a double-spaced printout by taking the cy component of the `GetTextExtent` call, doubling it (*2), and making that the new offset.

Pretty slick, huh? This will help us ensure that we don't have a problem with overlapping or poorly spaced headers and footers (otherwise known as an undocumented feature).

The last thing we need to do is change the `TOP_MARGIN` constant in HEXPADOC.H to 3. This will allow the spacing necessary so that the text won't overwrite the header on the page (remember that `TOP_MARGIN` is an offset from the top of the page).

Printing

Multiple Pages

Although we aren't going to implement multiple-page printing in this chapter, I would like to give you a few hints on where to look to get started. In the print loop in Figure 17.2, several of the steps come into play. You can override the OnPreparePrinting() call to set the length of the document if you know what it is. Fortunately, a call supported by the CScrollView class allows you to get the document size. Override the OnPrepareDC() call if you didn't set the length of the document, because you would check for the end of the document here. OnPrint() would be overridden to print a specified page of the document.

Some magic is needed in order to get all this to work. Many applications (including \MFC\SAMPLES\SUPERPAD\SUPERPAD.MAK) call their own functions instead of OnDraw when they're printing. This new function, possibly CHexpadView::PrintInsideRectangle, takes into account the ThePage variable (drawing area) we adjusted in the OnPrint() routine. This ensures that the printout won't run over the header/footer on the page. If you want to print a specific page, you need to figure out which lines of your document will go in that page and then print those lines only.

Additional material can be found in the class library reference manuals. Finally, don't forget to look at the CPrintInfo structure. It contains a wealth of information.

Summary

Printing isn't something for the faint of heart. I have tried to give a treatment to a subject that most books would ignore entirely. There are so many pitfalls and nuances to it that I wonder how applications like Microsoft Word can print at all! I have a healthy respect for Microsoft Word's printing capability now that I know what's involved, and I don't mind an occasional glitch as much as I used to.

I invite you to play with printing. It would be nice to have another person in the world who understands. Try changing the mapping modes and see what happens. Remember, though, that each mapping mode treats the axis coordinates differently. What was "down" yesterday could easily be "up" today. The next chapter moves on to OLE containers.

Q&A

Q Why is there a GetCurrentFont() call for the CFontDialog class if it works only while the dialog box is visible?

A This could be used in conjunction with the Apply button to get the user's current font selection and apply it to the specified text.

Q What do I have to take into account when printing a multiple-page document?

A Lots. One of the items most frequently overlooked is the sizing of data on the page. If the user requests only pages 13 and 14, you need to ensure that the records that would normally appear on those pages get printed. This is easy if each record is one line and there are 50 lines per page. It is more difficult if some of the records contain multiple-line comment fields and so on.

Workshop

Quiz

1. Which call actually brings up the Print dialog box?
2. Why is the axis a problem when changing mapping modes?
3. What function would we override to change DC attributes?
4. Which PrintInfo data member defines the currently usable page area?

Exercises

1. Change the footer on the CHexpadView printout to be a timestamp of when the document was printed.
2. Don't use m_lf to get the LOGFONT structure. Instead, use the member functions available in the CFontDialog class to retrieve font information a piece at a time. Then use the CreateFont() call instead of CreateFontIndirect() to create the printer font.

OLE Containers

WEEK 3

Day 18: OLE Containers

Thus far in our OLE programming experience, we have dealt only with the server side of OLE. In this chapter we will discuss containers. Happily, we will find that OLE containers are much easier to implement than the servers they contain. In a superficial description of a container, we could say that it is merely a box that can hold server applications. Of course, the average container you will meet on the street is much more than just a container; it too is an application of some sort that uses servers to enhance its utility.

Containers—by AppWizard

Let's let AppWizard do its thing and create a new application. Select the following options in the AppWizard dialog and create the application:

1. Enter `Wingrep` as the project name.
2. Select an appropriate project directory (C:\TYMFC, for example).
3. In the Options dialog, deselect the MDI option. (We want an SDI application.) Leave the rest of the selections in this dialog at their default settings.
4. Choose the container selection in the OLE Options dialog. This tells AppWizard to make the new application an OLE container.
5. Leave everything under Database Options and Classes at their default values.

Compile, link, and run the application. You should have a real-life OLE container application up and running before your eyes. Is it everything you dreamed of? No? Well, let's take it through some of its paces just the same. Pull down the Edit menu and you will see the typical grouping of OLE-esque menu items (see Figure 18.1).

Figure 18.1.
The default container with the Edit menu visible.

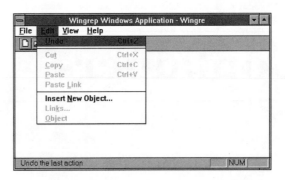

At the moment, only one of the OLE menu selections is active: Insert New Object. This selection will automatically bring up the OLE Insert Object dialog, from which you may choose any of the registered server applications available on your system. Naturally, this is the same thing we encountered when we were talking about servers in Chapter 16. There really is no difference. We're just looking at things from the other side of the OLE coin.

Go ahead and insert an object. Let's try a Windows Paintbrush object, just to get started. You'll note that Paintbrush objects don't support in-place editing, so the full-blown Paintbrush application is invoked. However, if you look at the Paintbrush window's title, you'll see that it tells you that this picture is embedded in "Wingre"—well, we know it means "Wingrep." Make some scribbles on the empty screen and close Paintbrush. You will be asked if you wish to update your changes to the embedded picture. Say yes. Alternatively, if you explicitly tell Paintbrush to update your current work by using the File | Update menu selection, you won't be interrogated on exit. At this point you should see your picture embedded in Wingrep, as shown in Figure 18.2.

Figure 18.2.
A Paintbrush picture embedded in Wingrep.

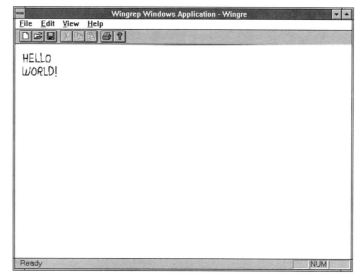

Not bad for a default container that we have yet to touch. But wait; there's more. Once a server item is embedded, how can we get access to it again? Typically, server access is provided through the mouse. A quick double-click on the picture's image should convince you that this particular feature is yet to be implemented. Not to fear: Mouse interaction will be fully functional before this chapter is over. But what do we do in the meantime? Lucky for us, AppWizard was thinking ahead. After an item is embedded and selected, we can give it simple commands (in OLE-speak, commands are called *verbs*) through the Edit menu. If you take another look at the Edit menu, you will see that it has changed. The last item in the menu used to be Object, but now, with a Paintbrush object embedded and selected, the last menu item is Paintbrush Picture Object. Wow! The menu text changes to reflect the particular selected server application object. Clicking on that last menu item brings up a submenu that enumerates the OLE verbs supported by Paintbrush. See Figure 18.3.

OLE Containers

Figure 18.3.
Wingrep with the Paintbrush Picture Object submenu displayed.

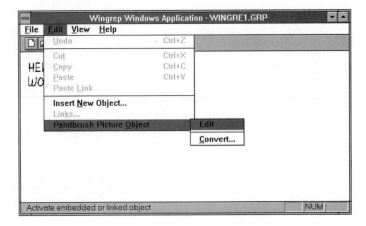

Paintbrush supports only two OLE verbs: Edit and Convert. Edit opens up the Paintbrush application and allows additional changes to be made to the original masterpiece, as shown in Figure 18.4.

Figure 18.4.
Wingrep with an open Paintbrush object.

Choosing the Convert selection brings up the Convert dialog, shown in Figure 18.5.

Figure 18.5.
Paintbrush's Convert dialog.

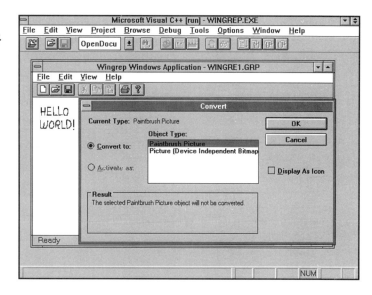

This dialog allows you to convert an OLE object into other server-supported forms. In the case of Paintbrush, you are given the following options:

- ☐ Convert the Paintbrush object into a DIB (device-independent bitmap). (See Chapter 14 for more on DIBs.)
- ☐ Leave the object alone, but change its representation in the container to an icon.
- ☐ Just leave the object alone—no changes will occur.

Different servers will present you with different conversion options, depending on their particular function. Experiment with the conversion options to see what trouble you can get yourself into.

In the larger scheme of things, different servers will present you with different OLE verbs, again depending on the server. These different verbs will manifest themselves in the Edit | Object menu option. Let's take a look at a different server in our Wingrep application. Choose Edit | Insert New Object to add an Excel 5.0 Worksheet object to our container. (If you don't have Excel 5.0, try to find another application that supports in-place editing. You could use the Hexpad application, for example.) At this point you should see something similar to Figure 18.6.

Note that a stand-alone instance of Excel 5.0 didn't get started. Excel is running as an embedded, in-place application. This tells us that Excel 5.0 supports in-place editing, whereas Paintbrush doesn't. This additional capability is also reflected in the verb list. But how do we get access to the verb list? With the Excel object embedded and open, we don't have access to Wingrep's full

OLE Containers

menu. This is because during an in-place editing session, the container's menu becomes merged with the server's menu. This facilitates in-place editing, but it can be confusing. In order to get back to a pure Wingrep menu, press the Escape key. This tells the container to close the currently open in-place server. Now we may look at the verb list for our Excel Worksheet object. Select Edit | Worksheet Object, and you will see the verb list shown in Figure 18.7.

Figure 18.6.
Excel 5.0 embedded and open in Wingrep.

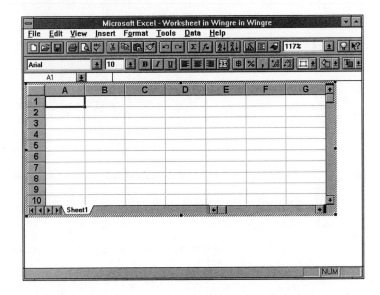

Figure 18.7.
Excel worksheet OLE verbs.

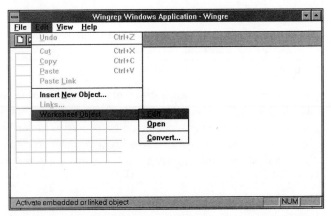

The Excel worksheet supports three verbs: Edit, Open, and Convert. Edit starts Excel as an in-place server—just as it was initially when we inserted it. Open causes Excel to be executed as a stand-alone application with our embedded worksheet loaded. Applying the Open verb to a server that supports in-place editing has the same effect that the Edit verb has on a server that doesn't support in-place editing: In both cases, the stand-alone version of the server application is launched. Finally, the Convert verb is also available. However, there's not much you can convert an Excel worksheet to, so the only option you have is to represent it as an icon in the container's display.

Speaking of the container's display, where did our Paintbrush object masterpiece go? Don't panic. Nothing happened to it. It didn't actually go anywhere; we just can't see it at the moment. It isn't currently visible because the default AppWizard container displays only the currently selected embedded object. The last OLE object embedded becomes the current selection. Of course, the user can change the current selection if such a selection process is provided (and yes, we'll get to that soon). The Paintbrush object might not be selected (and therefore is invisible), but it's still there.

Just as with Paintbrush, when the Excel server is closed, you can see the residual server item picture. This picture is the result of a C*XXX*ServerItem::OnDraw() call, as you might remember from Chapter 16. The Excel object is closed, but it is still the selected embedded server. Therefore, we may again bring up the in-place edit box for the Excel worksheet by selecting Edit | Worksheet Object | Edit. As you might also recall from Chapter 16, the thick border around our in-place server is the in-place frame window. This window may be moved and sized just like other windows. Doing so can result in a screen similar to Figure 18.8.

Figure 18.8.
An open worksheet in Wingrep with a ghost.

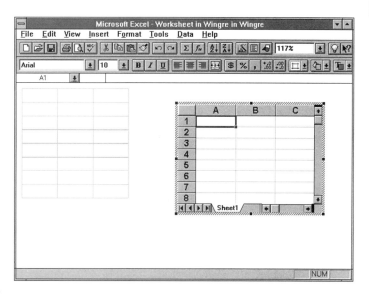

What's that in the upper-left corner? It's a ghost image of the server item. We didn't see anything like that when we were experimenting with Hexpad in Chapter 16! That's because we weren't dealing with a dumb container before. Yup, we've bumped up against one of the default

OLE Containers

container's limitations: It's stupid when it comes to server item placement. Well, you can't expect AppWizard to do everything. After all, this *is* a book on programming!

The default AppWizard container is quite a feat. I think that it's easily the most useful of the Wizard-generated applications. Without any modification, it will hold a server. It will provide OLE verb access to the currently selected server. It supports in-place editing of servers with that ability. And it automatically ties the server items into its serialization process. It does all of this right out of the AppWizard gate. Quite impressive. However, there are a few items that could stand some improvement. Phew, we still have a job!

The Whole Is More Than the Sum of Its Parts

Before we start writing code, let's first take a quick glimpse at the default application's structure. A default AppWizard-generated container application consists of the classes and associated files described in Table 18.1.

Table 18.1. The default container's classes.

AppWizard Class Built for Wingrep	Where It's Found	Class It's Derived From	Description
CWingrepApp	WINGREP.H, WINGREP.CPP	CWinApp	The usual core application class. AppWizard made only slight customizations to it for OLE.
CMainFrame	MAINFRM.H, MAINFRM.CPP	CFrameWnd	The usual SDI mainframe class. Nothing new.
CWingrepView	WINGRVW.H, WINGRVW.CPP	CView	The usual view class. However, AppWizard made extensive additions to it.
CWingrepDoc	WINGRDOC.H, WINGRDOC.CPP	COleDocument	Brand-new document class. This new document class keeps a list of the embedded OLE items.

AppWizard Class Built for Wingrep	Where It's Found	Class It's Derived From	Description
CWingrepCntrItem	CNTRITEM.H, CPPCNTRITEM.CPP	COleClientItem	Brand-new class. An object of this class will represent a server item in the container.

Each of these classes has its respective duties to perform so that the container will operate properly. Aside from their usual responsibilities, each class also has some small part to play in this new OLE drama. Of course, AppWizard did as much as it could to make the default implementations of these classes good enough to support OLE. Sometimes the OLE customizing is slight, and sometimes a major overhaul is necessary.

CWingrepApp needed only a minor modification. It is responsible for initializing the OLE libraries. This is accomplished through a single call to AfxOleInit() from CWingrepApp::InitInstance().

CMainFrame uses the same code as a non-OLE application. It's still just the outermost frame window of our application.

CWingrepView, an immediate descendent of CView, is central to some of the OLE issues. It therefore requires considerable additions by AppWizard to bring it up to OLE speed. We will discuss the OLEization of CView in a moment.

CWingrepDoc is the trivial descendent of the brand-new class COleDocument. COleDocument was derived from CDocument, so it's not too far from what we know. Actually, the additions to COleDocument are just what the doctor (or perhaps Wizard) ordered. The COleDocument class is so close to what we need that AppWizard has nothing to add to CWingrepDoc, at least with regard to OLE. The real changes that were made to CDocument (to get it to COleDocument) center around the idea of embedded items. COleDocument keeps a list of all its embedded items. These items, as far as a container is concerned, are COleClientItem objects.

CWingrepCntrItem is a direct descendent of COleClientItem, which is a brand-new class built especially for OLE projects. Objects of this class represent server items embedded in a container application. You can think of this class in terms of our server experience from Chapter 16. COleClientItem is to the container application what COleServerItem was to the server application. Both classes represent an embedded item from either side of the OLE container/server looking glass. Again, we will postpone the discussion of the particulars of this class.

Day 18

OLE Containers

Now that we have a general notion of what all the pieces of the default container application are, it's time to see how they fit together. Figure 18.9 shows how the container interacts with itself, as well as how it interacts with its servers.

Figure 18.9.
The SDI MFC container architecture.

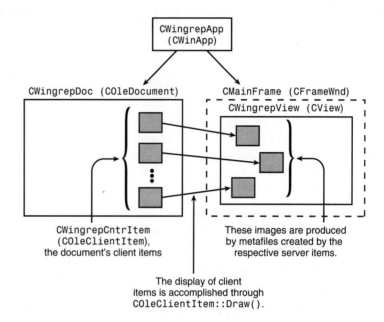

As you can see, the usual SDI architecture is very evident in the SDI container application. The `CWinApp`-derived class is the core class that creates instances and controls all the other classes. The `COleDocument`-derived class performs the duties of a usual document class, but it also holds (and provides access to) a list of client items that represent embedded server objects. Our old friend `CMainFrame` is unchanged. It is still the top frame window of the application and therefore, in an SDI application, it holds a single view class object. There is nothing too special about the `CView`-derived class other than the extensions built in by AppWizard to support the display of the embedded objects. The actual mechanics of client item display center around the concept of the metafile. A metafile is a recording of the `CDC` commands given to a display device. Once recorded, this file may be played on command, giving a rendering of the original screen image. This method is almost always more efficient than capturing and holding a screen image as a bitmap. A server item builds a metafile via a `COleServerItem::OnDraw()` call. This metafile is given to the appropriate `COleClientItem`-derived object, which uses it during a `COleClientItem::Draw()` function call.

The MDI version of Figure 18.9 isn't included here simply because it doesn't really add anything to the understanding of the OLE container. The extra clutter of multiple documents just adds more confusion. However, you don't have to worry about anything special when generalizing a container to an MDI environment—other than the usual MDI issues.

Now that we have some understanding of a container's building blocks and how they fit together, let's take a closer look at some of the principal players in the container application.

CWingrepCntrItem (Also Known as *COleClientItem*)

`CWingrepCntrItem` is a direct descendent of `COleClientItem`. However, these client items are very particular to the application in which they reside. They have to communicate/mediate between the server items and the container's document class and the container's view class. This is quite a responsibility, but fortunately much of this code can be abstracted into the `COleClientItem` class. In `CWingrepCntrItem`, all AppWizard has to do is make the proper connections into our application. The following is the interface to `CWingrepCntrItem`. Take a moment to note its structure.

```
// cntritem.h: Interface of the CWingrepCntrItem class
//
class CWingrepDoc;
class CWingrepView;
class CWingrepCntrItem : public COleClientItem
{
        DECLARE_SERIAL(CWingrepCntrItem)

// Constructors
public:
        CWingrepCntrItem(CWingrepDoc* pContainer = NULL);
                // Note: pContainer is allowed to be NULL to enable
                // IMPLEMENT_SERIALIZE.
                // IMPLEMENT_SERIALIZE requires that the class have
                // a constructor with zero arguments.  Normally, OLE
                // items are constructed with a non-NULL document
                // pointer.

// Attributes
public:
        CWingrepDoc* GetDocument()
        { return (CWingrepDoc*)COleClientItem::GetDocument(); }
        CWingrepView* GetActiveView()
        { return (CWingrepView*)COleClientItem::GetActiveView(); }

// Implementation
public:
        ~CWingrepCntrItem();
#ifdef _DEBUG
        virtual void AssertValid() const;
        virtual void Dump(CDumpContext& dc) const;
#endif
        virtual void Serialize(CArchive& ar);
        virtual void OnGetItemPosition(CRect& rPosition);
        virtual void OnDeactivateUI(BOOL bUndoable);
```

DAY 18

OLE Containers

```
protected:
    virtual void OnChange(OLE_NOTIFICATION wNotification, DWORD dwParam);
    virtual BOOL OnChangeItemPosition(const CRect& rectPos);
};
```

//

The first lines of this interface establish the view and document class prototypes. This allows the client item to reference the view and document classes in the interface. You might wonder why the usual include directive wasn't used. Well, the problem is that document and view must include the client item class in their interfaces too. Does the term *circular reference* ring any bells? The way around it is this prototype trick.

Once we get into the class interface itself, we see a constructor for the class. The constructor takes a single parameter, which is a pointer to the containing document. Nothing is out of the ordinary here. After all, we've been using and building constructors since the beginning of the book. However, the block of comments found immediately after the constructor must be there for a reason. The comment justifies why a NULL document pointer is a legitimate parameter. Normally, you would think that if you were constructing a client item, you would have to have a container in which to put it. But, as the comment explains, we must allow for a parameterless constructor so that serialization can be supported. Recall from Chapter 6 that serialization requires a parameterless constructor so that the load routines may construct the various items and fill them with data without having to know anything about them (such as what parameters their constructors require). If you're wondering why we would want to support client item serialization in the first place, think about it. Do you want to save the embedded objects as part of your container document? Of course you do, and serialization is the means to that end.

The next couple of functions, `GetDocument()` and `GetActiveView()`, are very similar to `CView`'s `GetDocument()` function. That is, they return a pointer to the associated document or view object, respectively. Just as `CView`'s `GetDocument()` function is used heavily, you'll see these two functions as a common fixture in many of your `COleClientItem`-derived class functions.

The next few functions should seem very familar. A destructor. A couple of diagnostic functions. The serialization function. All these functions are implemented just as you would think. Of course, a minor addition to the serialization function is made to call the base class. `COleClientItem::Serialize()` takes care of the serialization of the associated server item. This attachment makes the server items truly embedded in the document. When you save the container document, it saves its list of client items, and each client item saves the server item data. Naturally, all this saving is done through a `CArchive` object.

The last four functions in `CWingrepCntrItem`'s interface are completely new to us. Each one helps the client item deal with its role in OLE.

`OnGetItemPosition()` and `OnChangeItemPosition()` both deal with the position of the client item with respect to its view. It is through these functions that you may access the client item's position. However, note that `OnChangeItemPosition()` is protected; users of this class shouldn't be able to arbitrarily change the item's position. In the default application, client item positions are not tracked. Consequently, both of these calls do very little. This is an area where we will have some significant input.

`OnChange()` gets called by the framework whenever the user changes, saves, or closes the client item. `OnChange()` is called whenever the state or visual appearance of the client item needs updating. The default implementation of this function calls the parent `OnChange()` function and then instructs the document to update all its views.

`OnDeactivateUI()` is called by the framework when an active, embedded, in-place server item gets deactivated (for example, when you press the Escape key). The default implementation of this function simply deactivates the client item through the `COleClientItem::Deactivate()` function. This function shuts down the OLE item and frees any associated resources.

We will see more of these functions as we add functionality to Wingrep. But before we drift away from our discussion of client items, let's talk about their states, shown in Table 18.2.

Table 18.2. Client item states.

State	Description
`COleClientItem::emptyState`	The item has been created, but it contains nothing. It's not really a client item until it is loaded with OLE data.
`COleClientItem::loadedState`	The item is not only created, but it is also loaded with OLE data. It is now truly an OLE client item.
`COleClientItem::openState`	The associated server item is in the fully open configuration (not being edited in-place). It is customary to shade the client item rectangle with a crosshatch brush while in this state.
`COleClientItem::activeState`	When the item gets activated in-place, it passes through this state on its way to `activeUIState`.
`COleClientItem::activeUIState`	After the item is activated, the container menu and the embedded server menu are merged. Once this merging is complete, the item is in the `activeUIState`. Note that the `activeState` is usually just a transitional state.

When the client item is changed from one of these states to another, it is notified by the framework through its `OnChange()` function. And so we discover another stitch in the delicate fabric of the MFC. It's amazing how everything ties together so well—the mark of quality.

Day 18: OLE Containers

CWingrepView (Also Known as *CView* with an OLE Attitude)

As I stated earlier, there's nothing special about `CWingrepView`'s bloodline. It's an immediate descendent of `CView`—you can't get more common than that. However, just because greatness isn't in the blood doesn't mean that the class can't be special. After the class gets a complete makeover by AppWizard, it comes out with quite a few OLE additions (dare I say improvements?). So what are these additions? The interface to `CWingrepView` follows:

```cpp
// wingrvw.h: interface of the CWingrepView class
//
/////////////////////////////////////////////////////////////////////////////

class CWingrepCntrItem;

class CWingrepView : public CView
{
protected:  // Create from serialization only
    CWingrepView();
    DECLARE_DYNCREATE(CWingrepView)

// Attributes
public:
    CWingrepDoc* GetDocument();

    // m_pSelection holds the selection to the current
    // CWingrepCntrItem. For many applications, such a
    // member variable isn't adequate to represent a selection,
    // such as a multiple selection or a selection of objects
    // that are not CWingrepCntrItem objects. This selection
    // mechanism is provided just to help you get started.

    // TODO: Replace this selection mechanism with one appropriate
    //  to your app.
    CWingrepCntrItem* m_pSelection;

// Operations
public:

// Implementation
public:
    virtual ~CWingrepView();
    virtual void OnDraw(CDC* pDC);  // Overridden to draw this view
#ifdef _DEBUG
    virtual void AssertValid() const;
    virtual void Dump(CDumpContext& dc) const;
#endif

protected:
    virtual void OnInitialUpdate(); // Called first time after construct

    // Printing support
    virtual BOOL OnPreparePrinting(CPrintInfo* pInfo);
```

```
        virtual void OnBeginPrinting(CDC* pDC, CPrintInfo* pInfo);
        virtual void OnEndPrinting(CDC* pDC, CPrintInfo* pInfo);

        // OLE container support
        virtual BOOL IsSelected(const CObject* pDocItem) const;

// Generated message map functions
protected:
    //{{AFX_MSG(CWingrepView)
        // NOTE: ClassWizard will add and remove
        // member functions here. DO NOT EDIT what
        // you see in these blocks of generated code!
    afx_msg void OnSetFocus(CWnd* pOldWnd);
    afx_msg void OnSize(UINT nType, int cx, int cy);
    afx_msg void OnInsertObject();
    afx_msg void OnCancelEdit();
    //}}AFX_MSG
    DECLARE_MESSAGE_MAP()
};

#ifndef _DEBUG  // Debug version in wingrvw.cpp
inline CWingrepDoc* CWingrepView::GetDocument()
    { return (CWingrepDoc*)m_pDocument; }
#endif
```

//

AppWizard didn't completely transform the CView class, but there are some distinct additions that are not self-explanatory. Let's walk through the interface and examine the implementation when necessary.

The first addition we come across is a large block of commented notes followed by the new attribute m_pSelection—a pointer to a CWingrepCntrItem object. This attribute keeps track of the currently selected client item. The comment notes that this attribute is a starter attribute provided "just to help you get started." It explains that some applications will want support for multiple selections or other customization for which a single selection is not adequate. For our application, a single selection will be more than sufficient.

Below the declaration of the m_pSelection attribute, we find a glut of familiar functions: a destructor, OnDraw(), diagnostic routines, OnInitialUpdate(), and the printing functions. The implementation of these functions is also very familiar, with the possible exception of OnDraw(). The default implementation of OnDraw() does take into account the idea of client items, albeit crudely. Let's take a look.

```
void CWingrepView::OnDraw(CDC* pDC)
{
        CWingrepDoc* pDoc = GetDocument();
        ASSERT_VALID(pDoc);

        // TODO: Add draw code for native data here.
        // TODO: Also draw all OLE items in the document.

        // Draw the selection at an arbitrary position. This code should
        // be removed once your real drawing code is implemented.
```

Day 18

OLE Containers

```
    // This position corresponds exactly to the rectangle returned
    // by CWingrepCntrItem, to give the effect of in-place editing.

    // TODO: Remove this code when final draw code is complete.

    if (m_pSelection == NULL)
    {
        POSITION pos = pDoc->GetStartPosition();
        m_pSelection = (CWingrepCntrItem*)
                pDoc->GetNextClientItem(pos);
    }
    if (m_pSelection != NULL)
        m_pSelection->Draw(pDC, CRect(10, 10, 210, 210));
}
```

The `OnDraw()` function starts out as a thousand `OnDraw()`s did before it by declaring a document pointer and validating it. But here is where the familiarity ends. This function goes on into OLE-specific realms. AppWizard's comments again provide an explanation. They tell us that this `OnDraw()` function will draw the current selection at an arbitrary position. It goes on to say that unless you want your application to look stupid, you'd better customize this piece of code to draw the stuff particular to your application. Okay, that's a loose translation, but it's a relatively accurate assessment. As it stands, `OnDraw()` knows nothing of our application, so it draws the current selection in the hard-coded rectangle (10, 10, 210, 210). Egad, again with the hard-coding! This hard-coded client item position is the source for the ghost image we found in our experiments at the beginning of this chapter. No matter where the actual client item was, it was always drawn at (10, 10, 210, 210). Well, it does emphasize that you really must customize this function for your own purposes. If there is no current selection, it sets the current selection to the first client item in the document's list. Needless to say, we will modify this function!

The next function we find in the interface is `IsSelected()`. This function merely returns the current client item selected. In other words, it returns `m_pSelection`.

All that's left to explain in the interface is the message map functions: `OnSetFocus()`, `OnSize()`, `OnInsertObject()`, and `OnCancelEdit()`. Like all message map functions, each of these functions is called by the framework in response to some user event. The first two, `OnSetFocus()` and `OnSize()`, are inherited from `CWnd`. They are called when the window gains focus and when the window is resized, respectively. The second two, `OnInsertObject()` and `OnCancelEdit()`, are called when the user chooses Edit | Insert New Object and when the user presses the Escape key, respectively.

`OnSetFocus()` needs to be overridden due to the possibility of an active in-place server item. If this view has a server item currently active and in-place, the focus must be transferred to the in-place frame. Otherwise, `OnSetFocus()` might pass the call on to the base class.

`OnSize()` must be overridden to take into account the possibility of uncovering portions of an active, in-place object. If an active, in-place server is present, the default `CWingrepView::OnSize()` will tell it that its displayable size might have been altered. This is accomplished through the `COleClientItem::SetItemRects()` function.

`OnInsertObject()` is a rather involved function. It prompts the user with an Insert OLE Item dialog, which displays a list of the currently registered server types. It creates a client item attached to the document and associates it with the server type chosen. It then instructs the item to show itself for editing via the OLE verb `OLEIVERB_SHOW`. The result of this call is a new server item embedded in the container and ready to be edited. If both the container and server support in-place editing, the new client item will be in its `::activeUIState` and the server item will be in its in-place frame. Otherwise, the full-blown server item will be invoked and the client item will be in the `::openState`.

`OnCancelEdit()`, in response to the Escape key, closes the active in-place server item. If none of the embedded items are currently being edited in-place, the function does nothing. It's interesting to note that `OnCancelEdit()` has no representation on the menu. Its command ID, `ID_CANCEL_EDIT`, is found only in the keyboard accelerator resource, not in both places like many commands.

CWingrepDoc (Also Known as *COleDocument*)

As I mentioned earlier, AppWizard had very little to do to the `COleDocument`-derived class. This is because the original class was designed precisely for this purpose—to be a document for an MFC container. Just because there isn't much to talk about concerning `CWingrepDoc` doesn't mean that there isn't anything to say in this section. The base class `COleDocument` has ample topics of discussion.

So what's new in `COleDocument`? Table 18.3 shows some of the more pertinent new member functions.

Table 18.3. Selected `COleDocument` member functions.

Member Function	Description
GetPrimarySelectedItem	Returns a pointer to the currently selected item in the specified view. Returns NULL if no item is selected or if more than one item is selected.
GetInPlaceActiveItem	Returns a pointer to the active in-place item contained within the given CWnd object. Returns NULL if no item is active and in place.
GetStartPosition	Returns the first position in the document's item iterator. Returns NULL if the document has no items.
GetNextItem	Iterates through the document's list of items, returning a pointer to an item on each call. It takes a POSITION value

continues

Table 18.3. continued

Member Function	Description
	initialized in `GetStartPosition()` as an argument. The position is set to `NULL` when the iteration is complete.
`GetNextClientItem`	Same as `GetNextItem()`, except it's customized for client item iteration.
`GetNextServerItem`	Same as `GetNextItem()`, except it's customized for server item iteration.
`UpdateModifiedFlag`	Flags the document as modified. Call this function when an embedded item changes and is therefore in need of saving.
`AddItem`	Adds an item to the document. Called from the `COleServerItem` and `COleClientItem` constructors.
`RemoveItem`	Removes an item from the document. Called from the `COleServerItem` and `COleClientItem` destructors.

Most of these new member functions center around the new list of items that `COleDocument` must now manage. Note that these items can be either client items or server items. A given `COleDocument` object will not have both types of items. The `COleDocument` class serves as a base class for container documents as well as server documents. Both item types must therefore be supported. `COleDocument` uses the typical means of providing access to an underlying list—that's right, through our hero, the iterator. Iterators afford a great amount of flexibility while ensuring the integrity of the list.

We will see some of these functions in action very soon, when we start customizing our container. Excitement is in the air!

A Better Container

Okay, we've seen what the default container can do. We know how the default container was built. And we understand, at least in part, how the pieces interact. Now it's time to decide what our container should do and it will do it.

Despite its good points, the default container isn't quite up to anyone's expectations concerning a real-life container application. At the bare minimum, a nontrivial container application must

- [ ] draw all the embedded client items
- [ ] allow the user to mouse-select and move these items
- [ ] provide Edit, Open, and other OLE verb access to the items
- [ ] do application-specific manipulations to said items

Central to each of these tasks is the idea of keeping track of the objects and their respective positions. Fortunately, the `COleDocument` class object will automatically keep track of the client items. Each client item knows which server it represents. Adding knowledge of its physical position on-screen is very simple. All we have to do is add a `CRect` object to the `CWingrepCntrItem` interface and make sure it gets updated and referenced at the appropriate times.

Place the following line in the public attributes section of `CWingrepCntrItem`'s interface:

```
CRect m_rectPosition;    // Current position of the embedded item
```

This attribute must be initialized, so make the following changes to `CWingrepCntrItem`'s constructor:

```
CWingrepCntrItem::CWingrepCntrItem(CWingrepDoc* pContainer)
      : COleClientItem(pContainer)
{
      m_rectPosition.SetRect(10, 10, 210, 210);
}
```

Hey, if (10, 10, 210, 210) was good enough for the default application, it's good enough for the initial position of our new client items! Now we have to support both the changing and the retrieval of this position. This is accomplished through the following two functions:

```
BOOL CWingrepCntrItem::OnChangeItemPosition
            (const CRect& rectPos)
{
      ASSERT_VALID(this);

      CWingrepDoc* pDoc = GetDocument();

// During in-place activation, CWingrepCntrItem::OnChangeItemPosition
// is called by the server to change the position of the in-place
// window. Usually, this is a result of the data in the server
// document changing such that the extent has changed or a result
// of in-place resizing.
//
// The default here is to call the base class, which will call
// COleClientItem::SetItemRects to move the item to the new
// position.

      if (!COleClientItem::OnChangeItemPosition(rectPos))
            return FALSE;

      pDoc->UpdateAllViews(NULL);
      m_rectPosition = rectPos;
      pDoc->SetModifiedFlag(TRUE);

      return TRUE;
}

void CWingrepCntrItem::OnGetItemPosition(CRect& rPosition)
{
      ASSERT_VALID(this);
```

Day 18

OLE Containers

```
// During in-place activation, CWingrepCntrItem::OnGetItemPosition
// will be called to determine the location of this item. The default
// implementation created from AppWizard simply returns a hard-coded
// rectangle. Usually, this rectangle would reflect the current
// position of the item relative to the view used for activation.
// You can obtain the view by calling CWingrepCntrItem::GetActiveView.

        rPosition = m_rectPosition;
}
```

Both of these functions are pretty easy. `OnChangeItemPosition()` gets a new `CRect` item as a parameter that indicates the new position and size of the client item. Our job is to copy this into our attribute and alert the document to this change. `OnGetItemPosition()` is even simpler. All that is required is the passing back of our position rectangle. The last function in `CWingrepCntrItem` that must be altered to accommodate the new attribute is the `Serialize()` function. After all, the position of the client items in the view should be saved too.

```
void CWingrepCntrItem::Serialize(CArchive& ar)
{
        ASSERT_VALID(this);

        // Call base class first to read in COleClientItem data.
        // Since this sets up the m_pDocument pointer returned from
        // CWingrepCntrItem::GetDocument, it is a good idea to call
        // the base class Serialize first.
        COleClientItem::Serialize(ar);

        // Now store/retrieve data specific to CWingrepCntrItem
        if (ar.IsStoring())
        {
                ar << m_rectPosition;
        }
        else
        {
                ar >> m_rectPosition;
        }
}
```

Again, a trivial change in the default code does the trick. We are done with the client item class, yet if you compile, link, and run Wingrep, you won't see anything new. Of course not. We haven't changed the display code! Now doesn't that sound like our next topic?

Enhancing *WingrepView*

Before we go off the deep end and start rewriting the `OnDraw()` code (which is the next logical step), we should talk about another very useful item that will make our coding life much easier. `CRectTracker` is a handy little class that implements a floating tracking rectangle that automatically supports moving and resizing. Although this class came as a part of the OLE libraries, it is by no means restricted to OLE-only applications. In other words, everything we learn about `CRectTracker` can be put to use in any application that needs such an object. Table 18.4 lists the attributes of `CRectTracker`, and Table 18.5 lists its member functions.

Table 18.4. CRectTracker's attributes.

Attribute	Description
m_rect	The CRect position of the CRectTracker object. This position is in device units relative to the view window.
m_sizeMin	A CSize value holding the minimum possible size the CRectTracker object can become.
m_nHandleSize	The size, in device units, of the CRectTracker object's resize handles.
m_nStyle	The current style of the CRectTracker object. The possible values of this attribute are enumerated in the CRectTracker interface. They are solidLine, dottedLine, resizeInside, resizeOutside, hatchedBorder, and hatchInside.

Table 18.5. CRectTracker's member functions.

Member Function	Description
CRectTracker	Constructor.
Draw	Draws the tracker based on its attributes—especially m_nStyle.
GetTrueRect	Retrieves a pointer to a RECT structure containing the position and size of the outermost border of the tracker.
HitTest	Returns a value of an enumerated type that indicates the nature of a point hit. The enumerated type is found in the CRectTracker interface: hitNothing, hitTopLeft, hitTopRight, hitBottomRight, hitBottomLeft, hitTop, hitRight, hitBottom, hitLeft, hitMiddle.
NormalizeHit	Since Track() and TrackRubberBand() support inverted x- and y-axes, the HitTest() function can report inverted handle hits. The NormalizeHit() function converts the tracker hit obtained from HitTest() into a hit normalized to the screen.
SetCursor	Call this function from your view's SetCursor() function when over the tracker. This function sets the cursor shape to something appropriate for the tracker.
Track	Call this function when the left mouse button is pressed to start tracking the rectangle. This function will move or resize the rectangle visually while updating the object via the DrawTrackerRect() and OnChangedRect() functions, respectively.

OLE Containers

Table 18.5. continued

Member Function	Description
TrackRubberBand	Supplies the "rubber band" for rubber band selection. Call it when the left mouse button is pressed. It will draw a sizing rectangle based on your mouse dragging.
AdjustRect	Called by the framework when the tracker is being resized.
DrawTrackerRect	Called by the framework every time the tracker moves during a Track() or TrackRubberBand() call.
OnChangedRect	Called by the framework every time the tracker is resized during a Track() call.

You can see from these tables that the CRectTracker class could really come in handy in a number of instances. One instance that comes to mind is the moving of client items in an OLE container's view. Indeed, this is precisely the use to which we will put CRectTracker. However, we do need a helper function that will aid us in initializing a given CRectTracker. This function is based on the suggestions and sample code found in the OLE 2.0 Class Reference.

```
void CWingrepView::SetupTracker( CRectTracker* pTracker,
         CWingrepCntrItem* pItem, CRect* pTrueRect )
{
    ASSERT(pTracker != NULL);
    ASSERT(pItem != NULL);

    // Set minimum size for tracker
    pTracker->m_sizeMin.cx = 8;
    pTracker->m_sizeMin.cy = 8;

    // Initialize style to 0
    pTracker->m_nStyle = 0;

    // Initialize the tracker rectangle to our
    // client item's rectangle
    pTracker->m_rect = pItem->m_rectPosition;

    // Set the tracker's style based on the
    // nature of the client item

    // If the client item is currently selected,
    // let the tracker show it by displaying the
    // resize handles
    if (pItem == m_pSelection)
        pTracker->m_nStyle |= CRectTracker::resizeInside;

    // Set the border style based on the item type
    if (pItem->GetType() == OT_LINK)
        pTracker->m_nStyle |= CRectTracker::dottedLine;
    else
```

```
                pTracker->m_nStyle |= CRectTracker::solidLine;

        // Draw the item's interior hatched if the item is
        // open or active. Either way, the real drawing will
        // be done by the server. The client item shouldn't
        // show anything.
        if ( (pItem->GetItemState() == COleClientItem::openState) ||
             (pItem->GetItemState() ==
                    COleClientItem::activeUIState) )
        {
                pTracker->m_nStyle |= CRectTracker::hatchInside;
        }

        // Send back the true size of the tracker via pTrueRect
        if (pTrueRect != NULL)
                pTracker->GetTrueRect(pTrueRect);
}
```

All this function does is initialize the tracker object. The tracker's size and position data are initialized first, and then the tracker's style is configured to the client item's state. The style configuration algorithm we are using in this function is only suggested by Microsoft, but no doubt it will turn into a hard-and-fast standard. In short, the algorithm tells the tracker object to draw itself in the following manner:

- ☐ If the item is linked, draw a dashed border.
- ☐ If the item is embedded, draw a solid border.
- ☐ If the item is selected, draw the resize handles.
- ☐ If the item is open or in-place active, fill the interior with a hatched brush. In either of these cases, the server is in control again, so the client item representation of the server (the metafile) is, at least potentially, out-of-date! Hence, we shouldn't display it.

Note that the true size of the tracker is passed back through the pTrueRect parameter. We won't use this functionality, but it can be useful in certain instances. Recall that because of the extent of the resize handles, the true size of the tracker object can be larger than the client item rectangle. In our application, this is not a critical concern, but in other applications it can be.

Every time a CRectTracker object is declared, it must also be initialized to its associated client item. With the aid of the SetupTracker() function, we will be able rewrite the OnDraw() function.

```
void CWingrepView::OnDraw(CDC* pDC)
{
        CWingrepDoc* pDoc = GetDocument();
        ASSERT_VALID(pDoc);

        // Draw the OLE items in the document's list
        // using the item iterator
        POSITION pos = pDoc->GetStartPosition();
        while (pos != NULL)
        {
                // Get the client item...
                CWingrepCntrItem* pItem =
```

Day 18: OLE Containers

```
                (CWingrepCntrItem*)pDoc->GetNextItem(pos);
        // ...and draw it
        pItem->Draw(pDC, pItem->m_rectPosition);

        // Draw the tracker over the item
        CRectTracker tracker;
        CRect rectTrue;
        SetUpTracker(&tracker, pItem, &rectTrue);
        tracker.Draw(pDC);
    }
}
```

We enhance `OnDraw()` in two ways. First, we iterate through and draw all the client items instead of just drawing the first client item in the document's list. We also replace the hard-coded (10, 10, 210, 210) drawing rectangle with a tracker object initialized to each client item. The tracker object will indicate the state of the client item and further promote visual feedback to the user.

Hit Testing and Getting Mousy

Wingrep is now tracking client item positions and displaying the items correctly, but it supports no way of actually changing the positions. Therefore, our next move is to add the ability of client item manipulation via the mouse. Basically, this is done in the following fashion:

- ☐ Capture any left-button mouse clicks that occur in the view window.
- ☐ Check the point of click against the existing client item rectangles.
- ☐ Select the topmost client item under the click (if there are any).
- ☐ Construct a `CRectTracker` object to automate the client item movement.
- ☐ Invoke the `Track()` function.
- ☐ If the `Track()` was successful, update the client item position rectangle.

This to-do list might look a bit difficult at first, but everything in it is actually quite straightforward. Capturing left mouse button clicks is accomplished easily through ClassWizard. Instruct ClassWizard to build a `WM_LBUTTONDOWN` handler function in the `CWingrepView` class. Finding the top client item containing a specific point (the mouse hit) is also relatively easy, but because this functionality is commonly needed, we will make it a separate function: `GetItemContaining()`. Selecting this new item is a bit complicated, so it too requires a function of its own. The last three bulleted items can all be thrown in the `CRectTracker` pot; our tracker object will handle most of this work. So, in short, enabling the mouse is relatively easy! Our first job is to construct the function `GetItemContaining()`:

```
CWingrepCntrItem* CWingrepView::GetItemContaining(CPoint point)
{
    CWingrepDoc* pDoc = GetDocument();
    CWingrepCntrItem* pTestItem;
    CWingrepCntrItem* pHitItem = NULL;
```

```
        // Initialize the iterator
        POSITION pos = pDoc->GetStartPosition();
        while (pos != NULL)
        {
                // Iterate through the list, testing each item
                pTestItem = (CWingrepCntrItem*)pDoc->GetNextItem(pos);
                if (pTestItem->m_rectPosition.PtInRect(point))
                        pHitItem = pTestItem;
        }

        // Return the last item hit (this corresponds to
        // the topmost item containing the point)
        return pHitItem;
}
```

Like the OnDraw() function, this function makes good use of the client item iterator provided by COleDocument. It steps through the list of items, checking each one via the PtInRect() function to see if it contains the point in question. If it does, it keeps a copy of the item's pointer in the variable pHitItem. After all the client items have been visited, the last one hit will be returned. From this algorithm, you can discern that the items are stored in bottom-to-top order. The last item in the list is the topmost item in the view.

The second helper function we need is one that changes the view's selected client item to one we provide. This is just a bit involved, as you can see from the SetSelection() function:

```
void CWingrepView::SetSelection (CWingrepCntrItem* pNewSelection)
{
        CWingrepDoc* pDoc = GetDocument();
        ASSERT_VALID(pDoc);

        // If the new selection is already the current
        // selection, there is nothing for us to do
        if ( pNewSelection == m_pSelection )
                return;

        // Get the currently active item (if any)
        COleClientItem* pActiveItem = pDoc->GetInPlaceActiveItem(this);

        // If there is no active item, there is nothing to close. If the
        // active item is the "new" selection, there is nothing to do.
        if ( (pActiveItem != NULL) &&
                (pActiveItem != pNewSelection) )
        {
                // Close the active item and make sure it closed
                pActiveItem->Close();
                ASSERT(pDoc->GetInPlaceActiveItem(this) == NULL);
        }

        // Tell the view that it needs to be redrawn
        Invalidate();

        // Finally, update the selection
        m_pSelection = pNewSelection;
}
```

OLE Containers

This function takes, as its single parameter, a pointer to the proffered new selection. After verifying that there is something to do with this new selection, SetSelection() closes any currently active item, invalidates the window, and finally sets the view's selection to the new selection. This function has ample comments illuminating any dark crevices you happen to find.

Now that the GetItemContaining() and SetSelection() functions are built, we may work on the function that ClassWizard built for us that captures left mouse button clicks. The completed OnLButtonDown() function follows:

```
void CWingrepView::OnLButtonDown(UINT nFlags, CPoint point)
{
        CWingrepCntrItem* pHitItem = GetItemContaining(point);
        SetSelection(pHitItem);

        if (pHitItem != NULL)
        {
                // Initialize the tracker
                CRectTracker tracker;
                CRect rectTrue;
                SetupTracker(&tracker, pHitItem, &rectTrue);

                // Update the view before invoking Track()
                UpdateWindow();
                // Hand over control to the tracker
                if (tracker.Track(this, point))
                {
                        // If the tracker succeeds, save the new position
                        // and tell the document and view that things
                        // might have changed
                        pHitItem->m_rectPosition = tracker.m_rect;
                        GetDocument()->SetModifiedFlag();
                        Invalidate();
                }
        }

        // Finish up by calling the base class
        CView::OnLButtonDown(nFlags, point);
}
```

OnLButtonDown() is called every time the user single-clicks the left mouse button in this view. The first thing we do in this function is determine which (if any) client items were hit by the mouse click. The top hit is then passed to the SetSelection() function, which makes it the current selection in the view. If a client item was hit and selected, we construct and initialize a CRectTracker object. Calling Track() transfers control to this tracker object. The tracker will move or resize the client item as necessary. If the tracker succeeds in its tracking (that is, if the track wasn't aborted by an escape or a right mouse button click), we update the new position/size and tell the document and view that a change has occurred. This function isn't all that complicated, although it does rely heavily on two other functions we constructed as well as CRectTracker. Anyway, single-click mouse support is installed!

Hmmmm. Single-click mouse support implies that there should be double-click mouse support. Excellent deduction. You get an A for the day. What should a double-click do to a client item? The usual interpretation of a double-click on a client item is to activate the associated server. This is done through the use of OLE verbs. Let's take a look at a typical implementation. Have ClassWizard install a left-button double-click handler function in our view class. Fill out this handler as follows:

```
void CWingrepView::OnLButtonDblClk(UINT nFlags, CPoint point)
{
    // Take care of the selection process by calling
    // the single button click code
    OnLButtonDown(nFlags, point);

    // If the user double-clicked on a client item,
    // send it an appropriate OLE verb command
    if (m_pSelection != NULL)
    {
        LONG oleVerb;

        // If the Ctrl key is pressed when the double-click
        // occurs, force the server to be fully open. Otherwise,
        // activate the server using its primary verb.

        if (GetKeyState(VK_CONTROL) < 0)
            oleVerb = OLEIVERB_OPEN;
        else
            oleVerb = OLEIVERB_PRIMARY;

        m_pSelection->DoVerb(oleVerb, this);
    }

    // Finish by calling the base class
    CView::OnLButtonDblClk(nFlags, point);
}
```

This function traps any double-clicks that occur in the view's window. It then calls the single-click code. The reason for this is that we want all the selection code in `OnLButtonDown()` executed before we start our new double-click code. Because we activate the currently selected item, it's important that we select the appropriate client item first. This is easily done through `OnLButtonDown()`. Activating the associated server item is done through the `DoVerb()` function; however, which verb to choose can be confusing. Our code narrows the choices down to `OLEIVERB_OPEN` when the Ctrl key is pressed and `OLEIVERB_PRIMARY` otherwise. The OLE verbs are described in Table 18.6.

Day 18: OLE Containers

Table 18.6. Some often-used OLE verbs.

Verb	Value	Description
OLEIVERB_PRIMARY	0	Activates the server using its primary verb. The primary verb defined for the server is typically OLEIVERB_SHOW.
(No symbol)	1	Activates the server using its secondary verb. There is no standard for the secondary verb. It will be particular to the application.
OLEIVERB_SHOW	−1	Activates the server in its editing mode. If in-place editing is not supported, this verb is indistinguishable from the OLEIVERB_OPEN verb.
OLEIVERB_OPEN	−2	Opens the server as a stand-alone application.
OLEIVERB_HIDE	−3	Causes the object to be hidden from the user's view.

Note that other verbs are defined for objects. As if that weren't bad enough, the user can even define verbs particular to her application. Okay, we've gone the extra mile with verbs. Suffice it to say, the verbs in Table 18.6 will do the job nine times out of ten. So as long as you write only nine OLE applications, you should be fine.

Just one item of unfinished business is left. You might recall from earlier in the chapter I mentioned something about the mouse cursor changing when it's over the client items. This is kind of an important point. If the mouse cursor stays the same everywhere in the view, the user won't have any visual feedback concerning what he can or can't do while over a client item. Visual feedback is the heart and soul of Windows. We have to make the effort! Use ClassWizard to create a WM_SETCURSOR handler in CWingrepView, and implement it as shown:

```
BOOL CWingrepView::OnSetCursor(CWnd* pWnd, UINT nHitTest, UINT message)
{
    if ( (pWnd == this) && (m_pSelection != NULL) )
    {
        // Give the tracker for the selection a chance
        CRectTracker tracker;
        CRect rectTrue;
        SetupTracker(&tracker, m_pSelection, &rectTrue);
        if (tracker.SetCursor(this, nHitTest))
            return TRUE;
    }
```

```
        return CView::OnSetCursor(pWnd, nHitTest, message);
}
```

Basically, this function just transfers control to the good ol' `CRectTracker` object and lets it take care of the messy details when the cursor is over a client item.

Now compile, link, and run Wingrep! It's always amazing when these things work properly. As it stands, the application should load and keep track of server items. The server items will be represented in the container's view as client item rectangles that may be selected, invoked, and moved using the mouse. This is the core functionality for most OLE container applications. It might not be too fancy yet, but it does the job. In Chapter 19 we will fancy-up Wingrep. Stay tuned.

Summary

In this chapter we created a simple container application. We added functionality to the default AppWizard-generated application piece-by-piece until a recognizable OLE application stood before us. Each step in the process required quite a bit of background understanding of OLE technology. Much of this chapter, therefore, was dedicated to explaining OLE details.

Q&A

Q **Our Wingrep application doesn't "grep" anything. Am I missing something?**

A Nope. We'll discuss "grepping" in the next chapter.

Q **What's this business about inverted x- and y-axes in the `CRectTracker` discussion?**

A If you pass a `TRUE` Boolean value as the `bAllowInvert` parameter in a call to `Track()`, the tracker will allow you to invert the tracker's x- and y-axes. This could be done by resizing the tracker with the lower-right handle and dragging this handle diagonally up and to the left until it is past the upper-right handle. In a sense, you have turned the tracker rectangle inside out; both axes have been inverted. Because of this inversion, what was the lower-right handle has become the upper-left handle. This possibility of handle swapping generates the need for the `NormalizeHit()` function.

Q **During a `Track()` call, I can lose my client item off the edge of the application. Once it's lost, I can't get it back. Is it really gone?**

A No, it's still there. The value of the `m_rectPosition` attribute is set in a nondisplayable region. You could solve this problem any number of ways. You could add scrollbars so that you could always scroll to the new position. A better solution would be to impose a restriction on valid `m_rectPositon` values.

OLE Containers

Workshop

Quiz

1. What is the purpose of CWingrepCntrItem?
2. Describe the major difference between the CDocument class and the COleDocument class.
3. Is CRectTracker restricted to OLE applications?
4. Describe the difference between the OLE verbs OLEIVERB_SHOW and OLEIVERB_OPEN.

Exercises

1. Put the current state of the Wingrep application through the same paces that we put the default container through at the beginning of this chapter.
2. Think about how you would implement multiple selection support in Wingrep. Don't actually do it, because it would conflict with our additions in the next chapter.
3. Add client item removal to Wingrep. Make a working Edit | Delete Object menu item. Don't forget to implement the command UI handler. (You shouldn't be allowed to delete an object if no object is currently selected.)
4. Fix the problem alluded to in the last question of the Q&A section.

WEEK
3

Drag and Drop

Drag and Drop

OLE 2.0 drag and drop as we know it today represents a broad spectrum of data transfer. We think nothing of picking up an embedded OLE object and moving it to a completely different application. As long as both applications are willing, this procedure works famously. However, in the not-too-distant past (before OLE 2.0), this was unheard of. The closest we could get to this kind of support was through OLE's ancestors: File Manager drag and drop and the Clipboard.

File Manager drag and drop allows the user to drag files from the File Manager window to a prepared drop target. The drop target accepts the files and manipulates them according to its application. Two limitations made File Manager drag and drop less than ideal. First, only File Manager could be the source of drop files. Second, the only data being transferred were the filenames themselves. This restricted drag and drop technique only whetted people's appetite for the real OLE drag and drop that was to come.

The Clipboard was more flexible when it came to the actual data to be transferred, but it still had its restrictions. The major problem with the Clipboard was the awkwardness of using it. You had to use the cut-and-paste paradigm which, despite its utility, required the use of keyboard (or menu) commands. This was a glitch in the otherwise smooth user interface for which Windows was so touted. Don't get me wrong. The Clipboard was and is an amazing idea. I use it every day, without exception. But when you're moving otherwise autonomous blocks of data, the "point and shoot" beauty of OLE drag and drop wins hands down.

OLE drag and drop merges the wonderful user interface of File Manager drag and drop with the flexibility and utility of the Clipboard. The results of this marriage will astound you. Unfortunately, you will only get a glimpse of the big picture in this chapter. Even the drag and drop subset of OLE 2.0 is too big to see at one time—let alone in a single application.

The Grep Application

Our OLE container application will take on two duties: searching a selected set of files for a particular substring, and providing a means of viewing the files that contain this substring. The first task will involve directory and file manipulation in the searching of files and the building of a result list. The second task can be implemented in any number of ways. Of course, the method we will use embraces OLE and drag and drop.

We will first attack the problem of file selection, storing the selection list, and, of course, the actual searching of the files. Later we will come back to the drag and drop issues.

Before we do anything else, we must establish a structure in which we can store the filenames of the files to be searched. Naturally, we will use one of the MFC collection classes to store the filenames, but which one? Filenames can be thought of as simple strings, so the collection class we use to store the filenames can be one of the ones based on CString. There are only three CString collection classes: CStringArray, CStringList, and CMapStringToString. We will choose the CStringList collection because it's slightly more useful for our purposes.

Note: If you quickly peruse the existing MFC classes, you might note that five (not three) different collection classes involve CString. So why did I say that there were only three? The two collection classes that I snubbed were the map collections CMapStringToPtr and CMapStringToOb. These map classes use CStrings as indices to the real storage objects' void pointers or CObjects, respectively.

Add the following lines to the appropriate public sections of the CWingrepDoc interface:

```
CStringList m_lstFiles;

void SearchFiles(const char* lpszSubString);
```

The first line declares our storage structure. As advertised, we are using a list of CString structures to hold the list of filenames. The second line we added to CWingrep's interface is a function prototype for the routine that will handle the task of searching every file in the list for the specified substring. Searching a file for a substring could be a nice function to have on file in its own right, so we will break out that functionality. The file search code follows:

```
// Filename: filesrch.h

#ifndef __FILESRCH_H__
#define __FILESRCH_H__

BOOL Search (const char* lpszFilename, const char* pSubString,
             WORD wStringLen, LONG& lFoundAt, LONG lStartAt = 0);

// Returns TRUE if pSubString is found in lpszFilename

// File errors cause appropriate CFileExceptions to be thrown!

#endif

// Filename: filesrch.cpp

#include "stdafx.h"

BOOL Search (const char* lpszFilename, const char* pSubString,
             WORD wStringLen, LONG& lFoundAt, LONG lStartAt = 0)
{
    CFile fileToSearch;
    CFileException e;

    if ( !fileToSearch.Open(lpszFilename, CFile::modeRead, &e ) )
    {
        // If Open() fails, pass the problem to the caller
        THROW(&e);
    }

    TRY
    {
        // Seek to the starting position
```

Day 19 Drag and Drop

```
            fileToSearch.Seek(lStartAt, CFile::begin);
    }
    CATCH(CException, e)
    {
            // If lStartAt isn't a legitimate position,
            // our search finds nothing!
            fileToSearch.Close();
            return FALSE;
    }
    END_CATCH

    DWORD dwFilePos = fileToSearch.GetPosition();
    WORD wStringPos = 0;
    BOOL Found = FALSE;
    BYTE b;

    // Start searching the file
    while (fileToSearch.Read(&b, 1) == 1)
    {
            if (b == pSubString[wStringPos])
            {
                    wStringPos++;
                    if (wStringPos == wStringLen)
                            Found = TRUE;
                    continue;
            }
            if (wStringPos > 0)
                    fileToSearch.Seek(dwFilePos, CFile::begin);
            wStringPos = 0;
            dwFilePos++;
    }

    fileToSearch.Close();

    return Found;
}
```

With the actual search function completed, we may implement the `SearchFiles()` function:

```
void CWingrepDoc::SearchFiles(const char* lpszSubString)
{
    CString S;
    WORD wLen = strlen(lpszSubString);
    LONG lPos;
    POSITION posCurrent = m_lstFiles.GetHeadPosition();
    POSITION posOld;

    while (posCurrent != NULL)
    {
            posOld = posCurrent;
            S = m_lstFiles.GetNext(posCurrent);
            TRY
            {
                    // If the search was successful,
                    // leave the selection alone
```

```
                    if ( Search(S, lpszSubString, wLen, lPos) )
                            continue;
            }
            CATCH( CFileException, e )
            {
                    TRACE0(
                    "An exception was thrown during a file search.\n");
            }
            END_CATCH

            // If the search was unsuccessful, or if something
            // went wrong in the Search routine (evidenced by
            // an exception), remove the selection
            m_lstFiles.RemoveAt(posOld);
    }

    UpdateAllViews(NULL);
}
```

This function will search each of the files found in the `m_lstFiles` collection and remove them from the list if the substring is not found. Using this function while changing the search criteria, you can successively cull out more and more files from your list. In this way, you can do a compound search using a very simple search engine. Okay. Now that we have a search function, how do we attach it to the user interface? Using a new menu item, of course! Add the following new menu and new menu item to the `IDR_MAINFRAME` menu resource:

New Menu	Grep
New Menu Item	Grep	Search
ID	`ID_GREP_SEARCH`
Caption	`&Search`
Prompt	Search for the specified substring.

Use ClassWizard to create a handler for this menu item in the `CWingrepDoc` class. This handler is implemented as follows:

```
void CWingrepDoc::OnGrepSearch()
{
    // TODO: Make this search string an attribute of the document
    // and provide support for display and modification of this value
    const char* pString = "Test";

    SearchFiles(pString);
}
```

We have the search code working, but we still have two other file management tasks to take care of before we can move on to OLE drag and drop. Our first priority is to make visible what we have already built. In other words, we need to display the file list. The container's current view is cluttered with a hodgepodge of OLE items—it's a mess. What we need is a second view that is specialized to the needs of our file list. Ask and ye shall receive.

Drag and Drop

Two Views Are Better Than One

Wait a minute! We're working in an SDI application here, so how can we have two views? Well, this isn't as contradictory as it might seem. First, recall what SDI means: single-document interface. That puts no restriction on the number of views! However, as you know from our MDI work, a second view typically requires a second window, and a second window typically requires a second frame. In that situation, we need a frame window that provides for multiple child windows. Therefore, we are back to CMDIFrameWnd and hence MDI. A little trick that you have seen again and again in various Windows applications allows us to manage this seeming impossibility: splitter windows. Yes, I'm talking about the same splitter window found in applications ranging from File Manager to Excel. A splitter window allows you to display two (potentially far-flung) pieces of the same document or even two distinct and different views of the same document. That illusive splitter creature of myth and legend will soon be yours to wield.

Installing a splitter window is much easier than you might expect. Basically, all you have to do is tell your main frame window class that it now has a splitter window view instead of its normal view class. This is accomplished in two steps:

1. Place an object of the class CSplitterWnd in a protected section of the interface of CMainFrame.
2. Override the frame window's virtual function OnCreateClient() to install the view class(es) for each pane in the splitter window.

In most applications, this can be done by adding the following code to the interface of CMainFrame:

```
// mainfrm.h: Interface of the CMainFrame class
//
/////////////////////////////////////////////////////////////////////

class CMainFrame : public CFrameWnd
{
protected:  // Create from serialization only
        CMainFrame();
        DECLARE_DYNCREATE(CMainFrame)

// Attributes
protected:
        CSplitterWnd m_wndSplitter;

// Operations
public:

// Implementation
public:
        virtual ~CMainFrame();
        virtual BOOL OnCreateClient(LPCREATESTRUCT lpcs,
                    CCreateContext* pContext);
```

```
#ifdef _DEBUG
        virtual void AssertValid() const;
        virtual void Dump(CDumpContext& dc) const;
#endif

protected:  // Control bar embedded members
        CStatusBar  m_wndStatusBar;
        CToolBar    m_wndToolBar;

// Generated message map functions
protected:
        //{{AFX_MSG(CMainFrame)
        //}}AFX_MSG
        DECLARE_MESSAGE_MAP()
};

/////////////////////////////////////////////////////////////////////////////
```

Then you must implement OnCreateClient() as shown:

```
BOOL CMainFrame::OnCreateClient(LPCREATESTRUCT lpcs,
             CCreateContext* pContext)
{
        // Create the static splitter window with one row and
        // two columns (two panes side-by-side)
        if (!m_wndSplitter.CreateStatic(this, 1, 2))
        {
             TRACE("CreateStatic() failed.\n");
             return FALSE;
        }

        // Attach a newly created CFilesView to the first pane (0,0)
        if (!m_wndSplitter.CreateView(0, 0,
             RUNTIME_CLASS(CFilesView),
             CSize(200, 0), pContext))
        {
             TRACE("CreateView() failed on first pane.\n");
             return FALSE;
        }

        // Attach a newly created CWingrepView to the second pane (0,1).
        // CWingrepView is the default view of the application.
        if (!m_wndSplitter.CreateView(0, 1,
             pContext->m_pNewViewClass, CSize(0, 0), pContext))
        {
             TRACE("CreateView() failed on second pane.\n");
             return FALSE;
        }

        // Activate the default view. CWingrepView is the second pane.
        SetActiveView((CView*)m_wndSplitter.GetPane(0,1));

        return TRUE;

}
```

Drag and Drop

Note that this implementation creates a two-pane splitter window that holds a different view in each pane. This is slightly more complex than the splitter window implementation shown in the Scribble tutorial (found in your Visual C++ documentation), which uses the same view class for both panes. This implementation has quite a bit of new material in it, so we will go slowly.

The first block of code creates the splitter window through a call to m_wndSplitter.CreateStatic(). The this pointer parameter indicates that the CMainFrame window will be the parent of the splitter window. The next two parameters of CreateStatic() tell the splitter window the pane configuration. Using (1, 2) indicates that we will have one row and two columns. In other words, the parameters (1, 2) say that we want two panes side-by-side. If (2, 1) were passed, a two-pane splitter window would be created with two rows and one column (that is, its panes would be stacked above and below). This technique can be used to slice and dice our main frame window into quite a few little windows, each one of which could represent a unique view of the document. There is a limit, however. You're limited to a maximum of 16 rows and 16 columns. Such restrictions!

The next two blocks of code attach the view class objects to each pane of our splitter window. This is done through a call to m_wndSplitter.CreateView(). This function creates a new view window object based on the RUNTIME_CLASS information of the particular view class we wish to attach. In the first block of code, we explicitly give the function the runtime class information for CFilesView (a new class we will manufacture in a moment). In the second block of code, we use the default runtime class information embedded in the CCreateContext structure. This default view class is simply the view class created for our application by AppWizard: CWingrepView. In both cases, CreateView() needs a little more information to perform the view creation and attachment. It needs to know to which pane the view is to be attached; the first two parameters specify the pane coordinates. It needs to know the size of the view/pane in the frame window; the third parameter specifies the size of the pane. Note that this size information is used only when necessary. The last pane will reside in whatever is left of the window. Hence, the size of our second pane is ignored, so we set it to (0, 0). If we specified three panes side-by-side, the sizes of the first two must be specified, and the third would be determined by what's left in the window. Finally, CreateView() needs to know the miscellaneous information concerning the creation process; this information is held in the CCreateContext structure. The members of this structure are described in Table 19.1.

Table 19.1. The CCreateContext structure.

Member	Description
m_pNewViewClass	A pointer to the default runtime view class.
m_pCurrentDoc	A pointer to the current document object.
m_pNewDocTemplate	A pointer to the default document template.

Member	Description
m_pLastView	A pointer to the last view object on which other view windows can be modeled.
m_pCurrentFrame	A pointer to the current frame window on which other frame windows can be modeled.

You can see from this table that a lot of good information is held in the CCreateContext object. This data can be very handy during the view creation process. Is it any wonder that CreateView() would want it?

Now let's get back to an issue that we brushed past a few paragraphs ago. What is CFilesView? The simple answer to this question is that it is the view in the first pane of our splitter window. But we already knew that from our earlier discussion. The real answer to this question must place the class in the perspective of our application. This new view class will display a list of filenames that represent the results of a substring search over a set of files in a directory or directories. In UNIX, this type of search is accomplished through the use of the UNIX tool *grep*—hence the name of our application, "Wingrep."

Without further ado, let's create CFilesView. Bring up ClassWizard and click on the Add Class... button. In the Add Class dialog, create this new class with the following data:

Class Name	CFilesView
Class Type	CScrollView
Header File	FILESVW.H
Implementation File	FILESVW.CPP

Once ClassWizard puts the finishing touches on CFilesView, you must include this new class in the implementation file of CMainFrame:

```
#include "filesvw.h"
```

We are now ready to make the connection between the document file list and our new view. This connection is made through CFilesView::OnDraw():

```
void CFilesView::OnDraw(CDC* pDC)
{
    CWingrepDoc* pDoc = (CWingrepDoc*)GetDocument();
    POSITION pos = pDoc->m_lstFiles.GetHeadPosition();

    TEXTMETRIC tm;
    pDC->GetTextMetrics(&tm);
    int nCharHeight = tm.tmHeight + tm.tmExternalLeading;
    int nCharWidth = tm.tmAveCharWidth;
    int x = nCharWidth*LEFT_MARGIN;
    int y = nCharHeight*TOP_MARGIN;
```

Day 19: Drag and Drop

```
        if (pos == NULL)
                pDC->TextOut(x, y, "No files are selected.");

        while (pos != NULL)
        {
                pDC->TextOut(x, y, pDoc->m_lstFiles.GetNext(pos));
                y += nCharHeight;
        }
}
```

Note that we have defined the two constants TOP_MARGIN and LEFT_MARGIN in the interface of CFilesView. The actual values of these constants are immaterial, but if you really must know, we used the values 2 and 1, respectively.

That done, we're ready for a compile, link, run session. You should see a brand-new, fully-functional splitter window application. Try moving the splitter bar. It works! Isn't that cool? Of course, at the moment all we see in the left pane is No files are selected, but that's because no files are in our list. A way around this dilemma is to initialize the file list to arbitrary values. The following modifications to the document's constructor can make this happen:

```
CWingrepDoc::CWingrepDoc()
{
        // For most containers, using compound files is a good idea
        EnableCompoundFile();

        // Temporarily initialize the m_lstFiles collection
        // with a bunch of filenames
        CString S = "C:\\Test.txt";
        m_lstFiles.AddHead(S);
        S = "C:\\Test2.txt";
        m_lstFiles.AddHead(S);
        S = "C:\\Test3.txt";
        m_lstFiles.AddHead(S);
        S = "C:\\Test4.txt";
        m_lstFiles.AddHead(S);
}
```

This is kind of a cheesy way to fill the files list. If we learned anything over the last few chapters, we found out that hard-coded values aren't the best idea. There must be a better way. Hey, wouldn't it be great if we could just pop open File Manager and drag some files over and drop them into place? It sure would, so that's what we'll do.

File Manager Drag and Drop

Earlier in this chapter I neglected to mention one nice feature of File Manager drag and drop—it's very simple to implement a File Manager drop target.

The first thing you must do is make the CFilesView window a drop target for File Manager files. This is accomplished through the CWnd function DragAcceptFiles(). DragAcceptFiles()

registers the window as an official destination of File Manager files. Our `CFilesView` class can be so enhanced by the following modification of its `OnInitialUpdate()` function:

```
void CFilesView::OnInitialUpdate()
{
        // Make this window into a drop target for File Manager files
        DragAcceptFiles(TRUE);

        CScrollView::OnInitialUpdate();

        CSize sizeTotal;
        // TODO: Calculate the total size of this view
        sizeTotal.cx = sizeTotal.cy = 100;
        SetScrollSizes(MM_TEXT, sizeTotal);
}
```

The view will now accept the `WM_DROPFILES` message, but that's just half of the battle! We still have to process this new message. In order to process this message intelligently, we have to become familiar with a couple of new functions (Windows API calls, actually). The best place to see these functions in action is in the default `WM_DROPFILES` handler found in the implementation of `CWnd`. This function is as follows:

```
void CFrameWnd::OnDropFiles(HDROP hDropInfo)
{
        SetActiveWindow();   // Activate us first!
        UINT nFiles = ::DragQueryFile(hDropInfo, -1, NULL, 0);

        for (UINT iFile = 0; iFile < nFiles; iFile++)
        {
                char szFileName[_MAX_PATH];
                ::DragQueryFile(hDropInfo, iFile, szFileName, _MAX_PATH);
                AfxGetApp()->OpenDocumentFile(szFileName);
        }
        ::DragFinish(hDropInfo);
}
```

This function first activates its window. It then determines exactly how many files are being dropped by using the Windows API function `DragQueryFile()`. This new function allows the programmer to obtain information about the list of files being passed in the drag/drop. Using this information, the function can loop through the list, visiting each file. This function calls the `OpenDocumentFile()` function, which creates a new view and loads it with the specified file's data via the serialization paradigm. The function is completed through a call to the other new API function, `DragFinish()`. This function tells Windows that we don't need the drag/drop information anymore, so it can clean up the associated memory. The four new functions that we use in File Manager drag and drop are summarized in Table 19.2.

Drag and Drop

Table 19.2. File Manager drag and drop support functions.

Function	Description
`DragAcceptFiles`	A `CWnd` member function that registers that window as a File Manager drop target. `bAccept` is a Boolean value that turns the drop target on or off.
`::DragQueryFile`	Retrieves information about the list of files being dragged. `hDrop` is a handle to the block of memory containing the data. `iFile` is an index to the list of files. `lpszFile` is a pointer to the buffer that is to hold the filename. `cb` is the size of the buffer intended to contain the filename.
`::DragQueryPoint`	Retrieves the point where the files were dropped. `hDrop` is a handle to the block of memory containing the data. `lppt` is a pointer to the `POINT` structure in question.
`::DragFinish`	Notifies Windows that the drag/drop is over. This allows Windows to clean up the memory associated with the data. `hDrop` is a handle to the block of memory containing the data.

Use ClassWizard to create a `WM_DROPFILES` handler in `CFilesView`. Using `CWnd::OnDropFiles()` as a template, we will implement `CFilesView::OnDropFiles()` as follows:

```
void CFilesView::OnDropFiles(HDROP hDropInfo)
{
        CWingrepDoc* pDoc = (CWingrepDoc*)GetDocument();
        ASSERT_VALID(pDoc);

        // Activate this view window
        SetActiveWindow();

        // Determine how many files are being dragged
        UINT nFiles = ::DragQueryFile(hDropInfo, -1, NULL, 0);

        char strFilename[_MAX_PATH];
        CString S;
        for (UINT i = 0; i < nFiles; i++)
        {
                ::DragQueryFile(hDropInfo, i, strFilename, _MAX_PATH);
                S = strFilename;
                pDoc->m_lstFiles.AddTail(S);

                // TODO: Check for duplicate entries in the list.
                // There is no need to search a file more than once!
        }
```

```
        // Tell Windows to clean up after the
        // File Manager drag/drop event
        ::DragFinish(hDropInfo);

        // Tell the view(s) to refresh
        pDoc->UpdateAllViews(NULL);

        // Don't call the base class's OnDropFiles. We don't
        // want these files "Opened" in this application. We
        // just want the filenames themselves.
}
```

You will note that we don't call CWnd's OnDropFiles, nor do we call the CWingrepApp function OnOpenDocument(). We don't want to open the files that were dropped on the view! We just want the filenames themselves. The rest of the function is very similar to CWnd's function and is fully commented in any case.

Well, that's it for File Manager drag and drop. It's very easy to implement, but it does have those pesky limitations. For my next trick, I will show you how OLE 2.0 drag and drop can overcome these limitations. Unfortunately, this comes at the expense of an easy implementation. There is no free lunch!

OLE Drag and Drop

The File Manager technique might be simple, but it has the unfortunate consequence of not supporting the source side of the equation. In other words, there is no predefined way of becoming a source for File Manager file data objects. This limitation was just the way it was before the advent of OLE; you just had to accept it as a fact of Windows life. With the advent of OLE 2.0, we have the opportunity to make our applications much more general sources than File Manager ever hoped to be. Through OLE 2.0, we can transmit and receive all sorts of data. Even OLE server objects themselves may be passed around. Our current sights are somewhat lower. All we want to be able to do is provide a filename to another application in a meaningful manner. To accomplish this feat, we will utilize the OLE 2.0 drag and drop mechanism.

In order to play ball, we need two participants: one to throw and one to catch. Drag and drop is no different. It takes one object to supply the data to be dragged and another object to accept the dropped data. Because of this duality, we must alter both container and server in order to fully implement the specialized drag and drop we have been leading up to.

The MFC provides a few classes that aid us in our drag and drop endeavors. These classes are summarized in Table 19.3.

Day 19: Drag and Drop

Table 19.3. MFC data transfer support classes.

Class	Description
COleDataObject	A destination actor in OLE data transfer associated with the Clipboard or drag and drop.
COleDataSource	A source actor in OLE data transfer associated with the Clipboard or drag and drop.
COleDropTarget	Represents the destination window of a drag and drop operation. It determines whether a drop is acceptable.
COleDropSource	Represents the object of a drag and drop operation. It controls the visual feedback associated with potential drops.

In addition to these MFC classes, a few OLE structures provide a great deal of help in OLE data transfer. These structures are described in the following paragraphs.

The FORMATETC structure (which stands for "format, etc.") is an expansion of the normal Windows Clipboard format used in the transfer of data. Its definition follows:

```
typedef struct FARSTRUCT tagFORMATETC
{
        CLIPFORMAT              cfFormat;
        DVTARGETDEVICE FAR*     ptd;
        DWORD                   dwAspect;
        LONG                                    lindex;
        DWORD                   tymed;
} FORMATETC, FAR* LPFORMATETC;
```

The first member of this structure, cfFormat, is the Clipboard format of the data. However, it is a slightly extended version of the normal Windows Clipboard format. CLIPFORMAT variables can take on any of the following value types:

The Normal Windows Clipboard Formats

CF_BITMAP	CF_DIB
CF_DIF	CF_DSPBITMAP
CF_DSPMETAFILEPICT	CF_DSPTEXT
CF_METAFILEPICT	CF_OEMTEXT
CF_OWNERDISPLAY	CF_PALETTE
CF_PENDATA	CF_RIFF
CF_SYLK	CF_TEXT
CF_TIFF	CF_WAVE

Private, application-defined (programmer-defined) custom formats are particular to the defining application and other applications designed for compatibility. The following are the OLE Clipboard formats designed for OLE object transfer:

```
CF_EMBEDSOURCE          CF_LINKSOURCE
CF_CUSTOMLINKSOURCE     CF_EMBEDDEDOBJECT
CF_OBJECTDESCRIPTOR     CF_LINKSOURCEDESCRIPTOR
```

The second member attribute of FORMATETC, ptd, is a pointer to a structure holding information about the device for which the object was designed. If the nature of the actual device is immaterial to the object's display, you may indicate this by setting ptd to NULL.

The aspect of the object is contained in the third member attribute. Object aspects are enumerated in DVASPECT and can take on the values listed in Table 19.4.

Table 19.4. DVASPECT enumerated values.

Value	Description
DVASPECT_CONTENT	The normal, full view of the object. The typical view seen when the object is embedded and inactive.
DVASPECT_THUMBNAIL	A thumbnail sketch of the object. The typical view seen in a browsing tool.
DVASPECT_ICON	The iconized representation of the object.
DVASPECT_DOCPRINT	The printed-document view. The typical view you would see in a print preview screen.

Note: These values are mutually exclusive; you can't have an object with two or more of these aspects "on" at the same time.

In our application we will use only the DVASPECT_CONTENT aspect—the normal full view.

The next attribute of FORMATETC, lindex, is rather useless. It is keyed to the DVASPECT attribute. If dwAspect is content or docprint, lindex must be set to –1. Otherwise, lindex is ignored. So for all intents and purposes, simply setting lindex to –1 is a good general policy. Since we're only interested in the DVASPECT_CONTENT value, we have to use –1 for lindex anyway.

The last attribute of FORMATETC, TYMED, indicates the storage media type (TYMED stands for "type medium"). Using this member, you may communicate exactly what storage medium the object's data is being held in. Table 19.5 lists the potential values for TYMED.

Drag and Drop

Table 19.5. `TYMED` values.

Value	Description
TYMED_HGLOBAL	The data being passed is an HGLOBAL section of memory.
TYMED_FILE	The data being passed is a disk file.
TYMED_ISTREAM	The data is being passed through the OLE IStream interface.
TYMED_ISTORAGE	The data is being passed through the OLE IStorage interface.
TYMED_GDI	The data being passed is a GDI object.
TYMED_MFPICT	The data being passed is a metafile.
TYMED_NULL	No data is being passed.

Therefore, `FORMATETC` allows the passage of information concerning the format of passed data. However, the data itself also needs to be passed.

The storage medium structure, `STGMEDIUM`, is a standard means of transferring data within and between applications (typically, but not necessarily, OLE applications). The structure is defined as follows:

```
typedef struct tagSTGMEDIUM
{
        DWORD           tymed;

        union
        {
                HANDLE          hGlobal;
                LPSTR           lpszFileName;
                LPSTREAM            pstm;
                LPSTORAGE           pstg;
        };

        LPUNKNOWN       pUnkForRelease;

} STGMEDIUM;
```

This is a very interesting and advanced structure. The first member of the structure, `tymed`, indicates the type of medium on which the data is being sent. The second member of the structure is one of the four variables specified in the union. Yes, only one of these mutually exclusive variables. After all, if you pass the data via a file, what use do you have for an `hGlobal` handle? The recipient of an object of this structure will determine which one of the variables to use from the `tymed` attribute. Finally, the third and last member of the structure, `pUnkForRelease`, provides a means of media cleanup. If `pUnkForRelease` is `NULL`, the recipient owns the medium and must take responsibility for its memory management (that is, freeing its memory). If, on the other hand, `pUnkForRelease` is not `NULL`, the recipient of the medium will call the `pUnkForRelease->Release()` function, in which the caller will provide memory management for the medium. As I stated, this structure is interesting and uses some advanced techniques that you might not have seen until now. Make sure you understand the subtleties of this structure before moving on.

To sum up: An object of STGMEDIUM will have three member attributes. The first indicates the type of medium. The second points to an object of the medium of data storage. The third provides a callback mechanism for media memory management.

We will use this structure to transfer file information between our Wingrep application and Hexpad.

Bringing Wingrep and Hexpad Together

Why are we bringing Wingrep and Hexpad together? The dream application we're trying to build will search a bunch of files and then allow you to drag one of the searched files over to a Hexpad server, where it will be opened and displayed in either ASCII or hex.

Our first step in implementing OLE 2.0 drag and drop for the data transfer we have in mind is to get Wingrep ready to deliver some data. Of course, the data we will have Wingrep send will be just a filename—shades of File Manager drag and drop. Drag and drop almost always starts in an OnLButtonDown() function. In other words, drag and drop is initiated when the user clicks and drags a data object from one place to another. But before we start capturing mouse clicks, let's create a helper function that will translate mouse click positions into the appropriate filename shown in the display. This function, shown next, is analogous to the GetItemContaining() function we use in CWingrep's other view.

```
BOOL CFilesView::HitTestFiles (CPoint point, CString& strHit)
{
        CWingrepDoc* pDoc = (CWingrepDoc*)GetDocument();
        ASSERT_VALID(pDoc);

        // Construct and initialize a device context based on the view
        CClientDC dc(this);
        OnPrepareDC(&dc);

        // Calculate the character extents
        TEXTMETRIC tm;
        dc.GetTextMetrics(&tm);
        int nCharHeight = tm.tmHeight + tm.tmExternalLeading;
        int nCharWidth = tm.tmAveCharWidth;

        int index;
        // Convert device coordinates (point) into
        // character coordinates
        index = point.y/nCharHeight - TOP_MARGIN;

        if ( index < 0 )
                return FALSE;
```

Day 19: Drag and Drop

```
    // Translate the character index into a list position
    POSITION pos = pDoc->m_lstFiles.FindIndex(index);

    if (pos == NULL)
            return FALSE;

    // Return the filename that was hit via the strHit variable
    strHit = pDoc->m_lstFiles.GetAt(pos);

    return TRUE;
}
```

The only really tricky portion of this function is the device/character translation code. Remember that the point variable is in device units, so when we divide the y component of the position by the character height (also in device units), we get a resultant value in terms of character units. Then we have to shift the whole mess by the appropriate margin value. This will line our index value up with the list index. We exploit this fact in the remainder of the function.

One last item needs to be added to the CFilesView interface so that our OnLButtonDown() function will make sense. We must add the COleDataSource object to CFilesView's attributes. This object will be responsible for holding and transferring the data between this class and another class (or application, for that matter).

```
// Attributes
protected:
    COleDataSource m_dataSource;
```

Now we can have ClassWizard create a left button mouse click handler in CFilesView. Its implementation follows:

```
void CFilesView::OnLButtonDown(UINT nFlags, CPoint point)
{
    CWingrepDoc* pDoc = (CWingrepDoc*)GetDocument();
    ASSERT_VALID(pDoc);

    // Get the filename that was clicked on. If no
    // filename was clicked on, there is nothing to do!
    CString strFilename;
    if (!HitTestFiles(point, strFilename))
            return;

    int nLen = strFilename.GetLength() + 1;

    // Create a storage structure and fill it
    // with data (a filename)
    STGMEDIUM stgMedium;
    stgMedium.tymed = TYMED_HGLOBAL;
    stgMedium.hGlobal = GlobalAlloc(GHND, nLen);
    BYTE FAR* lpText = (BYTE FAR*)
                    GlobalLock(stgMedium.hGlobal);
    if (lpText == NULL)
            TRACE0("OnLButtonDown : GlobalLock failed.\n");
    _fmemcpy(lpText, (const char*)strFilename, nLen);
    TRACE1("Global Text is %Fs.\n", (char FAR*)lpText);
    GlobalUnlock(stgMedium.hGlobal);
```

```
            stgMedium.pUnkForRelease = NULL;

            // Transfer the storage structure into the
            // data source's cache
            m_dataSource.CacheData(CF_TEXT, &stgMedium,
                        &pDoc->m_fetcTransferProtocol);

            /*
            // Alternative method of sending a global memory block
            HGLOBAL hgData;
            hgData = GlobalAlloc(GHND, nLen);
            char FAR* lpText = (char FAR*)GlobalLock(hgData);
            _fmemcpy(lpText, (const char*)strFilename, nLen);
            TRACE1("Global Text is %Fs.\n", (char FAR*)lpText);
            GlobalUnlock(hgData);
            DWORD dwSize = GlobalSize(hgData);
            TRACE1("Size of global memory block = %ld.\n",dwSize);
            m_dataSource.CacheGlobalData(CF_TEXT, hgData,
                        &pDoc->m_fetcTransferProtocol);
            */

            if ( m_dataSource.DoDragDrop(DROPEFFECT_COPY)
                        == DROPEFFECT_NONE )
            {
                    TRACE0("DoDragDrop was incomplete.\n");
                    m_dataSource.Empty();
            }
            else
            {
                    TRACE0("DoDragDrop completed a transfer.\n");
            }

}
```

This function can be summarized as follows:

- Get the filename hit by the mouse click. If no filename was hit, abort the function.
- Using the filename as well as what we know about storage structures, fill a STGMEDIUM object with the data to be transferred.
- After the storage structure is filled, give it to the data source object, which stores it internally to itself.
- Call the DoDragDrop() function, which takes control much as the CRectTracker::Track() function did.

One other item might puzzle you. The reference to pDoc->m_fetcTransferProtocol is right out of the blue. This document attribute is defined as

FORMATETC m_fetcTransferProtocol;

and is initialized in the modified CWingrepDoc constructor:

```
CWingrepDoc::CWingrepDoc()
{
        // For most containers, using compound files is a good idea
```

Day 19: Drag and Drop

```
        EnableCompoundFile();

        // Initialize the transfer protocol between
        // the two kinds of windows used in the app
        m_fetcTransferProtocol.cfFormat = CF_TEXT;
        m_fetcTransferProtocol.ptd = NULL;
        m_fetcTransferProtocol.dwAspect = DVASPECT_CONTENT;
        m_fetcTransferProtocol.lindex = -1;
        m_fetcTransferProtocol.tymed = TYMED_HGLOBAL;

        // Temporarily initialize the m_lstFiles collection
        // with a bunch of filenames
        CString S = "C:\\Test.txt";
        m_lstFiles.AddHead(S);
        S = "C:\\Test2.txt";
        m_lstFiles.AddHead(S);
        S = "C:\\Test3.txt";
        m_lstFiles.AddHead(S);
        S = "C:\\Test4.txt";
        m_lstFiles.AddHead(S);
}
```

This is all there is to do on the drop source side of the fence. Building a drop target is a bit more involved. Before we modify Hexpad, let's try something a little easier—the other Wingrep view class. We have a splitter window. One pane can be an OLE drag and drop source, while the other is an OLE drag and drop target! Actually, each pane could behave as both a source and a target, but that gets a little complicated. Let's stick to the original plan. CFilesView already exports a drop source object, so all we have to do is make the modifications to CWingrepView that will allow it to accept dropped objects.

Just as in File Manager drag and drop, the first thing we must do is register the class as an OLE drag and drop target. This is similar to the File Manager drag and drop registration, but it's different. If you want a window to accept both types of drag and drop objects, you must make both registrations. In order to register a window for OLE drag and drop, you must make the following two additions to CWingrepView. Add the following line of code to CWingrepView's interface:

```
COleDropTarget m_dropTarget;
```

and add the following function to CWingrepView (via ClassWizard):

```
int CWingrepView::OnCreate(LPCREATESTRUCT lpCreateStruct)
{
        if (CView::OnCreate(lpCreateStruct) == -1)
                return -1;

        m_dropTarget.Register(this);

        return 0;
}
```

You can think of the COleDropTarget object as the catcher and the COleDropSource object found in CFileView as the pitcher. Actually, the COleDropSource object is more analogous to the ball than to the pitcher, but the pitcher/catcher metaphor is much better. What can you do?

Our CWingrepView object can now accept dropped OLE 2.0 data objects—or at least it could if we would get on the ball and override the view functions that notify our class of drag and drop events. The overrides for CWingrepView are provided as follows. Note that ClassWizard won't help you with these functions. You have to type in everything yourself, including the prototypes in the interface.

```
DROPEFFECT CWingrepView::OnDragEnter
            (COleDataObject* pDataObject, DWORD dwKeyState, CPoint point)
{
    TRACE0("OnDragEnter called!\n");
    return OnDragOver(pDataObject, dwKeyState, point);
}

void CWingrepView::OnDragLeave()
{
    TRACE0("OnDragLeave called!\n");
}

DROPEFFECT CWingrepView::OnDragOver
            (COleDataObject* pDataObject, DWORD dwKeyState, CPoint point)
{
    CWingrepDoc* pDoc = GetDocument();
    CLIPFORMAT clipFormat = pDoc->m_fetcTransferProtocol.cfFormat;
    DROPEFFECT de = DROPEFFECT_NONE;

    // Don't put trace call here since it will be called
    // continuously while the object is over the window
    //TRACE0("OnDragOver called!\n");

    if ( GetItemContaining(point) == NULL )
        return de;

    if ( pDataObject->IsDataAvailable(clipFormat,
                &pDoc->m_fetcTransferProtocol) )
    {
        TRACE0("Dropped format is acceptable!\n");
        de = DROPEFFECT_COPY;
    }

    return de;
}

BOOL CWingrepView::OnDrop(COleDataObject* pDataObject,
            DROPEFFECT dropEffect, CPoint point)
{
    TRACE0("OnDrop called!\n");

    CWingrepDoc* pDoc = GetDocument();
    CLIPFORMAT clipFormat = pDoc->m_fetcTransferProtocol.cfFormat;
```

Drag and Drop

```
        HGLOBAL hgData;
        char FAR* lpszData;
        CString strFileName;

        if ( pDataObject->IsDataAvailable(clipFormat,
                   &pDoc->m_fetcTransferProtocol) )
        {
             // Dropped format is acceptable!
             hgData = pDataObject->GetGlobalData(clipFormat,
                           &pDoc->m_fetcTransferProtocol);
             if (hgData == NULL)
             {
                   TRACE0("GetGlobalData() failed!\n");
                   return FALSE;
             }
             lpszData = (char FAR*)GlobalLock(hgData);
             if (lpszData == NULL)
             {
                   TRACE0("GlobalLock() failed!\n");
                   return FALSE;
             }

             TRACE1("The filename transferred is : %Fs.\n", lpszData);
             GlobalUnlock(hgData);

             return TRUE;
        }

        return FALSE;
}
```

The best way to understand how these functions interrelate is to run the application and watch the debug window while you're dragging and dropping files from the first pane to the second pane. You'll see that `OnDragEnter()` is called when the dragged object enters the view. `OnDragOver()` is called continuously while the object is being dragged over the view. `OnDragLeave()` is called whenever the object is dragged outside the view. And, surprisingly enough, `OnDrop()` is called when an object is dropped onto the view. They really are just that simple. All you have to do is put your application-specific code into the appropriate function, and you're home.

I will leave the final implementation of the Wingrep/Hexpad interaction as an exercise for you. But to get you thinking in the right vein, consider what is happening when you drag an object over an active client item versus over an inactive client item. This will lead you to proper steps on the client side. The server side is much easier. All you have to do is make Hexpad into a drop target and then load the file associated with the dropped filename.

It's important to realize that we chose one path through the forest of OLE. This is by far not the only route available. OLE is a huge technology. I have tried to present some topics that aren't as widely covered in other sources. However, these other sources (such as the OLE additions to Scribble and the sample applications that came with Visual C++) are of inestimable worth to you in your quest to understand OLE. Travel down as many paths through OLE as you can to gain a better feel for its terrain. It's a powerful technology that will be very helpful to understand in the near future.

Summary

In this chapter we looked at the two generally accepted forms of drag and drop: File Manager and OLE 2.0. We found that despite their similarity, a single application can benefit by employing both techniques. Certainly the File Manager drag and drop is the simpler of the two. Enabling an application with the File Manager variety of drag and drop is much easier than the more flexible OLE 2.0 variety.

In preparing for the implementation of OLE 2.0 drag and drop, we studied many different data transfer structures. Oddly enough, they were of considerable help in dragging and dropping.

Q&A

Q Why did we even discuss File Manager drag and drop? The OLE 2.0 way is much more flexible.

A Yes, it's true that OLE 2.0 drag and drop is much more flexible than its File Manager equivalent. However, the ease of implementation shouldn't be discounted. Besides, users are used to grabbing things from File Manager and dropping them on applications. Not supporting that standard would be unkind to your users.

Q I noticed that we do a `GlobalAlloc()` to allocate memory for parts of our `STGMEDIUM` object, yet we call `GlobalFree()` only under certain conditions. Aren't we ultimately responsible for the memory cleanup of this object?

A Sometimes. If the OLE drag and drop transfer is successful, the object belongs to the "dropee," and so it is responsible for memory cleanup. If the transfer is unsuccessful, the responsibility falls back on us.

Workshop

Quiz

1. How can you have two or more windows open at the same time in an SDI application?
2. What kind of splitter window would be created by the call `m_wndSplitter.CreateStatic(this, 2, 2)`?
3. What's the difference between File Manager drag and drop and OLE 2.0 drag and drop?
4. What's the difference in usage between `FORMATETC` and `STGMEDIUM`?

Drag and Drop

Exercises

1. Remove the hard-coded "Test" search string and add support for a user-defined and user-changeable search string.
2. Add scrolling support for the `CFilesView` class. Recall that we have already derived this class from `CScrollView`, so implementing the remainder of the scroll support is relatively easy.
3. Now that you have seen how one of our container views was made into a drop target for File Manager files, repeat the procedure for Hexpad.
4. Finish the application by making Hexpad a drop target. Have it take the filename proffered and load it automatically.

WEEK 3

Help Me

Help Me

Have you ever wondered who writes the lousy online help included with the product you just purchased? I have. It seems that either the help is organized incorrectly, or the content itself is poor, too brief, incomplete, or done with no pizzazz. This chapter shows you how to organize your help, construct the help file, and hook it into your C++ application using the MFC. Remember that your online help is the first line of defense between the user and your tech support number. And as a bonus, wouldn't it be nice to hear from your user base that your help was both useful and well done?

Introducing Help

I'm sure you've used the Windows help engine at least once. Windows help (WINHELP.EXE) has come a long way in giving us a standard interface to present help to the user. One use of help that is becoming more common is to use Windows help files to disseminate information completely independent of any application. In this chapter we will explore planning your help system, constructing topic files, graphics integration, macros, and compiling and testing your help files. After reading this chapter you will be able to construct your own help files for use in your MFC application or as a stand-alone help system.

Features of Help

Many features of help are a direct result of its being a Windows application. These include the ability to use multiple fonts, font sizes, and colors in your help screens. Other features include the ability to include graphics, especially bitmaps (BMPs) with multiple resolutions, and Windows metafiles (WMFs). We will deal with graphics later in this chapter. Macros are also accessible from the Windows help engine. These macros allow you to extend the functionality of your help system and automate tasks.

Keyword searches and hypergraphics that include multiple hotspots are some of the other features that are available to you as a developer. All of these features are available to you using only the help compiler and related applications provided with it.

Tools and Source Files

Several tools are provided that aid you in developing professional-quality help. They include the following:

- [ ] The Help Compiler (HC31.EXE). This application compiles your topic and graphics files into the finished Windows help file that can be used by WINHELP.EXE.
- [ ] The Hotspot Editor (SHED.EXE). SHED opens a bitmap or Windows metafile and allows you to define hotspots within that graphic. These hotspots are nothing more than areas on the graphic that get linked to a particular topic in your help file when the user clicks on them.

- The Multiple-Resolution Bitmap Compiler (MRBC.EXE). This program allows you to compile the same bitmap in several different resolutions into one file. This assists us greatly when showing a bitmap to the user, regardless of the resolution of the user's screen.

In addition to the tools just mentioned, you need to create and feed a number of source files to the help compiler. They result in the final product (MYHELP.HLP). These source files are listed in Table 20.1. Some are optional.

Table 20.1. The different files used in creating a Windows help file.

Source File	Extension	Description
Project	.HPJ	This file is central to all help projects. It holds a list of all graphics and text files necessary for creating the help file. It also retains the geometry (size and position) of all windows in the project. The help compiler uses this file in a way very similar to the MAKE file in C. There can be only one .HPJ file per project.
Topic	.RTF	This file of files (there can be several per project) holds the textual information contained in the help file. It also contains the codes necessary to link the topics, as well as the references to the graphics. These text files must be in RTF (rich text format) in order for the help compiler to be able to use them.
Bitmap	.BMP	These optional files contain a single graphical image in the Windows bitmap format. The graphics can be included directly in the .RTF file itself, or just referenced there. Programs such as Paintbrush can be used to create these files. An example is a screen capture used in a Windows help file.
Metafile	.WMF	These optional files contain a single graphical image in the Windows metafile format. The graphics can be included directly in the .RTF file itself, or just referenced there. Metafiles are an efficient means of storing graphical data and are much smaller than a comparable bitmap image.

continues

Help Me

Table 20.1. continued

Source File	Extension	Description
Hypergraphic	.SHG	This unique format contains a single bitmap or Windows metafile. This file has been altered to provide hotspots as generated by the Hotspot Editor (SHED.EXE).
Multiple-Resolution Bitmap	.MRB	To ensure that your help file graphics are consistent regardless of the user's screen resolution, this file contains several versions of the same bitmap at different resolutions. These files are generated by MRBC.EXE and are optional.

All the files listed here are combined to provide the finished product. Figure 20.1 illustrates the process of combining the files into that product.

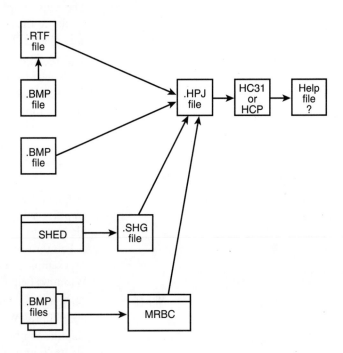

Figure 20.1.
The compilation process.

The Process

Creating the help file is a straightforward process. Here are the steps involved:

1. Gather the information you wish to relay to the user in the help file.
2. Determine the layout of the help system.
3. Construct the topic files from the information you have gathered.
4. Add additional control codes to the topic files.
5. (Optional) Create any graphics (screen shots and so on) that might be necessary. This also could include the creation of hotspot graphics (SHED).
6. (Optional) Create any macros.
7. Create the project (.HPJ) file that encompasses all the other files you have created to this point.
8. Test (and possibly debug) the help system.
9. Provide the hooks for the help in your final application.

Sounds easy, huh? Well, it is. The first time I created help for a Windows application, I had heard that the help system was hard to use and learn. It really isn't. A little later in this chapter I will talk about tools that can help you with the tasks just mentioned.

A User's Perspective

How does the user see help? You've been a user, and isn't it always about the same? Figure 20.2 shows a help screen you might encounter as a typical end user.

Figure 20.2.
Help from a user's perspective.

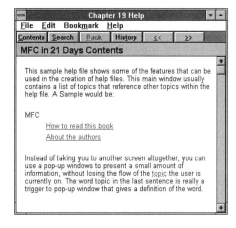

Day 20

Help Me

Your help might include a set of browse buttons, the ability to create bookmarks in help, and so on. You have at your disposal all the features the developer has enabled, including hotspots that take you to other topics, as well as pop-up windows showing definitions of terms or giving quick tips.

The user also might encounter secondary windows. A secondary window allows the developer to launch a completely new window to provide a new topic without forcing the user to drop the current one. This could be especially effective in presenting reference material (such as a glossary of terms) while letting the user have access to the original text she is reading.

A Developer's Perspective

What about a developer's view of help? It's less than glamorous. The heart of the help system is the .RTF file. This file looks like a very poorly constructed word processing file. It is in fact a carefully orchestrated set of command codes, interlaced with the text you wish to convey to the user. Figure 20.3 shows help from a developer's viewpoint.

Figure 20.3.
Help from a developer's perspective.

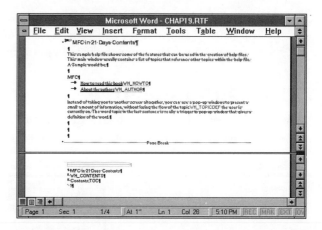

You can see text that is underlined and highlighted, as well as text that doesn't appear in the final product. These are the control codes I spoke of earlier. I will demonstrate some in a moment.

Planning is Everything

The most important step in developing your help system is the planning phase. If you don't spend the time to lay out how your help will look to the user, the end result might be reminiscent of the poor help systems you have seen in a number of products. Let's look at several key points you should consider when planning your help system.

Who Are You Helping?

First, who are you trying to help? You must understand your enemy before you can defeat him. You must also understand your user before you can help him. Consider these questions:

1. What is your user's expertise level? Novice? Pro?
2. What is your help intended to do? Should it be strictly an online reference manual, or a tutorial with extensive explanations and examples? If your users are pros, they will probably want only a quick reference, whereas a novice would want a tutorial with definitions of terms and examples of concepts.

If you can accurately assess your application's user base, you will serve your users better.

Batteries Not Included

Some help systems contain all the information you need except the one topic or function you need three times a day! It's like getting that new Sony Discman and forgetting to buy batteries!

Besides the core set of functions that should exist (Contents, Search, and About), you can also include features such as a complete alphabetical index, glossary, and maybe even a "How to Use Help" screen included in some of the better products. You should try to do a couple of things:

1. Keep the topic screens concise. There's nothing worse than a 10-page topic.
2. List the topics in the Contents screen in some sort of order—functional, reference, or by category of use.
3. Try to keep the entries in a list to seven, plus or minus two. Studies have shown that the human brain handles items best when dealing with five to nine items. Less is not enough information, and more is too much to take in at one time.
4. Try not to nest the topic too many levels into the "tree." If you make the user look too hard, he might give up.

These are just some things I have learned or been told during my stint as a software engineer.

The Forest for the Trees: Structuring Your Help

It's important to structure your help in such a way that the user will easily be able to navigate it by using the search facility or just the browse buttons. Structuring it in a "tree" fashion seems to provide the greatest ease of use. See Figure 20.4.

After arranging your topics, you can use browse sequence numbers that control the order in which the topics are displayed when the user clicks on the browse buttons. These browse sequence numbers allow you to redirect a user to your planned help chain if he wanders off the beaten path.

Help Me

Figure 20.4.
The help hierarchy.

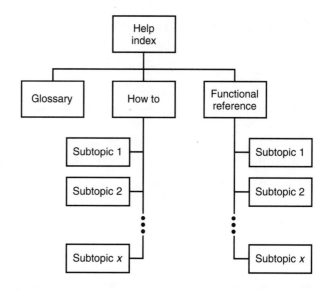

Be Sensitive

A big boon in many of today's applications is having context-sensitive help. When you're stuck at a particular data entry field, it's nice to press F1 and get help on that particular field as opposed to the whole form or application. Context-sensitive help relieves users from having to use the search engine to acquire the information they need to continue with the task at hand.

Near the end of this chapter I will show you how to tie your help file into your application using this context-sensitive method. It's not difficult (with planning), and it can improve the quality of your application dramatically.

Structural Engineering

As I stated earlier, you can put the text for your help project into one or more .RTF files. You might wonder why you should use more than one. Depending on the size of your project and the number of people working on it, you might want to divide the work up and assign the topics to the developers of that portion of the code.

This might not be necessary, but it allows for a great deal of flexibility. Remember that the help compiler takes all the topics from all the files and compiles them together. This means that you must make sure that all the links between topics (which are also between files) are there and are correct.

The total number of topics will be dictated by your application's features. The more complex your application, the more topics you will probably need. The larger the number of topics, the more helpful it will become to have more than one .RTF file. Figure 20.5 shows the topic file layout for a typical help file.

Figure 20.5.
The help topic file structure.

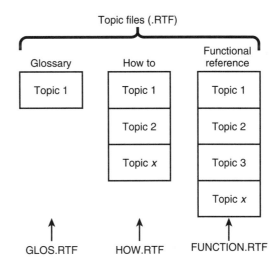

The topic should be one to two pages in length (Microsoft's recommendation), which is the screen width by 20 to 40 lines long. Try to avoid using jumps in the middle of a paragraph. This confuses users by not letting them finish the original text. Use a limited number of pop-up windows to define terms. The pop-up should occur only at the first instance of the word.

Designing the Text

When designing your text, you can utilize a number of features to improve the look and feel of your help. The use of colors, different fonts, and graphics aid in understanding. Here are some key points to remember:

1. Use short paragraphs. Avoid going on and on, talking forever about something that could be explained in a few short sentences, but you decide to write several pages of text that continue to belabor the point until there's almost nothing you haven't said about the subject... You get the point.

Help Me

2. Be consistent in your design. You want to maintain the same look and feel throughout the help system. If you define terms in pop-up windows, don't switch to secondary windows later.
3. Use white space effectively. You will find that isolating information has a dramatic effect. It helps emphasize items without needing additional support (shading, lines, and other separators that confuse the interface).
4. Speak English! If you're writing help for beginners, don't use terminology that only an expert would know. The fastest way to turn users off is to baffle them with terms and acronyms. One of the hardest skills to acquire is the ability to effectively communicate knowledge to those who know less than you. Pretend you're explaining jet propulsion to a 12-year-old.
5. Use highlighting sparingly. Have you ever seen help that is so bright that it looks like Chuckles the Clown exploded on it? The use of different colors and fonts can make help visually appealing as well as easier to read. Although you can change fonts to add appeal, I recommend that you stay with the fonts shipped with Windows 3.1. These effects, if used correctly and not overdone, can really spice up your help file.

Pictures, Pictures, Pictures

A picture is worth a thousand words. In Windows, that is no less true. Graphical images can add a new realm of understanding to an otherwise indescribable topic. Use graphics only when they help the user understand a function or concept. Graphics used for looks only just tend to confuse users. Later we will discuss actually creating and including graphics files in your project.

Managing Complexity

One of the hardest things in any medium-to-large help project is tracking browse sequences, context IDs, and other attributes within the help system. It is important to assure that

- ☐ all topics are included in the build
- ☐ every topic is assigned a context ID (if you're implementing context-sensitive help)
- ☐ the browse sequence is correct
- ☐ keywords are identified (the search capability will be lousy without them)

One technique that Microsoft suggests is creating a Word document (table) that shows topic, context ID, browse sequence number, and keywords for each entry. This simple method allows you to better plan your system and ensure that all the loose ends are tied up.

The Creation

Well, enough theory. Let's talk about how to implement what's in your head (and hopefully on paper too). The creation process is very straightforward. You need to create the .RTF files that contain the text.

Pick Your Poison

There are three categories of tools you can use to construct your help file. The first one is free, the second one is free if you already own Word, and the third one could get a little expensive.

The Hard Way

If you're a total masochist, you might prefer to write the .RTF with an ASCII editor such as Notepad. If you decide to go that route, you will have to learn the RTF language definition. It is fraught with strange control codes and makes little sense. Here is an example of an .RTF file:

```
{\rtf1\ansi \deff5\deflang1033{\fonttbl{\f3\fmodern\fcharset0\fprq1 Courier;}
{\f4\froman\fcharset0\fprq2 Times New Roman;}{\f5\fswiss\fcharset0\
fprq2 Arial;}{\f11\fmodern\fcharset0\fprq1 Courier New;}{\f18\fswiss\
fcharset0\fprq2 Arial Narrow;}}{\colortbl;\red0\green0\blue0;\red0\green0\
blue255;\red0\green255\blue255;\red0\green255\blue0;\red255\green0\blue255;\
red255\green0\blue0;\red255\green255\blue0;\red255\green255\blue255;\red0\
green0\blue128;\red0\green128\blue128;\red0\green128\blue0;\red128\green0\
blue128;\red128\green0\blue0;\red128\green128\blue0;\red128\green128\blue128;\
red192\green192\blue192;}{\stylesheet{\li120\sa60\sl-220\slmult1 \f5\fs20
\snext0 Normal;}{\s1\sb60\sl-240\slmult1\keepn \b\f5 \sbasedon0\snext0
heading 1;}{\s2\sb60\sa60\sl-240\slmult1 \b\f5\fs20 \sbasedon1\snext0
heading 2;}{\s3\li120\sb60\sa60\sl-240\slmult1 \b\f5\fs20 \sbasedon1\snext0
heading 3;}{\s4\fi-245\li360\sb120\sa60\sl-240\slmult1\f5\fs20 \sbasedon2\
snext4 heading 4;}{\s5\sb60\sa60\sl-240\slmult1 \b\f5\fs20\sbasedon2\snext0
heading 5;}{\s6\sb40\sl-238\slmult1\keepn\pvpara\posy0\absh255\dxfrtext130\
dfrmtxtx130\dfrmtxty0 \b\f5\fs21 \sbasedon1\snext15 heading 6;}{\s9\li115\
sa20\sl-240\slmult1\keepn\tx1440\tx2880 \f5\fs16 \sbasedon1\snext0 heading
9;}{\*\cs10 \additive Default Paragraph Font;}{\s15\sb40\sa160\sl-220\slmult1
\f5\fs21 \sbasedon0\snext0 H6p;}{\s16\fi-300\li420\ri140\sb100\sl-210\slmult1\
tx140\tx420\f18\fs19 \snext16 *Cbx;}{\s17\fi-300\li420\ri140\sb100\sa100\
sl-210\slmult1\tx140\tx420 \f18\fs19 \sbasedon16\snext0 *Cbxe;}{\s18\qc\fi-245\
li360\sl-360\slmult1\keepn\box\brdrs\brdrw15\brsp20\brdrcf8\pvpara\phpg\
absh-390\absw1460\dxfrtext220\dfrmtxtx220\dfrmtxty0 \shading6000\cfpat2 \f18\
cf8\up4 \sbasedon4\snext4 *hb1;}{\s19\ri120\sa60\sl-360\slmult1\keepn\box\
brdrs\brdrw15\brsp80\brdrcf8 \pvpara\phmrg\posxr\posy0\absh-390 \shading6000\
cfpat2\b\f18\cf8\up10 \sbasedon0\snext0 *hb2;}{\*\cs20 \additive\cf11\
sbasedon10 annotation reference;}{\s21\li120\sl-220\slmult1 \f5\cf11\
sbasedon0\snext21 annotation text;}{\s22\li115\sb120\sa120\tx120\tx480\tx840 \
f5\fs20 \sbasedon0\snext0 Art;}{\s23\sa120\keepn\tx120\tx480\tx840\tqr\
```

Help Me

```
tx1560\pvpara\phpg\posy0\absw1560\dxfrtext240\dfrmtxtx240\dfrmtxty0 \f5\fs20 \
sbasedon22\snext0 ArtSd;}{\s24\li120\sa240\sl-220\slmult1\tx120\tx480\tx840 \
b\f5\fs20 \sbasedon0\snext0 Cap;}{\s25\li120\sl-220\slmult1\tx120\tx480\
tx840\tqr\tx1560\pvpara\phpg\posy0\absw1560\dxfrtext240\dfrmtxtx240\dfrmtxty0 \
b\f5\fs20 \sbasedon24\snext0 CapSd;}{\s26\sb120\keepn \b\f5\fs28 \sbasedon1\
snext0 Ch;}{\s27\li-1800\sa280\sl-240\slmult1\keepn\caps\f4\expnd24\
expndtw120 \snext26 Cn;}{\s28\li440\sa80\sl-220\slmult1 \f5\fs20 \sbasedon0\
snext29 Def1;}{\s29\li120\sb20\sa20\sl-220\slmult1 \f5\fs20 \sbasedon0\snext28
Term1;}{\s30\li560\sa80\sl-220\slmult1 \f5\fs20 \sbasedon28\snext0 Def2;}{
\s31\sb60\sa60\sl-240\slmult1
```

The amount of "code" you have just seen is about 10 percent of what is necessary to set up the help screen shown in Figure 20.2. It is a miserable existence to use this method, and I don't recommend it.

The Free Way

Microsoft understood that the method just mentioned wouldn't win them any popularity contests. Therefore, Microsoft has provided a number of tools to assist in the development of help files. WHAT6 is an archive available free from Microsoft that provides a Word 6.0 template and some management tools to help you. This template adds several menu selections such as Insert Topic and Insert Jump. When selected, these functions bring up a dialog box that you fill in, and then Word builds the .RTF document for you. A sample dialog is shown in Figure 20.6.

Figure 20.6.
The Insert Topic dialog (WHAT6).

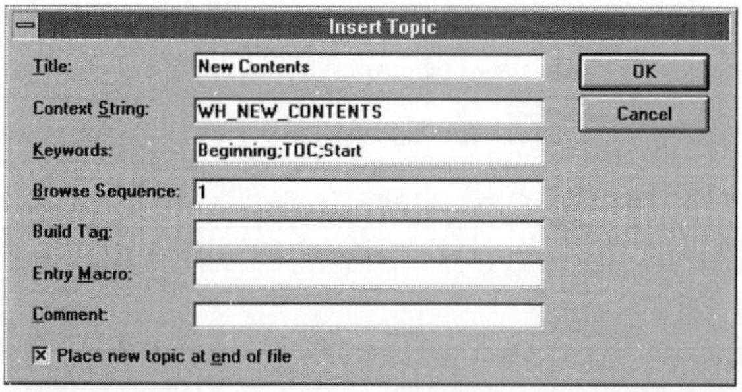

As you can see, the template provides a good interface for things such as topic creation.

I found the Windows help project editor (WHPE) included with the WHAT6 template to be lame and unreliable. This tool is supposed to help you build the .HPJ project file. It caused GPFs about every third time I ran it, and I found that if I made the smallest change to the .HPJ without WHPE, it wouldn't read the file the next time I ran WHPE. The project file is simple to construct, and I found this easier to do by hand.

The third tool I found turned out to be a real gem. It's called HULK (not Hogan). HULK is an unsupported tool written by Microsoft for its internal use. I found it on my MSDN CD subscription. This program is a front-end shell that helps you compile, syntax-check, generate maps for context IDs, and a number of other really cool things. Figure 20.7 shows a sample of the interface.

Figure 20.7.
The HULK interface.

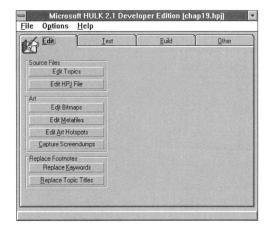

This is a jewel of a program. It has a screen-capture utility to help you include screen shots in your online help. It did everything for me except create the .HPJ file. I don't understand how this core function of creating the .HPJ file was left out! Oh well, maybe in the next version. HULK might be available from the Microsoft Download Service or CompuServe.

This was my quick, low-cost, sort-of-professional way to implement help. I have used the combination of WHAT6 (mostly the template), HULK, and WHPE (just to generate the initial .HPJ file). All the help files and examples for this book were created with this combination.

The Pay Way

The third way to do help is to pay for a tool (I hate it when that happens). A number of third-party tools help take the bother out of help file creation. The one I own is called RoboHelp. It's an overlay to Word 6.0 that provides cool floating toolbars with buttons to create topics and other things. It's a nice product, but I question the $400+ price tag. Others, such as ForeHelp, are also highly rated. Maybe the help projects I'm doing just aren't complex enough for me to realize the benefits of one of these expensive tools.

Another Language?

Even if you use a tool like Word that can save a file in RTF, you still need to know how to read the control codes in the document. You might have to manually "tweak" them after the document has been created. Let's look at some of the control codes.

Day 20

Help Me

Context Strings

The context string is the unique identifier that all help topics must have. This ID provides the handle for you to create the links in your help system. The context ID is denoted by a # in the footnote area, with the context ID itself following. An example would be

```
# WH_CONTENTS
```

This denotes our context ID for the Contents screen in the help file shown in Figure 20.2. (WH stands for Windows Help.)

Titles

The title I'm speaking of is the one displayed at the beginning of a particular topic. In Figure 20.2, it would be "MFC in 21 Days Contents." The title can be anything you wish, up to 128 characters. The title ID is denoted by a $ in the footnote. An example would be

```
$ MFC in 21 Days
```

Keywords

Keywords are the words that are placed in the search dialog box. These words are linked to your topic to help users find a topic when they're not sure what they're looking for. The keywords can be duplicated between topics. For example, the keyword "start" could apply to the Table of Contents topic and the Introduction topic. Keywords are denoted by a superscript K in the footnote. The K is followed by the keywords or phrases, separated by semicolons. An example would be

```
K TOC;Beginning;Introduction;Start;
```

Browse Sequences

The browse buttons in the Windows Help engine are a great way to peruse help when you're in the general area of the help you need. It allows you to see peripheral data around the current subject. The way this is presented is up to the Help developer. The browse sequence numbers assigned to each topic determine the order in which they are displayed. It's usually a good idea to assign the browse sequence numbers in increments of five. This allows you to insert additional topics later without having to shuffle all the browse sequence numbers. The browse sequence number is denoted by a + in the footnote area, followed by the browse sequence number. An example would be

```
+ 1
```

This is the browse sequence string for the Contents topic in Figure 20.2. It is the first topic in the sequence.

Linking Topics

We can link the topics in our help files by using jumps. There are several different kinds of jumps. Let's look at each one and its use.

Jumps Between Topics

The most fundamental of all jumps is the jump to a topic. This operation is used in about 80 percent of all help screens. You start with a contents topic screen that shows the help sections. When you choose something from that screen, you are teleported to a new topic in the help. This jump is achieved by double-underlining (or strikethrough) on the text that will be the jump text. This text will appear underlined in the end product. Following the jump text, the context ID of where you want to jump to is written in hidden text (see Figure 20.8). This hidden text appears to you (the developer) as red text with a dotted underline attribute. This is a simple and effective way of making link connections between topics.

Figure 20.8.
Hidden text after jump text.

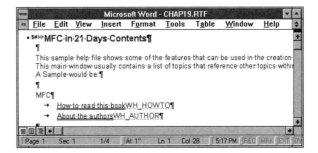

Jumps to Another Help File

Jumping to another help file is also possible. Your help system might be unusually complex or have a number of help files that can be used independently. If you have a shell that ties all the help files together, this type of jump becomes very useful. You format the jump just like the jump to topic we just discussed, except that you add the @ symbol followed by the help filename (either absolute or relative path). The syntax would be

`contextstring@c:\path\file.hlp`

Remember that once you lead the user down the garden path, the only way she can get back to her original help file is by using the history window or back button (or you could provide jump text back if appropriate). If you use no path in the jump statement, the current directory is assumed.

Help Me

Jumps to Secondary Windows

You can also jump to a secondary window. As I mentioned earlier, a secondary window can be useful if you need to relay more information than should be placed in a pop-up window but you would like the user to maintain his current position in the help file.

A prime example of this would be the user's being able to bring up a glossary window to look at term definitions while viewing the work in question in the original window as well. The syntax for the secondary window jump would be

`contextstring>windowname`

Combo Jumps

We can do combinations of jumps (no, this is not gymnastics) to get the user where we want him to be. If you combine syntax, you can jump to a secondary window in another help file quite easily. The syntax for a combo jump would be

`contextstring@c:\path\file.hlp>windowname`

Jumps to Pop-Up Windows

Pop-up windows can be a very effective means of presenting term definitions, tips, tricks, and other informative items that are fairly short. The syntax for jumping to a pop-up is nearly identical to a regular jump. In order for the help compiler to understand that you wish to generate a pop-up window as opposed to a jump to topic, the jump text must be single-underlined as opposed to double-underlined or strikethrough. The syntax for a combo jump would be

`contextstring`

Nonscrolling Regions

Some of the best help I have seen contains nonscrolling regions. This occurs when you scroll through a multiple-page help topic and the top portion of the screen remains in place while the rest of the screen scrolls to reveal the next page of information. A nonscrolling region always appears at the head or top of the topic. Placing it in the middle or on the bottom of the page would confuse the user.

By default, the nonscrolling region appears the same color as the rest of the help window (white). This appearance can be altered. I have found that a gray background is much more pleasing to the eye and gives your help a classier look. You change the default color setup in the .HPJ file, as we will discuss later. See Figure 20.9.

Figure 20.9.
The nonscrolling region.

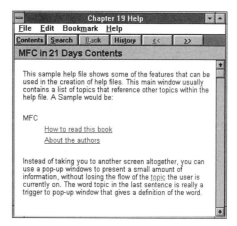

You create a nonscrolling region by typing the desired text and then formatting the paragraphs with the Keep with Next paragraph attribute.

Graphical Interpretation

Let's talk about how to add graphics to your help file. Some of the graphics I have seen are both entertaining and add real value to the end product. We will look at file formats, how to add graphics to your topic files, and creating hypergraphics and multiple-resolution bitmaps.

File Formats

In Table 20.1 we looked briefly at the different files used to create the .HLP file. Four of those files were graphics file formats. How is each of them created and used?

The bitmap file (.BMP extension) is used primarily for screen captures and other images that need a pixel-by-pixel duplicate of the original. Windows help is limited to displaying the 16 base colors in help. If you create or screen-capture a bitmap with more colors, the additional colors won't be displayed. All those unnecessary colors take up space in your help file (recall Table 13.3 in Chapter 13). You want to create or capture the bitmap at the same resolution the user will be displaying it.

The Windows metafile format (.WMF extension) is the other mainstay of the Windows graphics world. The metafile format is typically much smaller than the bitmap file. The metafile is a series of device-independent drawing commands (I think of it as a sort of PostScript). The advantage is twofold: It reduces the size of the graphics file, and there's no need to include one file for each display resolution.

Help Me

The hypergraphic (.SHG extension) is a bitmap file that has hotspots implanted on it. These hotspots are created by using the SHED.EXE program. These hotspots are the equivalent of jump text statements, just without the text! This allows pictures to be the table of contents. The user clicks on the part of the picture that represents the topic he wants help on, and he is transported to that topic. This is very useful in our WYSIWYG world.

The multiple-resolution bitmap format (.MRB extension) is generated by the Multiple-Resolution Bitmap Compiler (MRBC). These files solve the problem we discussed earlier of adding identical copies of a bitmap for each screen resolution to your help file. You can create the same bitmap in several sizes and compile all those "copies" into one file. When you include that file in your topic file, the Windows engine will use whichever bitmap is correct for the user's display.

Pasting Pictures

When it's time to integrate graphics into your topic files, there are two ways to do so—by reference or by value. What are the ups and downs of each method?

Including the bitmap by reference means including the file by adding a command in the .RTF file. There are three commands you can use to affect the alignment when placing a graphic by reference. See Table 20.2.

Table 20.2. Graphics commands.

Command	Description
bmc	Aligns the graphics as regular characters. The resulting help file will have a single copy of the file, separate from the help text itself.
bml	Aligns the graphics at the left edge of the page. All the text following the graphical reference will wrap along the graphic's right edge. There is still only a single copy of the graphics file, kept separate from the help text itself.
bmr	Aligns the graphics at the right edge of the page. All the text following the graphical reference will wrap along the graphic's left edge. There is still only a single copy of the graphics file, kept separate from the help text itself.

The inclusion by reference is done by using one of these three commands with the name of the graphics file. If no path is specified, the current directory is assumed. The syntax is

```
{bmc C:\WORK\BITMAPS\BUTTON.BMP}
```

If you choose to include the graphics file directly (by using the Insert | Graphic command in Word), the actual graphic will be placed in the text file. Tables 20.3 and 20.4 compare the advantages and disadvantages of inclusion by reference and inclusion by value.

Table 20.3. Graphics inclusion by reference.

Advantages	Disadvantages
You can use any text editor, even if it doesn't support graphics files.	You can't see the graphics while working on the .RTF file.
You can change the graphic without having to paste new instances of it into your document.	You must enter the location of the files in your .RTF file. There can be errors at compile time if the path is incorrect.
You can use hypergraphics in your help. These can be included by reference *only*.	
Multiple instances can be used in your help file, but only one copy of the file will actually be stored in the help file itself.	

Table 20.4. Graphics inclusion by value.

Advantages	Disadvantages
You can see the graphic as you work on the .RTF file. This might help you get a better feel for how the finished product will look.	You can use only Word for Windows to write the .RTF file.
You don't have to enter the absolute path to the graphic file. This helps avoid compilation errors later.	You can't change the graphics file inside Word. You must use an external program to edit it (although OLE helps with this).

Ooh, That's the Spot: Hotspots

Hotspots are fun! The Hotspot editor allows us to add embedded hotspots so that when the user clicks on that hotspot we can

- ☐ jump to another topic
- ☐ display a pop-up window
- ☐ run a help macro
- ☐ execute routines in an external DLL

Help Me

Using the Hotspot Editor

The Hotspot Editor, shown in Figure 20.10, allows you to bring in a standard bitmap image and add hotspot support to it. Then you save the file as an .SHG file to be used by the .RTF file later. You must include the context IDs or macros to execute at the time of the .SHG file creation. This means that you need to plan your attack first and then execute that plan.

Figure 20.10.
The Hotspot Editor in action.

You can add a hotspot by simply pressing the left mouse button and dragging the cursor to the spot you want to activate. A box will form that you can size appropriately. Then choose Edit | Attributes. The resulting dialog box, shown in Figure 20.11, allows you to define the context ID and whether this is a jump, pop-up, or execute macros reference. Additionally, you can specify whether or not the box that creates the bounded area is visible.

Figure 20.11.
The Hotspot Editor Attributes dialog.

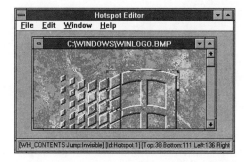

After completing the hotspot editing, save the bitmap file as an .SHG file. This file can be included by reference only in your .RTF file.

Any Size Will Do: MRBs

Wouldn't it be nice to have copies of a bitmap in all the different resolutions, so that no matter what resolution the user had, the bitmap would display properly sized? Well, your prayers have been answered. The Multiple Resolution Bitmap Compiler allows you to take existing bitmap

files (several copies of the same bitmap at different resolutions) and compile them into one graphics file. This file can then be included by reference in your .RTF file. When the help engine displays your help file, the engine will choose the bitmap that goes best with that user's screen resolution. At compile time, you need to specify the monitor type for each bitmap you wish to have included in the .MRB file.

MRBC is a DOS-based application that needs to be executed from within a DOS window. This tool can be very useful if you're creating help files that are used by a diverse crowd of users (diverse from a hardware perspective).

Macros

Macros are an important part of the Windows help system. Macros allow you to customize your help system by changing the functions of or adding buttons to the help screen. You can also execute applications from within help and execute functions in external DLLs.

Run on Open

If you include a macro definition in the [CONFIG] section of the .HPJ file, the macros will be executed when the help file is first brought up. A macro that will usually exist in your .HPJ file (if you use a tool to generate the file) is BrowseButtons(). When help is started, this macro places the browse forward and backward buttons in the help window. A number of help macros are available. I could use up 10 pages listing them, but in the interest of brevity, I will just say that you can find them in your C++ documentation.

Run on Topic

You can execute a macro when a topic is chosen. The macro is defined in the footnote section of the topic. It will be executed when the user clicks on a jump to the topic, clicks on the back or browse button and lands on the topic, or selects the topic from the Search list in the Search dialog box.

Run from Hotspot

You can run a macro from a hotspot. You set up the hotspot by selecting Macro from the Type dropdown box. Notice how the context ID data entry field has changed to the word "macro." Now type the name of the macro to be executed. When that hotspot is activated, the macro you named will be executed. Figure 20.12 shows the Attributes dialog box with the type set to Macro.

Help Me

Figure 20.12.
Defining a macro in the Hotspot Editor.

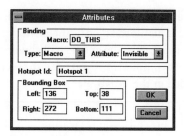

Rules of the Road for Coding

Here are some general rules of conduct for constructing macros:

1. Separate each macro with a semicolon. Remember, a single string can include more than one macro.
2. Macros aren't case-sensitive. Use capitalization that makes you happy!
3. When using special characters, place them in strings enclosed in quotation marks and prefaced by a backslash.
4. Macros can be used as parameters when calling other macros.
5. A macro must be 512 characters long or less.

If you remember these points, you should be able to create a veritable plethora of online wonders (or at least good help).

DLLs

You can call DLL routines from a Windows help file. Before you can use these routines, you must register them by adding an entry to the [CONFIG] section of the .HPJ file. The RegisterRoutine() macro is placed there for every DLL routine you wish to call. The format of this macro is

```
RegisterRoutine("DLLname", "FunctionName", "FormatSpecification")
```

The *FormatSpecification* parameter specifies the formats of the arguments to the DLL function. A complete list of the format specifiers is in the macro reference under RegisterRoutine.

Building Help

Now that you have seen the pieces of the puzzle, let's put the pieces into place and create the help file we've been working on.

Project Files

The project file (.HPJ) is the heart of the help project. The project file specifies a number of different attributes about your project and acts as a guide to the help compiler. The file is broken into sections. These sections are logical groupings of related items. Let's look at each section and the items that can be specified in that section.

Options

The [OPTIONS] section specifies options that control the build process. This entire section is optional. A number of items can be added or changed from their default behavior. Table 20.5 lists all the option entries.

Table 20.5. .HPJ [OPTIONS] section entries.

Option	Sample Use	Description
BMROOT	BMROOT=C:\BITMAPS	Names the directory where the help compiler can find the graphics file(s) named in the bml, bmc, or bmr entries in your topic files.
BUILD	BUILD=MYBUILD	Determines which topics to use in the build process. This is used in conjunction with BUILDTAGS.
COMPRESS	COMPRESS=HIGH	Defines the level of compression the help file will have. You can set this to low, medium, or high.
CONTENTS	CONTENTS=WH_CONTENTS	Specifies which topic will appear when the user clicks on the Contents button in help.
COPYRIGHT	COPYRIGHT=My Stuff, 1994	Places the copyright string you specify into the About box in Windows help. It can contain 35 to 70 characters.
ERRORLOG	ERRORLOG=C:\BUGS.TXT	Tells the help compiler to direct any errors in the build process to this file. You can then review the errors later.

continues

Help Me

Table 20.5. continued

Option	Sample Use	Description
FORCEFONT	FORCEFONT=ARIAL	Forces help to be displayed in the font you choose, no matter what font was used in the creation of the .RTF file.
ICON	ICON=MYICON.ICO	Specifies the icon that users see when they minimize the help window.
LANGUAGE	LANGUAGE=Scandinavian	Since Windows Help 3.1 supports only one other language sort ordering other than English, if you use this option, you must specify "Scandinavian."
MAPFONTSIZE	MAPFONTSIZE=8:12	Makes the font sizes in your development environment map to other sizes in production. The example makes all 8-point fonts in the .RTF file come out as 12-point fonts.
MULTIKEY	MULTIKEY=L	You can create additional keyword tables in Windows help. The MULTIKEY option determines the footnote character used as the additional keyword label. All keywords labeled with the MULTIKEY label will be placed in the additional keyword table.
REPORT	REPORT=ON	Turns on error reports during the build process. It shows the steps as they happen.
ROOT	ROOT=C:\HELP	Designates the directory where the help compiler should look for the .RTF files.
TITLE	TITLE=My Help System 1.00.00	Assigns the title that is displayed in the Windows help title bar. It can be up to 50 characters long.

Option	Sample Use	Description
WARNING	WARNING=3	Sets the amount of debugging information that is reported by the help compiler during the build. 1 = only severe errors, 2 = an intermediate number of errors, and 3 = all errors and warnings.
BUILDTAGS	BUILDTAGS=MYBUILD	Allows you to include only those topics necessary for this build. You can specify a build tag for each topic. This means that your help files can be built differently, depending on the topics you wish to include.

Aliases

Since every topic must have a unique context ID, it would prove difficult to map the three different context IDs to the same topic. By creating aliases, you could consolidate three topics into one and not have to recode your help. Simply map all three of the old context IDs to the same topic.

Context-Sensitive Mapping

The [MAP] section is where you connect the context IDs to the context numbers being passed to help from the parent application. Normally the parent application will call WinHelp and pass a number that corresponds to a help context number. This number must be resolved to a context ID string such as the WH_CONTENTS we used earlier. The map has a simple one-to-one correlation between the two items.

.BMP by Reference

If you included bitmaps by reference in your .RTF files, you must reference them in the [BITMAPS] section of the .HPJ file. If no absolute path is given, the BMROOT or ROOT path is assumed. Otherwise, use the absolute path.

Help Me

Window Attributes

The size and position of the help window(s) are adjustable. They are defined in the [WINDOWS] section of the .HPJ file. An entry in the [WINDOWS] section for the main menu would be in this format:

```
main="caption", (horizposition, vertposition, width, height), sizing,
clientRGB, nonscrollingRGB, topmost
```

The sizing parameter is 0 if you want the windows to open normally and 1 if you want them maximized. The RGB parameters are in the format (255,255,255). If topmost is set to 1, the secondary windows will always stay above the main window. This keeps the secondary windows from getting lost in the shuffle.

External Files

The [BAGGAGE] section of the .HPJ file allows you to include external files in the .HLP file. This is a more efficient way to access the files, because WinHelp doesn't have to go to the FAT to get the filenames. When you reference the files in the topic files, prefix them with an exclamation point (!). This tells the help compiler that the file is internal to the .HLP file. Use this in combination with the ROOT option so that you don't need to specify the absolute path to all the files. The baggage limit is 1,000 bitmap files.

Compiling Help Files

As soon as you have completed the .HPJ file and have the bitmap and .RTF files in the appropriate directories, the process of compiling them is simple. You invoke the help compiler by typing

```
HC31 myproj.hpj
```

or

```
HCP myproj.hpj
```

and pressing Enter.

Which one you type depends on which help compiler you're using. HC31 is not a standard compiler. HCP is an extended compiler that offers more efficient use of memory and the ability to compile large help files.

Testing and Debugging Help Files

Now that your help file is compiled, how do you know if it works? Your first clue should be the compiler's output. If you get several error messages, chances are things might not work that great. If you placed ERRORLOG=xxx.txt in your .HPJ file, the errors should be reflected in that file. If the error has the word ERROR in front of it, it's probably a fatal error. If it has the word WARNING in front of it, it might be less serious. The error numbers and help text for each reside in the BLDERROR.HLP file that is included in WHAT6. This help file alone is worth retrieving the whole WHAT6 package.

Integrating Help into Your Application

This is the final leg of our journey. If you selected context-sensitive help in the AppWizard Options dialog box, AppWizard will provide all the message map entries in your CWinApp-derived class that allow you to make the connections to the help system. AppWizard also creates a set of starter .RTF files and populates them with basic menu selections. Talk about giving you a head start! AppWizard even creates a \HLP directory under your project directory and populates it with bitmaps (the ones on the toolbar) that correspond to the functions described in the skeletal help files!

If you run the MAKEHELP.BAT program that comes with Visual C++ 1.5x, you will find that it generates a help mapping file (.HMO extension). It includes that file in the [MAP] section of your .HPJ file and then compiles the final .HLP file. When adding to the help file, you will want to use the context ID that is created with the message map file. This file is in the form described in the section "Context-Sensitive Mapping." Type

CONTEXT_ID

and press the Tab key and type

CONTEXTNUMBER

After running MAKEHELP.BAT, you should be left with a working .HLP file. All this functionality is part of the MFC and AppWizard and is provided at no cost to you.

Summary

We've looked at the elements in a help file and the support files you create during the "creative" stage, and we've seen how to compile the end product. Help files are an easy and inexpensive way to distribute information to your users. It's much cheaper to include five online help files than to print a 500-page manual. Remember that help files can accompany a product or be used as a stand-alone data source and can add real value.

Day 20: Help Me

Q&A

Q Why is Windows help limited to a 16-color display?

A The Windows help engine depends on a bare-bones installation of Windows and must operate on any system. The standard VGA driver is a 16-color driver. It must work within these confines.

Q Why would I need the *BUILDTAGS* option in my .HPJ file?

A The different build options could be used to include more topics if the user purchased the professional edition of your software and fewer topics if he purchased the entry-level edition. Great marketing scam, huh?

Workshop

Quiz

1. What's the difference between the HC31 and the HCP help compilers?
2. When should you not use graphics in your help file?

Exercises

1. Create a help file for an existing project (one that you haven't selected context-sensitive help options for).
2. Try adding some bitmapped hotspots to your existing help file. Use all three jump types: jump, pop-up, and macros.

WEEK 3

Future Topics

Future Topics

For our final chapter on the MFC, we will discuss the future. This includes all manner of computer-related topics, such as new operating systems, advancements in hardware, and up-and-coming software aids and techniques. You might wonder what these things have to do with the MFC. The answer is: nothing and everything. They do and they don't apply to the MFC. But enough riddles. One of the most important things a potential world-class software developer (yes, you) needs to do is to keep up on what the future holds. So I decided to take a little poetic license and discuss some of the things that are near and dear to our software engineering hearts.

The advances being made every day in the computer industry are staggering, and every one of them will eventually have an impact on your life as a software developer. I decided to give you some insight into what's on the horizon and why you should care. If you're part of the industry already, you're probably too busy to keep up with every nuance of the potential future, so this chapter can be of value to you as well. I will summarize what's happening and (in my opinion) how it affects us.

Windows 9x

I jest only slightly with the 9x name. At the time this was written, the delivery date for Windows 95 had slipped again. It's a pretty slick marketing move to attach a year to an operating system. As with your car, it gives you the feeling that you're always driving last year's model and should trade it in for a new one. The problem is, Microsoft now has to deliver the product in 1995. (I bet the developers aren't happy with the marketing folks because of the name.)

Windows 95 offers some interesting features (both documented and undocumented) and functionality for developers and users alike. Let's explore a few of them.

The Wicked Witch Is Dead

Do you remember those awful days of the 640K limit? You're probably still living in them. I know that with my Banyan drivers, FTP TCP/IP drivers, mouse, keyboard (MS Natural keyboard, of course), and ASPI SCSI drivers loaded, I can squeeze out a meager 430K of free base memory (on a good day). Programs don't load or run right sometimes, and DOS boxes under Windows hang the machine.

Microsoft told us they had killed the Witch. Windows 95 is a brave new world! (That's the default message in the Win95 screen saver.) The DOS 640K barrier is gone. What? A flat memory model? Memory available from here to the horizon? We're saved! Does this sound too good to be true? You bet. Adrian King's book *Inside Windows 95* (Microsoft Press) states that DOS has been eliminated from Win95. At the same time, Andrew Schulman, author of *Unauthorized Windows 95,* claims that Win95 uses real-mode DOS code (running in a protected-mode virtual 86 session) to perform some operations. In the end, Microsoft admitted this is true. The Witch is very much alive. And sadness again descended upon the land.

Why should we care? Well, the 640K limit has impeded our progress for a long time. You could almost make an occupation of performing memory management duties (or writing/selling software packages like QEMM). It's sad that such a petty and annoying problem couldn't be solved. Oh well, maybe in Windows 97. Just remember, the ISVs (independent software vendors) make a good living off of deficiencies in Microsoft's products. It almost makes me wonder if Microsoft flaws its products on purpose—almost.

The Windows 95 Logo Program

If you want to be a member of the elite Win95 Logo club, you'll have to work at it. There are sacrifices. The Windows 95 Logo program is designed to reward software and hardware developers who conform to what Microsoft thinks is a reasonable standard. Have you noticed that some software has the Windows logo on the outside of the box or manual? This is supposed to assure you that the product you are about to purchase will work well with Windows.

So how do you get your software product branded with the soon-to-be infamous (oops, I mean famous, of course) Win95 logo? Your software must meet seven requirements:

1. Your application must be a Win32 executable. It must be compiled with a 32-bit compiler that generates an executable of the Portable Executable (PE) file format. This fascinating subject (PE) is worthy of its own chapter (in someone else's book). Microsoft has developed this format based on the COFF (Common Object File Format) in the UNIX world, and bits of VMS and MVS are thrown in too. This file format organizes information very similarly to the way it will be structured when loaded into memory. This is very unlike Windows 3.1, which reads the executable in and changes the memory image into something completely different. The PE format means that an application exists in the same format on disk as it will in memory, so no "translation" from disk image to memory image is necessary.

2. Your application must conform to the Microsoft Windows User Interface Design Guide. This document makes many recommendations, but here are the minimum requirements you must meet:

    - ☐ You must register 16x16 and 32x32 pixel icons for each file type you generate and for your application. This allows Win95 to display your icons in the normal large format and have a 16x16 icon lying around for use in those mini toolbars.

    - ☐ Keep the look and feel of your program in line with the design guide I just mentioned. Microsoft strongly recommends that you use the common dialogs and controls if you're going to interact with files. Using these will keep the user in a single environment where everything looks the same.

    - ☐ Get the colors and metrics from the system if you're going to create your own dialogs and controls. There's nothing gaudier than a dialog that is way out of line with the colors the user chooses in Control Panel. What's the point of letting the user choose colors if applications ignore them?

Future Topics

- The right mouse button springs to life. This is something we Windows 3.1 users aren't used to. In Win95, the right mouse button is used for bringing up context menus. These menus bring up a menu with options specific to the item the cursor is over. Microsoft strongly recommends that you not use the right mouse button for anything other than context menus and that you implement context menus in your program.

- Follow the Win95 setup guidelines. This is probably the single greatest thing for people who load and unload a lot of software. Win95 setup guidelines require that you avoid putting entries in the WIN.INI and SYSTEM.INI files (it's about time). All applications should use the registry to store configuration information. You will need to use the Registry API to add or retrieve information. One of the most important gains for users is that an uninstall program is now required for each application. Remember when an application would dump 60 files into various directories on your hard drive, and you could never find them all? No more. Now the software manufacturer (that might be you) is responsible for his own mess.

  You might ask, "How am I going to get rid of common files that I might share with other applications?" I asked the same question. For shared items, you will have to increment the users field in the Registry. This field logs how many applications dependent on the shared component have been loaded. When you uninstall the application, you need to decrement the user counter by one. If the user counter is at zero, give the user the option of deleting the shared component. You will want to warn the user that the shared component might be needed by another program later, one that hasn't registered its need with the Registry. Registering your uninstall program will display your application in the list of the Uninstall page of the Add/Remove Program Utility included with Windows.

3. Your application must run successfully on Windows NT version 3.5. If your application uses Win95 APIs only, you will have access to some new features that aren't available in NT 3.5. These features won't be available until the release of NT 3.51. For now, it's necessary for your application to do version checking and, if you're on NT, fail in a graceful manner.

4. Long filename support: Yes, the world of "8.3" filenames (OURFILES.TXT, for example) is fading fast. Win95 and NT 3.5 support the use of 255-character filenames. Was that a cheer? This was one of the chief complaints from Mac users. They have enjoyed naming their files `My Resume to Jim` for a long time; now it's our turn. I was running out of creative filenames; how about you? When you display long filenames in your applications, remember to strip the three-letter extensions from the end. We want the names to look more human and readable. If you use the common dialogs to open and save files, you will also gain a lot of the functionality associated

with them. This includes direct network drive browsing, links, and other Win95 goodies.

5. Your application must support OLE 2. Microsoft really went nuts with OLE in Windows 95. This is good for application users. Now that OLE 2.0 class libraries and tools are widely available, it's also good for developers. Application users love drag and drop. Your application needs to be drag-and-drop-enabled. There are a number of samples in the OLE 2.0 SDK to get you started. If you've already implemented cut, copy, and paste, it's not that much more work to implement drag and drop.

    An application that works with files should

    - [ ] be a container or an object
    - [ ] support drag and drop
    - [ ] include OLE 2.0 compound file support with "document summary information" (this is strongly suggested)
    - [ ] support OLE 2.0 automation (this is strongly suggested)

6. Support for UNC paths: If your application uses files, it should support Universal Naming Convention (UNC) paths. The goal of Windows 95 is to be a universal network client that can connect anytime, from anyplace, to just about anything. Your application doesn't need to be network-enabled, but it does need to work seamlessly in a network environment. Support for long filenames will set you up for long filenames in the shell and on network operating systems such as Novell NetWare.

    UNC paths allow connections to network devices without the need to reference a network drive letter. The system will be able to locate the network server and path with the UNC name. To ensure that your application will work seamlessly in a network environment, open and save files with UNC paths to enable your user to browse the network directly. Display the friendly form in your title bar—for example, `My file on Gandalf`.

7. Support simple mail using a common messaging call API: Windows 95 will ship with the Microsoft Mail client, so you can add the Send Mail command as a menu option. Of course, the CMC API enables you to do all kinds of messaging support, but the minimum effort you need to expend here is to add the Send Mail command. Depending on your application and your target audience, you might want to add more than the minimum Mail functionality. There are `MAPISendMail` examples in the Microsoft Development Library, in the MAPI SDK samples, and in the Windows 95 SDK.

The logo program contains much more information than I have covered here. You might feel that some of the requirements are a little harsh on the developer. But it's really for your own good. Making developers responsible for what their applications do to the end user's system is necessary. The uninstall idea should have happened 10 years ago. My Windows directories get so clogged with junk that I have to periodically scrub the disk and start over. Hopefully, the uninstall idea will change things.

Future Topics

A Virtual World (VxDs)

This whole 640K thing really isn't so bad. If it's any consolation, Microsoft has decreased the reliance on that 640K. They've done it by using more virtual device drivers and fewer real-mode ones. You might ask, virtual what? We rely pretty heavily on drivers we load in our CONFIG.SYS and AUTOEXEC.BAT files. These drivers run our CD-ROM players, mice, scanners, and a number of other devices. The problem is that they generate "RAM cram." That 640K gets full pretty quickly. We compensate by loading drivers "high" using LoadHigh in DOS 6.x or QEMM. But that "high" memory has a finite limit too. Microsoft has found a better way.

The VxD was created as a way to virtualize a piece of hardware. But this original purpose had blossomed into much more. It's used for communication between VMM- (virtual machine manager) aware programs and other tasks. Windows 3.1 and Windows for Workgroups 3.11 contain many VxDs. The loading of these VxDs cuts down on our RAM cram considerably by allowing the VxDs to be loaded anywhere in memory. The benefits are obvious. If you have 16M of RAM, you can load the VxD nearly anywhere.

Today's VxD has two major limitations. It can't be loaded and unloaded dynamically, and it can't be paged out to virtual memory (your swap file on your hard disk). The first isn't really that big of a deal. After all, how many times are you going to disconnect your multi-I/O card while the computer is running? The second limitation is more of a problem.

In order for Windows to utilize memory more efficiently, it should have complete control over the memory's content and utilization. If Windows doesn't need a particular item in RAM at this time, it should page it out to virtual memory and give other applications room to play. The current VxD isn't pageable. The entire data and code segments need to reside in memory all the time. Even though a VxD might not be needed at a particular time, it's locked into memory for some mystical reason. We will talk about how Win95 overcame this limitation in a moment.

Plug and Play (PnP)

Another technology that relates heavily to VxDs is PnP (Plug and Play). I will explain why in a minute. PnP is the knight in shining armor that will save all of us techy types from the bane of hardware jumpers. I/O board jumper configuration has made computer setup and the addition of I/O boards an Olympic event. Knowing the IRQs, DMA channels, and base addresses of your own computer (much less figuring out someone else's) is less likely than winning the lottery.

PnP changes all that. PnP defines a standard by which all I/O boards interact with the motherboard (and hence the BIOS). The real benefit of this standard is that PnP I/O cards can be added to a PnP computer with the details hidden from the installer. A true PnP I/O card has no jumpers on it. No jumpers, you say? That's right. How is this possible?

PnP works around a resource arbitrator. At boot time, the BIOS queries each of the I/O cards to retrieve resource requirements. It then dishes out IRQs, DMA channels, and so on to the cards. If there is a conflict (two cards say they *must* have the same IRQ or DMA), the resource arbitrator comes in and decides who gets what. Sounds great, doesn't it? How could this fail? Well, in theory, it won't.

If we happen to stick a non-PnP card into our PnP machine, how will our system deal with it? The PnP BIOS will allow you to enter the card's requirements, and it will try to ensure that no one else conflicts with that card—even if it has to reassign the IRQ on the other PnP cards just to accommodate the non-PnP card. Not bad, huh? An external program that allows you to enter configuration data for the non-PnP device will probably be necessary.

PnP's big benefit is that you can hot-swap devices on your PC. Yes, I know this sounds dangerous. We have all tried to hot-swap something in our PC before (you remember the black smoke and the smell of burning plastic), but this can work. You can remove or add items in the PCMCIA slots (I'll talk about this in a moment) or connect/disconnect your laptop from the docking station without turning the power off. How do you think Windows 3.1 would react if you just ripped open your PC case and pulled out the internal modem or serial card? Not well. Win95 will react a lot better to dynamic changes in your system configuration. One mechanism that allows this newfound freedom is the VXDDLR.

The heart of hot-swapping is the VXDLDR. (See, I told you we would get back to VxD.) The VXDLDR is a VxD that provides for the dynamic loading and unloading of VxDs. This helps accomplish a great deal. We can now unload the virtual driver for our CD-ROM player (in our docking station) when we pull the laptop out of the docking station. Do you see the beauty of this? Imagine a PC that can adapt to the conditions and resources it is given. That's what the PnP specification is trying to accomplish.

There is a PnP specification for BIOS, ISA component interaction, and SCSI. These specifications provide the foundation for what PnP will be. You can find these specifications on the MSDN (Microsoft Developers' Network) CD.

In order for all this to work, we must be able to store lots of PnP information in the BIOS so that we can have a good working data repository. That's where another new technology, flash BIOS, comes in.

Flash BIOS

Flash BIOS is (like most of the topics in this chapter) the greatest thing since sliced bread. If you've ever had to live with a BIOS bug (you know, the one that locks up your computer every Tuesday at 3:12 p.m. for no apparent reason), you know what I'm talking about. The only answer to this problem was the replacement of the BIOS chip itself. There were two possible

Future Topics

sources: the manufacturer of the system BIOS, or a third-party company like Mr. BIOS. The replacement was usually expensive—almost the price of a new system board. The results were also unpredictable; the BIOS might add more problems than it solved (my experience). No more.

Flash BIOS is BIOS that is stored in a flash memory chip. Intel (and other companies) have been working hard on flash, which is the newest nonvolatile memory technology (it holds data even when the power is off). This flash memory comes in different sizes, depending on your needs. System board manufacturers are utilizing this technology to allow you to update your BIOS without having to replace the actual BIOS chip. How do you change the BIOS? With a floppy disk.

This software method allows you to receive BIOS updates electronically and then run the upgrade program, which downloads the BIOS update into flash memory permanently. The result is spectacular. My Intel motherboard has this feature. Intel provides BIOS upgrades free of charge via its electronic BBS service. What a concept. I upgraded the BIOS in two minutes with just a quick BBS download. The nice part is, the application allowed me to save the old BIOS to a disk file in case I didn't like the new BIOS. I could then load the old BIOS back into the flash and be back where I started. A backout plan is always a must.

Flash also allows you to add information about the PnP items into its memory. The BIOS now becomes a repository of information related to the condition and configuration of the entire machine.

PCMCIA

PCMCIA (Personal Computer Memory Card International Association) is an acronym no one can say three times fast (or slowly, for that matter). However, everyone likes it, especially if they own a laptop. This bus standard was developed to allow for a uniform set of memory and peripheral card add-ons. The cards come in three distinct sizes and have one of the standard physical dimensions shown in Table 21.1.

Table 21.1. PCMCIA card sizes.

Card Type	Width	Length	Height
Type I	54 mm	85.6 mm	3.3 mm
Type II	54 mm	85.6 mm	5 mm
Type III	54 mm	85.6 mm	10.5 mm

However, provisions are made for a maximum length of 135.6 mm to allow for any external connectors or interfaces. These are credit-card-size accessories that plug into your computer.

They can be memory cards, LAN adapters, hard drives, or almost anything. Most, if not all, of the new laptop PCs come with at least one (but usually two) PCMCIA slots. The reason this is significant for the software developer is that with PCMCIA cards and PnP rolled up together, you will find that your application needs to become more aware of its surroundings. No longer can you assume anything. Your application will now have to get the lay of the land again and again to make sure it's up-to-date on the resources and conditions that might have changed during its execution.

Win32 and Win32s

In the beginning there was DOS, when dinosaurs roamed and birds flew. Worms crawled, fish swam, and computers were named after fruit. After DOS, the Win16 API was developed. This API was fairly well documented in a set of Microsoft manuals and provided a set of system-level calls to help us retrieve or set information in the Windows 3.1 operating system. This API served us well, but it lacked some of the fundamental things necessary for our distributed, corporate world. So, as the next step in the evolutionary process, the Win32 API was developed. This API includes a rich complement of calls to give the software developer access to the insides of a 32-bit operating system such as Windows NT. It covers a great deal of ground in the areas of security, new GDI functions, and networking. This new API filled the gaps left by the Win16 API and allowed the developer access to things that could make his or her application useful in the distributed corporate arena.

The Win32s API is a subset (hence the "s") of the functionality provided by Win32. Win32s was developed as a layered product to ride on top of the Win16 API present in Windows 3.1. Win32s allows Windows 3.1 users to run Win32 code on their machines. All of the functions available under the Win32 API are also available under the Win32s API. What's the point of having two APIs, then? Well, in Win32s, many of the functions are merely stubbed out. It would be kind of hard to create a new thread of execution in Windows 3.1, so when you call `CreateThread`, it returns 0. The 0 simply means that a new thread could not be created. This is a graceful way for the Win32s kernel to let a Win32 application down. The result is a shell by which most Win32 applications can be run on a Windows 3.1 platform, with the Win32s extensions installed. The differences in features are shown in Table 21.2.

Table 21.2. API features.

Feature	Windows NT	Win95	Windows 3.11/Word for Windows 3.11
32-bit memory management	☐	☐	☐
File mapping	☐	☐	☐

continues

Future Topics

Table 21.2. continued

Feature	Windows NT	Win95	Windows 3.11/Word for Windows 3.11
Networking	☐	☐	☐
OLE 2.0	☐	☐	☐
Win32 threading	☐	☐	
Mailslot and named pipes	☐	☐	
Advanced GDI (Béziers and paths)	☐	☐	
RPC (remote procedure calls)	☐	☐	
GDI transforms	☐		
Event logging	☐		
Security	☐		
UNICODE	☐		

Notice that Win95 supports a superset of Win32s and yet a subset of Windows NT. Microsoft implemented the functionality that seemed appropriate for the desktop. Remember that all functionality takes RAM to implement. Microsoft had promised Win95 to run in only 4M of RAM—a tall order considering Windows 3.1 doesn't even run well without 8M (16M if you're doing any real work and don't want your hard drive to sound like a blender, paging memory in and out). The Win32 Programmer's Reference manuals are a good source of information on how to use the API calls.

Windows NT 3.5

Windows NT is probably the biggest single advance Microsoft has ever made. This particular product will help define how network servers and high-end workstations will work well into the future. Many of us have had to deal with UNIX systems because UNIX was the only operating system that could handle multiple multithreaded applications. NT wants to change all that.

Now we can have the power of UNIX without having to deal with its cryptic interfaces. You no longer have to be a systems god to get a system like NT up and running. The first time I set up an NT 3.5 workstation, I had it up and running on the network in less than 30 minutes—and I *never* read instructions! Try that with System V Release 4. If you read some of the Windows tabloids (such as *Windows Sources*), there have been many articles comparing NT to UNIX. The results have been mixed. Although I will be the first to admit that a couple of powerful UNIX features are missing from NT, I am porting UNIX C applications over to NT using Visual C++ 2.1 as fast as I can code.

Let's look at the design goals for Windows NT. This might give you a better idea of what Microsoft was trying to accomplish. The four main design goals were

- Extensibility
- Portability
- Reliability
- Compatibility

Extensibility: Windows NT is a modular operating system. This modularity is based on the object-oriented mentality that has proven very effective at reducing coupling (the dependency of one module of code on another) and increasing code cohesion (the tightness and efficiency of a module of code). By making a piece of code generic, we allow it to perform the same function on many different types of objects. A piece of code that destroys objects can destroy many types of objects, not just one. The modularity of the code will also allow modules to be rewritten or replaced altogether without modifying or breaking the other modules in the system.

Portability: One of the things that Microsoft had to do was keep NT compatible with the existing installed base of applications. That means it needs to run on an x86 platform. At the same time, you don't want to alienate users who might be running Alpha, MIPS, or PowerPC systems. NT needs to be the server and high-end workstation for the masses—in other words, available to everyone regardless of the hardware they are running. This way, the product will have the widest possible distribution. How did Microsoft accomplish this? First, they wrote all the code in a high-level language that runs across many processors. They then isolated all the hardware-dependent code and made a connection layer that helps the independent code interface to the dependent code. This layer is called the Hardware Abstraction Layer (HAL). (No, it's not HAL2000, although that would have been a cool name.) HAL virtualizes hardware interfaces and provides transparency to the NT kernel. Quite an accomplishment. The result is an operating system in which only the device-dependent code needs to be adapted, while the rest is unaffected.

Reliability: If there's one thing I can't stand, it's an operating system that crashes for no apparent reason or one that is brought to its knees by one sinister, memory-hogging, CPU-cycle-sucking, screen-blanking program. Windows NT solves this problem by having every application run in its own protected address space. While the application is running, it can mess with only its own memory, not that of other applications. So the worst damage it can do is kill itself. This gives the OS much more control over what happens. Another feature that is giving the people in your Information Security department a warm fuzzy is that Microsoft has applied for a C2 security rating for NT. This security rating would mean that NT could be used in government networks that require advanced security. Another plus for the marketing folks to plug.

Day 21: Future Topics

Compatibility: There is always the duality of trying to keep up with advances in technology and staying compatible with old technology. This battle of conscience was true in the design of NT as well. Microsoft is driven to keep up with Intel's promise of "doubling performance every 18 months." Microsoft has more CPU horsepower to work with, but at the same time it wants to maintain compatibility with the older processors. One of the things NT did give up (from a legacy perspective) was real mode. Now it can take advantage of the true power of the processor. As consolation for this, they did add compatibility for OS/2 1.x character-based programs, POSIX 1003.1, and most MS-DOS and Windows 16-bit applications. The really nice part of this from your programming perspective is that if you write your application to the Win32 API, you will have source code compatibility between all NT platforms. The same code recompiled with the MIPS, x86, Alpha, or PowerPC version of Visual C++ will give you the ported application.

NT 3.5 comes in two flavors: workstation and server. The workstation is much more than the name implies. It provides a rich environment including FTP connectivity, TCP/IP, NetBIOS, and IPX network protocols. It also provides a set of administrative tools for managing your fixed disks and users, as well as a performance monitor. The NT diagnostics tool is provided for people raised on MSD. By the way, probably the most useful tool is the SCSI audio CD player (my personal favorite).

NT server has the same features as the workstation, plus a few more. It provides tools for monitoring all the NT machines in your domain (yes, NT server is a domain controller also), and it can also act as a WINS (Windows Internet Name Service) and DHCP (Dynamic Host Configuration Protocol) server as well. Both of these are related to the distribution and assignment of IP addresses and names on a network. One NT server can be the cornerstone of a good-sized office network, and several of them can run a small corporation.

Windows NT 4.0 (Cairo)

Cairo is a word so secret that Microsoft employees whisper it even *inside* their building. It's the code word for Windows NT 4.0. Cairo will be the next step on the evolutionary scale for NT 3.5. From what I have heard and read, Cairo will have the same interface as Win95. The days of Program Manager as the default interface are numbered. Cairo will also provide closer links with OLE. Right now, OLE 2.0 implements a compound file structure. In Cairo, that implementation will be replaced with a more efficient native file system implementation. You will hear more about Cairo in the press, but it might be quite a while before the product is on the shelf. I can hardly wait, but then, I am a technology addict.

WOSA

Have you ever tried to write a program that interfaces directly to Oracle (a popular database server)? How about taking that same application and tuning it to talk to Sybase System 10 (a different popular database server)? One of the things I don't relish is the thought of rewriting a piece of code over again just because I want to talk to a different brand of network object than I was talking to before. The time and energy spent doing this work could be better utilized (by a game of Doom II, for example).

The WOSA (Windows Open Services Architecture) was developed to provide a set of tools that allow for a single open-ended interface to your corporate computing environment. Most large companies have a large number of systems, all of them different and incompatible (funny how that happens). Probably the best thing, from the users' perspective, is to have their desktop PC be the universal interface to these systems. The next logical step (especially in Microsoft's eyes) is to make the Windows line of operating systems the center of this connectivity dance.

One of the key benefits of a single point of entry into the enterprise is that even though the enterprise might change, the single point of entry does not. This removes from the software developer the burden of learning all the interfaces to all the machines on the network.

Let's look at the services provided by WOSA. They are divided into three categories:

- Common application services
- Communication services
- Vertical market services

The following sections examine each category and its components.

Common Application Services

Common application services include components that allow Windows-based applications to seamlessly connect with different vendor implementations of information services.

- Open Database Connectivity (ODBC) allows seamless access across dissimilar database systems from within Windows-based applications. You have already used the power of ODBC to access the FoxPro database from the Family Tree application. Remember from the setup of that ODBC source that choosing the database you wanted (for example, FoxPro, Paradox, Btrieve) was nothing more than a mouse click away. That's what I mean by true database connectivity through a single interface.

Day 21: Future Topics

- Messaging Application Program Interface (MAPI) allows mail-enabled Windows-based applications to communicate and interoperate with multiple mail services. Of course, the main use for this would be mail. More and more mail systems are starting to provide a MAPI interface to their product. This enables people who have Microsoft Mail to communicate with new or legacy systems via gateways or translation packages. But there is another use for MAPI and Mail. Mail-enabled applications (MEAs) are popping up all over the place. Microsoft's Schedule+ will send meeting requests via Mail and get the replies to verify your schedule. Word 6 now allows you to mail a document directly from the File menu. MEAs are something that top companies are looking at to solve the "kill a tree a day" paper problem. Look for much more in the future about this topic.

- Windows Telephony (TAPI) allows desktop applications to access corporate telephone networks regardless of the type of telephone network or PC-telephone connection. I've been waiting for the day when Windows will answer the phone for me (silently), use caller ID to find out who is on the line, announce the caller through my Sound Blaster card (in the language of my choice), and then allow me to answer the call or have the PC take a digitized message (saved to the hard drive, of course). The technology is here, and TAPI is a key player.

- License Service Application Program Interface (LSAPI) makes it easier for corporations to implement centralized software license management. It's not too difficult to keep track of 20 applications on 20 machines in a small company, but when you are a company the size of WordPerfect Corp., for example, how do you control or even know how many copies of Word 6.0 you have? This is a monumental problem. And a company the size of WordPerfect Corp. can't claim ignorance when audited. That's where the LSAPI comes in. By allowing license management, you can better keep track of the number of people using a product. It's even possible to save money this way. You might be paying for a 500-copy site license of Word when only 250 users are ever using it at any given time. (Time to renegotiate that site license, huh?)

Communication Services

WOSA communication services give applications standard access to network communications. There are three types: mainframe connectivity, TCP/IP (socket) connectivity, and RPC.

- Windows SNA (System Network Architecture) API standardizes a corporation's method of host connectivity by providing open access to IBM SNA API categories. It provides a standard method of communicating with legacy mainframe systems. This use of the word "mainframe" doesn't refer to the `CMainFrame` class that we have used to create our applications, but to the big, slow, power-sucking refrigerators that adorn museums, cost a bundle to operate and maintain, and are manned by COBOL lovers.

- Windows Sockets allows Windows-based applications to access network services across multiple transport protocols such as TCP/IP, IPX/SPX, and AppleTalk. The WINSOCK.DLL file in your Windows directory provides a gateway to connectivity outside your machine. Companies such as FTP Software were providing proprietary solutions for connectivity. Now they're moving toward developing applications that rely on the Windows Sockets interface. This way, their applications can run on all systems, not just systems using their proprietary TCP stacks.

- Microsoft RPC is a remote procedure call facility that is compatible with the Open Software Foundation's DCE RPC. Microsoft rewrote the RPC to be more efficient under Windows. RPC is a mechanism that allows your machine to execute code on another machine. In a network containing a number of dissimilar systems, this can be a real plus. Why have your PC do your Fourier transform when you can use RPC to call your Cray to do it, and then have it pass the answer back to you? (Of course, we don't all have a Cray sitting around, but the principle is valid.)

Vertical Market Services

WOSA vertical market services enable Windows-based applications to access specialized services found in specific vertical markets. These services are geared toward the world of finances and stocks.

- WOSA Extensions for Financial Services provide Windows-based applications with a standard interface to services common in the banking industry. These services are being developed by the Banking Systems Vendor Council. They will define standard interfaces for dealing with items specific to banking, such as magnetic card readers, PIN pads, receipt printers, and so on. Other topics and needs will be addressed as the standard evolves.

- WOSA Extensions for Real-Time Market Data allow Windows-based applications to receive live market data from many different sources. This standard is being developed by the Open Market Data Council. This standard will work to develop means to exchange live data such as stock quotes and news.

The nine WOSA components just discussed make Windows a central connectivity point for enterprise-wide applications that allow the PC to be an active participant, not just a spectator.

MFC 3.x and OLE

This book has covered many aspects of the MFC. We have focused on the MFC version 2.5 because this is the version that shipped with Visual C++ version 1.5. Microsoft is continually improving the MFC (many sub-versions have come and gone during the writing of this book).

Day 21: Future Topics

The 32-bit version of Visual C++ 2.1 uses the MFC 3.1. The MFC 3.1 supports even more of the environment, including many of the new common controls (which you will see used in Win95):

- ☐ Tree view
- ☐ Sliders
- ☐ Tab control
- ☐ Header control
- ☐ Status bar control
- ☐ List view
- ☐ ToolTips control (my personal favorite)
- ☐ Progress control
- ☐ Animation control (animated cursors help pass the time)
- ☐ Hot key control
- ☐ Spin button
- ☐ Image list

As you can see, the MFC has a wealth of enhancements. But it doesn't stop there. For LAN developers, the MFC also supports MAPI and Windows Sockets through new 32-bit MFC classes and AppWizard.

The point I'm trying to make here is that the MFC is an evolutionary beast. It will grow and evolve. However, Microsoft has promised to keep it backwardly compatible to reassure us that what we develop today will not be lost tomorrow.

OpenGL

OpenGL was originally developed by Silicon Graphics Inc. (SGI), the originator of many really great graphics. You might have seen the magic of SGI in *Jurassic Park*. The dinosaurs were all created on SGI workstations. I have worked with SGI Indigo and Iris workstations, and I give them my highest fun rating. SGI developed OpenGL for its graphics workstations. It lets their applications create high-quality color images regardless of the windowing system, OS, or hardware used.

A governing body, the OpenGL Architecture Review Board (ARB), is responsible for defining OpenGL. There are some heavy hitters on this board, including SGI, Microsoft, Intel, IBM, and DEC. OpenGL was developed as a software interface for graphics hardware and is used primarily to render two- and three-dimensional objects into a frame buffer. We describe these objects in two ways—as sequences of vertices (geometric objects) and as pixels (image definition). OpenGL does the rest and turns your objects into pictures on-screen.

OpenGL libraries come free with Windows NT. This is a big bonus in my mind because it opens the door to letting you do great graphics programming without needing to buy an SGI machine.

WinG

I first heard about WinG while reading a prominent software publication. It stated that Microsoft had come out with a new programming API to assist Windows programmers in doing high-speed animation on the PC. Since graphics is my primary love, I investigated. It turns out that Microsoft's Advanced Consumer Technology Group did in fact create this API and make it available for free. This was Microsoft's attempt to evangelize Windows as a platform for writing cool video games (Tie Fighter under NT 3.5 sounds great to me).

What is great about WinG is that when a WinG application first starts up, it runs profiling code to determine how to best display graphics on your system. It then picks the best method for your platform and applies it. The WinG toolkit is available through the standard Microsoft channels and, of course, on the MSDN CD.

WinToon

So you like Bugs Bunny cartoons, huh? Well, how would you like to make your own? Now you can. WinToon is a set of extensions for Video for Windows that allows you to play back cartoons. The frames of the cartoons are played back on top of a bitmap background. This is the "blue screen" method. You can create .AVI files and play those back. The WinToon SDK is another piece of freeware from Microsoft. Now, if only I could draw....

Microsoft Network

So you think Bill Gates (hereafter referred to as Mr. GATE$) is happy with just owning your desktop and all the applications in it? Well, he's not. With the acquisition of Intuit, he wants to own your checkbook. He's working on deals with banks and credit card companies to help him own your online banking too. Well, there's one more thing he wants—your online services.

Microsoft Network (previously named Marvel) is an ambitious project to compete with other service providers such as CompuServe, America Online, and Prodigy. And why not! CompuServe is nice but very expensive (if you really use it). As for the others, let's just say that flashy graphics do not an online service make. Microsoft Network will integrate directly into the Win95 desktop. The services will look like files and folders, and you will be able to use the right mouse button to bring up a context menu describing the service, its address on the network, and how much it costs. The beauty is that Microsoft Network just looks like part of your desktop.

Future Topics

It had been rumored that the servers for this distributed network were going to be NT servers. Who would have guessed? Well, if we can have forums on everything from animation to home schooling, why not? Competition is always healthy, and this will be an incentive for other online services to give you more for your buck. Good luck, Mr. GATE$.

Intel's P6 and Beyond

Here is a subject near to our hearts (if you don't know why, read the About the Authors section). The Intel processor has helped drive us to where we are today. Think of the processor as the egg and the software as the chicken. As software becomes more complex, it requires yet a bigger processor to drive it. With the addition of multimedia, video conferencing, and powerful 3D rendering tools, the need for speed is even greater. The Pentium processor is in use on more desktops every day. Intel has also announced the P6 processor and deemed it 200 percent faster than a Pentium at the same clock speed. This is Intel owning up to doubling processing power every 18 months.

Intel has also signed an agreement with Hewlett-Packard to co-develop the next generation of processor beyond the P6. So if you think for a moment that the fat lady is singing, don't. Don't expect anything soon out of this relationship, but when it does come, it will be great.

The other evolving technology that will drive us to even faster processors is the integration of peripheral devices into the CPU. Why do we need Sound Blaster cards in our computers? Couldn't we just put the physical connectors on the back of the motherboard and do all the sound synthesis in software? Yes. The CPU could be everything from a modem to sound cards. This is also the wave of the future. Why should you have to buy a new sound card to upgrade from a Sound Blaster 16 to a Sound Blaster AWE32? Just pay Creative Labs for a diskette or an automatic upgrade via modem (although you should read about the conspiracy theory in the last section of this chapter) and upgrade the sound software. Sounds wonderful, doesn't it? It's coming, so get ready.

Delphi

Borland's Delphi product, nicknamed "the Visual Basic killer" by the press, might make its mark on the business of writing software. Just as Visual Basic brought closet Windows programmers out into the open, so might Delphi allow these same programmers to take an even bigger step toward "nerdvana."

One of the most straightforward languages to program in is Borland's Turbo Pascal. Delphi binds Object Pascal (a totally revamped version of Pascal) and couples it with a truly "visual" development environment similar to Visual Basic's. From all the reviews written, it seems that Delphi might have a bright future. I have seen true VB zealots defect and become Delphi addicts.

The promise of a true executable without the need for VBRUN300.DLL to accompany it sounds tantalizing. At the time this was written, Delphi did not support OCXs (a real bummer) and a few other necessities, but fixes were promised. We can only worry about the possible discord between Borland and Microsoft. People who wish to use all Microsoft products except Delphi might have to work with one product not supporting the other. I know that if Delphi doesn't support Access database files, I'll be bumming.

Conspiracy Theory

I have a conspiracy theory I would like to share with you. I heard it from a paranoid friend. Have you ever noticed that many products allow you to register your software electronically? Do you know how easy it would be for someone to gather information about what software is on your system during the electronic registration program's initialization and relay that information to the vendor when the electronic registration takes place? Think of the competitive edge a company could gain from knowing exactly what software you have on your PC. Also think of the copyright police bursting into your house with a computer printout of all the illegal software you have on your computer. I don't condone theft, but I also don't condone an invasion of privacy. Just something to think about while trying not to become roadkill on the information superhighway. Anybody have Oliver Stone's phone number?

Summary

This chapter tried to show you the tip of a wonderful iceberg. There is more than a lifetime's worth of information to be learned. I have bitten off only a small chunk (over the last 15 years), and it has been far too big to swallow.

Workshop

Exercises

1. Examine the applications on your system and try to decide how the future topics discussed in this chapter will affect the look and feel of your current setup. Do any of your existing application already have some of these future enhancements?
2. Future technologies have a tendency to change considerably by the time users actually gets their hands on them. Your mission, should you decide to accept it, is to grab the most recent issue of your favorite computer magazine and see how many of the topics in this chapter are discussed and how they differ from my description.
3. Think up a name for the P6 processor (and not Sextium; I've already thought of that).
4. Calculate Mr. GATE$' net worth. Make sure you have a calculator that supports scientific notation.

Answers to Quiz Questions

Answers to Quiz Questions

Chapter 1

1. `CWinApp`, `CFrameWnd`, `CDocument`, and `CView`.
2. `CView` displays data, and it acquires it from `CDocument`.
3. The `CDocTemplate`-derived class is the glue that binds the other classes together.
4. One implementation is for the debug version of the application, and the other is for the runtime version.
5. The application object creates and initializes the document template during its `InitInstance()` function. The document template creates the document, view, and frame window when `OnFileNew()` or `OnFileOpen()` is called.

Chapter 2

1. We would want to place code in the constructor that is executed only once during the program's execution. The code we place in `OnNewDocument()` will be executed every time the user creates a new document, which could be a large number of times per application execution.
2. All iterators consist of three parts: an iterator object, an initialization function, and an iteration function. The iterator object acts like a bookmark, holding your place in the iteration. The initialization function places your bookmark at the beginning of the set over which you're iterating. The iteration function increments your bookmark to the next logical position in the set.
3. `LineTo()` draws a straight line from the current point to the point specified in the parameters. A second `CDC` function, `MoveTo()`, allows you to change the current point.
4. `UpdateAllViews()` informs the document's associated views that the stored data has changed. The views, in turn, update the display with fresh data from the document.

Chapter 3

1. A message ID, which identifies the message. `WParam` and `LParam`, which can hold message data.
2. The `WM_COMMAND` message is special because it is the carrier of commands. It's really a message within a message.
3. Messages relay information, whereas commands direct action.
4. `AfxGetApp()` returns a pointer to the application object. Cursor ownership is critical to cursor management because only certain windows will properly display cursors they own.
5. No.

Chapter 4

1. `UpdateAllViews(NULL)` instructs the document's views to update their displays with new data. A `NULL` parameter will tell `UpdateAllViews()` to send an update message to all views, including the one that originated the change. If you're not careful in your `OnUpdate` function, where this message is processed, you could wind up in an endless loop.

2. `CWindowDC` is used to access the entire screen. `CClientDC` is used to access the client area of one window.

3. The first two parameters specify the ellipse on which the shape will be based. The second two parameters specify the section of the ellipse that defines the extent of the shape.

4. The `WINDING` polygon fill mode uses the concept of how many times the polygon winds around a given area to determine if it is filled. The `ALTERNATE` polygon fill mode simply fills alternate polygon cells, much like a multicolored map.

Chapter 5

1. `AnsiToOem()` and `OemToAnsi()` provide additional support for internationalization. They allow conversion between the normal ANSI character set we use in Windows and the character set installed with MS-DOS, identified by Windows as the OEM (Original Equipment Manufacturer) character set.

2. `AfxMessageBox()` is a global function (as are all `Afx` functions) and therefore can be used anywhere in your program. `MessageBox()` is a member function of the class `CWnd` and therefore can be called only from a `CWnd`-derived class.

3. The key idea in exception handling is an alternate flow of control. When an exception is encountered in a program unit, the sequential flow within that unit is halted. A separate flow is started—that of exception processing. If no handlers are found, the exception propagates to the MFC framework, where the exception becomes an error. An error message is displayed and your program remains halted (or, more appropriately, dead). The whole idea of exception handling is to catch these exceptions before they reach the framework (and hence become errors).

4. The `ASSERT` macro is used in the debug version of the Visual C++ environment to validate variable values. If the Boolean expression passed to `ASSERT` is true, program control proceeds as normal. If, on the other hand, a false expression is passed to `ASSERT`, the program halts and a diagnostic message is displayed. Liberal use of the `ASSERT` macro can assure a higher level of program robustness.

5. No.

Answers to Quiz Questions

Chapter 6

1. For tracking down errors and general troubleshooting.
2. `Dump()` will now display the true class name in the output window.
3. Every class derived from `CObject` has an associated `CRuntimeClass` object that holds runtime class information. The parameters passed to the macros indicate the current class and the immediate ancestor class. This information is transferred to the associated `CRuntimeClass` object.
4. I like to think of the schema number as the version number of your class. It's used during the load process to distinguish between objects of the same class but different versions.

Chapter 7

1. A Windows dialog consists of three parts: the dialog window, the dialog resource, and the dialog code. The dialog window holds the graphical elements of the dialog (the dialog controls) during runtime. The dialog resource is the information held in the resource file that specifies which graphical elements are to be included and where they are to be placed within the dialog. The dialog code is the brains behind the dialog. This is where the dialog is given life. In terms of the MFC, the dialog code resides primarily in the `CDialog` class.
2. `CListBox` is a selection box with multiple text selections for the user. `CComboBox` is an editable selection box and a hybrid of edit and list box controls.
3. With a modal dialog box, the user must respond to the dialog before the proper conditional branch may be determined. Modeless dialogs can be placed in the background, and processing continues.
4. We wait until after the base class call because it is only then that the data transfer has taken place.

Chapter 8

1. A table holds one or more records. A record is composed of one or more fields. A field holds a single piece of data.
2. A database can be sorted on only one field. This field is called the primary key. Only one primary key can exist in a database.

   Indexes are used in much the same way as book indexes. They give you an additional, usually alternative, way of referencing the information in question. They greatly facilitate the searching process. Unlike book indexes, you may define multiple secondary indexes for different search and sort orderings.

3. Normalized databases eliminate redundant data and assure data integrity. Remember, there should be only one producer of data and many consumers.
4. The ODBC Administrator displays and helps you register data sources for your system.
5. No. Even the text in a static text box can be changed during the execution of a program.

Chapter 9

1. `CRecordView` is a `CFormView` with `CRecordset` functionality built in. `CFormView` is a hybrid of the `CView` and `CDialog` classes. `CFormView` is merely a `CView` class with aspects of a dialog.
2. The default record set resides in the document class. It is the data item, so it belongs where all data belongs in an MFC application—in the document. The record set object is opened in the `CRecordView::OnInitialUpdate()` implementation; the view class opens the record set.
3. Although queries are invoked during both an `Open()` and a `Requery()` function call, a query is constructed only in a call to `Open()`.
4. `m_strFilter` is a string specifying the filter that includes/excludes records and is used in the SQL WHERE clause. The `m_strSort` parameter string specifies the sort order of the query results and is used in the SQL ORDER BY clause.
5. Through the `IsFieldNull()` function, we can determine if field variables are valid. Remember, database NULL and C++ NULL are two different things! You can't determine if a field variable is NULL by comparing it to the C++ NULL constant! Only passing the address of the record set's field member variable to the `IsFieldNull()` function will determine if the database field is NULL.

Chapter 10

1. The `Fail()` function is called whenever a transfer fails. The `Fail()` function, in turn, aborts the transfer and positions the input focus at the offending dialog control. Using the `Fail()` function in your transfer functions is a big responsibility. Poor usage of `Fail()` can cause the user to be trapped in a dialog. Another dangerous aspect of using the `Fail()` function is the fact that it generates an exception.
2. Each of these controls has two means of finding a particular string in their list. One method is searching for a prefix of a string. This will find the first string that has this prefix. The other method (which is available only on Windows 3.1 and later) is an exact-match method. With this method, only exact matches of the string are found.

Answers to Quiz Questions

As you have probably guessed, the "exact" string transfer functions select strings in the combo or list boxes only when an exact match is made. The "normal" string transfer functions select the first element in the list that has the appropriate prefix.

3. `CTime` has that little problem of not supporting dates prior to 1970. Therefore, it's not of much use for birthdays of people 20-something and older! `CTime` also has a problem with memory leaks—at least with one version of the compiler.

4. You might see both types of transfers occurring in a single ODBC application. There isn't a restriction on either one or the other because they serve two different purposes. The first method is the ordinary `CDialog` data transfer, and the second is the `CRecordset`/`CDialog` data transfer. You certainly can have both a normal dialog and a record set enhanced dialog in the same application.

Chapter 11

1. You can abort an `AddNew()` or `Edit()` by moving to another record without calling the `Update()` function. There is no way to abort a `Delete()`.

2. The `AddString()` function is used to add a new item to a list box. The `SetItemData()` function is used to attach an associated number to a list box item.

3. If you require an expression to be evaluated for the proper functioning of your application, either evaluate the expression outside of the `ASSERT` macro and pass the result to `ASSERT`, or call the `VERIFY` macro. `VERIFY` will always evaluate its expression and then act on the result in the same way as `ASSERT` does. In other words,

   ```
   VERIFY (expression);
   ```

   is equivalent to

   ```
   BOOL bTemp = expression;
   ASSERT (bTemp);
   ```

Chapter 12

1. Yes. Both multiple documents and multiple views are given to us in the default application. The term "multiple" just means several copies of the same document or view.

2. The main difference is that a single document may have many different views attached to it, whereas every view object has one and only one document object.

3. The resource ID, the document class, the view class, and the `CMDIChildWnd` frame class.

4. Document template objects are used to create those other classes, so they can't be placed within the mainframe, document, or view classes without causing a circular reference. We also place the document template pointers in the interface of our

application so that they will be visible and available for use from anywhere in the application.

5. They are worlds apart. `CTreeDoc` holds a reference to a changing database. The user has full access to move through and change the records in the database. This functionality is mirrored in the menu resource. What is the charter for `CAhnenDoc`? It is a static structure that holds the ancestry construction built from the database. No record scrolling or changing is allowed—what you see is what you get! Therefore, many of the menu items from the default resource are out of context when used with a `CAhnenDoc` document. A new menu, and potentially many other resource items, obviously are needed.

Chapter 13

1. $((420 \times 551) \times 8\text{bpp}) / 8 = 231{,}420$ bytes (the division by 8 gets us from bits to bytes).

2. No. A color palette can contain only a small subset of relevant colors. This feature allows the sharing of a single palette with multiple applications. Each application "registers" only the colors it needs, leaving room in the palette for others.

3. Yes. You can be rude and simply call `RealizePalette()`. This will ensure that your palette becomes the current one, period.

4. In order to effectively parse the actual bitmap data, we need to know how many bits of data represent each pixel. Without this information (`bmBitsPixel`), we wouldn't know how to parse the data.

Chapter 14

1. The two types of DIBs discussed were the Windows DIB and the Presentation Manager (PM) DIB. The principal difference between the two is that the Windows DIB is 32-bit and the PM DIB is 24-bit.

2. The `CDIBitmap` functions `LoadFromHandle()` and `SaveToHandle()` load DIBs from and save DIBs to `CLongBinary` objects.

3. Objects of the `CLongBinary` class serve as temporary holders for potentially large blocks of information passing between an ODBC-enabled application and a database. This class is a thin shell of functionality over a handle to a global block of memory.

4. A Windows DIB file can be broken into the following parts: a `BITMAPFILEHEADER`, which contains information about the DIB file; a `BITMAPINFOHEADER`, which contains information about the bitmap; a color table, which consists of a series of `RGBQUAD` structures containing color code information; and finally the bits themselves.

Answers to Quiz Questions

Chapter 15

1. Linking an object simply places a pointer to the object in the document, whereas embedding actually places an instance of the object into the document.
2. VBX technology is a wonderful tool for the Visual Basic programming world. The problem is that the technology doesn't port to a 32-bit world. The OLE custom control (OCX) doesn't have that limitation.

Chapter 16

1. The new OLE classes that are of consequence to a server application are

CIPFrameWnd	The window frame for an in-place server.
COleServerItem	The base class for your server-side objects that provide for embedding and linking.
COleServerDoc	The base class for your server document.
COleTemplateServer	The document template class for your server application.
COleDocument	The base class for both server and container documents.

2. The server needs the first `OnDraw()` function to act as the usual `CView`-style `OnDraw()`. The second `OnDraw()` is intended to produce the metafile object that the container application uses to display the embedded item.

Chapter 17

1. The line `CFontDialog dlg(plf, CF_PRINTERFONTS, pDC);` sets up the dialog box for use, and the line `if (dlg.DoModal() == IDOK)` actually invokes the dialog box to appear on-screen.
2. The axis is a problem because the orientation of the axis changes depending on the mapping mode chosen.
3. You would override the `OnPrepareDC()` function.
4. The `m_RectDraw` data member holds the current drawable area for the page.

Chapter 18

1. `CWingrepCntrItem` (also known as `COleClientItem`) is the container-side manifestation of a server item.
2. The biggest difference between `CDocument` and `COleDocument` is the list of container items maintained by `COleDocument` and the associated maintenance functions.

3. No. `CRectTracker` can be used in any application. However, in order to get at the actual `CRectTracker` code, you must include the appropriate OLE libraries.
4. `OLEIVERB_SHOW` instructs the server to activate in in-place editing mode. `OLEIVERB_OPEN` instructs the server to activate as a stand-alone application. If either the server or the container doesn't support in-place editing, both verbs have the same result.

Chapter 19

1. A splitter window makes this possible.
2. This call would create a static splitter window with four panes—two rows and two columns.
3. File Manager drag and drop has a number of restrictions. The primary limitation is that the only data that can be transferred is filenames. OLE 2.0 drag and drop, on the other hand, has very few limitations, but it has the flaw of being much more complicated to program. Such is the price of flexibility.
4. `FORMATETC` is a structure that holds information concerning the data being transferred. `STGMEDIUM` holds the data and is the actual structure being transferred.

Chapter 20

1. HC31 is the standard compiler. It works well for small-to-medium help files. HCP should be used when you're compiling medium-to-large help projects. It makes more efficient use of memory.
2. You shouldn't use graphics in your help file when they don't add to the understanding of the topics being explained. I love graphics more than most people, but I must admit that sometimes they just clutter things up.

Hungarian Notation

Hungarian Notation

The peculiar nature of Windows gave rise to a peculiar, but valuable, notation named for the Microsoft programmer Charles Simonyi. Windows variables and your variables can be identified as to their type by the prefixes they sport. Hungarian notation can be invaluable in your programming efforts, since you can deduce considerable information about a variable just from its name. This reduces coding errors, increases understanding, and provides uniformity in your code. However, you're not required to utilize this strategy. You might decide to use it for public variables only and use your old familiar notation for variables local to functions. This approach isn't wrong, but once you adopt Hungarian notation, you will find yourself using it everywhere. You'll find that practically all the variables in Windows practice this convention. It seems to be a Windows house rule. Don't despair; you'll soon get used to it. In time, you'll even come to like it!

Table B.1. The prefixes of Hungarian notation.

Prefix	Description	Example
a	Array of variables	anTotals, awValues
b	Boolean type: BOOL	bDone
by	8-bit unsigned type: BYTE	byHiWord
C	Name of a foundation class or derivative	CDocument
c	Character type: char	cStatus
cx, cy	x-, y-length variables: short	cxLength, cyHeight
dw	Double word type: DWORD	dwData
f	Float	m_fDistance
fn	Function	fnGetTime
h	Handle to an object	hInstance
i	Integer type: int	iAge
l	Long integer type: LONG	lParam
m_	Class member variable	m_bFound
n	Integer type: int or short	nCount
p	Pointer type	pDC
s	String type (not null-terminated)	sBuffer
sz	String terminated by a null (\0)	szName
w	Unsigned word (or int): WORD (or UINT)	wParam
x,y	Coordinate pair: short	x,y

These prefixes aren't mutually exclusive. You can have a variable that's a long pointer to a null-terminated string. So which prefix would you choose? All of them! Mix and match prefixes. Use any or all that are necessary. The variable just mentioned would have a prefix of lpsz—actually, quite a common prefix in the Windows world.

Don't feel constrained to this list. It's abbreviated anyway. At some point you might want to refer to a complete list of Hungarian notation in order to find a prefix for a variable that's not found here. But don't view the "Complete Hungarian Notation" as a sacred work. It's merely an accepted standard in Windows. In certain cases, you might opt to invent your own prefixes. After all, you make your own types through the class structure, so why not make your own prefixes? However, when you do construct your own prefixes, take care in choosing them and, once you've chosen them, make sure you use them consistently. Hungarian notation is more than just a list of prefixes. It's really the idea of using prefixes consistently to convey information about the variable.

Use the Source

Use the Source

One of the most valuable lessons about programming the MFC (or programming in general, for that matter) is how and where to look up information. This book is a good start, but it's more along the lines of a tutorial. When you're working on a large program, you will invariably need facts on how to do a specific task. This kind of computer lore typically is found in the references that come with your compiler. But the references are big, dense, and usually lacking in concrete examples. When such a circumstance arises, you're usually in too much of a hurry to pore over the references, hoping for a glimmer of understanding. Don't get me wrong. The references are irreplaceable resources for your programming work. It's just that sometimes they're too general to be of much help. In some circumstances, they're worthless. What should you do? If you're programming at work, there are usually a number of computer wizards roaming around, looking for someone (such as you) to inundate with their guruness. You used to be able to find gurus very easily. They left behind a trail of Cheese Doodle wrappers and laughed distinctively whenever a line from *Star Trek* was misquoted. You would find them hacking away through the night on software only gurus would understand. Sadly, times have changed. I have seen gurus in suits. They drive "Beemers" now and have 2.3 kids. Some even go home to their families at night. It's tragic. So what if you can't find your neighborhood computer genius, or worse, you *are* the local guru? How do you find the answer to your problem? Use the Source, Duke!

When in doubt as to what a particular MFC function does or, more importantly, how it does what it's supposed to do, go to the source. All the foundation classes are represented with source code in the MSVC\MFC\SRC directory. Notice that I didn't say that *all* the source code for the MFC is contained in the specified directory. That's because the actual source code for the MFC might differ from that provided. In other words, there is no guarantee that the source code supplied is the same source code used in generating the libraries. The supplied code is for instructional purposes only! But that's okay. That's really the only reason we would want it anyway. Surely you don't want to recompile the MFC libraries when you can use inheritance to get the same utility! Don't recompile the MFC in any case. Take advantage of the MFC as a stable, maintained platform. But also take advantage of the educational opportunities afforded by the supplied MFC code. The remainder of this appendix is an index to the supplied MFC source.

All interface files are contained in the MSVC\MFC\INCLUDE directory, and all implementation source code files are contained in the MSVC\MFC\SRC directory.

Table C.1. A guide to class implementation.

MFC Name	Interface	Implementation
CArchive	AFX.H	ARCCORE.CPP
CArchiveException	AFX.H	ARCEX.APP
CBEdit	AFXPEN.H	PENCNTRL.CPP
CBitmap	AFXWIN.H	WINGDI.CPP

MFC Name	Interface	Implementation
CBitmapButton	AFXEXT.H	WINBTN.CPP
CBrush	AFXWIN.H	WINGDI.CPP
CButton	AFXWIN.H	WINCNTRL.CPP
CByteArray	AFXCOLL.H	ARRAY_B.CPP
CClientDC	AFXWIN.H	WINGDI.CPP
CCmdTarget	AFXWIN.H	CMDTARG.CPP
CCmdUI	AFXWIN.H	CMDTARG.CPP
CColorDialog	AFXDLGS.H	DLGCLR.CPP
CComboBox	AFXWIN.H	WINCNTRL.CPP
CControlBar	AFXEXT.H	WINFRM.CPP
CCreateContext	AFXEXT.H	DOCTEMPL.CPP
CDatabase	AFXDB.H	DBCORE.CPP
CDataExchange	AFXWIN.H	DLGDATA.CPP
CDBException	AFXDB.H	DBCORE.CPP
CDC	AFXWIN.H	WINGDI.CPP
CDialog	AFXWIN.H	DLGCORE.CPP
CDialogBar	AFXEXT.H	BARDLG.CPP
CDocItem	AFXOLE.H	OLEDOC1.CPP
CDocTemplate	AFXWIN.H	DOCTEMPL.CPP
CDocument	AFXWIN.H	DOCCORE.CPP
CDumpContext	AFX.H	DUMPCONT.CPP
CDWordArray	AFXCOLL.H	ARRAY_D.CPP
CEdit	AFXWIN.H	WINCNTRL.CPP
CEditView	AFXEXT.H	VIEWEDIT.CPP
CException	AFX.H	EXCEPT.CPP
CFieldExchange	AFXDB.H	DBCORE.CPP
CFieldInfo	AFXDB.H	DBCORE.CPP
CFile	AFX.H	FILECORE.CPP
CFileDialog	AFXDLGS.H	DLGFILE.CPP
CFileException	AFX.H	FILEX.CPP
CFindReplaceDialog	AFXDLGS.H	DLGFR.CPP

continues

Use the Source

Table C.1. continued

MFC Name	Interface	Implementation
CFont	AFXWIN.H	WINGDI.CPP
CFontDialog	AFXDLGS.H	DLGFNT.CPP
CFormView	AFXEXT.H	VIEWFORM.CPP
CFrameWnd	AFXWIN.H	WINCORE.CPP
CGdiObject	AFXWIN.H	WINGDI.CPP
CHEdit	AFXPEN.H	PENCNTRL.CPP
CListBox	AFXWIN.H	WINCNTRL.CPP
CLongBinary	AFXDB.H	DBRFX.CPP
CMapPtrToPtr	AFXCOLL.H	MAP_PP.CPP
CMapPtrToWord	AFXCOLL.H	MAP_PW.CPP
CMapStringToOb	AFXCOLL.H	MAP_SO.CPP
CMapStringToPtr	AFXCOLL.H	MAP_SP.CPP
CMapStringToString	AFXCOLL.H	MAP_SS.CPP
CMapWordToOb	AFXCOLL.H	MAP_WO.CPP
CMapWordToPtr	AFXCOLL.H	MAP_WP.CPP
CMDIChildWnd	AFXWIN.H	WINMDI.CPP
CMDIFrameWnd	AFXWIN.H	WINMDI.CPP
CMemFile	AFX.H	FILEMEM.CPP
CMemoryException	AFX.H	EXCEPT.CPP
CMemoryState	AFX.H	AFXMEM.CPP
CMenu	AFXWIN.H	WINMENU.CPP
CMetaFileDC	AFXEXT.H	DCMETA.CPP
CMultiDocTemplate	AFXWIN.H	DOCMULTI.CPP
CNotSupportedException	AFX.H	EXCEPT.CPP
CObArray	AFXCOLL.H	ARRAY_O.CPP
CObject	AFX.H	OBJCORE.CPP
CObList	AFXCOLL.H	OBJCORE.CPP
COleBusyDialog	AFXODLGS.H	OLEDLGS2.CPP
COleChangeIconDialog	AFXODLGS.H	OLEDLGS1.CPP
COleClientItem	AFXOLE.H	OLEDOC1.CPP

MFC Name	Interface	Implementation
COleConvertDialog	AFXODLGS.H	OLEDLGS1.CPP
COleDataObject	AFXOLE.H	OLEDOBJ1.CPP
COleDataSource	AFXOLE.H	OLEDOBJ2.CPP
COleDialog	AFXODLGS.H	OLEDLGS2.CPP
COleDispatchDriver	AFXDISP.H	OLEDISP2.CPP
COleDispatchException	AFXDISP.H	OLEDISP1.CPP
COleDocument	AFXOLE.H	OLEDOC1.CPP
COleDropSource	AFXOLE.H	OLEDROP1.CPP
COleDropTarget	AFXOLE.H	OLEDROP2.CPP
COleException	AFXOLE.H	OLEMISC.CPP
COleInsertDialog	AFXODLGS.H	OLEDLGS1.CPP
COleIPFrameWnd	AFXOLE.H	OLEIPFRM.CPP
COleLinkingDoc	AFXOLE.H	OLECLI1.CPP
COleLinksDialog	AFXODLGS.H	OLEDLGS1.CPP
COleMessageFilter	AFXOLE.H	OLEMSGF.CPP
COleObjectFactory	AFXDISP.H	OLEFACT.CPP
COlePasteSpecialDialog	AFXODLGS.H	OLEDLGS1.CPP
COleRectTracker	AFXEXT.H	OLEMISC.CPP
COleResizeBar	AFXOLE.H	OLEBAR.CPP
COleServerDoc	AFXOLE.H	OLESVR1.CPP
COleServerItem	AFXOLE.H	OLEDOC1.CPP
COleStreamFile	AFXOLE.H	OLESTRM.CPP
COleTemplateServer	AFXDISP.H	OLETSVR.CPP
COleUpdateDialog	AFXDLGS.H	OLEDLGS1.CPP
CPaintDC	AFXWIN.H	WINGDI.CPP
CPalette	AFXWIN.H	WINGDI.CPP
CPen	AFXWIN.H	WINGDI.CPP
CPoint	AFXWIN.H	WINGDI.CPP
CPrintDialog	AFXDLGS.H	DLGPRNT.CPP
CPrintInfo	AFXEXT.H	VIEWPRNT.CPP
CPrintPreviewState	AFXEXT.H	VIEWPRNT.CPP

continues

Use the Source

Table C.1. continued

MFC Name	Interface	Implementation
CPtrArray	AFXCOLL.H	ARRAY_P.CPP
CPtrList	AFXCOLL.H	LIST_P.CPP
CRecordset	AFXDB.H	DBCORE.CPP
CRecordsetStatus	AFXDB.H	DBVIEW.CPP
CRecordView	AFXDB.H	DBVIEW.CPP
CRect	AFXWIN.H	WINGDIX.CPP
CRectTracker	AFXEXT.H	TRCKRECT.CPP
CResourceException	AFXWIN.H	WINGDI.CPP
CRgn	AFXWIN.H	WINGDI.CPP
CRuntimeClass	AFX.H	ARCCORE.CPP
CScrollBar	AFXWIN.H	WINCNTRL.CPP
CScrollView	AFXWIN.H	VIEWSCRL.CPP
CSingleDocTemplate	AFXWIN.H	DOCSINGL.CPP
CSize	AFXWIN.H	VIEWCORE.CPP
CSplitterWnd	AFXEXT.H	VIEWCORE.CPP
CStatic	AFXWIN.H	WINCNTRL.CPP
CStatusBar	AFXEXT.H	BARCORE.CPP
CStdioFile	AFX.H	FILETXT.CPP
CString	AFX.H	STRCORE1.CPP
CStringArray	AFXCOLL.H	ARRAY_S.CPP
CStringList	AFXCOLL.H	LIST_S.CPP
CTime	AFX.H	TIMECORE.CPP
CTimeSpan	AFX.H	TIMECORE.CPP
CToolBar	AFXEXT.H	BARTOOL.CPP
CUIntArray	AFXCOLL.H	ARRAY_U.CPP
CUserException	AFXWIN.H	WINGDI.CPP
CVBControl	AFXEXT.H	VBCNTRL.CPP
CView	AFXWIN.H	WINFRM.CPP
CWinApp	AFXWIN.H	APPCORE.CPP
CWindowDC	AFXWIN.H	WINGDI.CPP
CWnd	AFXWIN.H	BARCORE.CPP
CWordArray	AFXCOLL.H	ARRAY_W.CPP

printf Format Codes

printf Format Codes

I've provided this appendix so that you won't have to run to the reference manuals for every little thing. I use `printf` often and would have liked this in the back of the books I was reading!

For detailed information, see page 441 of the *Run-Time Library Reference*.

Form

`%[Flags][Width][.Precision][{F¦N¦h¦l¦L}]type`

Arguments

Flags	Optional characters that affect the form of numeric types.
Width	Specifies the minimum allowed output width in characters.
Precision	Specifies the exact number of characters to be printed (truncation might occur).
F, N	Indicators for FAR or NEAR, respectively.
h, l, L	Indicators for short, long integer, or long double, respectively.
type	The actual type to be output.

Types

d, i	Signed decimal integer.
u	Unsigned decimal integer.
o	Unsigned octal integer.
x	Unsigned hexadecimal integer using "abcdef."
X	Unsigned hexadecimal integer using "ABCDEF."
f	Double (floating-point) value.
e	Double value in scientific notation using e (for example, 3.55e4 = 35500).
E	Double value in scientific notation using E (for example, 3.55E4 = 35500).
g	Double value using f or e format, whichever is more compact.
G	Double value using f or E format, whichever is more compact.
c	Character.
s	String (printed until a \n is reached).
n	Pointer to integer.
p	Far pointer to void.

Windows Types and Constants

Windows Types and Constants

The Visual C++ environment has a number of predefined types that aid in Windows programming. This appendix lists these definitions.

Table E.1. Windows types.

Name	Description
BOOL	`typedef int`: Boolean type (true or false) zero or nonzero.
BSTR	A 32-bit character pointer.
BYTE	`typedef unsigned char`: 8-bit computer unit 0 to 255.
COLORREF	A 32-bit value used as a color value.
WORD	`typedef unsigned short`: 16-bit double-byte 0 to 65,535.
UINT	`typedef unsigned int`: System-dependent.
LONG	`typedef long`: 32-bit long integer. −2,147,483,648 to +2,147,483,647.
DWORD	`typedef unsigned long`: 32-bit double word. 0 to 4,294,967,295.
LPARAM	A 32-bit value passed as a parameter to a window procedure or callback function.
LPSTR	`typedef char FAR*`: Far pointer to a string.
LPCSTR	`typedef const char FAR*`: Far pointer to a constant string.
LPVOID	A 32-bit pointer to an unspecified type.
LRESULT	A 32-bit value returned from a window procedure or callback function.
UINT	A 16-bit unsigned integer on Windows versions 3.0 and 3.1. A 32-bit unsigned integer on Win32.
WNDPROC	A 32-bit pointer to a window procedure.
WORD	A 16-bit unsigned integer.
WPARAM	A value passed as a parameter to a window procedure or callback function. 16 bits on Windows versions 3.0 and 3.1. 32 bits on Win32.
Data Types Unique to the Microsoft Foundation Class Library	
POSITION	A value used to denote the position of an element in a collection. Used by Microsoft Foundation collection classes.
LPCRECT	A 32-bit pointer to a constant (nonmodifiable) `RECT` structure.

Table E.2. Windows constants.

Name	File	Description
TRUE	AFX.H	Defined to be 1 (Boolean true).
FALSE	AFX.H	Defined to be 0 (Boolean false).
NULL	AFX.H	Defined to be 0.

ANSI Chart

ANSI Chart

Dec	Hex	Char	Dec	Hex	Char	Dec	Hex	Char
†000	00		040	28	(	080	50	P
†001	01		041	29	)	081	51	Q
†002	02		042	2A	*	082	52	R
†003	03		043	2B	+	083	53	S
†004	04		044	2C	,	084	54	T
†005	05		045	2D	-	085	55	U
†006	06		046	2E	.	086	56	V
†007	07		047	2F	/	087	57	W
†008	08		048	30	0	088	58	X
†009	09		049	31	1	089	59	Y
†010	0A		050	32	2	090	5A	Z
†011	0B		051	33	3	091	5B	[
†012	0C		052	34	4	092	5C	\
†013	0D		053	35	5	093	5D	]
†014	0E		054	36	6	094	5E	^
†015	0F		055	37	7	095	5F	_
†016	10		056	38	8	096	60	`
†017	11		057	39	9	097	61	a
†018	12		058	3A	:	098	62	b
†019	13		059	3B	;	099	63	c
†020	14		060	3C	<	100	64	d
†021	15		061	3D	=	101	65	e
†022	16		062	3E	>	102	66	f
†023	17		063	3F	?	103	67	g
†024	18		064	40	@	104	68	h
†025	19		065	41	A	105	69	i
†026	1A		066	42	B	106	6A	j
†027	1B		067	43	C	107	6B	k
†028	1C		068	44	D	108	6C	l
†029	1D		069	45	E	109	6D	m
†030	1E		070	46	F	110	6E	n
†031	1F		071	47	G	111	6F	o
032	20		072	48	H	112	70	p
033	21	!	073	49	I	113	71	q
034	22	"	074	4A	J	114	72	r
035	23	#	075	4B	K	115	73	s
036	24	$	076	4C	L	116	74	t
037	25	%	077	4D	M	117	75	u
038	26	&	078	4E	N	118	76	v
039	27	'	079	4F	O	119	77	w

Dec	Hex	Char	Dec	Hex	Char	Dec	Hex	Char
120	78	x	160	A0		200	C8	È
121	79	y	161	A1	¡	201	C9	É
122	7A	z	162	A2	¢	202	CA	Ê
123	7B	{	163	A3	£	203	CB	Ë
124	7C	|	164	A4	¤	204	CC	Ì
125	7D	}	165	A5	¥	205	CD	Í
126	7E	~	166	A6	¦	206	CE	Î
†127	7F		167	A7	§	207	CF	Ï
†128	80		168	A8	¨	208	D0	Ð
†129	81		169	A9	©	209	D1	Ñ
130	82	‚	170	AA	ª	210	D2	Ò
131	83	ƒ	171	AB	«	211	D3	Ó
132	84	„	172	AC	¬	212	D4	Ô
133	85	…	173	AD	-	213	D5	Õ
134	86	†	174	AE	®	214	D6	Ö
135	87	‡	175	AF	¯	215	D7	×
136	88	ˆ	176	B0	°	216	D8	Ø
137	89	‰	177	B1	±	217	D9	Ù
138	8A	Š	178	B2	²	218	DA	Ú
139	8B	‹	179	B3	³	219	DB	Û
140	8C	Œ	180	B4	´	220	DC	Ü
†141	8D		181	B5	µ	221	DD	Ý
†142	8E		182	B6	¶	222	DE	Þ
†143	8F		183	B7	·	223	DF	ß
†144	90		184	B8	¸	224	E0	à
145	91	'	185	B9	¹	225	E1	á
146	92	'	186	BA	º	226	E2	â
147	93	"	187	BB	»	227	E3	ã
148	94	"	188	BC	¼	228	E4	ä
149	95	•	189	BD	½	229	E5	å
150	96	–	190	BE	¾	230	E6	æ
151	97	—	191	BF	¿	231	E7	ç
152	98	˜	192	C0	À	232	E8	è
153	99	™	193	C1	Á	233	E9	é
154	9A	š	194	C2	Â	234	EA	ê
155	9B	›	195	C3	Ã	235	EB	ë
156	9C	œ	196	C4	Ä	236	EC	ì
†157	9D		197	C5	Å	237	ED	í
†158	9E		198	C6	Æ	238	EE	î
159	9F	Ÿ	199	C7	Ç	239	EF	ï

# ANSI Chart

Dec	Hex	Char	Dec	Hex	Char	Dec	Hex	Char
240	F0	ð	246	F6	ö	252	FC	ü
241	F1	ñ	247	F7	÷	253	FD	ý
242	F2	ò	248	F8	ø	254	FE	þ
243	F3	ó	249	F9	ù	255	FF	ÿ
244	F4	ô	250	FA	ú			
245	F5	õ	251	FB	û			

ASCII (Also Known as OEM) Chart

ASCII (Also Known as OEM) Chart

Dec	Hex	Char	Dec	Hex	Char	Dec	Hex	Char
000	00	NUL	040	28	(	080	50	P
001	01	SOH	041	29	)	081	51	Q
002	02	STX	042	2A	*	082	52	R
003	03	ETX	043	2B	+	083	53	S
004	04	EOT	044	2C	,	084	54	T
005	05	ENQ	045	2D	-	085	55	U
006	06	ACK	046	2E	.	086	56	V
007	07	BEL	047	2F	/	087	57	W
008	08	BS	048	30	0	088	58	X
009	09	HT	049	31	1	089	59	Y
010	0A	LF	050	32	2	090	5A	Z
011	0B	VT	051	33	3	091	5B	[
012	0C	FF	052	34	4	092	5C	\
013	0D	CR	053	35	5	093	5D	]
014	0E	SO	054	36	6	094	5E	^
015	0F	SI	055	37	7	095	5F	_
016	10	DLE	056	38	8	096	60	`
017	11	DC1	057	39	9	097	61	a
018	12	DC2	058	3A	:	098	62	b
019	13	DC3	059	3B	;	099	63	c
020	14	DC4	060	3C	<	100	64	d
021	15	NAK	061	3D	=	101	65	e
022	16	SYN	062	3E	>	102	66	f
023	17	ETB	063	3F	?	103	67	g
024	18	CAN	064	40	@	104	68	h
025	19	EM	065	41	A	105	69	i
026	1A	SUB	066	42	B	106	6A	j
027	1B	ESC	067	43	C	107	6B	k
028	1C	FS	068	44	D	108	6C	l
029	1D	GS	069	45	E	109	6D	m
030	1E	RS	070	46	F	110	6E	n
031	1F	US	071	47	G	111	6F	o
032	20	SP	072	48	H	112	70	p
033	21	!	073	49	I	113	71	q
034	22	"	074	4A	J	114	72	r
035	23	#	075	4B	K	115	73	s
036	24	$	076	4C	L	116	74	t
037	25	%	077	4D	M	117	75	u
038	26	&	078	4E	N	118	76	v
039	27	'	079	4F	O	119	77	w

Dec	Hex	Char	Dec	Hex	Char	Dec	Hex	Char
120	78	x	160	A0	á	200	C8	╚
121	79	y	161	A1	í	201	C9	╔
122	7A	z	162	A2	ó	202	CA	╩
123	7B	{	163	A3	ú	203	CB	╦
124	7C	|	164	A4	ñ	204	CC	╠
125	7D	}	165	A5	Ñ	205	CD	=
126	7E	~	166	A6	ª	206	CE	╬
127	7F	DEL	167	A7	º	207	CF	╧
128	80	Ç	168	A8	¿	208	D0	╨
129	81	ü	169	A9	⌐	209	D1	╤
130	82	é	170	AA	¬	210	D2	╥
131	83	â	171	AB	½	211	D3	╙
132	84	ä	172	AC	¼	212	D4	╘
133	85	à	173	AD	¡	213	D5	╒
134	86	å	174	AE	«	214	D6	╓
135	87	ç	175	AF	»	215	D7	╫
136	88	ê	176	B0	░	216	D8	╪
137	89	ë	177	B1	▒	217	D9	┘
138	8A	è	178	B2	▓	218	DA	┌
139	8B	ï	179	B3	│	219	DB	█
140	8C	î	180	B4	┤	220	DC	▄
141	8D	ì	181	B5	╡	221	DD	▌
142	8E	Ä	182	B6	╢	222	DE	▐
143	8F	Å	183	B7	╖	223	DF	▀
144	90	É	184	B8	╕	224	E0	α
145	91	æ	185	B9	╣	225	E1	ß
146	92	Æ	186	BA	║	226	E2	Γ
147	93	ô	187	BB	╗	227	E3	π
148	94	ö	188	BC	╝	228	E4	Σ
149	95	ò	189	BD	╜	229	E5	σ
150	96	û	190	BE	╛	230	E6	µ
151	97	ù	191	BF	┐	231	E7	τ
152	98	ÿ	192	C0	└	232	E8	Φ
153	99	Ö	193	C1	┴	233	E9	Θ
154	9A	Ü	194	C2	┬	234	EA	Ω
155	9B	¢	195	C3	├	235	EB	δ
156	9C	£	196	C4	─	236	EC	∞
157	9D	¥	197	C5	┼	237	ED	ø
158	9E	₧	198	C6	╞	238	EE	ε
159	9F	ƒ	199	C7	╟	239	EF	∩

ASCII (Also Known as OEM) Chart

Dec	Hex	Char	Dec	Hex	Char	Dec	Hex	Char
240	F0	≡	246	F6	÷	252	FC	η
241	F1	±	247	F7	≈	253	FD	²
242	F2	≥	248	F8	°	254	FE	■
243	F3	≤	249	F9	•	255	FF	
244	F4	⌠	250	FA	·			
245	F5	⌡	251	FB				

Index

:: (scope resolver)

Symbols

:: (scope resolver), 59
<< (storage) operator, 147-148
>> (retrieval) operator, 147-148
? (question mark) in SQL statements, 248-249
640K limit, 556-559

A

aborting functions, 378
abstraction, xxi
accelerator table editor, 64-66
Add Member Variable dialog box, 169
Add( ) function, 136-137
AddDay( ) function, 134-136
AddDocTemplate( ) function, 339
AddItem( ) function, 490
AddNew( ) function, 288-289
AdjustRect( ) function, 494
Administrator application (ODBC), 208-213
AfxGetApp( ) function, 57
AfxMessageBox( ) function, 112-115
AHNENDOC.CPP implementation file, 332-335
AHNENDOC.H header file, 331-335
ahnentafel listings, 198-199
    CAhnenDoc class, 330
    creating documents for, 331-339
algorithms
    drawing, 76
    game strategy, 33-38
aliases (help files), 551
allocating memory, exception handling, 119-121
AnalyzeBoard( ) function, 36-38
AND_CATCH macro, 117
AnimatePalette( ) function, 349
ANSI character set
    chart, 602-604
    converting with ASCII character set, 108-109
AnsiToOem( ) function, 107-109

appending strings, 104-105
applications
    Administrator (ODBC), 208-213
    connecting help files, 553
    CWinApp class, 8-14
    Family Tree, *see* Family Tree application
    Hexpad, *see* Hexpad server application
    internationalization, 66
    minimal, creating, 4-7
    mouse support, adding, 42-45
    OOSS (object-oriented system software), Microsoft technology strategy, 399-400
    Paint, 77-96
    pointers to, 57
    Query (ODBC), 213-219
    Software Lister, 161-190
    Tic-Tac-Toe, *see* Tic-Tac-Toe game
    Wingrep, *see* Wingrep application
AppStudio editors
    accelerator table, 64-66
    cursor, 58-60
    dialog, 231-232
    icon, 56-58
    menu, 60-64
    string table, 66-68
AppWizard
    adding database support to applications, 219-225
    classes and files, 7-8
    minimal applications, creating, 4-7
    OLE containers, 474-480
    printing support, 453-455
    server applications, 416-418
Arc( ) function, 76, 82-83
array collection classes, 176
ASCII
    character set
        chart, 606-608
        converting with ANSI character set, 108-109
    editors, writing .RTF files, 537-538
    file viewer, *see* Hexpad server application
ASSERT macro, 103, 142-143, 306

ASSERT_VALID macro, 142-143
AssertValid( ) function, 14-15, 139-140, 142-143
assignment operators, 104-105
attributes
    CDataExchange class, 261
    CDBException class, 309-310
    CFieldExchange class, 268
    CLongBinary class, 381
    CPrintInfo class, 455
    CRecordset class, 240-242
    CRectTracker class, 493
    CRuntimeClass class, 144
    drawing attributes of DCs, 88-90
    help file windows, 552
    strings, 101-102
AutoCorrect( ) function, 109
automation (OLE), 402

B

backgrounds
    colors/modes, 88
    drawing, 87
BEGIN_MESSAGE_MAP( ) macro, 52
BeginWaitCursor( ) function, 255
binary large objects (BLOBs), 381
BIOS, flash, 561-562
BitBlt( ) function, 358
bitmap (.BMP) file format, 543
bitmap files, 529
    hypergraphic files, 544
    multiple-resolution, 530, 544, 546-547
    referencing, 551
bitmap resources, creating, 358-360
BITMAP structure, 351-352
BITMAPCOREHEADER structure, 366
BITMAPFILEHEADER structure, 365
BITMAPINFOHEADER structure, 367
bitmaps, 351-358
    DDBs (device-dependent bitmaps), 352
        disadvantages, 361

classes

DIBs (device-independent bitmaps), 364
  drawing, 385-388
  formats, 365-368
  I/O and display, 371-375
  in Family Tree application, 388-392
  loading from files, 375-380
  memory management, 368-370
  saving and loading to/from CLongBinary objects, 382-385
  temporary storage, 381
  transferring to/from files, problems, 364
BLOBs (binary large objects), 381
BMIColorCount( ) function, 379-380
.BMP file extension, 529
BOOL data type, 598
Borland's Delphi, 572-573
boundary checking (Dialog Data Validation), 265-266
browse sequences (help), 540
BrowseButtons( ) macro, 547
brushes, 84-96
BSTR data type, 598
buffering, CString, 110-112
button controls, 157-158
  radio, adding to dialog boxes, 296-297
BYTE data type, 598

C

CAhnenDoc class, 330-336
CAhnenView class, 336-337
Cairo (Windows NT 4.0), 566
calculations, win line sums, 33-38
CanAppend( ) function, 243, 289
Cancel( ) function, 292
CanRestart( ) function, 243
CanScroll( ) function, 243
CanTransact( ) function, 243
CanUpdate( ) function, 243, 290
capitalization conversions, 108
CArchive class, 147-150
CArchiveException class, 116

cards
  PCMCIA, 562-563
  video, colors, 346-347
cartoons, playing, 571
CATCH macro, 117
CBitmap class, 353-358
CBrush class, 87
CButton class, 155, 157-158
CByteArray class, 176
CClientDC class, 73, 96-97
CCmdTarget class, xxii
CCmdUI class, 63-64
CComboBox class, 155, 159-160
CCreateContext class, 510-511
CDatabase class, 207
CDataExchange class, 261-265
CDate class, 130-139
  data transfer utility file, 272-277
  DDX date transfer function, 277
  DDX_Field date transfer function, 277
  installing support, 279-283
  RFX date transfer function, 278-279
CDBException class, 116, 207, 309-311
CDC class, 72-73, 75-84
  mapping mode functions, 429-430
  unit conversion functions, 432
CDC objects, creating/destroying, 96-97
CDDBitmap class, 355-358
  installing support, 359-360
CDialog class, 155, 171-175
CDIBitmap class, 371-380, 385-388
CDocument class, 26-29
CDWordArray class, 176
CEdit class, 155-157
CEdit control preparation, 262
CException class, 116-121
CFieldExchange class, 207, 268-271
CFileException class, 116
CFilesView class, 511-512
CFont class, 456-458
CFontDialog class, 458-464
CFontDialog( ) function, 462-464
CFormView class, 231-232

character sets
  ANSI (chart), 602-604
  ASCII (chart), 606-608
  converting between ASCII and ANSI, 108-109
check box controls, adding to dialog boxes, 166
CheckDlgButton( ) function, 297
CheckRadioButton( ) function, 297
CHelloApp class, 8-14
CHelloView class, 14-18
CHexpadApp class, 420
CHexpadDoc class, 420
  drawing code, 422-423
CHexpadSrvrItem class, 420-422
CHexpadView class, 420
  fonts, 456-468
choose-font flags, 459-461
Chord( ) function, 76, 82-83
CInPlaceFrame class, 421
CIPFrameWnd class, 418
circular references, 484
classes, 7-8
  CAhnenDoc, 330-336
  CAhnenView, 336-337
  CArchive, 147-150
  CArchiveException, 116
  CBitmap, 353-358
  CBrush, 87
  CButton, 155, 157-158
  CByteArray, 176
  CClientDC, 73, 96-97
  CCmdTarget, xxii
  CCmdUI, 63-64
  CComboBox, 155, 159-160
  CCreateContext, 510-511
  CDatabase, 207
  CDataExchange, 261-265
  CDate, 130-139, 272-283
  CDBException, 116, 207, 309-311
  CDC, 72-73, 75-84
    mapping mode functions, 429-430
    unit conversion functions, 432
  CDDBitmap, 355-360
  CDialog, 155, 171-175
  CDIBitmap, 371-380, 385-388

611

classes

CDocument, 26-29
CDWordArray, 176
CEdit, 155-157
CException, 116-121
CFieldExchange, 207, 268-271
CFileException, 116
CFilesView, 511-512
CFont, 456-458
CFontDialog, 458-464
CFormView, 231-232
CHelloApp, 8-14
CHelloView, 14-18
CHexpadApp, 420
CHexpadDoc, 420
   drawing code, 422-423
CHexpadSrvrItem, 420-422
CHexpadView, 420
   fonts, 456-468
CInPlaceFrame, 421
CIPFrameWnd, 418
CListBox, 155, 158-159
CLongBinary, 207, 381-385
CMainFrame, 420, 480-481
CMapPtrToPtr, 177
CMapPtrToWord, 177
CMapStringToOb, 177
CMapStringToPtr, 177
CMapStringToString, 177
CMapWordToOb, 177
CMapWordToPtr, 177
CMDIFrameWnd, 323-324
CMemoryException, 116
CNotSupportedException, 116
CObArray, 176
CObject, xxi-xxii, 128-150
CObList, 176
COleBusyDialog, 419
COleChangeIconDialog, 419
COleClientItem, 418, 483-485
COleConvertDialog, 419
COleDataObject, 419, 516
COleDataSource, 419, 516
COleDialog, 419
COleDispatchException, 420
COleDocItem, 419
COleDocument, 419, 489-490
COleDropSource, 419, 516
COleDropTarget, 419, 516
COleException, 116, 420
COleInsertDialog, 419

COleLinkingDoc, 418
COleLinksDialog, 419
COleMessageFilter, 420
COleObjectFactory, 418
COlePasteSpecialDialog, 419
COleResizeBar, 418
COleServerDoc, 418
COleServerItem, 418
COleStreamFile, 420
COleTemplateServer, 418
COleUpdateDialog, 419
collection, 175-182
CPaintDC, 73
CPalette, 349-351
CPen, 85-86
CPersonDlg, 281-283
CPersonView, 321-329
CPoint, 77
CPrintInfo, 454-455
CPtrArray, 176
CPtrList, 176
CRecordset, 207, 236-247,
   288-295
CRecordView, 207, 232-236
CRect, 81
CRectTracker, 418, 492-496
CResourceException, 116
CRuntimeClass, 144, 147
CScrollBar, 155, 160
CScrollView, printing support
   functions, 452-453
CSingleDocTemplate, 12-13
CSize, 469
CSplitterWnd, 508
CStatic, 155, 156
CString, 100-112
CStringArray, 176, 330
CStringList, 176, 179-182
CSWAddDlg, 168-169
CSWListerDoc, 178
CTextLine, 434-440
CTime, 121-124
CTreeSet, 249-251
CTreeView, 237, 251-252
CTTTDoc, 26-29
CTTTView, 38-41
CUnionSet, 298-300
CUserException, 116
CVBControl, 155, 161
CView, 14-18
   OLE containers, 486-489

CWinApp, 8-14
CWindowDC, 73, 96-97
CWingrepApp, 480-481
CWingrepCntrItem, 481,
   483-485, 490-492
CWingrepDoc, 480-481,
   489-490
CWingrepView, 480-481,
   486-489, 492-496
CWnd, xxii-xxiii, 296-297
CWordArray, 176
dialog, transferring data between
   dialog windows and, 260-265
names, changing in minimal
   applications, 24-26
ODBC classes, 206-207
source files, 590-594
Wingrep application, 480-483
**ClassWizard, adding mouse
support for classes, 42-45**
cleaning up memory, 185-186
client items, 483-485
   customizing, 490-492
Clipboard, 504
CListBox class, 155, 158-159
CLongBinary class, 207, 381-385
Close( ) function, 237
CMainFrame class, 420, 480-481
CMapPtrToPtr class, 177
CMapPtrToWord class, 177
CMapStringToOb class, 177
CMapStringToPtr class, 177
CMapStringToString class, 177
CMapWordToOb class, 177
CMapWordToPtr class, 177
**CMDIFrameWnd class message
map, 323-324**
CMemoryException class, 116
**CMultiDocTemplate class
constructor, 337-338**
**CNotSupportedException
class, 116**
**CNTRITEM.H header file,
483-484**
CObArray class, 176
CObject class, xxi-xxii
   deriving classes from, 130-139
   diagnostic services, 139-143
   dynamic creation of objects, 146
   runtime information support,
   143-146

CreateObject ( ) function

serialization, 146-150
uses, 128-130
CObList class, 176
COleBusyDialog class, 419
COleChangeIconDialog class, 419
COleClientItem class, 418, 483-485
COleConvertDialog class, 419
COleDataObject class, 419, 516
COleDataSource class, 419, 516
COleDialog class, 419
COleDispatchException class, 420
COleDocItem class, 419
COleDocument class, 419, 489-490
COleDropSource class, 419, 516
COleDropTarget class, 419, 516
COleException class, 116, 420
COleInsertDialog class, 419
COleLinkingDoc class, 418
COleLinksDialog class, 419
COleMessageFilter class, 420
COleObjectFactory class, 418
COlePasteSpecialDialog class, 419
COleResizeBar class, 418
COleServerDoc class, 418
COleServerItem class, 418
COleStreamFile class, 420
COleTemplateServer class, 418
COleUpdateDialog class, 419
Collate( ) function, 103-104
collection classes, 175-182
color palettes, video memory, 347-351
COLORREF data type, 598
colors
    DDBs (device-dependent bitmaps), 361
    dithering, 346
    drawing, 84-96
    pixels, 345-347
combo box controls, 159-160
    storing data, 303
commands, 53-55
    UPDATE_COMMAND_UI, 63
common application services (WOSA), 567-568
communication services (WOSA), 568-569
Compare( ) function, 103-104

CompareNoCase( ) function, 103-104
comparison operators, 103-104
    adding to CDate class, 137
compiling help files, 552
completeness, xxi
component management (OLE), 404
Component Object Model (COM), 401-402
composite fields, 203
compound documents (OLE Documents), 404-406
computers, history, xix-xxi
concatenation operators, 104-105
configuring help files, 549-552
confirmability, xxi
connecting
    help files to applications, 553
    record sets to record views, 247-248
conserving
    memory, 66
    resources, 74
conspiracy theory, 573
const char* operator, 111-112
constants
    declaring, 38-39
    naming, 31
    Windows, 599
constructors
    CDate class, 133-134
    CDialog class, 172-173
    CMultiDocTemplate class, 337-338
    CRecordset class, 237
    CString class, 101
    CTime class, 122
    CWingrepDoc class, 512, 521-522
    versus InitInstance( ) function, 9-10
containers
    classes, 418-419, 480-483
    client items, 483-485
        customizing, 490-492
    default AppWizard application, 474-480
    documents, 489-490
    drag and drop, File Manager files, 512-515

files, searching, 504-507
mouse support, 496-501
splitter windows, 508-512
views, 486-489
    customizing, 492-496
context strings (help), 540
context-sensitive help, 534
    mapping, 551
control codes (help), 539-540
control variables, 169
controls
    button, adding to dialog boxes, 165-166
    combo box, adding to dialog boxes, 165
    dialog, 155 161
        adding to dialog boxes, 163-167
        CWnd functions for, 296-297
        IDs, 166-167
    double-click support, 304-309
    list box, adding to dialog boxes, 164-165
    OLE custom, 403
converting
    between mapping mode units, 431-432
    OLE objects, 405
    strings, 107-109
copying directory contents, 55
corruption (data), default multiple views, 317-321
CPaintDC class, 73
CPalette class, 349-351
CPalette( ) function, 349
CPen class, 85-86
CPersonDlg class, 281-283
CPersonView class, 321-329
CPoint class, 77
CPrintInfo class, 454-455
CPtrArray class, 176
CPtrList class, 176
CreateBitmap( ) function, 353
CreateBitmapIndirect( ) function, 353
CreateCompatibleBitmap( ) function, 354
CreateDiscardableBitmap( ) function, 354
CreateObject( ) function, 147

613

CreatePalette( ) function

CreatePalette( ) function, 349-350
CRecordset class, 207, 236-247, 288-295
CRecordView class, 207, 232-236
CRect class, 81
CRectTracker class, 418, 492-496
CRectTracker( ) function, 493
CResourceException class, 116
CRuntimeClass class, 144, 147
CScrollBar class, 155, 160
CScrollView class, printing support functions, 452-453
CSingleDocTemplate class, 12-13
CSize class, 469
CSplitterWnd class, 508
CStatic class, 155-156
CString class, 100-112
CStringArray class, 176, 330
CStringList class, 176, 179-182
CSWAddDlg class, 168-169
CSWListerDoc class, 178
CTextLine class, 434-440
CTime class, 121-124
CTreeSet class, 249-251
CTreeView class, 251-252
  pointers to CRecordset-derived objects, 237
CTTTDoc class, 26-29
CTTTView class, 38-41
Cue Cards window, 214
CUnionSet class, 298-300
current date/time, 123
cursor, changing when over client items, 500-501
cursor editor, 58-60
CUserException class, 116
custom controls (OLE), 403
CVBControl class, 155, 161
CView class, 14-18
  OLE containers, 486-489
CWinApp class, 8-14
CWindowDC class, 73, 96-97
CWingrepApp class, 480-481
CWingrepCntrItem class, 481, 483-485, 490-492
CWingrepDoc class, 480-481, 489-490
CWingrepView class, 480-481, 486-489, 492-496
  as drop target, 522-524

CWnd class, xxii-xxiii
  functions for dialog controls, 296-297
CWordArray class, 176

D

data
  connecting to views, 38-41
  corruption, default multiple views, 317-321
  storing, 30-32
  visibility, implementing, 300-304
data members, CPrintInfo class, 455
data sources, construction, 207-213
data transfer
  between databases and record sets, 267-271
  between dialog windows and dialog classes, 260-267
  data transfer process (dialog boxes), 182-187
  DDX date transfer function, 277
  DDX_Field date transfer function, 277
  drag and drop
    File Manager, 512-515
    OLE, 515-519
  RFX date transfer function, 278-279
  routes, 271-272
  support classes, 419, 516
  utility files, CDate class, 272-277
data types
  enumerated, RFX_Operation, 270-271
  ODBC SQL, 209-212
  Windows (lising of), 598
database drivers, 209-212
database management systems (DBMSs), 201
database theory, 201-206
databases, 201
  adding support to applications, 219-225
  data source construction, 207-213

exceptions, 309-311
  transferring data between record sets and, 267-271
DATE_STRUCT structure, defining, 278
dates
  CDate class, 130-139
  CTime class, 121-124
DateString( ) function, 138-139
DATEUTIL.CPP implementation file, 273-277
DATEUTIL.H header file, 272-273
DaysInMonth( ) function, 134-135
DBMSs (database management systems), 201
DCs (device contexts), 72-75
  drawing attributes, 88-90
DDBITMAP.CPP implementation file, 355-356
DDBITMAP.H header file, 355
DDBs (device-dependent bitmaps), 352
  disadvantages, 361
DDV (Dialog Data Validation), 265-266
DDV_MaxChars( ) function, 266
DDV_MinMaxByte( ) function, 266
DDV_MinMaxDouble( ) function, 266
DDV_MinMaxDWord( ) function, 266
DDV_MinMaxFloat( ) function, 266
DDV_MinMaxInt( ) function, 266
DDV_MinMaxLong( ) function, 266
DDV_MinMaxUInt( ) function, 266
DDX (Dialog Data eXchange), 260-265
  functions, 277
  interacting directly with record sets, 266-267
DDX_CBIndex( ) function, 264
DDX_CBString( ) function, 264-265
DDX_CBStringExact( ) function, 264-265
DDX_Check( ) function, 264

614

drag and drop

DDX_Control( ) function, 263-264
DDX_Field*XXX*( ) functions, 266-267, 277
DDX_LBIndex( ) function, 264
DDX_LBString( ) function, 264-265
DDX_LBStringExact( ) function, 264-265
DDX_Radio( ) function, 264
DDX_Text( ) function, 264
debugging
    functions for, 14-15
    help files, 553
declarations, constants, 38-39
DECLARE_DYNAMIC macro, 143-144
DECLARE_DYNCREATE macro, 27, 146
DECLARE_SERIAL macro, 149
default
    AppWizard OLE containers, 474-480
    AppWizard printing support, 453-455
    AppWizard server applications, 416-418
    file loading, 440-442
    mapping mode, 427
    multiple documents, 330-331
    multiple views, 317-321
defining
    BITMAP structure, 351
    DATE_STRUCT structure, 278
    FORMATETC structure, 516
    LOGFONT structure, 459
    LOGPALETTE structure, 350
    PALETTEENTRY structure, 350
    STGMEDIUM structure, 518
Delete( ) function, 288, 290-291
DeleteContents( ) function, 442, 444
DeleteObject( ) function, 360
Delphi (Borland), 572-573
destroying CDC objects, 96-97
destructors
    CSWAddDlg class, 185-186
    CSWListerDoc class, 178
device-dependent bitmaps (DDBs), 352

device-independent bitmaps, *see* DIBs
diagnostic services, CObject class, 129, 139-143
dialog boxes
    Add Member Variable, 169
    AppWizard, 4-7
    calling from applications, 187-190
    Classes, 24-26
    collecting/storing data, 175-182
    components, 155-161
    creating, 161-169
    data transfer process, 182-187
    Family Tree application main
        adding static controls, 219-225
        setting up, 228-231
    font selection, 458-464
    initializing, 171-175
    message boxes, 112-115
    modal, 154
    modeless, 154
    OLE Options, 412
    Person Data, 280-283
    radio buttons, adding, 296-297
    support classes (OLE), 419
    terminating, 173
dialog code, 155
dialog controls, CWnd functions for, 296-297
Dialog Data eXchange (DDX), 260-265
    interacting directly with record sets, 266-267
Dialog Data Validation (DDV), 265-266
dialog editor, 231-232
dialog resources, 155
dialog windows, 155
DIBITMAP.CPP implementation file, 372-375
DIBITMAP.H header file, 371-372
DIBs (device-independent bitmaps), 364
    drawing, 385-388
    formats, 365-368
    I/O and display, 371-375
    in Family Tree application, 388-392
    loading from files, 375-380

    memory management, 368-370
    saving and loading to and from CLongBinary objects, 382-385
    temporary storage, 381
directories, copying contents, 55
DisplayStatus( ) function, 40-41, 57, 67-68
dithering, 85, 346
DlgDirList( ) function, 297
DlgDirListComboBox( ) function, 297
DlgDirSelect( ) function, 297
DlgDirSelectComboBox( ) function, 297
DLLs (Dynamic Linked Libraries), calling from Windows help files, 548
document templates, 317
    registering objects, 339
documents, 22
    adding headers/footers, 467-468
    CDocument class, 26-29
    data
        connecting to views, 38-41
        storing, 30-32
    multiple, 330-339
    OLE containers, 489-490
    OLE Documents, 404-406
    serializing, 442-445
    views, 14, 445-447
DoDataExchange( ) function, 260-263, 267
DoFieldExchange( ) function, 250-251, 269, 299-300
DoModal( ) function, 171-175
DoPreparePrinting( ) function, 452, 454
DoPromptFileName( ) function, 440-441
double-click support, 304-309
    OLE containers, 499
DoVerb( ) function, 499
dpi (dots per inch), 345
DPtoHIMETRIC( ) function, 432
DPtoLP( ) function, 432
drag and drop
    File Manager, 504, 512-515
    OLE, 404, 515-519
    Wingrep searched files to Hexpad application, 519-524

615

DragAcceptFiles( ) function

DragAcceptFiles( ) function, 512, 514
DragFinish( ) function, 513-514
DragQueryFile( ) function, 513-514
DragQueryPoint( ) function, 514
Draw( ) function, 493
DrawBoard( ) function, 39-40
DrawFocusRect( ) function, 76
DrawIcon( ) function, 57
drawing
    colors, 84-96
    DIBs (device-independent bitmaps), 385-388
drawing attributes of DCs, 88-90
drawing code, 422-426
drawing functions, 75-84
drawing objects, 73-74
DrawList( ) function, 445-446
DrawO( ) function, 39-40
DrawOnDC( ) function, 357, 385
DrawPoint( ) function, 79
DrawStuff( ) function, 422-423, 432-433
DrawTrackerRect( ) function, 494
DrawX( ) function, 39-40
drivers
    database, 209-212
    virtual (VxD), 560
drop-down combo boxes, 159
drop-down list boxes, 159
Dump( ) function, 14-15, 139-143
DWORD data type, 598
dynamic creation of objects, CObject class, 129, 146
dynaset record sets, 238

E

edit controls, 156-157
    adding to dialog boxes, 164
Edit( ) function, 288, 290
EditCurrentPerson( ) function, 283, 291
editing
    record sets, 288-295
    visual (OLE), 404-405
editors
    accelerator table, 64-66

ASCII, writing .RTF files, 537-538
cursor, 58-60
dialog, 231-232
Hotspot Editor (SHED.EXE), 528, 546
icon, 56-58
menu, 60-64
string table, 66-68
Windows help project (WHPE), 538
Ellipse( ) function, 40, 76, 81
e-mail, Windows 95 support, 559
empty record sets, determining, 246-247
Empty( ) function, 102
Enable( ) function, 64
END_CATCH macro, 117
EndDialog( ) function, 173
EndDoc( ) function, 464
EndWaitCursor( ) function, 255
enumerated data types, RFX_Operation, 270-271
events, 50
    OLE custom controls, 403
exception handling, 115-121
exceptions, databases, 309-311
ExitInstance( ) function, 327-328
extracting strings, 105-107

F

Fail( ) function, 261-262
Family Tree application
    ahnentafel listings (CAhnenDoc class), 330
    double-click support, 304-309
    Gender radio buttons, 296-297
    Info menu, 244-247
    installing CDDBitmap support, 359-360
    main view/dialog
        adding static controls, 219-225
        setting up, 228-231
    multiple documents, 331-339
    multiple views, creating, 321-329
    Person Data dialog box, creating, 280-283

Person database table, 204
Portrait menu, 388-392
Record menu, 282-283, 292-295
records, adding/editing, 288-295
reflecting familial relations in record view, 247-255
registering document template objects, 339
Unions database table, 205
    installing support, 298-304
fields, 202
    composite, 203
    multiple-word names, 250-251
    primary keys, 202
File Manager drag and drop, 504, 512-515
files, 7-8
    data transfer utility, CDate class, 272-277
    drag and drop from Wingrep to Hexpad, 519-524
    extensions
        .BMP, 529
        .HMO, 553
        .HPJ, 529
        .MRB, 530
        .OCX, 403
        .RTF, 529
        .SHG, 530
        .WMF, 529
    header, see header files
    help, see help files
    implementation, see implementation files
    loading, default, 440-442
    long filenames, Windows 95 support, 558-559
    searching, 504-507
FILESRCH.CPP implementation file, 505-506
FILESRCH.H header file, 505
filling polygon fill mode, 88
FillSpouses( ) function, 304
Find( ) function, 109
FindOneOf( ) function, 109-110
fixed-scale mapping modes, 430
flags, choose-font, 459-461
flash BIOS, 561-562
floating tracking rectangle, 492-496

functions

font selection dialog boxes, 458-464
fonts, printing, 456-468
footers
    adding to documents, 467-468
    spacing, 468-469
format codes, printf( ) function, 596
Format( ) function, 123-124
FORMATETC structure, 516-518
FormatGmt( ) function, 123-124
formats
    date and time, 123-124
    DIBs (device-independent bitmaps), 365-368
    help file graphics, 543-544
    PE (Portable Executable), 557
frameworks, registering document template objects, 339
free( ) function, 370
FromHandle( ) function, 349, 354
full servers, 413
FullName( ) function, 251
functions
    aborting, 378
    Add( ), 136-137
    AddDay( ), 134-136
    AddDocTemplate( ), 339
    AddItem( ), 490
    AddNew( ), 288-289
    AdjustRect( ), 494
    AfxGetApp( ), 57
    AfxMessageBox( ), 112-115
    AnalyzeBoard( ), 36-38
    AnimatePalette( ), 349
    AnsiToOem( ), 107-109
    Arc( ), 76, 82-83
    AssertValid( ), 14-15, 139-140, 142-143
    AutoCorrect( ), 109
    BeginWaitCursor( ), 255
    BitBlt( ), 358
    BMIColorCount( ), 379-380
    CanAppend( ), 243, 289
    Cancel( ), 292
    CanRestart( ), 243
    CanScroll( ), 243
    CanTransact( ), 243
    CanUpdate( ), 243, 290
    CFontDialog( ), 462-464

CheckDlgButton( ), 297
CheckRadioButton( ), 297
Chord( ), 76, 82-83
Close( ), 237
Collate( ), 103-104
Compare( ), 103-104
CompareNoCase( ), 103-104
CPalette( ), 349
CreateBitmap( ), 353
CreateBitmapIndirect( ), 353
CreateCompatibleBitmap( ), 354
CreateDiscardableBitmap( ), 354
CreateObject( ), 147
CreatePalette( ), 349-350
CRectTracker( ), 493
DateString( ), 138-139
DaysInMonth( ), 134-135
DDV_MaxChars( ), 266
DDV_MinMaxByte( ), 266
DDV_MinMaxDouble( ), 266
DDV_MinMaxDWord( ), 266
DDV_MinMaxFloat( ), 266
DDV_MinMaxInt( ), 266
DDV_MinMaxLong( ), 266
DDV_MinMaxUInt( ), 266
DDX (Dialog Data eXchange), 277
DDX_CBIndex( ), 264
DDX_CBString( ), 264-265
DDX_CBStringExact( ), 264-265
DDX_Check( ), 264
DDX_Control( ), 263-264
DDX_Field*XXX*( ), 266-267, 277
DDX_LBIndex( ), 264
DDX_LBString( ), 264-265
DDX_LBStringExact( ), 264-265
DDX_Radio( ), 264
DDX_Text( ), 264
Delete( ), 288, 290-291
DeleteContents( ), 442, 444
DeleteObject( ), 360
DisplayStatus( ), 40-41, 57, 67-68
DlgDirList( ), 297
DlgDirListComboBox( ), 297
DlgDirSelect( ), 297
DlgDirSelectComboBox( ), 297
DoDataExchange( ), 260-263, 267

DoFieldExchange( ), 250-251, 269, 299-300
DoModal( ), 171-175
DoPreparePrinting( ), 452, 454
DoPromptFileName( ), 440-441
DoVerb( ), 499
DPtoHIMETRIC( ), 432
DPtoLP( ), 432
DragAcceptFiles( ), 512, 514
DragFinish( ), 513-514
DragQueryFile( ), 513-514
DragQueryPoint( ), 514
Draw( ), 493
DrawBoard( ), 39-40
DrawFocusRect( ), 76
DrawIcon( ), 57
DrawList( ), 445-446
DrawO( ), 39-40
DrawOnDC( ), 357, 385
DrawPoint( ), 79
DrawStuff( ), 422-423, 432-433
DrawTrackerRect( ), 494
DrawX( ), 39-40
Dump( ), 14-15, 139-143
Edit( ), 288, 290
EditCurrentPerson( ), 283, 291
Ellipse( ), 40, 76, 81
Empty( ), 102
Enable( ), 64
EndDialog( ), 173
EndDoc( ), 464
EndWaitCursor( ), 255
ExitInstance( ), 327-328
Fail( ), 261-262
FillSpouses( ), 304
Find( ), 109
FindOneOf( ), 109-110
Format( ), 123-124
FormatGmt( ), 123-124
free( ), 370
FromHandle( ), 349, 354
FullName( ), 251
GetAt( ), 102
GetBitmapBits( ), 354
GetBitmapDimension( ), 354
GetBkColor( ), 88
GetBkMode( ), 88
GetBuffer( ), 110-111
GetBufferSetLength( ), 110-111
GetCheckedRadioButton( ), 297

617

functions

GetCurrentPosition( ), 76
GetCurrentTime( ), 123
GetDefID( ), 174
GetDlgItemInt( ), 297
GetDlgItemText( ), 297
GetDocSize( ), 447
GetDocument( ), 14, 16
GetInPlaceActiveItem( ), 489
GetItemContaining( ), 496-497
GetItemData( ), 309
GetLength( ), 102
GetMapMode( ), 429
GetMappingMode( ), 430
GetMomDad( ), 252-254
GetNearestPaletteIndex( ), 350
GetNextClientItem( ), 490
GetNextDlgGroupItem( ), 297
GetNextDlgTabItem( ), 297
GetNextItem( ), 489
GetNextServerItem( ), 490
GetPalette( ), 386-388
GetPaletteEntries( ), 349
GetPixel( ), 76
GetPolyFillMode( ), 88
GetPrimarySelectedItem( ), 489
GetRecordCount( ), 243, 246
GetROP2( ), 88
GetRuntimeClass( ), 145-146, 336
GetSQL( ), 243
GetStartPosition( ), 489
GetStatus( ), 243, 246
GetTableName( ), 243
GetTextExtent( ), 468-469
GetTrueRect( ), 493
GetUniqueRandomID( ), 294-295
GetViewportExt( ), 429
GetViewportOrg( ), 429
GetWindowExt( ), 429
GetWindowOrg( ), 429
GotoDlgCtrl( ), 174
HIMETRICtoDP( ), 432
HIMETRICtoLP( ), 432
HitTest( ), 493
HitTestFiles( ), 519-520
InitInstance( ), 9-10, 12-13, 295, 327-328, 337
InitModalIndirect( ), 173
IsBOF( ), 243, 246-247
IsDeleted( ), 243

IsDlgButtonChecked( ), 297
IsEmpty( ), 102
IsEOF( ), 243, 246-247
IsEquivalent( ), 110
IsFieldType( ), 269-270
IsFirstRecord( ), 232
IsLastRecord( ), 232-233
IsLeapYear( ), 134-135
IsLoading( ), 147
IsOpen( ), 243
IsSelected( ), 488
IsStoring( ), 147
IsValid( ), 137-138
KindOf( ), 145-146
Left( ), 105-106
LineTo( ), 38, 40, 76
LoadAncestry( ), 336
LoadBitmap( ), 353
LoadCursor( ), 59
LoadFromDIB( ), 375-380
LoadFromHandle( ), 381-384
LoadIcon( ), 57-58
LoadOEMBitmap( ), 353
LoadStandardCursor( ), 60
LPtoDP( ), 432
LPtoHIMETRIC( ), 432
MakeLower( ), 107-108
MakeReverse( ), 107-108
MakeUpper( ), 107-108
MakeValid( ), 137-138
malloc( ), 369
memcmp( ), 370
memcpy( ), 370
memset( ), 370
MessageBox( ), 112-115
Mid( ), 105-106
Move( ), 242
MoveFirst( ), 242
MoveLast( ), 242
MoveNext( ), 242
MovePrev( ), 242
MoveTo( ), 38, 40, 76, 305-306
NewPen( ), 86
NextDlgCtrl( ), 174
NextWinSum( ), 34-36
NormalizeHit( ), 493
OemToAnsi( ), 107-109
OffsetViewportExt( ), 429
OffsetViewportOrg( ), 429
OffSetWindowOrg( ), 429
OnAppAbout( ), 8, 14

OnBeginPrinting( ), 452, 462, 465-466
OnCancel( ), 174-175
OnCancelEdit( ), 488-489
OnChange( ), 485
OnChangedRect( ), 494
OnChangeItemPosition( ), 484-485, 491-492
OnCmdMsg( ), 54
OnCreate( ), 59, 522
OnCreateClient( ), 509
OnDeactivateUI( ), 485
OnDragEnter( ), 524
OnDragLeave( ), 524
OnDragOver( ), 524
OnDraw( ), 14, 17-18, 41, 75, 78-79, 81-84, 95-96, 323, 336-337, 359-360, 391-392, 422-424, 432, 487-488, 495-496, 511-512
OnDrop( ), 524
OnDropFiles( ), 513-515
OnEndPrinting( ), 452, 464-465
OnEndPrintPreview( ), 452
OnFileNew( ), 13
OnFileOpen( ), 440
OnGetExtent( ), 422
OnGetItemPosition( ), 484-485, 491-492
OnGetRecordset( ), 232, 234
OnGrepSearch( ), 507
OnInfoRecordset( ), 244-245
OnInitDialog( ), 174-175, 183-185
OnInitialUpdate( ), 448, 513
OnInsertObject( ), 488-489
OnLButtonDblClk( ), 306-308, 499
OnLButtonDown( ), 43-45, 78, 498, 520-521
OnMove( ), 232, 234-235, 318-321
OnNewDocument( ), 27-28, 31-32, 78, 90, 335
OnOK( ), 174, 183-185
OnOpenDocument( ), 441-442
OnOptionsDrawpoints( ), 80
OnPaint( ), 75
OnPrepareDC( ), 452, 464-467
OnPreparePrinting( ), 452, 454
OnPrint( ), 452, 467-468

GetNextItem( ) function

OnRecordAdd( ), 293-294
OnRecordDelete( ), 292-293
OnSetCursor( ), 500-501
OnSetFocus( ), 488
OnSize( ), 488
OnUpdate( ), 448
OnUpdateOptionsDrawpoints( ), 80
OnUpdate*XXXX*( ), 63, 189-190
OnVScroll( ), 186-187
OnWindowNew( ), 324-325
OnWindowNewdatawindow( ), 326
OnWindowNewrelativewindow( ), 325-326
On*XXXX*( ), 81
Open( ), 237-239, 249
OpenDocumentFile( ), 513
operator[ ], 102
Pie( ), 76, 82-83
Polygon( ), 76, 84
Polyline( ), 76, 84
PolyPolygon( ), 76
PrepareCtrl( ), 261-262
PrepareEditCtrl( ), 261-262
PrepareVBCtrl( ), 261
PrevDlgCtrl( ), 174
printf( ), format codes, 596
rand( ), 295
Read( ), 439
ReadFromArchive( ), 435, 439-440, 443-444
RealizePalette( ), 350
realloc( ), 370
Rectangle( ), 76, 81-82
ReleaseBuffer( ), 110-111
RemoveItem( ), 490
Requery( ), 237, 248-249, 293
ResetStrings( ), 253
ResizePalette( ), 350
ResizeScrollBars( ), 447-448, 466
ReverseFind( ), 109
RFX (Record Field eXchange), 278-279
RFX_type( ), 250
Right( ), 105-106
RoundRect( ), 76, 81-82
SaveToHandle( ), 381, 384
ScaleWindowExt( ), 430
SearchFiles( ), 506-507
SelectStockObject( ), 86

SendDlgItemMessage( ), 297
Serialize( ), 27, 147-150, 178, 422, 444, 492
SetAt( ), 102
SetBitmapBits( ), 354
SetBitmapDimension( ), 354
SetBkColor( ), 88
SetBkMode( ), 88
SetCheck( ), 64
SetClassWord( ), 59-60
SetCursor( ), 493
SetDefID( ), 174
SetDlgItemInt( ), 297
SetDlgItemText( ), 297
SetFieldType( ), 269-270
SetHelpID( ), 174
SetItemData( ), 303
SetLockingMode( ), 288
SetMapMode( ), 429
SetMappingMode( ), 430
SetPaletteEntries( ), 349
SetPixel( ), 76
SetPolyFillMode( ), 88
SetRadio( ), 64
SetROP2( ), 88
SetSelection( ), 497
SetText( ), 64
SetupTracker( ), 494-495
SetViewportExt( ), 429
SetViewportOrg( ), 429
SetWindowExt( ), 430
SetWindowOrg( ), 429
SpanExcluding( ), 105-107
SpanIncluding( ), 105-106
SQLError( ), 310
srand( ), 295
StretchBlt( ), 357-358
StretchDIBits( ), 386
StretchOnDC( ), 357, 385-386
strftime( ), 139
Strip( ), 107
SubClassDlgItem( ), 297
SubtractDay( ), 134-136
Track( ), 493, 498
TrackRubberBand( ), 494
Update( ), 288
UpdateAllViews( ), 45
UpdateData( ), 174-175, 235, 260, 320
UpdateModifiedFlag( ), 490

UpdateRelatives( ), 236, 252, 254-255
Write( ), 439
WriteToArchive( ), 435, 439-440, 443-444

G

games
 strategy algorithms, 33-38
 Tic-Tac-Toe, see Tic-Tac-Toe game
genealogy, 196-201
GetAt( ) function, 102
GetBitmapBits( ) function, 354
GetBitmapDimension( ) function, 354
GetBkColor( ) function, 88
GetBkMode( ) function, 88
GetBuffer( ) function, 110-111
GetBufferSetLength( ) function, 110-111
GetCheckedRadioButton( ) function, 297
GetCurrentPosition( ) function, 76
GetCurrentTime( ) function, 123
GetDefID( ) function, 174
GetDlgItemInt( ) function, 297
GetDlgItemText( ) function, 297
GetDocSize( ) function, 447
GetDocument( ) function, 14, 16
GetInPlaceActiveItem( ) function, 489
GetItemContaining( ) function, 496-497
GetItemData( ) function, 309
GetLength( ) function, 102
GetMapMode( ) function, 429
GetMappingMode( ) function, 430
GetMomDad( ) function, 252-254
GetNearestPaletteIndex( ) function, 350
GetNextClientItem( ) function, 490
GetNextDlgGroupItem( ) function, 297
GetNextDlgTabItem( ) function, 297
GetNextItem( ) function, 489

619

GetNextServerItem( ) function

GetNextServerItem( ) function, 490
GetPalette( ) function, 386-388
GetPaletteEntries( ) function, 349
GetPixel( ) function, 76
GetPolyFillMode( ) function, 88
GetPrimarySelectedItem( ) function, 489
GetRecordCount( ) function, 243, 246
GetROP2( ) function, 88
GetRuntimeClass( ) function, 145-146, 336
GetSQL( ) function, 243
GetStartPosition( ) function, 489
GetStatus( ) function, 243, 246
GetTableName( ) function, 243
GetTextExtent( ) function, 468-469
GetTrueRect( ) function, 493
GetUniqueRandomID( ) function, 294-295
GetViewportExt( ) function, 429
GetViewportOrg( ) function, 429
GetWindowExt( ) function, 429
GetWindowOrg( ) function, 429
GotoDlgCtrl( ) function, 174
graphics
  help files
    file formats, 543-544
    hotspots, 545-546
    inclusion by reference versus by value, 544-545
    multiple-resolution bitmap files, 546-547
    planning, 536
  WinG graphics API, 571
Grep menu (Wingrep application), 507

H

handling exceptions, 115-121
hatch brushes, 87
HC31.EXE (Help Compiler), 528
header files
  AHNENDOC.H, 331-335
  CNTRITEM.H, 483-484
  DATEUTIL.H, 272-273
  DDBITMAP.H, 355
  DIBITMAP.H, 371-372
  FILESRCH.H, 505
  HELLO.H, 8-9
  HELLOVW.H, 14-15
  HEXPADVI.H, 456-458
    listing of, 590-594
  MAINFRM.H, 508-509
  PERSONVI.H, 321-322
  SRVRITEM.H, 421-422
  TEXTLINE.H, 434-435
  TTTDOC.H, 26-27
  WINGRVW.H, 486-487
headers
  adding to documents, 467-468
  spacing, 468-469
Hello application
  HELLO.CPP implementation file, 9-12
  HELLO.H header file, 8-9
  HELLOVW.CPP implementation file, 15-17
  HELLOVW.H header file, 14-15
  minimal application, 4-7
help
  features, 528
  Help Compiler (HC31.EXE), 528
  Hotspot Editor (SHED.EXE), 528
  Multiple-Resolution Bitmap Compiler (MRBC.EXE), 529
  planning phase, 532-536
  source files, 529-530
  user interface, 531-532
Help Compiler (HC31.EXE), 528
help files
  compiling, 552
  configuring, 549-552
  connecting to applications, 553
  control codes, 539-540
  creating
    process, 531
    writing .RTF files, 537-539
  graphics
    file formats, 543-544
    hotspots, 545-546
    inclusion by reference versus by value, 544-545
    multiple-resolution bitmap files, 546-547
    linking topics, 541-542
  macros, 547-548
  nonscrolling regions of scrollable windows, 542-543
  testing/debugging, 553
help project editor (WHPE), 538
Hexpad menu (Hexpad server application), 446-447
Hexpad server application
  classes, 420-422
  converting between mapping mode units, 431-432
  creating, 412-416
  default AppWizard printing support, 453-455
  documents
    serializing, 442-445
    viewing, 445-447
  drawing code, 422-426
  dynamic character extent and coordinate axis direction, 432-433
  fonts (CHexpadView class), 456-468
  mapping modes, printing, 456
  opening/displaying searched files from Wingrep application, 519-524
  preparing data destinations, 434-440
  scroll view, 447-449
  text dimensions, determining for printing, 468-469
HEXPADDOC.CPP implementation file, 466-467
HEXPADVI.H header file, 456-458
hiding information, xxi
HIMETRICtoDP( ) function, 432
HIMETRICtoLP( ) function, 432
HitTest( ) function, 493
HitTestFiles( ) function, 519-520
.HMO file extension, 553
hot keys, attaching to menu items, 64-66
Hotspot Editor (SHED.EXE), 528, 546
hotspots
  cursor, 58
  help, 545-546
    running macros from, 547

.HPJ file extension, 529
HULK application, 538-539
Hungarian notation, 586-587
hypergraphic (.SHG) file
    format, 544
hypergraphic files, 530

I

icon editor, 56-58
icon resources, CAhnenDoc
    documents, 338
icons, Run (toolbar), 7
IDs
    context strings (help), 540
    creating with random numbers,
        294-295
    dialog controls, 166-167
        person data, 281-282
    main view/dialog control,
        229-230
    messages, 50-51
    standard cursors, 60
IMPLEMENT_DYNAMIC macro,
    143-144
IMPLEMENT_DYNCREATE
    macro, 146
IMPLEMENT_SERIAL
    macro, 149
implementation files
    AHNENDOC.CPP, 332-335
    DATEUTIL.CPP, 273-277
    DDBITMAP.CPP, 355-356
    DIBITMAP.CPP, 372-375
    FILESRCH.CPP, 505-506
    HELLO.CPP, 9-12
    HELLOVW.CPP, 15-17
    HEXPADDOC.CPP, 466-467
    listing of, 590-594
    PERSONVI.CPP, 322-323
    TEXTLINE.CPP, 435-439
    TTTDOC.CPP, 28-29
in-place activation, 405
indexes, secondary, 203
Info menu (Family Tree application), 244-247
information hiding, xxi
InitInstance( ) function, 9-10,
    12-13, 295, 327-328, 337
InitModalIndirect( ) function, 173

input, adding mouse support,
    42-45
Intel P6 processor, 572
interdependencies of classes, 8
internationalization of applications, 66
IsBOF( ) function, 243, 246-247
IsDeleted( ) function, 243
IsDlgButtonChecked( )
    function, 297
IsEmpty( ) function, 102
IsEOF( ) function, 243, 246-247
IsEquivalent( ) function, 110
IsFieldType( ) function, 269-270
IsFirstRecord( ) function, 232
IsLastRecord( ) function, 232-233
IsLeapYear( ) function, 134-135
IsLoading( ) function, 147
IsOpen( ) function, 243
IsSelected( ) function, 488
IsStoring( ) function, 147
IsValid( ) function, 137-138
iterators, 34

J–K

jumps (help), 541-542

keys (shortcut), attaching to menu
    items, 64-66
keywords
    help files, 540
    private, 27
    protected, 27
KindOf( ) function, 145-146

L

Left( ) function, 105-106
License Service Application
    Program Interface (LSAPI), 568
lines, drawing, 85-86
LineTo( ) function, 38, 40, 76
linking help topics, 541-542
links, storage-independent
    (OLE), 406
list box controls, 158-159
    drop-down, 159
    storing data, 303

list collection classes, 176
LoadAncestry( ) function, 336
LoadBitmap( ) function, 353
LoadCursor( ) function, 59
LoadFromDIB( ) function,
    375-380
LoadFromHandle( ) function,
    381-384
LoadIcon( ) function, 57-58
loading
    DIBs (device-independent
        bitmaps)
        from files, 375-380
        to and from CLongBinary
            objects, 382-385
    files, default, 440-442
LoadOEMBitmap( ) function, 353
LoadStandardCursor( )
    function, 60
localization, xxi
LOGFONT structure, 459
LOGPALETTE structure, 350
LONG data type, 598
lowercase, converting to, 108
LPARAM data type, 598
LPCRECT data type, 598
LPCSTR data type, 598
LPSTR data type, 598
LPtoDP( ) function, 432
LPtoHIMETRIC( ) function, 432
LPVOID data type, 598
LRESULT data type, 598
LSAPI (License Service Application
    Program Interface), 568

M

macros
    ASSERT, 103, 142-143, 306
    ASSERT_VALID, 142-143
    BEGIN_MESSAGE_MAP( ), 52
    DECLARE_DYNAMIC,
        143-144
    DECLARE_DYNCREATE,
        27, 146
    DECLARE_SERIAL, 149
    exception handling, 117
    IMPLEMENT_DYNAMIC,
        143-144

macros

IMPLEMENT_DYNCREATE, 146
IMPLEMENT_SERIAL, 149
in help files, 547-548
message map, 52
ON_COMMAND( ), 64
ON_COMMAND_EX, 234
ON_UPDATE_COMMAND_UI( ), 64
RGB (red, green, and blue), 85
THROW, 121
THROW_LAST, 121
TRACE, 143
mail, Windows 95 support, 559
main view/dialog control IDs, 229-230
MAINFRM.H header file, 508-509
MakeLower( ) function, 107-108
MakeReverse( ) function, 107-108
MakeUpper( ) function, 107-108
MakeValid( ) function, 137-138
malloc( ) function, 369
map collection classes, 177
MAPI (Messaging Application Program Interface), 568
mapping context-sensitive help, 551
mapping modes, 426-431
converting between units, 431-432
MM_ANISOTROPIC, 424
printing, 456
MDI (Multiple Document Interface), 316-317
document templates, 317
multiple documents, 330-339
multiple views
creating, 321-329
default, 317-321
registering document template objects, 339
member functions, *see* **functions**
member variables, associated with view/dialog controls, 230
memcmp( ) function, 370
memcpy( ) function, 370
memory
allocation, exception handling, 119-121
clean-up, 185-186
conserving, 66

exceptions, handling, 118
leaks, 120
management, DIBs (device-independent bitmaps), 368-370
video, 347-351
memset( ) function, 370
menu editor, 60-64
menu resources, CAhnenDoc documents, 338
menus
Grep (Wingrep application), 507
Hexpad (Hexpad server application), 446-447
Info (Family Tree application), 244-247
Portrait (Family Tree application), 388-392
Record (Family Tree application), 282-283, 292-295
Shapes, 79-84
message boxes, 112-115
message IDs, 50-51
message maps, 52-55
CMDIFrameWnd class, 323-324
MessageBox( ) function, 112-115
messages
CEdit control notification, 157
in MFC, 52-55
in Windows, 50-51
list box notification, 158-159
UPDATE_COMMAND_UI, 63
vertical scroll bar notification, 160
WM_COMMAND, 51
Messaging Application Program Interface (MAPI), 568
metafiles, 529
methods (OLE custom controls), 403
MFC (Microsoft Foundation Class) Library
CArchive class, 147-150
CArchiveException class, 116
CBitmap class, 353-358
CBrush class, 87
CButton class, 155, 157-158
CByteArray class, 176
CClientDC class, 73, 96-97
CCmdTarget class, xxii
CComboBox class, 155, 159-160
CDatabase class, 207

CDataExchange class, 261-265
CDBException class, 116, 207, 309-311
CDC class, 72-84, 429-430, 432
CDialog class, 155, 171-175
CDocument class, 26-29
CDWordArray class, 176
CEdit class, 155-157
CException class, 116-121
CFieldExchange class, 207, 268-271
CFileException class, 116
CFont class, 456-458
CFontDialog class, 458-464
CFormView class, 231-232
CIPFrameWnd class, 418
CListBox class, 155, 158-159
CLongBinary class, 207, 381
CMapPtrToPtr class, 177
CMapPtrToWord class, 177
CMapStringToOb class, 177
CMapStringToPtr class, 177
CMapStringToString class, 177
CMapWordToOb class, 177
CMapWordToPtr class, 177
CMemoryException class, 116
CNotSupportedException class, 116
CObArray class, 176
CObject class, xxi-xxii, 128-150
CObList class, 176
COleBusyDialog class, 419
COleChangeIconDialog class, 419
COleClientItem class, 418, 483-485
COleConvertDialog class, 419
COleDataObject class, 419, 516
COleDataSource class, 419, 516
COleDialog class, 419
COleDispatchException class, 420
COleDocItem class, 419
COleDocument class, 419, 489-490
COleDropSource class, 419, 516
COleDropTarget class, 419, 516
COleException class, 116, 420
COleInsertDialog class, 419
COleLinkingDoc class, 418
COleLinksDialog class, 419

COleMessageFilter class, 420
COleObjectFactory class, 418
COlePasteSpecialDialog class, 419
COleResizeBar class, 418
COleServerDoc class, 418
COleServerItem class, 418
COleStreamFile class, 420
COleTemplateServer class, 418
COleUpdateDialog class, 419
collection classes, 175-182
CPaintDC class, 73
CPalette class, 349-351
CPen class, 85-86
CPoint class, 77
CPrintInfo class, 454-455
CPtrArray class, 176
CPtrList class, 176
CRecordset class, 207, 236-247, 288-295
CRecordView class, 207, 232-236
CRectTracker class, 418
CResourceException class, 116
CScrollBar class, 155, 160
CScrollView class, 452-453
CSize class, 469
CStatic class, 155-156
CString class, 100-112
CStringArray class, 176, 330
CStringList class, 176
CTime class, 121-124
CUserException class, 116
CVBControl class, 155, 161
CView class, 14-18, 486-489
CWinApp class, 8-14
CWindowDC class, 73, 96-97
CWnd class, xxii-xxiii, 296-297
CWordArray class, 176
messages, 52-55
MFC 3.x, 569-570
ODBC classes, 206-207
OLE 2.0 support versus OLE API, 407-409
requirements, xix
Microsoft Network (Marvel), 571-572
Microsoft tools, writing .RTF files, 538-539
Mid( ) function, 105-106

minimal applications, creating, 4-7
    Tic-Tac-Toe game, 24-26
MM_ANISOTROPIC mapping mode, 424, 426
MM_HIENGLISH mapping mode, 426
MM_HIMETRIC mapping mode, 426
MM_ISOTROPIC mapping mode, 426
MM_LOENGLISH mapping mode, 426
MM_LOMETRIC mapping mode, 426
MM_TEXT mapping mode, 426-427
MM_TWIPS mapping mode, 426
modal dialog boxes, 154
modeless dialog boxes, 154
modes
    background, 88
    mapping, 426-431
        converting between units, 431-432
        MM_ANISOTROPIC, 424
        printing, 456
    polygon fill, 88
    ROP2 (binary raster operation), 89-90
modularity, xx
mouse
    OLE container support, 496-501
    support, adding, 42-45
mouse cursor, changing when over client items, 500-501
Move( ) function, 242
MoveFirst( ) function, 242
MoveLast( ) function, 242
MoveNext( ) function, 242
MovePrev( ) function, 242
MoveTo( ) function, 38, 40, 76, 305-306
moving with floating tracking rectangle, 492-496
.MRB file extension, 530
MRBC.EXE (Multiple-Resolution Bitmap Compiler), 529, 546-547
Multiple Document Interface, see MDI
multiple documents, 330-339

multiple views
    creating, 321-329
    default, 317-321
multiple-page printing, 470
multiple-resolution bitmap (.MRB) format, 544
Multiple-Resolution Bitmap Compiler (MRBC.EXE), 529, 546-547
multiple-resolution bitmap files, 530, 546-547

N

names
    classes, changing in minimal applications, 24-26
    constants, 31
    fields, multiple-word names, 250-251
    long filenames, Windows 95 support, 558-559
    variables, Hungarian notation, 586-587
navigating records, 242-243
nesting OLE objects, 405
NewPen( ) function, 86
NextDlgCtrl( ) function, 174
NextWinSum( ) function, 34-36
non-CEdit control preparation, 262
nonscrolling regions of scrollable help windows, 542-543
normalization, 203-205
NormalizeHit( ) function, 493
notification messages
    CEdit control, 157
    list box, 158-159
    vertical scroll bar, 160
numbers (random), creating IDs with, 294-295

O

objects, xxii
    CDC, creating/destroying, 96-97
    dynamic creation (CObject class), 129, 146

objects

storage, optimized (persistent), 406
.OCX file extension, 403
ODBC (Open Database Connectivity), 196, 567
    Administrator application, 208-213
    classes, 206-207
    Query application, 213-219
OEM (original equipment manufacturer) character set, see ASCII
OemToAnsi( ) function, 107-109
OffsetViewportExt( ) function, 429
OffsetViewportOrg( ) function, 429
OffSetWindowOrg( ) function, 429
OLE (Object Linking and Embedding)
    automation, 402
    classes, 419-420
    component management, 404
    Component Object Model (COM), 401-402
    containers
        classes, 480-483
        client items, 483-485, 490-492
        default AppWizard application, 474-480
        documents, 489-490
        mouse support, 496-501
        searching files, 504-507
        splitter windows, 508-512
        views, 486-489, 492-496
    custom controls, 403
    Documents, 404-406
    drag and drop, 404, 515-519
        File Manager files, 512-515
        Wingrep searched files to Hexpad application, 519-524
    OLE 1.0, 400-401
    OLE API versus MFC, 407-409
OLE Options dialog box, 412
OLEIVERB_HIDE verb, 500
OLEIVERB_OPEN verb, 500
OLEIVERB_PRIMARY verb, 500
OLEIVERB_SHOW verb, 500
ON_COMMAND( ) macro, 64
ON_COMMAND_EX macro, 234

ON_UPDATE_COMMAND_UI( ) macro, 64
OnAppAbout( ) function, 8, 14
OnBeginPrinting( ) function, 452, 462, 465-466
OnCancel( ) function, 174-175
OnCancelEdit( ) function, 488-489
OnChange( ) function, 485
OnChangedRect( ) function, 494
OnChangeItemPosition( ) function, 484-485, 491-492
OnCmdMsg( ) function, 54
OnCreate( ) function, 59, 522
OnCreateClient( ) function, 509
OnDeactivateUI( ) function, 485
OnDragEnter( ) function, 524
OnDragLeave( ) function, 524
OnDragOver( ) function, 524
OnDraw( ) function, 14, 17-18, 41, 75, 78-79, 81-84, 95-96, 323, 336-337, 359-360, 391-392, 422-424, 432, 487-488, 495-496, 511-512
OnDrop( ) function, 524
OnDropFiles( ) function, 513-515
OnEndPrinting( ) function, 452, 464-465
OnEndPrintPreview( ) function, 452
OnFileNew( ) function, 13
OnFileOpen( ) function, 440
OnGetExtent( ) function, 422
OnGetItemPosition( ) function, 484-485, 491-492
OnGetRecordset( ) function, 232, 234
OnGrepSearch( ) function, 507
OnInfoRecordset( ) function, 244-245
OnInitDialog( ) function, 174-175, 183-185
OnInitialUpdate( ) function, 448, 513
OnInsertObject( ) function, 488-489
OnLButtonDblClk( ) function, 306-308, 499
OnLButtonDown( ) function, 43-45, 78, 498, 520-521
online services, Microsoft Network (Marvel), 571-572

OnMove( ) function, 232, 234-235, 318-321
OnNewDocument( ) function, 27-28, 31-32, 78, 90, 335
OnOK( ) function, 174, 183-185
OnOpenDocument( ) function, 441-442
OnOptionsDrawpoints( ) function, 80
OnPaint( ) function, 75
OnPrepareDC( ) function, 452, 464-467
OnPreparePrinting( ) function, 452, 454
OnPrint( ) function, 452, 467-468
OnRecordAdd( ) function, 293-294
OnRecordDelete( ) function, 292-293
OnSetCursor( ) function, 500-501
OnSetFocus( ) function, 488
OnSize( ) function, 488
OnUpdate( ) function, 448
OnUpdateOptionsDrawpoints( ) function, 80
OnUpdate*XXXX*( ) functions, 63, 189-190
OnVScroll( ) function, 186-187
OnWindowNew( ) function, 324-325
OnWindowNewdatawindow( ) function, 326
OnWindowNewrelativewindow( ) function, 325-326
On*XXXX*( ) functions, 81
OOP (object-oriented programming), Microsoft technology strategy, 398-399
OOSS (object-oriented system software), Microsoft technology strategy, 399-400
Open Database Connectivity (ODBC), 196, 567
Open( ) function, 237-239, 249
OpenDocumentFile( ) function, 513
OpenGL libraries, 570-571
opening
    help files, running macros from, 547
    projects, 56
    record sets, 237-240

operator[ ] function, 102
operators
    << (storage), 147-148
    >> (retrieval), 147-148
    assignment, 104-105
    comparison, 103-104
        adding to CDate class, 137
    concatenation, 104-105
    const char*, 111-112
optimized (persistent) object storage, 406

P

P6 processor (Intel), 572
Paint application, 77-96
painting, 72
PALETTEENTRY structure, 350-351
palettes, video memory, 347-351
palindromes, 108
parameterization of record sets, 248-255
PCMCIA (Personal Computer Memory Card International Association), 562-563
PE (Portable Executable) file format, 557
pens, 84-96
persistent (optimized) object storage, 406
Person Data dialog box, creating, 280-283
person data dialog control IDs, 281-282
Person database table (Family Tree application), 204
Personal Computer Memory Card International Association (PCMCIA), 562-563
PERSONVI.CPP implementation file, 322-323
PERSONVI.H header file, 321-322
Pie( ) function, 76, 82-83
pixels, 344
    colors, 345-347
planning phase of help, 532-536
playing cartoons, 571
Plug and Play (PnP), 560-561

PM DIB file format, 365-368
pointers
    to applications, 57
    to CRecordset-derived objects, 237
polygon fill mode, 88
Polygon( ) function, 76, 84
Polyline( ) function, 76, 84
PolyPolygon( ) function, 76
Portable Executable (PE) file format, 557
Portrait menu (Family Tree application), 388-392
POSITION data type, 598
predefined cursors, 60
PrepareCtrl( ) function, 261 262
PrepareEditCtrl( ) function, 261-262
PrepareVBCtrl( ) function, 261
prepending strings, 104-105
PrevDlgCtrl( ) function, 174
primary keys, 202
printf( ) function format codes, 596
printing
    CScrollView support functions, 452-453
    default AppWizard support, 453-455
    fonts, 456-468
    mapping modes, 456
    multiple pages, 470
    text dimensions, determining, 468-469
private keyword, 27
project files (help), 529, 549-552
projects, opening, 56
properties (OLE custom controls), 403
protected keyword, 27
public attributes, *see* attributes

Q-R

Query application (ODBC), 213-219
query languages, 205-206
question mark (?) in SQL statements, 248-249

radio button controls, 165-166, 169
    adding to dialog boxes, 296-297
rand( ) function, 295
random numbers, creating IDs with, 294-295
range checking (Dialog Data Validation), 265-266
Read( ) function, 439
ReadFromArchive( ) function, 435, 439-440, 443-444
RealizePalette( ) function, 350
realloc( ) function, 370
Record Field eXchange (RFX), 267-271
Record menu (Family Tree application), 282-283, 292-295
record sets
    adding records, 288-295
    connecting to record views, 247-248
    creating, 298-300
    CRecordset class, 236-247
    dynaset, 238
    editing, 288-295
    empty, determining, 246-247
    interacting with DDX (Dialog Data Exchange), 266-267
    opening, 237-240
    parameterization, 248-255
    snapshot, 238
    status, determining, 243-246
    transferring data between databases and, 267-271
records, 202
    navigating, 242-243
Rectangle( ) function, 76, 81-82
registering document template objects, 339
RegisterRoutine( ) macro, 548
relational database systems, 201
ReleaseBuffer( ) function, 110-111
remote procedure call (RPC) facility, 569
RemoveItem( ) function, 490
Requery( ) function, 237, 248-249, 293
ResetStrings( ) function, 253
ResizePalette( ) function, 350
ResizeScrollBars( ) function, 447-448, 466

625

resizing with floating tracking rectangle

resizing with floating tracking rectangle, 492-496
resource-based dialog box construction, 172
resources
　bitmap, creating, 358-360
　conserving, 74
　dialog, 155
retrieval (>>) operator, 147-148
return codes (CDBException class), 309-310
ReverseFind( ) function, 109
RFX (Record Field eXchange), 267-271
　functions, 278-279
RFX_Operation enumerated type, 270-271
RFX_type( ) functions, 250
RGB (red, green, and blue) macro, 85
RGBQUAD structure, 367-368
RGBTRIPLE structure, 368
Right( ) function, 105-106
RoboHelp third-party tool, 539
ROP2 (binary raster operation) mode, 89-90
RoundRect( ) function, 76, 81-82
RPC (remote procedure call) facility, 569
.RTF file extension, 529
.RTF files, writing
　with ASCII editors, 537-538
　with Microsoft tools, 538-539
　with third-party tools, 539
Run icon (toolbar), 7
runtime class support, xxi-xxii
runtime information support (CObject class), 129, 143-146

S

SaveToHandle( ) function, 381, 384
saving DIBs (device-independent bitmaps) to/from CLongBinary objects, 382-385
ScaleWindowExt( ) function, 430
scope resolver (::), 59

scroll bar controls, 160
　activating, 186-187
　adding to dialog boxes, 166
scroll view (Hexpad server application), 447-449
SearchFiles( ) function, 506-507
searching
　files, 504-507
　　drag and drop from Wingrep to Hexpad, 519-524
　strings, 109-110
secondary indexes, 203
selectors, 132-133
SelectStockObject( ) function, 86
SendDlgItemMessage( ) function, 297
serialization, xxii
　CObject class, 129, 146-150
　documents, 442-445
Serialize( ) function, 27, 147-150, 178, 422, 444, 492
servers
　default AppWizard applications, 416-418
　full, 413
　Hexpad, see Hexpad server application
　support classes, 418-419
SetAt( ) function, 102
SetBitmapBits( ) function, 354
SetBitmapDimension( ) function, 354
SetBkColor( ) function, 88
SetBkMode( ) function, 88
SetCheck( ) function, 64
SetClassWord( ) function, 59-60
SetCursor( ) function, 493
SetDefID( ) function, 174
SetDlgItemInt( ) function, 297
SetDlgItemText( ) function, 297
SetFieldType( ) function, 269-270
SetHelpID( ) function, 174
SetItemData( ) function, 303
SetLockingMode( ) function, 288
SetMapMode( ) function, 429
SetMappingMode( ) function, 430
SetPaletteEntries( ) function, 349
SetPixel( ) function, 76
SetPolyFillMode( ) function, 88
SetRadio( ) function, 64

SetROP2( ) function, 88
SetSelection( ) function, 497
SetText( ) function, 64
SetupTracker( ) function, 494-495
SetViewportExt( ) function, 429
SetViewportOrg( ) function, 429
SetWindowExt( ) function, 430
SetWindowOrg( ) function, 429
Shapes menu, creating, 79-84
SHED.EXE (Hotspot Editor), 528, 546
.SHG file extension, 530
shortcut keys, attaching to menu items, 64-66
Simonyi, Charles, 586
single document templates, 12-13
skeletal applications, creating, 4-7
SNA (System Network Architecture) API, 568
snapshot record sets, 238
Sockets (Windows), 569
software engineering, xx-xxi
Software Engineering Principles, xx
Software Lister application, 161-169
　calling dialog boxes, 187-190
　collecting/storing data, 175-182
　data transfer process, 182-187
　initializing dialog boxes, 171-175
solid brushes, 87
source files, 590-594
　help, 529-530
　see also header files; implementation files
spacing (text dimensions), determining for printing, 468-469
SpanExcluding( ) function, 105-107
SpanIncluding( ) function, 105-106
spell checking, 109
splitter windows, 508-512
SQL (Structured Query Language), 205-206
　ODBC data types, 209-212
SQLError( ) function, 310
srand( ) function, 295
SRVRITEM.H header file, 421-422
standard cursors, 60

TTTDOC.CPP implementation file

static controls, 156
  adding to dialog boxes, 163
  adding to Family Tree application main view/dialog, 219-225
status of record sets, determining, 243-246
STGMEDIUM structure, 518-519
stock pens and brushes, 85-86
storage
  data, 30-32
  DIBs (device-independent bitmaps), temporary, 381
  optimized (persistent) object, 406
storage (<<) operator, 147-148
storage-Independent OLE links, 406
strategies, games, 33-38
StretchBlt( ) function, 357-358
StretchDIBits( ) function, 386
StretchOnDC( ) function, 357, 385-386
strftime( ) function, 139
string resources (CAhnenDoc documents), 338-339
string table editor, 66-68
strings
  assigning, 104-105
  attributes, 101-102
  comparing, 103-104
  concatenating, 104-105
  converting, 107-109
  extracting, 105-107
  searching, 109-110
Strip( ) function, 107
Structured Query Language (SQL), 205-206
  ODBC data types, 209-212
structures
  BITMAP, 351-352
  BITMAPCOREHEADER, 366
  BITMAPFILEHEADER, 365
  BITMAPINFOHEADER, 367
  DATE_STRUCT, 278
  FORMATETC, 516-518
  LOGFONT, 459
  LOGPALETTE, 350
  PALETTEENTRY, 350-351
  RGBQUAD, 367-368
  RGBTRIPLE, 368

  STGMEDIUM, 518-519
SubClassDlgItem( ) function, 297
SubtractDay( ) function, 134-136
system modal dialog boxes, 154
System Network Architecture (SNA) API, 568
system software
  Component Object Model (COM), 401-402
  OOSS (object-oriented system software), Microsoft technology strategy, 399-400

T

tab order, dialog box components, 167
tables
  accelerator, editor, 64-66
  databases, 201-202
    creating, 213-219
    normalization, 203-205
    Person (Family Tree application), 204
    Unions (Family Tree application), 205, 298-304
  string, editor, 66-68
TAPI (Windows Telephony), 568
templates
  document, 317
    registering objects, 339
    single document, 12-13
  help, 538
terminating dialog boxes, 173
testing help files, 553
text
  dimensions, determining for printing, 468-469
  dynamic character extent and coordinate axis direction, 432-433
  help files, planning, 535-536
TEXTLINE.CPP implementation file, 435-439
TEXTLINE.H header file, 434-435
THROW macro, 117, 121
THROW_LAST macro, 117, 121
thumb, 160

Tic-Tac-Toe game
  adding mouse support, 42-45
  attaching shortcut keys to menu items, 64-66
  building minimal application, 24-26
  designing, 23
  drawing board, 38-41
  editing icon, 56-58
  game strategy and win evaluation, 33-38
  menus, 60-64
  storing game moves, 30-32
  string tables, 66-68
time (CTime class), 121-124
titles (help), 540
toolbar, Run icon, 7
topic files, 529
topics (help)
  aliases, 551
  linking, 541-542
  running macros from, 547
TRACE macro, 143
Track( ) function, 493, 498
tracking rectangle, floating, 492-496
TrackRubberBand( ) function, 494
transferring data
  between databases and record sets, 267-271
  between dialog windows and dialog classes, 260-267
  bitmaps to/from files, problems, 364
  DDX date transfer function, 277
  DDX_Field date transfer function, 277
  dialog-box data transfer process, 182-187
  drag and drop
    File Manager, 512-515
    OLE, 515-519
  RFX date transfer function, 278-279
  routes, 271-272
  utility files (CDate class), 272-277
TRY macro, 117
TTTDOC.CPP implementation file, 28-29

627

TTTDOC.H header file

TTTDOC.H header file, 26-27
tutorials, Query application (ODBC), 214

U

UINT data type, 598
UNC (Universal Naming Convention) paths, Windows 95 support, 559
uniformity, xxi
Unions database table (Family Tree application), 205
  installing support, 298-304
Update( ) function, 288
UPDATE_COMMAND_UI command, 63
UpdateAllViews( ) function, 45
UpdateData( ) function, 174-175, 235, 260, 320
UpdateModifiedFlag( ) function, 490
UpdateRelatives( ) function, 236, 252, 254-255
uppercase, converting to, 108
user interface
  help, 531-532
  update commands, 63

V

validation
  date data, 137-138
  DDV (Dialog Data Validation), 265-266
value variables, 169
variable-scale mapping modes, 430
variables
  control, 169
  member, associated with view/dialog controls, 230
  names, Hungarian notation, 586-587
  value, 169
VBXs, 403
verbs (OLE), 475, 500
vertical market services (WOSA), 569

video cards, colors, 346-347
video memory, 347-351
viewing documents, 445-447
views, 14-18
  CFormView class, 231-232
  connecting document data to, 38-41
  containers, 486-489
    customizing, 492-496
  CRecordView class, 232-236
  Family Tree application main
    adding static controls, 219-225
    setting up, 228-231
  multiple
    creating, 321-329
    default, 317-321
  painting, 75
  pairing with documents in document templates, 317
  record, connecting record sets to, 247-248
  scroll (Hexpad server application), 447-449
virtual device drivers (VxD), 560
visibility to data, implementing, 300-304
visual editing (OLE), 404-405

W-Z

WHAT6 archive, 538
wildcards, matching to strings, 110
win evaluation, 33-38
win line sums, 33-38
win lines, 33
Win32 API, 563-564
Win32s API, 563-564
Win95 Logo program, 557-559
Windows
  constants, 599
  data types (lising of), 598
  DIB file format, 365-368
  future, xxiii
  help project editor (WHPE), 538
  metafile (.WMF) format, 543
  Open Services Architecture (WOSA), 567-569
  Sockets, 569
  Telephony (TAPI), 568

windows, xxii
  Cue Cards, 214
  dialog, 155
    transferring data between dialog classes and, 260-265
  help, nonscrolling regions, 542-543
  splitter, 508-512
Windows 95, 556-557
Windows NT 3.5, 564-566
Windows NT 4.0, 566
WinG graphics API, 571
Wingrep application
  classes, 480-483
  client items, 483-485
    customizing, 490-492
  default AppWizard application, 474-480
  documents, 489-490
  drag and drop
    File Manager files, 512-515
    searched files to Hexpad application, 519-524
  files, searching, 504-507
  mouse support, 496-501
  splitter windows, 508-512
  views, 486-489
    customizing, 492-496
WINGRVW.H header file, 486-487
WinToon, 571
Wizards
  AppWizard, see AppWizard
  ClassWizard, 42-45
WM_COMMAND message, 51
.WMF file extension, 529
WNDPROC data type, 598
WORD data type, 598
WOSA (Windows Open Services Architecture), 567-569
WPARAM data type, 598
Write( ) function, 439
WriteToArchive( ) function, 435, 439-440, 443-444
writing .RTF files
  with ASCII editors, 537-538
  with Microsoft tools, 538-539
  with third-party tools, 539

Add to Your Sams Library Today with the Best Books for Programming, Operating Systems, and New Technologies

The easiest way to order is to pick up the phone and call
1-800-428-5331
between 9:00 a.m. and 5:00 p.m. EST.
For faster service please have your credit card available.

ISBN	Quantity	Description of Item	Unit Cost	Total Cost
0-672-30370-1		Visual C++ 4 Developer's Guide (book/disk)	$49.95	
0-672-30493-7		What Every Visual C++ 2 Programmer Should Know	$29.99	
0-672-30279-9		C++ Programming PowerPack (book/disk)	$24.95	
0-672-30030-3		Windows Programmer's Guide to Serial Communications (book/disk)	$39.95	
0-672-30097-4		Windows Programmer's Guide to Resources (book/disk)	$34.95	
0-672-30226-8		Windows Programmer's Guide to OLE/DDE (book/disk)	$34.95	
0-672-30236-5		Windows Programmer's Guide to DLLs and Memory Management (book/disk)	$34.95	
0-672-30239-X		Windows Developer's Guide to Application Design (book/disk)	$34.95	
0-672-30364-7		Win32 API Desktop Reference (book/CD)	$49.95	
0-672-30295-0		Moving into Windows NT Programming (book/disk)	$39.95	
0-672-30338-8		Inside Windows File Formats (book/disk)	$29.95	
0-672-30299-3		Uncharted Windows Programming (book/disk)	$34.95	

❏ 3 ½" Disk

❏ 5 ¼" Disk

	Shipping and Handling: See information below.	
	TOTAL	

Shipping and Handling: $4.00 for the first book, and $1.75 for each additional book. Floppy disk: add $1.75 for shipping and handling. If you need to have it NOW, we can ship product to you in 24 hours for an additional charge of approximately $18.00, and you will receive your item overnight or in two days. Overseas shipping and handling adds $2.00 per book and $8.00 for up to three disks. Prices subject to change. Call for availability and pricing information on latest editions.

201 W. 103rd Street, Indianapolis, Indiana 46290

1-800-428-5331 — Orders   1-800-835-3202 — FAX   1-800-858-7674 — Customer Service

Book ISBN 0-672-30462-7

GET CONNECTED
to the ultimate source of computer information!

The MCP Forum on CompuServe

Go online with the world's leading computer book publisher! Macmillan Computer Publishing offers everything you need for computer success!

Find the books that are right for you!

A complete online catalog, plus sample chapters and tables of contents give you an in-depth look at all our books. The best way to shop or browse!

➤ Get fast answers and technical support for MCP books and software

➤ Join discussion groups on major computer subjects

➤ Interact with our expert authors via e-mail and conferences

➤ Download software from our immense library:
  ▷ Source code from books
  ▷ Demos of hot software
  ▷ The best shareware and freeware
  ▷ Graphics files

Join now and get a free CompuServe Starter Kit!

To receive your free CompuServe Introductory Membership, call **1-800-848-8199** and ask for representative #597.

The Starter Kit includes:
➤ Personal ID number and password
➤ $15 credit on the system
➤ Subscription to *CompuServe Magazine*

Once on the CompuServe System, type:

GO MACMILLAN

for the most computer information anywhere!

　　　　　CompuServe

PLUG YOURSELF INTO...

The Macmillan Information SuperLibrary™

Free information and vast computer resources from the world's leading computer book publisher—online!

FIND THE BOOKS THAT ARE RIGHT FOR YOU!

A complete online catalog, plus sample chapters and tables of contents give you an in-depth look at *all* of our books, including hard-to-find titles. It's the best way to find the books you need!

- **STAY INFORMED** with the latest computer industry news through our online newsletter, press releases, and customized Information SuperLibrary Reports.
- **GET FAST ANSWERS** to your questions about MCP books and software.
- **VISIT** our online bookstore for the latest information and editions!
- **COMMUNICATE** with our expert authors through e-mail and conferences.
- **DOWNLOAD SOFTWARE** from the immense MCP library:
    - Source code and files from MCP books
    - The best shareware, freeware, and demos
- **DISCOVER HOT SPOTS** on other parts of the Internet.
- **WIN BOOKS** in ongoing contests and giveaways!

TO PLUG INTO MCP: ➤ **WORLD WIDE WEB: http://www.mcp.com**

GOPHER: gopher.mcp.com
FTP: ftp.mcp.com